Justice and the Legal System

ANDERSON'S
Law School Publications

APPELLATE ADVOCACY: PRINCIPLES AND PRACTICE
Cases and Materials
by Ursula Bentele and Eve Cary

CASES AND PROBLEMS IN CRIMINAL LAW
by Myron Moskovitz

A CONTRACTS ANTHOLOGY
by Peter Linzer

CRIMINAL LAW: CASES AND MATERIALS
by Arnold H. Loewy

EFFECTIVE INTERVIEWING
by Fred. E. Jandt

ENDING IT: DISPUTE RESOLUTION IN AMERICA
Descriptions, Examples, Cases and Questions
by Susan M. Leeson and Bryan M. Johnston

ENERGY LAW AND POLICY
by Joseph P. Tomain and James E. Hickey, Jr. with Sheila S. Hollis

ENVIRONMENTAL LAW
by Jackson B. Battle and Mark Squillace

FEDERAL RULES OF EVIDENCE
Rules, Legislative History, Commentary and Authority
by Glen Weissenberger

HARD ROCK MINING
by Michael Braunstein

INTERNATIONAL HUMAN RIGHTS: LAW, POLICY AND PROCESS
Problems and Materials
by Frank Newman and David Weissbrodt

INTRODUCTION TO THE STUDY OF LAW: CASES AND MATERIALS
by John Makdisi

JUSTICE AND THE LEGAL SYSTEM
A Coursebook
by Anthony D'Amato and Arthur J. Jacobson

THE LAW OF DEFAMATION, PRIVACY, PUBLICITY AND "MORAL RIGHTS"
Cases and Materials on Protection of Personality Interests
by Sheldon W. Halpern

LEGAL RESEARCH, WRITING AND ADVOCACY, SECOND EDITION
by Welsey Gilmer, Jr.

PATIENTS, PSYCHIATRISTS AND LAWYERS
Law and the Mental Health System
by Raymond L. Spring, Roy B. Lacoursiere, M.D., and Glen Weissenberger

PROBLEMS AND SIMULATIONS IN EVIDENCE
by Thomas F. Guernsey

SPORTS LAW: CASES AND MATERIALS
by Raymond L. Yasser, James R. McCurdy and C. Peter Goplerud

TRIAL PRACTICE
Text by Lawrence A. Dubin and Thomas F. Guernsey
Problems and Case Files with *Video* Presentation
by Edward R. Stein and Lawrence A. Dubin

Justice and the Legal System

A COURSEBOOK

by

ANTHONY D'AMATO

Judd & Mary Morris Leighton
Professor of Law, Northwestern University

and

ARTHUR J. JACOBSON

Max Freund Professor of Litigation and Advocacy,
Benjamin N. Cardozo School of Law, Yeshiva University

CINCINNATI
ANDERSON PUBLISHING CO.

We dedicate this book

to

Norma D'Amato Kraus,
always cheerful through the long, debilitating pain;

to

Harold Jacobson, and to the memory of Ruth Jacobson, loving parents.

D'AMATO & JACOBSON, JUSTICE AND THE LEGAL SYSTEM: A COURSEBOOK

© 1992 by Anderson Publishing Co.

Library of Congress Cataloging-in-Publication Data

D'Amato, Anthony A.
    Justice and the legal system : a coursebook / by Anthony D'Amato
and Arthur J. Jacobson
        p.   cm.
    Includes bibliographical references.
    ISBN 0-87084-447-4
    1. Justice, Administration of—United States.   2. Justice
Administration of—United States—Cases—Cases.   3. Justice.   I. Jacobson,
Arthur J.   II. Title.
KF386.D28   1992
347.73—dc20
[347.307]
                                                                91-39634
                                                                      CIP

Contents

CHAPTER 2—*concluded*

CHAPTER 3   A Fair Judge

3.1   Do judges ever decide "according to law"?

3.2   Judicial bias: Framework

3.3   Judicial bias: Applications

3.4   Judicial partiality toward substantive law

Table of Cases

Preface

This new coursebook is designed for a one-semester law school course for students at any level. For the first-year curriculum, *Justice and the Legal System* may serve as a text for existing courses in Introduction to Law, Legal Method, Legal Process, The Legal System, and Elements of Law, or any other introductory course. We have taught these materials in such "slots." In upper levels the coursebook may serve as a text for courses in Jurisprudence, Legal Philosophy, and related courses. It could also be used as an in-class text for externship or clinical courses. An especially desirable combination would be to offer *Justice and the Legal System* in the fall semester and Legal Ethics or Professional Responsibility in the spring semester. The present coursebook introduces some questions of judicial ethics that may serve as a springboard to the required course in professional ethics.

We focus on justice; more precisely, we study and examine lawyers' arguments about justice. Several decades ago, law professors were heard in class to dismiss any discussion about justice or fairness as "irrelevant" to legal thinking. One famous professor's answer to a student's question whether a decision was just, was "If it's justice you're looking for, you should have gone to divinity school." Fortunately, these attitudes no longer obtain. Justice considerations are more and more the subject of discussion in every law-school classroom. The present coursebook can be viewed simply as a way of putting those considerations together in one relatively coherent and relatively comprehensive package. We attempt to fill a gap in the law-school curriculum that is no longer controversial—the need for direct and focused examination of arguments about fairness and justice.

We have collected a host of varied and provocative teaching materials. We use transcripts of oral arguments; we use cases that quote extensively from trial-court transcripts; we use materials from foreign legal systems such as the Nuremberg judgment; we even include the transcript of a classroom dialogue when we once co-taught this course at the Cardozo School of Law. We present numerous questions to challenge the intellect and help students to learn to think effectively about the normative arguments that win cases. We focus much more on the litigation process at the pre-trial and trial stages than upon appellate court opinions. We believe that law is designed to solve real-life problems, and hence we steer away from doctrinal discussion. Although our subject-matter ranges over the entire curriculum, we do not attempt to instruct the student in any particular legal subjects.

We are not unmindful of the claim that justice cannot be taught because it is so elusive, or because in a pluralist society there are so many versions of justice. Indeed, these competing views of justice can be found throughout the materials in this coursebook. These competing views of justice must be addressed on their merits. An attorney is an advocate; just because one side has made a claim about justice is no reason for the other side to give up and be silent. Our point is that a law student should be conversant with various ways of thinking about justice in order to effectively answer—or introduce—a claim based on justice.

A judge will invariably have his or her own vision of justice. A judge will try to be just. Surely it is part of the professional responsibility of a well-trained advocate to address, and even help shape, the judge's concern for doing what is fair and just. Justice arguments are as much a stock in trade of the good lawyer as legal arguments.

However, focusing upon justice as part of the lawyer's stock in trade does not ensure that justice can work for any client irrespective of the merits of his or her case. Rather, if the client's situation is unjust (and the client will probably know this as well as the attorney), the good lawyer should whenever possible offer to assist the client in settling or dropping the case. But by the same token, the good attorney should never refuse to take on a just case that appears legally hopeless. The real test of lawyering is to help a client win who ought to win, even if the law seems hopelessly stacked against that client.

But above and beyond advocacy, justice as an intellectual matter animates all law in all legal systems. One cannot understand law without understanding where its normative power comes from. All persuasive legal argumentation turns out, upon inspection, to be structured upon perceived commonalities of justice and fairness. The relation between law and justice is never either/or. Rather, law bereft of justice is only words—words on paper that lack a sense of conviction.

This coursebook reflects our belief that the role of the law-school professor is to teach students how to teach themselves the law. Each student bears the primary responsibility for his or her own legal education—an education in law that starts in law school and never stops thereafter. Law school is simply an initiation into self-training in the law that continues unabated in the productive life of any lawyer after law school—in judicial clerkships, pro bono practice, law firm apprenticeship and eventually partnership, law teaching, government work, or any of the other myriad careers and opportunities to do justice that the law provides. The first year of law school, from this point of view, is just the initial context in which students are actually engaging in legal practice. We believe that law-school education itself constitutes a rudimentary practice.

Learning is best when it is fun. Indeed, the fun of learning is the most important motivation to learn. Of all the many classes we have taught in law school, neither of us have ever had as rewarding an experience as we have experienced in our classes on *Justice and the Legal System*. Even though we have used xeroxed materials that underwent constant revision as we distributed them—and hoped for the day when we would see this coursebook published—our students have understood our project and have been superbly patient. Many students have contributed newspaper clippings and references that have found their way in some form or other into this coursebook. We have hardly ever had a class when all the students left the room at the end of the hour; invariably, a group of students remains, arguing and continuing the dialogue among themselves. The arguments are sometimes heated but always cordial. We have found, simply, that law students *love* to argue about justice.

We have omitted ellipses and many footnotes from cases and quoted materials in order to avoid unnecessary distractions. The scholar who may use this book should, of course, consult original texts.

The book could not have been completed without assistance from several endowments: the Perkins-Bauer Teaching Professorship at Northwestern University, and the Stanford Clinton Sr. Research Professorship at Northwestern University. Nor could the book have been completed without the invitation by Dean Monroe Price of the Cardozo School of Law for us to co-teach the new Justice course during a visit to Cardozo in the Fall of 1986.

We would like to thank Joni Corn and David Katz, students at the Cardozo School of Law, for their indefatigable research assistance, and Jerry Ritthaler at Northwestern for his superb administrative help. Professor Stewart Sterk of the Cardozo School of Law gave us precious guidance on Chapter 6. We would also like to thank the students at the Cardozo School of Law and Northwestern Law School who have used and helped us shape the materials that now assume printed form. We hope that the joy we have experienced in trying to persuade them, and in turn being persuaded by them, blooms through the printed words.

Acknowledgments

We appreciate the permission of the following authors, periodicals, and publishers to reprint excerpts from their publications:

James A. Acker, *Exercising Peremptory Challenges After* Batson. Reproduced with permission from 24 Criminal Law Bulletin 187 (May–June 1988). Warren, Gorham & Lamont, Inc., 210 South Street, Boston, MA 02111. Copyright 1988. All rights reserved.

Ruggiero J. Aldisert, *Philosophy, Jurisprudence and Jurisprudential Temperament,* 20 Indiana L. Rev. 453 (1987). Excerpt reprinted with permission of the Trustees of Indiana University.

Albert W. Altschuler, *Courtroom Misconduct by Prosecutors and Trial Judges,* 50 Texas L. Rev. 629 (1972). Excerpt reprinted with permission of the publisher.

Aristotle, *Nicomachean Ethics* (W.D. Ross trans.), Oxford, 1941: Oxford University Press. Excerpts reprinted with permission of the publisher.

John H. Baker, *An Introduction to English Legal History* (2d ed.), London, 1979: Butterworths. Excerpts reprinted with permission of the publisher.

Boris I. Bittker, *The Case for Black Reparations,* New York, 1973: Random House. Excerpts reprinted with permission of the author.

Zechariah Chafee, Jr., *Some Problems of Equity* (Thomas M. Cooley Lecture Series), Ann Arbor, 1950: University of Michigan Law School. Excerpt reprinted with permission of the publisher.

Felix Cohen, *Transcendental Nonsense and the Functional Approach.* Copyright © 1935 by the Directors of the Columbia Law Review Association, Inc. All Rights Reserved. This article originally appeared at 35 Colum. L. Rev. 809 (1935). Reprinted by permission.

Anthony A. D'Amato, *Is Equality a Totally Empty Idea?,* 81 Mich. L. Rev. 600 (1983). Excerpt reprinted with permission of the publisher.

Anthony A. D'Amato, *Rethinking Legal Education,* 74 Marquette L. Rev. 1 (1991). Excerpts reprinted with permission of the publisher.

Patrick Devlin, *The Enforcement of Morals,* Oxford, 1965: Oxford University Press. Excerpts reprinted with permission of the publisher.

William F. Duker, *A Constitutional History of Habeas Corpus,* Westport, 1980: Greenwood Press. Excerpt reprinted with the permission of the publisher.

Leonard Emmerglick, *A Century of the New Equity,* 23 Texas L. Rev. 244 (1945). Excerpt reprinted with permission of the publisher.

Edwin B. Firmage, *Religion and the Law,* 12 Cardozo L. Rev. 765 (1991). Excerpt reprinted with permission of the author and the publisher.

Stanley Fish, *Doing What Comes Naturally: Change, Rhetoric, and the Practice of Theory in Literary and Legal Studies,* Durham, 1989: Duke University Press. Excerpt reprinted with permission of the author and the publisher.

Jerome Frank, *What Courts Do in Fact,* 26 Ill. L. Rev. (Northwestern University School of Law) 645 (1932). Excerpt reprinted with permission of the publisher.

Thomas A. Green, *Verdict According to Conscience,* Chicago, 1985: University of Chicago Press. Excerpt reprinted with permission of the author and the publisher.

Friedrich A. Hayek, *Law, Legislation and Liberty,* Vol. 2: *The Mirage of Social Justice,* Chicago, 1976: University of Chicago Press. Excerpts reprinted with permission of the author and the publisher.

Joseph Hutcheson, Jr., *The Judgment Intuitive,* 14 Cornell L.Q. 274 (1929). Excerpts reprinted with permission of the publisher.

Susan Jacoby, *Wild Justice,* New York, 1983: HarperCollins Publishers. Excerpt reprinted with permission of the publisher.

M. Janofsky with Peter Alfano, *System Accused of Failing Test Posed by Drugs,* November 17, 1988, p. 1, copyright © 1988 by The New York Times. Excerpt reprinted with permission of the publisher.

Hans, Kelsen, *General Theory of Law and State.* Reprinted by permission of the publishers from *General Theory of Law and State* by Hans Kelsen, Cambridge, Mass.: Harvard University Press, copyright © 1945 by the President and Fellows of Harvard College.

Hans Kelsen, *What is Justice?* Berkeley, 1957: The University of California Press. Excerpts reprinted with permission of the publisher.

John Leubsdorf, *Theories of Judging and Judge Disqualification,* 62 N.Y.U. L. Rev. 237 (1987). Excerpt reprinted with permission of the publisher.

David J. Luban, *Some Greek Trials: Order and Justice in Homer, Hesiod, Aeschylus and Plato.* The full text of this article appears at 54 Tennessee L. Rev. 279 (1987) and is excerpted by permission of the author and the Tennessee Law Review Association, Inc.

Steven Lubet, *Judicial Impropriety and Reversible Error,* 3 Crim. Justice 26 (1988), American Bar Association Section of Criminal Justice. Excerpt reprinted with permission of the author.

David B. Lyons, *The New Indian Claims and Original Rights to Land, Social Theory and Practice,* Vol. 4, No. 3 (1977): Department of Philosophy, Florida State University. Excerpts reprinted with permission of the author.

David Miller, *Social Justice,* Oxford, 1976: Oxford University Press. Excerpts reprinted with permission of the publisher.

David Moskowitz, *The Prediction Theory of Law,* 39 Temple L. Q. 413 (1966). Excerpt reprinted with permission of the publisher.

Thomas Nagel, *Equal Treatment and Compensatory Discrimination,* 2 Philosophy and Public Affairs 357 (1973): Princeton University Press. Excerpt reprinted with permission of the publisher.

Chaim Perelman, *The Idea of Justice and the Problem of Argument* (J. Petrie trans.), London, 1944: Allen & Unwin (Routledge Chapman & Hall). Excerpt reprinted with permission of the publisher.

Plato, *The Republic* (Allan Bloom trans.), New York, 1968: Basic Books (HarperCollins Publishers. Excerpts reprinted with permission of the publisher.

Karl Popper, *The Open Society and Its Enemies,* Vol. 1: The Spell of Plato (5th rev. ed.), Princeton, 1966: Princeton University Press. Excerpt reprinted with permission of the publisher.

Richard A. Posner, *The Concept of Corrective Justice in Recent Theories of Tort Law,* 10 J. Legal Studies 187 (1981): University of Chicago Press. Excerpt reprinted with permission of the author and the publisher.

John Rawls, *A Theory of Justice.* Reprinted by permission of the publishers from *A Theory of Justice* by John Rawls, Cambridge, Mass.: Harvard University Press, copyright © 1971 by the President and Fellows of Harvard College.

Sixty Minutes, December 6, 1987, *Justice For Sale?* CBS News. Excerpts reprinted with permission of CBS.

Robert M. Veatch, *The Foundations of Justice: Why the Retarded and the Rest of Us Have Claims to Equality,* New York, 1986: Oxford University Press. Excerpts reprinted with permission of the author and the publisher.

Peter Westen, *The Empty Idea of Equality,* 95 Harv. L. Rev. 537 (1982). Excerpts reprinted with permission of the publisher.

Introduction

Like any other law-school coursebook, the book you are holding in your hands has lots of cases in it. Cases and problems from the lives of real people caught up in a conflict situation. We will look at these cases from the perspective of justice.

When we do so, we soon realize—like Moliere's character who realized that all his life he was speaking "prose"—that every case is a case about justice. Not just the cases in this book, but every case in every law book. Not all cases will precisely articulate the conception of justice that made a difference in the decision that was reached, but justice arguments were there anyway—in the background when not in the foreground.

But if cases are not always articulate about justice, good lawyers must always be. A lawyer cannot be effective in practice today without knowing what kinds of arguments to make to support claims of fairness and justice. Law schools can no longer afford the indifference that Harold Berman reminds us was their attitude decades ago:[1]

> Oliver Wendell Holmes, Jr., once said: "I hate justice, which means that I know if a man begins to talk about that, for one reason or another he is shirking thinking in legal terms."[2] It was in those days that a Harvard Law School student asked in class, "But sir, is that just?" and the professor replied, "If it's justice you're looking for, you should have gone to divinity school!"

But today's practicing lawyer would make as grave an argumentative error to *ignore* justice considerations as a lawyer decades ago would have made to *emphasize* such considerations in front of a judge such as Justice Holmes.

We believe that this new course on *Justice and the Legal System* may help in actualizing a lifelong perspective that justice, after all, is what law is all about. Not simply doing justice, though that is of immense importance, but also arguing about justice. The most important task of a lawyer—the thing he or she can do best of all—is to articulate and present as powerfully as possible the justice of the client's position.[3] The lawyer must appeal

---

[1] Berman, *Toward an Integrative Jurisprudence: Politics, Morality, History*, 76 Cal. L. Rev. 779, 784 (1988).

[2] O.W. Holmes, His Book Notices and Uncollected Letters and Papers 201 (H. Shriver ed. 1936).

[3] If the client's position appears to be unjust, a good attorney will work with that client to modify the position such as making a bona fide offer of settlement to the other side. Often, however, further investigation of the client's position will reveal that the client acted out of his or her own sense of justice. Such further investigation may prove to be the decisive factor in structuring a legal argument that will present the client's fact situation in terms of societal fairness and justice that may appeal to the judge or decisionmaker.

to the sense of fairness of the tribunal that is charged with passing upon the merits of the client's case. If the client can be shown to *deserve* to win the argument, then the lawyer's job is nearly finished. What remains is the presentation of a justificatory legal argument. Even then, the degree of persuasiveness of the legal argument overtly or covertly derives from the soundness of its foundation in the justice of the client's cause.

We are not saying that arguments about law are unimportant compared to arguments about justice. Far from it. A naked appeal to justice in the course of an argument or negotiation is almost always a tip-off to the decisionmaker that the arguer is resorting to "justice" to get around what the law clearly demands. The frank, even if heartfelt, appeal to justice alone is often a losing strategy—this is the "lesson" of the previous quotation from Oliver Wendell Holmes. Rather, the attorney must show that the client's position is just and right *within the law* properly interpreted. The present course on *Justice and the Legal System* is addressed primarily to accomplishing this task. The materials you will be reading involve the intersection of justice and law. You will find that justice is not something apart from the law; rather, justice informs the law.

We offer this new course to you in the faith that you share with us the intellectual challenge and excitement that comes from examining the deepest foundations of the legal system and attempting to put into words the sense of justice that we all have and that we dedicate our professional lives toward helping to achieve.

Anthony D'Amato

Arthur Jacobson

What Is Justice?

CHAPTER ONE

1.1 Property, friendship and power

The Republic[1]

Plato

SOCRATES. Shall we simply assert that [justice] is the truth and giving back what a man has taken from another, or is to do these very things sometimes just and sometimes unjust? Take this case as an example of what I mean: everyone would surely say that if a man takes weapons from a friend when the latter is of sound mind, and the friend demands them back when he is mad, one shouldn't give back such things, and the man who gave them back would not be just, and moreover, one should not be willing to tell someone in this state the whole truth.

CEPHALUS. What you say is right....

THRASYMACHUS. I say that the just is nothing other than the advantage of the stronger. Well, why don't you praise me? But you won't be willing.

SOCRATES. First I must learn what you mean. For, as it is, I don't yet understand. You say the just is the advantage of the stronger. Whatever do you mean by that, Thrasymachus?

THRASYMACHUS. Don't you know that some cities are ruled tyrannically, some democratically, and some aristocratically?

SOCRATES. Of course.

THRASYMACHUS. In each city, isn't the ruling group master?

SOCRATES. Certainly.

THRASYMACHUS. And each ruling group sets down laws for its own advantage; a

---

[1] THE REPUBLIC OF PLATO, Book I, 331c–331d, 338c, 338d–340a (Allan Bloom trans. 1968). For the sake of clarity, we have put the dialogue into direct discourse. [Editors]

democracy sets down democratic laws; a tyranny, tyrannic laws; and the others do the same. And they declare that what they have set down—their own advantage—is just for the ruled, and the man who departs from it they punish as a breaker of the law and a doer of unjust deeds. This is what I mean: in every city the same thing is just, the advantage of the established ruling body. It surely is master; so the man who reasons rightly concludes that everywhere justice is the same thing, the advantage of the stronger.

SOCRATES. Now I understand what you mean. Whether it is true or not I will try to find out. Now, you too answer that the just is the advantageous, Thrasymachus—although you forbade me to give that answer. Of course, "for the stronger" is added on to it.

THRASYMACHUS. A small addition, perhaps.

SOCRATES. It isn't plain yet whether it's a big one. But it is plain that we must consider whether what you say is true. That must be considered, because, while I too agree that the just is something of advantage, you add to it and assert that it's the advantage of the stronger, and I don't know whether it's so.

THRASYMACHUS. Go ahead and consider.

SOCRATES. That's what I'm going to do. Now, tell me: don't you say though that it's also just to obey the rulers?

THRASYMACHUS. I do.

SOCRATES. Are the rulers in their several cities infallible, or are they such as to make mistakes too?

THRASYMACHUS. By all means, they certainly are such as to make mistakes too.

SOCRATES. When they put their hands to setting down laws, do they set some down correctly and some incorrectly?

THRASYMACHUS. I suppose so.

SOCRATES. Is that law correct which sets down what is advantageous for themselves, and that one incorrect which sets down what is disadvantageous?—Or, how do you mean it?

THRASYMACHUS. As you say.

SOCRATES. But whatever the rulers set down must be done by those who are ruled, and this is the just?

THRASYMACHUS. Of course.

SOCRATES. Then, according to your argument, it's just to do not only what is advantageous for the stronger but also the opposite, what is disadvantageous.

THRASYMACHUS. What do you mean?

SOCRATES. What you mean, it seems to me. Let's consider it better. Wasn't it agreed that the rulers, when they command the ruled to do something, sometimes completely mistake what is best for themselves, while it is just for the ruled to do whatever the rulers command? Weren't these things agreed upon?

THRASYMACHUS. I suppose so.

SOCRATES. Well, then, also suppose that you're agreed that it is just to do what is disadvantageous for those who are the rulers and the stronger, when the rulers unwillingly command what is bad for themselves, and you assert it is just to do what they have commanded. In this case, most wise Thrasymachus, doesn't it necessarily follow that it is just for the others to do the opposite of what you say? For the weaker are commanded to do what is doubtless disadvantageous for the stronger.

POLEMARCHUS. Yes, by Zeus, Socrates, most clearly.

Notes and Questions

1. Cephalus is an old man. He is also a man of property. Socrates offers him a definition of justice a property owner would appreciate: speaking the truth and giving back what one takes. Property owners limit justice to matters like paying debts, not committing theft or fraud. Children understand this idea of justice first, in the playground—don't lie, don't take what's mine. So Cephalus' is the first idea of justice in the *Republic*.[2] Let us call it *justice as property.*

2. Rousseau fashioned his own critique of Cephalus' principle in the *Discourse on the Origin and Foundations of Inequality Among Men.* He argues that property makes people unequal, that being unequal causes them infinitely more misery than the happiness they get from property:[3]

> The first, who having enclosed a plot of land, presumed to say, *this is mine,* and found people simple enough to believe it, was the true founder of civil society. What crimes, what wars, what murders, what miseries and horrors would the human species have been spared by one who, uprooting the stakes or filling in the ditch, had cried out to his fellows: Defend yourselves from listening to this imposter; you are lost if you forget that the fruits belong to all, and the earth to no one.

> From the cultivation of land necessarily followed its partition; and from property, once recognized, the first rules of justice. For in order to give each his own, everyone must be able to have something.

Socrates too believes that inequality causes misery and turmoil. Cephalus' idea of justice

---

[2] *"Kephalaios"* means "head" or "chief." See An Intermediate Greek-English Lexicon, Founded Upon the Seventh Edition of Liddell and Scott's Greek-English Lexicon 430 (1889) ("Liddell and Scott"). The definition Socrates offers Cephalus forms the "head" of the dialogue. Cephalus was the "head" of his family, the owner of the family property.

Actually, Plato draws one picture of justice and one of injustice before Cephalus and Socrates join together to define justice as property. These pictures are so primitive that we don't even define them. The picture of justice is *respect for elders* (Socrates speaks respectfully to Cephalus at the beginning of the dialogue. 328e.) Socrates' talk with Cephalus shows the problem with this picture of justice: once we start dealing with elders on a level footing, we can't hold them in awe just because they are elders, as we did when we were children. The picture of injustice is growing old and decrepit—more broadly, *natural endowments* and *needs.* 329a-d. The rest of the dialogue deals intensively with these silent, omnipresent forces in human existence.

[3] J.J. Rousseau, Oeuvres Completes, Tome III, 164, 173 (1964). Translated by the editors.

works, Socrates teaches, only when people are pretty well satisfied with their property, and only when they ignore other obligations, such as those of citizens.

Socrates "takes back" from Cephalus the definition of justice he just gave him. Cephalus himself, Socrates points out, does not ruthlessly treat justice as property. He would not, for example, return property to a friend who would use it to hurt himself. Cephalus leaves out from justice what everyone leaves out who stops at property: friends and citizens.

3. In a portion of the dialogue we have omitted, Cephalus' son and heir, Polemarchus, intervenes at this point. Unlike his father, Polemarchus is willing to pursue more warlike and political arguments: justice is doing good to friends and harm to enemies.[4] Children understand this idea of justice shortly after they understand justice as property, when they begin to make friends. Let us call this conception *justice as friendship*.

In the next portion of the dialogue (which we have omitted), Socrates shows Polemarchus why equating justice with friendship is insufficient. The physician does good to patients, he says, not because they are friends, but because they pay him.[5] If physicians worked for friendship, not for pay, then we should really have to fear them. Most people, after all, are liable to make mistakes, to choose bad people as friends. To be truly just is to do good for just people, because they are just and not because they are friends, and to do harm to unjust people, because they are unjust, not because they are enemies. Friendship is irrelevant to justice.

4. Now we meet Thrasymachus, whom Socrates describes as a "wild beast."[6] He was a teacher of rhetoric, a sophist. Professional rhetoricians in Athens wrote speeches for litigants to read to juries. Writing these speeches was the only "legal" task performed by paid specialists.[7] Other than rhetoricians (who functioned only on this narrow task), Athens had no professional cadre of lawyers.

Thrasymachus considers justice nothing but rhetoric, which rulers use to keep people in order. Justice is the advantage[8] of the stronger. It is just the opposite of friendship: the stronger call looking to their own advantage "justice," where a friend calls looking to a friend's advantage "justice."

To say that justice is the advantage of the stronger is to say there is no justice. This is the point of view of the sophist. Thrasymachus introduces the sophist's point of view

---

[4] The Polemarch was the third of nine archons, or chief magistrates, who presided in the court in which the causes of metics were tried. Polemarchus' father was a metic, a foreigner living in Athens as a guest. So Polemarchus was a judge in the very court in which his father would have brought actions to defend his property. In earlier times the Polemarch was the commander-in-chief of the army. See LIDDELL & SCOTT 653, definition of "*poleuarchos*."

[5] The same holds true for lawyers. For a different and much criticized view, *see* Fried, *The Lawyer as Friend: The Ethical Foundations of the Lawyer-Client Relation*, 85 YALE L.J. 1060 (1976).

[6] "*Thrasos*" means courage or boldness; in a bad sense—overboldness, rashness, audacity, impudence. See LIDDELL & SCOTT 368.

[7] And the propriety of even this limited function was in doubt. See R. BONNER & G. SMITH, THE ADMINISTRATION OF JUSTICE FROM HOMER TO ARISTOTLE II, ch. 2 (1938).

[8] Other translators use the word "interest" for "advantage." These words carry along with them very different views of social life. Can you characterize the difference?

into the discussion of justice. Let us call it *justice as rhetoric*. Plato devotes the rest of the dialogue to refuting it.

Justice as rhetoric equates justice with emotion. (Rhetoric is an appeal to emotion.) Lawyers use justice talk to win arguments before juries. Clever lawyers sometimes distract juries from following law.

Note the view of law that creeps into the discussion of justice as rhetoric. Consider the following passage, from a modern Thrasymachan tract, Hans Kelsen's *What is Justice?*:[9]

There is in traditional jurisprudence a terminological tendency to identify law and justice, to use the term law in the sense of just law, and to declare that a coercive order which on the whole is effective and therefore a valid positive law, or a single norm of such a social order, is no "real" or "true" law if it is not just. This use of the term "law" has the effect that any positive law, or single norm of a positive law is to be considered at first sight as just, since it presents itself as law and is generally called "law." It may be doubtful whether it deserves to be termed law, but it has the benefit of the doubt. He who denies the justice of such "law" and asserts that the so-called law is no "true" law, has to prove it; and this proof is practically impossible since there is no objective criterion of justice. Hence the real effect of the terminological identification of law and justice is an illicit justification of any positive law.

There is not, and cannot be, an objective criterion of justice because the statement "something is just or unjust" is a judgment of value referring to an ultimate end, and these value judgments are by their very nature subjective in character, because based on emotional elements of our mind, on our feelings and wishes. They cannot be verified by facts, as can statements about reality. Ultimate value judgments are mostly acts of preference; they indicate what is better rather than what is good; they imply the choice between two conflicting values, as for instance the choice between freedom and security. Whether a social system that guarantees individual freedom but no economic security is preferable to a social system that guarantees economic security but no individual freedom, depends on the decision whether freedom or security is the higher value. It is hardly possible to deny that there exists a definite difference between the statement that freedom is a higher value than security, or vice versa, and the statement that water is heavier than wood. There are individuals who prefer freedom to security because they feel happy only if they are free, and hence prefer a social system and consider it just only if it guarantees individual freedom. But others prefer security because they feel happy only if they are economically secure, and hence consider a social system just only if it guarantees economic security. Their judgments about the value of freedom and security and hence their idea of justice are ultimately based on nothing but their feelings. No objective verification of their respective value judgments is possible. And since men differ very much in their feelings, their ideas of justice are very different. This is the reason why in spite of the attempts made by the most illustrious thinkers of mankind to solve the problem of justice, there is not only no agreement but the most passionate antagonism in answering the question of what is just. Quite different is the situation with respect to statements about reality. The statement that water is heavier than wood can be verified by experiment, showing that the statement conforms to facts. Statements about facts are based, it is true, on the perception of our senses controlled by our reason, and hence are in a certain sense subjective too. But the perceptions of our senses are in a much higher degree under the control of our reason than are our feelings, and as a matter of fact nobody doubts that water is heavier than wood. Even if we accept

---

[9] 295–97 (1957).

a philosophy of radical subjectivism and admit that the universe exists only in the mind of man, we must nevertheless maintain the difference which exists between value judgments and statements about reality. The difference may be relative only as a difference between degrees of subjectivity ("objective" meaning the lowest possible degree of subjectivity). But the relative difference is considerable enough to justify the differentiation between a judgment about what is just and a statement about what is the law, the positive law. "Positive" law means that a law is created by acts of human beings which take place in time and space, in contradistinction to natural law, which is supposed to originate in another way. Consequently, the question of what is the positive law, the law of a certain country or the law in a concrete case, is the question of a law creating act which has taken place at a certain time and within a certain space. The answer to this question does not depend on the feelings of the answering subjects; it can be verified by objectively ascertainable facts, whereas the question of whether a law of a certain country or the decision of a certain court is just, depends on the idea of justice presupposed by the answering subject, and this idea is based on the emotional function of his mind.

5. Socrates' argument against Thrasymachus resembles his argument against Polemarchus: the stronger may mistake their advantage. Socrates does not disagree that the stronger rule. He is realistic. He does disagree, however, that the advantage of the stronger is whatever they feel it is. Justice, according to Socrates, requires knowledge of advantage.

In the balance of the dialogue Socrates describes the conditions under which rulers can accurately perceive their advantage. The first and most important condition, from which all the rest flow, is that each person must do only one job, "that one for which his nature made him naturally most fit."[10] Merchants, like Cephalus, must be only merchants, and not claim that owning property gives them the right to govern. The army must not use arms to steal our property or to take over the job of government. Rulers must be rulers only, and not own property, as if they were merchants.

Only a city in which each person "minds his own business" can be a city where rulers accurately perceive their advantage, a just city. And it will be a city incorporating and perfecting the primitive conceptions of justice, each in its own proper sphere: property for merchants, friendship for auxiliaries (or warriors), and the advantage of the stronger for guardians (or rulers). This is Socrates' definition of justice: *minding one's own business.*[11]

Socrates' definition contradicts the primitive conceptions of justice in only one respect: the imaginary just city must be founded on a "noble lie," that the class structure of the city reflects differences in the composition of the bodies of its citizens (gold, silver, and iron/bronze).[12] Cephalus, remember, said that justice meant not lying. We think *equality* involves something of a lie. Socrates felt that *inequality* involves a lie! So the just city is based on a lie—the lie of inequality.

Surely Socrates' vision is attractive in many respects.[13] We want judges to behave as if they were Platonic rulers, considering their advantage only in the most enlightened sense.

---

[10] 433a. Also, 370b.

[11] 433a.

[12] 414c–415d.

[13] For a recent defense, see M. WALZER, SPHERES OF JUSTICE: A DEFENSE OF PLURALISM AND EQUALITY (1983).

We want generals to be friends, not enemies; merchants to rule markets, not governments. But Socrates' vision also has its unattractive side. Consider the following passages from Karl Popper's defense of equality and freedom, *The Open Society and Its Enemies*:[14]

What did Plato mean by "justice"? I assert that in the *Republic* he used the term "just" as a synonym for "that which is in the interest of the best state." And what is in the interest of the best state? To arrest all change, by the maintenance of a rigid class division and class rule. If I am right in this interpretation, then we should have to say that Plato's demand for justice leaves his political programme at the level of totalitarianism.

The city is founded upon human nature, its needs, and its limitations. "We have stated, and you will remember, repeated over and over again that each man in our city should do one work only; namely, that work for which his nature is naturally best fitted." From this Plato concludes that everyone should mind his own business; that the carpenter should confine himself to carpentering, the shoemaker to making shoes. Not much harm is done, however, if two workers change their natural places. "But should anyone who is by nature a worker (or else a member of the money-earning class)...manage to get into the warrior class; or should a warrior get into the class of the guardians, without being worthy of it;...then this kind of change and of underhand plotting would mean the downfall of the city." From this argument which is closely related to the principle that the carrying of arms should be a class prerogative, Plato draws his final conclusion that any changing or inter-mingling within the three classes must be injustice, and that the opposite, therefore, is justice: "When each class in the city minds its own business, the money-earning class as well as the auxiliaries and the guardians, then this will be justice." This conclusion is reaffirmed and summed up a little later: "The city is just...if each of its three classes attends to its own work." But this statement means that Plato identifies justice with the principle of class rule and class privilege. For the principle that every class should attend to its own business means, briefly and bluntly, that *the state is just if the ruler rules, if the worker works, and if the slave slaves*.[15]

The humanitarian theory of justice makes three main demands or proposals, namely, (a) the equalitarian principle proper, i.e., the proposal to eliminate "natural" privileges, (b) the general principle of individualism, and (c) the principle that it should be the task and the purpose of the state to protect the freedom of its citizens. To each of these political demands or proposals there corresponds a directly opposite principle of Platonism, namely, (a1) the principle of natural privilege, (b1) the general principle of holism or collectivism, and (c1) the principle that it should be the task and the purpose of the individual to maintain, and to strengthen, the stability of the state.

6. We shall consider closely the relations among equality, freedom and justice—whether justice makes freedom impossible, in what sense justice supports or detracts from equality. For now, Plato has thrown down the gauntlet: for justice.

7. Though Thrasymachus means his definition to be an attack against anyone who takes justice seriously, there is a sense in which Thrasymachus, too, is serious about justice.

Justice, he says first, is the advantage of the stronger; only boobs are taken in by

---

[14] Volume 1, THE SPELL OF PLATO 89, 90, 94 (5th ed. revised 1966).

[15] Plato does not say much about slaves in the *Republic*, although what he says is significant enough; but he dispels all doubts about his attitude in the *Laws*.... [Popper's observation should be taken with caution. Plato's attitude towards slavery has been fiercely debated. In the *Statesman*, to cite another dialogue, Plato makes it clear that he considers slavery wrong.—Eds.]

justice talk. But then, when Socrates asks him to explain what he means by this, Thrasymachus says that the ruling group in each city sets down *laws* for its advantage. Socrates confounds Thrasymachus by arguing, as we have seen, that rulers can mistake their advantage. But there is a related way to confound him, which Socrates misses, because he, like his contemporaries in Greece, regards law as something objective, to be found by the jury as if it were fact.[16] Socrates could have said that those who enforce and administer the law may mistake the commands of the rulers. At the least, even on Thrasymachus' own terms, the laws' enforcers can be just only by enforcing laws as the ruling group *meant* them to be enforced.

Neither Thrasymachus nor Socrates considered enforcement to be problematic. Assuming they know their advantage in gross, the ruling group knows exactly what to do in every case to pursue it. Unless the advantage of the rulers always coincides with a law, ordinary citizens could say: You told us yesterday your advantage is X. Today you tell us it is Y. Please be consistent, so we can know what to do. If you're inconsistent, then surely you are being unjust to us.[17]

Modern Thrasymachans, for whom the enforcement of law is problematic, have an alternative to considering justice only as emotion. Consider, again, Kelsen. One possible meaning of justice, he says, is *justice under the law*:[18]

> "Justice" in this sense means legality; it is "just" for a general rule to be actually applied in all cases where, according to its content, this rule should be applied. It is "unjust" for it to be applied in one case and not in another similar case. And this seems "unjust" without regard to the value of the general rule itself, the application of which is under consideration.

A contemporary of Kelsen, Chaim Perelman, developed a more general version of Kelsen's idea, the notion of *formal justice*:[19]

> Is there a conceptual element common to all the formulas of justice? Apparently, yes. In effect, we all agree on the fact that to be just is to treat in equal fashion. Unfortunately, difficulties and controversies arise as soon as precision is called for. Must everyone be treated in the same way, or must we draw distinctions? And if distinctions must be drawn, which ones must we take into account in administering justice? Each man puts forward a different answer to these questions. Each man advocates a different system. No system is capable of securing the adherence of all. Some say that regard must be had to the individual's merits. Others that the individual's needs must be taken into consideration. Yet others say it is impossible to disregard origin, rank, etc.
>
> But despite all their differences, they all have something in common in their attitude. He who requires merit to be taken into account wants the same treatment for persons having equal merits. A second wants equal treatment to be provided for persons having the same

---

[16] For an account of law as evidence in Greek procedure, see A. HARRISON, THE LAW OF ATHENS 134–35 (1971).

[17] Lon Fuller proposed the idea that law has a necessary moral structure, including the regularity of official action, in THE MORALITY OF LAW 79–91 (1964).

[18] H. KELSEN, GENERAL THEORY OF LAW AND STATE 14 (1945).

[19] C. PERELMAN, THE IDEA OF JUSTICE AND THE PROBLEM OF ARGUMENT 15–16 (J. Petrie trans., 1944).

needs. A third will demand just, that is, equal, treatment for persons of the same social rank and so on. Whatever, then, their disagreement on other points, they are all agreed that to be just is to give the same treatment to those who are equal from some particular point of view, who possess one characteristic, the same, *and the only one to which regard must be had in the administration of justice*. Let us qualify this characteristic as *essential*. If the possession of any characteristic whatever always makes it possible to group people in a class or category defined by the fact that its members possess the characteristic in question, people having an essential characteristic in common will form part of one and the same category, the same essential category.

We can, then, define formal or abstract justice as *a principle of action in accordance with which beings of one and the same essential category must be treated in the same way*.

8. Other than formal justice or justice under law, the modern champions of Thrasymachus argue, we must keep justice and law entirely separate. Kelsen, again:[20]

[T]he Pure Theory of Law insists upon a clear separation of the concept of law from that of justice, be it called natural, true, or objective law, and . . . renounces any justification of positive law by a kind of superlaw, leaving that problematical task to religion or social metaphysics.

One question we will be asking you to keep in mind throughout the course is whether separation between law and justice is possible.

9. Cephalus' idea of property is *not* a legal idea. Cephalus never mentions law or lawbreaking in describing the advantages of property. (Thrasymachus, we have seen, is the first to mention law, almost as an afterthought, explaining his notion of justice to Socrates.) We have the idea of property long before we know anything about law. Justice as property is a *moral* idea, which informs our thinking about law, but also about many other subjects.

The modern critique attacks justice as property from a perspective very different from Socrates'. Socrates, remember, attacked property as an *insufficient*, not an immoral account of justice. The modern critique, beginning with Hobbes,[21] running through Rousseau to Rawls,[22] attacks the property principle as unprincipled, and not simply as insufficient.

Thinkers who attack the property principle as immoral often adopt a principle of *contract* as the model for justice, as the source of law, and as the highest expression of human association. The values embedded in contract are exactly the ones Socrates (if not Plato) found so problematic: freedom and equality. (Rousseau expressed the value of equality in the passage in Note 2 above.) The vision of association based on contract is very different from the one based on property. So too is the role of law. Think about these differences as we proceed through our inquiry.[23] When listening to justice arguments, it is always helpful to understand whether the moral idea animating it is property or contract.

---

[20] H. Kelsen, What Is Justice? 301–02 (1957).

[21] T. Hobbes, Leviathan 110–12 (1909) [1651] (justice is keeping covenants).

[22] J. Rawls, A Theory of Justice 15–17 (1971) ("justice as fairness" is a contract theory of justice).

[23] For more on the relations between contract as justice and justice as contract, *see* Rosenfeld, *Contract and Justice: The Relation Between Classical Contract Law and Social Contract Theory*, 70 Iowa L. Rev. 769 (1985).

1.2 Distributive and corrective justice

In any society, the basic principles of justice are open to contention. Different people assert different claims to the distribution of goods, and different reasons for protecting the existing distribution against the takings of others. It is to these claims and these reasons in ordinary societies which we must now turn—issues of distributive and corrective justice.

A Theory of Moral Sentiments[24]

Adam Smith

There can be no proper motive for hurting our neighbor, there can be no incitement to do evil to another which mankind will go along with, except just indignation for evil which that other has done to us. To disturb his happiness merely because it stands in the way of our own, to take from him what is of real use to him merely because it may be of equal or of more use to us, or to indulge, in this manner, at the expense of other people, the natural preferences which every man has for his own happiness above that of other people, is what no impartial spectator can go along with. Every man is, no doubt, by nature, first and principally recommended to his own care; and as he is fitter to take care of himself than of any other person, it is fit and right that it should be so. Every man, therefore, is much more deeply interested in whatever immediately concerns himself, than in what concerns any other man: and to hear, perhaps, of the death of another person, with whom we have no particular connection, will give us less concern, will spoil our stomach, or break our rest much less than a very insignificant disaster which has befallen ourselves. But though the ruin of our neighbor may affect us much less than a very small misfortune of our own, we must not ruin him to prevent that small misfortune, nor even to prevent our own ruin. We must here, as in all other cases, view ourselves not so much according to that light in which we may naturally appear to ourselves, as according to that in which we naturally appear to others. Though every man may, according to the proverb, be the whole world to himself, to the rest of mankind he is a most insignificant part of it. . . . In the race for wealth, and honors, and preferments, he may run as hard as he can, and strain every nerve and every muscle, in order to outstrip all his competitors. But if he should jostle, or throw down any of them, the indulgence of the spectators is entirely at an end. It is a violation of fair play, which they cannot admit of.

---

[24] Pp. 161–62, from Part I, Section II, Chapter 2, OF THE SENSE OF JUSTICE, OF REMORSE, AND OF THE CONSCIOUSNESS OF MERIT (1969) [1853].

What Is Justice?[25]

Hans Kelsen

The longing for justice is men's eternal longing for happiness. It is happiness that man cannot find alone, as an isolated individual, and hence seeks in society. Justice is social happiness. It is happiness guaranteed by a social order. In this sense Plato, identifying justice with happiness, maintains that only a just man is happy, and an unjust man unhappy. The statement that justice is happiness is evidently not a final answer; it is only shifting the question. For, now, we must ask: What is happiness?

It is obvious that there can be no "just" order, that is, one affording happiness to everyone, as long as one defines the concept of happiness in its original, narrow sense of individual happiness, meaning by a man's happiness, what he himself considers it to be. For it is then inevitable that the happiness of one individual will, at some time, be directly in conflict with that of another. For example, love is one of the most important sources of happiness as well as of unhappiness. Let us suppose that two men are in love with one and the same woman, and each believes, rightly or wrongly, that he cannot be happy without having this woman exclusively for his own wife. However, according to law and perhaps also according to her own feelings, a woman can be only the wife of one of them. Hence, the happiness of the one is inevitably the unhappiness of the other. No social order can solve this problem in a satisfactory, that is to say, in a just way, guaranteeing the happiness of both—not even the famous judgment of the wise King Solomon. He decided, as will be remembered, to divide into two parts a child which each of two women claimed as her own; but he was willing to attribute the child to the one who should withdraw her claim in order to avoid the death of the child, because—so the king assumed—she truly loved the child. If the Solomonic judgment was just at all, it was so only under the condition that one woman only loved the child. If both loved the child, which is quite possible and even quite probable since both wished to have it, and if both had withdrawn their claim, the dispute would have remained undecided; and if, despite the fact that both women waived their claim, the child had been awarded one of them, the judgment would certainly not have been just, since it would have made one party unhappy. Our happiness very often depends on the satisfaction of needs which no social order can satisfy.

Another example: The commander-in-chief of the army shall be appointed. Two men are in competition, but only one can be appointed. It seems to be evident that it is just to appoint the one who is more fit for the office. But what if the two are equally fit? Then, no just solution is possible. Let us suppose that the one is considered to be better than the other because he is tall and handsome, and has an impressive personality, whereas the other, although professionally absolutely equal, is small and plain and looks insignificant. If the first one gets the job, the other will not feel that the decision was just. He will ask, "Why am I not tall and handsome as the other, why has nature given me a less attractive body?"

[25] 2–3 (1957).

And, indeed, if we judge nature from the point of view of justice, we must admit that nature is not just; it makes the one healthy, and the other sick, the one intelligent, the other stupid. No social order can compensate for the injustice of nature.

General Theory of Law and State[26]

Hans Kelsen

Nor is a just order . . . possible even on the supposition that it is trying to bring about not the individual happiness of each, but the greatest possible happiness of the greatest possible number of individuals. The happiness that a social order can assure can be happiness in the collective sense only, that is, the satisfaction of certain needs, recognized by the social authority, the law-giver, as needs worthy of being satisfied, such as the need to be fed, clothed, and housed. But which human needs are worthy of being satisfied, and especially what is their proper order of rank? These questions cannot be answered by means of rational cognition. The decision of these questions is a judgment of value, determined by emotional factors, and is, therefore, subjective in character, valid only for the judging subject and therefore relative only. It will be different according to whether the question is answered by a believing Christian, who holds the good of his soul in the hereafter more important than earthly goods, or by a materialist who believes in no afterlife; and it will be just as different according to whether the decision is made by one who considers personal freedom as the highest good, i.e. by liberalism, or by one for whom social security and the equality of all men is rated higher than freedom, by socialism.

---

[26] P. 6 (1945).

Questions

1. Kelsen says that no principle of justice can determine which of the two men should be allowed to marry the woman. Is this true?

2. Kelsen says that if the handsomer man is appointed to the army position, the unattractive man will feel that justice was not done. Why? What if the appointer was looking to select an unattractive man for the position—perhaps because he is jealous of handsome ones? Then wouldn't the handsomer man feel that justice was not done? But isn't that, ultimately, Kelsen's point? Or does Kelsen himself have a bias toward the handsomer man? What would Smith say?

3. A mother of two children cuts the dessert cake; she hands a large piece to Jane and a small piece to Tom. Is our sense of justice offended?

Suppose you ask the mother why she did this. Consider the following set of possible answers. How does each of them comport with your sense of justice?

(a) "I like Jane more."
(b) "Jane is a girl."

(c) "Jane is cute; Tom is plain looking."

(d) "The doctor put Tom on a low sugar diet."

(e) "Because it's Tuesday."

(f) "Tom hates cake."

(g) "They've got to learn that the world isn't fair."

4. This is not a coursebook in "social justice." We are not *directly* concerned whether, in our society or in any given society, goods and values have been justly distributed and allocated to all persons. Yet, is it possible to "assume away" all questions of social justice whenever there is a lawsuit between individuals? Does litigation take place on a morally level playing field? Or are "social justice" concerns a part of every case?

Aristotle first talked of two kinds of justice: distributive (or "social") justice, and rectificatory (or "corrective") justice. Consider the following excerpt from Aristotle's *Nichomachean Ethics*, then what Posner has to say about it. Can we ever keep distributive justice considerations *completely out* of a lawsuit? How and when can we let them in? On what terms? Would letting them in be fair to both parties? Think about these questions now, but keep an open mind about them, as they will come up in specific contexts throughout this course.

Nicomachean Ethics[27]

Aristotle

Of particular justice[28] and that which is just in the corresponding sense, (A) one kind is that which is manifested in distributions of honour or money or the other things that fall to be divided among those who have a share in the constitution (for in these it is possible for one man to have a share either unequal or equal to that of another), and (B) one is that which plays a rectifying part in transactions between man and man. . . .

3(A) . . . The [distributively] just, therefore, involves at least four terms; for the persons for whom it is in fact just are two, and the things in which it is manifested, the objects distributed, are two. And the same equality will exist between the persons and between the things concerned; for as the latter—the things concerned—are related, so are the former; if they are not equal, they will not have what is equal, but this is the origin of quarrels and complaints—when either equals have and are awarded unequal shares, or unequals equal shares. Further, this is plain from the fact that awards should be "according to merit"; for all men agree that what is just in distribution must be according to merit in some sense, though they do not all specify the same sort of merit, but democrats identify it with the

---

[27] The selections are from Book V, Chapters 2, 3 and 4 (R. McKeon ed., W.D. Ross trans., 1941).

[28] As opposed to the justice "which answers to the whole of virtue." Here Aristotle discusses justice and injustice only in terms of what is lawful and fair, unlawful and unfair. [Eds.]

status of freeman, supporters of oligarchy with wealth (or with noble birth), and supporters of aristocracy with excellence.

The just, then, is a species of the proportionate. . . . [T]he unjust is what violates the proportion. Hence one term becomes too great, the other too small, as indeed happens in practice; for the man who acts unjustly has too much, and the man who is unjustly treated too little, of what is good. . . .

This, then, is one species of the just.

4(B) The remaining one is the rectificatory, which arises in connection with transactions both voluntary and involuntary. This form of the just has a different specific character from the former. For the justice which distributes common possessions is always in accordance with the kind of proportion mentioned above (for in the case also in which the distribution is made from the common funds of a partnership it will be according to the same ratio which the funds put into the business by the partners bear to one another); and the injustice opposed to this kind of justice is that which violates the proportion. But the justice in transactions between man and man is a sort of equality indeed, and the injustice a sort of inequality; not according to that kind of proportion [the ratios in distributive justice], however, but according to arithmetical proportion. For it makes no difference whether a good man has defrauded a bad man or a bad man a good one, nor whether it is a good or a bad man that has committed adultery; the law looks only to the distinctive character of the injury, and treats the parties as equal, if one is in the wrong and the other is being wronged, and if one inflicted injury and the other has received it. Therefore, this kind of injustice being an inequality, the judge tries to equalize it; for in the case also in which one has received and the other has inflicted a wound, or one has slain and the other been slain, the suffering and the action have been unequally distributed; but the judge tries to equalize things by means of the penalty, taking away from the gain of the assailant. For the term "gain" is applied generally to such cases, even if it be not a term appropriate to certain cases, e.g. to the person who inflicts a wound—and "loss" to the sufferer; at all events when the suffering has been estimated, the one is called loss and the other gain.

The Concept of Corrective Justice in Recent Theories of Tort Law[29]

Richard Posner

[These] points should be noted about Aristotle's concept of corrective [rectificatory] justice:

1. The duty to rectify is based not on the fact of injury but on the conjunction of injury and wrongdoing. The injurer must do wrong (*adikei*) as well as do harm (*eblapsen*), and the victim must be wronged (*adiketei*) as well as harmed (*beblaptai*). Not all departures from distributive justice call for correction. Someone who voluntarily makes a bad bargain

---

29 10 J. LEGAL STUD. 187, 190–91 (1981).

may end up worse off than the principles of distributive justice would, but for the bad bargain, dictate. But he has not been wronged, and he is not entitled to rectification. Moreover, what is wrongful or unjust—*adikos*—is not defined in Chapter 4; it is assumed. In Chapter 8 of Book V we learn that "Whether an act is or is not one of injustice (or of justice) is determined by its voluntariness or involuntariness." But even within the class of voluntary acts, only those that are deliberate can be acts of injustice. Those done by misadventure (where "the injury takes place contrary to reasonable expectation") or by mistake (where, for example, "he threw not with intent to wound but only to prick") are not.

2. The idea that distributive considerations do not count in a setting of corrective justice ("it makes no difference whether a good man has defrauded a bad man or a bad man a good one...") is a procedural principle. It is not equivalent to saying that distributive notions should not affect the definition of rights or even that they should not enter into the determination what sorts of acts are unjust or wrongful. The point, rather, is that the judge is interested only in the character—whether it is wrongful—of the injury, rather than in the character of the parties apart from that of the injury: "the moral worth of persons... is ignored."[30]

---

[30] 2 THE ETHICS OF ARISTOTLE 113 n. 3 (Alexander Grant ed., 4th rev. ed. 1885).

Questions

1. Suppose a law professor asks the students in her seminar on "Justice" to turn in a paper which will determine the final grade in the seminar. The paper should be at least 10 pages long. It should be a critical analysis of the legal philosophy—or any aspect thereof—of Hans Kelsen. Monica turns in a carefully typed 50-page paper with 120 footnotes, exhaustively surveying the voluminous writings, both in German and English, of Kelsen on law and justice and showing in detail how his thoughts on the subject of justice developed over time. Elizabeth turns in a hurriedly typed 10-page paper with one footnote, arguing that an inconsistency in one paragraph of Kelsen's writings could only be avoided if Kelsen were to change the conception of justice that the seminar has been attributing to him.

The law professor reads the papers and tentatively decides to give Monica a grade of C+ and Elizabeth a grade of A+. Would the grades be just?

2. Suppose a law professor announces to her first-year class that in determining final grades, she will read each student's application for admission to the law school and determine the student's financial status. Then she will add extra points to the final grade for students who come from disadvantaged or poor families, or who are on scholarships, and take away some points from students who come from professional or highly prosperous families. Is her plan just or unjust?

3. Same facts as in the preceding question. A student challenges the professor to explain the rationale for her grading plan. She replies as follows:

In this society there are great disparities of economic wealth and privilege. A baby coming into the world has no choice of who its parents will be and has done nothing to deserve being in one family rather than another. Yet some babies achieve the windfall of great wealth and privilege, while other babies—indistinguishable from the first group on any theory of justice—are born into poor and underprivileged families. For hundreds of years this society has talked about these issues, yet today the gap between rich and poor is just about as large as it has ever been.

If I were President, I would do what I could to alleviate this unjust economic disparity. I am not President; I am merely a law professor. But as a law teacher, I have the same obligation to do everything I can to alleviate the unjust economic disparity that I would have if I were President. Since it is within my power to take this small step to contribute toward social justice, I feel obliged to hand in final grades that tend to redress the unjust disparity between rich and poor.

Does this response change your answer to the preceding question? Has the law professor made a persuasive argument? Can it be refuted? How?

4. Suppose at the end of the first year of law school two students get such low grades that they are flunked out of school. However, in some cases, readmission (on probation status) is possible. They petition the faculty for readmission.

Richard says: "I worked extremely hard. I went to every class, took extensive notes, studied them after class, and rewrote them into a separate notebook with excerpts from the cases. I briefed each and every case before each class. Whenever the casebook cited a law-review article, I went to the library and read it. I averaged about five and a half hours of sleep per night. I never took a vacation. I never interviewed for a job. I worked through every weekend and every vacation. Although our midterm grades are only practice exams and not officially recorded, I'm glad that I had low grades on them because I was spurred on to even greater effort as a result. I studied intensively for the finals with my study group. My notes were so complete that everyone wanted to exchange notes with me. I did my very best and I desperately want to finish law school. My parents are counting on me. I don't know why I did so badly on the finals; maybe I had a kind of mental logjam because I had crammed so much material into my head."

Kenneth says: "I didn't take the first year of law seriously; I didn't study, and I didn't do my homework. In the middle of the school year I got into a heavy relationship with a woman who dumped me a week before the finals. I couldn't study and couldn't see straight, and blew every one of my final exams. However, when I took the midterm practice exams I got straight A's. I hadn't studied for them either."

The university administration informs the faculty that they can readmit only one of these students due to overenrollment the next year. The faculty decides to readmit Kenneth. Was this decision just?

5. Why don't we simply say, "justice consists in giving each person his due?" Is that a good definition? Does it *explain* what justice is? Consider the following.

Social Justice[31]

David Miller

The most valuable general definition of justice is that which brings out its distributive character most plainly: justice is *suum cuique*, to each his due. The just state of affairs is that in which each individual has exactly those benefits and burdens which are due to him by virtue of his personal characteristics and circumstances. We have yet to inquire what those characteristics and circumstances may consist in, but the general definition conveniently leaves this question open.

Our definition of justice has two important corollaries. First, it implies that where two men are equal in the relevant respects (so that their "dues" are the same) they should be treated in the same way. This principle ("Treat equals equally" or "Treat men equally except where there are relevant differences between them") has often been proposed as a general characterization of justice, but it seems to me inferior to the one I have given. This is mainly because it presents the relation between the concepts of justice and equality in a misleading way. The principle embodies only a weak sense of equality, whose connection with our general definition of justice is obviously close; but it may also encourage the false belief that justice is conceptually tied to a stronger notion of equality. Rather than justice necessarily being egalitarian, equality in the strong sense constitutes *one* way of interpreting justice which may either be accepted or rejected. It is therefore better to regard "treat equals equally" simply as a corollary of the more fundamental principle "render to each his due." The second corollary of this principle is perhaps only a corollary in a loose sense, but it does appear to be suggested by the original formula: this is the principle of proportion. Such a principle applies in cases where a person's due depends upon an attribute which can be quantified. We then have the principle that the amount of benefit he enjoys or the amount of burden he suffers should be proportional to the quantity of the relevant attribute which he possesses. Thus if the relevant attribute were "gravity of crime committed" (calculated, let us suppose, on the basis of the total amount of pain produced), we would have the principle that the amount of punishment inflicted on each man should be proportional to the gravity of the crime which he has committed. The principle of proportion allows us to deal not only with cases in which "dues" are identical, but with cases in which "dues" are different, and yet can be expressed as quantities of the same attribute.

The notion of conservative justice can be derived from the general formula by interpreting a man's due as that to which he has a right or is entitled. It may thus be expressed in the form "to each according to his rights." In order to put such a conception of justice into practice, it is of course necessary to know what each man's rights are. The rights in question may be legal rights, institutional rights, or certain types of moral right, such as the rights one derives from a promise or other non-legal agreement. Rights generally derive from publicly acknowledged rules, established practices, or past transactions: they do not depend upon a person's current behavior or other individual qualities. For this reason it is

---

[31] Pp. 20–21, 25–27 (1976).

appropriate to describe this conception of justice as "conservative." It is concerned with the continuity of a social order over time, and with ensuring that men's expectations of one another are not disappointed.

Although we generally think that the protection of individuals' rights is an important matter of justice, we do not usually believe that it exhausts that concept, for the distribution of rights can itself be assessed from the point of view of justice, as Sidgwick saw. To do this we must switch to a different interpretation of justice, termed by Sidgwick "ideal" and by Raphael "prosthetic" justice. What is the principle of ideal justice? In Sidgwick's view it was the principle of desert: men ought to be rewarded according to their deserts. This is evidently another way in which the general formula of justice can be filled out, a man's due here being taken to mean his deserts. "Desert" in turn may be interpreted in a number of ways, although it always depends upon the actions and personal qualities of the person said to be deserving. Thus a man's deserts may be measured by his moral virtue, his productive efforts, his capacities, and so on.

It is fairly clear that justice as the protection of rights, and justice as desert are conflicting values. We have no reason to believe in general that individuals' rights, which are to be protected by conservative justice, correspond to their deserts. To take one obvious example from our own society, an individual has a right to inherit wealth, that is to say a right to whatever amount of money another may leave him, once taxes have been deducted; yet he can hardly be said to deserve money so received, unless he has actually earned his benefactor's gratitude through services performed prior to his death. There is a conflict here between conservative justice, which insists that an individual's right to inherit be protected, and justice as desert, which demands that a man should earn whatever benefits he receives. This conflict recurs in many other cases.

Does the principle of desert exhaust ideal justice? Sidgwick believed so—but Raphael, writing nearly a century later, argues that the criterion of need is more central to prosthetic (ideal) justice than the notion of desert. If we take up Raphael's suggestion, we have a third interpretation of justice to contend with, a third rendering of the general formula "to each his due." The concept of need must be distinguished from the concept of desert, for when we speak of a man deserving something we have in mind some favorable attribute which we think ought to bring him a benefit, whereas when we speak of him needing something we are thinking of a lack or deficiency on his part—for instance we may say that a man needs food, meaning that it is necessary to him, that it will be injurious to him not to have it.

Questions

1. Do you agree with Miller that there are three and only three distinct kinds of distributive justice: (a) to each according to his or her legal rights, (b) to each according to whether he or she deserves it, and (c) to each according to his or her needs? Which one, or more, of these would Kelsen have chosen? Perelman?

2. Consider the following argument made by St. Thomas Aquinas in the Eleventh

Article of his masterwork, *Summa Theologica*:[32]

> It would seem that the act of justice is not to render to each one his due. For Augustine ascribes to justice the act of succoring the needy. Now, in succoring the needy, we give them what is not theirs but ours. Therefore, the act of justice does not consist in rendering to each one his due.

Does St. Thomas' argument in effect show that Miller's third category of distributive justice is incompatible with either of the other two categories?

3. Do you personally believe in social (distributive) justice? Consider the following.

---

[32] AQUINAS, SUMMA THEOLOGICA, Pf. II, Q. 58, Art. 11, Obj. 1.

Law, Legislation, and Liberty[33]

Friedrich A. Hayek

What I hope to have made clear is that the phrase 'social justice' is not, as most people probably feel, an innocent expression of good will towards the less fortunate, but that it has become a dishonest insinuation that one ought to agree to a demand of some special interest which can give no real reason for it. If political discussion is to become honest it is necessary that people should recognize that the term is intellectually disreputable, the mark of demagogy or cheap journalism which responsible thinkers ought to be ashamed to use because, once its vacuity is recognized, its use is dishonest. I may, as a result of long endeavors to trace the destructive effect which the invocation of 'social justice' has had on our moral sensitivity, and of again and again finding even eminent thinkers thoughtlessly using the phrase, have become unduly allergic to it, but I have come to feel strongly that the greatest service I can still render to my fellow men would be that I could make the speakers and writers among them thoroughly ashamed ever again to employ the term 'social justice.'

We are not familiar with the concept of non-viable systems of morals and certainly cannot observe them anywhere in practice since societies which try them rapidly disappear. But they are being preached, often by widely revered saintly figures, and the societies in decay which we can observe are often societies which have been listening to the teaching of such moral reformers and still revere the destroyers of their society as good men. More often, however, the gospel of 'social justice' aims at much more sordid sentiments: the dislike of people who are better off than oneself, or simply envy, that 'most anti-social and evil of all passions' as John Stuart Mill called it, that animosity towards great wealth which represents it as a 'scandal' that some should enjoy riches while others have basic needs unsatisfied, and camouflages under the name of justice what has nothing to do with justice. At least all those who wish to despoil the rich, not because they expect that some more

---

[33] Vol. 2, THE MIRAGE OF SOCIAL JUSTICE, pp. 97, 98-100 (1976).

than deserving might enjoy that wealth, but because they regard the very existence of the right as an outrage, not only cannot claim any moral justification for their demands, but indulge in a wholly irrational passion and in fact harm those to whose rapacious instincts they appeal.

There can be no moral claim to something that would not exist but for the decision of others to risk their resources on its creation. What those who attack great private wealth do not understand is that it is neither by physical effort nor by the mere act of saving and investing, but by directing resources to the most productive uses that wealth is chiefly created. And there can be no doubt that most of those who have built up great fortunes in the form of new industrial plants and the like have thereby benefited more people through creating opportunities for more rewarding employment than if they had given their super-fluity away to the poor. The suggestion that in these cases those to whom in fact the workers are most indebted do wrong rather than greatly benefit them is an absurdity. Though there are undoubtedly also other and less meritorious ways of acquiring large fortunes (which we can hope to control by improving the rules of the game), the most effective and important is by directing investment to points where they most enhance the productivity of labour—a task in which governments notoriously fail, for reasons inherent in non-competitive bureau-cratic organizations.

But it is not only by encouraging malevolent and harmful prejudices that the cult of 'social justice' tends to destroy genuine moral feelings. It also comes, particularly in its more egalitarian forms, into constant conflict with some of the basic moral principles on which any community of free men must rest. This becomes evident when we reflect that the demand that we should equally esteem all our fellow men is irreconcilable with the fact that our whole moral code rests on the approval or disapproval of the conduct of others; and that similarly the traditional postulate that each capable adult is primarily responsible for his own and his dependants' welfare, meaning that he must not through his own fault become a charge to his friends or fellows, is incompatible with the idea that 'society' or government owes each person an appropriate income.

Though all these moral principles have also been seriously weakened by some pseudo-scientific fashions of our time which tend to destroy all morals—and with them the basis of individual freedom—the ubiquitous dependence on other people's power, which the enforcement of any image of 'social justice' creates, inevitably destroys that freedom of personal decisions on which all morals must rest. In fact, that systematic pursuit of the ignis fatuus of 'social justice' which we call socialism is based throughout on the atrocious idea that political power ought to determine the material position of the different individuals and groups—an idea defended by the false assertion that this must always be so and socialism merely wishes to transfer this power from the privileged to the most numerous class. It was the great merit of the market order as it has spread during the last two centuries that it deprived everyone of such power which can be used only in arbitrary fashion. It has indeed brought about the greatest reduction of arbitrary power ever achieved. This greatest triumph of personal freedom the seduction of 'social justice' threatens again to take from us. And it will not be long before the holders of the power to enforce 'social justice' will entrench themselves in their position by awarding the benefits of 'social justice' as the remuneration for the conferment of that power and in order to secure to themselves the support of a praetorian guard which will make it certain that their view of what is 'social justice' will prevail.

1.3   Vengeance

Wild Justice[34]

Susan Jacoby

Justice is a legitimate concept in the modern code of civilized behavior. Vengeance is not. We prefer to avert our eyes from those who persist in reminding us of the wrongs they have suffered—the mother whose child disappeared three years ago on a New York street and who, instead of mourning in silence, continues to appear on television and appeal for information about her missing son; the young Sicilian woman who, instead of marrying her rapist as ancient local custom dictates, scandalizes the town by bringing criminal charges; the concentration-camp survivors who, instead of putting the past behind them, persist in pointing their fingers at ex-Nazis living comfortable lives on quiet streets. Such people are disturbers of the peace; we wish they would take their memories away to a church, a cemetery, a psychotherapist's office and allow us to return justice and vengeance to the separate compartments they supposedly occupy in twentieth-century life.

---

34 S. JACOBY, WILD JUSTICE pp. 1–2 (1983).

Payne v. Tennessee

111 S. Ct. 2597
United States Supreme Court
June 27, 1991

Petitioner [Pervis Tyrone] Payne was convicted by a Tennessee jury of the first-degree murders of Charisse Christopher and her 2-year-old daughter [Lacie], and of first-degree assault upon, with intent to murder, Charisse's 3-year-old son Nicholas. The brutal crimes were committed in the victims' apartment after Charisse resisted Payne's sexual advances. During the sentencing phase of the trial, Payne called his parents, his girlfriend, and a clinical psychologist, each of whom testified as to various mitigating aspects of his background and character. The State called Nicholas' grandmother, who testified that the child missed his mother and baby sister. In arguing for the death penalty, the prosecutor commented on the continuing effects on Nicholas of his experience and on the effects of the crimes upon the victims' family. The jury sentenced Payne to death on each of the murder counts.

CHIEF JUSTICE REHNQUIST delivered the opinion of the court.

[Nicholas survived, despite several wounds inflicted by a butcher knife that completely penetrated through his body from front to back. Charisse had sustained 42 direct knife wounds and 42 defensive wounds on her arms and hands. The wounds were caused by 41 separate thrusts of a butcher knife. Lacie had suffered stab wounds to the chest, abdomen, back, and head.

[During the sentencing hearing, the prosecutor said to the jury: "Somewhere down the road Nicholas is going to grow up, hopefully. He's going to want to know what happened. And he is going to know what happened to his baby sister and his mother. He is going to want to know what type of justice was done. He is going to want to know what happened. With your verdict, you will provide the answer. No one will ever know about Lacie Jo because she never had the chance to grow up. Her life was taken from her at the age of two years old. So, no there won't be a high school principal to talk about Lacie Jo Christopher, and there won't be anybody to take her to her high school prom. And there won't be anybody there— there won't be her mother there or Nicholas' mother there to kiss him at night. His mother will never kiss him good night or pat him as he goes off to bed, or hold him and sing him a lullaby."]

We granted certiorari . . . to reconsider our holdings in *Booth* and *Gathers*[35] that the Eighth Amendment prohibits a capital sentencing jury from considering "victim impact" evidence relating to the personal characteristics of the victim and the emotional impact of the crimes on the victim's family.

We are now of the view that a State may properly conclude that for the jury to assess meaningfully the defendant's moral culpability and blameworthiness, it should have before it at the sentencing phase evidence of the specific harm

---

[35] Booth v. Maryland, 482 U.S. 496 (1987); South Carolina v. Gathers, 490 U.S. 805 (1989). [Eds.]

caused by the defendant. "The State has a legitimate interest in counteracting the mitigating evidence which the defendant is entitled to put in, by reminding the sentencer that just as the murderer should be considered as an individual, so too the victim is an individual whose death represents a unique loss to society and in particular to his family." *Booth,* 482 U.S. at 517 (White, J., dissenting). By turning the victim into a "faceless stranger at the penalty phase of a capital trial," Booth deprives the State of the full moral force of its evidence and may prevent the jury from having before it all the information necessary to determine the proper punishment for a first-degree murder.

Reconsidering [*Booth* and *Gathers*] now, we conclude . . . that they were wrongly decided and should be, and now are, overruled.

JUSTICE MARSHALL, with whom JUSTICE BLACKMUN joins, dissenting.

[A]dmission of victim-impact evidence creates an unacceptable risk of sentencing arbitrariness. As Justice Powell explained in Booth, the probative value of such evidence is always outweighed by its prejudicial effect because of its inherent capacity to draw the jury's attention away from the character of the defendant and the circumstances of the crime to such illicit considerations as the eloquence with which family members express their grief and the status of the victim in the community.

Questions

1. Is the decision in *Payne* a return to the notion of "vengeance" described by Susan Jacoby?

2. Should a "hit-man" for the "Mob," who kills a rival criminal boss, be entitled to argue that he should be given a very light sentence because he removed an undesirable person from society?

3. Consider the "victim-impact" approach in ordinary civil litigation. Suppose a poor mother with three children, whose husband has left her, is unable to come up with the rent for January. Would it be just for the landlord to evict her? Should the landlord be allowed to evict her immediately for non-payment of rent? Should the landlord be allowed to evict her after a period of time?

4. Would the following consideration be *relevant* in the (a) legal and (b) moral senses of "relevant": the landlord herself has been left with two children, is renting out one room in her house and desperately needs the rent to make payments on the mortgage, and without the rent will lose her house to the bank? If your answer differs between (a) and (b), what background considerations played a role in your mind in leading to that difference?

5. Suppose the agent for an insurance company tells the victim of an automobile accident, who is badly crippled, that the most that his company will pay as compensation for this kind of accident is fifty thousand dollars, that if the victim wants a penny more the company will litigate the case and drag it out in court for years, and that at the end the victim won't get any more than fifty thousand dollars anyway and will have all of it eaten up in legal costs. Suppose the victim does not consult with a lawyer, but rather asks her family and her friends, and they tell her that she had better take the settlement. She does. Later she meets a lawyer who tells her that if she had threatened to litigate, the insurance company would have easily given her half a million dollars, and she could have won at least two million if she had gone ahead and litigated. Was it unjust for the insurance agent to make the representations he made to the victim? Can he argue that if the victim wasn't clever enough to see through his self-serving threats, she doesn't deserve more than what his company paid her?

6. What if the agent for the insurance company was a lawyer? Does a lawyer have responsibilities for the administration of justice an ordinary agent does not have? This is the question we address in the following section.

1.4 Lawyering and justice

Do the state and the organized bar have an interest in justice? In practice, might it not turn out that they have an interest only in the appearance of justice? Is it not *always* in the interest of rulers to convince the public that justice is being done, irrespective of reality? Kelsen says that legislators and judges *always* say that the law they enact or apply is in conformity with justice. What would Plato say?

What Is Justice?[36]

Hans Kelsen

Plato advocates the opinion that a just man—that means in this connection, a man who obeys the law—and only a just man, is happy; whereas an unjust man—a man who violates the law—is unhappy. Plato says, that "the most just life is the most pleasant."[37] Plato, however, admits that perhaps in one case or another the just man may be unhappy

---

[36] 6–7 (1957).

[37] PLATO, THE LAWS, 662b.

and the unjust man happy. But, asserts the philosopher, it is absolutely necessary that the individuals, subject to the legal order, believe in the truth of the statement that only the just man is happy, even if it should not be true; for otherwise nobody would obey the law. Consequently the government has, according to Plato, the right to spread among the people by means of propaganda the doctrine that the just are happy and the unjust unhappy, even if this doctrine be a lie. If this is a lie, says Plato, it is a very useful lie, for it guarantees obedience to the law. "Could a law giver, who was worth his salt, find any more useful lie than this, or one more effective in persuading all men to act justly in all things willingly and without constraint? ... If I were a legislator, I should endeavour to compel the poets and all the citizens to speak in this sense [that the most just life is the happiest]."[38] The government, then, is fully justified in making use of a useful lie. Plato places justice—and that means here, what the government considers to be justice, namely, lawfulness—above truth; but there is no sufficient reason not to place truth above lawfulness and to repudiate as immoral a governmental propaganda based on lies, even if it serves a good purpose.

Some Greek Trials: Order and Justice In Homer, Hesiod, Aeschylus and Plato[39]

David Luban

Hesiod's view of the primacy of justice appears [in Plato's *The Laws*] as an exoteric, or public, doctrine, promulgated to maintain a city organized esoterically along the lines of the Homeric notion that stability and civic friendship are primary and justice merely secondary. [The quest for justice] is honored in myth even as it is denied in practice.

Plato, I believe, put his finger on an immensely important problem of political psychology. On the Aeschylean elaboration of Homer's view, institutions of justice exist (paradoxically) to stabilize a society rather than to do justice. But if people believe that these institutions do not do justice, if they believe the Aeschylean view [that the institutions exist to promote social order], then they will not respect those institutions, and the institutions will break down—they (paradoxically) will not stabilize the society. Hence the Aeschylean view must remain esoteric, and most people must instead be made to believe in the justice of those institutions.

This is a very contemporary dilemma. The American Bar Association Code of Professional Responsibility requires that "a lawyer should avoid even the appearance of professional impropriety," and explains:

> Continuation of the American concept that we are to be governed by rules of law requires that people have faith that justice can be obtained through our legal system. A lawyer should promote public confidence in our system and in the legal profession.[40]

---

[38] PLATO, THE LAWS, II, par. 663.

[39] 54 TENN. L. REV. 279, 321-24 (1987).

[40] MODEL CODE OF PROFESSIONAL RESPONSIBILITY Canon 9 and EC 9-1 (1979).

This is a troubling rule. Suppose a lawyer is convinced that the legal system does not *deserve* confidence, that it is profoundly corrupt: it sounds as though the lawyer could be disciplined for making these suspicions too public. The rule quotes a judicial opinion: "Confidence in our law, our courts, and in the administration of justice is our supreme interest."[41] If confidence is the *supreme* interest, it follows that it is more important than our law, courts and administration of justice really *deserving* this confidence. One may object that the court could not mean to be saying this, but it is in fact a logical consequence of legal instrumentalism, the view that stability is more important than justice. For stability comes from public confidence in our institutions, whether they deserve it or not; justice, by contrast, means that they deserve it. As Karl Llewellyn wrote, defending an instrumentalist view:

> An impressive ceremonial has a value in making people *feel* that something is being done; this holds, whether the result is right or wrong; and there is some value in an institution which makes men content with fate, whatever that fate may be.[42]

The lawyer must therefore uphold the ceremonial "whether the result is right or wrong," and keep up public confidence in justice even if that confidence is misplaced. The lawyer must join in deceiving the public. Or, in the words of H.L. Mencken, "bosh is the right medicine for boobs."[43]

I believe that the Platonic apotheosis of legal instrumentalism is its refutation. The defining fact about legal institutions that do not do justice is that *they create innocent victims*.

---

[41] Erwin M. Jennings Co. v. DiGenova, 107 Conn. 491, 141 A. 866, 868 (1928), quoted in MODEL CODE OF PROFESSIONAL RESPONSIBILITY Canon 9 n.2 (1979).

[42] Llewellyn, *On Reading and Using the Newer Jurisprudence,* 40 COLUM. L. REV. 610 (1940).

[43] H.L. MENCKEN, *Gamalielese Again, in* A CARNIVAL OF BUNCOMBE 43 (1956).

Questions

1. What is the difference between what is fair and what is perceived to be fair?

2. Do you agree with Luban that lawyers' associations seem to be more concerned with the appearance of justice than with its actuality? What would motivate a professional organization to have this overriding concern?

3. A lawyer is an officer of the court. He or she is required to faithfully observe rules of procedure and rules governing the representation of clients. What if some of those rules lead to an injustice? Should an attorney ever disobey a law because obeying it would cause an injustice to a client?

Utilitarianism[44]

John Stuart Mill

In most if not in all languages, the etymology of the word which corresponds to "just" points distinctly to an origin connected with the ordinances of law. *Justum* is a form of *jussum*, that which has been ordered. *Dikaion* comes directly from *dike*, a suit at law. *Recht*, from which came *right* and *righteous*, is synonymous with law. The courts of justice, the administration of justice, are the courts and the administration of law. *La justice*, in French, is the established term for judicature. I am not committing the fallacy, imputed with some show of truth to Horne Tooke, of assuming that a word must still continue to mean what it originally meant. Etymology is slight of evidence of what the idea now signified is, but the very best evidence of how it sprang up. There can, I think, be no doubt that the *idée mère*, the primitive element, in the formation of the notion of justice was conformity to law. It constituted the entire idea among the Hebrews, up to the birth of Christianity; as might be expected in the case of a people whose laws attempted to embrace all subjects on which precepts were required, and who believed those laws to be a direct emanation from the Supreme Being. But other nations, and in particular the Greeks and Romans, who knew that their laws had been made originally, and still continued to be made, by men, were not afraid to admit that those men might make bad laws; might do, by law, the same things, and from the same motives, which if done by individuals without the sanction of law would be called unjust. And hence the sentiment of injustice came to be attached, not to all violations of law, but only to violations of such laws as *ought* to exist, including such as ought to exist but do not and to laws themselves if supposed to be contrary to what ought to be law. In this manner the idea of law and of its injunctions was still predominant in the notion of justice, even when the laws actually in force ceased to be accepted as the standard of it.

Rethinking Legal Education[45]

Anthony D'Amato

Many clear-minded lay observers throughout history have concluded that justice and injustice are all that matter in a legal system. The person on the street is apt to be skeptical about lawyers who simply know how to twist the meaning of words. Underworld slang for attorney is "mouthpiece." Many novelists have shown how legalism can be employed in the service of state oppression. Historians have explained how the arcane processes of trials and inquisitions have been perverted to serve the ends of the state—or, more specifically, the ends of a group of persons who are in effective control of the state at a given time.

---

[44] From J.S. MILL, UTILITARIANISM, ON LIBERTY, ESSAY ON BENTHAM 302–03 (M. Warnock ed. 1962)(from ch. 5, On the Connection Between Justice and Utility).

[45] 74 MARQUETTE L. REV. 1, 30, 35, 47 (1990).

The grossest forms of injustice can be given the patina of legality by the solemnities of law-words spoken in official settings.[46] Public prosecutors and defense attorneys can lose sight of justice, and in cowardice induced by the relativity of law-words can become capable of unfairness so perverse that they fail to recognize how unfair they have become.

The change I advocate, stated in its simplest and perhaps most controversial manner, is that law schools should stop teaching law. Instead we should teach justice. Justice is the purpose and goal of law. It is the reason law exists. It animates and breathes life into the law. The professional calling of a lawyer is to help achieve justice in society. The skill of an advocate is the ability to convince a judge that his client's cause is a just one and his client should win the lawsuit. The role of a judge is to decide cases justly. Since the judge is presented with plausible legal arguments from both sides, the judge will usually pick the side that she believes *ought* to win.[47] This "ought" is a *moral* imperative; it is part of her sense of justice. It is not a *legal* imperative except to the extent that the judge feels that one side's interpretation of the law is coincident with the dictates of justice. When the judge couches her opinion in terms of "law" (which is indeed the presently acceptable way of presenting a judicial opinion to the legal community), we can interpret her opinion as showing that she has chosen the more deeply sound *legal* position by using justice as a guide to the choice between the two conflicting legal arguments presented by the parties to the court.

Teaching *justice* is a *way* to teach law. Since law is taught by the mental operation of similarity and analogy, and since common law depends on precedents, the legal process works when we compare past decisions to present ones. All we have to add is the normative component: that we *ought* to decide present cases similarly to the way past cases were decided. And this "ought" is provided by the consideration of justice. Justice requires the perpetuation of precedents because that is the only way to treat present litigants fairly. As the old cliche puts it, justice means treating like cases alike. This is not a tautology; it is a profound truth. It is a tautology only at the *verbal* level, but since (I claim that) justice notions are pre-verbal, what case is "like" another is a primitive pre-verbal notion that cannot be defeated by verbal logic constructs.

In order to study whether a past decision is similar to a present case, we have to know the facts of the past decision and compare it to present facts. Legal *training* thus consists in reading hundreds and hundreds of cases and comparing them with each other and with present fact situations. In doing this work, we will sharpen our sense of justice by honing

---

[46] Compare what Judge Richard Posner says about the role of a judge. A judge is "a decision maker in a system of government, and such a decision maker must be concerned not only with doing substantive justice in the case at hand but also with maintaining a legal fabric that includes considerations of precedent, of legislative authority, of the framing of issues by counsel, of the facts of record, and so forth." R. Posner, The Problems of Jurisprudence 156–57 (1990).

[47] Of course, judges do not necessarily decide cases according to their sense of justice. The possibility always exists that bribery, corruption, political dealing, conflict of interest, and prejudice can eclipse for a judge the dictates of justice. *See* G. Spence, With Justice For None 101–02 (1989) ("I saw a judge throw out the just case of a widow whose husband had been murdered, because the jury's verdict would have been an embarrassment to the governor who had appointed him. I saw a judge permit the prosecution of an innocent man because the man was unpopular in the judge's club.")

our ability to recognize patterns of factual similarity and analogy.

Teaching justice instead of "law" does not entail wholesale jettisoning of existing courses or casebooks. I am talking about a change of focus, of emphasis—but it is a change that would reverberate in every course and in every class session. The question we should ask of every case is not, "what is the rule of law that this case lays down?" but rather, "was justice done to the parties?" If we find that justice was not done, we should examine how the legal system went wrong. Perhaps it went wrong because of bad lawyering. Perhaps the "rule" that the case could be said to exemplify should have been interpreted differently by the court. Perhaps certain facts were not adduced in court because a lawyer thought that those facts were not legally relevant. Indeed, bad lawyering—a not surprising product of the way law schools train future lawyers—is often associated with blunders at the trial level concerning the introduction of evidence; the incompetent attorney is too readily convinced of the legal irrelevancy of potent evidence. Yet if we are trying to achieve justice, we may find that facts that appeared to be legally irrelevant are significant from a justice standpoint. Since the rules of evidence are intended in the aggregate to promote justice, any one of them is open to challenge or reinterpretation.

Questions

1. Recall Kelsen's position that doing justice is deciding a case according to the law. What if "the law" leads to an unjust result? Imagine a judge in a country (it could be any country, including your own) who, in deciding a case, finds that in her own view, the law clearly points to a particular decision. But also in her view, the law is clearly unjust. Should she decide the case according to the law or according to justice? (We will return to this question in the last chapter.)

2. Which of the following reasons more closely reflects your own decision to become a lawyer: (a) to faithfully serve the law of the land? (b) to help achieve justice in society?

A Fair Jury

CHAPTER TWO

2.1 Improper argument

There is a common saying, "Justice is blind." What does it mean? Is the person making the statement *criticizing* justice? Or *praising* it? *Should* justice be blind? If not entirely, should justice *wear blinders*?

Laypersons as well as lawyers are well aware, from television shows such as *Perry Mason* and *L.A. Law* and from numerous books and magazines, that there are strict controls over what can be said in a courtroom. Lawyers are always saying, "Objection, your honor!" and the judge often says, "Objection sustained. The jury is instructed to disregard the preceding remarks."

There are lengthy and detailed rules of evidence that govern what can be said and what can't be said in court. What is the point of all of this? Why can't people just say what they want to say? Why isn't a litigant allowed to make any argument whatsoever that she believes would be helpful to her case? Why isn't the other side given the same degree of latitude?

In fact, the rules of evidence impose strict "blinders" on the jury. The jury is not allowed to hear everything a litigant wants it to hear, because of the fear that injustice might result. We apparently want a jury with blinders and earmuffs.

But how narrowly should the jury's vision be constrained with those blinders? How much or how little should the jury be permitted to hear? Should the jury be allowed to *see* the litigants and the witnesses? Should the jury be allowed to discover anything about the case outside the courtroom?

Should courtrooms try to depersonalize lawsuits? Recall that in English courts the judges and the advocates wear wigs. Do the wigs tend to depersonalize the judges and lawyers, so that less attention will be drawn to their personal characteristics with greater resulting attention paid to the quality of their arguments? If so, might this not have a detrimental effect upon litigants who need emotional and empathetic understanding in order to persuade the fact-finder of the merits of their cause? Or, on the contrary, does it contribute to an "even playing field"?

When we consider how little or how much the jury can be told about a case, we have to consider not only *factual* material (such as the reputation and character of the witnesses), but also *legal* material, such as the legal rules that apply to the case. To a large extent, we want juries to decide *facts* and not law. But is it possible to confine the jury's role to fact-finding? Doesn't the underlying law of a case *characterize* the facts? And, in turn, doesn't the underlying justice of a case characterize the law?

At the end of each trial, the opposing lawyers are permitted to make "closing arguments" to the jury. The attorneys sum up their views of the evidence that the jury has seen and heard, characterizing that evidence in the light most favorable to their own clients' interest. The moment of legal decision is almost at hand. The jury is about to retire into a secure and secluded room. Everything that has been said at the trial about facts, and everything that has been said about the law, now boil down just to assertions and rhetoric. It is up to the jury to render a verdict based upon justice.

But how can a jury know what justice is when, in the name of justice, they have not been allowed to see or hear certain things? This question is equivalent to using "justice is blind" as a *criticism*. Maybe we should ask the opposite question: can a jury deliver a just verdict *only* when what it has seen and what it has heard has not been contaminated by irrelevant and prejudicial evidence?

Questions such as these have been asked throughout the history of legal systems. The answers may change as perceptions about justice change. The questions in a sense are more enduring than the answers. Yet questions are worthless unless we *try* to answer them. In the cases and materials that follow, you are invited to reflect upon how the present legal system in the United States has attempted to answer—or perhaps in some instances to avoid answering—these and related questions.

Rojas v. Richardson (Rojas I)

703 F.2d 186
United States Court of Appeals,
Fifth Circuit
April 21, 1983
Rehearing Granted Aug. 29, 1983

Gregory L. Ceshker, Julianne May Young, Dallas, Texas, for plaintiff-appellant.

Richard Grainger, Tyler, Texas, for defendants-appellees.

Appeal from the United States District Court for the Eastern District of Texas.

Before RUBIN, JOHNSON and WILLIAMS, Circuit Judges.

JERRE S. WILLIAMS, Circuit Judge.

Paulino Izaguirre Rojas worked as a ranch hand for Robert Richardson, a partner in the M and R Cattle Company along with Kenneth McGee. On December 4, 1980, Rojas met with Richardson and another employee for the day's work. Richardson furnished Rojas with a horse named Jet. Rojas had ridden this horse a few times before. When Rojas mounted Jet, the horse began bucking and running. Rojas finally was thrown from the horse and severely injured. Rojas later filed this suit in federal district court against Richardson, McGee, and the partnership, invoking diversity jurisdiction, 28 U.S.C. § 1332(a)(2). Rojas claimed negligence in furnishing an inadequately broken horse with a dangerous bridle. In addition, he claimed a failure to give reasonable warnings regarding the dangers of the horse or its bridle. In the alternative, he sought payment of his medical expenses under the terms of his oral employment contract. The defendants denied these claims and countered with a defense of contributory negligence. After a full trial, the jury returned a verdict for the defendants.

Rojas brings a timely appeal, primarily seeking a new trial based on irreparable jury prejudice from the defense counsel's reference during closing argument to Rojas as an illegal alien. . . . We reverse and remand on the basis of defense counsel's incendiary remarks to the jury during closing argument.

Objections to Closing Argument

Rojas' major argument is that defense counsel tainted the propriety of the trial by reference to Rojas as an illegal alien. Rojas claims that identification as an illegal alien was unsupported in the evidence, completely irrelevant to the issues before the court, and inherently prejudicial to a full and fair hearing on the merits. Rojas asserts the emotional weight of the remark by pointing out that the public education for undocumented aliens case, *Doe* v. *Plyler*, 628 F.2d 448 (5th Cir. 1980), *aff'd*, 457 U.S. 202 (1982), dealt with the school district from Tyler, Texas, where the trial in this case was held. *Doe* v. *Plyler* was pending in the United States Supreme Court when the trial was held. Rojas urges that the improper argument was directed especially toward the jury foreman, an employee of the Tyler Independent School District. He urges that any general prejudice of the jurors toward undocumented workers likely would have operated against him in this civil trial.

The employers have no serious counter to the substance of these charges. Rather, they claim that this issue was not preserved for appeal because no objection was made in the district court to use of the term "illegal alien."

We have checked the trial record carefully, and indeed find no objection during trial to use of the term "illegal alien." Rojas directs our attention to his request for a motion in limine made before trial.[1] Paragraphs 2 and 3 of this motion

in limine would have barred the use of testimony concerning the status of Rojas as a "wetback" or illegal alien, and the presentation of any evidence that the witnesses in the case ever employed undocumented workers.[2] These two paragraphs of the motion in limine were denied.[3] Rojas claims, first, that the denial of the motion in limine is an appealable error in its own right, and, second, that the request for the motion in limine should be sufficient to preserve the error regarding defense counsel's use of the term illegal alien.

First, we conclude that the denial of the motion in limine is not a sufficient ground for reversal in this case. Denial of a motion in limine rarely imposes a serious hardship on the requesting party, since the affected party can make a subsequent objection if the evidence is ever offered at trial. That later objection is the better time to evaluate the possible exclusion of testimony because it is at that time that the claims of prejudice and irrelevance move out of the abstract context of a motion in limine into the real world of an actual speaker and a specific statement. In the case before us, there is no particular injury claimed from the denial of the motion in limine other than that connected with the admission of later statements referring to Rojas as an illegal alien. We find the issue better framed by the "actual—instead of hypothetical—circumstances at trial." *Collins* v. *Wayne Corp.*, 621 F.2d 777,

---

[1] A "motion in limine" is a pre-trial request for an order to suppress evidence at trial. Advance suppression of evidence requires blanket exclusion, since the judge is not ruling in response to an actual objection to a single question. Authority for the motion in limine cannot be found in any of the published rules governing federal civil procedure—either the Federal Rules of Civil Procedure or local rules promulgated by each panel of United States district courts. The motion belongs instead to the vast non-statutory ("common") law of procedure. [Eds.]

[2] The pertinent part of plaintiff's first motion in limine provided:

II

Whether the Plaintiff was or ever has been in the United States illegally, was a "wetback" or has ever been in the United States without proper authorization and/or documentation or the mode or manner in which he physically came into the United States prior to his injuries made the basis of this suit.

III

Whether any witness employs or has employed workers who are illegal aliens, "wetbacks" or are in the United States illegally or without proper authorization and/or documentation.

[3] All other portions of the plaintiff's motion in limine, and all parts of the defendants' motion in limine, were granted. These portions of the motions are not at issue in this case.

784 (5th Cir. 1980). Consequently, we look at the error, if any, committed when the actual statements regarding alienage were admitted, rather than when the blanket hypothetical requests to limit such statements were denied during pretrial motions.

Rojas urges that the motion in limine itself was a sufficient presentation of his concerns to the district court to preserve the assignment of error on appeal. This Circuit, however, has held otherwise. In *Collins v. Wayne Corp.*, *supra*, the defendant corporation in a products liability action had cross-examined the plaintiff's expert witness regarding his fees in prior cases. No objection was made at trial, although the plaintiffs had tried to suppress such testimony through a pretrial motion in limine. Judge Johnson stated the general rule that an overruled motion in limine does not preserve error on appeal.

> Plaintiff's counsel never objected to cross-examination of Severy about fees he had earned in prior cases. Plaintiffs therefore cannot predicate error on this cross-examination. Fed.R.Evid. 103(a)(l). The overruling of a motion in limine is not reversible error; only a proper objection at trial can preserve error for appellate review. Motions in limine are frequently made in the abstract and in anticipation of some hypothetical circumstance that may not develop at trial. When a party files numerous motions in limine, the trial court may not pay close attention to each one, believing that many of them are purely hypothetical. Thus, a party whose motion in limine has been overruled must object when the error he sought to prevent with his motion is about to occur at trial. This will give the trial court an opportunity to reconsider the grounds of the motion in light of the actual—instead of hypothetical—circumstances at trial.

Id. at 784.

The general rule is that where "no good reason is shown for the failure of appellant's trial counsel to object to the admission of evidence, the objection is deemed to have been waived." [Citing cases]

Rojas relies upon the case of *Reyes v. Missouri Pac. R.R. Co.*, 589 F.2d 791 (5th Cir. 1979), in an attempt to carve a broad exception out of *Collins*. In *Reyes*, the plaintiff brought negligence claims against a railroad after he was run over by a train. The railroad claimed that Reyes was drunk on the night in question and had fallen asleep on the tracks. During pretrial proceedings, Reyes made a motion in limine to exclude evidence relating to four prior convictions for public intoxication. The motion was denied. Reyes then presented that evidence himself to the jury and later appealed the use of that evidence at trial.

This Circuit allowed such an appeal, rejecting the railroad's suggestion that *Reyes* had waived error by volunteering the information rather than objecting at trial. "After the trial court refused to grant Reyes' motion *in limine* to exclude the evidence, he had no choice but to elicit this information on direct examination in an effort to ameliorate its prejudicial effect. Error was sufficiently preserved by making the motion *in limine*. See Fed.R.Evid. 103, 28 U.S.C.A." *Id*. at 793 n.2.

Reyes, however, stands only as an example of the general rule, not as a departure. Objection must be made in the trial court unless a good reason exists not to do so. In *Reyes*, the good reason was a valid trial strategy to attempt to soften the blow of damaging information by delivering the independent punch to the jury. An objection to one's own testimony is an absurdity. It is impossible. This Circuit consequently found the offensive use of damaging information to fall outside the general rule requiring a timely objection.

Rojas, however, offers no justification for his failure to object. He made no offensive use of his status within this country, whatever that status may be. He makes no other claim of good cause for not raising the objection at trial. In the absence of such a showing we have no choice but to find that he cannot claim an objection was lodged to the use of the phrase "illegal alien." Fed.R.Evid. 103(a)(l). *See Brown & Root, Inc. v. Big Rock Corp.*, 383 F.2d 662 (5th Cir. 1967) ("improper" and "inexcusable" appeals to sympathy and sectional prejudices of the jury are not appealable absent a timely objection at trial). Rojas' only possible recourse is establishing "plain error."[4]

Closing Argument as Plain Error

Even if Rojas has waived his right to appeal the use of the phrase "illegal alien", however, this Court is not precluded from reviewing the use of the phrase at trial. Fed.R.Evid. 103(d) provides: "Nothing in this rule [requiring objection to preserve appealability] precludes taking notice of plain errors affecting substantial rights although they were not brought to the attention of the court."[5] Our authority to review, we note, is limited to "plain errors," and the errors must affect "substantial rights." We find that allegations unsupported by the record that Rojas was an illegal alien might well have a serious and negative effect on his substantial right to an impartial jury. The only serious issue is whether the allegations rise to the level of "plain error."

The plain error rule is "not a run-of-the-mill remedy." [Citing cases] It is invoked "only in exceptional circumstances to avoid a miscarriage of justice." [Citing cases] The exact delineation of plain error is difficult to articulate. We have defined plain error as error which is "both obvious and substantial." [Citing cases] But such elegant phraseology yields little guidance. The determination still rests ultimately on the facts of each case.

Perhaps the most telling guidelines were laid down by Justice Stone in 1936, when he wrote:

> In exceptional circumstances, especially in criminal cases, appellate courts, in the public interest, may, of their motion, notice errors to which no exception has been taken, if the errors are obvious, or if they otherwise seri-

ously affect the *fairness, integrity, or public reputation of judicial proceedings*.

United States v. Atkinson, 297 U.S. 157, 160, 56 S.Ct. 391, 392, 80 L.Ed. 555 (1936) (emphasis added). Following the clarion call of Justice Stone's words, we must hold that the "fairness, integrity, or public reputation" of the proceedings in this case were adversely affected by the closing jury argument of defense counsel. The closing remarks included this paragraph:

> I hope—I hope—that you don't, because Mr. Rojas is an alien, give him any more benefit than you would any United States citizen who comes in this Court. If the situation were reversed and you or I were in Mexico— were illegal aliens in Mexico—I would hope Mexico would open up their Courts, would open up their job market, would open up their public schools, would open up their State hospitals, as we have in this country for Mr. Rojas. Certainly he is—I'm not saying we shouldn't do those things, but he shouldn't be entitled to any extra benefits because he is an illegal alien in this country than would any other citizen of the United States be entitled.

These remarks prejudiced the jury on two counts. First, by introducing irrelevant and unproven allegations that Rojas was an illegal alien, the defense clearly was appealing to the prejudice and bias of members of the jury on the basis of national origin. Although there was justification for presenting Rojas' Mexican citizenship to the jury to establish diversity jurisdiction, 28 U.S.C. §1332(a)(2), his status as an "illegal" alien was completely irrelevant to the negligence claims the jury was to evaluate. Furthermore, the closing reference to "illegal alien" could have placed a prejudicial gloss on the many references throughout trial to Rojas as an "alien." Having laid a strong foundation through use of the term "alien" throughout trial, even counsel's single reference to the incendiary, derogatory expression "illegal alien" is prejudicial. Finally, the allegation that Rojas was in the country illegally is unsupported in the record.

Texas courts have found plain error in jury remarks that appeal to racial or ethnic bias. *Penate v. Berry*, 348 S.W.2d 167 (Tex.Civ.App.—El Paso 1961, *writ ref'd n.r.e.*), involved remarks to

---

[4] Judge Rubin joins in this opinion because *Collins* is the law of the circuit. However, should the issue be again properly presented, he would vote to reconsider *Collins*. Objections in limine, fully briefed and argued at a time when they can be given adequate consideration by both counsel and the court, deserve to be encouraged, in preference to the cryptic objections hurriedly argued and hastily ruled on at trial, unless the circumstances are such that a ruling can properly be made only at the trial.

[5] The rule has its source in Rule 52(b) of the Federal Rules of Criminal Procedure. Advisory Committee Notes, FED. R. EVID. 103.

the jury that an alien has no right to "come into court and reach your hands into the pockets of an *American* citizen. . . ." The court reversed and remanded for new trial, despite absence of a timely objection at trial. *See also Texas Employers' Insurance Ass'n v. Jones*, 361 S.W.2d 725 (Tex. Civ.App.—Waco 1962, *writ ref'd n.r.e.*) (claims to racial or religious prejudice justify new trial).

Second, these remarks were an impermissible invocation of the "golden rule" argument. As we recently explained,

> What every lawyer should know is that a plea to the jury that they "should put themselves in the shoes of the plaintiff and do unto him as they would have done unto them under similar circumstances. . . ." [is] improper because it encourages the jury to depart from neutrality and to decide the case on the basis of personal interest and bias rather than on the evidence.

Loose v. Offshore Navigation, Inc., 670 F.2d 493, 496 (5th Cir. 1982) . . . . The fact that the statement in this case was an inverse incantation of this golden rule is insufficient to validate the partiality inherent in the argument. *Loose, supra.* The "golden rule" argument, while not plain error, is normally ground for new trial. *Id.*

The closing remarks of defense counsel were highly prejudicial and a blatant appeal to jury bias. Although the district court gave a jury instruction emphasizing equal access to justice, even this instruction was ambiguous. The jury was instructed:

> You are instructed that all persons are equal before the law, and this case should be considered and decided by you as an action between persons of equal standing in the community, of equal worth, and holding the same or similar stations in life. The law is no respecter of persons. All persons, including partnerships, and other lawful organizations, stand equal before the law, and are

to be dealt with as equals in a Court of Justice.

While its wording might have been adequate to indicate that aliens must be treated equally, it was not adequate to tell the jury that "illegal aliens" are "equal before the law." A jury could readily conclude that someone who is "illegal" is not "equal before the law" to law abiding citizens and jurors. We are not convinced that the jury instruction could rebuild the "fairness, integrity, or public reputation of jury proceedings" that Justice Stone admonished us to protect, see *Atkinson*, 297 U.S. at 160, 56 S.Ct. at 392. As we first noted in *Dunn v. United States*, 307 F.2d 883, 887 (5th Cir. 1962), "if you throw a skunk into the jury box, you can't instruct the jury not to smell it." Some references are so prejudicial that it is difficult for curative instructions to resuscitate fairness. See *e.g.*, *Pride Transport Co. v. Hughes*, 591 S.W.2d 631 (Tex.Civ.App.—Eastland 1979, *writ ref'd n.r.e.*) (disclosure of defendant's insurance coverage can be grounds for mistrial in Texas). Even assuming that a proper jury instruction could have cured prejudice, this instruction did not do so.

We hold that the obvious and blatant appeal in this case to racial and ethnic prejudice is plain error. In consideration of this impropriety, combined with an additional "golden rule" appeal to the jury's partiality, we must reverse the judgment of the district court and order a new trial.

Conclusion

We have examined other exceptions to the manner in which the trial was conducted and find no further grounds for reversal. There is substantial evidence to support the jury verdict in this case. However, on the basis of the defendants' closing references to Rojas as an "illegal alien" and their appeal to jury prejudice, we must reverse the judgment of the district court and remand for new trial.

REVERSED AND REMANDED.

Rojas v. Richardson (Rojas II)

713 F.2d 116
United States Court of Appeals,
Fifth Circuit
August 29, 1983

Appeal from the United States District Court for the Eastern District of Texas.

Before RUBIN, JOHNSON and WILLIAMS, Circuit Judges.

ON PETITION FOR REHEARING

JERRE S. WILLIAMS, Circuit Judge.

This suit involves a claim by Paulino Izaguirre Rojas, who worked as a ranchhand for Robert Richardson, a partner in the M and R Cattle Company. On December 4, 1980, while at work, Rojas was thrown from the horse he was riding and severely injured. He brought this suit in federal court invoking diversity jurisdiction. He claimed negligence in furnishing him with a dangerous horse and bridle. After a full trial, the jury returned a verdict denying him recovery.

In our prior opinion [*Rojas I*] we reversed the district court and remanded for a new trial on the ground that counsel for the defendant in closing argument made reference to Rojas as an "illegal alien," coupling that argument with the Golden Rule argument: "If the situation were reversed and you or I were in Mexico—were illegal aliens in Mexico—I would hope Mexico would open up their Courts, would open up their job market, would open up their public schools, would open up their State hospitals, as we have in this country for Mr. Rojas." He then went on to say that Mr. Rojas "shouldn't be entitled to any extra benefits because he is an illegal alien in this country than would any other citizen of the United States be entitled."

It was known throughout the trial that Rojas was a citizen of Mexico since the jurisdiction of the court was based upon this fact. But as the case was presented to this Court by the briefs of both parties, the entire trial was devoid of any reference to Rojas being an "illegal alien" until the closing argument of the counsel for the defense. Under these circumstances, we found the argument detailed above so highly prejudicial to the jury that we reversed and remanded for a new trial even though no objection had been made by the plaintiff's counsel at the time the argument was advanced. To reach this result, therefore, we had to find that allowing the argument to go to the jury was "plain error" on the part of the district court. On motion for rehearing, defendant Richardson brings to our attention an important aspect of this case which was not in the record and was not referred to in the briefs, although the briefs focused upon the reference to "illegal alien." The defendant on rehearing supplemented the record with the transcript of the proceedings on voir dire. Those proceedings made clear that it was made known to the prospective jurors at that time that plaintiff, Rojas, was an "illegal alien."

The sequence of events under which this occurred is revealed by the supplemented record. The trial court overruled the plaintiff's motion in limine to bar reference to plaintiff as an illegal alien at the trial. No exception was taken to this ruling by plaintiff's counsel. The voir dire began immediately, on the same day. It appears clear that as a matter of tactics, the plaintiff's attorney himself brought to the attention of the jury the fact that the plaintiff was an illegal alien as an obvious means of heading off a later dramatic presentation of this fact by the defendant. The motion for rehearing also points out that there was one brief mention during trial of the fact that Rojas was an alien "without papers" and, therefore, was "as we say 'an illegal alien.'" This one brief and casual mention in the record is the only reference to the fact that plaintiff was an undocumented alien in the entire record after the voir dire until the closing argument by counsel for the defendant.

The critical point, however, is that contrary to the way the case was presented to the panel in the briefs of the parties, the jury was aware throughout the entire case that the plaintiff Rojas was an "illegal alien." The major ground upon which we found the argument so prejudicial as to be plain error thus has been removed by the supplementing of the record and our consideration of the voir dire examination.

In our prior opinion we referred to the argument as "highly prejudicial and a blatant appeal to jury bias." We still characterize this argument with these terms. But in view of the knowledge which the jury had throughout the trial as to plaintiff's legal status, we cannot find that in the absence of objection by plaintiff's counsel this argument was so prejudicial as to be plain error, even when coupled with the Golden Rule argument. Plain error is not a "run of the mill remedy". *United States v. Gerald*, *supra*, 624 F.2d at 1299. It is invoked "only in exceptional circumstances to avoid a miscarriage of justice." *Eaton v. United States*, 398 F.2d 485, 486 (5th Cir.), *cert. denied*, 393 U.S. 937. We cannot find exceptional circumstances once it is shown to us on rehearing that the jury knew throughout the trial that Rojas had the status of an illegal alien.

We therefore GRANT the motion for rehearing, and upon rehearing we set aside our earlier decision and AFFIRM the judgment of the district court.

AFFIRMED.

Federal Rules of Evidence

Rule 401. Definition of "Relevant Evidence"

"Relevant evidence" means evidence having any tendency to make the existence of any fact that is of consequence to the determination of the action more probable or less probable than it would be without the evidence.

Rule 402. Relevant Evidence Generally Admissible; Irrelevant Evidence Inadmissible

All relevant evidence is admissible, except as otherwise provided by the Constitution of the United States, by Act of Congress, by these rules, or by other rules prescribed by the Supreme Court pursuant to statutory authority. Evidence which is not relevant is not admissible.

Rule 403. Exclusion of Relevant Evidence on Grounds of Prejudice, Confusion, or Waste of Time

Although relevant, evidence may be excluded if its probative value is substantially outweighed by the danger of unfair prejudice, confusion of the issues, or misleading the jury, or by considerations of undue delay, waste of time, or needless presentation of cumulative evidence.

Notes and Questions

1. Rojas was in Mexico when he filed his action against Richardson. The ranchers—Robert Richardson and Kenneth McGee—are prominent citizens in Tyler. Rojas worked as a ranchhand for their firm, the M and R Cattle Company. Work on a ranch, unlike a farm, is not seasonal. Some ranchhands stay for a month or two; others stay for years.

Undocumented aliens earn wages that average considerably lower than documented aliens or citizens. The average annual income of an undocumented alien, at the time of the Rojas case, was $7,000.[6]

2. Appellate courts are reluctant to order a new trial when counsel does not make a contemporaneous objection to the alleged error. Yet trial lawyers often dislike objecting frequently in front of jurors, who may get the impression from the objections that the lawyer is uncooperative, has something to hide, or is generally an unpleasant person. Moreover, an objection denied draws attention to the response to the question. Jurors may give more weight to the response—listen more carefully to it, think of it as especially relevant. Yet every American system of procedure requires lawyers to object to questions in order to preserve the right to appeal a judge's error in permitting the question.

Consider the costs of re-trying a case. Had the lawyer made a timely objection, the judge could have corrected error in the proceedings right then and there. Failure to object wastes scarce resources. Also, if the appeals court reverses a decision where prejudicial evidence came up at trial but was not objected to by the party who now complains on appeal about the prejudice, then future attorneys will be encouraged not to make objections at trial. Will they not calculate that (l) the jury may give them the decision anyway, and (2) if the jury doesn't, they can always appeal the case on the ground of prejudice? Doesn't allowing an appeal without objection permit attorneys to "play both sides of the street"?

3. What was the role of the "motion in limine"? Judges disfavor such motions, which ask them to rule wholesale on testimonial admissibility in advance of trial. They prefer instead, as Judge Williams explains in *Rojas*, to rule retail on actual objections to single questions in a concrete line of questions. Only a line of questions in flight reveals exactly where the testimony they elicit is landing. Even so, orders in limine are appropriate for two purposes:

(1) to sharpen or clarify terms of the pre-trial order—the screenplay judges compose beforehand to set down the roles witnesses and documents will play at trial so that there will be no surprise.[7] A lawyer concerned that a pre-trial order will permit his adversary to ask irrelevant and injurious questions uses a motion in limine to have the scope of the pre-trial order narrowed. The pre-trial order states what testimony the judge will permit; the order in limine, the testimony she will not permit out of all the testimony she is permitting;

(2) to forbid questions designed to elicit testimony that will prejudice a party. Unanswered questions accomplish prejudice simply by inducing an adversary to object to them on the grounds of prejudice.

4. Rojas' attorney was familiar with the *Reyes* precedent.[8] Were Rojas' rights clear

---

[6] *See* E. HARWOOD, IN LIBERTY'S SHADOW 14 (1986).

[7] Rule 16(e) of the Federal Rules of Civil Procedure requires federal trial judges to issue a pre-trial order on the eve of trial after conferring with the parties, listing documents each party plans to introduce, witnesses each will examine, and summarizing testimony each party expects to elicit from the witnesses. Parties may not casually depart from the scenario of the order.

[8] In a telephone conversation on August 3, l987, Rojas' trial lawyer, Gregory Ceshker, Esq., told one of the authors that he made a deliberate decision not to raise an objection to his opponent's inflammatory argument to the jury, relying consciously and directly on *Reyes*.

under *Reyes*? Can we distinguish *Rojas*? In *Rojas II* why didn't Judge Williams also revisit the *Reyes* branch of *Rojas I*? Is the reliability of the *Reyes* exception to the rule in *Collins* clear after *Rojas II*?

Should the appeals court have overruled *Reyes*? Or *Collins*? (Note Judge Rubin's suggestion in a Note in *Rojas I*.) Suppose your answer is "Yes, *Reyes* should have been overruled." Where does that leave Rojas? Isn't he being sacrificed just because his case happens to be the occasion by which the court wants to announce its overruling of *Reyes*? Would that be fair?

Should your answer turn on Rojas' reasonable expectations? Did his attorneys reasonably expect to be able to rely on *Reyes*? Should they have known that *Reyes* was an inherently unstable case, one that would be overruled as soon as the court realized that it allowed attorneys to play both sides of the street? But shouldn't attorneys always be allowed to rely on direct precedent? Should a court ever overrule one of its precedents? We will be taking up these and related questions in a later chapter on Retroactivity.

5. Can we explain the result of *Rojas II* simply on the ground that the appeals court was so upset that counsel had not told the court all the facts during *Rojas I* (i.e., the facts about the voir dire) that the court decided to "punish" Rojas' attorneys by reversing *Rojas I*? If so, was Rojas the victim of a different kind of prejudice—intellectual prejudice by the judges on the Court of Appeals? Or *should* the judges have properly been upset by this failure of disclosure?

Why should Rojas' attorneys be "punished" at all? Wasn't it primarily the fault of the *defendant's* attorneys that they did not tell the Court of Appeals in *Rojas I* that the issue of illegal alienage came up during the voir dire? Wasn't it their burden to argue that their closing argument was not prejudicial because of what had happened during voir dire? If so, why did the Court "reward" them by rescinding its previous order for a new trial?

Should justice to a client depend so directly on procedural decisions a lawyer has made or failed to make? On broader and subtler differences of lawyering? Is the court's role to supervise the rules of a game, whose results we support because the game has been played correctly? Or to find the truth about the dispute between parties, even though their lawyers misplay the game?[9]

6. Was the argument of the ranchers' lawyer objectionable simply because he referred to Rojas as an "illegal alien," or because he made *statements* about illegal aliens that were calculated to inflame the prejudice of the jury? If the latter, should the jurors' awareness of Rojas' status as a result of the voir dire render the appeal to prejudice less harmful?

7. In *Rojas I* Judge Williams quotes Justice Stone's "guidelines" for appellate courts "noticing" errors to which no exception has been taken. Appellate courts may notice error

---

[9] As you analyze the ranchers' lawyer's argument in terms of Rule 403 of the Federal Rules of Evidence, consider whether the argument was at all relevant. Prior to 1952 Rojas' status as an undocumented alien might have been relevant, because some courts were refusing the requests of undocumented aliens to enforce contracts. Then, Richardson might have defended on the ground that Rojas lacked the capacity to sue. In 1952 Congress ended the debility under contract, in part because employers (against whom sanctions were heavy) out of wages. By 1983 testimony about Rojas' status would not have been relevant to determining the *validity* of his contract of employment with Richardson. Would it have been relevant to the *contents* of the contract?

only "[i]n exceptional circumstances . . . in the public interest." In other words, when the sole consequence of tolerating error is unfairness to a litigant whose lawyer failed to object, the appeals court won't save the lawyer's skin by noticing error. Why not?

A further condition on the appeals court's power, according to Justice Stone, is that errors must either be obvious or they must "seriously affect the fairness, integrity, or public reputation of judicial proceedings." Whether or not the error in Rojas' trial was obvious (why should "obviousness" be a criterion?), Judge Williams holds "that the fairness, integrity, or public reputation of the proceedings in this case were adversely affected by the closing jury argument of the defense counsel." Isn't the judge deciding in the first opinion to send the case back to trial in Tyler, not because the argument of the ranchers' lawyer harmed Rojas, but because arguments of the sort he made "seriously affect the fairness, integrity, or public reputation of judicial proceedings"? The plain error rule, remember, does not save parties for their own sake, but for the sake of the "public reputation of judicial proceedings."

Why then in the rehearing opinion does Judge Williams conclude that "[w]e cannot find exceptional circumstances once it is shown to us on rehearing that the jury knew throughout the trial that Rojas had the status of an illegal alien"?

8. Would Judge Williams have preferred to destroy all copies of his first opinion, and simply issue a new one that would be published for the world to read?

In a celebrated case involving claims against a psychotherapist, the California Supreme Court issued a full opinion, reported as *Tarasoff v. Regents of Univ. of Cal.*, 529 P.2d 553, 118 Cal. Rptr. 129 (1974), then granted a rehearing and issued a full opinion two years later, reported in 17 Cal.3d 425, 551 P.2d 334, 131 Cal. Rptr. 14 (1976). As you can see from these citations, the first opinion was not printed in the official reports of the California Supreme Court whereas the second opinion was. Interestingly, the second opinion makes no mention of or reference to the first. To be sure, the second opinion is not a drastic departure; it retains the basic holding, but with some differences, including a change from liability to no-liability of the California police who were one of the defendants. Apparently the California Supreme Court used its authority to keep the first opinion out of the official state Supreme Court reports, but could not undo the fact that the first opinion had been reported in the commercial reporter systems.

Should courts ever have the power to delete a prior opinion from the public records? Should they have the power, which apparently many courts exercise today, to withhold an opinion from publication entirely?

9. Rojas became a quadriplegic as a result of his accident.[10] Though the University of Texas hospital at Tyler cared for him, Texas and federal medical assistance programs do not reimburse hospitals for the treatment of undocumented aliens.[11] The hospital would thus have put a "hospital lien" on any judgment Rojas won against the ranchers. The hospital's "shadow" on the litigation made settlement all the more difficult.

---

[10] Telephone conversation of August 3, 1987 with Gregory Ceshker, Esq.

[11] Local hospitals in Tyler, as in other parts of the country, never ask questions about residency status. According to a physician practicing in Tyler, hospitals never turn in patients known to be undocumented aliens.

10. Was justice done to Rojas? To the ranchers?

Comment on Procedural Justice, Queues and Lotteries

You may have been surprised how little in the two *Rojas* opinions seemed to turn on dispensing justice to Rojas as an individual. You will meet this attitude of proceduralism over and over in your practice of law: law often seems to tell us only *how* to make decisions about disputes but not *what* decisions. The way to whether a decision is correct is to scrutinize the application of procedures the legal system uses for deciding disputes of the kind involved in that decision. If the legal personnel—lawyers and judges—correctly follow the procedures, then the decision is legally correct, even if we have independent reason to know that it is not correct. If the legal personnel do not correctly follow the procedures, then the decision is incorrect, even if, for example, they departed from the procedures only to get information assuring us that the procedurally flawed decision is correct.

John Rawls has distinguished three sorts of procedural justice.[12] Perfect procedural justice assumes an independent criterion for deciding whether a result is just, and also a procedure that is sure to give the just result. "To illustrate [perfect procedural justice]," he writes,[13]

> consider the simplest case of fair division. A number of men are to divide a cake: assuming that the fair division is an equal one, which procedure, if any, will give this outcome? Technicalities aside, the obvious solution is to have one man divide the cake and get the last piece, the others being allowed their pick before him. He will divide the cake equally, since in this way he assures for himself the largest share possible.

Imperfect procedural justice assumes an independent criterion for correct outcomes, but no feasible procedure which is sure to reach them. Rawls says that legal trials exemplify this sort of procedural justice. Pure procedural justice assumes that there is no independent criterion for the right result. All we have is a correct or fair procedure. Gambling, according to Rawls, is an example of this sort of procedural justice.

Actually, two compelling notions of justice, which Rawls does not mention, flow from or are associated with pure procedural justice. These are the *justice of lotteries* and the *justice of queues*—two procedures for allocating scarce goods that seem to assume that there is no independent criterion for the right result.

Queues dominate everyday life—lining up to buy theater tickets in Manhattan, or some consumer goods in the Soviet Union (the Soviets have a journal devoted to the mathematical study of queues). But queues also work powerfully in our legal system. "First in time first in right" can be found everywhere in property law and in other guises, such as "priority" in bankruptcy.[14]

---

[12] *See* J. RAWLS, A THEORY OF JUSTICE 85–86 (1971).

[13] *Ibid.*, at 85.

[14] *See, e.g.*, Symposium, *Time, Property Rights, and the Common Law,* 64 WASH. U.L.Q. 661 (1986).

The justice of queues, it is said, protects expectations that accumulate around the undisturbed possession or use of a right over time. But doesn't this beg the question? Why do expectations accumulate? Also, queues protect priorities even when expectations may not have time to accumulate, as when one title holder just beats out another to the registry to record a deed.

One possibility is that queues promote desirable social policies. Take the race to record a deed. Deed-holders who do not record are making it possible for dishonest grantors to defraud some future victim. We want to reward deed-holders who record and punish those who don't. First-in-time is a sensible policy to accomplish just that. One can often come up with social policy explanations of this sort. Often one can't, however. And even when one can, social policy is never the whole story. Look again at the race to the registry. The race recording statutes give no mercy to an infant deed-holder, an infirm deed-holder, a deed-holder whose car breaks down on the way to the registry, and so forth. Why not? Is the social policy of cutting off the odd-ball fraud stronger than any excuse for not showing up at the registry? Or, does the race statute also reflect a powerful vision of justice?

Another possibility is that queues form when we simply have no other rational way of allocating a scarce resource. How could a theater rationally decide who gets in to see the 8:30 performance of a popular movie?[15] The queue solves that problem. Queues are also useful when a rational way of allocating a resource exists, but doing the allocation is too costly, or more costly than the aggregate cost to the recipients of lining up. Or, an allocator uses queues to shift the cost of allocation to recipients, making them spend time lining up, even though their aggregate cost may be greater than the cost of rational allocation.

Another possibility is that queue justice supplies its own rational standard, appealing on its own terms, competing with other standards. Lotteries, by contrast, are used when we are frightened to make rational distinctions or do not believe that we can agree on the distinctions, as, for example, when we allocate kidney dialysis. Lotteries provide a procedure for maintaining equality—an equality of chances, when we cannot provide equality of results.[16] (Remember lotteries when we consider *Bakke* in Chapter 5.)

Courtroom Misconduct by Prosecutors and Trial Judges

Albert W. Altschuler[17]

I believe that misconduct by a defense attorney can sometimes justify prosecutorial behavior that would otherwise be improper. The test should not be whether the prosecutor

---

[15] One possibility is the quasi-illegal phenomenon known as "scalping." In some popular events, a customer can show up at the last minute and buy a designated-seat ticket from a "ticket scalper" who charges an inflated price (and thereby makes a profit) for the "convenience."

[16] On these matters, *see* Kornhauser and Sager, *Just Lotteries*, 27 Social Science Information 483 (1988).

[17] 50 Texas L. Rev. 629, 637 (1972).

was "provoked" but whether the prosecutor's action was reasonably designed to remedy the wrong perpetrated by the defense.

Ordinarily, for example, it would be improper for a prosecutor to express his personal belief in the defendant's guilt or to suggest that the defense attorney had been biased by his fee. Suppose, however, that a defense attorney had improperly told the jury that he knew in his heart that the defendant was innocent, and that he would blame his own inadequacies and never again enjoy a good night's sleep if the defendant were convicted. It would be unfair to confine the remedy for this misconduct to an instruction to the jury, and to inform the prosecutor that he could not mention the incident at all in his own remarks. The prosecutor should be able to go beyond the court's formal instruction in explaining why the defense attorney's misconduct should be disregarded. Indeed, in the course of his argument, I think that the prosecutor should be permitted to mention his own belief in the defendant's guilt and to suggest that the defense attorney had, after all, been paid to think as favorably of the defendant as he could. It should be incumbent upon the prosecutor, if he chose this course, to make it clear to the jurors that he was not urging conviction on the basis of his personal opinions, but merely illustrating why full responsibility for the ultimate decision belonged to the jury alone.

Notes and Questions

1. The brief excerpt you have just read raises many issues. First, why is it ethically improper for an attorney to tell the jury what she personally believes? An attorney has, after all, studied with great care the case she is presenting in court. She has probably formed some definite opinions. Why is it normally improper for an attorney—whether in a criminal case or a civil case—to tell the jury what she personally thinks?

2. If your answer to Question 1 is something along this line—that it is improper for an attorney to voice her personal opinion to the jury because that would simply invite the attorney on the opposite side to voice his personal opinion to the jury—why isn't it a net gain for the cause of justice to allow *both* attorneys to express their personal beliefs?

3. If, instead, your answer to Question 1 is something along this line—that what attorneys believe is irrelevant to the law—what is it about "law" that should exclude the personal belief of attorneys? Isn't that what might be *wrong* with the law?

4. Perhaps, instead, your answer to Question 1 was that a trial should not be a sincerity contest between opposing attorneys. Jurors should not be swayed by what the attorneys believe, because the attorney who gives the appearance of being the more sincere will be the one who prevails. A trial should be a search for truth, and not a contest as to who is the better actor.[18]

Suppose, then, that this was your answer to Question 1. If so, how would you criticize Altschuler's argument that if the defense attorney tells the jury what he believes, then the

---

[18] Marlon Brando is reported to have made the following remark about theatrical acting ability: "What you need to be a great actor is realism, sincerity, honesty, and truth. If you can fake these things, you've got it made."

prosecutor should also be allowed to tell the jury what *he* believes? (Most courts, by the way, have allowed the prosecutor to make improper arguments in retaliation for improper remarks by defense counsel under what has come to be known as the "invited response" rule.)

Suppose we know nothing about the comparative acting abilities of prosecutor and defense counsel. Nevertheless, who is more *likely* to convince a jury of the sincerity of his or her belief? Isn't the jury *almost always* more likely to believe the *prosecutor*? The prosecutor, after all, is a public servant. As such, she would not be "wasting her time" prosecuting this defendant if she did not believe that the defendant was guilty. If she *tells* the jury that she believes the defendant is in fact guilty, isn't the jury more likely to believe her? Juries, after all, know that criminal defendants can hire their own counsel (maybe with funds that they have illegally acquired). So aren't juries more likely to discount what the defense counsel believes than discount what the prosecutor believes?

5. Altschuler obviously doesn't want the prosecutor to go too far in mentioning his own belief of the defendant's guilt as an "invited response" to the defense attorney's tactics. Altschuler says that the prosecutor should mention to the jury that he is not in fact urging conviction on the basis of his personal opinion. Is the jury likely to understand this kind of hedging on the part of the prosecutor?

What if the prosecutor goes too far? What if the prosecutor simply waits for the defense attorney to make a slip, and then uses the "invited response" doctrine to launch into a prejudicial tirade against the defendant? In a recent case, a defendant was on a weekend furlough from prison when a brutal crime was committed. The defendant was prosecuted for the crime. The prosecutor argued to the jury that the jury should vote for the death sentence because that would be the only guarantee that this defendant would not be furloughed again and commit another murder. The prosecutor said to the jury:

> I will ask you to advise the Court to give him death. That's the only way that I know that he is not going to get out on the public. It's the only way I know. It's the only way I can be sure of it. It's the only way that anybody can be sure of it now.

The Supreme Court, however, sustained the conviction on a broad reading of the "invited response" theory. *Darden v. Wainwright*, 477 U.S. 168 (1986).

6. Clearly, a prosecutor can go too far. Suppose, for example, a prosecutor says to the jury during closing argument: "We've shown you a lot of evidence that proves this defendant guilty. But I can tell you that I've seen a lot more evidence than we've had time to show you in court, a lot of additional evidence, and other eyewitnesses to the crime, and that evidence conclusively shows, and those eyewitnesses conclusively proved to me, that the defendant is guilty beyond any doubt whatsoever." This kind of statement, under present law, will probably be held to constitute a denial of due process. If the jury convicts the defendant, a reviewing court will probably reverse the conviction and remand for a new trial.

Now, suppose a defense attorney tells the jury the following during closing argument: "The evidence shows that the defendant was not at the scene of the crime when the murder was committed. Well, where was he, then? I can tell you where he was. He was at O'Hare Airport, in a conference room, participating in an interdenominational seminar on the future of religion in the United States. With him at the seminar were a priest, a deacon, and a rabbi. These three gentlemen subsequently went back to their home states—California, Louisiana, and Massachusetts. They couldn't be at this trial today because of their work on behalf of God. But I met with each of them, and they swore to me that the defendant on trial today was with them all during that seminar, which was at the exact hour and minute and second that the murder was being committed fifty miles away from O'Hare Airport. I met with Father William O'Shamrock in Boston, I met with Rabbi Israel Ginzburg in Los Angeles, and I talked for an hour and a half on the phone with Deacon Percival Parker from Baton Rouge, and each of them swore to me that this defendant was with them on the fateful morning of the crime."

Suppose the jury acquits the defendant. Now what? The answer is—nothing. There can be no reversal on appeal because of the prejudicial and improper remarks by defense counsel, because under the American legal system,[19] once a jury has rendered a verdict of acquittal, a defendant cannot be tried again for the same crime.

Thus, while the case reports contain many cases of *prosecutorial misconduct*, there is very little mention of the misconduct of defense counsel. When defense counsel behaves improperly at trial and nevertheless the defendant is convicted, defense counsel can hardly urge on appeal that his own misbehavior should constitute grounds for reversal! And on the other hand, when the defendant is acquitted, that's the end of the story—there is no further appeal. That is why many cases have been appealed on the ground of prosecutorial misconduct, but none on the ground of defense counsel misconduct.

Now, reconsider your answers to Questions 4 and 5. Does justice require that some additional leeway be given to prosecutors to redress the imbalance caused by the fact that misbehavior on the part of defense counsel cannot be corrected on appeal? Or would you say that the danger of convicting an innocent person must be avoided at all costs, even if it means giving defense counsel strategic advantages at the trial?

7. Respecting the efficacy of curative instructions, suppose two police officers burst through a suspect's door without a warrant, punch him, handcuff him, and ransack his apartment. The suspect sues the police for conducting an illegal search. The officers' attorney mentions to the jury that the search revealed evidence of heroin trafficking. The judge orders the jurors to disregard the statement.

A study by the American Bar Foundation and Northwestern University, reported in the Wall Street Journal,[20] used this and other fictional cases, and found that mock jurors who didn't hear about the drugs were nearly twice as likely to award punitive damages to the victim as those who did.

Commenting to the Wall Street Journal on judges' instructions to disregard evidence, Professor Michael Saks of the University of Iowa said, "It's laughable, because juries don't disregard it. They do the rational thing instead of the just thing." Do you agree with Saks' distinction between the "just" and the "rational"?

---

[19] Not all legal systems follow the American legal system in this regard. Some countries routinely allow appeals by either the prosecution or by the defense.

[20] WALL STREET JOURNAL, January 25, 1988, p. 31.

8. Reference to wealth by a prosecutor—potentially explosive as turning a jury of average means against a rich litigant—has sometimes led to reversal. In *Read v. United States*[21] a Special Assistant to the Attorney General of the United States had argued to the jury in a criminal trial for misapplication of bank funds:[22]

> The entire Read fortune grew up out of and had its origin in the First National Bank of Shenandoah, Iowa, and if my information is correct, it is a very substantial fortune. I think the law of the sea should prevail in a case of this kind the same as it does at sea. The law of the sea requires that the captain of the ship, in case of disaster, shall stay on the bridge of his ship until every passenger who has entrusted himself to his care shall have reached safety before the captain himself shall seek safety, otherwise the captain must go down with his ship. The Read family, and by the 'Read family' I mean every member of the Read family, should have turned over their entire fortune to pay the depositors of this bank every cent that they had entrusted to the care of the Read's [*sic*] bank. The Read women should have stripped their jewels from their persons, and not a shingle should have been left over their heads, unless and until every depositor was paid in full.

The defendants were subsequently convicted. The appellate court reversed:[23]

> The argument of counsel for defendants is not in the record; therefore we are unadvised as to whether this was said in reply to some argument advanced by said counsel. There was no evidence that the Read family had a fortune, or that the Read women had any jewels. Latitude must be allowed for the effect upon a prosecution of the heat engendered during the trial of a case, but argument must be restrained within reasonable limits. This case was well and skillfully prosecuted. It is apparent from the affidavits in the record of various parties that feeling against the Reads was running high. Prejudice against them was intense, and it was difficult for defendants in this atmosphere to secure a fair trial. Parties who see their lifelong savings lost in a bank failure are not in a condition of mind to do justice to those whom they believe may have caused that loss, and deep-seated prejudice against officers of a failed bank is most natural. It is the duty of a prosecuting attorney to assist in giving a fair trial to a defendant. The government cannot afford to convict its citizens by unfair means. The argument referred to was a subtle and powerful appeal to the prejudice of a jury. Counsel went outside of the evidence to convey to the jury the idea that the Reads had a fortune; that they kept it while innocent depositors suffered; that they saved themselves, contrary to the law of the sea, and did not go down with the ship, but continued to possess their jewelry and fortune. Such an argument was clearly prejudicial. The case was a close one on the facts, as is evidenced by the various verdicts of the jury on different counts of the indictments. This appeal was undoubtedly a most persuasive influence with the jury to convict the defendants on some count, and was such prejudicial error as to make the trial, in our judgment, an unfair one.

Note the court's emphasis on the failure of counsel to prepare the closing argument by introducing evidence to support it at trial. Hence, the closing argument was not only inherently inflammatory, it was also not "fair comment" on the evidence.

Is "wealth" included in the limited list of improper references (including race, region,

---

[21] 42 F.2d 636 (8th Cir. 1930).

[22] 42 F.2d at 645.

[23] *Id. But compare* Gilman v. City of Laconia, 51 A. 631 (N.H. Sup. Ct., Belknap 1902), where the court more charitably interpreted a subtler appeal against wealth, albeit in a civil case.

and religion) because we can expect, as a general rule, that most juries most of the time will be composed of persons who are not at all wealthy? And what about the question whether a litigant is covered by insurance? Insurance, after all, makes a litigant quite "wealthy"—any adverse verdict will be paid not by the litigant but by a "deep pocket" insurance company. We take up the "insurance" question in Section 2.2.

2.2   Truths we don't want jurors to hear (mostly about defendants)

In the sections that follow we will consider two examples of rules requiring a trial judge to exclude evidence about matters jurors might consider very important in deciding whether to judge a defendant innocent or guilty. You should ask yourself two general questions about the cases that follow in these sections. First, what is the relevance, if any, of the excluded evidence? In other words, what vision of justice would admission of the evidence promote? Second, what is the interest of justice in each case in excluding evidence assumed to be relevant?

Questions

1. Imagine you are a juror in a negligence case. The plaintiff was injured while driving to her art gallery in her late-model Mercedes; she was taken to a hospital for minor injuries and released after two days. She is suing for $55,000 damage to her car, $85,000 pain and suffering, and $9,000 in hospital bills and related medical costs. The judge has instructed the jury that if it finds for the plaintiff, then the plaintiff will be entitled as a matter of law to the $55,000 for car damages and the $9,000 for hospital bills, but the jury will be able to assess and fix the amount of damages for pain and suffering, from zero to $85,000.

The defendant was driving a six-year-old Ford. The defendant was trying to make a turn but was distracted by his children who were in the front seat; he didn't see the plaintiff's car and, although he tried to avoid her car, failed at the last minute and hit it. You are convinced that the plaintiff's injuries were the result of the defendant's negligence. But the defendant is a widower with three small children at home whom he is taking care of while also working in a factory. He owns the house the family lives in which has a present market value of $35,000, owns his car worth $1,500, and he has no other significant assets or savings.

Assuming you are in a jurisdiction where drivers are not required to carry automobile insurance, would you be interested, before retiring to the jury room, in knowing whether the defendant was insured?

2. Could you say that knowing whether the defendant was insured might help you decide whether the defendant was negligent? Is it likely that people who are careless tend to take out insurance policies, whereas people who are careful do not? Or, the converse? Would you have any other reason for finding a connection between whether the defendant is insured and whether he was negligent?

3. Could you say that knowing whether the defendant was insured might help you ascertain how the verdict in this case might affect you personally? If the defendant is not insured, then it wouldn't matter to you whether you voted for his total liability for all damages. But if the defendant is insured, then voting for liability would mean that the insurance company would pay, and as a result the insurance company would raise everyone's premium, including your own.

4. However you answered Question 3, do you think it is ever fair for a decision-maker—in this case, a juror—to calculate whether the decision in the case will have any personal impact, however slight? Would calculating such an impact be a sign of prejudice? Or just common sense and prudence? If a juror is concerned about the rising costs of insurance, how can the juror put that concern to one side in the jury room?

5. The preceding questions ask us to examine possible prejudices that we may have, or possible theories of justice that we may have. Is it important for us to know our own prejudices and/or our own theories of justice before passing judgment upon the prejudices and/or theories of justice of others?

Jessup v. Davis

211 N.W. 190
Supreme Court of Nebraska
Nov. 19, 1926

EBERLY, J. This action was brought by Esther M. JESSUP, as administratrix of the estate of her deceased husband, Ursa S. Jessup, to recover damages for his death, alleged to have been caused by the negligence of defendant in so operating his automobile, while her husband was riding therein as an invited guest, as to cause the car to skid and overturn, thereby inflicting fatal injuries on Mr. Jessup. This court divides in this case solely upon the question of adherence to the doctrine announced in *Miller v. Central Taxi Co.*, 110 Neb. 306, 193 N.W. 919, stated as follows:

> Where a plaintiff in a personal injury action seeks by appropriate interrogatories[24] on the cross-examination to discover whether the defendant is indemnified from loss by an insurance company, it is error for the court to sustain an objection to interrogatories which tend to develop the fact on that question.

[24] By "interrogatories" the court means questions by counsel at the trial. [Eds.]

The district court failed to follow the rule above announced, and the plaintiff urges this fact as ground for reversal. Plaintiff's contentions are controverted not only by the defendant, but the interests and viewpoint of liability insurance companies generally in opposition thereto, have been most ably presented in oral argument and by three written briefs filed by amici curiae.

On the part of the insurer is necessarily involved, from the nature of the business in which it is engaged, its maintenance of a staff of attorneys, investigators and experts; on occurrence of an accident in which its policyholder is involved, upon "immediate notice" received, the prompt appearance of its efficient and paid investigators upon the scene, thorough investigation of the facts, interviews with all parties (if possible) and of all persons having knowledge of facts and full reports of the same, together with measures taken to preserve and secure favorable evidence, maps and photos. Thereafter the insurer settles or litigates, as the conditions of the accident, the situation and standing of the parties involved, views of monetary considerations, may deem wise.

If litigation follows, the defense is to be conducted "in the name of the defendant," it is true, but by the insurer's attorneys, along lines wholly determined by the insurer, and to the extent that the insurer's interests may determine. The witnesses, whose testimony may be used in behalf of the defendant, are exclusively selected by the insurer, and are all obtained by efforts of its agents, and are necessarily in many cases employees, employed for the purpose of assuring success in expected litigation. If the resulting decision be finally adverse, to the extent of the policy, the insurer satisfies the judgment and defrays the cost of attorneys and expenses of litigation. Indeed, after the occurrence of the accident and notice to the insurer, the entire matter is within the absolute control of the insurance company. It litigates or settles as its interests may determine. The assured has, by his agreement, waived all right to object, influence, or in any manner control the ensuing proceedings whether of litigation or settlement. He thereafter acts and participates only to the extent and in the manner the insurer may request or direct.

The acid test of truth in judicial proceedings is cross-examination. It is admittedly the most efficacious agency which the law has devised for the discovery of truth. The ordinary rule is, by cross-examination, the situation of the witness with respect to the parties in interest, and to the subject of litigation, his interest, his motives, his inclination and prejudices, may all be fully investigated and ascertained, and submitted to the consideration of the jury before whom he has testified, and who have had the opportunity of observing and determining the just weight and value of his testimony.

We have a [statute] providing that all actions shall be prosecuted by the real parties in interest. The reason for such a [statute] is so that the actual status of the case may be apparent to the entire court, including the jury. If this is the reason, then why is it not just as important that the real parties in interest as defendants shall appear? We have heretofore arrived at the conclusion that the contract of insurance between the insurance company and the insured, in such a case as this, makes the insurance company the unquestioned party in interest, and, not only that, but the unqualified, controlling party interested in the defense. The sole object of such a contract as that existing between the insurance company and the insured, as well as the principle now contended for, is that the case may proceed in the name of an ostensible party controlled and directed by the insurance company, both as to himself and his witnesses, as well as the attorneys, and yet the court and the jury shall be wholly oblivious of that fact.

If motives, bias and interest of witnesses, and the situation of witnesses, with respect to parties and the subject of litigation, are each a proper and necessary subject for consideration of juries, cross-examination must proceed upon the basis of the actual facts of the case as to the real parties in interest who will be substantially affected by the outcome. What may be essential to the true development of the actual facts, in order that these actual relations may be shown, certainly is proper cross-examination. It would seem, therefore, that questions eliciting the fact of the existing insurance and the relations sustained by each witness to the insurance company must be permitted. If they are not permitted, the ordinary right of cross-examination is denied, and a litigant is thus deprived of his "rights of proof" to which the ordinary application of the rule entitles him.

In the form of the proceeding before us the real defendant, though unnamed apparently, as a matter of fact, seeks to avail himself of the benefit of the vouchments of the ostensible party defendant. Under the terms of the contract of insurance, it cannot be said that the witness apparently called and vouched for, as to veracity and standing by the apparent defendant, is in fact, his witness, when he is actually selected and called as the witness of the real party in interest, the insurance company, and entitled to no other vouchment. Indeed, the entire theory of legal procedure outlined in these contracts for liability insurance contemplates a proceeding carried on secretly, by a real, though unknown, party in interest, making use of concealment and deception. Its essential nature is therefore incompatible with an "open court" and judgments publicly and openly arrived at. To compel and permit such proceeding is to countenance and participate in what is tantamount to fraud.

Lastly, it is thought the procedure contemplated in these liability insurance contracts, whereby the defense, though actually made and controlled by the insurance company, is concealed by the name of the ostensible defendant, is opposed to a just and enlightened public policy. It is certainly patent that for courts to encourage, recognize, enforce and aid, especially by means of a benevolent concealment, the carrying out of this portion of the contracts of insurance companies is to judicially invite, conceal and promote [evils] into the liability insurance world. In addition, the invitation thus extended would carry with it assurance to those tempted to wrong that there would be no relief for the unfortunates, and no retribution for the wrongdoer, because the wrongdoers would judicially be concealed, and in the records of our courts their names would not appear or be known. Still, underneath the veil of procedure, or behind the mask, maintained by precedent, will inevitably be developed in truth, with passing time, the same vexatious and oppressive resisting of payments, justly due, the same persistent endeavor to secure for themselves, under and in the name and shadow of the assured, an escape from just liability that characterized the fire insurance business of the recent past.

It would seem that the doctrine of "Open Court" with judgments openly arrived at, and also "Equality before the law" are principles that public good cannot permit to be limited, qualified, or abandoned, openly or in secret, judicially or otherwise.

And, indeed, on broader grounds, when we consider the enhanced efficiency of the automobile, the ever-increasing numbers in active use, the increased improvements of our highways, and the increase in the number of protective policies of insurance issued to automobile owners, and then call to mind the astounding list of casualties on our public roads, we are impelled to seek for the cause of this wreckage of property and destruction of life and limb. It cannot be the automobile, or the highway, alone. If not there, may it not rest in those who operate these machines of pleasure and usefulness on our public thoroughfares? The ever-increasing casualties are all out of proportion to the increasing number of automobiles used. Are we not thus driven to conclude that, when such insurance is arranged for, the feeling of liability, as well as responsibility, on the part of the individual insured is lessened, and that thereby recklessness or lack of ordinary care is bred, rather than ordinary care held in statu quo or greater care promoted? Should not such question be one for the jury or court trying the case as any other fact submitted for consid-

eration, not as a question of intent on the part of the party causing the claimed injury, but as such fact may bear on the question of his care or lack of care or negligence in the particular case?

It follows that the judgment of the district court is reversed and remanded for further proceedings in conformity with this opinion.

Reversed.

GOOD, J. (dissenting). For the reasons hereinafter set forth, I cannot concur in that part of the majority opinion which holds:

> Where a plaintiff in a personal injury action seeks by appropriate interrogatories on the cross-examination to discover whether the defendant is indemnified from loss by an insurance company, it is error for the court to sustain an objection to interrogatories which tend to develop the fact on that question.

It is true that this rule was previously announced in *Miller v. Central Taxi Co.*, 110 Neb. 306, 193 N.W. 919. In that case, however, no reason for the rule was given save that it was supposedly based on the holding of this court in *Egner v. Curtis, Towle & Paine Co.*, 96 Neb. 18, 146 N.W. 1032, L.R.A. 1915A, 153. In the latter case it was ruled that it is proper to inquire of the jurors, on their voir dire, if they are stockholders or otherwise interested in a company, carrying insurance indemnifying defendant against loss from the accident or transaction out of which the action arose. This was on the theory that such information was necessary to enable plaintiff to prudently exercise his challenges. With that ruling I am in entire accord. The point decided, however, has no bearing on the question under consideration and is not authority for the rule announced in *Miller v. Central Taxi Co.* I do not wish to be understood as contending that it is in no case proper to bring before the jury evidence that defendant carries indemnity insurance. Cases may arise where such disclosure may be proper, for the purpose of showing the interest or bias of witnesses, who may be stockholders, officers, agents or employees of the company carrying the indemnity insurance for defendant.

I have made a painstaking examination of the authorities upon the question and find that, where the precise question has been presented, a view, contrary to that expressed in the majority opinion, has been taken in practically every jurisdiction that has passed upon the question, save that of Nebraska. The courts of 27 of our sister states and the federal courts take a contrary view to that of the majority opinion. Among the decisions holding that it is error to permit the plaintiff, in an action for personal injuries, to offer evidence or make argument to the jury that the defendant in the action is protected by indemnity insurance, are the following: [citing many cases].

What was the purpose sought to be attained in offering such evidence to the jury? I think that all know that the purpose of the offer was not to elucidate any issue involved, but for the effect that it might have on the jury in rendering a verdict for plaintiff.

It is suggested in the majority opinion that the insurance company is the real party defendant, at least to the extent of the insurance carried by the defendant. This is mere assumption, based upon nothing appearing in the record. It also assumes that defendant will be able to recover his loss in an action against his insurer. This is mere assumption again.

It is further suggested that the insurance company is responsible for the entire conduct of the defense and calls such witnesses as it pleases, and that the party calling the witnesses vouches for their veracity; that therefore the jury should know that the insurance company is the one who vouches for the veracity of the witnesses called. It is a new doctrine to me that the veracity of a witness should be determined by the person who calls him. It may sometimes happen that a person of poor reputation or standing for veracity and probity may call as a witness one of high character and probity. On the other hand, a party of high character and standing may, by the exigencies of the situation, be required to call as a witness one who is not of that character. In the latter case, is, then, the witness to be given faith and credit because a person of high standing calls him as a witness; or is a reputable witness of high character and probity to be given little credence because of the character of the person who calls him as a witness? Certainly no such rule obtains. Besides, the majority opinion assumes that the insurance company, or those who control its policies and actions, are not of high character and standing. Again this is mere assumption, not based upon any fact disclosed by the record.

I respectfully submit that the trial court's ruling in sustaining the objection is right. I think the correct rule should be that, unless there are disclosed good reasons for offering such evidence, it should be excluded, and if it is brought to the attention of the jury they should be instructed as to the purpose for which it was admitted, and to consider it for that purpose alone.

ROSE and DAY, JJ., concur in this dissent.

Fielding v. Publix Cars

265 N.W. 726
Supreme Court of Nebraska
March 13, 1936

Where the plaintiff shows that defendant carries liability insurance, when it is not relevant to some issue in the case, we have come to the conclusion that it is inadmissible. Such evidence can have no relevancy to the question of negligence. It cannot be disputed that there are cases where liability insurance may be the subject of evidence, or the object of interrogatories, if the fact of insurance bears upon an issue in the case. In other words, if the evidence is properly admissible for any purpose, it cannot be excluded for the reason that it tends to prejudice the defendant because it shows or tends to show that he carries liability insurance. We have examined with care the opinion in the case of *Jessup v. Davis*, [130 Neb. 576, 211 N.W. 190], as well as the opinions of the court of appeals of the District of Columbia, three circuit courts of appeal and the courts of last resort in 40 sister states, all holding to the contrary. We will not take the space to quote from each of these holdings. A discussion of a large number of cases contrary to *Jessup v. Davis, supra,* and supporting the rule we now believe to be the correct one, will accomplish no good purpose.

Against this array of authority, we have failed to find a single case supporting the rule announced by our court in *Miller v. Central Taxi Co.,* [110 Neb. 306, 193 N.W. 919], and *Jessup v.*

Davis, supra. The authorities are unanimous in supporting a contrary view. In addition to the great weight of authority being against the rule heretofore existent in Nebraska, we feel that reason and logic also support the majority view.

It is therefore ordered that the rule of practice promulgated in *Jessup v. Davis, supra,* and heretofore followed by this court, is revoked, such revocation to be effective in all cases tried after 20 days from the date of the release of this opinion, and that on and after said date, this rule and the holdings of this court based thereon shall cease to be authoritative.

For the reasons herein stated, the judgment of the trial court is reversed, and the cause is remanded.

Reversed.

Notes and Questions

1. The Nebraska Supreme Court's view in 1926 was strongly expressed: to allow courts to conceal from the jurors the fact that the defendant is insured "is to countenance and participate in what is tantamount to fraud." What exactly are the frauds? (There are more than one.) What are the interests of justice in preventing them? After all, we permit "softcore" frauds in other contexts: sales talk, cult solicitations, promises by candidates for office.[25] Why forbid it here?

2. Suppose a developer wishes to build a shopping center one interchange away from an already established shopping center on an interstate. The owners of the established shopping center secretly supply funds to a citizens group who wish to challenge the proposed shopping center on environmental grounds. The purpose of the funds is to pay counsel fees. Should the law allow the donation?

Should public interest law firms be required to disclose their funding sources?

3. Should a major corporation be permitted to assemble small parcels of land through nominee corporations? If law suits result from such transactions, should the law require disclosure of the ownership of the nominees?

4. The majority writes about the insurance company operating "underneath the veil of procedure, or behind the mask." Presumably justice requires ripping off masks, exposing exactly who are the "real parties in interest." At the same time, however, we believe that, "The law is no respecter of persons." Are these thoughts consistent?

5. Ten years later, when the Nebraska Supreme Court overruled its decision of 1926, it made no mention of the phrase "tantamount to fraud." Was that because in the ten years between 1926 and 1936, vastly more cars were sold, huge insurance conglomerates sprung up, and the "insurance lobby" successfully pressured legislatures and courts to keep the mention of insurance out of negligence cases? Because automobile insurance was becoming the norm? Because the tort of vehicular negligence was changing?

In thinking about this question, consider who, in the following four cases, would be hurt, as between all plaintiffs, insurance companies (assuming policy amounts entirely cover judgments), and uninsured motorists:

---

[25] On these matters, and many more, *see* A. Leff, Swindling and Selling (1976).

(1) the court lets in evidence about insurance, and people assume motorists have insurance;

(2) the court keeps out evidence about insurance, and people assume motorists have insurance;

(3) the court lets in evidence about insurance, and people do *not* assume motorists have insurance;

(4) the court keeps out evidence about insurance, and people do *not* assume motorists have insurance.

Holding steady the assumption that people do *not* assume motorists have insurance, which class would you prefer to see disadvantaged? Holding steady the assumption that people do assume motorists have insurance, which class would you prefer to see disadvantaged? Do your answers shed light on the transformation in the views of the Nebraska Supreme Court between 1926 and 1936?

6. If the 1926 Nebraska view had prevailed and become the dominant national approach, what would be the economic effect on the automobile insurance companies? On the public?

7. So far, which view makes more sense to you—the 1926 or the 1936 view? Consider the cases that follow.

Brown v. Walter

62 F.2d 798
Circuit Court of Appeals, Second Circuit
Jan. 16, 1933

L. HAND, Circuit Judge.

The defendant's chief complaint is in the persistent effort of the plaintiff to get and keep before the jury the fact that he was insured; especially in his summation, which charged that the insurer had suborned the defendant and his companions in the car to perjure themselves. This issue requires us to go into a little detail. The plaintiff called the defendant as his witness, and after getting his story, asked whether he had made a report to the state inspector, which was already in evidence, following this by inquiring whether he had not been interviewed by one Aikey, an insurance agent. As there was no attempt to establish any contradiction between what he said to the agent and what he said on the stand, the evidence was clearly incompetent, and could only have been meant to introduce a forbidden element into the case. The plaintiff's wife was then called, and testified that after the accident the defendant was at a house where she was being revived, and where among other things the defendant had said that the car belonged to his father and was insured. This again, though not shown to be deliberate, was extremely prejudicial, and the defendant objected at once, but the judge would not exclude it. When later the witness repeated it, the judge again allowed the testimony to stand, contenting himself with an admonition that the jury should hold itself impartial in spite of the defendant's insurance. The same testimony came out from the plaintiff while he was on the stand; this time, the defendant unsuccessfully moved for a mistrial.

We should therefore hardly have passed the verdict, had the matter rested there; but the injustice became much more serious, when the plaintiff came to sum up. Then he spun a web of suspicion of which there was no warrant whatever. He argued with much warmth that the whole defense had been fabricated by the insurer—transparently veiled by such provocative phrases as an "unseen hand," and an "unseen force," and the like. This had not the slightest support in the evidence; it was unfair to the last degree. Nobody can read the summation without being satisfied that the real issues were being suppressed, and the picture substituted of an alien and malevolent corporation, lurking in the background and contriving a perjurious defense. A judge, at least in a federal court, is more than a moderator; he is affirmatively charged with securing a fair trial, and he must intervene sua sponte to that end, when necessary. It is not always enough that the other side does not protest; often the protest will only serve to emphasize the evil. Justice does not depend upon legal dialectics so much as upon the atmosphere of the court room, and that in the end depends primarily upon the judge.

It is, indeed, not common to reverse for such reasons, but here we must intervene. While it is quite true that there are jurisdictions which allow the inquiry, we cannot agree. There can be no rational excuse, except the flimsy one that a man is more likely to be careless if insured. That is at most the merest guess, much more than outweighed by the probability that the real issues will be obscured. In the case at bar, save for the cross-examination of the doctor, there was no excuse for even an intimation that the defendant was insured; if that witness is not called upon the next trial, there will be none whatever, and unless the insurance is scrupulously kept from the jury, a mistrial should be declared. The prevalent knowledge that in such cases insurance is usually taken, is a hard enough handicap at best; it is difficult in any event to get a decision on the real issues.

Judgment reversed; new trial ordered.

Smith v. Raup

296 Ill. App. 171
Appellate Court of Illinois, Second District
June 22, 1938

DOVE, Presiding Justice.

Counsel for appellant called appellee as an adverse witness and during the course of his examination he testified without objection that after the accident and before starting for the hospital, appellant asked him if he carried insurance. Upon his direct examination, when called as a witness in his own behalf, appellee testified that before starting for the hospital the only remark appellant made was to inquire of him whether he had insurance, her attorney objected and the court stated that the witness had already testified to the same thing upon cross-examination. The objection was overruled and appellee answered that in reply to appellant's inquiry as to whether he had insurance, he said "No."

Counsel for appellant, in their argument, state that counsel for appellee began at an early stage of the trial and persisted in, during the course of the trial, a determined effort to inform the jury that appellee carried no liability insurance on his automobile and argue that judgments have frequently been reversed when testimony has been introduced which informs the jury that one of the parties has or has not liability insurance. [Citing cases] These cases hold that it is improper to show that the defendant is insured against loss in case of a recovery against the defendant on account of his negligence. What is said in those cases and many others that might be cited has no application here. Indemnity insurance is very generally carried by automobile owners and drivers. In the instant case, the jury learned of the fact that appellee did not carry such insurance as a result of appellee and his daughter testifying as to the reply which appellee made to an inquiry of appellant. If appellee had not been permitted to state his answer to appellant's question, the jury could have inferred that any verdict which they returned, if in favor of appellant, would have to be paid by an insurance company. This court recognizes that the belief is prevalent and widespread that in cases of this character the defendant is really the nominal party in interest and that the real defendant whose pecuniary interest is at stake is an insurance carrier and no valid reason has been suggested by counsel or occurs to us why appellee, in the instant case, should be precluded from proving, if such was a fact, that he himself would be pecuniarily affected by any verdict that might be returned against him. The trial court committed no error in admitting this evidence.

We have read all the evidence as abstracted by counsel for appellant. The issues made by the pleadings were submitted to the jury under proper instructions. In our opinion the verdict was warranted by the evidence. The trial court approved it. No reversible error is found in the record and the judgment will therefore be affirmed.

Judgment affirmed.

WOLFE and HUFFMAN, JJ., concur.

Questions

1. If Judge Hand could find a way to prevent the jurors from bringing into the courtroom their prior knowledge that drivers tend to be insured, would he do so? Can you think of any way to do it? Could the prospective jurors be asked on voir dire if they have any idea of what "insurance" is? What if twelve jurors could be found who have never heard of "insurance"? How representative would such jurors be of the general community?

2. How would Judge Hand criticize Judge Dove? Does Judge Dove make *too much* use of the fact that jurors come into the courtroom with prior knowledge about the prevalence of insurance?

3. Do you agree or disagree with the following general rule: "Justice requires that if the defendant has insurance, it would be reversible error to allow evidence into the courtroom of that fact. However, justice also requires that if the defendant is uninsured, it would be reversible error to *disallow* evidence into the courtroom of that fact."

4. To what extent would Judge Dove have to accept the general rule spelled out in Question 3?

5. Think back to the questions that opened this section on insurance. Suppose you are representing the rich plaintiff with the Mercedes. You are fearful that the jury will be reluctant to find that the defendant was negligent even if the jury believes the defendant was negligent—because the judgment would impoverish him while simply adding more money to the plaintiff's coffers. Yet you cannot omit the fact of your client's wealth from the case—at the very least, the jury will know that she was driving a very expensive Mercedes. Is there any argument you can make to the judge that might justify your deliberate introduction into the evidence of the fact that the defendant is insured?

Consider the following array of possible cases:

1) RICH PLAINTIFF v. POOR DEFENDANT
2) RICH PLAINTIFF v. RICH DEFENDANT
3) POOR PLAINTIFF v. POOR DEFENDANT
4) POOR PLAINTIFF v. RICH DEFENDANT

Now consider what prejudice would result from introducing evidence that the defendant is insured:

1) What effect does evidence of insurance have here?
2) In this case, evidence of insurance unfairly biases the result;
3) In this case as well, evidence of insurance unfairly biases the result;

4) Also in this case, evidence of insurance unfairly biases the result.

Is it not true that in 3 out of the 4 possible cases, whatever the underlying equities of the case might be, the introduction of evidence of insurance would *unfairly* prejudice the jury against the defendant?

Now, what about Case 1? Here, as in the other cases, the introduction of insurance evidence will bias the case against the defendant. But, unlike the other three cases, is it not possible here to argue that the bias is a *necessary corrective* to the injustice that otherwise would obtain? Would any court accept such an argument? Is there any harm trying? If you represented the defendant, what argument would you make in rebuttal?

King v. Starr

260 P.2d 351
Supreme Court of Washington
Aug. 20, 1953
Rehearing Denied Oct. 19, 1953

On July 6, 1950, Carol King, who subsequently married Robert Gaddis, was employed by respondents to work on their farm during the haying season. While working on a hay baling machine she was somehow precipitated into the moving parts of the machinery and suffered very severe injuries. The complaint which instituted this action alleged that these injuries were proximately caused by the defendants' negligence.

On March 18, 1952, this case came on for trial. Before the jury was impaneled counsel for both parties appeared before the trial judge in his chambers for the purpose of disposing of certain preliminary matters.

The following then occurred:

MR. GAVIN. One other item. There is evidently going to be an issue, and I think it is proper to suggest it to Your Honor at this time. We will take the position that it will be improper for the defense to show anything of the defendants' financial condition.

THE COURT. That is not an element.

MR. GAVIN. Or particularly whether they are covered by insurance or not.

THE COURT. Neither of those have any place in the thing.

MR. GAVIN. If it was made an issue we would be compelled to move for a mistrial

and we don't want to do it.

THE COURT. Their financial condition is no part of this case. That has no bearing here.

MR. HUTCHESON. We don't think there is any motion of that kind made at this time.

THE COURT. There is no harm done talking about it, but we don't want it in the case at all.

Immediately thereafter a jury was selected and the trial commenced. After appellant's counsel made his opening statement, counsel for respondents then made his opening statement. Near the end of that statement he said:

The testimony will show that the defendants here—they are suing among other things for medical expenses. The testimony will show that the defendants have paid almost all the plaintiff's hospital and medical expenses that were incurred in Goldendale. The defendants have no insurance here.

He was then interrupted by appellant's counsel who objected to the statement. The court twice stated that the remark was objectionable and instructed the jury to disregard the statement of counsel. Respondents' counsel then continued his statement and concluded without further reference to the matter of insurance.

As soon as the opening statements were completed counsel again retired to the judge's chambers where appellant's counsel moved for a mistrial on the ground that respondents' counsel had mentioned to the jury that respondents were not covered by insurance in this case and that under the circumstances the remark was improper and prejudicial and could not be cured by an instruction to disregard it. The judge heard arguments from both sides and then ruled that, while the remark was improper and "absolutely uncalled for," it was not prejudicial since he had promptly admonished the jury to disregard the statement and in his opinion they would do so. He then denied the motion for a mistrial and appellant assigns this ruling as error.

The rule is well established in this jurisdiction that in personal injury cases the fact that the defendant carries liability insurance is entirely immaterial, and the deliberate or wanton injection of this matter into the case by plaintiff is ground for reversal.

Where the fact that the defendant is covered by insurance is brought before the jury inadvertently and it appears that neither the attorney nor the witness connected with the case deliberately, willfully or collusively injected such fact into the case in the presence of the jury, a mistrial will not be granted.

> The gravamen of the offense is not in the disclosure of a collateral fact, but in the manner of its disclosure; that is, the misconduct of counsel. *Jensen v. Schlenz* [89 Wash. 268, 154 P. 160].

The question whether a defendant can deliberately inject into a personal injury case the fact that he has no insurance, has never before been directly presented to this court.

In other jurisdictions the rule is that where, as here, nothing has been done or said from which the jury might infer that defendant is protected by liability insurance it is improper for defendant to show that he does not have insurance protec-

tion. Indeed some courts have even excluded evidence that the defendant is not insured although there is already evidence in the case from which it may be inferred that he is insured. The reason evidence that the defendant is not covered by insurance is excluded by the courts is that it is immaterial and does not pertain to any issues in the cases.

We believe that these decisions from other jurisdictions adequately dispose of respondents' contentions, as set forth in their brief in this court, to the effect that it was entirely proper for their counsel to inject the fact that they had no liability insurance coverage in this case.

Respondents cite *Fine v. Parella,* 92 N.H. 81, 25 A.2d 121, 123. However, in the last paragraph of the *Fine* case [the New Hampshire] court said:

> The rule in *Piechuck v. Magusiak,* remains in force. The case was decided in 1926 and the general increase of motor vehicle liability insurance since then as matter of common knowledge might serve to make evidence of it less likely to provoke prejudice. But the converse of evidence of no insurance is so interrelated with that of carriage of insurance that the evidence in either situation ought not to be unnecessarily received. It remains as immaterial with some chance of its use for a legally harmful purpose. It does no good and may do harm.

The deliberate reference to the fact that respondents carried no insurance, made in the presence of the jury and in violation of the court's previous ruling that such information had no part in the case, was improper and the prejudicial effect was not eradicated by the prompt action of the trial judge who instructed the jury to disregard it. For this reason the trial judge was in error in refusing to grant the motion for mistrial and in subsequently denying the motion for a new trial.

Reversed and remanded with directions to grant appellant a new trial.

Hoover v. Gregory

253 N.C. 452, 117 S.E.2d 395
Supreme Court of North Carolina
Nov. 30, 1960

HIGGINS, Justice.

The plaintiffs' only assignments of error challenge the following portion of the court's charge:

There is one other matter that I must call to your attention, and of which the court takes judicial notice. And of which, as I say, is a matter of common knowledge to all people, that in North Carolina in 1958 every person who owned and operated a motor vehicle in North Carolina was required to do one of two things, that is provide some sort of liability insurance or post some sort of a bond. You are not concerned with that fact even though you may know about it. You would violate your oaths and would not be fit to serve on a jury if you would let that fact have any bearing upon your verdict in this case, that is, you should not speculate about whether the parties are insured or not insured. You know if a plaintiff in a suit, and this has nothing to do with this case, if a person is prudent enough to take out some insurance and gets hurt in some sort of accident whether it is an automobile or some other accident and his insurance company pays him, that does not prevent him from suing another for negligence and recovering. So, this matter of having liability insurance in North Carolina must be faced by all of our people, jurors, litigants, judges and lawyers and everybody else, and we must be mindful that this fact has no place in the jury box. Premiums are determined upon the losses and liabilities suffered by insurance companies which we all must bear, but nevertheless, that should not enter into a jury's verdict. It would be just as bad to let that enter into one's verdict as it would to say on the other hand that a person has insurance. You first got to determine in cases like this whether or not there is liability, and then if there is liability, what is the damage that naturally and proximately flow and have been suffered by the parties, and whether they have insurance or don't have insurance has nothing in the world to do with the case.

In this case the learned and painstaking judge, after delivering clear and correct instructions, added at the end the portion to which the assignments of error are addressed. His purpose in doing so is not apparent. If the jury accepted the court's admonition to disregard liability insurance, neither party was prejudiced. If it did not accept the admonition, the existence of insurance might have prejudiced the defendant. The verdict cured any such harmful effect. However, the plaintiffs contend the jury might have been influenced by the court's remark about insurance rates being determined by losses and liabilities. Both before and after the remark, the judge cautioned the jury not to let such matters enter into the verdict. The effect of one accident on any juror's future insurance premium would be too insignificant, it seems to us, to overcome the judge's positive instructions as to the rule of damages and that insurance had nothing to do with the case.

This opinion goes no further than to hold that on the facts here disclosed the plaintiffs have failed to show prejudicial error.

No error.

PARKER, Justice (dissenting).

The trial judge's totally irrelevant statement about automobile liability insurance in his charge to the jury is set forth in the majority opinion.

Centuries ago the son of David, king in Jerusalem, wrote "there is no new thing under the sun." Ecclesiastes, Chapter 1, Verse 9. So far as a diligent search by myself and my law clerk discloses the quoted part of the charge is a new thing under the sun. I am fortified in my opinion by the fact that the majority opinion and the briefs of counsel cite nothing like it from the thousands of volumes of reported cases from the Courts of the lands where the English tongue is spoken.

The trial judge charged the jury that they, the defendant, and all other persons in North Carolina, who own and operate automobiles, were required to have automobile liability insurance or post a bond, and then specifically charged, "premiums are determined upon the losses and liabilities suffered by insurance companies, which we all must bear."

The majority opinion states this was not prejudicial, because the judge charged before and after this specific statement about premiums not to let insurance enter into their verdict, and because "the effect of one accident on any juror's future insurance premium would be too insignificant, it seems to us, to overcome the judge's positive instructions as to the rule of damages, and that insurance had nothing to do with the case." To this reasoning, I do not agree.

What the trial judge charged the jury about the determination of the size of the insurance premiums was prejudicial to plaintiffs, in my opinion, and nothing he said before and after that specific statement about premiums could undo the damage done them.

What was the probable effect of the judge's charge in respect to the determination of the size of premiums for automobile liability insurance on the minds of the jury? The majority opinion states the effect of the one case here would be too insignificant to affect their verdict. My mind reaches a different conclusion. I think the probable effect was highly prejudicial to plaintiffs, because the jury would probably believe that to award plaintiffs substantial damages or any damages at all might tend to increase the size of the premiums they would be required to pay under our State statute for automobile liability insurance to operate their automobiles, and, therefore, might probably cause them to award plaintiffs nothing as damages, which they in fact did. The reluctance of people to pay insurance premiums increased in size is known to all.

Justice Walker said for the Court in *Withers v. Lane*, 144 N.C. 184, 56 S.E. 855:

> The judge should be the embodiment of even and exact justice. He should at all times be on the alert, lest, in an unguarded moment, something be incautiously said or done to shake the wavering balance which, as a minister of justice, he is supposed, figuratively speaking, to hold in his hands. Every suitor is entitled by the law to have his cause considered with the 'cold neutrality of the impartial judge' and the equally unbiased mind of a properly instructed jury. This right can neither be denied nor abridged.

I vote for a new trial.

MOORE, J., joins in dissent.

Questions

1. What seemed to animate the *King* court more—the general principle about avoiding reference to insurance, or the misbehavior of the defendant-appellee Starr's counsel?

2. If misbehavior of Starr's counsel was the reason for the reversal, was it fair to Starr to force him to undergo attorneys' fees a second time when the fault was his counsel's?

3. Consider Question 2 carefully. On the assumption that Starr's lawyer misbehaved, why did the lawyer misbehave? What was the effect of the misbehavior? Who profited from it? How fully, how comprehensively, does a lawyer represent the interests of a client?

4. In *Hoover*, do you agree with Judge Higgins or Judge Parker? Does their reasoning change your earlier answer to Questions 4 and 5 at the outset of this section?

5. Was Judge Higgins reluctant to have the state incur the expense of retrying the case? If this is a "justice" factor and we plug it in to the equation, is the result

Higgins + expense factor = Parker?

In other words, are Higgins and Parker really quite close together? Are they both seeking the just result? If you feel they are far apart even without the "expense factor," is only one of them trying to do justice? If they are far apart and both are trying to do justice, can only one of them—or can both—succeed?

6. In the cases you have read so far, do the judges appear to be more concerned about fairness to the litigants (either the plaintiff or defendant) or fairness to insurance companies?

Federal Rules of Evidence

Rule 411. Liability Insurance

Evidence that a person was or was not insured against liability is not admissible upon the issue whether the person acted negligently or otherwise wrongfully. This rule does not require the exclusion of evidence of insurance against liability when offered for another purpose, such as proof of agency, ownership, or control, or bias or prejudice of a witness.

Question

How effective do you think Rule 411 will be in preventing the fact of insurance from being mentioned in trials held in federal court and thus prejudicing the jury?

2.3   Truths we don't want jurors to hear (about accusers)

United States v. Kasto

584 F.2d 268
United States Court of Appeals, Eighth Circuit
Decided Sept. 18, 1978
Rehearing Denied Oct. 13, 1978

Terry L. Pechota, Mission, S.D., for appellant.

Gary G. Colbath, Asst. U.S. Atty., Sioux Falls, S.D., for appellee.

Before HEANEY, BRIGHT and STEPHENSON, Circuit Judges.

HEANEY, Circuit Judge.

Abraham Kasto appeals from his conviction of rape in violation of 18 U.S.C. §§ 1153 and 2031. The primary issue raised on appeal is whether the District Court erred in prohibiting the introduction of evidence as to the reputation of the prosecutrix for unchastity, as to her specific prior acts of sexual intercourse with men other than the defendant, and as to the fact that she was wearing an intrauterine contraceptive device at the time of the incident. We hold that the exclusion of this evidence was not an abuse of discretion.

Beth Renee Jennings, the prosecutrix, was an Iowa State University student who was living on the Cheyenne River Indian Reservation in

South Dakota. She came to South Dakota on March 20, 1977, as a participant in a cultural exchange program sponsored by the University and the Cheyenne River Indian Reservation YMCA. At about 11:00 P.M. on March 27, 1977, Jennings was awakened at her residence by Kasto, who had been previously introduced to her as a representative of the YMCA. She turned on the lights, let Kasto in and engaged in casual conversation with him for about forty-five minutes. Kasto then asked her to take a ride with him in his truck. During the ride, Kasto drank whiskey while they discussed the YMCA program on the reservation. After a few minutes, Kasto stopped the truck. Jennings asked to be taken home, but Kasto refused. A scuffle ensued, during which Jennings was pulled from the truck and raped by Kasto on the ground. He then drove her to his house, where he raped her twice. She escaped from the house and went to the home of neighbors who took her to a local hospital. She was treated for skin abrasions and a laboratory examination revealed the presence of sperm in her vagina. Jennings was the only witness to testify as to the events surrounding the rapes.

Prior to trial, the government moved for a court order prohibiting the defense from making any reference at trial to any sexual activities which Jennings may have had with men other than Kasto, and from making any reference to the fact that she was wearing an intrauterine contraceptive device at the time of the alleged rape. The District Court granted the motion on the basis that a rape victim's reputation for unchastity and evidence of her specific acts of sexual intercourse with men other than the defendant are irrelevant to either her general credibility as a witness or to the issue of her consent to intercourse with the defendant on the date charged.

Kasto challenges this ruling on two grounds. First, he argues that, under *Packineau v. United States,* 202 F.2d 681 (8th Cir. 1953), evidence of Jennings' reputation for unchastity or prior acts of sexual intercourse with men other than the defendant, and evidence of her use of an intrauterine contraceptive device, were relevant to the issue of her consent to have intercourse with him. He argues that, under Fed.R.Evid. 401, the fact that Jennings may have consented to sexual intercourse with others, and wore a contraceptive device ostensibly for that purpose, would make the consequential fact of her consent to inter-

course with him more likely.

In *Packineau v. United States, supra,* the Court held that the trial court's ruling which prohibited cross-examination of the prosecutrix as to her cohabitation with a young man a few months before the alleged rape was prejudicial error requiring a new trial. *Id.* at 685. The Court reasoned that such evidence was necessary to reasonably test the credibility of the prosecutrix. In the view of the majority,

> That her story of having been raped would be more readily believed by a person who was ignorant of any former unchaste conduct on her part than it would be by a person cognizant of the unchaste conduct defendants offered to prove against her seems too clear for argument. * * * To an ordinary person called on to make an appraisal of [the prosecutrix's] accusation that one of the young men with whom she was out for dalliance on this night had raped her, the reaction would certainly be very different if it were known that she had been openly cohabiting with a young man only a few months before than it would be if she were the unsophisticated young lady she appeared to be.

Id. at 685–686.

Judge Sanborn dissented. In his view, the trial court did not err in limiting such cross-examination of the prosecutrix because the evidence which the defense sought to introduce was "incompetent, irrelevant and immaterial and had no bearing whatever upon any issue in the case." *Id.* at 688–689. He reasoned that any woman, even one who may have engaged in consensual, extramarital sexual activities with other men, "has some freedom of selection, and consent obtained from such a woman by a stunning blow on the jaw is no consent at all." *Id.* at 689.

We believe that Judge Sanborn's dissent has withstood the test of time and is supported both in logic and in human experience. The fact that a rape victim has engaged in consensual sexual relations with the defendant in the past under similar conditions may have some logical relevance to the question of consent to the act charged, and evidence of prior sexual activity with the defendant under dissimilar circumstances may also have some logical relevance, but "[w]hen both identity of persons and similarity of circumstances are removed, * * * probative value all but disappears." Ordover, *Admissibility of Patterns of Similar Sexual Conduct: The Unlamented Death of Character for Chastity,* 63 Cornell L.Rev. 90, 106 (1977). Although Judge Sanborn's dissenting views were limited to the elicitation of such evidence during the cross-examination of the prosecutrix, we feel that the same logic applies to direct examination testimony sought to be introduced by the defense. We, therefore, conclude that absent circumstances which enhance its probative value,[26] evidence of a rape victim's unchastity, whether in the form of testimony concerning her general reputation or direct or cross-examination testimony concerning specific acts with persons other than the defendant, is ordinarily insufficiently probative either of her general credibility as a witness[27] or of her

---

[26] Such circumstances might include where the evidence is explanative of a physical fact which is in evidence at trial, such as the presence of semen, pregnancy, or the victim's physical condition indicating intercourse, *see* State v. Cosden, 18 Wash. App. 213, 219, 568 P.2d 802, 806 (1977); State v. McDaniel, 204 N.W.2d 627, 629 (Iowa 1973), or where the evidence tends to establish bias, prejudice, or an ulterior motive surrounding the charge of rape. *See* Shoemaker v. State, 58 Tex. Cr. R. 518, 126 S.W. 887, 889 (1910). Sexual history might also be relevant where the victim has engaged in a prior pattern of behavior clearly similar to the conduct immediately in issue. *See Ordover, supra* at 93–94, 110–119.

[27] Some cases have held that evidence of a rape victim's unchastity is admissible for the sole purpose of impeaching the rape victim's credibility as a witness, on the theory that a woman of bad moral character is less likely to speak the truth than is a woman of good moral character. This thinking is reflected in State v. Coella, 3 Wash. 99, 28 P. 28, 29 (1891):

> She [the prosecutrix] could not have ruthlessly destroyed that quality [chastity] upon which most other good qualities are dependent, and for which, above all others, a woman is reverenced and respected, and yet retain her credit for truthfulness unsmirched * * *.

[Citing cases] Other courts have repudiated such views. It is obvious that the mere fact of unchastity of a victim has no relevance whatsoever to her credibility as a witness. Such a proposition would "necessarily imply the absurd [corollary] that the extramarital sexual history of a female witness would be admissible to impeach her credibility in any case in which she testified." [Citing cases]

consent to intercourse with the defendant on the particular occasion charged to outweigh its highly prejudicial effect. [Citing cases] To the extent that the majority opinion in *Packineau v. United States, supra,* is inconsistent with this conclusion, that case is hereby overruled.[28]

The weighing of the probative value of such evidence against its prejudicial effect is, of course, entrusted to the broad discretion of the trial judge. *See* Fed.R.Evid. 401, 403. Our examination of the record in the instant case satisfies us that the ruling by the District Court prohibiting any reference to any sexual activity which Jennings may have had with men other than Kasto, and to the fact that she was wearing an intrauterine contraceptive device at the time of the incident, was not an abuse of discretion. Any relevance which this evidence may have had to the issue of her consent to sexual relations with Kasto was outweighed by its prejudicial effect. Since we agree with the District Court that the evidence sought to be introduced by Kasto fails the threshold test of relevancy, we need not reach his contentions that the admission of this evidence would have been permitted by Fed.R.Evid. 404 and 608.

Kasto also argues that his inability to cross-examine Jennings as to her prior sexual activities and her use of an intrauterine contraceptive device denied him his Sixth Amendment right to confront the witness against him. This claim is without merit. The Sixth Amendment right to confrontation and the Fifth Amendment right to due process of law require only that the accused be permitted to introduce all relevant and admissible evidence. *See United States v. Nixon,* 418 U.S. 683, 711 (1974). Since we have upheld the District Court's determination that the proffered evidence was irrelevant to the issue of Jennings' consent to sexual relations with Kasto, its exclusion deprived him of no constitutional right.

Kasto next contends that he was impermissibly denied the opportunity to cross-examine Jennings as to any sexual activities which she may have had immediately prior to the alleged rape, which may have been relevant to the source of the

---

[28] This opinion was circulated to all judges in regular active service and a majority of the Court has expressly approved this panel decision overruling Packineau v. United States, 202 F.2d 681 (8th Cir. 1953).

semen found in her subsequent medical evaluation. Although the sexual activities of a prosecutrix immediately prior to an alleged rape may be a relevant area for cross-examination by the defense, our reading of the record convinces us that the failure of defense counsel to pursue this line of inquiry was not the result of any express prohibition on such questioning by the District Court. Prior to trial, the government stated that it intended to ask Jennings at trial whether she had intercourse with anyone within forty-eight hours of the alleged incident, and requested a ruling from the court as to whether such a question would open the door to inquiry by the defense as to any sexual activities which Jennings may have had at other times with other men. When, however, defense counsel stated that he had no evidence that Jennings had intercourse with anyone within forty-eight hours of the alleged rape, the government agreed not to ask the question at trial, and no ruling on the implications of its asking was made by the District Court. Later, when Jennings was examined *in camera,* she stated in response to the government's question, that she had had no sexual relations with anyone from the time of her arrival in South Dakota until the incident with Kasto on the night of March 27. The defense did not cross-examine Jennings as to the truth of this statement.

Kasto also argues that he should have been permitted to question Jennings and the examining physician as to the type of contraceptive device that she was wearing at the time of rape. We find no merit to this contention. The defense was permitted to question Jennings *in camera* as to the type of device she was wearing, and there was no evidence from her testimony that it was other than an intrauterine contraceptive device. Although the defense had access to the physician's report prior to trial, no request was made to question the physician about this issue until after the government had rested and the witness had been dismissed. Under these circumstances, any right which the defense might have had to make an offer of proof on the basis of the physician's testimony was waived.

Kasto also contends that he has been deprived of equal protection of law since, as an Indian charged with the rape of a non-Indian under 18 U.S.C. §§ 1153 and 2031, he was subject to a maximum penalty of life imprisonment upon conviction, while a non-Indian charged with the same offense under South Dakota law would be subject to a maximum of only twenty years' imprisonment. In *United States v. Antelope,* 430 U.S. 641, 97 S.Ct. 1395, 51 L.Ed.2d 701 (1977), the Supreme Court held that it is of no constitutional significance that a federal scheme for the punishment of a particular offense differs from a state criminal code otherwise applicable within the boundaries of the state where the reservation lies. *Id.* at 648–650, 97 S.Ct. 1395. We are bound by that decision.

The judgment is affirmed.

Notes and Questions

1. Can you find language in the court's opinion that evidence of prior sexual activity the prosecutrix may have had with other men is flat-out irrelevant to the issue of consent in a rape case? Can you also find language that although such evidence is not irrelevant, introducing it would be too prejudicial to the prosecutrix? What is the court's holding on this issue? If the court switches ground, try to locate the exact moment and say why.

2. Kasto was convicted of a crime to which life imprisonment attaches. Should *all* unconsensual intercourse, no matter what the context, be punished by life imprisonment? Was the real problem that Kasto's defense attorney faced the fact that there were no statutory *degrees* of rape? Should there be? Would you expect higher conviction rates if there were?

What would be the reason justifying degrees of rape? Degrees of moral culpability of the offense? Trustworthiness of testimony about consent in different contexts? Is the latter a proper consideration in defining what is and what is not criminal behavior?

What is the justification for *not* having degrees of rape?

3. As you can see from the case, Kasto violated a *federal* statute against rape. The federal statute applied to him because he was an Indian on an Indian reservation, hence state law did not apply to him. Do you agree with the court that Kasto has not been denied equal protection of the laws even though were a non-Indian to commit rape on the same reservation the laws of South Dakota would apply and the maximum penalty would only be 20 years?

4. Consider further the importance of the reservation. Suppose Kasto was acting toward Jennings in a manner he had been brought up to think was natural or inevitable. Imagine a culture in which it would have been reasonable for Kasto to believe Jennings had consented. If Indian culture was in fact such a culture, is it fair for the United States to superimpose on the reservation its *own* laws as to rape and its *own* courts to adjudicate such cases? Is that cultural imperialism? Even if not, does it do justice to the question of consent?

5. What about the issue whether Jennings' decision to live for a while on the reservation—as part of a "cultural exchange program" sponsored by Iowa State University—obliges her to familiarize herself with possible differences in perception regarding matters such as sexual intercourse on the part of Indians living on the reservation? Can Kasto make out a credible case of "provocation"?

Federal Rules of Evidence

Rule 412.[29] Rape Cases; Relevance of Victim's Past Behavior

(a) Notwithstanding any other provision of law, in a criminal case in which a person is accused of rape or of assault with intent to commit rape, reputation or opinion evidence of the past sexual behavior of an alleged victim of such rape or assault is not admissible.

(b) Notwithstanding any other provision of law, in a criminal case in which a person is accused of rape or of assault with intent to commit rape, evidence of a victim's past sexual behavior other than reputation or opinion evidence is also not admissible, unless such evidence other than reputation or opinion evidence is—

(1) admitted in accordance with subdivisions (c)(1) and (c)(2) and is constitutionally required to be admitted; or

(2) admitted in accordance with subdivision (c) and is evidence of—

(A) past sexual behavior with persons other than the accused, offered by the accused upon the issue of whether the accused was or was not, with respect to the alleged victim, the source of semen or injury; or

(B) past sexual behavior with the accused and is offered by the accused upon the issue of whether the alleged victim consented to the sexual behavior with respect to which rape or assault is alleged.

---

[29] The Federal Rules of Evidence were first adopted by Congress in 1975. Rule 412 was adopted later, in Pub. L. No. 95-540 § 2(a)(October 28, 1978), two weeks after the rehearing was denied in *Kasto*.

(c)(1) If the person accused of committing rape or assault with intent to commit rape intends to offer under subdivision (b) evidence of specific instances of the alleged victim's past sexual behavior, the accused shall make a written motion to offer such evidence not later than fifteen days before the date on which the trial in which such evidence is to be offered is scheduled to begin, except that the court may allow the motion to be made at a later date, including during trial, if the court determines either that the evidence is newly discovered and could not have been obtained earlier through the exercise of due diligence or that the issue to which such evidence relates has newly arisen in the case. Any motion made under this paragraph shall be served on all other parties and on the alleged victim.

(2) The motion described in paragraph (1) shall be accompanied by a written offer of proof. If the court determines that the offer of proof contains evidence described in subdivision (b), the court shall order a hearing in chambers to determine if such evidence is admissible. At such hearing the parties may call witnesses, including the alleged victim, and offer relevant evidence. Notwithstanding subdivision (b) of rule 104, if the relevancy of the evidence which the accused seeks to offer in the trial depends upon the fulfillment of a condition of fact, the court, at the hearing in chambers or at a subsequent hearing in chambers scheduled for such purpose, shall accept evidence on the issue of whether such condition of fact is fulfilled and shall determine such issue.

(3) If the court determines on the basis of the hearing described in paragraph (2) that the evidence which the accused seeks to offer is relevant and that the probative value of such evidence outweighs the danger of unfair prejudice, such evidence shall be admissible in the trial to the extent an order made by the court specifies evidence which may be offered and areas with respect to which the alleged victim may be examined or cross-examined.

(d) For purposes of this rule, the term "past sexual behavior" means sexual behavior other than the sexual behavior with respect to which rape or assault with intent to commit rape is alleged.

Questions

1. Does Rule 412 take any positions that do not square with a possible application of the other evidence rules, specifically Rules 401, 403, and 404(a) (evidence of a person's character is not admissible to show that he acted in conformity with it)? If not, what purpose can we ascribe to Congress in enacting Rule 412 along with the others? In other words, what, if anything, does Rule 412 accomplish?

2. The public tends to react to publicity about major crimes by demanding an increase in the severity of penalties. Rape is a major crime, but is an increase in the severity of punishment a productive way of reducing the incidence of sexual crimes? Even if it isn't productive, should penalties be increased anyway in order to make a statement about society's condemnation of sexual crimes?

If your answer to the first of these questions is No, and your answer to the second is Yes, what will happen to societal perceptions in the long run?

In Saudi Arabia, the penalty for the crime of adultery is death by stoning if the adulterer is a woman, and death by beheading if the adulterer is a man. Sandra Mackey reports that in the past twenty years in Saudi Arabia, only one woman is known to have been stoned to death for adultery.[30] Consider the degree of evidentiary proof needed to convict a person of adultery in Saudi Arabia. There must be eyewitness evidence of the adultery by either four male witnesses or eight female witnesses.[31] It is not enough that the witnesses see the accused couple naked and in an embrace; the witnesses must witness the actual penetration.

Is it fair to say that in Saudi Arabia there is a direct relation among (a) the severity of the sentence, (b) the degree of evidence required, and (c) the frequency of convictions?

---

[30] S. Mackey, The Saudis: Inside the Desert Kingdom 289 (1990).

[31] In the *sharia* law of Saudi Arabia, throughout all cases, it takes the testimony of two women to equal the testimony of one man.

Comment on the Federal Rules of Evidence and the Liberal Theory of Justice

The common theme of Rule 412 and related rules (Rules 404 to 412) is that persons should be judged only by the actions they do and only inasmuch as those very actions are the ones for which the court is seeking to determine whether they are legally—civilly or criminally—liable. Some of the rules in the series are calculated to protect the actions persons take in the course of litigation (Rule 408 on compromise and offers to compromise; Rule 410 on pleas). Others deal with collateral issues (Rule 407 on subsequent remedial measures; Rule 409 on payment of medical expenses occasioned by an injury; Rule 411 on liability insurance). The main rules in the series, however, focus on character (Rule 404; Rule 405 on methods of proving character when it is admissible; and Rule 412 on the special version of character relevant to rape cases).

But isn't the main difficulty with evidence about a person's character, apart from prejudice, the fact that no one understands "character" enough to be able to specify when character evidence is relevant to establishing character? Indeed, the only sure way we know to talk about character is to ask about reputation or to deliver conclusory statements in the form of opinion.

The Federal Rules indicate that the law is suspicious about character evidence. But this attitude is by no means inevitable. After all, ordinary people make decisions on the basis of character all the time. The bias against character evidence thus cannot be traced to a common opinion that evidence about character is fundamentally unreliable, or more unreliable than any other sort of evidence. If we are to find the roots of the bias against character evidence, we must turn to considerations other than reliability.

We suggest that the bias against character evidence has its origins in the theory of justice that dominates both common opinion and the legal system. We call it the liberal theory of justice. The theory holds that just treatment of persons focuses on what persons do, not who they are or what circumstance they find themselves in.

The source of the modern liberal theory of justice and social organization is the notion of freedom. Only when we judge persons by what they do, not who they are or what circumstance they find themselves in, can we consider persons juridically free. Otherwise, if we judge them by who they are or by their circumstance, we cannot hold them responsible for their actions, which we must do if we are to consider them juridically free. The great modern theorist of liberty, Friedrich Hayek, refers to the main purpose of a legal system as creating an "order of actions," that is, a realm in which it is legitimate to hold persons responsible for their actions and thus consider them juridically free.[32]

Character evidence is evil, from this point of view, not because it is unreliable, but because it threatens any legal order in which it is legitimate to hold persons juridically responsible for their actions. Perhaps the legal fear is summarized in the French saying, "to know all is to forgive all." If the jury knows *too much* (that is, legally too much) about a defendant, the jury might sympathize with the defendant rather than finding him guilty.

The only fact we know for sure about character is that one cannot freely choose one's own character. If one could act voluntarily to get a character, then the possession of certain undesirable characteristics would itself be criminal.

The flaw in the liberal theory of justice, which emphasizes freedom as the highest value, is the difficulty of believing that any person is actually free. Freedom is a value; it may not be a fact. People do commit crimes, and we do not suppose they always freely do so. If one is born poor, male and black in the United States, one is more likely, as a matter of statistical fact, to commit a violent crime than if one is born wealthy, female and white. We treat people *as if* they are free, always wondering whether doing so is legitimate.

Legal argument recognizes the hortatory character of the liberal theory of justice. We make ordinary judgments on the basis of character and circumstance, and we make legal judgments on the same basis, albeit reluctantly and with a consciousness that we are perhaps betraying our fundamental values.

At the very least, we constantly find lawyers and factfinders making judgments about the character of persons from their actions, and judgments about the actions of persons from their characters. How can we justifiably separate the two?[33]

The Federal Rules of Evidence wrestles with the dilemma of modernity, that persons wish to be free but fear they are not. Character evidence is necessary, but detested. Many of the paradoxes of the rules governing character evidence—its inconsistencies, loopholes, and deceptions that we do not here explore[34]—stem from the dilemmas of the liberal theory of justice.

---

[32] See F. HAYEK, LAW, LEGISLATION AND LIBERTY, VOL. I, RULES AND ORDER, ch. 5; NOMOS: THE LAW OF LIBERTY, 98–101 (1973).

[33] *See* Chaim Perelman's essay, *Act and Person in Argument,* in THE IDEA OF JUSTICE AND THE PROBLEM OF ARGUMENT (1963). For a classic battle of the giants over the questions, *see* People v. Zackowitz, 254 N.Y. 192, 172 N.E. 466 (1930) (Cardozo against character evidence, Pound for).

[34] For a full account of the extraordinary array, *see* 1A WIGMORE ON EVIDENCE §§ 52 *et seq.* (P. Tillers rev. 1983).

2.4 The composition of juries

The jury introduces average community sentiment into the adjudicatory process. But problems can arise when a particular jury that is empaneled is not representative of the community. Not many years ago, juries were selected from voter registration lists from predominantly white communities; hence blacks were systematically underrepresented on juries. In large metropolitan areas, many criminal cases involving black defendants were decided by all-white juries. And years before that, juries were all-male. However, as a matter of current constitutional law, a strong statistical showing that jury lists do not represent the community (because they may be biased in favor of whites or males, for example) is sufficient to require reversal of the jury's verdict. Even more recently, prosecutorial use of peremptory challenges (a right to excuse some prospective jurors without stating a reason) have been invalidated when the prosecutor's purpose can be demonstrated to have been the exclusion of jurors because of race. It may not be long before gender-based peremptory challenges are also held unconstitutional.

Our purpose here is not to reexamine constitutional requirements. Rather, the present section is designed to raise questions about the justice of certain kinds of juror-exclusion procedures.

Legal literature is practically silent about the empaneling experience from the juror's point of view. In a large city like Chicago, a citizen gets a summons in the mail to appear for jury call. The notice is well in advance of the call, so that the citizen can make arrangements to set aside two weeks. On Monday of the first week, he or she shows up at 9 a.m. in the courthouse auditorium. Numbers are assigned by lottery to all of the 500 to 700 prospective jurors. The numbers are called—thirty at a time—and persons with those numbers are led to a courtroom where they are subject to voir dire questioning. Those who survive the questioning process remain, the others go back to the auditorium.

In the auditorium, TV sets blare out the day's soap operas. People read books or sit silently. There is a room in the back for nonsmokers who want privacy. All day long numbers are called. Some people are afraid they will get selected for a long trial—because, once selected, they may have to appear daily in the jury for weeks or months. So some devise procedures for avoiding selection—thus ensuring that their maximum time spent will be the two weeks "waiting" to be called. These procedures are fairly sophisticated. Information is exchanged on how to demonstrate "bias" when questioned by the attorneys. Some prospective jurors say they are prepared to lie so that they are not selected. The day drags on. At 4:30 p.m., all the persons in the auditorium who haven't been selected for a jury are dismissed and told to come back the next day at 9 a.m. They have to return to the courthouse auditorium for nine more consecutive weekdays.

Many persons waiting in the courthouse auditorium consider the entire procedure to be a gross imposition on their time. Many complain of loss of income; although employers are required to continue paying a salary to employees who are called to jury duty, a number of persons are self-employed and hence the approximately $16 per day that they are paid to wait on call constitutes a severe economic loss for them. But some prospective jurors are anxious to get selected for an interesting case. They devise strategies to "hide" any biases they might have so that they will be selected. If they are rejected from several jury panels early in their two-week call, they become progressively better at answering questions in their succeeding calls so that they will not again be rejected. They learn to give ambiguous or evasive answers. The cleverest learn to appear sympathetic when questioned by the attorneys for both sides, so that neither plaintiff nor defendant will reject them.

Exercising Peremptory Challenges After *Batson*[35]

James A. Acker

[Lawyers who want to know which prospective jurors to accept or reject start by commissioning a demographic analysis.] A description typically is made of the general characteristics of the population in the community in which the trial is to be held. This demographic analysis includes information about the age structure of the community, its racial composition, and aggregate data concerning political and religious affiliations, occupations, education levels, income, and so forth.

This is followed by more complete telephone or face-to-face interviews with a sample of the population. The survey collects descriptive information about the respondents, and also elicits their opinions and attitudes on a variety of topics relevant to the case, crime and criminal justice generally, and other information that could provide insights about their likely performances as jurors. The demographic and attitudinal variables are then analyzed for significant correlations. The analysis may suggest, for example, that younger jurors, the more highly educated, religious agnostics, people who read *The New York Times*, or people who drive pickup trucks might make more or less desirable jurors for the particular impending trial.

Profiles are then generated of "ideal" jurors for the case. Although such portraits might be developed with greater specificity and somewhat greater colorable validity than lawyers arrive at through common sense and intuition, they nevertheless are based on the same group stereotyping condemned by *Batson*[36] and related cases. The juror profiles, however, are but a single stream of information relied on in systematic jury selection and provide a foundation and starting point for the subsequent voir dire of individual prospective jurors in the courtroom.

If possible, information is compiled about the individual members of the venire who have been summoned for jury duty. This may be accomplished informally, through local networking, or more systematically, through access to the questionnaires completed by the members of the jury panel before reporting to court. The attorneys thus commence their voir dire armed with general information about the community and the venire, about the veniremembers, and with a series of questions that both relate to and go beyond the

---

[35] 24 CRIM. L. BULL. 187, 206–208 (1988).

[36] Batson v. Kentucky, 90 L. Ed. 2d 69 (1986) (prosecutor may not exercise peremptory challenges against black prospective jurors to achieve a nonblack jury).

foundation provided by the demographic and attitude survey.

Voir dire questioning then elicits important descriptive information from the individual prospective jurors, including basic demographic characteristics, hobbies and uses of recreational time, preferred reading material, membership in groups, clubs and voluntary organizations, and the like. The attorneys also probe more deeply into attitudes relevant to jury service. They may seek to identify "authoritarian" value systems, belief in a "just world," and other such general orientations that may help determine perceptions and attitudes important to veniremembers' potential performance as jurors. Social science indices designed to evaluate people on such dimensions are typically integrated with a lawyer's questioning on voir dire for this purpose.

The nonverbal behavior of prospective jurors might also be assessed as a part of systematic jury selection. The eye and hand movements of veniremembers, their shifts in posture, speech inflections, and other "body language" might yield information about their candor and affinity toward the attorneys representing the different parties to a case. Members of the panel are evaluated not only as individuals, but according to how they would likely fit with other jurors during group decision making. Potential leaders and followers might be identified, likely cliques and coalitions predicted, and attorneys generally might have to be attentive to the composition of the jury as a group, rather than simply considering the individual members of it.

A lawyer faithful to such procedures would only make a decision about exercising peremptory challenges after these numerous pieces of information about a case, the community, and prospective jurors were combined and evaluated. Unless racial identity or other group membership were considered such a dominant characteristic as to dwarf the other ostensibly relevant attributes of a "good" or "bad" juror, reliance on systematic jury selection techniques should effectively discourage lawyers from acting on the sorts of racial assumptions condemned in *Batson* and related cases. The larger question, however, is whether these techniques are apt to contribute affirmatively to a lawyer's objectives in selecting a jury, an issue on which the evidence is mixed.

Notes and Questions

1. Do you consider these systematic juror selection procedures to be a triumph of good litigation skills or an impediment to the just resolution of disputes?

2. Would the legal system be better off if jurors were asked no questions at all, there were no dismissals of jurors for cause, and all peremptory challenges were eliminated?

3. No matter what an individual juror's background, education, and general attitudes may be, is it not possible that he or she has a particular bias relating to the facts of the case? If the bias is personal—for example, the juror knows one of the parties—then the judge will typically dismiss the juror "for cause." But a juror may also be biased because of a particular personal experience. For example, a juror who was once the victim of an automobile accident is generally considered dismissible "for cause" in a tort case involving an automobile accident. Doesn't the exclusion of such jurors destroy the "representativeness" of the jury panel in the community?

4. Suppose you are a prospective juror in a murder case. You are told that the defendant has been indicted for first-degree murder and that the state is asking for the death penalty. Then the prosecutor asks you on voir dire whether you are opposed to capital punishment. How would you respond? Consider the following Letter to the Editor of *The Chicago Lawyer*:[37]

DALEY'S OFFICE BLASTED FOR ASSAILING
DISSENTING JUROR IN DEATH PENALTY CASE

To the Editor of *Chicago Lawyer:*

As members of the Chicago legal community, we strongly condemn statements issued publicly by the Cook County state's attorney's office expressing the intent to prosecute, for perjury, a juror who voted against the death penalty in a recent case.

In December, a jury convicted Miriam Watt of murdering her two-year-old granddaughter. The prosecution requested the death penalty. After five hours of deliberations, the jury voted 11 to 1 in favor of death. Because a death verdict must be unanimous, Watt's life was spared. The state's office, upset that the 12 jurors did not march lockstep to the death chamber, now has threatened to prosecute an individual of conscience.

Immediately after the verdict, the prosecutor accused the dissenting juror of "sabotaging the system." Supervising Assistant State's Attorney Robert Clifford announced to the press that his office was contemplating prosecuting the juror for perjury on the ground that the juror, when questioned before the trial, stated that he could consider imposing a death sentence, yet refused to do so during the jury's deliberations.

Clifford should be reminded that in a democracy, the voice of dissent is not sabotage, but a necessary and valuable part of the "system." Clifford's statements constitute not only a blatant threat to punish a juror for depriving the state's attorney's office of a death verdict, but an insidious attempt to intimidate future jurors with the specter of prosecution for disagreement with the government. Such threats and intimidation have no place in our criminal justice system.

Jury deliberations are sacrosanct. No juror ever need justify his or her vote in a criminal case. The dissenting juror in the Watt case, for whatever reason, concluded that the defendant should not be sentenced to death. Perhaps the juror felt lingering doubt about Watt's guilt, since the evidence against her was completely circumstantial. Perhaps the juror felt the evidence did not warrant the death penalty. Perhaps the juror chose to extend mercy to Watt. Any of these reasons is completely legitimate and above questioning or criticism.

Moreover, even if the juror in the Watt case simply refused to consider the death penalty, there was no "perjury" involved. The decision to sentence a fellow human being to death is unlike any other. A potential juror being questioned before a trial may sincerely believe that he could, under the proper circumstances, sentence someone to death. Yet that same juror, after hearing the evidence and considering the sentence in deliberations, may find himself unable to do so. Such a good faith realization by a juror is no crime.

Our jury system will cease to work if jurors are forced to worry that they may be

[37] CHICAGO LAWYER, February 1989, at p. 10. The letter was signed by: Randolph N. Stone, Public Defender of Cook County; Robert P. Isaacson, Chief, Appeals Division, Cook County Public Defender's Office; Kyle Wesendorf, Assistant Public Defender; Steven Clark and Charles Hoffman, Assistant Defenders, Supreme Court Unit, Office of the State Appellate Defender; Standish Willis, Co-Chair, Chicago Conference of Black Lawyers; Jed Stone, Member, Board of Directors, Illinois Attorneys for Criminal Justice; Douglass W. Cassel Jr., President, Chicago Chapter, National Lawyers Guild; Peter J. Schmiedel, Peoples Law Office; Benjamin Wolf, Staff Attorney, ACLU.

punished for their decisions. State's Attorney Daley should immediately and publicly retract the threat to prosecute the dissenting juror in the Watt case, and insure that similar threats are not repeated by his assistants in the future.

5. Suppose you are asked the question on voir dire, and you say that you are opposed to capital punishment. You will be dismissed "for cause." So will every juror who so responds. The empaneled jury will be made up only of citizens who are *not* opposed to capital punishment. Would such a jury be "representative of the community"?

6. Is a person who is in favor of the death penalty a person who is more likely to find the defendant guilty? Or does a juror's verdict on the facts bear no necessary relationship to the juror's beliefs about the propriety or impropriety of capital punishment?

7. Do you agree with the writers of the letter that jury deliberations are "sacrosanct"? If so, why? If not, why not?

United States v. Dougherty

473 F.2d 1113
United States Court of Appeals,
District of Columbia Circuit
June 30, 1972
Rehearing Denied October 26, 1972

Before BAZELON, Chief Judge, LEVEN-THAL, Circuit Judge, and ADAMS, Circuit Judge, United States Court of Appeals for the Third Circuit.

LEVENTHAL, Circuit Judge:

Seven of the so-called "D.C. Nine" bring this joint appeal from convictions arising out of their unconsented entry into the Washington offices of the Dow Chemical Company, and their destruction of certain property therein. On February 11, 1970, after a six-day trial, the seven were each convicted of two counts of malicious destruction. The jury acquitted on the burglary charges but convicted on the lesser-included offense of unlawful entry.

Appellants urge [among other contentions, that] the judge erroneously refused to instruct the jury of its right to acquit appellants without regard to the law and the evidence, and refused to permit appellants to argue that issue to the jury.

[Appellants] say that the jury has a well-recognized prerogative to disregard the instructions of the court even as to matters of law, and

that they accordingly have the legal right that the jury be informed of its power. We turn to this matter in order to define the nature of the new trial permitted by our mandate.

There has evolved in the Anglo-American system an undoubted jury prerogative-in-fact, derived from its power to bring in a general verdict of not guilty in a criminal case, that is not reversible by the court. The power of the courts to punish jurors for corrupt or incorrect verdicts, which persisted after the medieval system of attaint by another jury became obsolete, was repudiated in 1670 when Bushell's Case, 124 Eng.Rep. 1006 (C.P. 1670) discharged the jurors who had acquitted William Penn of unlawful assembly. Juries in civil cases became subject to the control of ordering a new trial; no comparable control evolved for acquittals in criminal cases.

The pages of history shine on instances of the jury's exercise of its prerogative to disregard uncontradicted evidence and instructions of the judge. Most often commended are the 18th century acquittal of Peter Zenger of seditious libel, on the plea of Andrew Hamilton, and the 19th century acquittals in prosecutions under the fugitive slave law. The values involved drop a notch when the liberty vindicated by the verdict relates to the defendant's shooting of his wife's paramour, or purchase during Prohibition of alcoholic beverages.[38]

Even the notable Dean Pound commented in 1910 on positive aspects of "such jury lawlessness."[39] These observations of history and philosophy are underscored and illuminated, in terms of the current place of the jury in the American system of justice, by the empirical information and critical insights and analyses blended so felicitously in H. Kalven and H. Zeisel, The American Jury.[40]

Reflective opinions upholding the necessity for the jury as a protection against arbitrary action, such as prosecutorial abuse of power, stress fundamental features like the jury "common sense judgment" and assurance of "community participation in the determination of guilt or innocence."[41] Human frailty being what it is, a prosecutor disposed by unworthy motives could likely establish some basis in fact for bringing charges against anyone he wants to book, but the jury system operates in fact, (see note [40]) so that the jury will not convict when they empathize with the defendant, as when the offense is one they see themselves as likely to commit, or consider generally acceptable or condonable under the mores of the community.

The existence of an unreviewable and unreversible power in the jury, to acquit in disregard of the instructions on the law given by the trial judge, has for many years co-existed with legal practice and precedent upholding instructions to

---

[38] Kalven and Zeisel, op. cit. *infra* note [40], at p. 310 (Fugitive Slave Law), at p. 292, note 10 (Prohibition acquittals statistics, showing variation by districts).

[39] See R. Pound, *Law in Books and Law in Action,* 44 Am. L. Rev. 12, 18 (1910): "Jury lawlessness is the greatest corrective of law in its actual administration. The will of the state at large imposed on a reluctant community, the will of a majority imposed on a vigorous and determined minority, find the same obstacle in the local jury that formerly confronted kings and ministers." Pound comments that the law as written, and invoked by prosecutors, "demands conviction of persons whom local or even general opinion does not desire to punish," and adds that "the law is often too mechanical at a point requiring nicety of adjustment."

[40] (Pub. Little, Brown 1966). The study of the American jury system, undertaken at the University of Chicago Law School, is a complete analysis of 3576 criminal jury trials, with particular focus on the 1063 instances where the judge reported that he disagreed with the jury verdict, and why. Half these cases present an apparent difference between judge and jury on "sentiments on the law."

The study supports in depth the conclusion that the jury is likely to call on its prerogative of lenity and equity, contrary to the judge's instruction, when the case is one where it can empathize with the defendant, feeling either that the jurors might well have been or come to be in the same position, or that in the large the defendant's conduct is not so contrary to general conduct standards as to be condemned as criminally deviate conduct. From a study teeming with illustrations, the following are cited as examples.

The authors broadly discern that "in cases having a de minimis cast or a note of contributory fault or provocation * * * the jury will exercise its de facto powers to write these equities into the criminal law" (p. 285) and "an impatience with the nicety of the law's

boundaries hedging the privilege of self-defense" (p. 241). (E.g., acquittal for retaliation following assaults, or even harassment and provocation, without present danger; for violence erupting after domestic strife, or unfaithfulness of spouse; for fraud of a victim still the seller's friend; for statutory rape of a girl unchaste; for sale of liquor to a minor who is a member of the armed forces).

Perhaps most relevant is ch. 19 on Unpopular Laws, p. 286 et seq. Though the authors discerned no law prompting a jury revolt comparable to the historic acquittals on charges of violation of seditious libel or fugitive slave laws, or even Prohibition, the data indicate that the historic role of the jury as a bulwark against official tyranny is "amply evident in its contemporary role as a moderate corrective against undue prosecutions for gambling, game and liquor violations and, to some extent, drunken driving" (p. 296), the jury's traditional hostility to sumptuary legislation being "keyed to its perception that . . . widespread violation is tolerated" so that prosecution of a particular defendant is contrary to the principle of evenhanded justice (p. 287). And so in some counties "people generally do not like the game law" (p. 288). In counties where jurors play the numbers they acquit broadly in gambling cases (p. 289) etc. When the jurors "feel the same thing could happen to them," they will acquit even of negligent manslaughter charges, as in running a red light, though there are more convictions in cases involving extreme speed. (Ch. 24).

[41] *See* Duncan v. Louisiana, 391 U.S. 145, 156 (1968).

the jury that they are required to follow the instructions of the court on all matters of law. There were different soundings in colonial days and the early days of our Republic. We are aware of the number and variety of expressions at that time from respected sources—John Adams; Alexander Hamilton; prominent judges—that jurors had a duty to find a verdict according to their own conscience, though in opposition to the direction of the court; that their power signified a right; that they were judges both of law and of fact in a criminal case, and not bound by the opinion of the court.

The rulings did not run all one way, but rather precipitated "a number of classic exchanges on the freedom and obligations of the criminal jury."[42] This was, indeed, one of the points of clash between the contending forces staking out the direction of the government of the newly established Republic, a direction resolved in political terms by reforming but sustaining the status of the courts, without radical change.[43] As the distrust of judges appointed and removable by the king receded, there came increasing acceptance that under a republic the protection of citizens lay not in recognizing the right of each jury to make its own law, but in following democratic processes for changing the law.

The crucial legal ruling came in United States v. Battiste, 2 Sum. 240, Fed.Cas. No. 14,545 (C.C.D.Mass. 1835). Justice Story's strong opinion supported the conception that the jury's function lay in accepting the law given to it by the court and applying that law to the facts. This considered ruling of an influential jurist won increasing acceptance in the nation. The youthful passion for independence accommodated itself to the reality that the former rebels were now in control of their own destiny, that the practical needs of stability and sound growth outweighed the abstraction of centrifugal philosophy, and that the judges in the courts, were not the colonial appointees projecting royalist patronage and influence but were themselves part and parcel of

the nation's intellectual mainstream, subject to the checks of the common law tradition and professional opinion, and capable, in Roscoe Pound's words, of providing "true judicial justice" standing in contrast with the colonial experience.[44]

The tide was turned by *Battiste,* but there were cross-currents. At mid-century the country was still influenced by the precepts of Jacksonian democracy, which spurred demands for direct selection of judges by the people through elections, and distrust of the judge-made common law which enhanced the movement for codification reform. But by the end of the century, even the most prominent state landmarks had been toppled; and the Supreme Court settled the matter for the Federal courts in Sparf v. United States, 156 U.S. 51, 102 (1895) after exhaustive review in both majority and dissenting opinions. The jury's role was respected as significant and wholesome, but it was not to be given instructions that articulated a right to do whatever it willed. The old rule survives today only as a singular relic.

Since the jury's prerogative of lenity, in Learned Hand's words, introduces a "slack into the enforcement of law, tempering its rigor by the mollifying influence of current ethical conventions," it is only just, say appellants, that the jurors be so told. It is unjust to withhold information on the jury power of "nullification," since conscientious jurors may come, ironically, to abide by their oath as jurors to render verdicts offensive to their individual conscience, to defer to an assumption of necessity that is contrary to reality.

This so-called right of jury nullification is put forward in the name of liberty and democracy, but its explicit avowal risks the ultimate logic of anarchy. This is the concern voiced by Judge Soboloff in United States v. Moylan, 417 F.2d 1002, 1009 (4th Cir. 1969), cert. denied, 397 U.S. 910 (1970):

> To encourage individuals to make their own determinations as to which laws they will obey and which they will permit themselves as a matter of conscience to disobey is to invite chaos. No legal system could long sur-

---

[42] M. R. Kadish & S. H. Kadish, *On Justified Rule Departures by Officials,* 59 Calif. L. Rev. 905, 914 (1971).

[43] A. Ellis, The Jeffersonian Crisis (Oxford Press, 1971).

[44] *See* IV Pound, Jurisprudence (West Pub. Co. 1959) pp. 8–9.

vive if it gave every individual the option of disregarding with impunity any law which by his personal standard was judged morally untenable. Toleration of such conduct would not be democratic, as appellants claim, but inevitably anarchic.

The statement that avowal of the jury's prerogative runs the risk of anarchy, represents, in all likelihood, the habit of thought of philosophy and logic, rather than the prediction of the social scientist. But if the statement contains an element of hyperbole, the existence of risk and danger, of significant magnitude, cannot be gainsaid. In contrast, the advocates of jury "nullification" apparently assume that the articulation of the jury's power will not extend its use or extent, or will not do so significantly or obnoxiously. Can this assumption fairly be made? We know that a posted limit of 60 m.p.h. produces factual speeds 10 or even 15 miles greater, with an understanding all around that some "tolerance" is acceptable to the authorities, assuming conditions warrant. But can it be supposed that the speeds would stay substantially the same if the speed limit were put: Drive as fast as you think appropriate, without the posted limit as an anchor, a point of departure?

Our jury system is a resultant of many vectors, some explicit, and some rooted in tradition, continuity and general understanding without express formulation. A constitution may be meaningful though it is unwritten, as the British have proved for 900 years.

The jury system has worked out reasonably well overall, providing "play in the joints" that imparts flexibility and avoids undue rigidity. An equilibrium has evolved—an often marvelous balance—with the jury acting as a "safety valve" for exceptional cases, without being a wildcat or runaway institution. There is reason to believe that the simultaneous achievement of modest jury equity and avoidance of intolerable caprice depends on formal instructions that do not expressly delineate a jury charter to carve out its own rules of law.

The way the jury operates may be radically altered if there is alteration in the way it is told to operate. The jury knows well enough that its prerogative is not limited to the choices articulated in the formal instructions of the court. The jury gets its understanding as to the arrangements in the legal system from more than one voice. There is the formal communication from the judge. There is the informal communication from the total culture—literature (novel, drama, film, and television); conversation; and, of course, history and tradition. The totality of input generally convey adequately enough the idea of prerogative, of freedom in an occasional case to depart from what the judge says. Even indicators that would on their face seem too weak to notice—like the fact that the judge tells the jury it must acquit (in case of reasonable doubt) but never tells the jury in so many words that it must convict—are a meaningful part of the jury's total input. Law is a system, and it is also a language, with secondary meanings that may be unrecorded yet are part of its life.

When the legal system relegates the information of the jury's prerogative to an essentially informal input, it is not being duplicitous, chargeable with chicane and intent to deceive. The limitation to informal input is, rather a governor to avoid excess: the prerogative is reserved for the exceptional case, and the judge's instruction is retained as a generally effective constraint. We "recognize a constraint as obligatory upon us when we require not merely reason to defend our rule departures, but damn good reason."[45] The practicalities of men, machinery and rules point up the danger of articulating discretion to depart from a rule, that the breach will be more often and casually invoked. We cannot gainsay that occasionally jurors uninstructed as to the prerogative may feel themselves compelled to the point of rigidity. The danger of the excess rigidity that may now occasionally exist is not as great as the danger of removing the boundaries of constraint provided by the announced rules.

Rules of law or justice involve choice of values and ordering of objectives for which unanimity is unlikely in any society, or group representing the society, especially as diverse in cultures and interests as ours. To seek unity out of diversity, under the national motto, there must be a procedure for decision by vote of a majority or prescribed plurality—in accordance with democratic philosophy. To assign the role of mini-legislature

---

45 Kadish & Kadish, *supra,* note [42], 59 CALIF. L. REV. at 926.

to the various petit juries, who must hang if not unanimous, exposes criminal law and administration to paralysis, and to a deadlock that betrays rather than furthers the assumptions of viable democracy.

Moreover, to compel a juror involuntarily assigned to jury duty to assume the burdens of mini-legislator or judge, as is implicit in the doctrine of nullification, is to put untoward strains on the jury system. It is one thing for a juror to know that the law condemns, but he has a factual power of lenity. To tell him expressly of a nullification prerogative, however, is to inform him, in effect, that it is he who fashions the rule that condemns. That is an overwhelming responsibility, an extreme burden for the jurors' psyche. And it is not inappropriate to add that a juror called upon for an involuntary public service is entitled to the protection, when he takes action that he knows is right, but also knows is unpopular, either in the community at large or in his own particular grouping, that he can fairly put it to friends and neighbors that he was merely following the instructions of the court.

In the last analysis, our rejection of the request for jury nullification doctrine is a recognition that there are times when logic is not the only or even best guide to sound conduct of government. For machines, one can indulge the person who likes to tinker in pursuit of fine tuning. When men and judicial machinery are involved, one must attend to the many and complex mechanisms and reasons that lead men to change their conduct—when they are told of the consequences of their conduct; and when conduct exercised with restraint as an unwritten exception is expressly presented as a legitimate option.

What makes for health as an occasional medicine would be disastrous as a daily diet. The fact that there is widespread existence of the jury's prerogative, and approval of its existence as a "necessary counter to case-hardened judges and arbitrary prosecutors," does not establish as an imperative that the jury must be informed by the judge of that power. On the contrary, it is pragmatically useful to structure instructions in such wise that the jury must feel strongly about the values involved in the case, so strongly that it must itself identify the case as establishing a call of high conscience, and must independently initiate and undertake an act in contravention of the established instructions. This requirement of independent jury conception confines the happening of the lawless jury to the occasional instance that does not violate, and viewed as an exception may even enhance, the over-all normative effect of the rule of law. An explicit instruction to a jury conveys an implied approval that runs the risk of degrading the legal structure requisite for true freedom, for an ordered liberty that protects against anarchy as well as tyranny.

BAZELON, Chief Judge, dissenting in part:

My disagreement with the Court concerns the issue of jury nullification. As the Court's opinion clearly acknowledges, there can be no doubt that the jury has "an unreviewable and unreversible power * * * to acquit in disregard of the instructions on the law given by the trial judge * * *." More important, the Court apparently concedes—although in somewhat grudging terms—that the power of nullification is a "necessary counter to case-hardened judges and arbitrary prosecutors," and that exercise of the power may, in at least some instances, "enhance, the over-all normative effect of the rule of law." We could not withhold that concession without scoffing at the rationale that underlies the right to jury trial in criminal cases, and belittling some of the most legendary episodes in our political and jurisprudential history.

The sticking point, however, is whether or not the jury should be told of its power to nullify the law in a particular case. Here, the trial judge not only denied a requested instruction on nullification, but also barred defense counsel from raising the issue in argument before the jury. The majority affirms that ruling. I see no justification for, and considerable harm in, this deliberate lack of candor.

At trial, the defendants made no effort to deny that they had committed the acts charged. Their defense was designed to persuade the jury that it would be unconscionable to convict them of violating a statute whose general validity and applicability they did not challenge. An instruction on nullification—or at least some argument to the jury on that issue—was, therefore, the linchpin of the defense.

[W]e are left with a doctrine that may "enhance the over-all normative effect of the rule of law," but, at the same time, one that must not only be concealed from the jury, but also effectively condemned in the jury's presence. Plainly, the justification for this sleight-of-hand lies in a fear that an occasionally noble doctrine will, if acknowledged, often be put to ignoble and abusive purposes—or, to borrow the Court's phrase, will "run the risk of anarchy." A breakdown of the legal order is not a result I would knowingly encourage or enjoy. But the question cannot be resolved, at least at this stage of the argument, by asking if we are for or against anarchy, or if we are willing to tolerate a little less law and order so that we can permit a little more jury nullification. No matter how horrible the effect feared by the Court, the validity of its reasoning depends on the existence of a demonstrable connection between the alleged cause (a jury nullification instruction or argument to the jury on that issue) and the effect. I am unable to see a connection.

To be sure, there are abusive purposes, discussed below, to which the doctrine might be put. The Court assumes that these abuses are most likely to occur if the doctrine is formally described to the jury by argument or instruction. That assumption, it should be clear, does not rest on any proposition of logic. It is nothing more or less than a prediction of how jurors will react to the judge's instruction or argument by counsel. And since we have no empirical data to measure the validity of the prediction, we must rely on our own rough judgments of its plausibility.

The Court reasons that a jury uninformed of its power to nullify will invoke that power only where it "feel[s] strongly about the values involved in the case, so strongly that it [will] itself identify the case as establishing a call of high conscience * * *." In other words, the spontaneous and unsolicited act of nullification is thought less likely, on the whole, to reflect bias and a perverse sense of values than the act of nullification carried out by a jury carefully instructed on its power and responsibility.

It seems substantially more plausible to me to assume that the very opposite is true. The juror motivated by prejudice seems to me more likely to make spontaneous use of the power to nullify, and more likely to disregard the judge's exposition of the normally controlling legal standards. The conscientious juror, who could make a careful effort to consider the blameworthiness of the defendant's action in light of prevailing community values, is the one most likely to obey the judge's admonition that the jury enforce strict principles of law.

Moreover, if it were true that nullification which arises out of ignorance is in some sense more worthy than nullification which arises out of knowledge, the Court would have to go much further. For under the Court's assumption, the harm does not arise because a jury is *told* of its power to disregard the law, but because it *knows* of its power. Logically construed, the Court's opinion would seem to require the disqualification at voir dire of any prospective juror who admitted to knowledge of the doctrine.[46] By excluding jurors with knowledge of the doctrine the Court could insure that its invocation would be spontaneous. And yet, far from requiring the exclusion of jurors who are aware of the power, the Court takes comfort in the fact that informal communication to the jury "generally convey[s] adequately enough the idea of prerogative, of freedom in an occasional case to depart from what the judge says." One cannot, it seems to me, have the argument both ways. If, as the Court appears to concede, awareness is preferable to ignorance, then I simply do not understand the justification for relying on a haphazard process of informal communication whose effectiveness is likely to depend, to a large extent, on whether or not any of the jurors are so well-educated and astute that they are able to receive the message. If the jury should know of its power to disregard the law, then the power should be explicitly described by instruction of the court or argument of counsel.

My own view rests on the premise that nullification can and should serve an important function in the criminal process. I do not see it as a doctrine that exists only because we lack the power to punish jurors who refuse to enforce the law or to re-prosecute a defendant whose acquittal cannot be justified in the strict terms of law. The doctrine permits the jury to bring to bear on the criminal process a sense of fairness and particularized justice. The drafters of legal rules cannot anticipate and take account of every case where a defendant's conduct is "unlawful" but not blameworthy, any more than they can draw a bold line to mark the boundary between an accident and negligence. It is the jury—as spokesman for

---

[46] Would this be possible? If a juror knows nothing about nullification, wouldn't *asking* her if she is aware of it give her the very information she lacked?—Eds.

the community's sense of values—that must explore that subtle and elusive boundary.

Admittedly, the concept of blameworthiness does not often receive explicit recognition in the criminal process. But it comes very close to breaking through the surface in cases where the responsibility [*mens rea*] defense is raised. [Citing cases] More than twenty-five years ago this Court recognized "[o]ur collective conscience does not allow punishment where it cannot impose blame."[47] And the Supreme Court, in a well-known opinion by Justice Jackson, has pointed out that

> courts of various jurisdictions, and for the purposes of different offenses, have devised working formulae, if not scientific ones, for the instruction of juries around such terms as "felonious intent," "criminal intent," "malice aforethought," "guilty knowledge," "fraudulent intent," "wilfulness," "scienter," to denote guilty knowledge, or "*mens rea*," to signify an evil purpose of mental culpability. By use or combination of these various tokens, they have sought to *protect those who were not blameworthy in mind from conviction of infamous common-law crimes.*[48]

The very essence of the jury's function is its role as spokesman for the community conscience in determining whether or not blame can be imposed.

---

[47] Holloway v. United States, 80 U.S. App. D.C. 3, 4–5, 148 F.2d 665, 666–667 (1945), quoted in Durham v. United States, 94 U.S. App. D.C. 228, 242, 214 F.2d 862, 876 (1954).

[48] Morissette v. United States, 342 U.S. 246, 252 (1952) (emphasis supplied). *See also* United States ex rel. McCann v. Adams, 126 F.2d 774, 775–776 (2d Cir. 1942) (L. Hand, J.), *rev'd on other grounds,* 317 U.S. 269 (1962); Hart, *The Aims of the Criminal Law,* 23 Law & Contemp. Probs. 401 (1958).

The nullification doctrine derives from the same moral principles as the *mens rea* or responsibility defense. But in view of my conclusion that the trial judge should have granted a nullification instruction, it is unnecessary for me to decide whether reversal would be required on the theory that the instruction that was offered effectively directed the jury to make a finding that the defendant possessed the necessary *mens rea.*

I do not see any reason to assume that jurors will make rampantly abusive use of their power. Trust in the jury is, after all, one of the cornerstones of our entire criminal jurisprudence, and if that trust is without foundation we must re-examine a great deal more than just the nullification doctrine. Nevertheless, some abuse can be anticipated. If a jury refuses to apply strictly the controlling principles of law, it may—in conflict with values shared by the larger community—convict a defendant because of prejudice against him, or acquit a defendant because of sympathy for him and prejudice against his victim. Our fear of unjust conviction is plainly understandable. But it is hard for me to see how a nullification instruction could enhance the likelihood of that result. The instruction would speak in terms of acquittal, not conviction, and it would provide no comfort to a juror determined to convict a defendant in defiance of the law or the facts of the case. Indeed, unless the jurors *ignored* the nullification instruction they could not convict on the grounds of prejudice alone. Does the judge's recitation of the instruction increase the likelihood that the jury will ignore the limitation that lies at its heart? I hardly think so.

As for the problem of unjust acquittal, it is important to recognize the strong internal check that constrains the jury's willingness to acquit. Where defendants seem dangerous, juries are unlikely to exercise their nullification power, whether or not an explicit instruction is offered. Of course, that check will not prevent the acquittal of a defendant who may be blameworthy and dangerous except in the jaundiced eyes of a jury motivated by a perverse and sectarian sense of values. But whether a nullification instruction would make such acquittals more common is problematical, if not entirely inconceivable. In any case, the real problem in this situation is not the nullification doctrine, but the values and prejudice that prompt the acquittal. And the solution is not to condemn the nullification power, but to spotlight the prejudice and parochial values that underlie the verdict in the hope that public outcry will force a re-examination of those values, and deter their implementation in subsequent cases. Surely nothing is gained by the pretense that the jurors lack the power to nullify, since that pretense deprives them of the opportunity to hear the very instruction that might compel them to confront their responsibility.

One often-cited abuse of the nullification power is the acquittal by bigoted juries of whites who commit crimes (lynching, for example) against blacks. That repellent practice cannot be directly arrested without jeopardizing important constitutional protections—the double jeopardy bar and the jury's power of nullification. But the revulsion and sense of shame fostered by that practice fueled the civil rights movement, which in turn made possible the enactment of major civil rights legislation. That same movement spurred on the revitalization of the equal protection clause and, in particular, the recognition of the right to be tried before a jury selected without bias. The lessons we learned from these abuses helped to create a climate in which such abuses could not so easily thrive.

Moreover, it is not only the abuses of nullification that can inform our understanding of the community's values and standards of blameworthiness. The noble uses of the power—the uses that "enhance the over-all normative effect of the rule of law"—also provide an important input to our evaluation of the substantive standards of the criminal law. The reluctance of juries to hold defendants responsible for unmistakable violations of the prohibition laws told us much about the morality of those laws and about the "criminality" of the conduct they proscribed. And the same can be said of the acquittals returned under the fugitive slave law as well as contemporary gaming and liquor laws. A doctrine that can provide us with such critical insights should not be driven underground.

On remand the trial judge should grant defendants' request for a nullification instruction. At the very least, I would require the trial court to permit defendants to argue the question before the jury. But it is not at all clear that defendants would prevail even with the aid of an instruction or argument. After all, this case is significantly different from the classic, exalted cases where juries historically invoked the power to nullify. Here, the defendants have no quarrel with the general validity of the law under which they have been charged. They did not simply refuse to obey a government edict that they considered illegal, and whose illegality they expected to demonstrate in a judicial proceeding. Rather, they attempted to protest government action by interfering with others—specifically, the Dow Chemical Company. This is a distinction which could and should be explored in argument before the jury. If revulsion against the war in Southeast Asia has reached a point where a jury would be unwilling to convict a defendant for commission of the acts alleged here, we would be far better advised to ponder the implications of that result than to spend our time devising stratagems which let us pretend that the power of nullification does not even exist.

Moot Court Exercise

Elect one student to play the role of judge, another to play the role of prosecutor, and a third to play the role of attorney for the defendants.

The scene takes place out of the hearing of the jury. The prosecutor has asked the judge to instruct the jury as follows: "If your find beyond a reasonable doubt that the defendants have in fact obstructed entrance to the Kittridge Abortion Clinic, and have in fact physically stood in the way of doctors and nurses and staff members, employed by the Clinic, who were attempting to gain entrance to the Clinic, then the law requires you to find the defendants guilty of trespass and battery."

The defense attorney objects to this instruction unless it is coupled with the following instruction: "However, if finding the defendants guilty would be genuinely offensive to your conscience as jurors, this court will not require you to render such a decision."

The Kittridge Abortion Clinic is a small building in a neighborhood near your law school. For four hours one Friday morning, a group of persons carrying placards proclaiming "Right to Life" physically obstructed and in fact prevented entrance into the Abortion Clinic of doctors, nurses, and staff members working there. The police were called and ordered the "Right to Life" picketers to carry on their picketing peacefully and in a way that would not physically obstruct persons who wanted to gain entrance into the Clinic. The "Right to Life" picketers refused and then resisted arrest. Eventually, they were all arrested and charged with trespass and battery.

At the trial, the testimony was conclusive that the defendants obstructed entrance to the abortion clinic. In fact, the prosecutor showed the jurors a videotape of the scene in front of the clinic where the defendants were blocking the staff members from entering the clinic. The defense attorney managed to get into the record expert testimony about the evils of abortion, and some photographs, shown to the jurors, of fetuses that were killed as a result of abortions.

(1) The student who is playing the role of defense attorney should begin by making an argument to the judge that the additional instruction should be granted. The judge may interrupt with questions.

(2) The student who is playing the role of prosecutor should then make an argument to the judge that the additional instruction should be denied. The judge may interrupt with questions.

(3) The judge may then freely ask questions of both defense attorney and prosecuting attorney.

(4) The judge should leave the classroom for five or ten minutes of private deliberation. In the meantime, the two attorneys should discuss with the class the strategic choices they made in presenting their arguments, and the class should comment thereon.

(5) The judge should then return and deliver the decision of the court regarding the suggested instructions, and indicate the court's reasoning.

(6) The formal session is now over. The class may ask the judge to explain in greater depth the reasons that led to the judge's decision.

(7) The larger question posed by the case—jury nullification in the context of the abortion debate—may now be examined by the class in a general discussion.

Note

In a history of jury nullification in English courts, Thomas Green suggests one source of the practice in English history:[49]

> Students of Tudor and early Stuart England have pointed to the fit between, on the one hand, a system of criminal justice that announced legal imperatives in definitive terms but provided abundant opportunities for bestowing mercy and, on the other, a religious ethic that portrayed all men as sinners, as subject to temptation and transgression, but proffered opportunities for redemption to all but the worst of the fallen. Legal and religious systems of maintaining order and saving souls, they have asserted, in reality constituted a single system. Not only did society at large see the matter in this fashion, but authorities also explained it in these terms. Professor Herrup has developed this argument with particular force, characterizing Elizabethan and Jacobean enforcement of the criminal law as part of a religion-based process of rehabilitation, or moral regeneration. This seems to me, in fact,

---

[49] T. Green, Verdict According to Conscience: Perspectives on the English Criminal Trial Jury 1200–1800, 376–77 (1985).

a plausible way of understanding the practical application of legal rules across the entire period, 1200–1800.

My own study of the history of the criminal trial jury points to some contours of the evolution of this worldview that, in some dimension, is with us still. The tendency to assimilate the law to prevailing religious notions is undoubtedly age-old. Religious and secular norms were not viewed as separate in the Middle Ages. Post-Reformation Puritanism intensified belief in the omnipresence of sin and the capacity for moral regeneration, but it did not mark a new departure in the identification of serious criminal offenses with breaches of divine command. The royal pardon had always carried with it—or was supposed to carry with it—the imprimatur of Godly Mercy; the refusal to forgive an offender, and the ritual of execution, were imbued with the notion that the offender was in the eyes of God beyond earthly redemption.

It may be that from the outset of the common-law period it was assumed that a variety of institutions, the jury included, would apply the law in a merciful fashion. We simply do not know how far authorities countenanced such behavior. At the very least, if authorities did believe that prosecutors, grand jurors, and trial jurors should conform to the formal rules of law, they also believed that the Crown should apply those rules in accordance with the standards of divine justice. I have suggested that society's reluctance to adhere to formal rules was far greater than authorities had at the outset assumed it would be. Indeed, society's disposition was apparently more merciful than that of the Crown, for early on the Crown left itself relatively few opportunities to intercede to prevent executions. Social (including religious) attitudes that were themselves in part—but only in part—engendered by secular and religious authorities combined with the relative lack of royal institutions of mitigation to produce a powerful degree of community intercession.

Is nullification from motives of mercy inappropriate in a democracy, where there is no religious consensus? Is mercy inappropriate when the law being applied is a just law? Consider these questions as you read the following materials.

Religion and the Law:
The Mormon Experience in the Nineteenth Century[50]

Edwin Firmage[51]

George Reynolds was an English immigrant, private secretary to Brigham Young, and a polygamist. In October 1874, he was indicted under the Morrill Act, and subsequently convicted of polygamy on the testimony of his polygamous wife. On appeal to the Utah Supreme Court, Reynolds argued that the grand jury that had indicted him had been constituted improperly. The Utah Supreme Court agreed and reversed Reynolds' conviction because the trial court followed federal rather than territorial law in fixing the size of the grand jury. [*United States* v. *Reynolds,* 1 Utah 226 (1875)]

In October 1875, Reynolds was indicted again for violating the Morrill Act. This time, in accordance with Utah law, the indictment was handed down by a grand jury of fifteen men, seven Mormons and eight non-Mormons. Reynolds was convicted again and sentenced

---

[50] 12 Cardozo L. Rev. 765, 772 (1991).

[51] Professor of Law, University of Utah College of Law.

to two years' hard labor and a $500 fine. The Utah Supreme Court sustained his conviction.

United States v. Reynolds[52]

1 Utah 319
Supreme Court of the Territory of Utah, 1876

BOREMAN, J., delivered the Opinion of the Court:

The Defendant was indicted for the crime of bigamy or polygamy, found guilty and sentenced to imprisonment in the penitentiary, and to pay a fine. He appeals to this Court.

It is alleged as error that the Court below, sustained the challenges of the prosecution to the several jurors who appeared to be otherwise qualified, but who refused to answer a question to criminate themselves. The question was asked as follows: "Are you living in polygamy?"

The Court cautioned the jurors that they need not answer, if the answer would tend to incriminate them. They declined, upon that ground, to answer. The inevitable conclusion is that these jurors were guilty of the crime of polygamy. This is not like asking a juror on a trial for larceny, whether he had stolen anything, or on a trial for murder, if he had ever committed murder. The question is not, "Did you ever commit the crime of polygamy?" But it was, "Are you now doing so?" They virtually admit that they are. Would such men make impartial jurors, or such as the law requires? They cannot be such if they are at that very moment practicing the same crime as that charged upon the prisoner. A murderer will never be convicted, if those engaged in committing murder are the jurors—they cannot be impartial, and it was not necessary that the disqualification of the jurors should be shown by extrinsic evidence, when they, in effect, admitted it themselves.

Upon the whole case, therefore, we can perceive that no error was committed in the Court below. It is therefore ordered that the judgment of the Court below be affirmed.

---

[52] The following is an excerpt from the opinion in Reynolds' second appeal.

Reynolds v. United States

98 U.S. 145
United States Supreme Court, 1878

ERROR to the Supreme Court of the Territory of Utah.

This is an indictment found in the District Court for the third judicial district of the Territory of Utah, charging George Reynolds with bigamy, in violation of sect. 5352 of the Revised Statutes, which, omitting its exceptions, is as follows:—

"Every person having a husband or wife living, who marries another, whether married or single, in a Territory, or other place over which the United States have exclusive jurisdiction, is guilty of bigamy, and shall be punished by a fine of not more than $500, and by imprisonment for a term of not more than five years."

The [trial] court also, when Homer Brown was called as a juror, allowed the district attorney to ask him the following questions: Q. "Are you living in polygamy?" A. "I would rather not answer that." The court instructed the witness that he must answer the question, unless it would criminate him. By the district attorney: "You understand the conditions upon which you refuse?" A. "Yes, sir." Q. "Have you such an opinion that you could not find a verdict for the commission of that crime?" A. "I have no opinion on it in this particular case. I think under the evidence and the law I could render a verdict accordingly." Whereupon the United States challenged the said Brown for favor, which challenge was sustained by the court, and the defendant excepted.

John W. Snell, also a juror, was asked by the district attorney on *voir dire:* Q. "Are you living in polygamy?" A. "I decline to answer that question." Q. "On what ground?" A. "It might criminate myself; but I am only a fornicator." Whereupon Snell was challenged by the United States for cause, which challenge was sustained, and the defendant excepted.

MR. CHIEF JUSTICE WAITE delivered the opinion of the court.

The questions raised upon these assignments of error are not whether the district attorney should have been permitted to interrogate the jurors while under examination upon their *voir dire* as to the fact of their living in polygamy. No objection was made below to the questions, but only to the ruling of the court upon the challenges after the testimony taken in answer to the questions was in. From the testimony it is apparent that all the jurors whom the challenges related were or had been living in polygamy. It needs no argument to show that such a jury could not have gone into the box entirely free from bias and prejudice. [T]he jurors were incompetent and properly excluded.

[The Court went on to hold that the statute prohibiting polygamy in the Territory of Utah was constitutional.]

Congress cannot pass a law for the government of the Territories which shall prohibit the free exercise of religion. The first amendment to the Constitution expressly forbids such legislation.

Polygamy has always been odious among the northern and western nations of Europe, and, until the establishment of the Mormon Church, was almost exclusively a feature of the life of Asiatic and of African people. At common law, the second marriage was always void (2 Kent, Com. 79), and from the earliest history of England polygamy has been treated as an offence against society.

In our opinion, the statute immediately under consideration is within the legislative power of Congress. It is constitutional and valid as prescribing a rule of action for all those residing in the Territories, and in places over which the United States have exclusive control. This being so, the only question which remains is, whether those who make polygamy a part of their religion are excepted from the operation of the statute. If they are, then those who do not make polygamy a part of their religious belief may be found guilty and punished, while those who do, must be acquitted and go free. This would be introducing a new element into criminal law. Laws are made for the government of actions, and while they cannot interfere with mere religious belief and opinions, they may with practices. Suppose one believed that human sacrifices were a necessary part of religious worship, would it be seriously contended that the civil government under which he lived could not interfere to prevent a sacrifice? Or if a wife religiously believed it was her duty to burn herself upon the funeral pile of her dead husband, would it be beyond the power of the civil government to prevent her carrying her belief into practice?

So here, as a law of the organization of society under the exclusive dominion of the United States, it is provided that plural marriages shall not be allowed. Can a man excuse his practices to the contrary because of his religious belief? To permit this would be to make the professed doctrines of religious belief superior to the law of the land, and in effect to permit every citizen to become a law unto himself. Government could exist only in name under such circumstances.

Notes and Questions

1. Reynolds had more than one wife. He was entitled to have more than one wife under the Mormon religion which he practiced. Indeed, the religion taught him—and his wives—that polygamy was desirable in the eyes of God.

Reread the statute under which Reynolds was convicted. It says that "Every person having a husband or wife living, who marries another, whether married or single . . . is guilty of bigamy." If marrying another person is criminal and hence illegal under this statute, how was it possible for Reynolds to "marry another"? Wasn't the second marriage impossible as a matter of law? Could Reynolds have argued that he was not "married" a second time *as far as the statutory definition of "marriage" was concerned* because any such second marriage would have been a legal impossibility? Could Reynolds have argued that, irrespective of the relationship that he might have with the second woman who went through a particular Mormon ceremony with him, that relationship could not possibly be called "marriage" under the federal statute?

How could Reynolds have been successfully prosecuted for "bigamy"? How can anyone ever be successfully prosecuted for "bigamy"? Isn't the argument of the last paragraph a possible one for all "bigamists"?

2. Why did the prospective jurors (Brown and Snell) decline to answer the prosecutor's question whether they were living in polygamy? Could they not have mentally applied a variation on the reasoning in the preceding question? Could they not have said to themselves that of course they are not living in "polygamy" because second marriages are illegal and hence, under the civil law, they could not possibly be validly married more than once? Could they have answered, "No, I am not living in polygamy"?

3. Would such an answer have been dishonest? As a literal matter? As an interpretive matter? As a common-sense matter?

4. Is it not clear that if either Brown or Snell had been on the jury, the jury would not have convicted Reynolds? Recall that *Reynolds* was the very first "test" of the new statute. There was a substantial argument that could be made that the statute violated the First Amendment of the Constitution in that it deprived consenting adult Mormons of the possibility of faithfully exercising their religious beliefs. Hence, if the only juries that could be "representative of the community" in Utah included some jurors who were practicing polygamists, those jurors—by invariably voting for acquittal—would have been able to frustrate the statute entirely. Wouldn't they thus have ensured their own freedom to go on living in polygamy? Wasn't Reynolds convicted precisely because some members of the community—namely, practicing polygamists—were excluded from the jury?

5. Were the Supreme Court of the Territory of Utah and the U.S. Supreme Court correct in analogizing the disqualification of Brown and Snell to the disqualification of murderers or larcenists on juries in murder or larceny cases? Isn't murder or larceny clearly a crime? Why did both Courts say that polygamy was a crime? If your answer to this last question is, "because Congress made it a crime," consider whether Congress had the *power* to make it a crime. If outlawing polygamy was unconstitutional as a violation of the First Amendment, then Congress did not have the power to make it a crime.

But didn't the Supreme Court already know that it was going to hold, later in its opinion, that Congress *did* have that power, and wasn't this foreknowledge the reason that the Court said that the jurors could be excluded because of the reasonable suspicion that they were polygamists?

6. Yet didn't the statute outlaw *bigamy* and not *polygamy*? The Mormon religion said nothing about "bigamy." Presumably the Mormon religion would have been totally opposed to bigamy, with its connotation of fraud.[53] The Mormon religion was in favor of "polyg-amy"—plural wives with the full consent of all parties (indeed, the first wife could "veto" any individual subsequent wife under the Mormon practice at the time).[54]

When the prosecutor asked "Are you living in polygamy?" could Snell have given any of the following impertinent answers:

(a) No, I'm living in Salt Lake City.
(b) I don't know what you mean by "polygamy."
(c) What do you mean by "polygamy"?
(d) I thought this case was about "bigamy."
(e) Ask the Elders of my religion.
(f) Ask my lawyer.
(g) Ask my live-in female roommates.

Maybe his actual answer was the most impertinent of all: "I am only a fornicator."

But *whatever* answer Snell might have given, isn't it clear that the judge would have dismissed him for cause anyway?

7. Suppose you are a prospective juror and the prosecutor asks you whether you are morally opposed to capital punishment. Suppose further that you *are* in general opposed to capital punishment, *but* in your mind you are willing to make at least one exception: you are in favor of capital punishment for a criminal who has been sentenced to life imprisonment who murders a prison guard. You are in favor of this exception because you believe that otherwise there would be no deterrence at all against the murder of prison guards by prisoners who have been sentenced to life imprisonment.

The prosecutor asks you, "Are you morally opposed to capital punishment?" Would you answer "No"? Why? Why not?

Concluding Questions

1. The present-day legal systems of China and the Soviet Union routinely admit any and all character evidence in criminal trials. Sometimes the evidence is nothing more than uncorroborated neighborhood gossip about the accused. But the goal of criminal trials in those systems is not punishment; rather, it is rehabilitation. A person found guilty is not a "criminal" so much as a "deviant." Rehabilitation, then, consists of forceful attempts to change the deviant's character so that he will better "adjust" to his community. Are those systems a desirable alternative to the American system?

2. Can the prejudices of juries in the American system of law ever be eliminated? Should they be?

---

[53] The classic bigamist is the person who marries a second time without the second spouse knowing about the first marriage.

[54] There were economic and political reasons in favor of polygamy. Economically, the Mormons believed that only the wealthiest persons should have more than one wife. In this fashion, the wealth was "distributed" to more persons than it would have been under a monogamous system. With respect to other political issues, the Mormons were decades ahead of the rest of the country in advocating voting rights and full political participation for women.

3. Is it reasonable to suppose that juries can "apply the law" to the facts of a case, armed with nothing more than the judge's "instructions to the jury"? Judge Jerome Frank quotes another judge, Judge Curtis Bok, as saying:[55]

> Juries have the disadvantage . . . of being treated like children while the testimony is going on, but then being doused with a kettlefull of law, during the charge [the judge's instructions], that would make a third-year law student blanch.

Judge Frank adds that a case was reported in which the jurors later explained their verdict as follows:[56]

> We couldn't make head or tail of the case, or follow all the messing around the lawyers did. None of us believed the witnesses on either side, anyway, so we made up our minds to disregard the evidence on both sides and decide the case on its merits.

4. In each of the cases we have studied, the trial judge ruled or should have ruled on the admissibility of testimony or evidence that was arguably prejudicial. Doesn't this assume that the trial judge has no prejudice of his or her own? Further, aren't we assuming that when the trial judge rules on admissibility, he or she will somehow avoid being unduly swayed in the very process of hearing about the arguably prejudicial testimony or evidence? Keep these questions in mind as we examine the role of the judge in Chapter 3.

---

[55] J. FRANK, COURTS ON TRIAL 117 (1949).

[56] *Id.* at 114.

A Fair Judge

CHAPTER THREE

3.1 Do judges ever decide "according to law"?

The Judgment Intuitive: The Function of the "Hunch" in Judicial Decision[1]

Joseph C. Hutcheson, Jr.[2]

I remember once, in the trial of a patent case, where it was contended with great vigor on the one side that the patent evidenced invention of the highest order, and with equal vigor on the other that the device in question was merely a mechanical advance, I announced, almost without any sense of incongruity, that I would take the case under advisement, and after "having well and exactly seen and surveyed, overlooked, reviewed, read and read over again" etc.,[3] all of the briefs, authorities and the record, would wait awhile before deciding to give my mind a chance to hunch it out, for if there was the flash of invention in the device my mind would give back an answering flash; while if there were none my mind would in a dully cogitative way, find only mechanical advance.

One of the lawyers, himself a "huncher," smiled and said—"Well, Your Honor, I am very grateful to you for having stated from the Bench what I have long believed, but have hesitated to avow, that next to the pure arbitrament of the dice in judicial decisions, the best chance for justice comes through the hunch." The other lawyer, with a different type of mind only looked on as though impatient of such foolery.

But I, proceeding according to custom, got my hunch, found invention and infringement, and by the practice of logomachy[4] so bewordled my opinion in support of my hunch that I found myself in the happy situation of having so satisfied the intuitive lawyer by the correctness of my hunch, and the logomachic lawyer by the spell of my logomachy, that both sides accepted the result and the cause was ended.

---

[1] 14 CORNELL L.Q. 274, 280, 282, 284–85, 286–87 (1929).

[2] United States District Judge for the Southern District of Texas.

[3] The quotation is from Rabelais.

[4] From the Greek *logos* (speech, words) and *mache* (battle). Hence, an argument about words. [-Eds.]

Collision cases in admiralty furnish excellent illustrations of the difficulty of arriving at a sound fact conclusion by mere reasoning upon objective data. In these cases, as every trier knows, the adherents of the respective ships swear most lustily in true seagoing fashion for their side, and if a judge were compelled to decide the case by observing the demeanor of the witnesses alone, he would be in sad plight, for at the end of eleven years upon the Bench I am more convinced than ever that the shrewdest, smartest liars often make the most plausible and satisfactory witnesses, while the humblest and most honest fellows often, upon the witness stand, acquit themselves most badly.

Judges who have tried many patent cases, who have heard the testimony of experts, the one affirming the matter to be merely an advance in mechanical steps, the other to be invention of the highest order; the one affirming prior use, the other denying it; the one affirming it to be the flight of genius into new fields, the other, the mere dull trudging of an artisan, know that for a just decision of such causes no objective criteria can be relied on. They well know that there must be in the trier something of the same imaginative response to an idea, something of that same flash of genius that there is in the inventor, which all great patent judges have had, that intuitive brilliance of the imagination, that luminous quality of the mind, that can give back, where there is invention, an answering flash for flash.

Time was when judges, lawyers, law writers and teachers of the law refused to recognize in the judge this right and power of intuitive decision. It is true the trial judge was always supposed to have superior facilities for decision, but these were objectivized in formulas, such as: the trial judge has the best opportunity of observing the witnesses, their demeanor; the trial judge can see the play and interplay of forces as they operate in the actual clash of the trial.

Under the influence of this kind of logomachy, this sticking in the "skin" of thought, the trial judge's superior opportunity was granted, but the real reason for that superior position, that the trial creates an atmosphere springing from but more than the facts themselves, in which and out of which the judge may get the feeling which takes him to the desired end, was deliberately suppressed.

Later writers, however, not only recognize but emphasize this faculty, nowhere more attractively than in Judge Cardozo's lectures in 1921[5] while Max Radin, in 1925, in a most sympathetic and charming way, takes the judge's work apart, and shows us how his wheels go round.[6]

He tells us, first, that the judge is a human being; that therefore he does not decide causes by the abstract application of rules of justice or of right, but having heard the cause and determined that the decision ought to go this way or that way, he then takes up his search for some category of the law into which the case will fit.

He tells us that the judge really feels or thinks that a certain result seems desirable, and he then tries to make his decision accomplish that result. "What makes certain results seem desirable to a judge?" he asks, and answers his question that that seems desirable to

---

[5] B. Cardozo, The Nature of the Judicial Process (1921).

[6] Radin, *Theory of Judicial Decision* 2 A.B.A.J. 359 (1925).

the judge which, according to his training, his experience, and his general point of view, strikes him as the jural consequence that ought to flow from the facts, and he advises us that what gives the judge the struggle in the case is the effort so to state the reasons for his judgment that they will pass muster.

Now what is he saying except that the judge really decides by feeling, and not by judgment: by "hunching" and not by ratiocination, and that the ratiocination appears only in the opinion?

Now what is he saying but that the vital, motivating impulse for the decision is an intuitive sense of what is right or wrong for that cause, and that the astute judge, having so decided, enlists his every faculty and belabors his laggard mind, not only to justify that intuition to himself, but to make it pass muster with his critics?

There is nothing unreal or untrue about this picture of the judge, nor is there anything in it from which a just judge should turn away. It is true, and right that it is true, that judges really do try to select categories or concepts into which to place a particular case so as to produce what the judge regards as a righteous result, or, to avoid any confusion in the matter of morals, I will say a "proper result."

This is true. I think we should go further, and say it ought to be true. No reasoning applied to practical matters is ever really effective unless motivated by some impulse.

If the judge sat upon the Bench in a purely abstract relation to the cause, his opinion in difficult cases would be worth nothing. He must have some motive to fire his brains, to "let his mind be bold."

By the nature of his occupation he cannot have advocacy for either side of the case as such, so he becomes an advocate, an earnest one, for the—in a way—abstract solution. Having become such advocate, his mind reaches and strains and feels for that result. He says with Elihu, the son of Barachel, the Buzite, of the family of Ram—"There is a spirit in man, and the breath of the Almighty giveth him understanding. It is not the great that are wise, nor the aged that understand justice.—Hearken to me; I also will show mine opinion. For I am full of matter; the spirit within me constraineth me. Behold my belly is as wine which hath no vent. Like new wineskins it is ready to burst."[7]

And having travailed and reached his judgment, he struggles to bring up and pass in review before his eager mind all of the categories and concepts which he may find useful directly or by analogy, so as to select from them that which in his opinion will support his desired result.

For while the judge may be, he cannot appear to be, arbitrary. He must at least appear reasonable, and unless he can find a category which will at least "semblably" support his view, he will feel uncomfortable.

---

[7] *Job,* 32: 9, 10, 18, 19.

What Courts Do in Fact[8]

Jerome Frank[9]

But talks with candid judges have begun to disclose that, whatever is said in opinions, the judge often arrives at his decision before he tries to explain it. With little or no preliminary attention to legal rules or a definite statement of facts, he often makes up his mind that Jones should win the lawsuit, not Smith; that Mrs. White should have the custody of the children; that McCarthy should be reinstated as keeper of the dog pound. After the judge has so decided, then the judge writes his "opinion."

The judge's opinion makes it *appear* as if the decision were a result solely of playing the game of law-in-discourse. But this explanation is often truncated, incomplete. Worse, it is frequently unreal, artificial, distorted. It is in large measure an after-thought. It omits all mention of many of the factors which induced the judge to decide the case.[10] Those factors (even to the extent that the judge is aware of them) are excluded from the opinion. So far as opinions are concerned, those factors are tabu, unmentionables.

Opinions, then, disclose but little of how judges come to their conclusions. The opinions are often ex post facto; they are *censored expositions*. To study those eviscerated expositions as the principal bases of forecasts of future judicial action is to delude oneself. It is far more unwise than it would be for a botanist to assume that plants are merely what appears above the ground, or for an anatomist to content himself with scrutinizing the outside of the body.

It is helpful for the lawyer to borrow the point of view of the political scientist and look at the judge as one kind of governmental official. When William Howard Taft, as President, gave his reasons for recommending or vetoing a bill, urging the adoption of a treaty, espousing a higher tariff, or finding that charges against his Secretary of the Interior were groundless, many wise students of government recognized that his explanations were sometimes artificial or incomplete and that sometimes he formulated them long after he had reached the decisions which he formally explained. If William Howard Taft, when on the bench, followed a not unlike course, he was adopting the admitted practice of some of the ablest of those governmental officials we call judges. One recalls the story about Marshall (recently quoted by Llewellyn): "Judgment for the plaintiff; Mr. Justice Story will furnish

---

[8] 26 ILL. L. REV. 645, 653–55 (Northwestern Law School, 1932).

[9] In 1941 Jerome N. Frank became a United States Circuit Court Judge.

[10] The artificial character of opinions is usually not due to hypocrisy or intellectual or moral dishonesty. As I have devoted a considerable portion of a book to pointing out the unconscious self-deception involved in many judicial opinions, I shall not redevelop that thesis here. *See* FRANK, LAW AND THE MODERN MIND 37, 120, 144–147, 152–153, 362 (1930).

the authorities."[11] Chancellor Kent, when off the bench, explained that in arriving at a judicial decision he first made himself "master of the facts." That done, he wrote,

> I saw where justice lay, and the moral sense decided the court half the time. I then sat down to search the authorities ... I might once in a while be embarrassed by a technical rule, but I almost always found principles suited to my view of the case.

A member of an upper court once told me that the chief justice said to him after the oral argument of a case, "We'll have to lick plaintiff somehow and it's up to you to find some theory and authorities that will help us to it." The chief justice of another important upper court recently wrote a friend of mine that in his court it was the usual practice for the judges first to determine the "abstract justice" of a case and then to examine the "law."

Transcendental Nonsense and the Functional Approach[12]

Felix S. Cohen

The "hunch" theory of law, by magnifying the personal and accidental factors in judicial behavior, implicitly denies the relevance of significant, predictable, social determinants that govern the course of judicial decision. Those who have advanced this viewpoint have performed a real service in indicating the large realm of uncertainty in the actual law. But actual experience does reveal a significant body of predictable uniformity in the behavior of courts. Law is not a mass of unrelated decisions nor a product of judicial bellyaches. Judges are human, but they are a peculiar breed of humans, selected to a type and held to service under a potent system of governmental controls. Their acts are "judicial" only within a system which provides for appeals, re-hearings, impeachments, and legislation. The decision that is "peculiar" suffers erosion—unless it represents the first salient manifestation of a new social force, in which case it soon ceases to be peculiar. It is more useful to analyze a judicial "hunch" in terms of the continued impact of a judge's study of precedents, his conversations with associates, his reading of newspapers, and his recollections of college courses, than in strictly physiological terms.

---

[11] Put that story in a formal-law speech and it reads: "The general rule of law to be applied to a particular case must be conceived as existing before the particular concrete case to which it is applied occurred." Cf. *Zane* "German Legal Philosophy" (1918) 16 MICH. LAW REV. 287 at 311. Zane also says (338): "The rule of law and its application may be reached in a thousand different ways, but a judgment of a court is always this pure deduction. Now it must be apparent to any one who is willing to admit the rules governing rational mental action that unless the rule of the major premise exists as antecedent to the ascertainment of the fact or facts put into the minor premise, there is no judicial act in stating the judgment."

Of course, the mere fact that the reason given for an act or a judgment is ex post facto does not invalidate that reason. Jones may hit Smith, or vote for Hoover, or make love to a girl, or explore the arctic without reflecting on his conduct. When asked to explain or justify his acts he may give excellent reasons which are entirely satisfactory. But sometimes it is impossible to ascertain the soundness of those reasons because it is impossible to ascertain the truth of the facts asserted in his fact premise. This is peculiarly true of judicial opinions because the facts stated in the judge's fact premise are often "subjective."

[12] 35 COLUM. L. REV. 809, 843 (1935).

Law and the Modern Mind[13]

Jerome Frank

Once trapped by the belief that the announced rules are the paramount thing in the law, and that uniformity and certainty are of major importance, and are to be procured by uniformity and certainty in the phrasing of rules, a judge is likely to be affected, in determining what is fair to the parties in the unique situation before him, by consideration of the possible, yet scarcely imaginable, bad effect of a just opinion in the instant case on possible unlike cases which may later be brought into court. He then refuses to do justice in the case on trial because he fears that "hard cases make bad laws." And thus arises what may aptly be called "injustice according to law."

---

[13] P. 154 (1930).

Notes and Questions

1. The excerpts from articles you have just read were written between 1929 and 1935 as part of the movement in American law called "legal realism." The realists believed that legal rules, legal principles, and legal theory have no direct effect upon a judicial decision. The decision is not "constrained" by law; rather, law is a collection of words that can be drawn upon to rationalize decisions that have already been reached for other reasons. (For more on "constraint," see the Fish excerpt in Section 3.)

As you can well expect, realism was a radical position in its time. Its influence in American legal studies was at its strongest in—roughly speaking—the 1930s and 1940s. With the 1950s as a kind of transitional period, American legal scholarship took a theoretical turn. In the 1960s and 1970s, theorizing about law flourished in books and journals, and judges cited theories in their court opinions. However, in the 1980s, we have seen a turn back to legal realism among some of the writers (certainly not all) that have become associated with the movement called "critical legal studies." In addition, since the 1930s, developments in the related fields of philosophy and literary interpretation have reinforced the intellectual soundness of the legal realist position.

Although the jurisprudential debate whether law and theory constrain judicial decisions is not itself the subject of this course, the following questions ask you to think about the relation of law to justice in the context of the role of the judge.

2. Frank says that it is helpful for the lawyer to "look at the judge as one kind of governmental official." What are the relevant similarities and differences? Should a lawyer act toward a judge the way a lobbyist acts toward a government official? Doesn't the lobbyist sometimes suggest, or at least strongly imply, the promise of political help toward the official's next re-election campaign?[14] Federal judges do not run for re-election, but some

---

[14] Later in this chapter we will look at the Texaco-Pennzoil dispute in Texas, where judges were accused of favoring lawyers who made large contributions to their election campaigns.

state judges do. Would the "lobbyist" approach to state judges ever be justified?

3. Cohen asserted, as you have read, that there is "a significant body of predictable uniformity in the behavior of courts. Law is not a mass of unrelated decisions nor a product of judicial bellyaches." Do you agree? If so, what accounts for the uniformity—the law itself, or theories of law, or what Cohen calls "social determinants"? How would Hutcheson and Frank answer Cohen?

4. Is it possible that the uniformity Cohen talks about is only an illusory uniformity—that if we construct legal theories of sufficient vagueness and generality, then many cases can be subsumed under them, leading us to conclude that there is uniformity? Is it possible that the closer we look at the facts of any two cases, the less we are able to construct a legal theory or point to a legal rule that applies to both cases? Consider the relation between the *Reyes* case (cited in *Rojas I*) and *Rojas II*. Are the two results consistent or inconsistent? Does your answer depend on which facts you select as a description of each case? If so, what theory or law guided you in your selection of those particular facts? Why did you omit other facts? How did the courts know which facts to mention and which to omit, considering that there was a world of facts to choose from?

5. Suppose a judge, looking at the facts of a case, sees that the "application" of a given rule of law would tend to lead to an unjust result in that case. What would Hutcheson and Frank do with the rule? Would they ignore it? Would they say it doesn't apply? Would they find new facts to show that the rule doesn't apply? Would they say that no rule ever applies, and hence this one doesn't? Would they *say* the same thing that they *do*? Or would they do one thing and rationalize it by saying something else?

6. Justice Brandeis is said to have remarked: "To be effective in this world you have to decide which side is probably right; and, once you decide, you must act as if it were one hundred per cent right." [15]

Is this what judges really do? If so, should they? Is doing it a matter of justice, or of the appearance of justice?

7. Keep your answers to Question 5 in mind as you read the following excerpts and cases. Note especially that the second case was decided by Judge Frank, the same judge who a decade earlier wrote the article and book from which you have read excerpts.

---

[15] This was purportedly an oral remark by Justice Brandeis to Thomas Corcoran, who repeated it to Nathaniel Nathanson, who repeated it to John Coons. *See* Coons, *Compromise as Precise Justice*, 68 CAL. L. REV. 250, 260 n.13 (1980).

3.2   Judicial bias: Framework

Berger v. United States

255 U.S. 22
Supreme Court of the United States
Certificate from the Circuit Court of Appeals for
the Seventh Circuit
January 31, 1921

MR. JUSTICE MCKENNA delivered the opinion of the court.

Section 21 of the Judicial Code provides as follows:

"Whenever a party to any action or proceeding, civil or criminal, shall make and file an affidavit that the judge before whom the action or proceeding is to be tried or heard has a personal bias or prejudice either against him or in favor of any opposite party to the suit, such judge shall proceed no further therein, but another judge shall be designated in the manner prescribed in the section last preceding, or chosen in the manner prescribed in section twenty-three, to hear such matter. Every such affidavit shall state the facts and the reasons for the belief that such bias or prejudice exists, [and shall be filed not less than ten days before the beginning of the term at which the proceeding is to be heard, or good cause shall be shown for failure to file it within such time]. No party shall be entitled in any case to file more than one such affidavit; and no such affidavit shall be filed unless accompanied by a certificate of counsel of record that such affidavit and application are made in good faith. The same proceedings shall be had when the presiding judge shall file with the clerk of the court a certificate that he deems himself unable for any reason to preside with absolute impartiality in the pending suit or action."

February 2, 1918, there was returned into the District Court of the United States for the Northern District of Illinois, an indictment against plaintiffs in error (it will be convenient to refer to them as defendants), charging them with a violation of the Act of Congress of June 15, 1917, known as the Espionage Act, c.30, 40 Stat. 217.[16] In due time they invoked § 21 by filing an affidavit charging Judge Landis, who was to preside at the trial, with personal bias and prejudice against them, and moved for the assignment of another judge to preside at the trial. The motion was denied and upon the trial defendants were convicted and each sentenced to twenty years' imprisonment. From the judgment and sentence they took the case to the United States Circuit Court of Appeals for the Seventh Circuit. That court, reciting that certain questions of law under § 21 have arisen upon the affidavit and motion upon which the court is in doubt and upon which it desires the advice and instructions of this court, certifies questions of the sufficiency of the affidavit and of the duty of the judge thereunder, and also certifies the affidavit and other proceedings upon such motion.

The affidavit, omitting formal and unnecessary parts, is as follows: Petitioners (defendants) represent "that they jointly and severally verily believe that His Honor Judge Kenesaw Mountain Landis has a personal bias and prejudice against certain of the defendants, to wit: Victor L. Berger, William F. Kruse and Adolph Germer, defendants in this cause, and impleaded with J. Louis Eng-

---

[16] "Whoever, when the United States is at war, shall willfully make or convey false reports or false statements with intent to interfere with the operation or success of the military or naval forces of the United States or to promote the success of its enemies and whoever, when the United States is at war, shall willfully cause or attempt to cause insubordination, disloyalty, mutiny, or refusal of duty, in the military or naval forces of the United States, or shall willfully obstruct the recruiting or enlistment service of the United States, shall be punished. . . ."

dahl and Irwin St. John Tucker, defendants in this case. That the grounds for the petitioners' beliefs are the following facts: That said Adolph Germer was born in Prussia, a state or province of Germany; that Victor L. Berger was born in Rehback, Austria; that William F. Kruse is of immediate German extraction; that said Judge Landis is prejudiced and biased against said defendants because of their nativity and in support thereof the defendants allege, that, on information and belief, on or about the 1st day of November said Judge Landis said in substance: 'If anybody has said anything worse about the Germans than I have I would like to know it so I can use it.' And referring to a German who was charged with stating that 'Germany had money and plenty of men and wait and see what she is going to do to the United States,' Judge Landis said in substance: 'One must have a very judicial mind, indeed, not to be prejudiced against the German Americans in this country. Their hearts are reeking with disloyalty. This defendant is the kind of a man that spreads this kind of propaganda and it has been spread until it has affected practically all the Germans in this country. This same kind of excuse of the defendant offering to protect the German people is the same kind of excuse offered by the pacifists in this country, who are against the United States and have the interests of the enemy at heart by defending that thing they call the Kaiser and his darling people. You are the same kind of a man that comes over to this country from Germany to get away from the Kaiser and war. You have become a citizen of this country and lived here as such, and now when this country is at war with Germany you seek to undermine the country which gave you protection. You are of the same mind that practically all the German-Americans are in this country, and you call yourselves German-Americans. Your hearts are reeking with disloyalty. I know a safeblower, he is a friend of mine, who is making a good soldier in France. He was a bank robber for nine years, that was his business in peace time, and now he is a good soldier, and as between him and this defendant, I prefer the safeblower.'

"These defendants further aver that they have at no time defended the Kaiser, but on the contrary they have been opposed to an autocracy in Germany and every other country; that Victor L. Berger, defendant herein, editor of the Milwaukee Leader, a Socialist daily paper; Adolph Germer, National Secretary of the Socialist party; William F. Kruse, editor of the Young Socialists Magazine, a Socialist publication; and J. Louis Engdahl disapproved the entrance of the United States into this war.

"Your petitioners further aver that the defendants Tucker and Engdahl were born in the United States and were not born in enemy countries, and are not immediate descendants of persons born in enemy countries, but verily believe because they are impleaded with Berger, Kruse and Germer that they as well as Berger, Germer and Kruse can not receive a fair and impartial trial, and that the prejudice of said Judge Landis against said Berger, Germer and Kruse would prejudice the defense of said defendants Tucker and Engdahl impleaded in this case."

The affidavit was accompanied by the certificate of Seymour Stedman, attorney for defendants, that the affidavit and application were made in good faith.

The questions certified are as follows:

(1) Is the aforesaid affidavit of prejudice sufficient to invoke the operation of the act which provides for the filing of affidavit of prejudice of a judge?

(2) Did said Judge Landis have the lawful right to pass upon the sufficiency of the said affidavit of his prejudice, or upon any question arising out of the filing of said affidavit?

(3) Upon the filing of the said affidavit of prejudice of said Judge Landis, did the said Judge have lawful right and power to preside as judge on the trial of plaintiffs in error upon said indictment?

The basis of the questions is § 21, and the primary question under it is the duty and power of the judge—whether the filing of an affidavit of personal bias or prejudice compels his retirement from the case or whether he can exercise a judgment upon the facts affirmed and determine his qualification against them and the belief based upon them?

These alternatives present the contentions in the case. Defendants contend for the first; the United States contends for the second. The assertion of defendants is that the mandate of the section is not subject to the discretion or judgment of the judge. The assertion of the United States is that the motion and its supporting affidavit, like other motions and their supporting evidence, are submitted for decision and the exercise of the judicial judgment upon them. In other words, the action of the affidavit is not "automatic," to quote the Solicitor General, but depends upon the substance and merit of its reasons and the truth of its facts, and upon both the judge has jurisdiction to pass. The issue is, therefore, precise, and while not in broad compass is practically of first impression as now presented.

In *Glasgow v. Moyer*, 225 U.S. 420, the section was referred to but not passed upon. In *Ex parte American Steel Barrel Co.*, 230 U.S. 35, the phase of the section presented here was not presented. There proceedings in bankruptcy had progressed to a decree of adjudication, and the judge who had conducted them was charged by certain creditors with bias and prejudice based on his rulings in the case. Such use of § 21 was disapproved. "It was never intended," it was said, "to enable a discontented litigant to oust a judge because of adverse rulings made, for such rulings are reviewable otherwise, but prevent his future action in the pending cause." As pertinent to the comment and to the meaning of § 21, we may say, that Judge Chatfield, against whom the affidavit was directed, said that he felt that the intention of § 21 was "to cause a transfer of the case, without reference to the merits of the charge of bias," and he did so immediately, in order, as he said, "that the application of the creditors" might "be considered as speedily as possible by such Judge as" might "be designated." Another judge was designated and to restrain action by the latter and vacate the orders that he had made, and to command Judge Chatfield to resume jurisdiction, mandamus was sought. It was denied. The case establishes that the bias or prejudice which can be urged against a judge must be based upon something other than rulings in the case.

The cases at circuit in which § 21 was considered have not much guidance. They, however, deserve attention. *Ex parte N.K. Fairbank Co.*, 194 Fed. Rep. 978, may be considered as expressing power in the presiding judge to pass upon the sufficiency of the facts affirmed. In *Ex parte Glasgow*, 195 Fed. Rep. 780, the question came up upon an application for a writ of *habeas corpus* and it appeared that the affidavit of bias was not filed until after trial of the case and when the court was about to pass upon a motion in arrest of judgment and new trial. It was held that § 21 was not applicable at such stage of the proceedings. *Henry* v. *Speer*, 201 Fed. Rep. 869, was a petition for mandamus to require an affidavit of bias against District Judge Speer to be certified to the senior circuit judge that the latter might determine its sufficiency, and to restrain Judge Speer from exercising jurisdiction of the case. The writ was refused on the ground that the affidavit did not conform to § 21 in that it omitted to charge "personal" bias, a charge of such bias, it was held, being a necessary condition. The court, (Circuit Court of Appeals for the Fifth Circuit), by Judge Meek, said, "Upon the making and filing by a party of an affidavit under the provisions of section 21, of necessity there is imposed upon the judge the duty of examining the affidavit to determine whether or not it is the affidavit specified and required by the statute and to determine its legal sufficiency. If he finds it to be legally sufficient then he has no other or further duty to perform than that prescribed in section 20 of the Judicial Code. He is relieved from the delicate and trying duty of deciding upon the question of his own disqualification." This comment sustains defendants' view of § 21 and marks a distinction between determining the legal sufficiency of the affidavit and passing upon the truth of its statements, a distinction to which we shall presently advert.

The cases (one being excepted) to the extent they go, militate against the contention of the Government and they have confirmation in the words of the section. Their declaration is that "whenever a party to any action or proceeding, civil or criminal, shall make and file an affidavit that the judge before whom the action or proceeding is to be tried or heard has a personal bias or prejudice either against him or in favor of any opposite party to the suit, such judge shall proceed no further therein, but another judge shall be designated . . . to hear such matter." There is no ambiguity in § 21 and seemingly nothing upon which construction can be exerted—nothing to qualify or temper its words or effect. It is clear in its permission and direction. It permits an affidavit of personal bias or prejudice to be filed and upon its filing, if it be accompanied by certificate of counsel, directs an immediate cessation of action by the judge whose bias or prejudice is averred, and in his stead, the designation of another judge. And there is purpose in the conjunction; its elements are complements of each other. The exclusion of one judge is emphasized by the requirement of the designation of another.

But it is said that there is modification of the absolutism of the quoted declaration in the succeeding provision that the "affidavit shall state the facts and the reasons for the belief" of the existence of the bias or prejudice. It is urged that the purpose of the requirement is to submit the reality and sufficiency of the facts to the judgment of the judge and their support of the averment or belief of the affiant. It is in effect urged that the requirement can have no other purpose, that it is idle else, giving an automatism to the affidavit which overrides everything. But this is misunderstanding of the requirement. It has other and less extensive use as pointed out by Judge Meek in *Henry* v. *Speer, supra.* It is a precaution against abuse, removes the averments and belief from the irresponsibility of unsupported opinion and adds to the certificate of counsel the supplementary aid of the penalties attached to perjury. Nor do we think that this view gives room for frivolous affidavits. Of course the reasons and facts for the belief the litigant entertains are an essential part of the affidavit, and must give fair support to the charge of a bent of mind that may prevent or impede impartiality of judgment. The affidavit of defendants has that character. The facts and reasons it states are not frivolous or fanciful but substantial and formidable and they have relation to the attitude of Judge Landis' mind toward defendants.

It is, however, said that the assertion and the facts are stated on information and belief and that hence the affidavit is wholly insufficient, § 21 requiring facts to be stated "and not merely belief." The contention is that "the court is expected to act on the affidavit itself" and that, therefore "the act of Congress requires facts—not opinions, beliefs, rumors, or gossip." *Ex parte American Steel Barrel Co., supra,* is cited for the contention. We do not know what counsel means by "opinions, beliefs, rumors, or gossip." The belief of a party the section makes of concern and if opinion be nearer to or farther from persuasion than belief, both are of influence and universally regarded as of influence in the affairs of men and determinative of their conduct, and it is not strange that § 21 should so regard them.

We may concede that § 21 is not fulfilled by the assertion of "rumors or gossip" but such disparagement cannot be applied to the affidavit in this case. Its statement has definite time and place

and character, and the value of averments on information and belief in the procedure of the law is recognized. To refuse their application to § 21 would be arbitrary and make its remedy unavailable in many, if not in most, cases. The section permits only the affidavit of a party, and *Ex parte American Steel Barrel Co., supra,* decides, that it must be based upon facts antedating the trial, not those occurring during the trial. In the present case the information was a definite incident, and its time and place were given. Besides, it cannot be the assumption of § 21 that the bias or prejudice of a judge in a particular case would be known by everybody, and necessarily, therefore, to deny to a party the use of information received from others is to deny to him at times the benefit of the section.

We are of opinion, therefore, that an affidavit upon information and belief satisfies the section and that upon its filing, if it show the objectionable inclination or disposition of the judge, which we have said is an essential condition, it is his duty to "proceed no further" in the case. And in this there is no serious detriment to the administration of justice nor inconvenience worthy of mention, for of what concern is it to a judge to preside in a particular case; of what concern to other parties to have him so preside? And any serious delay of trial is avoided by the requirement that the affidavit must be filed not less than ten days before the commencement of the term.

Our interpretation of § 21 has therefore no deterring consequences, and we cannot relieve from its imperative conditions upon a dread or prophecy that they may be abusively used. They can only be so used by making a false affidavit; and a charge of, and the penalties of, perjury restrain from that — perjury in him who makes the affidavit, connivance therein of counsel thereby subjecting him to disbarment. And upon what inducement and for what achievement? No other than trying the case by one judge rather than another, neither party nor counsel having voice or influence in the designation of that other; and the section in its care permits but "one such affidavit."

But if we concede, out of deference to judgments that we respect, a foundation for the dread, a possibility to the prophecy, we must conclude Congress was aware of them and considered that there were countervailing benefits. At any rate we can only deal with the act as it is expressed and enforce it according to its expressions. Nor is it our function to approve or disapprove it; but we may say that its solicitude is that the tribunals of the country shall not only be impartial in the controversies submitted to them but shall give assurance that they are impartial, free, to use the words of the section, from any "bias or prejudice" that might disturb the normal course of impartial judgment. And to accomplish this end the section withdraws from the presiding judge a decision upon the truth of the matters alleged. Its explicit declaration is that, upon the making and filing of the affidavit, the judge against whom it is directed "shall proceed no further therein, but another judge shall be designated in the manner prescribed in the section last preceding, or chosen in the manner prescribed in section twenty-three, to hear such matter." And the reason is easy to divine. To commit to the judge a decision upon the truth of the facts gives chance for the evil against which the section is directed. The remedy by appeal is inadequate. It comes after the trial and, if prejudice exist, it has worked its evil and a judgment of it in a reviewing tribunal is precarious. It goes there fortified by presumptions, and nothing can be more elusive of estimate or decision than a disposition of a mind in which there is a personal ingredient.

After overruling the motion of defendants for his displacement, Judge Landis permitted to be filed a stenographic report of the incident and language upon which the motion was based. We, however, have not discussed it because under our interpretation of § 21 it is excluded from consideration.

We come then to the questions certified, and to the first we answer, Yes, that is, that the affidavit of prejudice is sufficient to invoke the operation of the act. To the second we answer that, to the extent we have indicated, Judge Landis had a lawful right to pass upon the sufficiency of the affidavit. To the third we answer, No, that is, that Judge Landis had no lawful right or power to preside as judge on the trial of defendants upon the indictment.

So ordered.

MR. JUSTICE DAY, dissenting.

As this case is to settle the practice for this and similar cases which may arise in the federal courts, and as the opinion does not consider some aspects of the record, I venture to state the reasons which impel me to reach a different conclusion than that announced by the majority.

An examination shows that statutes exist in a number of States covering the subject under consideration. These statutes vary in character, and in the requirements for establishing the bias or prejudice of the judge which may require him to abstain from sitting at the trial of a particular case. In some of them an affidavit of belief of prejudice, or that a fair trial cannot be had before a particular judge, is sufficient to disqualify him. Other statutes require supporting affidavits and the certificate of counsel, and provide for a hearing on the matter of disqualification.

The federal statute, now under consideration, had its origin in an amendment to the Judicial Code, introduced in the House of Representatives when the adoption of the Code was under consideration. As adopted in the House, the affidavit was required to set forth the reasons for the belief that personal bias or prejudice existed against the party, or in favor of the opposite party to the suit. . . .

When the bill came before the Senate the section was amended so as to require the facts, and the reasons for the belief that bias or prejudice existed, to be set forth, and the affidavit is required to be accompanied by a certificate of counsel of record that it and the application are made in good faith. . . . It is thus apparent that the section in the form in which it finally became part of the Judicial Code intended that the bias or prejudice which should disqualify a judge should be personal against the objecting party, and that it should be established by an affidavit which should set forth the reasons and facts upon which the charge of bias or prejudice was based. The evident purpose of this requirement was to require a showing of such reasons and facts as should prevent imposition upon the court, and establish the propriety of the affidavit of disqualification. "It is not sufficient," said the late Mr. Justice Brewer, when a member of the Supreme Court of Kansas, in *City of Emporia* v. *Volmer*, 12 Kansas 627, "that a *prima facie* case only be shown, such a case as would require the sustaining of a challenge to a juror. It must be strong enough to overthrow the presumption in favor of the trial-judge's integrity, and of the clearness of his perception."

I accept the opinion of the majority that the

judge under the requirements of this statute may pass upon the sufficiency of the affidavit, subject to a review of his decision by an appellate court, and, if it be sufficient to show personal bias and prejudice, the judge should not try the case. But I am unable to agree that in cases of the character now under consideration the statement of the affidavit, however unfounded, must be accepted by the judge as a sufficient reason for his disqualification, leaving the vindication of the integrity and independence of the judge to the uncertainties and inadequacy of a prosecution for perjury should it appear that the affidavit contains known misstatements.

Notwithstanding the filing of the affidavit purporting compliance with the statute, the court has a right to use all reasonable means to protect itself from imposition. *Davis* v. *Rivers*, 49 Iowa 435. The personal bias or prejudice of the judge against the defendants in this case is said to be established by language imputed to the judge as his utterances concerning the attitude of the German people during the progress of the war.

The affidavit filed contained a statement of alleged language of the judge, concerning a German who was "charged" with making the statements set forth. Counsel in open court admitted that the offending language was used in passing sentence after conviction in Weissensel's case.

Moreover, upon the affidavit being filed, and after this admission of counsel, the District Attorney offered in evidence a transcript of what took place and what was in fact said upon the sentencing of Weissensel.

This stenographic report, sent up with the certificate and made part of it, and which there is no reason to believe fails to state accurately what took place, is in marked contrast with statements of the affidavit which the defendants made when seeking the disqualification of the Judge. The Judge in speaking of the convicted defendant said that he was of the type of man who branded almost the whole German-American population, and that one German-American, such as the defendant, talking such stuff did more damage to his people than thousands of them could overcome by being good and loyal citizens; and that he, the defendant, was an illustration of the occasional American of German birth whose conduct had done so much to damn the whole ten million in America. While this language might have been more temperate, there does not appear to be any-

thing in it fairly establishing that the Judge directed his observations at the German people in general, but rather that his remarks were aimed at one convicted as was the defendant, of violation of law.

As I understand the opinion of the court, notwithstanding the admissions of counsel, and the sworn stenographic report of what took place, the affidavit must be accepted, and, if it discloses matters, which if true, would tend to establish bias and prejudice, the same must be given effect and the judge be disqualified. It does not seem to me that this conclusion comports with the requirements of the statute that reasons and facts must be set forth for the consideration of the judge. It places the federal courts at the mercy of defendants who are willing to make affidavits as to what took place at previous trials in the court, which the knowledge of the judge, and the uncontradicted testimony of an official report may show to be untrue, and in many districts may greatly retard the trial of criminal causes.

While, as I have said, in sentencing Weissensel the Judge might have been more temperate in his observations, I am unable to find that the statements of the affidavit, when read in connection with the admissions of counsel and the established facts as to what took place as gathered from the stenographic report, showed such evidence of personal bias or prejudice against the defendants as required the Judge upon the mere filing of this affidavit to permit its misleading statements to be placed of record, and to proceed no further with the case.

It does not appear that the trial judge had any acquaintance with any of the defendants, only one of whom was of German birth, or that he had any such bias or prejudice against any of them as would prevent him from fairly and impartially conducting the trial. To permit an *ex parte* affidavit to become in effect a final adjudication of the disqualification of a judge when facts are shown, such as are here established, seems to me to be fraught with much danger to the independent discharge of duties by federal judges, and to open a door to the abuse of the privilege which is intended to be conferred by the statute in question. . . .

MR. JUSTICE PITNEY concurs in this dissent.

MR. JUSTICE MCREYNOLDS, dissenting.

I am unable to follow the reasoning of the opinion approved by the majority or to feel fairly certain of its scope and consequence. If an admitted anarchist charged with murder should affirm an existing prejudice against himself and specify that the judge had made certain depreciatory remarks concerning all anarchists, what would be the result? Suppose official stenographic notes or other clear evidence should demonstrate the falsity of an affidavit, would it be necessary for the judge to retire? And what should be done if dreams or visions were the basis of an alleged belief?

The conclusion announced gives effect to the statute which seems unwarranted by its terms and beyond the probable intent of Congress. Bias and prejudice are synonymous words and denote "an opinion or leaning adverse to anything without just grounds or before sufficient knowledge"—a state of mind. The statute relates only to adverse opinion or leaning towards an individual and has no application to the appraisement of a class, e.g., revolutionists, assassins, traitors.

To claim personal bias without more is insufficient; "the facts and the reasons for the belief that such bias or prejudice exists" must be set out, and plainly, I think, this must be done in order that the judge or any reviewing tribunal may determine whether they suffice to support honest belief in the disqualifying state of mind.

Defendants' affidavit discloses no adequate ground for believing that personal feeling existed against any one of them. The indicated prejudice was towards certain malevolents from Germany, a country then engaged in hunnish warfare and notoriously encouraged by many of its natives who, unhappily, had obtained citizenship here. The words attributed to the judge (I do not credit the affidavit's accuracy) may be fairly construed as showing only deep detestation for all persons of German extraction who were at that time wickedly abusing privileges granted by our indulgent laws.

Of course, no judge should preside if he entertains actual personal prejudice towards any party and to this obvious disqualification Congress added honestly entertained belief of such prejudice when based upon fairly adequate facts and circumstances. Intense dislike of a class does not render the judge incapable of administering complete justice to one of its members. A public officer who entertained no aversion towards disloyal German immigrants during the late war was simply unfit for his place. And while "An overspeaking judge is no well tuned cymbal" neither is an amorphous dummy unspotted by human emotions a becoming receptacle for judicial power. It was not the purpose of Congress to empower an unscrupulous defendant seeking escape from merited punishment to remove a judge solely because he had emphatically condemned domestic enemies in time of national danger. The personal concern of the judge in matters of this kind is indeed small, but the concern of the public is very great.

In my view the trial judge committed no error when he considered the affidavit, held it insufficient, and refused to retire.

Notes and Questions

1. Do the dissenting judges differ between themselves whether Judge Landis showed bias toward German-Americans as a class? Do they agree that Judge Landis showed no personal bias toward the defendants in *Berger*?

2. In his dissent Justice Day argues that any bias Judge Landis' statements may have shown was not *personal* bias against Berger, since the statements had been made in sentencing Weissensel, who had already been tried and convicted of violating the Espionage Act. Justice McReynolds states in his dissent:

> The statute [Section 21 of the Judicial Code, now 28 U.S.C. 144] relates only to adverse opinion or leaning towards an individual and has no application to the appraisement of a class, *e.g.*, revolutionists, assassins, traitors.

One possible meaning of "bias" is treating a person as a member of a disfavored class rather than as an individual with merits and demerits having nothing to do with the class. Do the dissenting justices *exclude* this sort of bias from coverage under the statute? Justice McReynolds insists that the "bias" forbidden by the statute is "personal bias": it "relates only to adverse opinion or leaning towards an individual." Do you agree?

3. Justice McReynolds also states: "Intense dislike of a class does not render the judge incapable of administering complete justice to one of its members." Does it not matter exactly *why* the judge "dislikes" the class? Is it obvious what it means for an individual to be a "member" of a class? Shouldn't we want to know the purpose of the litigation?

4. Judge Landis was, in the words of the dissent, "an overspeaking judge." He said what was on his mind; he was ingenuous. Suppose he had kept his opinions to himself—he still would have been just as biased as the Supreme Court said he was. But now, as the result of the *Berger* decision, judges will learn not to say what is on their mind. Won't that drive bias and prejudice underground? Judges will be as biased as they ever were; they just won't *admit* it. Is that a desirable outcome of the *Berger* litigation? What else can the judicial system do to protect against judicial bias?

5. Perhaps Judge Landis was not biased against one class, but rather against the intersection of two classes: (1) Germans in the United States, and (2) persons disloyal to the United States. The defendants certainly fit into (1); but did they fit into (2)? Wouldn't the answer to that question depend on how the facts came out at the trial? If so, can we say that Judge Landis was not biased at all? Consider the following questions:

A. Suppose a judge announces at the beginning of a criminal case: "I hereby disclose my total and complete prejudice against Chicanos who deal in cocaine and crack, because Latin America is growing the stuff and shipping it here and destroying the lives of our youth in the process." Suppose that the trial is against a defendant who is a Chicano accused of selling cocaine. Should the judge be dismissed from the case on the authority of *Berger*? What prejudice does the judge show against the defendant? Can't the judge say that if the defendant turns out to be innocent, he then is *not* a Chicano who deals in cocaine, and hence is *not* the object of the judge's prejudice? Can't the judge say further that all judges should be prejudiced against guilty cocaine dealers?

B. Same hypothetical as in the previous question. Can we argue that the judge is predisposed toward finding this defendant guilty because the judge wants to "send a message" to the Chicano community to stay away from dealing in cocaine? If the judge wants to "send messages," can such a judge be fair toward this defendant? Is this a case where bias against a class boils down to a presumption against a particular member of that class?

6. Imagine a white racist judge presiding over a court in Mississippi in the 1930s. Should that judge be barred from hearing either of the following cases (each involving alleged negligence on the part of the defendant causing injury to the plaintiff)?

A. A black plaintiff sues a black defendant.

B. A white plaintiff sues a white defendant.

Theories of Judging and Judge Disqualification[17]

John Leubsdorf

The list of disqualifying factors has expanded since the eighteenth century, when financial interest was the sole ground for recusal. Legislation played an important part in this evolution. Congress has supplemented its original disqualification statute of 1792 five times, in each instance expanding the scope of disqualification. The Supreme Court has read the Constitution to forbid decision makers to hear cases when they have a personal stake in the result, become personally embroiled with a party, or were involved in the litigated incidents. The organized bar has similarly expanded its standards.

Except for Chief Justice Rehnquist, every commentator who has critically analyzed disqualification in the federal courts has supported its expansion. The 1974 disqualification legislation did not end this trend; commentators continue to seek further enlargements, often supporting automatic disqualification when a party files a conclusory affidavit of bias.

The obvious explanation for these developments is a shift in society's view of judicial psychology, and of psychology in general: from the eighteenth century's economic man, susceptible only to the tug of financial interest, to today's Freudian person, awash in a sea of conscious and unconscious motives. Alternatively, one might view the law as developing out of a paradigm of disqualification when a judge is "judge in his own case"—a disqualification perhaps grounded less on the likelihood of impartial decision than on the inconsistency between the roles of judge and party. Today, disqualification law is clearly directed at the likelihood of warped judgment, with a judge's financial or familial stake in the case as just one circumstance from which to infer such a likelihood.

However, it is an oversimplification to conclude that a growing belief in the influence of emotional and unconscious drives led to more judicial disqualification. After all, the eighteenth century also disqualified witnesses for interest, yet later generations have abandoned rather than expanded this practice. Freud or no Freud, no one today proposes to disqualify congressmen from voting or scientific researchers from researching because of their emotions. On the other hand, eighteenth-century lawyers and judges knew that motives other than financial or personal interest could warp judgment. They often disqualified jurors under circumstances that created a suspicion of partiality, such as belonging to the same society as a party or opposing a party in an unrelated suit. Joseph Chitty (not a pioneer of psychology) mentioned long before Freud that jurors could be "unconsciously" influenced. Bentham reminded lawyers that nonfinancial motives can sway judges, but he did not discover that truth. Indeed, the Talmud had recognized the precariousness of impartiality when it said: "Every judge who judges a case with complete fairness even for a single hour is credited by the Torah as though he had become a partner to the Holy One, Blessed Be He, in the work of creation."

---

[17] 62 N.Y.U.L. REV. 237, 246–50 (1987).

Increasing doubts that correct answers exist for legal questions underlie the growth of disqualification. Barbara Shapiro relates the seventeenth century's concern for judicial impartiality, as shown in efforts to make judicial tenure more secure, to that period's doubts about the availability of unquestionable knowledge. For a long time, lawyers and judges were able to limit these doubts or believed that they could preserve credibility by hiding them from the public and suppressing public criticism. However, as reaching an objectively correct legal decision came to seem a more Herculean task, people went to greater lengths to prevent extraneous motives from inhibiting the delicate feat.

An increased sense of the role of policy in adjudication may also have spotlighted disqualification problems. Martin Shapiro and Owen Fiss have suggested that the root concept of traditional litigation is the selection by two disputants of a third person to resolve their dispute. The disputants, presumably, would choose an arbiter who had never commented on the matters in dispute, was unaligned with either party, and embodied a system of values to which they both adhered. A judge might well meet these requirements; if so, courts adjudication would be much like arbitration. But over the years it has become clearer that judges do not simply resolve private disputes, but also shape and enforce governmental policy. That gives litigants more reason to distrust even a judge with no stake in the result. It also gives the government and citizens more reason to ensure that its judges will enforce rather than undermine the correct policies.

Although these developments have made people more concerned about disqualification, they have also threatened to undermine any disqualification rules. If unconscious motives sway everyone, how can one find a judge who is free of them? If only Hercules can find the correct result—or if there is no correct result—how can we say that one judge is better suited to decide a case than another? If judges are molders of policy, why should anyone promote a judicial ideal that is more than an array of the promoter's own preferred policies? As Kenneth Davis has said, "Almost any intelligent person will initially assert that he wants objectivity, but by that he means biases that coincide with his own biases."

Judge Jerome Frank wrestled with these questions at a deeper level than any of his contemporaries who wrote about disqualification. The decision in *In re Linahan* did not call for much agony, because the only evidence of bias presented was that a Master, after hearing the evidence, had ruled against one party, and that some of those rulings were reversed on appeal. But the case must have challenged Judge Frank to show that, as a judge, he could acknowledge and yet confine his earlier assertions that the judge's personality shapes judicial decisions more than impersonal law.

He posed the problem squarely.

In re J.P. Linahan

138 F.2d 650
Circuit Court of Appeals, Second Circuit
Nov. 8, 1943

FRANK, Circuit Judge.

Appellants complain that the District Court, having appointed Referee Olney as Special Master in Chapter X proceeding begun by involuntary petition and contested by appellants, denied appellants' application to remove that Special Master because of bias. Appellants point to matters alleged to show such bias, most of which are so frivolous as to deserve no discussion. Special emphasis is put on these facts: The Master has heretofore entered orders, accompanied by findings adverse to appellants; the District Court's orders, approving these orders of the Master, were, in some instances, reversed by this court on previous appeals; some of the findings of the Special Master are alleged to have been, at least by inference, disapproved on these appeals and, in one instance, to have been based on hearsay. These facts do not call for removal of the Special Master. Appellants entertain a fundamentally false notion conception [*sic*] of the prejudice which disqualifies a judicial officer.

Democracy must, indeed, fail unless our courts try cases fairly, and there can be no fair trial before a judge lacking in impartiality and disinterestedness. If, however, "bias" and "partiality" be defined to mean the total absence of preconceptions in the mind of the judge, then no one has ever had a fair trial and no one ever will. The human mind, even at infancy, is no blank piece of paper. We are born with predispositions; and the process of education, formal and informal, creates attitudes in all men which affect them in judging situations, attitudes which precede reasoning in particular instances and which therefore, by definition, are prejudices. Without acquired "slants," preconceptions, life could not go on. Every habit constitutes a prejudgment; were those prejudgments which we call habits absent in any person, were he obliged to treat every event as an unprecedented crisis presenting a wholly new problem he would go mad. Interests, points of view, preferences, are the essence of living. Only death yields complete dispassionateness, for such dispassionateness signifies utter indifference. "To

live is to have a vocation, and to have a vocation is to have an ethics or scheme of values, and to have a scheme of values is to have a point of view, and to have a point of view is to have a prejudice or bias * * *"[18] An "open mind," in the sense of a mind containing no preconceptions whatever, would be a mind incapable of learning anything, would be that of an utterly emotionless human being, corresponding roughly to the psychiatrist's descriptions of the feeble-minded. More directly to the point, every human society has a multitude of established attitudes, unquestioned postulates. Cosmically, they may seem parochial prejudices, but many of them represent the community's most cherished values and ideals. Such social preconceptions, the "value judgments" which members of any given society take for granted and use as the unspoken axioms of thinking, find their way into that society's legal system, become what has been termed "the valuation system of the law." The judge in our society owes a duty to act in accordance with those basic predilections inhering in our legal system (although, of course, he has the right, at times, to urge that some of them be modified or abandoned). The standard of dispassionateness obviously does not require the judge to rid himself of the unconscious influence of such social attitudes.[19]

In addition to those acquired social value judgments, every judge, however, unavoidably has many idiosyncratic "leanings of the mind,"

---

[18] KENNETH BURKE, PERMANENCE AND CHANGE 329 (1936).

[19] A word of caution is needed here. These social value judgments are often said to be a product of the "spirit of the times." One may doubt, however, whether, in any period, there is a single time spirit or, to use a common phrase, a single "climate of opinion." The "time spirit" is often differently interpreted by different judges: "In every court there are likely to be as many estimates of the 'Zeitgeist' as there are judges on its bench." CARDOZO, THE NATURE OF THE JUDICIAL PROCESS 174 (1920).

uniquely personal prejudices, which may interfere with his fairness at a trial. He may be stimulated by unconscious sympathies for, or antipathies to, some of the witnesses, lawyers or parties in a case before him. As Josiah Royce observed, "Oddities of feature or of complexion, slight physical variations from the customary, a strange dress, a scar, a too-steady look, a limp, a loud or deep voice, any of these peculiarities . . . may be, to one, an object of fascinated curiosity; to another . . . an intense irritation, an object of violent antipathy."[20] In *Ex parte Chase*, 43 Ala. 303, Judge Peters said he had "known a popular judicial officer grow quite angry with a suitor in his court, and threaten him with imprisonment, for no ostensible reason, save the fact, that he wore an overcoat made of wolf skins," and spoke of "prejudice, which may be swayed and controlled by the merest trifles—such as the toothache, the rheumatism, the gout, or a fit of indigestion, or even through the very means by which indigestion is frequently sought to be avoided." "Trifles," he added, "however ridiculous, cease to be trifles when they may interfere with a safe administration of the law." Frankly to recognize the existence of such prejudices is the part of wisdom. The conscientious judge will, as far as possible, make himself aware of his biases of this character, and, by that very self-knowledge, nullify their effect.[21]

Much harm is done by the myth that, merely by putting on a black robe and taking the oath of office as a judge, a man ceases to be human and strips himself of all predilections, becomes a passionless thinking machine.[22] The concealment of the human element in the judicial process allows that element to operate in an exaggerated manner; the sunlight of awareness has an antiseptic effect on prejudices. Freely avowing that he is a human being, the judge can and should, through self-scrutiny, prevent the operation of this class of biases.[23] This self-knowledge is needed

---

[20] Royce, Race Questions, Provincialism and Other American Problems 47–52 (1908).

[21] One of the subtlest tendencies which a conscientious judge must learn to overcome is that of "leaning over backwards" in favor of persons against whom his prejudices incline him. Pascal wrote of some men who have been unjust in their efforts to exclude bias: "The sure way of losing a just cause is to get it recommended to these men by their near relatives." Pascal, *Pensees*, No. 82.

[22] "The judicial mind is subject to the laws of psychology like any other mind. When the judge assumes the ermine he does not divest himself of humanity. He has sworn to do justice to all men without fear or favour, but the impartiality which is the noble hallmark of our Bench does not imply that the judge's mind has become a mere machine to turn out decrees; the judge's mind remains a human instrument working as do other minds, though no doubt on specialized lines and often characterized by individual traits of personality, engaging or the reverse." Lord Macmillan, Law and Other Things 202 (1937).

[23] There would have been no disqualification of the trial judge in Berger v. United States, 255 U.S. 22, if he had said, not that he was virtually incapable of being fair to German American citizens during World War I, but that he was aware of his prejudice against them and could therefore discount it.

The unrecognized, unspoken, bias is dangerous. Darwin said that he found it so easy to pass over cases opposed to his favorite generalizations that he made it a habit to jot down every exception which he observed or thought of, as otherwise he would be almost sure to forget it. It is difficult to agree with Rohrlich (17 Am. Bar Assn. J. 481) that it is wise for judges to suppress the expression of certain factors in the process of decision-making, that such suppression tends "to reduce the influence of those factors."

What Herbert Spencer said as to more general preconceptions has a bearing here: "The only reasonable hope is, that here and there one may be led, in calmer moments to remember how largely his beliefs about public matters have been made for him by circumstances, and how probable it is that they are either untrue or but partially true. When he reflects on the doubtfulness of the evidence which he generalizes, collected hap-hazard from a narrow area—when he counts up the perverting sentiments fostered in him by education, country, class, party, creed—when, observing those around, he sees that from other evidence selected to gratify sentiments partially unlike his own, there result unlike views; he may occasionally recollect how largely mere accidents have determined his convictions. Recollecting this, he may be induced to hold these convictions not quite so strongly; may see the need for criticism of them with a view to revision; and, above all, may be somewhat less eager to act in pursuance of them." Spencer, Study of Sociology 356–357 (1873).

in a judge because he is peculiarly exposed to emotional influences; the "court room is a place of surging emotions . . . the parties are keyed up to the contest, often in open defiance; and the topics at issue are often calculated to stir up the sympathy, prejudice, or ridicule of the tribunal."[24] The judge's decision turns, often, on what he believes to be the facts of the case. As a fact-finder, he is himself a witness—a witness of the witnesses; he should, therefore, learn to avoid the errors which, because of prejudice, often affect those witnesses.

But, just because his fact-finding is based on his estimates of the witnesses, of their reliability as reporters of what they saw and heard, it is his duty, while listening to and watching them, to form attitudes towards them. He must do his best to ascertain their motives, their biases, their dominating passions and interests, for only so can he judge of the accuracy of their narrations. He must also shrewdly observe the stratagems of the opposing lawyers, perceive their efforts to sway him by appeals to his predilections.[25] He must cannily penetrate through the surface of their remarks to their real purposes and motives.[26] He

---

[24] WIGMORE, PRINCIPLES OF JUDICIAL PROOF 960 (2d ed. 1931).

[25] It will repay any judge to re-read carefully Aristotle's *Rhetoric,* which, in large part, is a manual on how to win a law suit, telling in detail the numerous ways to appeal to a judge's prejudices.

It is not without interest that one of the much-quoted statements in the *Rhetoric* on "natural" or "universal" law is contained in a passage in which Aristotle advises that, if the written law is against a litigant, he should urge that the case is governed by unwritten "universal law," but that, if the written law is in his favor, he should dwell on the dangers of resorting to such unwritten principles. See ARISTOTLE, RHETORIC, Book I, Chapter 15.

[26] Some lawyers are seductively persuasive, recalling Plutarch's report of a remark of a contemporary about Pericles: "Whenever I throw him in wrestling, he disputes the fall, and carries his point, and persuades the very men who saw him fall."

has an official obligation to become prejudiced in that sense. Impartiality is not gullibility. Disinterestedness does not mean child-like innocence. If the judge did not form judgments of the actors in those court-house dramas called trials, he could never render decisions.

His findings of fact may be erroneous, for, being human, he is not infallible; indeed, a judge who purports to be superhuman is likely to be dominated by improper prejudices. When upper court judges on an appeal decide that the findings of a trial judge are at fault because they—correctly or incorrectly—[27]think those findings insufficiently supported by relevant and competent evidence, that appellate decision does not brand him as partial and unfair. When, his decision reversed because of errors in his findings of fact or conclusions of law, the case comes back to his court for a further hearing, he will not, if he is the kind of person entitled to hold office as a judge, permit his previous decision in the case control him.

These comments dispose of the issue here. Referee Olney has honorably discharged the duties of his office for many years. Nothing in his official career or in the record of this case justifies the suggestion that he did not and will not conform to the judicial standards of fairness as we have defined them. Judge Coxe, one of our ablest and most experienced trial judges, has refused to remove Referee Olney as Master in these proceedings. We see nothing to warrant us in interfering with Judge Coxe's discretion. Indeed, had he ruled otherwise, we would have been strongly inclined to reverse him.

Affirmed.

---

[27] Judicially, they are deemed to be correct. In fact, being human, they too may err.

Notes and Questions

1. To what extent can we account for the difference in result in *Berger* and *Linahan* by the fact that in *Berger* the judge's prejudicial statements were made before trial whereas in *Linahan* the prejudice came out during the proceedings?

2. Is Justice McReynolds in his dissent to *Berger* simply prefiguring Judge Frank's model of the judicial temperament in *Linahan*: awareness of one's prejudices and preparedness to act contrary to them? Do you believe that some people, at least, possess such an ability to overcome their own known prejudices?

3. In Note 21 to his opinion in *Linahan* [Note 6 in the original] Judge Frank describes a tendency in some people to decide opposite to their inclinations to prove to themselves and the world either that they do not have the inclination or that they are able to act contrary to it. We have some famous examples of Supreme Court justices—Frankfurter, Warren—who confounded the expectations of their political sponsors once they started work on the bench. Can we ever tell whether a judge is setting aside a bias or acting in accordance with Judge Frank's phenomenon? Can we decide such a question about ourselves?

4. Does the following assertion go too far? "The very deepest prejudices we have do not seem like prejudices to us; we call them facts."

5. Comment upon the following assertion: "Faith is what we know on the basis of evidence we have not seen."

6. Judge Frank said that the trial judge must observe witnesses at a trial very closely, for it is his duty "to form attitudes toward them. He must do his best to ascertain their motives, their biases, their dominating passions and interests, for only so can he judge of the accuracy of their narrations." Do you agree? Is it possible for a judge to "ascertain" "motives"? Assuming it is, what is more likely—that the judge will *accurately* ascertain such motives or *inaccurately* do so? When engaging in something as elusive as the ascertainment of the motives of other persons, is there not room for prejudice and bias to creep in?

7. May a judge go outside the trial to ascertain the motives and biases of witnesses? May he discuss the case with other judges? With attorneys at the local bar association? Should he inquire in his community as to the motives and biases of witnesses who are appearing or will appear in trials that he is conducting? Suppose his son goes to the same school as the daughter of a witness in a trial; should he ask his son to ask the witness's daughter certain things about her father, his friends, his habits, or his beliefs?

Except for consulting with other judges (which is expressly allowed by the Code of Judicial Conduct of the American Bar Association), any such deliberate forays by a judge outside of the trial itself would be considered improper under the standards of judicial ethics. In *Price Brothers Co. v. Philadelphia Gear Corp.*, 629 F.2d 444 (6th Cir. 1980), it was alleged that the trial judge sent his law clerk to view the subject matter of the litigation. The Sixth Circuit held that this was so potentially "destructive of the appearance of impartiality" that the case was remanded for a hearing on the truth of the allegation.

8. Some litigations are huge and extend over many years. One of the biggest of these was the government's antitrust case against IBM, in which the trial judge heard 10,000 motions! IBM claimed that the judge was biased because he ruled against them on 86% of the 10,000 motions. The appellate court held that adverse rulings alone do not create the appearance of partiality. *In re International Business Machines Corp.*, 618 F.2d 923, 929 (2d Cir. 1980) ("A trial judge must be free to make rulings on the merits without the apprehension that if he makes a disproportionate number in favor of one litigant, he may have created the impression of bias.") Do you agree?

9. What light does Judge Frank's account of judging in *Linahan* shed on the model of judging implicit in legal realism? Should we be concerned not with judicial bias, but with the degree of judicial bias? If so, how could it be measured?

Federal Statutes on Judicial Bias

28 U.S.C. § 144

[We encountered the precursor to this statute in the *Berger* case. It disqualifies district court judges for personal bias or prejudice as alleged in a party's affidavit.]

28 U.S.C. § 455

(a) Any justice, judge, or magistrate of the United States shall disqualify himself in any proceeding in which his impartiality might reasonably be questioned.

(b) He shall also disqualify himself in the following circumstances:

(1) Where he has a personal bias or prejudice concerning a party, or personal knowledge of disputed evidentiary facts concerning the proceeding;

(2) Where in private practice he served as lawyer in the matter in controversy, or a lawyer with whom he previously practiced law served during such association as a lawyer concerning the matter, or the judge or such lawyer has been a material witness concerning it;

(3) Where he has served in governmental employment and in such capacity participated as counsel, adviser or material witness concerning the proceeding or expressed an opinion concerning the merits of the particular case in controversy;

(4) He knows that he, individually or as a fiduciary, or his spouse or minor child residing in his household, has a financial interest in the subject matter in controversy or in a party to the proceeding, or any other interest that could be substantially affected by the outcome of the proceeding;

(5) He or his spouse, or a person within the third degree of relationship to either of them, or the spouse of such a person:

(i) Is a party to the proceeding, or an officer, director, or trustee of a party;

(ii) Is acting as a lawyer in the proceeding;

(iii) Is known by the judge to have an interest that could be substantially affected by the outcome of the proceeding;

(iv) Is to the judge's knowledge likely to be a material witness in the proceeding.

(c) A judge should inform himself about his personal and fiduciary financial interests, and make a reasonable effort to inform himself about the personal financial interests of his spouse and minor children residing in his household.

(d) For the purposes of this section the following words or phrases shall have the meaning indicated:

(1) "proceeding" includes pretrial, trial, appellate review, or other stages of litigation;

(2) the degree of relationship is calculated according to the civil law system;

(3) "fiduciary" includes such relationships as executor, administrator, trustee, and guardian;

(4) "financial interest" means ownership of a legal or equitable interest, however small, or a relationship as director, adviser, or other active participant in the affairs of a party, except that:

(i) Ownership in a mutual or common investment fund that holds securities is not a "financial interest" in such securities unless the judge participates in the management of the fund;

(ii) An office in an educational, religious, charitable, fraternal, or civic organization is not a "financial interest" in securities held by the organization;

(iii) The proprietary interest of a policyholder in a mutual insurance company, of a depositor in a mutual savings association, or a similar proprietary interest, is a "financial interest" in the organization only if the outcome of the proceeding could substantially affect the value of the interest;

(iv) Ownership of government securities is a "financial interest" in the issuer only if the outcome of the proceeding could substantially affect the value of the securities.

(e) No justice, judge, or magistrate shall accept from the parties to the proceeding a waiver of any ground for disqualification enumerated in subsection (b). Where the ground for disqualification arises only under subsection (a), waiver may be accepted provided it is preceded by a full disclosure on the record of the basis for disqualification.

(f) Notwithstanding the preceding provisions of this section, if any justice, judge, magistrate, or bankruptcy judge to whom a matter has been assigned would be disqualified, after substantial judicial time has been devoted to the matter, because of the appearance or discovery, after the matter was assigned to him or her, that he or she individually or as a fiduciary, or his or her spouse or minor child residing in his or her household, has a financial interest in a party (other than an interest that could be substantially affected by the outcome), disqualification is not required if the justice, judge, magistrate, bankruptcy judge, spouse or minor child, as the case may be, divests himself or herself of the interest that provides the grounds for the disqualification.

Notes and Questions

1. The versions of Sections 144 and 455 in force when *Berger* and *Linahan* were decided were enacted by Congress as Sections 21 and 20 respectively of the Act of March 3, 1911, c.231, 36 Stat. 1090. Both sections then applied only to district court judges. Section 20 (now 28 U.S.C. § 455) was revised in 1948 to be applicable to all justices and judges of the United States.[28] Section 21 (now 28 U.S.C. § 144) is still applicable only to district court judges.

The version of Section 455 in force at the time of *Berger* and *Linahan* read somewhat differently than the current version:

> Sec. 20. Whenever it appears that the judge of any district court is in any way concerned in interest in any suit pending therein, or has been of counsel or is a material witness for either party, or is so related to or connected with either party as to render it improper, in this opinion, for him to sit on the trial, it shall be his duty, on application by either party, to cause the fact to be entered on the records of the court; and also an order that an authenticated copy thereof shall be forthwith certified to the senior circuit judge for said circuit then present in the circuit; and thereupon such proceedings shall be had as are provided in section fourteen [permitting the designation by a circuit judge of a district judge from any other district in the same circuit[29]].

The 1948 "broadening" of Section 455 to apply to all judges, also eliminated the application procedure found in the original statute, stating only that the justice or judge "shall disqualify himself."[30] The current, substantively expanded version arose in a major amendment to Section 455 in 1974.[31] To the relatively narrow grounds for recusal contemplated in the pre-1974 version of the statute, the amended statute added notions of "impartiality" and "personal bias or prejudice."

2. Section 455 asks a judge to recuse herself for any of several listed conditions. Some of the conditions are clearly objective, such as having a spouse who is a party to the litigation. Some are objective in form only, such as, "in which his impartiality might reasonably be questioned." Others are subjective, such as a judge becoming aware (whether others are aware or not) that she has a "personal bias" against a party. Is it realistic to expect a judge to recognize conditions that are either subjective or are objective in form only? Is it realistic to expect appellate judges to review a trial judge's response to a motion for recusal based upon subjective factors?

3. Should we be more careful about financial interests and blood relationships because we find them easier to identify than other interests and relationships? Because we think they are more potent? Or, should we be less careful about them?

---

[28] June 25, 1948, c.646, § 1, 62 Stat. 908.

[29] Section 21 provided for designation of another judge within the same district. Why the difference?

[30] "Any justice or judge of the United States shall disqualify himself in any case in which he has a substantial interest, has been of counsel, is or has been a material witness, or is so related to or connected with any party or his attorney as to render it improper, in his opinion, for him to sit on the trial, appeal, or other proceeding therein."

[31] Pub. L. No. 93–512, § 1, 88 Stat. 1609 (Dec. 5, 1974).

4. In *United States* v. *Will*, 449 U.S. 200 (1980), the Supreme Court considered a challenge to Congress' power to repeal or modify a statutorily defined formula for annual cost-of-living increases in the salary of federal judges. Even the justices who ruled on this case had a direct personal financial interest in the outcome! The Court found a way around the ethical requirement—the "rule of necessity." This court-made rule states that no judge is required to disqualify himself if the basis for the disqualification would require every judge to disqualify himself. Can you see why this "rule of necessity" would be relevant to interpreting Section 455? The Court held that Section 455 was designed to guarantee litigants a fair forum in which to pursue their claims. The "rule of necessity" thus makes it possible for all litigants to have *a* forum.

5. Is our judicial system biased in favor of capitalism? If so, is it a matter for concern? (Consider these questions when you read the next case and the "60 Minutes" excerpt below.) Is there a difference between a judge's bias and widely held beliefs about social policy? What if society is torn on an issue of policy? What if a judge considers widely held beliefs to be evil? (We will take up these questions in Section 4.)

3.3 Judicial bias: Applications

United States v. Fiat Motors

Background

On January 4, 1980, the Government charged Fiat with violating the National Traffic and Motor Vehicle Safety Act. 15 U.S.C. §§ 1381, *et seq*. The complaint charged Fiat with failing to remedy safety defects on several models of its motor vehicles. The Government alleged that certain designated Fiat models were subject to severe rust and corrosion of critical undercarriage components, which in turn affected their operational safety, more particularly the problem of control or lack of control of the motor vehicle. On the same day that the complaint was filed, the National Highway Traffic Safety Administration issued a final order requiring Fiat to recall those vehicles. In this proceeding the Government sought enforcement of that recall order. . . .

Nearly fourteen months after the Government brought this suit, Fiat filed a motion seeking the disqualification of Judge Barrington D. Parker from further presiding over the matter, or, alternatively, that he exercise his discretion and transfer the matter to the Calendar Committee for reassignment to another judge.

IN THE UNITED STATES DISTRICT COURT FOR THE DISTRICT OF COLUMBIA

THE UNITED STATES OF
AMERICA
     Plaintiff,

    -vs.-

FIAT MOTORS OF
NORTH AMERICA, INC.,
    Defendant

Civil Action No. 80–25

Washington, D.C. Friday, April 3, 1981

The above-captioned action came on for motion for disqualification of trial judge before the Honorable BARRINGTON D. PARKER, United States District Court Judge, in Courtroom 19, commencing at approximately 9:20 o'clock a.m.

APPEARANCES:

For the Plaintiff:
SURELL BRADY, ESQ.
Department of Justice, Room 3535
10th Street and Constitution Avenue, NW.
Washington, D.C. 20530

ROBERT NESLER, ESQ.
Department of Justice, Room 3334
10th Street and Constitution Avenue, NW.
Washington, D.C. 20530

DAVID ALLEN, ESQ.
Department of Transportation
National Highway Safety Administration
400 Seventh Street, SW.
Washington, D.C. 20590

For the Defendant:

JOHN H. KORNS, ESQ.
HARRY W. CLADOUHOS, ESQ.
PAUL M. LAURENZA, ESQ.
Cladouhos & Brashares
1750 New York Avenue, NW.
Washington, D.C. 20006

THE COURT. Mr. Korns, you may proceed, sir.

I may say that I received the letter of counsel for Fiat in which they suggested that this matter be held in chambers. I felt it was a rather curious observation and request, and you may if you want to—you can address that, too, Mr. Korns.

Of course, I have made the decision. The decision is I would hear it in open court.

MR. KORNS. Certainly, Your Honor.

ORAL ARGUMENT ON BEHALF OF THE DEFENDANT

MR. KORNS. Your Honor, I wouldn't want the Court to misunderstand our position. We were not requesting the hearing in chambers. We were just indicating that if the Court desires such a hearing, we had no objection to it.

THE COURT. Why would you even make that proffer?

MR. KORNS. Fiat was not urging a hearing in chambers, Your Honor.

The only point we were making was that since we were raising considerations about which the Court might very well feel sensitive, and which we felt were delicate matters, that the Court might feel more comfortable having the hearing in chambers.

THE COURT. Well, I certainly appreciate your interest in the Court being comfortable. There are a number of cases—as a matter of fact there are a legion of cases dealing with a disqualification of recusal, and as I read them, they all reported, and they all suggest—there is nothing to the con-trary—they all suggest that everything is ventilated on the record in open court.

Can you point to any situation where a so-called sensitive matter relating to a judge's disqualification or recusal is held in chambers?

MR. KORNS. Your Honor, we were not urging this. Truly we were not urging the matter. We simply were pointing out if the Court wanted to do so, we had no objection and, in fact, the papers in the Branson case, if I recall, or the transcript—I don't recall now which—the U.S. Attorney made the identical suggestion that if the Court wished, he would be happy to have the hearing in chambers.

THE COURT. Counsel, the situation in the Branson case, since you bring it up, is remarkably in contrast and different from this.

MR. KORNS. If the Court feels so, that is fine, Your Honor. We were not urging the matter, and we are not urging the matter—

THE COURT. I will tell you quite frankly I was surprised. I wasn't annoyed at all, but I was just curious as to just what was the thinking of your sending such a letter.

You have explained it. You may proceed with your argument.

MR. KORNS. Thank you, Your Honor.

Your Honor, there are a couple of points I would like to make preliminarily.

The first is that I would like the Court to understand that no lawyer, no member of our firm has ever filed a motion for disqualification before. We undertake this matter not lightly, not as a matter of course of litigation tactic. We undertake it in all good faith, feeling that under the law that it is a very appropriate motion.

THE COURT. Mr. Korns, I don't go beyond your certificate of counsel, so you needn't—I am sure you do it in good faith—

MR. KORNS. Thank you, Your Honor.

THE COURT. —as represented in the certificate of counsel.

MR. KORNS. And that it is a situation in which the client feels with justification, I submit, that there are questions as to the ability of any person in the Court's position to be truly impartial, questions that can never be answered fully in advance as to which nobody could give an exact answer at this point in a case, and that under the law the party in this very, very important case should not have to take the risk of influence on the Court's mind from the Court's own very unfortunate experience.

That is one point I would like to make, Your Honor.

There are no dispositive cases on the issue. It is a very small point, and what I would suggest is this: The statutory language says that the Court shall disqualify itself if there is reason to question the Court's impartiality, and in legislative history the terms were used "if reasonable factual basis for having doubts about the Court's ability to be impartial," therefore the standard is not whether the Court is, in fact, biased.

The standard is not whether a reasonable man would find the Court biased. The question is whether there is a reasonable factual basis for having concerns, questions, doubts about the ability of the Court or of any person in the Court's situation to be impartial.

Your Honor, we would just submit that in all sincerity we think that any person on the street, that any litigant in a similar situation would have doubts about any person's ability to be impartial in such a situation, and we think that it is a situation that is not something that speaks to this Court's particular capabilities, Your Honor, in any way, but it is an inherent fact that any person who has been through the very unfortunate situation that you have would have problems being truly impartial and rising above that experience.

That is our point, Your Honor, and we think that since the standard of the law speaks not to what is inside the Court's head, but speaks to an objective standard, what people on the street would think, what common litigants would think that the only reasonable conclusion is to say, yes, people would have doubts.

Even if you think that you know that those doubts are unfounded, that, in fact, people knowing the public circumstances would have doubts, and that is our only point, Your Honor.

Thank you. I would like to reserve time to respond to any points the Government might have to—

THE COURT. Very well.

ORAL ARGUMENT ON BEHALF OF THE PLAINTIFF

MS. BRADY. Good morning, Your Honor. Surell Brady of the Justice Department for the plaintiff.

I would just like to respond very briefly to several points made by Mr. Korns and made by Fiat's motion for disqualification.

We feel that the only issue before the Court on the motion for disqualification is whether Fiat has established either of the standards for disqualification under 28 U.S.C. section 144 or 28 U.S.C. section 455.

In this case they have not even minimally approached those standards. Each of those statutes require that there be facts set forth showing either a judge's actual bias or actual facts from which a person could infer that judge's impartiality could reasonably be questioned. There are no such facts in this case.

The sole and only basis for Fiat's motion is that Your Honor was injured by an automobile in 1975, period. There is nothing more to their assertions than that.

There is no proof. There are no allegations that Your Honor has any animosity or bias toward Fiat. The accident in no way involved Fiat or a manufacturer, and the only point that they make is the inference they wish to draw and they alone that because of the serious injuries suffered by Your Honor, Your Honor would be unable to sit fairly and impartially in this case.

However, that is simply not sufficient. The case law explains that disqualification statutes are quite clear, that mere inference or speculation is not enough. There must be absolute and grounded facts which would cause a person or the Court to conclude that the Court is, in fact, biased.

The purpose of the affidavit which is submitted in support of section 144 is to set forth those facts from which the Court could determine whether or not it has a bias against one of the parties to the proceeding or to the subject matter of the proceeding.

The affidavit filed by Fiat here is abysmally absent in those qualifications. Mr. Fallon's affidavit states only that Your Honor was injured by a car and sets forth the circumstances and facts of that injury, nothing more. There are no facts, no allegations of bias or animosity towards Fiat, and on that basis alone the motion is groundless and should be denied.

The standard defendant will seek to assert under 455 is that the severity of a judge's experience would require his disqualification, and in this case the severity of your injuries would disqualify you from sitting in this case because it tangentially involves auto safety.

However, that is not the standard under the statute. Again facts must be shown showing that you do, indeed, as a result of a personal, extra judicial experience have a bias against Fiat, and that has been markedly absent here.

The logical extension of the arguments made here by Fiat would be that any negative or serious experience suffered by a Federal judge would be sufficient or, indeed, would require his disqualification.

As your Honor is aware, none of the cases hold that, and indeed accepting that proposition would certainly turn judicial experience on its head.

The cases, however, do recognize that judges come to the Bench and come to proceedings before them cloaked with all the normal experiences of life which do include serious injuries.

As regards Fiat's assertion that the public interest here—that the public interest would not be harmed in any way by Your Honor's disqualification, we submit that it would and that this case and others like it would suffer supreme prejudice.

THE COURT. Why would the public interest be harmed?

MS. BRADY. The public interest would be harmed because it is our position that standards for disqualification have not been met. However, Fiat would have Your Honor, nonetheless, step aside.

If that were the case, it would be possible in any case on such groundless assertions of bias for a Federal judge to step down, and despite Fiat's claims that there would be no rescheduling problems or no date problems, we submit that having the case transferred to a totally unknown judge, to a totally unknown schedule could not but inject at least some level of uncertainty to the normal progress of this case.

But a more important point is that as the plaintiff in this case and as parties to many similar suits like this, the United States certainly has an interest in having the statutory standards for the qualification of Federal judges met, and in a case such as this where they are simply not met, the public interest requires that those statutes be adhered to and that the judge step down if those statutes cannot be met.

And on that basis alone we feel also the public interest requires that unless Your Honor can make a determination that statutory standards for bias are not met in this case, that he continue to preside over this case.

Unless Your Honor has questions, I have no further comments at this time.

REBUTTAL ARGUMENT ON BEHALF OF THE DEFENDANT

MR. KORNS. Your Honor, just a couple of very brief points.

Your Honor, the first point I would like to make is that Miss Brady suggests to the Court that one can never draw inferences about partiality problems. One must always find evidence of partiality to require disqualification.

I submit that is clearly wrong. The statute, for instance, sets up a number of kinds of situations where judges are required to disqualify themselves. For instance, if a judge has some relationship to one of the parties, or in the Potashnick case the judge had a business transaction with one of the counsel in the case.

Now, Your Honor, in both of those cases the Court recognizes that the judges are probably not partial at all, that there is no indication that, in fact, those experiences and relationships make them unable to handle the case in an impartial manner, but there is a common perception that those things endanger impartiality and cause doubt about impartiality, and, therefore, a judge proceeding in such a case, even if he knows in his own mind that he personally is free of bias, he has to deal with the fact that people out there who don't know the judge personally, who only know the gross facts that X, Y and Z happened, or that the judge at such and such a place, their reaction is to have doubts about the ability of the Court to be impartial, and I submit that is the case here, Your Honor.

We do not point to, and I am not going to urge here that we are pointing to some specific act and saying, "See, the Court is not impartial."

What we are saying is, we are going to have a long trial in this case. This case is going to go on for a long time. It is a very complicated case, and—

THE COURT. Mr. Korns?

MR. KORNS. Yes, Your Honor.

THE COURT. That is your—I don't know what you mean by "We are going to have a long trial in this case. The case is going to go on for a long time."

You are not warranted in that characterization.

MR. KORNS. Let me restate it, Your Honor. This is a complicated case with a lot of factual questions in it, and the only point I wanted to bring to the Court's attention is that Fiat feels—and I think most people out there would feel that with the same kind of case before a court, which has had such a personal experience, it is just not fair for the litigant to have concerns, good-faith serious concerns, about whether any such person having those experiences can be truly impartial, truly a peer situation in his own mind about those experiences.

Your Honor, I would also point out that the cases on which the Government relies Miss Brady cites as for the proposition that the experiences the Court brings to the Bench do not disqualify the Court; that all of those cases involve very different experiences, mild, every-day, typical experiences.

They do not involve serious personal injuries, every-day problems inflicted by those injuries, and there is no case law. The fact is there is no case that controls this issue.

We have not found any that support us, and we don't think the cases cited by the Government support their position. This is a question for the Court to determine solely under the statutory standards, and, your honor, the last point I would make is that, as we have submitted on our papers, Judge Oberdorfer reached the conclusion that he had discretion under Local Rule 305a, and we submit that is correct, that under the local rule the Court has discretion for a broad variety of reasons, unlimited variety of reasons within the Court's sound discretion to transfer the case to the Calendar Committee, and that Judge Oberdorfer found that an appropriate thing to do knowing the vast number of judges here qualified to handle this case, and we submit that if the Court has any doubts about Fiat having made a sufficient case to require disqualification, that the Court should exercise its very sound discretion to transfer this case to rid this case of any such issues, to make this case free of any doubts of any concerns by litigants about the impact on the case.

Whichever way this case comes out, it should not be tainted by concerns, good-faith concerns about any person's ability to rise above these issues.

Thank you Your Honor.

THE COURT. Very well.

MS. BRADY. Your Honor, may I make two brief comments regarding counsel's argument?

THE COURT. Brief, Miss Brady.

MS. BRADY. Very brief.

REBUTTAL ARGUMENT ON BEHALF OF THE PLAINTIFF

MS. BRADY. With regard to defendant's assertions that there is some independent basis for Your Honor stepping down, such as a discretionary transfer of this case as was done by Judge Oberdorfer in the Flood case, as we pointed out again, and that supports our position, facts are necessary for a transfer or disqualification in a case such as this.

In that case Judge Oberdorfer had termed that as a prior employee of the Justice Department he had had personal involvement with the defendant, the very defendant sitting before him in the criminal case, and as a former employee of the Justice Department he was aware of internal Justice Department documents which could not be made part of the public record in the criminal case then pending before him.

We submit to you that under all of the cases that there were facts showing the relationship in which a judge's impartiality was reasonably questioned, and those such facts are missing here.

Thank you.

MR. KORNS. Your Honor—

THE COURT. Mr. Korns, I have to exercise some discretion and the discretion is that I won't hear any more.

MR. KORNS. Your Honor, as the moving party, may we make just two brief points?

THE COURT. You have had your opportunity for rebuttal. Do you want to make a rebuttal to rebuttal?

MR. KORNS. Well, Your Honor, as far as I am aware, it is usually the moving party that has the—

THE COURT. All right. Come to the lectern.

MR. KORNS. Very, very briefly, Your Honor.

The point about what Judge Oberdorfer did, Your Honor,—

THE COURT. Counsel, I have read Judge Oberdorfer's opinion, and, as a matter of fact, I have talked with him about it. I don't think there is anything you can add in clarification of what he did or why he did it, but I will hear you.

MR. KORNS. Your Honor, I would submit that the public perception of that opinion would be that Judge Oberdorfer knew in his heart that he was not biased and that under the standards he need not disqualify himself, but because he could

not make that clear to the public by releasing documents to prove it, he thought it was a better part of valor to step aside, and we would submit that a similar kind of standard here, Your Honor, suggests that the Court exercise its discretion.

Thank you. I apologize for taking the additional time.

THE COURT. Very well. I am ready to rule in this case.

United States v. Fiat Motors

512 F. Supp. 247
United States District Court,
District of Columbia
April 15, 1981

BARRINGTON D. PARKER, District Judge:

[Background above]

After a full consideration of the parties' memoranda of points and authorities, and the argument of counsel, I conclude that Fiat's motion is frivolous and must be denied. The factual basis for the motion is weak; the legal authority is tenuous. In sum, the motion is devoid of merit.

Fiat's counsel asserts several grounds as the basis for disqualification. First, he claims that it was only recently learned that in 1975 I was involved in an automobile accident from which I sustained permanent, severe, crippling injuries and loss; that it is alleged in the Government's complaint that certain of defendant's vehicles contain safety defects; that in this nonjury case I will rule on a number of factual questions and legal issues all related to motor vehicle safety and risks of accident. Fiat's counsel then arrives at the conclusion that it does not believe that any human being who has suffered such serious injuries and loss by an automobile, as I have, can determine such issues impartially and under the circumstances that it would be unreasonable to compel their company to run the substantial risk of partiality—and expose them to potential liability in staggering amounts. The company states that since my impartiality may reasonably be questioned, it should not be required to run that risk gauntlet and that I should be disqualified.

Secondly, Fiat claims that at a recent January

23, 1981 hearing, I made a comment which clearly indicates that I prejudged an issue in this proceeding—relating to the state of the art at the time that the vehicles involved in this litigation were produced and the corrosion experience of other motor vehicle manufacturers. It is claimed that this, too, demonstrates my bias against Fiat Motors.

In October 1975, as a pedestrian, I was involved in an automobile accident. I sustained injury to my left leg and other minor losses. Later, I underwent surgery and an amputation above the left knee. I returned to duty in the early spring of 1976 and have since continued without incident or interruption.

The defendant's motion has been certified as to good faith by its counsel as required by the statute. The motion is supported by a seven-page affidavit of Gerald Fallon, Fiat's General Counsel and Vice President. Several documents are attached to Mr. Fallon's affidavit: the official police accident report on the 1975 automobile accident; a news article of November 11, 1979, written several years later after I had resumed my judicial responsibilities: and a third attachment, a 1975 release of the National Highway Traffic Safety Administration. Several footnotes to the affidavit refer to the negligence litigation I pursued in the District of Columbia Superior Court, a civil proceeding seeking damages arising from the injuries I sustained in 1975. The 1979 news article is of questionable relevancy.

In advancing the motion, Fiat relies on sections 144 and 455 of Title 28 U.S.C., as well as the Court's inherent authority to exercise discretion and to voluntarily relinquish the assignment. Section 144 requires the trial court to withdraw from a proceeding whenever a party "files a timely and sufficient affidavit that the judge before whom the matter is pending has a personal bias or prejudice either against him or in favor of an adverse party." It is clear that where, as here, such an affidavit is filed, accompanied by a good-faith certificate of counsel, the Court must accept the affiant's statement of facts as true and pass only on their legal sufficiency in demonstrating bias or prejudice. *Berger v. United States*, 255 U.S. 22, 36 (1921) (applying this standard to section 21 of the Judicial Code, the precursor to section 144). It is also well-settled that a section 144 affidavit mandates a judge's disqualification only if the reasons and facts set out for the belief "give fair support to the charge of bent of mind that may prevent or impede impartiality of judgment." Only under those circumstances is recusal or disqualification required. *Berger*, 255 U.S. at 33–34.

I turn now to the Fallon supporting affidavit. It falls far short in satisfying the criteria and standard imposed by § 144. It is factually and legally deficient and otherwise flawed. The relied-upon "facts" are a mere recitation of the events chronicled in the 1975 accident report, the civil complaint later filed on my behalf, excerpts from depositions in that proceeding, and excerpts from the questionable news article. The affidavit does refer to the serious injuries and losses I sustained in the accident.

The most notable flaw in Fallon's affidavit is that it fails to point to any fact bearing on this litigation or any extrajudicial attitude or statement that I have ever made or directed toward Fiat or North America or any of its corporate affiliations. He does not state that my complaint for damages involved any claim of automobile safety and defects. He does not state that a Fiat motor vehicle was involved in my accident or that the civil complaint filed by me as a result of the accident involved any automobile manufacturer or any liability on the part of a manufacturer. The reason for such omissions is, of course, obvious. The several paragraphs of the affidavit which attempt to link my injuries with a "bent of mind" against the defendant are no more than speculative and unsupported assertions. He then advances an unwarranted conclusion that, because I sustained

loss of a limb in an automobile accident, I would be unable to preside in an impartial manner and without bias in litigation involving automobile safety.

The outer limits of a supporting affidavit have been defined by our Court of Appeals; the affidavit must "show a true personal bias, and must allege specific facts and not mere conclusions or generalities." *Brotherhood of Locomotive Firemen and Enginemen v. Bangor and Aroostook Ry. Co.*, 380 F.2d 570, 576 (D.C.Cir. 1967). The Fallon affidavit fails to meet this minimum standard. Moreover, a trial judge is presumed to be impartial and the affiant assumes a heavy burden in demonstrating the contrary.

Indeed, the logical extension and result of Fiat's argument would require my disqualification in a substantial number of other proceedings. If, in fact, my injuries and losses would cause a reasonable person to question my ability to render impartial judgments on questions of automobile safety and defects, would it not also lead a litigant to raise questions about my impartiality in any personal injury litigation involving an automobile? If the defendant's position were accepted, would it be proper for me to preside in any trial involving a serious personal claim, whether it stems from a motor vehicle collision, an aircraft disaster, an industrial explosion or any of an endless list of other types of accidents resulting in serious personal injury?

While Fiat's argument may at first blush seem to have a surface allure, on close examination and careful analysis it soon unravels. The unfortunate incident which I experienced several years ago is, of course, lasting in nature, but is no more lasting than some of the personal and background experiences of other trial judges where disqualification attempts were advanced by a litigant and denied. As Fiat's counsel has pointed out, no case authority directly on point or similar to the situation here, involving disqualification or recusal, has been found. However, several recent cases have presented factual situations in which a litigant has focused on a particular background characteristic of personal experiences of the presiding judge.

In *Parrish v. Board of Commissioners,* 524 F.2d 98 (5th Cir. 1975) (en banc) (Tuttle, Goldberg, dissenting, Wisdom separately dissenting), cert. denied, 425 U.S. 944 (1976), the Fifth Circuit upheld the denial of a recusal motion under sections 144 and 455. The plaintiffs sought to disqualify a district court judge who was a former officer and still maintained membership in the Alabama State Bar Association which once barred blacks. They claimed that he could not rule in a case alleging that the Bar Association discriminated against blacks. The majority held that the affidavit in that case, like the one here, only set out general facts regarding the judge's background and was insufficient and fell short of making the required showing of personal bias. In *Paschall v. Mayone,* 454 F.Supp. 1289, 1299–1301 (S.D.N.Y. 1978), a case involving alleged prison beatings in violation of the plaintiff's civil rights, the defendants moved to disqualify the trial judge because of his frequent representation of prisoners in civil rights cases while an active litigator with the NAACP Legal Defense Fund. The trial judge denied the motion, rejecting the claim that his prior litigation experience gave rise to any appearance of impartiality. Judge Constance Motley, also a NAACP litigator, denied efforts to secure her disqualification in a class action charging sex discrimination under Title VII of the Civil Rights Act of 1964. *Blank v. Sullivan & Cromwell,* 418 F. Supp. 1, 4 (S.D.N.Y. 1975). She rejected defendant's argument under sections 144 and 455 that her strong identification with the victims of discrimination provided any showing that she would be biased in the case against that law firm. Judge Leon Higginbotham, as a trial judge, denied a recusal motion based on similar allegations in *Commonwealth of Pennsylvania v. Local 542 International Union of Operating Engineers,* 388 F.Supp. 155 (E.D.Pa. 1974). There a labor union charged with racial discrimination in the construction industry claimed that he could not decide the case impartially because of his long identification as a spokesperson for racial integration and because of a speech he had recently given before a predominantly black historical group. These facts, Judge Higginbotham concluded, showed only the "ordinary results" of experiences in "this day and generation" and did not in any way demonstrate bias.

The personal background and experience of a trial judge has also been found legally insufficient for disqualification in a variety of other situations. For example, in *United States v. Clark,* 398 F.Supp. 341, 361–63 (E.D.Pa. 1975), aff'd without opinion, 532 F.2d 748 (3rd Cir. 1976), Judge Herbert Fogel, of the Eastern District of Pennsylvania, denied the recusal motion based on his personal friendship with a kidnap victim in a criminal proceeding where the defendant was charged with a bank robbery by taking a hostage. Also, in *State of Idaho v. Freedman,* 478 F.Supp. 33 (D.Idaho 1979), Judge Marion Callister denied the recusal motion in a case challenging the ratification process for the Equal Rights Amendment because of his "prominent position" in the Mormon Church.

Fiat's second argument, not urged or addressed at the April 3rd hearing, will nonetheless be considered. The claim that I had personal knowledge of disputed evidentiary facts is based on my comment at a recent January 23rd status conference—that problems of rust and corrosion by other automobile manufacturers similar to those alleged to have been experienced by Fiat in this case have not been a matter of the public's attention. Fiat argues that this comment shows prejudice and a prejudgment of an issue in the case; that the comment demonstrates that because of my injuries I have taken a peculiar and particular interest in matters involving automobile defects and consequently I have personal knowledge of evidentiary matters in this case.

Fiat has inflated the significance of that statement. It was no more than a comment at a discovery motion hearing as to my knowledge of the state of the record and the pleadings, as then developed by the parties. The suggestion that I made an evaluation of relevant evidence outside the scope of this proceeding and the suggestion that I had made a prejudgment of material, factual or legal issues is misplaced, exaggerated and a gross misunderstanding of the Court's comment. Standing alone, or in context, the statement does not show a fixed opinion or a closed mind on the merits. In any event, the statement was made in open court and on the record. Under the statute "alleged bias and prejudice to be disqualifying must stem from an extrajudicial source and result in an opinion on the merits of some basis other than what the judge learned from his participation in the case." *United States v. Grinnel Corp.,* 384 U.S. 563, 583 (1966).

In conclusion, putting aside all that has been said—the repetitive statements, the comments and concerns set out in Fallon affidavit about my injuries—Fiat fails to identify or to state that I have exhibited any personal bias or prejudice against their company. The affidavit does not contain one unequivocal allegation of bias or prejudice attributed to me, nor can it, for none exists. Nor is the affidavit sufficient to fairly support any such inferences. Further, I know of nothing that would lead a reasonable person to question my interest in this case.

My only concerns with this proceeding are that all the relevant facts be fully revealed; that the law be applied correctly and evenhandedly and that this litigation advance through the discovery and pretrial stages without unnecessary and unwarranted delay. Fiat must, indeed, recognize that auto safety is an issue of general concern in this country, and that, in fact, was recognized by the Congress when it enacted the statute at issue in this case. This proceeding has been assigned to me for trial, and that is the extent of my interest. The attempt to exaggerate any generalized interest in auto safety into a specific bias by citing injuries sustained is simply insufficient on its face.

The present efforts of Fiat rest on a crimped and distorted consideration of the facts and a superficial analysis of the applicable law. The defendant's motion is baseless and it is denied.

Notes and Questions

1. Recall *Berger,* where the dissenting justices said that Judge Landis' bias against Germans as a class did not prove that he was biased against the particular defendants before him. Isn't Judge Parker making the same argument? Judge Parker states that the "most noticeable flaw" in the defense attorney's affidavit is that "it fails to point to any fact bearing on this litigation or any extrajudicial attitude or statement that I have ever made or directed toward Fiat." How do you reconcile *Berger* and *Fiat*? What does it mean to be biased against an individual? Is it *possible* to understand "personal bias" without reference to a disfavored category of which the individual is a member?

2. Is Judge Parker's reasoning persuasive—that although he lost a leg in an automobile accident, he wasn't run over by a Fiat? What would we say of a judge who owns substantial equity in apartment buildings—should she recuse herself from cases where tenants are suing landlords of buildings she does not own?

United States v. Holland

655 F.2d 44
United States Court of Appeals,
Fifth Circuit
Aug. 31, 1981

PER CURIAM:

This is the second appeal to this court of this case. George Holland was indicted on four counts of interstate transportation and concealment of stolen vehicles in violation of 18 U.S.C. §§ 2312, 2313. Holland was first tried before a jury on July 25, 1979 and was found guilty on the two concealment counts and not guilty on the interstate transportation counts. He was sentenced to three years imprisonment on each of the two counts, the sentences to run concurrently. After this conviction Holland employed new counsel to represent him on appeal. The principal issue on that first appeal was the propriety of an unrecorded conversation between the trial judge and the jury in the jury room. After an hour of deliberation the jury had sent a note to the trial judge asking for help in filling out the verdict forms.

When the trial judge told the government and defense attorneys that he was going into the jury room there was no objection from Holland's attorney. On appeal we reversed and remanded for a new trial because we found that Holland had been denied his right to a complete trial transcript.

The case was tried again before the same judge in the fall of 1980. When the jury retired to deliberate, the judge commented on his belief that Holland had "broken faith" with the court at his first trial by consenting to the judge visiting the jury room but then raising the issue on appeal. Following several exchanges between the judge and defense counsel, defense counsel moved for a mistrial. The motion was denied. The judge then stated for the record that he intended to increase Holland's sentence because of the incident which he had described. The following occurred outside the presence of the jury:

> THE COURT. Now Mr. Holland, the last time we tried this case I asked you and your lawyer if you had any problems with the correspondence I had with the jury. I offered to let you and your lawyer go back with me to the jury room and in my judgment you declined to go. You declined to object to what I offered to do. I was simply trying to save time for you, the Government and everybody else. Now, you took advantage of that on your appeal. You implied that you didn't agree to that. Is there anything about this trial that you haven't agreed to that you want to voice now either through yourself or your counsel and you may consult with your counsel and let him express it for you if you would like.
>
> DEFENSE COUNSEL. Your Honor, I frankly don't understand.
>
> THE COURT. You talk to him and see. I don't care if you understand or not.
>
> DEFENSE COUNSEL. Is there anything that you want to tell the Judge about?
>
> THE COURT. You talk to him quietly so he will have a private opportunity.
>
> DEFENSE COUNSEL. Other than the objections I have already made and noted for the Record, Mr. Holland doesn't know what to say, he is not a lawyer.
>
> THE COURT. Well, he knew what to say or not to say last time and he chose not to say anything until the appeal. I think he broke faith with the Court frankly and I want to be sure that if he has anything to say this time that he says it. I don't criticize your efforts but I do feel that he understood very well what was going on last time and he sat there and said nothing and his lawyer passedly [sic] agreed to my proposal and then raised it on - somebody raised it on appeal. I don't know or care who it was, it wasn't the fault of the lawyer. He had a duty to raise whatever he could as far as I was concerned. But when somebody agrees with the Court about something and then refuses to abide by it, I think I have the duty to consider that and to guard against it on the next trial. And that is all I am trying to do. If Mr. Holland has something that is bothering him I want to know about it. If he has something that he thinks I have done wrong about I want to know about it and I want to know now before we finally submit this matter to the jury because I don't want to treat him wrongly but I don't want him wasting thousands of dollars of the Government's money getting a new trial about something that he doesn't point out to the trial Court initially. I want to be sure he has an opportunity to point out any problems he may have.
>
> DEFENSE COUNSEL. Your Honor, Defendant Holland is concerned that the Court, in imposing a sentence in this case if he is found guilty, the Court has already expressed to him that you feel like he broke faith with the Court and that you resent what happened and he tells me that he didn't even know what was going on about this conference with the jury.
>
> THE COURT. It all took place in his presence. He was represented, his lawyer sat there and as far as the Record shows said nothing. I am almost certain that the lawyer, by action at least, in nodding agreed to it because I was talking to all of the lawyers and they all indicated their assent in one way or another. If they didn't they should have accepted [sic] to anything they felt the Court was doing wrong about. And I do feel that he broke faith with the Court but I feel that

he has received a fair trial in this case and the Record stands for that.

DEFENSE COUNSEL. Well, I would move for a mistrial in light of the Court's apparent belief that the Defendant has somehow quote, broken faith with the Court.

THE COURT. All right, you move for a mistrial and that motion is overruled: denied. It there any other problem?

DEFENSE COUNSEL. No, sir, not with that, Your Honor.

THE COURT. All right. Frankly, I have expressed this on the Record for the specific purpose of letting it appear clearly why I intend to increase his sentence unless something appears in the probation file that was not in it before. I have a duty not to increase it unless there is something that justifies an increase in it that I did not have before me on the other occasion. And I do have this matter before me that was not before me when I sentenced him before and I have a duty to consider it in my judgment but I want it on the Record so that it shows clearly my thinking about it. I think it does.

After the jury returned a verdict of guilty, the trial judge again stated his reason for increasing Holland's sentence. The judge made the following comments:

> THE COURT. . . . On the jury verdict of guilty against you on counts two and four, I sentence you to four years on count two and four years on count four with those sentences to run concurrently with each other. Now, you will notice that I have increased the amount of your sentence. I think that I have made plain for the Record why I have. I know, as well as I can know, that you agreed with me and your lawyer agreed with me at the time of your last trial that I might step into the jury room and answer a question which could not damage you in any way and when you agree with me on something, I think that if you dishonor that agreement that I have a duty to consider that in your sentence if that agreement comes about and that dishonor comes about after the matters that I considered in your first sentence. I think you show by what you have done in implying that this Court did not give you

every opportunity to object to what I did in that proceeding, that you are trying to take advantage of somebody else. The fact that it is the Court is material only in that I understand precisely what happened. If it was somebody else I still would have an obligation in my judgment to take it into consideration. That is the reason I have added one year to your total sentence. I have added one year to each of the counts but those are to be served concurrently so it would be a total addition of only one year.

He then announced that the sentence would be increased to four years.

On appeal Holland contends that (1) the trial judge displayed such bias and prejudice as to require a new trial before a different judge and that (2) the trial judge committed error in increasing the defendant's sentence after the second trial. Our holding with respect to the first contention makes consideration of the second contention unnecessary.[32]

The relevant statutory provision governing disqualification of federal judges is 28 U.S.C. § 455. Paragraph (a) of section 455 provides that a judge "shall disqualify himself in any proceeding in which his impartiality might reasonably be questioned." This section imposes a reasonable man standard in determining whether a judge should recuse himself. [Citing cases] Additionally paragraph (b)(1) provides that a judge should disqualify himself "where he has a personal bias or prejudice concerning a party. . . ." The general rule is that bias sufficient to disqualify a judge must stem from an extrajudicial source. [Citing cases] In *Davis v. Board of School Commissioners,* 517 F.2d 1044 (5th Cir. 1975), cert. denied, 425 U.S. 944 (1976), however, we recognized that

> there is an exception where such pervasive bias and prejudice is shown by otherwise judicial conduct as would constitute bias against a party.

Id. at 1051. Accord, *Whitehurst v. Wright,* 592 F.2d 834, 837 (5th Cir. 1979) (noting that "the single fact that the judge's remarks were made in

---

[32] We note, however, that North Carolina v. Pearce, 395 U.S. 711 (1969), requires a judge to base a more severe sentence on objective reasons.

a judicial context does not prevent a finding of bias").

Applying this standard to the trial judge's conduct, we conclude that a reasonable man would be convinced that the trial judge's impartiality might be questioned. The trial judge's remarks also reflect a personal prejudice against Holland for successfully appealing his conviction on the basis of the judge's actions during the prior trial. The fact that these comments were made in a judicial context outside the presence of the jury does not prevent a finding of bias.[33] A "defendant is entitled to a trial before a judge who is not biased against him at any point of the trial...."

United States v. Thompson, 483 F.2d 527, 529 (3d Cir. 1973). Accordingly, the judgment of conviction is reversed and the case remanded for a new trial before a different judge.

REVERSED and REMANDED.

---

[33] We reject the government's argument that there was no bias because the trial judge's comments were made outside the presence of the jury. We also reject a similar argument that the appellant did not demonstrate any prejudicial comments or rulings. Section 455 does not require such a showing.

Notes and Questions

1. After the first trial, when Holland got a new lawyer for the appeal, he won a reversal on the issue of denial of a trial transcript. But his lawyer also argued the matter of the judge going into the jury room. Was Holland "breaking faith" by following the advice of his new lawyer in arguing this latter issue on appeal? Had Holland waived his right?

2. Let's say Holland did "break faith" with the trial judge. Why shouldn't the judge use Holland's behavior during the trial as relevant information for sentencing? Does taking the information into account show bias or prejudice? Does talking about taking it into account show bias or prejudice?

3. The trial judge displayed his "bias" or "prejudice" in the course of the second trial. Should the Court of Appeals give more latitude to trial judges' behavior during trial than outside of trial (cf. *Linahan*)? Did the Court of Appeals?

4. The trial judge raised his displeasure with Holland only after the jury verdict, during sentencing. Does the appeals court cite any evidence of unfairness toward Holland during the trial? If not, could we say that the judge kept his bias or prejudice against Holland in check during trial, and thus his bias or prejudice did not cause Holland any injury? Does the opinion appear to depend, after all, on a finding of bias or prejudice or some other finding based on different premises?

5. Recall that Judge Frank said that a trial judge whose decision is reversed on appeal, and who gets the case back on remand, remains impartial. Judge Frank was stating a widely held belief that if a trial judge is proven to have been wrong on the law, the judge will simply learn what the new law is and apply it fairly to both sides. How realistic is Judge Frank's position? Suppose, after a lengthy civil litigation, the trial judge awards a contract decision to the corporate defendant against the complaining plaintiff. Then the plaintiff manages to get the case reversed and remanded on appeal. Back the plaintiff goes into the same courtroom, against the same corporation, in front of the same judge. Would you say that there is absolutely no basis for the plaintiff to suspect that the trial judge will be angry at the plaintiff for having gotten the case reversed on appeal? Would you say that there is absolutely no basis for the plaintiff to suspect that the same reasons and motivations that animated the judge in the first trial to hold for the corporation will be operative again on remand? Is it fair for the law to lay down what amounts to a conclusive presumption that no trial judge will be biased against a plaintiff on this set of facts (That is, without an actual comment by the judge indicating bias, as in the *Holland* case)?

"60 Minutes"

December 6, 1987

Justice For Sale?

MIKE WALLACE. Is justice for sale in Texas? Some recent headlines might make you wonder. *The Wall Street Journal* has called the decision of one Texas court "a national embarrassment." *The New York Times* editorialized that the conduct of the Texas courts is "reminiscent of what passes for justice in small countries run by colonels in mirrored sunglasses." What triggered this barrage of criticism? The Texaco-Pennzoil dispute and the 10 and a half billion dollar verdict that a Houston jury rendered against Texaco, a verdict permitted to stand last month by the Texas Supreme Court. But the issue at the heart of the controversy is not which of the giant oil companies should have won the case. Instead, it is about the fact that in Texas, where judges are elected to office like politicians, their biggest campaign contributors are the lawyers who practice before the very judges they help elect.

WALLACE [voice-over]. Case in point, Joe Jamail, the legendary Texas trial lawyer who represented Pennzoil and now prides himself on being the man who bankrupted Texaco.

WALLACE [voice-over]. Joe Jamail was not so circumspect when we asked him in Corpus Christi what people should think about his large campaign contributions to Judge Mauzy.

MR. JAMAIL. Well, who else would help? I know him about as well as anybody. I know what his philosophy is. You know, is he going to go to his enemies? Are they going to give him campaign contributions? That's bull[expletive] and naive. You know it and I know it. And—tell me, first off, our laws permit this. And not just in Texas but every elective state that uses the elective system. So I don't know what they think. They would think he would be a fool if he didn't ask. And incidentally, he never had to ask.

WALLACE. And how much did Jamail give?

MR. JAMAIL. I don't remember what it was.

JUDGE MAUZY. Twenty-five.

MR. JAMAIL. I think it was $25,000. It may have been mo—I think it's 25,000. But you see, that's not unusual for me. I think that's the same contribution I've given to all of the Supreme Court justices, Gonzales everybody.

WALLACE [voice-over]. Actually, Jamail gave Judge Mauzy some $45,000 and was one of a group of lawyers who guaranteed a $225,000 loan to the judge.

MR. JAMAIL. To run for statewide office now, as you know, with television and what have you requires a good deal of money. Most of that money, I'd say 95% of it, comes from lawyers. Because who else—the citizen isn't going to—he doesn't particularly give a damn.

JUDGE JACK POPE. I think the giving and the acceptance of these unseemly sums of money is wrong.

WALLACE [voice-over]. Judge Jack Pope retired as chief justice of the Texas Supreme Court three years ago.

[interviewing] One would think, that common sense indicates, the justices, the judges are going to look kindly on those lawyers who have given them the biggest contributions.

JUDGE POPE. Mr. Wallace, I'm not defending the system. I'm just reporting to you what the facts are. Pigs is pigs.

WALLACE. Does the Texas Supreme Court have a credibility problem in the Pennzoil-Texaco case because of the massive contributions given by lawyers on both sides?

JUDGE POPE. Well, I suppose anybody can answer that question, and I—

WALLACE. Sounds like you're saying, you're damn right.

JUDGE POPE. Well I am—I am saying that if I were walking into the courthouse to try a lawsuit before a judge that I knew had been heavily financed in a successful campaign, I would be worried about the case.

WALLACE. Case in point, during the Texaco-Pennzoil case, Joe Jamail representing Pennzoil, gave a $10,000 campaign contribution to the original trial judge. Anthony Farris. Jamail's contribution to the now-deceased Judge Farris was given just four weeks after Judge Farris had been assigned the case. Judge Farris himself, in this letter, called the $10,000 contribution "a princely sum." And he sought Joe Jamail's help to raise more money. As the case proceeded, Jamail did just that, soliciting his lawyer friends to pony up at least a thousand dollars apiece to Farris' campaign. Texaco, citing the size, nature and the timing of these contributions, attempted to disqualify the judge. But Judge Farris successfully argued, to Texaco's astonishment, that, "mere bias or prejudice" is not grounds in Texas for a judge to disqualify himself.

[voice-over] When the jury returned its unanimous verdict, Pennzoil and Jamail emerged victorious, the winner of the largest jury verdict in history. Texaco promptly appealed. And when the appeals court turned them down, they moved to the court of last resort in Texas, the Texas Supreme Court.

TV ANNOUNCER. Ted Robertson, a judge to be proud of.

WALLACE [voice-over]. The case before the court involved Judge Robertson's main campaign contributor, Texas oil millionaire Clinton Manges, who has given the judge over $120,000 in contributions at a time when Manges had a major case before the court. Initially, Robertson said he would not vote on the case, but he changed his mind when the then-Chief Justice announced that, for want of one vote, Mr. Manges was about to lose.

JUDGE POPE. When that happened, he then reconsidered, and he did vote five to four.

WALLACE. How long did it take him to reconsider, Judge Pope?

JUDGE POPE. About as long as you and I have been asking the question.

WALLACE. In other words, Robertson changed his mind.

MR. ARMSTRONG. In a heartbeat, he did. And after that, there was this sort of quiet that settled over the room while everybody tried to figure out exactly what had happened.

WALLACE. And they realized what had happened, that this man, in effect, seemed at least to be voting his pocketbook instead of his conviction.

MR. ARMSTRONG. I think if you'd taken a poll of the people in that room that day, that's exactly what you would have found out. I don't think somebody's conscience changes that quickly.

WALLACE [voice-over]. A year later, when the case came under review and his vote was no longer the decisive one, Robertson voted with seven other justices against Manges. Because he declined to talk to us, we were unable to ask him why, when the court's decision had hung on his one vote, he had sided with the man who had contributed $120,000 to his campaign.

WALLACE. Judge Mauzy, let's say that Joe Jamail or almost anybody has given you a big campaign contribution, and he comes before you, let's say he's given you $50,000, and he comes before you with a case, do you feel no obligation to recuse yourself, to take yourself off that case?

JUDGE MAUZY. No, I wouldn't feel any obligation to.

WALLACE. Because?

JUDGE MAUZY. Because that contribution I look on just like it was given to me. Anyone who's ever contributed to me knows this. That money is accepted to help me get elected to office. It is not accepted for the purpose of influencing me on anything that I'm going to say.

JUDGE MAUZY. Well, you'll have to ask him what he gave it for.

WALLACE [voice-over]. Texaco's lawyers have indeed made sizable contributions since losing the jury trial. But to date, as best we can tell from the records, Jamail and Pennzoil have out-contributed Texaco by almost a three-to-one margin. Again, the sitting Chief Justice of the Texas Supreme Court, John Hill.

[interviewing] Three-quarters of a million dollars has been given—from both sides, both Texaco and Pennzoil, to various judges. Does this not corrupt the process? Does it not stand a chance of corrupting the process?

JUDGE HILL. I think again that it's perceived by people. They look and see the amounts of money that's been given by litigants, be it these two litigants or others. They focus on that. They wonder why. They get confused. They read stories. It breaks down confidence.

SEN. TEJEDA. There may be so much taint, deservedly or undeservedly, because of the large amounts of contributions that have been given by both sides, but particularly by Pennzoil attorneys, that I think no matter what happens in that case, the perception, the appearance will always be there that it was bought by one side or the other.

WALLACE. On November 2, the Texas Supreme Court turned down Texaco's appeal. Texaco is now preparing a final appeal to the United States Supreme Court in Washington.

Notes and Questions

1. The Pennzoil-Texaco lawsuit resulted in the largest damages award by any jury, over 10 billion dollars. Texaco had to seek bankruptcy court protection pending appeals. A few weeks after the "60 Minutes" program, a settlement was reached in which Texaco agreed to pay Pennzoil 3 billion dollars. Texaco had asked the United States Supreme Court for a writ of certiorari, but there was considerable doubt whether the Court would grant the writ. Given this doubt, Texaco agreed to the settlement.

The dispute concerned the competition between Texaco and Pennzoil to purchase the assets of Getty Oil. Let us oversimplify the figures involved to give an idea of the basic issues. Assume the following figures:

$10 billion = asset value of Getty Oil
$ 9 billion = amount Texaco offered to buy Getty Oil
$ 8 billion = amount Pennzoil bid to buy Getty Oil

Also assume that Pennzoil had a signed deal to buy Getty Oil at Pennzoil's price of $8 billion, and that Texaco wrongfully interfered with this deal and purchased Getty Oil for itself for $9 billion. Texaco answered that Getty and Pennzoil had only reached an "agreement in principle," and not an actual contract. The question whether Texaco wrongfully interfered with an actual deal, or whether Texaco properly competed for an asset that had not yet gone to contract, was, as you might imagine, intensely litigated. However, as you will see, it was not the most financially important issue in the case. In awarding decision to Pennzoil, the jury found that Texaco had wrongfully interfered. Let us take that assumption as given.

The financially significant issue is the amount of damages due Pennzoil. One might think that ordinary calculation would produce the following amount of damages:

$10 billion (asset value)
- 8 billion (Getty's offering price)

$ 2 billion (Pennzoil's bargained-for actual damages)

What the Texas jury instead did was to award Pennzoil the full amount of Getty's asset value: $10 billion dollars. Did the jury think that Texaco deprived Pennzoil of the opportunity of getting Getty *for free*? They must have believed that Texaco's wrongdoing cost Pennzoil the chance to acquire for free an asset worth $10 billion dollars, instead of what Pennzoil bargained for—a $10 billion dollar asset in exchange for $8 billion.

Is there any way that what the jury did could make sense? It happened largely because of an enormous strategic mistake that the highly-paid Texaco lawyers committed during the trial: they failed to dispute the obviously erroneous calculation of damages that attorney Jamail presented to the jury on Pennzoil's behalf, because they were afraid that if they got into a dispute about damages, the jury might be confused into thinking that Texaco had in fact conceded the primary question of Texaco's liability for interference in Pennzoil's deal.

Texaco thought that the trial judge, after the jury's verdict had come in, would revise this obvious error on damages. But the trial judge explicitly refused to do so. Texaco appealed the case to the Texas Supreme Court. Not only didn't the Texas Supreme Court reverse the case or even simply revise the gigantic error as to the computation of damages, but the Court dismissed the appeal with practically no comment. The $10 billion judgment against Texaco was allowed to stand, and plunged that company into bankruptcy.

Texaco was left with the real problem of whether relief was possible from the U.S. Supreme Court. Their attorneys figured that if the Supreme Court heard the case, the Justices would surely reverse the jury's error on damages if not reverse the entire case (because Texaco had a strong defense on the merits). But the question was whether the Supreme Court would hear the case at all. Texaco had no statutory right of appeal to the Supreme Court; it could only hope that four Justices out of the nine on the Court would accept Texaco's petition for certiorari. The Supreme Court has adopted a wholly discretionary approach to certiorari questions. There is no way to tell in advance whether the Court will accept or turn down a certiorari request.

Under pressure from its stockholders Texaco decided to pay Pennzoil $3 billion rather than risk a denial of certiorari. If certiorari were granted, Texaco felt that the verdict could be substantially reduced, if not wiped out. Between a potential victory of $0 in the U.S. Supreme Court and a potential loss of $10 billion (plus interest), Texaco agreed to pay $3 billion. The uncertainty engendered by the Supreme Court's discretionary approach to reviewing cases on certiorari cost Texaco $3 billion.

Does it matter that the income alone from $3 billion could have financed all the election campaigns for all Texas judges in all Texas courts for decades to come?

2. The Wall Street Journal reported that Baker & Botts, the Houston firm which represented Pennzoil, paid Solomon Casseb Jr. $25,000 eight months before he was named to hear Pennzoil's suit against Texaco. He replaced the original trial judge, who had become ill. "At the time, Mr. Casseb was a retired judge and practicing lawyer, and had no connection with the Texaco-Pennzoil case. He was reimbursed for helping Baker & Botts in unrelated litigation over an oil and gas field near Laredo, Texas, the law firm said."[34] Judge Casseb was the first judge to rule on the damage issue.

3. After the 1988 Olympic games in Seoul, Korea, the New York Times reported that at least half of the 9,000 athletes who competed there used anabolic steroids in training to enhance their performance:[35]

> Although Ben Johnson of Canada, the world's fastest sprinter, and nine others were expelled from the Summer Games for using substances banned by the International Olympic Committee, as many as 20 other athletes tested positive and were not disqualified, said Dr. Park Jong Sei, the director of the Olympic drug-testing lab in Seoul. Estimates of how many Olympic athletes used steroids in training range from 10 percent to 99.9 percent. Most

---

[34] WALL STREET JOURNAL, April 30, 1990.

[35] *System Accused of Failing Test Posed by Drugs,* by Michael Janofsky with Peter Alfano, THE NEW YORK TIMES, November 17, 1988, at p. 1, col. 1.

experts interviewed, including Dr. Robert Voy, the chief medical officer of the United States Olympic Committee, agreed the figure is above 50 percent. An athlete like Johnson, they say, was caught because of his failure to stop using drugs before they were eliminated from his body.

Dr. Voy suggested that some athletic federations may prolong the appeal process so that athletes can compete, and even win medals and set records, before their appeals conclude. Other cases, like the unannounced positives in Seoul, are disposed of in the athletes' favor before appeal is necessary.

"A lot of appeals are based on technicalities," Dr. Voy said in an interview early this month at his home in Colorado Springs. "Usually, the athlete is guilty as sin. Positive urine is still positive urine."

These kinds of discrepancies add to a perception of impropriety, as does the fact that individual sports test their own athletes. In essence, the same people who sell the television rights and the tickets and who, in some cases, pay appearance fees to the athletes, are also serving as judge and jury in cases involving test results.

"You can't have a sport test itself and be trustworthy," Dr. Voy said. "It's like the fox guarding the henhouse. You can't depend on it."

4. Refer back to Section 455, quoted earlier. Do any of the practices in Texas as recounted by the "60 Minutes" interviews appear to violate Section 455?

United States v. Murphy
768 F.2d 1518

United States Court of Appeals,
Seventh Circuit
July 19, 1985
Rehearing and Rehearing En Banc
Denied Sept. 27, 1985

Anna R. Lavin, Edward V. Hanrahan, Chicago, Ill., for defendant-appellant.

Daniel C. Murray, Asst. U.S. Atty., Chicago, Ill., for plaintiff-appellee.

Before CUDAHY and EASTERBROOK, Circuit Judges, and SWYGERT, Senior Circuit Judge.

EASTERBROOK, Circuit Judge.

John M. Murphy was an Associate Judge of the Circuit court of Cook County from 1972 until 1984. He was indicted in 1983 and charged with accepting bribes to fix the outcome of hundreds of cases, from drunk driving to battery to felony theft. Some of the counts on which he was convicted grew out of contrived cases staged by the FBI and federal prosecutors as part of Operation Greylord, an investigation of the Cook County courts.

The charges spanned many years and many statutes. Part I of this opinion sets out the background. [The middle parts, not reproduced here, address Murphy's challenge to Operation Greylord, Murphy's arguments under particular statutes, and the conduct of the trial.] [P]art V [looks] at the decision of the district judge not to recuse himself.

I

The evidence at trial, which we now view in the light most favorable to the prosecution, showed several categories of cases in which Murphy took bribes. We separate the evidence into several groups: traffic court, "hustling," fixed felony offenses, and the cases that were contrived as part of the investigation. We omit a great deal of the evidence and describe only enough to give the general picture. Some of the events we recount are pertinent to other Greylord cases still in litigation. Our statement of the evidence and the inferences the jury could draw about Murphy's conduct is not meant to prejudge those cases.

Traffic court. The Cook County courts are organized into divisions, and supervisory judges assign other judges to particular divisions or courtrooms. From 1972 to early 1981 Murphy was assigned to traffic court, which has courtrooms for major offenses (driving while intoxicated, leaving the scene of an accident, and so on) and minor offenses (such as running a red light). Judge Richard LeFevour was the Supervising Judge of traffic court; he had the authority to decide whether Murphy and other judges would hear major or minor cases.

Officer James LeFevour of the Chicago police, Richard LeFevour's cousin, was assigned to traffic court from 1969 through 1980. James LeFevour testified for the prosecution as part of an agreement under which the Government limited its charges against him to three tax offenses. He testified that beginning in 1975 he met regularly with Melvin Cantor, who would give him a list of his cases that day. James LeFevour would take the list to Judge Richard LeFevour; Judge LeFevour would assign Murphy to hear some of Cantor's cases. James LeFevour would present Murphy the list of Cantor's cases. Murphy then would find the defendants not guilty or sentence them to "supervision," an outcome defendants favored. Later in each day Cantor would give James LeFevour money to pass to Judge LeFevour and some for James to keep for a "tip."

Although Richard LeFevour kept the bribes for these cases, he put Murphy in a position to "earn" his own bribes. Richard LeFevour would assign to major cases, on a regular basis, only those judges who would "see" James LeFevour. Lawyers then would bribe some of the judges assigned to the major courtrooms. Murphy was in a major courtroom more often than most other judges.

Lawyers known as "miracle workers" occasionally met with James LeFevour and with Joseph Trunzo, another police officer assigned to traffic court. The lawyers would tell Officer LeFevour or Officer Trunzo which defendants they represented; the officers would pass the information to Murphy; after the defendant had prevailed, the lawyer would hand an envelope to the officer with $100 per case for Murphy and another $10 or so for the officer; the officer would pass the envelope to Murphy. Prosecutors testified that although they won as many as 90% of their major traffic cases against public defenders, they almost never won a case in which the defendant was represented by one of the "miracle workers."

The testimony at the trial of this case concerned unidentified cases in traffic court. But some plays stood out, even though the players were anonymous. A prosecutor recalled one drunk driving case in which the defendant was represented by Harry Kleper, a miracle worker. The arresting police officer testified that the defendant failed the usual roadside tests of drunkenness and admitted drinking beer before driving. The defendant took the stand and did not deny imbibing; she said only that the liquor did not affect her ability to drive. Under cross-examination she admitted "feeling" the beer; the prosecutor then asked: "And don't you think it is fair to say that you were under the influence of intoxicating liquor?", to which she replied, "Yes, I guess that is a fair thing to say." Judge Murphy threw up his hands and called a recess, turning to Kleper with the remark: "Counselor, I suggest you talk to your client." As Murphy left the bench, the prosecutor heard Murphy yell down the hall to the judges' chambers: "You won't believe this. The State's Attorney just got the defendant to admit she was drunk." A few minutes later Murphy reconvened the court. Kleper asked the defendant whether she was drunk; she said no. In closing argument the prosecutor stressed the defendant's admission. Kleper did not give a closing argument. Murphy ruled: "I still have a reasonable doubt. Not guilty."

Hustlers. In 1981 Judge LeFevour became Presiding Judge for Cook County's First Municipal District court, which has a general jurisdiction. Many of the branch courts had been frequented by "hustlers." "Hustlers" are lawyers who stand outside the courtroom and solicit business from the people about to enter. Ethical rules long have prohibited such solicitations, and every appearance form in Circuit Court contains a representation that solicitation did not occur. Hustling is a profitable business nonetheless, and people find ways to pursue the profits of illegitimate enterprise with the same vigor they devote to lawful activities.

The profit in hustling comes from the bail system in Illinois. A defendant required to post bail may do so by depositing 10% of the bail in cash. If the defendant is discharged, the case deposit (less the clerk's handling fee) is returned. This payment, called the cash bond refund (CBR), also may be assigned to the defendant's lawyer as compensation for legal services. Assignment requires the approval of the court. Hustlers make their money by persuading defendants to hire them and assign the CBR, then persuading the judge to release the CBR to them.

Judge Thaddeus L. Kowalski, who presided over the court known as Branch 29 from June 1980 to March 1981, believed that hustlers cheated their clients at the same time as they violated ethical rules. Often the hustlers appeared as counsel only when the case was bound to be dismissed anyway, as they well knew. Their "representation" of the defendants simply diverted the CBRs from the defendants to the lawyers. Judge Kowalski addressed hustling in the most effective way—by eliminating its profitability. He refused to permit the hustlers to collect the CBRs. They soon deserted Branch 29. When Richard LeFevour became the presiding judge of the first district, Judge Kowalski explained to Judge LeFevour how he had cut down on hustling. Judge LeFevour praised Judge Kowalski and promptly transferred him from Branch 29 to the East Chicago Avenue Police Court, which handles criminal cases originating in the Cabrini Green housing project. Judge LeFevour replaced Kowalski with Murphy.

Hustlers flourished under Murphy, who routinely permitted them to collect the CBRs. The hustlers showed appropriate gratitude. Every month the lawyers, collectively known as the Hustlers Club, paid James LeFevour $2500. James kept $500 and gave the rest to Richard. (The sums were reduced for some months when the hustlers' take fell. Murphy was incapacitated by a broken ankle, and his replacement was apparently less compliant.) After a hustler made a certain amount, he paid an additional sum to the judge of the particular court. James LeFevour told Murphy of the Hustlers Club and Richard LeFevour's approval. Murphy told James LeFevour that he approved too.

Although Richard LeFevour kept the principal bribe, there were still rewards for Murphy. As at traffic court, Murphy was free to establish his own stable of bribe-givers. The Chicago Bar Association (CBA) maintains a Lawyer Referral Service. This service screens lawyers and assigns them to branch courtrooms to be of service to unrepresented defendants. These lawyers are potential competitors of the hustlers, and Murphy apparently cultivated them as independent sources of revenue.

Arthur Cirignani participated in the CBA's program. (The evidence at the trial casts no shadows on the integrity of the CBA itself.) From June 1980 through the end of 1983 he was assigned to a courtroom three to four times a month. Whenever he was assigned to Branch 29, he paid Judge Murphy to assign cases to him rather than to continue the proceedings and allow the hustlers to claim the CBRs.

Fixed cases. Murphy threw business to lawyers; he also threw cases. Arthur Cirignani, who testified under an arrangement that he would not be prosecuted if he told the truth, described one such case. Cirignani represented Arthur Best, charged with felony theft. The police had seized evidence from the grounds of Best's house under authority of a warrant, and Cirignani moved to suppress the evidence. On the day of the suppression hearing Cirignani visited Murphy's chambers before court began and while they were alone told Murphy that he had a "good" motion to suppress. Murphy promised to "take a look at it." Judge Murphy later granted the motion to suppress, giving no reasons. The prosecutor then dismissed the case against Best. Before leaving the courthouse Cirignani gave Murphy an envelope containing $300. Cirignani received a CBR of $1800 in the case, and the client also paid $700 directly.

Greylord cases. Most of the evidence about fixed cases was presented by witnesses who had concocted the cases for the purpose of the Greylord investigation. Terrence Hake, an agent of the FBI posing as a corrupt lawyer, would represent the defendants in ghost-written cases. Agents would file complaints and testify about made-up events.

In one case two agents of the FBI, posing as "Norman Johnson" and "John Stavros," claimed to have had a violent encounter in which Johnson injured Stavros. Hake represented Johnson, the "defendant." Wearing a tape recorder, Hake privately visited Judge Murphy's chambers on the morning the case was set for hearing. He introduced himself as Johnson's lawyer and said he wanted a verdict of not guilty. Murphy replied: "I'll throw the fucker out the window." Hake mentioned dealings with Joseph Trunzo and suggested that Trunzo would make arrangements; Murphy said: "That's okay, everything's alright." Murphy found Johnson not guilty. But things were not well. After the trial Hake gave $300 to Officer Joseph Trunzo ($200 for Murphy, $100 for Joseph and his twin brother Jim). They did not deliver the $200 to Murphy; they apparently planned to fleece Hake (a novice at corruption) by keeping the money, leaving Hake to face an angry judge. Murphy told Hake the following week that he had not seen either Trunzo. A few days later Murphy visited traffic court, still the assignment of both Trunzos, looking for them. Joseph Trunzo then gave Murphy the $200 he had received from Hake, explaining to Murphy that "I got busy and forgot to call you." (In the other trials Joseph Trunzo kept Hake's money and Murphy did not get paid, but so far as the record shows Murphy did not know the money in these cases had been meant for him.)

Hake represented the "defendants" in several other cases fabricated by the FBI. The payoffs went more smoothly. On each occasion the "defendant" was discharged, and Hake paid Officer James LeFevour, apparently a more honest criminal than the brothers Trunzo. James LeFevour passed most of the money to Richard LeFevour and told Murphy that Judge LeFevour wanted verdicts of not guilty. Hake had some additional recorded ex parte conversations with Murphy. In one Hake conceded that his client was guilty but said he needed a verdict of not guilty; Murphy said "it'll be discharged that's all" and later acquitted the "defendant."

The outcome. The jury convicted Murphy on 24 of the 27 counts in the indictment. The counts involved four legal theories. Some counts charged violations of the mail fraud statute, 18 U.S.C. § 1341. The checks constituting the CBRs were mailed to the attorneys, and each mail fraud count was based on the mailing of one CBR. The "fraud" was one committed by Murphy on the people of Cook County, who lost his honest services. Some counts were based on the Hobbs Act, 18 U.S.C. § 1951(a), which prohibits extortion affecting interstate commerce. The extortion lay in the solicitation and receipt of the bribes. Some counts were based on the theory that Murphy aided and abetted others who violated the Hobbs

Act. The remaining count was based on the Racketeer Influenced and Corrupt Organizations Act (RICO), 18 U.S.C. § 1962(d), which prohibits the operation of an "enterprise" in interstate commerce through a "pattern" (two or more events) of "racketeering" (the violation of specified state or federal laws). The "enterprise" here was the Cook County Circuit Court.

The district court imposed 24 concurrent sentences. The longest, ten years, are based on the RICO and Hobbs Act counts. The court did not impose a fine or a forfeiture.

[In sections of the opinion not reproduced here, the court of appeals found without merit Murphy's legal objections to the statutes under which he was convicted. Further, the court found that the trial judge did not commit reversible error in his supervision of the trial.]

V

This leaves for consideration the most difficult and troubling question: whether the district judge was required to recuse himself.

The principal lawyer for the United States at trial was Dan K. Webb, then the U.S. Attorney. Webb and Judge Kocoras are the best of friends. They met when both were Assistant United States Attorneys in Chicago between 1971 and 1975. Judge Kocoras stated that "our professional relationship developed into a social friendship as well." Immediately after Judge Kocoras sentenced Murphy on August 8, 1984, Judge Kocoras, Dan Webb, and the Kocoras and Webb families repaired to the Calloway Gardens Resort, Pine Mountain, Georgia. They resided there in adjoining cottages. The trip had been planned before the trial, and Judge Kocoras advanced the date of sentencing so that he could wrap up the Murphy case before going on vacation with the Webb family. This was not an isolated event. The Webbs and Kocorases had vacationed together at Calloway Gardens in 1982.

Counsel for Murphy learned of the 1984 vacation for the first time after Judge Kocoras had sentenced Murphy. In February 1985 counsel filed a motion seeking Judge Kocoras's recusal under 28 U.S.C. § 455(a), which provides that a judge "shall disqualify himself in any proceeding in which his impartiality might reasonably be questioned." Judge Kocoras denied the motion.

Neither the close friendship between Kocoras and Webb nor either of the vacations was disclosed on the record. Yet the statute places on the judge a personal duty to disclose on the record any circumstances that may give rise to a reasonable question about his impartiality. Although a judge may accept a waiver of disqualification under § 455(a), the "waiver may be accepted [only if] it is preceded by a full disclosure on the record of the basis of the disqualification." 28 U.S.C. § 455(e).

Murphy contends that the vacation plans give rise to a reasonable question about any judge's ability to remain impartial. No one doubts that Judge Kocoras was in fact impartial; his reputation for integrity and impartiality is outstanding. Yet the statutory test is not actual impartiality but the existence of a reasonable question about impartiality. When a question arises about friendship between a judge and a lawyer, "[t]he two fold test is whether the judge feels capable of disregarding the relationship and whether others can reasonably be expected to believe that the relationship is disregarded." Advisory Opinion No. 11, Interim Advisory Committee on Judicial Activities (1970).

The statutory standard puts to the judge a question about the objective state of the legal and lay culture. The court must consider whether an astute observer in either culture would conclude that the relation between judge and lawyer (a) is very much out of the ordinary course, and (b) presents a potential for actual impropriety if the worst implications are realized. The inquiry is entirely objective, see *Pepsico, Inc.* v. *McMillen*, 764 F.2d 458, 460–461 (7th Cir. 1985), and is divorced from questions about actual impropriety.

The existence of a "reasonable question" varies from time to time as ordinary conduct of lawyers and judges changes. When John Marshall was the Chief Justice, the Justices and many of the lawyers who practiced in the Supreme Court lived in the same boarding house and took their meals together. Washington, D.C., was still a small town and neither justices nor counsel lived there year-round. See G. Edward White, *The Working Life of the Marshall Court, 1815–1835*, 70 Va.L. Rev. 1 (1984). It is accepted today for a judge in the United Kingdom to hear a case in which his sibling or child is an advocate. The ordinary standards of conduct of the legal profession reflect judgments about the likelihood of actual impropriety in a particular case. Unless the conduct is substantially out of the ordinary, it is

unnecessary to pursue the further question whether the conduct presents the appearance of impropriety—although it is always possible to inquire into actual impropriety no matter how common the conduct may be.

In today's legal culture friendships among judges and lawyers are common. They are more than common; they are desirable. A judge need not cut himself off from the rest of the legal community. Social as well as official communications among judges and lawyers may improve the quality of legal decisions. Social interactions also make service on the bench, quite isolated as a rule, more tolerable to judges. Many well-qualified people would hesitate to become judges if they knew that wearing the robe meant either discharging one's friends or risking disqualification in substantial numbers of cases. Many courts therefore have held that a judge need not disqualify himself just because a friend—even a close friend—appears as a lawyer. [Citing cases]

These cases also suggest, however, that when the association exceeds "what might reasonably be expected" in light of the associational activities of an ordinary judge, the unusual aspects of a social relation may give rise to a reasonable question about the judge's impartiality. The relation between Judge Kocoras and U.S. Attorney Webb was unusual. These close friends had made arrangements before the trial began to go off to a vacation hideaway immediately after sentencing.

Most people would be greatly surprised to learn that the judge and the prosecutor in a trial of political corruption had secret plans to take a joint vacation immediately after trial. An objective observer "might wonder whether the judge could decide the case with the requisite aloofness and disinterest." The test for an appearance of partiality in this circuit is "whether an objective, disinterested observer fully informed of the facts underlying the grounds on which recusal was sought would entertain a significant doubt that justice would be done in the case." That hypothetical observer would be troubled by what happened in this case.

This is not an occasion on which to lay down rules for the permissible extent of social ties between judge and counsel. Social relations take so many forms that it would be imprudent to gauge all by a single test. We decide only the case before us. But with appreciation for both the difficulty of deciding how much is too much, and deference to the contrary judgment of a careful and upright judge, we conclude that an objective observer reasonably would doubt the ability of a judge to act with utter disinterest and aloofness when he was such a close friend of the prosecutor that the families of both were just about to take a joint vacation. A social relation of this sort implies extensive personal contacts between judge and prosecutor, perhaps a special willingness of the judge to accept and rely on the prosecutor's representations. The U.S. Attorney lays his own prestige, and that of his office, on the line in a special way when he elects to try a case himself. By acting as trial counsel he indicates the importance of the case and of a conviction, along with his belief in the strength of the Government's case. It is a particular blow for the U.S. Attorney personally to try a highly visible case such as this and lose. A judge could be concerned about handing his friend a galling defeat on the eve of a joint vacation. A defendant especially might perceive partiality on learning of such close ties between prosecutor and judge.

Yet this conclusion does not lead to a decision in Murphy's favor. Although perhaps 999 of 1000 observers would have been stunned to discover that judge and prosecutor were about to go on a joint vacation, the remaining one of the thousand was on Murphy's defense team. Matthias Lydon, the principal trial lawyer for Murphy, had been in the U.S. Attorney's office at the same time as Dan Webb and Judge Kocoras. Lydon and Webb later were partners in private practice. All three were friends and remained so. Judge Kocoras stated that "my professional relationship with [Lydon] developed into a social friendship as well, and no less than that with Mr. Webb. Those friendships developed [at the U.S. Attorney's office] and continue to the present day." The vacation at Calloway Gardens Resort in 1982 had included Lydon and his family as well as the Webb and Kocoras families. Although Lydon has filed an affidavit stating that he did not know of the plans for the 1984 vacation, he admitted that he knew of the close relation between Webb and Kocoras and did not deny the probability of future vacations at what is apparently the favorite resort of former members of the U.S. Attorney's office in Chicago. Murphy himself filed an affidavit conceding that he knew that Lydon, Webb, and Judge Kocoras are close friends, although Murphy denied knowledge of both vacations.

Lydon's friendship with Judge Kocoras removes some of the sting from the revelation about the vacation plans of the judge and the prosecutor. The defense camp's knowledge did not abrogate any obligation to spread the information on the record and seek Murphy's consent to his participation in the case, however. Section 455(e) requires waiver on the record, not waiver by implication. This court said in *SCA Services, Inc.* v. *Morgan*, 557 F.2d 110, 117–18 (7th Cir. 1977), that there is no time limit on a motion for recusal. The principal disqualification statute in effect before § 455 was amended in 1974 had contained a time limit for motions, and the Department of Justice asked Congress to put such a limit in the new § 455 as well. Congress did not, and the court concluded in *Morgan* that this implies the absence of a time limit.

Our decision stands alone, however. The Fifth Circuit has called the discussion in *Morgan* dicta and rejected the conclusion on the merits, reasoning that Congress did not put a time limit in § 455 because time limits were already so firmly fixed in both statute and common law that there was no need to add another. [Citing cases]

We need not decide whether to reconsider *Morgan* in light of [later cases]. It would be difficult to find a "waiver" on this record because neither Murphy nor Lydon knew before sentencing of the vacation plans, the only source of the appearance of impropriety. We believe, however, that the absence of a waiver is not dispositive. The question here is not really whether Judge Kocoras was required to recuse himself when Murphy filed his motion. Judge Kocoras already had imposed sentence; there were no further proceedings from which Judge Kocoras could be recused. What Murphy wants is not recusal from future proceedings but the nullification of everything that went before. We concluded that this is not the appropriate consequence of a recusal for appearance of impropriety.

In cases decided under § 455(a), disqualification runs from the time the motion was made or granted. In *Pepsico*, our most recent case under § 455(a), the court ordered the district judge to stand aside from the time a party filed the motion for recusal; we did not vacate all of the judge's earlier orders and require the new judge to start afresh. Our research has not turned up any case involving mere appearance of impropriety in which the court set aside decisions that had been taken by the district judge before any party asked for recusal.[36]

The statute requiring recusal when the judge's impartiality might reasonably be questioned vindicates interests of the judicial system as a whole. It is important to the administration of justice that judges both be and appear to be impartial. When a question about impartiality reasonably arises, the judge must stand aside in order to preserve public confidence in the courts. But this does not imply that a judge who is a close friend of counsel will provide an unjust disposition; if it implied that, the question would be one of actual impropriety rather than the "appearance" of impropriety. No one thinks that Chief Justice Marshall acted with actual impropriety when he heard arguments from lawyers with whom he shared a boarding house. The rule of § 455(a) is designed to put an extra measure of safety into the system. When that extra measure fails, the result is regrettable, and the judicial system as a whole suffers, but this does not mean that the parties actually received an unjust trial.

The waiver provision of § 455(e), which applies to the "appearance" of impropriety issues under § 455(a) but not to any actual conflict of interest under § 455(b), reinforces our conclusion that § 455(a) is concerned with perceptions rather than actual defects in the administration of justice. Under § 455(a) and (e) a party may stand on his right to a judge about whom no reasonable question may be asked; yet the possibility of waiver implies that the judge can provide a fair trial even if such questions may be asked. Section 455(e) gives a party an absolute right to remove a judge (by declining to waive), but it necessarily implies that conduct after a waiver (and therefore before one, too) does not automatically deprive the party of substantial personal rights. The many

cases in other circuits holding that "appearance" questions are waived if not timely asserted—so the judge may continue to sit even after the motion—also show that appearance of impropriety does not undercut personal rights. And unless an error affects substantial rights, it is not a basis of reversal. 28 U.S.C. § 2111; Fed.R.Crim.P. 52(a).

It is important in criminal cases especially to induce defendants to present their claims in a timely fashion. A battery of rules—from contemporaneous objection rules to forfeiture rules such as Fed.R.Crim.P. 12(f)—requires defendants to present claims while there is still time to eliminate the problem and avoid a needless trial. If they fail to do so, the claim is forfeit. [Citing cases] Forfeiture may occur even in the absence of an explicit time limitation if the right is knowable in advance and exercise of the right would prevent repetitious litigation. [Citing cases and] Peter Westen, *Away from Waiver: A Rationale for the Forfeiture of Constitutional Rights in Criminal Procedure*, 75 Mich.L.Rev. 1214, 1254–59 (1977). Only if the accused could not have known of the right or some other "cause" impedes a defendant from standing on his rights will a court permit the defendant to have two trials when a timely assertion of the right would have held the number to one.

Certainly a request for recusal before trial would have avoided any possibility of retrial. Murphy might have given a formal waiver on the record; Judge Kocoras might have recused himself; U.S. Attorney Webb might have stepped aside and allowed the case to be tried by a member of his office. Murphy had all the information he needed to initiate inquiry. Although according to the affidavits of Lydon and Murphy the defense camp did not know of the vacation plans for 1984, Lydon knew of the actual vacation in 1982, and Murphy knew of the longstanding friendship among Lydon, Webb, and Judge Kocoras. This was more than enough to put a reasonable person on notice of the potential gains from further inquiry, perhaps believing that an ethical judge such as Judge Kocoras would bend over backward to avoid favoring the prosecutor in such a case and that the defense therefore had more to gain from the Kocoras-Lydon friendship than it had to lose from the Kocoras-Webb friendship. The defendant is bound by a tactical choice such as this may have been, whether or not he participated

---

[36] Hall v. SBA, 695 F.2d 175 (5th Cir. 1983), comes the closest. In *Hall* a magistrate's law clerk accepted employment with the plaintiff's law firm and thereafter worked on the magistrate's opinion. The clerk also had been a member of the plaintiff class. The court thought this required the magistrate's opinion to be set aside, although no motion was made until after the opinion was released. We think that *Hall* is best understood as a case of actual bias (of the clerk) imputed to the court, not simply as an "appearance" case.

personally in that choice. [Citing cases]

Ultimately, however, we do not rest on the fact that Lydon, Webb, and Judge Kocoras went on vacation together in 1982. A detailed inquiry into what the defense camp knew and when is not essential when the motion under § 455(a) is filed as late as this was. A criminal trial is too serious and too costly to permit a defendant to sit on possible errors, hoping to have a crack at an acquittal (or low sentence) and then still a second trial. If a defendant wants a judge to stand aside under § 455(a), he must make the appropriate motion. Judicial acts taken before the motion may not later be set aside unless the litigant shows actual impropriety or actual prejudice; appearance of impropriety is not enough to poison the prior acts. See *Margoles* v. *Johns*, 660 F.2d 291 (7th Cir. 1981), cert. denied, 455 U.S. 909 (1982) (appearance of impropriety, and perhaps even actual impropriety, may not be raised for the first time on collateral attack); *Barry* v. *United States* 528 F.2d 1094, 1100 (7th Cir.), cert. denied, 429 U.S. 826 (1976) (when the trial is "impeccably fair and just" an erroneous failure to recuse is harmless error).

A judicial impropriety serious enough, and secret enough, to escape everyone's notice before trial probably also would be serious enough to create an actual conflict of interest. By the time the time the trial has been completed, an appearance of impropriety may have ripened into an actual impropriety. If it did not, and if no one asked for recusal before trial, then there is no need for still another trial to vindicate the concerns that underlie § 455(a).

It is regrettable that the vacation plans were not disclosed. This cast an unfortunate light on what was otherwise a well-handled trial. Judges and counsel should keep in mind the need to disclose unusual degrees of social as well as professional affiliation. The Webb-Kocoras vacation plans should have been disclosed. As it turns out, the silence did not adversely affect any substantial rights of Murphy. He could have protected himself fully by acting on the information he and Lydon possessed. At all events any appearance of impropriety under § 455(a) is not actual impropriety, so that recusal does not retroactively invalidate judicial acts that preceded the motion Murphy filed.

Both the circumstances concerning the vacation plans of the judge and the prosecutor, and the unavailability of a transcript of the conference on the jury instructions, have led us to resolve all ambiguities in favor of Murphy. After this review we are confident that Judge Kocoras was scrupulously impartial in fact and conducted this trial in accord with the highest standards of the bench. Murphy has had a fair trial, and the judgment is just.

AFFIRMED

SWYGERT, Senior Circuit Judge, concurring specially.

With respect to the recusal issue, I can concur only in the result ultimately reached by the court. I do not believe that a discussion of the merits of the recusal issue is necessary. Whether, at least in hindsight, the judge and prosecutor exercised poor judgment is irrelevant because the motion for recusal was untimely and waived.

The motion was filed several months after Murphy was sentenced. As such, it should be treated as a Fed.R.Crim.P. 33 motion for a new trial on the basis of newly-discovered evidence. In this circuit, such a motion could properly be entertained by the district court even though an appeal was pending. [Citing cases] Given defense counsel's close relationship and past vacation trips with the prosecutor and judge, the evidence supporting the recusal motion was not "newly-discovered evidence" within the meaning of Rule 33; had counsel exercised due diligence, the facts surrounding the relationship between the prosecutor and judge would have come to light much earlier. Given this failure to exercise due diligence, Murphy has waived his right to present the merits of his recusal motion. In short, the defendant's strategy was to "lay in the weeds," a tactic that should have and did backfire.

Such a holding would not contradict the strict waiver and timeliness rules announced by this court in *SCA Services, Inc.* v. *Morgan*, 557 F.2d 110 (7th Cir. 1977). There, the petitioner's right to be in court to present the recusal motion was not in question: the motion was filed in reference to a civil case pending trial. The issue here is whether the petitioner, subsequent to his conviction and sentence, has "waived" his right to get back in court to present new evidence. This is a distinct issue from whether, assuming the petitioner has a right to be in court in the first place, his right to require recusal has been "waived." *Morgan* applies only in the latter context; the case

says nothing about the law of waiver and timeliness in the context of postconviction proceedings.

Judicial Impropriety and Reversible Error[37]

Steven Lubet

The *Murphy* court made its greatest mistake in conflating the concepts of impropriety and partiality, treating the two terms as virtually interchangeable. This allowed the court to conclude that, because no demonstrated impropriety occurred, the appearance of partiality was irrelevant.

In truth, partiality ought to be understood as a distinct and particularly baneful subcategory of impropriety. The larger concept includes many forms of misconduct that do not necessarily imply unfairness. For example, impatience, discourtesy, delay, lack of diligence, undignified conduct, distraction from duty, public comment on pending litigation, and collateral misuse of office may all give rise to the appearance of impropriety. In the absence of some prejudice to a litigant, however, it is unlikely that any of these forms of behavior would be considered an actual impropriety sufficient to void a decision.

Impartiality, though, is a far more elusive concept. In the course of a significant trial a federal district court judge will make a nearly limitless number of discretionary decisions, most of which are neither subject to nor capable of meaningful review. The interplay of subtle factors on human choice is a subject that baffles psychologists, much less appellate court judges. It is for that reason that a prophylactic standard—the appearance of partiality—is most often substituted for actual evidence of bias.

The *Murphy* court also recognized the problem of subliminal motivation:

> A social relation of this sort implies extensive personal contacts between judge and prosecutor, perhaps a special willingness of the judge to accept and rely on the prosecutor's representations . . . A judge could be concerned about handing his friend a galling defeat on the eve of a joint vacation. 768 F.2d 1538.

The court went on, however, to conclude, presumably after searching the record, that "No one doubts that [the judge] was in fact impartial; his reputation for integrity and impartiality is outstanding." This is a non-sequitur. If the judge's conduct gave rise to the appearance of partiality, then someone must *doubt* that he was in fact impartial. How can it be otherwise? We may have no doubt that the judge committed no distinct reversible error. We may have no doubt (and I myself have no doubt) that the judge made every possible conscious effort to be scrupulously fair to the defendant. But on the subconscious or subliminal level neither we, nor the judge himself, can know what motivated each of the judge's hundreds of discretionary decisions. Of course, it is always the case that many of a judge's motivations will be unknown, but here we have an additional factor, a factual reason to doubt. Therefore, we must doubt.

---

[37] 3 CRIM. JUST. 26, 28–29 (1988).

The Seventh Circuit dismissed this problem as the "mere appearance of impropriety," that never ripened into actual prejudice. 768 F.2d at 1539, 1541. It is not so much their analysis as their taxonomy that is in error. Substitute partiality for impropriety and there can be nothing "mere" about it.

Notes and Questions

1. Do you agree with Lubet's distinction between impropriety and partiality? Does his distinction help to explain previous cases in this Chapter as well as *Murphy*?

2. The *Murphy* case was headline news in Chicago for many days. Judging from the news stories, the public was shocked and concerned that Judge Kocoras and Prosecutor Webb went on a vacation together right after the trial. Suppose that, at the time the Court of Appeals' decision was handed down affirming Murphy's conviction, you were asked to write a newspaper article stating the possible reasons the Court could have for its decision. Which of the following reasons appear plausible and which do not?

(a) It's perfectly all right for a judge and the chief prosecutor in a trial to go on vacation together right after the trial.

(b) Although sometimes a judge might be suspected of partiality if the judge were the sort of person who "could be concerned about handing his friend a galling defeat on the eve of a joint vacation" (as the *Murphy* decision put it), this particular judge—Judge Kocoras—is above that sort of thing. How do we know? The judges on the Court of Appeals tell us so. (In Chicago, the judges of the Court of Appeals work on the upper floor of the same building which houses the federal district judges' courtrooms.)

(c) Despite the appearance of partiality, the Court of Appeals found that the trial was fair, and so defendant Murphy wasn't hurt by the apparent prejudice.

(d) Defendant Murphy's own counsel also was friendly with Judge Kocoras, and therefore the prejudice evened out.

(e) The defendant's counsel knew all along about the close relationship between chief prosecutor and trial judge, and if they had brought a recusal motion at the beginning of the trial, Judge Kocoras would clearly have been forced to step down. But the defendant's counsel wanted a heads-I-win-tails-you-lose situation. They figured either that Murphy would be acquitted at trial, or if not, they could then charge that Judge Kocoras was unfair and maybe get a new trial. And it is this strategy, and this alone, that the Court of Appeals would not countenance.

3. If we are concerned about the *public appearance* of partiality, then how can the public really be expected to understand a complex motivation such as explanation (e) in the previous question? Can we even expect newspaper and TV reporters to convey the strategic situation clearly? If not, isn't *public appearance* a poor test for actual impropriety? Or is explanation (e) above *not* an answer to partiality at all, but rather a *competing consider-*

ation—one having to do with the efficient operation of the court system and the need to have counsel object to matters in a timely fashion in order to avoid unnecessary retrials?

3.4 Judicial partiality toward substantive law

This section is devoted not to judicial partiality toward the parties in one case, but to the preferences of judges toward the content of the law, hence toward classes of parties who are treated the same according to law.

The Enforcement of Morals[38]

Patrick Devlin[39]

In 1958 I was invited to deliver the second Maccabaean Lecture in Jurisprudence of the British Academy, the first having been delivered by Lord Evershed, then Master of the Rolls. It was an honour not to be declined but yet to be accepted only with much misgiving. A man who has passed his life in the practice of the law is not as a rule well equipped to discourse on questions of jurisprudence and I was certainly no exception to that rule. Fortunately, as it seemed to me, there was a subject which was both topical and within my powers to handle. In September 1957 the Wolfenden Committee had made its report recommending that homosexual practices in private between consenting adults should no longer be a crime. I had read with complete approval its formulation of the functions of the criminal law in matters of morality.

I had in fact given evidence before the Committee. Lord Goddard, then Lord Chief Justice, thought it desirable that evidence should be given by one judge of the Queen's Bench who thought that the law should not be altered and by another who was in favour of reform. I was in favour of reform. I agree with everyone who has written or spoken on the subject that homosexuality is usually a miserable way of life and that it is the duty of society, if it can, to save any youth from being led into it. I think that that duty has to be discharged although it may mean much suffering by incurable perverts who seem unable to resist the corruption of boys. But if there is no danger of corruption, I do not think that there is any good the law can do that outweighs the misery that exposure and imprisonment causes to addicts who cannot find satisfaction in any other way of life. Punishment will not cure and because it is haphazard in its incidence I doubt if it deters. Those who are detected and prosecuted are unlucky; and the full offence is frequently proved only because one or the other in his weakness confesses. I do not think that any judge now imposes a severe sentence in such cases. I cannot myself recollect ever having passed a sentence of imprisonment at all.

There is to my mind only one really powerful argument against reform and I put it in the form of a question. Can homosexuals be divided into those who corrupt youth and

---

[38] Pp. v–x, 4–24 (1965).

[39] Judge of the Queen's Bench, 1948–1960; Lord of Appeal, 1961–.

those who do not? If they cannot, is there a danger that the abolition of the offence between consenting adults might lead to an increase in corruption? The Wolfenden Committee thought that there was a division of this sort. Some judges of great experience for whose views I have a deep respect think otherwise. There is room for a more comprehensive study of case histories on this point than has, so far as I know, yet been made.

At any rate what I proposed to the Committee was one of those illogical compromises that would be rejected out of hand in any system of law that was not English. I suggested that, while the full offence of buggery should be retained, the lesser offences of indecent assault and gross indecency should be abolished unless the acts were committed on youths. It seemed to me that this compromise might go some way towards meeting the fears of those who thought that the repeal of the Act would be an admission that buggery should be tolerated. It would afford time to see whether offences against youths increased and, if it were found to be so, the way back would be less difficult than if the Act had been totally repealed. It would result, I thought, in prosecutions for buggery being brought only in clear and flagrant cases, since the alternative of a conviction for the lesser offence would no longer be available. Anyway, it seemed to me as much as public opinion would be at all likely to support. The proposal was not favoured by the Committee and I dare say they were quite right.

I must disclose at the outset that I have as a judge an interest in the result of the inquiry which I am seeking to make as a jurisprudent. As a judge who administers the criminal law and who has often to pass sentence in a criminal court, I should feel handicapped in my task if I thought that I was addressing an audience which had no sense of sin or which thought of crime as something quite different. Ought one, for example, in passing sentence upon a female abortionist to treat her simply as if she were an unlicensed midwife? If not, why not? But if so, is all the panoply of the law erected over a set of social regulations? I must admit that I begin with a feeling that a complete separation of crime from sin (I use the term throughout this lecture in the wider meaning) would not be good for the moral law and might be disastrous for the criminal.

[Some people argue that] a function for the criminal law independent of morals must be found. This is not difficult to do. The smooth functioning of society and the preservation of order require that a number of activities should be regulated. The rules that are made for that purpose and are enforced by the criminal law are often designed simply to achieve uniformity and convenience and rarely involve any choice between good and evil. Rules that impose a speed limit or prevent obstruction on the highway have nothing to do with morals. Since so much of the criminal law is composed of rules of this sort, why bring morals into it at all? Why not define the function of the criminal law in simple terms as the preservation of order and decency and the protection of the lives and property of citizens, and elaborate those terms in relation to any particular subject in the way in which it is done in the Wolfenden Report? The criminal law in carrying out these objects will undoubtedly overlap the moral law. Crimes of violence are morally wrong and they are also offences against good order; therefore they offend against both laws. But this is simply because the two laws in pursuit of different objectives happen to cover the same area. Such is the argument.

[My position is that] if the criminal law were to be reformed so as to eliminate from it everything that was not designed to preserve order and decency or to protect citizens (including the protection of youth from corruption), it would overturn a fundamental principle. It would also end a number of specific crimes. Euthanasia or the killing of another at his own request, suicide, attempted suicide and suicide pacts, duelling, abortion, incest between brother and sister, are all acts which can be done in private and without offence to others and need not involve the corruption or exploitation of others. Many people think that the law on some of these subjects is in need of reform, but no one hitherto has gone so far as to suggest that they should all be left outside the criminal law as matters of private morality. They can be brought within it only as a matter of moral principle. It must be remembered also that although there is much immorality that is not punished by the law, there is none that is condoned by the law. The law will not allow its processes to be used by those engaged in immorality of any sort. For example, a house may not be let for immoral purposes; the lease is invalid and would not be enforced. But if what goes on inside there is a matter of private morality and not the law's business, why does the law inquire into it at all?

I think that it is not possible to set theoretical limits to the power of the State to legislate against immorality. It is not possible to settle in advance exceptions to the general rule or to define inflexibly areas of morality into which the law is in no circumstances to be allowed to enter. Society is entitled by means of its laws to protect itself from dangers, whether from within or without. The law of treason is directed against aiding the king's enemies and against sedition from within. The justification for this is that established government is necessary for the existence of society and therefore its safety against violent overthrow must be secured. But an established morality is as necessary as good government to the welfare of society. Societies disintegrate from within more frequently than they are broken up by external pressures. There is disintegration when no common morality is observed and history shows that the loosening of moral bonds is often the first stage of disintegration, so that society is justified in taking the same steps to preserve its moral code as it does to preserve its government and other essential institutions. The suppression of vice is as much the law's business as the suppression of subversive activities; it is no more possible to define a sphere of private morality than it is to define one of private subversive activity. It is wrong to talk of private morality or of the law not being concerned with immorality as such or to try to set rigid bounds to the part which the law may play in the suppression of vice. There are no theoretical limits to the power of the State to legislate against treason and sedition,[40] and likewise I think there can be no theoretical limits to legislation against immorality. You may argue that if a man's sins affect only himself it cannot be the concern of society. If he chooses to get drunk every night in the privacy of his own home, is any one except himself the worse for it? But suppose a quarter or a half of the population got drunk every night, what sort of society would it be? You cannot set a theoretical limit to the number of people who can get drunk before society is

---

[40] Note that Great Britain, unlike the United States, does not have a written Constitution limiting the power of the government. In the United States, the First Amendment guarantees of freedom of speech, press, and assembly may be interpreted to set limits on sedition laws. [-Eds.]

entitled to legislate against drunkenness. The same may be said of gambling.

How is the law-maker to ascertain the moral judgements of society? It is surely not enough that they should be reached by the opinion of the majority; it would be too much to require the individual assent of every citizen. English law has evolved and regularly uses a standard which does not depend on the counting of heads. It is that of the reasonable man. He is not to be confused with the rational man. He is not expected to reason about anything and his judgement may be largely a matter of feeling. It is the viewpoint of the man in the street—or to use an archaism familiar to all lawyers—the man in the Clapham omnibus. He might also be called the right-minded man. For my purpose I should like to call him the man in the jury box, for the moral judgement of society must be something about which any twelve men or women drawn at random might after discussion be expected to be unanimous. This was the standard the judges applied in the days before Parliament was as active as it is now and when they laid down rules of public policy. They did not think of themselves as making law but simply as stating principles which every right-minded person would accept as valid. It is what Pollock called "practical morality," which is based not on theological or philosophical foundations but "in the mass of continuous experience half-consciously or unconsciously accumulated and embodied in the morality of common sense." He called it also "a certain way of thinking on questions of morality which we expect to find in a reasonable civilized man or a reasonable Englishman, taken at random."[41] It is not nearly enough to say that a majority dislike a practice; there must be a real feeling of reprobation. Those who are dissatisfied with the present law on homosexuality often say that the opponents of reform are swayed simply by disgust. If that were so it would be wrong, but I do not think one can ignore disgust if it is deeply felt and not manufactured. Its presence is a good indication that the bounds of toleration are being reached. Not everything is to be tolerated. No society can do without intolerance, indignation, and disgust; they are the forces behind the moral law, and indeed it can be argued that if they or something like them are not present, the feelings of society cannot be weighty enough to deprive the individual of freedom of choice. I suppose that there is hardly anyone nowadays who would not be disgusted by the thought of deliberate cruelty to animals. No one proposes to relegate that or any other form of sadism to the realm of private morality or to allow it to be practiced in public or in private. It would be possible no doubt to point out that until a comparatively short while ago nobody thought very much of cruelty to animals and also that pity and kindliness and the unwillingness to inflict pain are virtues more generally esteemed now than they have ever been in the past. But matters of this sort are not determined by rational argument. Every moral judgement, unless it claims a divine source, is simply a feeling that no right-minded man could behave in any other way without admitting that he was doing wrong. It is the power of common sense and not the power of reason that is behind the judgements of society. But before a society can put a practice beyond the limits of tolerance there must be a deliberate judgement that the practice is injurious to society. There is, for example, a general abhorrence of homosexuality. We should ask ourselves in the first instance whether, looking at it calmly and dispassionately,

---

[41] Essays in Jurisprudence and Ethics 278, 353 (1882).

we regard it as a vice so abominable that its mere presence is an offence. If that is the genuine feeling of the society in which we live, I do not see how society can be denied the right to eradicate it. Our feeling may not be so intense as that. We may feel about it that, if confined, it is tolerable, but that if it spread it might be gravely injurious; it is in this way that most societies look upon fornication, seeing it as a natural weakness which must be kept within bounds but which cannot be rooted out. It becomes then a question of balance, the danger to society in one scale and the extent of the restriction in the other. On this sort of point the value of an investigation by such a body as the Wolfenden Committee and of its conclusions is manifest.

The limits of tolerance shift. This is supplementary to what I have been saying but of sufficient importance in itself to deserve statement as a separate principle which law-makers have to bear in mind. I suppose that moral standards do not shift; so far as they come from divine revelation they do not, and I am willing to assume that the moral judgements made by a society always remain good for the society. But the extent to which society will tolerate—I mean tolerate, not approve—departures from moral standards varies from generation to generation. It may be that over-all tolerance is always increasing. The pressure of the human mind, always seeking greater freedom of thought, is outwards against the bonds of society forcing their gradual relaxation. It may be that history is a tale of contraction and expansion and that all developed societies are on their way to dissolution. I must not speak of things I do not know; and anyway as a practical matter no society is willing to make provisions for its own decay. I return therefore to the simple and observable fact that in matters of morals the limits of tolerance shift. Laws, especially those which are based on morals, are less easily moved. It follows as another good working principle that in any new matter of morals the law should be slow to act. By the next generation the swell of indignation may have abated and the law be left without the strong backing it needs. But it is then difficult to alter the law without giving the impression that moral judgement is being weakened. This is now one of the factors that is strongly militating against any alteration to the law on homosexuality.

The machinery which sets the criminal law in motion ends with the verdict and the sentence; and a verdict is given either by magistrates or by a jury. As a general rule, whenever a crime is sufficiently serious to justify a maximum punishment of more than three months, the accused has the right to the verdict of a jury. The result is that magistrates administer mostly what I have called the regulatory part of the law. They deal extensively with drunkenness, gambling, and prostitution, which are matters of morals or close to them, but not with any of the graver moral offences. They are more responsive than juries to the ideas of the legislature; it may not be accidental that the Wolfenden Report, in recommending increased penalties for solicitation, did not go above the limit of three months. Juries tend to dilute the decrees of Parliament with their own ideas of what should be punishable. Their province of course is fact and not law, and I do not mean that they often deliberately disregard the law. But if they think it is too stringent, they sometimes take a very merciful view of the facts. Let me take one example out of many that could be given. It is an offence to have carnal knowledge of a girl under the age of sixteen years. Consent on her part is no defence; if she did not consent, it would of course amount to rape. The law makes special provision for the situation when a boy and a girl are near age. If a man under twenty-four can prove that he had reasonable cause to believe that the girl was over the age of sixteen years, he has a good defence. The law regards the offence as sufficiently serious to make it one that is triable only by a judge at assizes. "Reasonable cause" means not merely that the boy honestly believed that the girl was over sixteen but also that he must have had reasonable grounds for his belief. In theory it ought not to be an easy defence to make out but in fact it is extremely rare for anyone who advances it to be convicted. The fact is that the girl is often as much to blame as the boy. The object of the law, as judges repeatedly tell juries, is to protect young girls against themselves; but juries are not impressed.

The part that the jury plays in the enforcement of the criminal law, the fact that no grave offence against morals is punishable without their verdict, these are of great importance in relation to the statements of principle that I have been making. They turn what might otherwise be pure exhortation to the legislature into something like rules that the law-makers cannot safely ignore. The man in the jury box is not just an expression; he is an active reality. It will not in the long run work to make laws about morality that are not acceptable to him.

The law should enforce public morality not by the formulation of hard and fast rules, but by a judgement in each case taking into account the sort of factors I have been mentioning. The line that divides the criminal law from the moral is not determinable by the application of any clear-cut principle. It is like a line that divides land and sea, a coastline of irregularities and indentations. There are gaps and promontories, such as adultery and fornication, which the law has for centuries left substantially untouched. Adultery of the sort that breaks up marriage seems to me to be just as harmful to the social fabric as homosexuality or bigamy. The only ground for putting it outside the criminal law is that a law which made it a crime would be too difficult to enforce; it is too generally regarded as a human weakness not suitably punished by imprisonment. All that the law can do with fornication is to act against its worst manifestations; there is a general abhorrence of the commercialization of vice, and that sentiment gives strength to the law against brothels and immoral earnings. There is no logic to be found in this. The boundary between the criminal law and the moral law is fixed by balancing in the case of each particular crime the pros and cons of legal enforcement in accordance with the sort of considerations I have been outlining. The fact that adultery, fornication, and lesbianism are untouched by the criminal law does not prove that homosexuality ought not to be touched. The error of jurisprudence in the Wolfenden Report is caused by the search for some single principle to explain the division between crime and sin. The Report finds it in the principle that the criminal law exists for the protection of individuals; on this principle fornication in private between consenting adults is outside the law and thus it becomes logically indefensible to bring homosexuality between consenting adults in private within it. But the true principle is that the law exists for the protection of society. It does not discharge its function by protecting the individual from injury, annoyance, corruption, and exploitation; the law must protect also the institutions and the community of ideas, political and moral, without which people cannot live together. Society cannot ignore the morality of the individual any more than it can his loyalty; it flourishes on both and without either it dies.

I have said that the morals which underlay the law must be derived from the sense of right and wrong which resides in the community as a whole; it does not matter whence the community of thought comes, whether from one body of doctrine or another or from the knowledge of good and evil which no man is without. If the reasonable man believes that a practice is immoral and believes also—no matter whether the belief is right or wrong, so be it that it is honest and dispassionate—that no right-minded member of his society could think otherwise, then for the purpose of the law it is immoral. This, you may say, makes immorality a question of fact—what the law would consider as self-evident fact no doubt, but still with no higher authority than any other doctrine of public policy. I think that that is so, and indeed the law does not distinguish between an act that is immoral and one that is contrary to public policy. But the law has never yet had occasion to inquire into the differences between Christian morals and those which every right-minded member of society is expected to hold. The inquiry would, I believe, be academic. Moralists would find differences; indeed they would find them between different branches of the Christian faith on subjects such as divorce and birth-control. But for the purpose of the limited entry which the law makes into the field of morals, there is no practical difference. It seems to me therefore that the free-thinker and non-Christian can accept, without offence to his convictions, the fact that Christian morals are the basis of the criminal law and that he can recognize, also without taking offence, that without the support of the churches the moral order, which has its origin in and takes its strength from Christian beliefs, would collapse.

Questions

1. A public prosecutor might choose not to prosecute certain offenses, such as a neighborhood poker game. Yet if there is a law against gambling, why shouldn't the prosecutor be obliged to prosecute all gamblers? Is there a fear that if the prosecutor did, society would demand the decriminalization of gambling? Who would be hurt if society did demand it?

2. A judge is in a different position from a prosecutor. A judge *must* rule as to a defendant who has been charged with committing a crime. Yet isn't Lord Devlin saying that the judge is in the same position as a prosecutor: a judge can acquit a defendant, or give a very light sentence (a rap on the knuckles) to a gambler? Is this a proper conception of judicial office?

3. Is Lord Devlin saying that it is worse for a judge to attempt to enforce moral laws that no longer have the support of society (such as minor gambling) than not to enforce them?

4. Is Lord Devlin saying that a judge ought to enforce moral laws that have the support of society (ascertained through the "man in the Clapham omnibus" or jury) even if "enlightened" public opinion (as expressed through the Wolfenden report, for example) is opposed?

5. Does Lord Devlin follow two principles as a judge: (1) the activity must be criminal, according to legislation; AND (2) a majority of people must want the law to enforce it? If so, when (2) changes even though (1) remains the same, would Lord Devlin change his own thinking and throw the case out of court?

6. Why does Lord Devlin feel that *he* ought to enforce the law against homosexuality when defendants charged with homosexual practices are brought before him?

7. Suppose that today, in the United States, a doctor is prosecuted for aborting a fetus. Suppose that the mother is thirteen years old, unmarried, does not know who the father is, and says that she simply did not want a baby. The doctor concedes that there was no threat to the health of the mother and that the fetus was normal. Now suppose that this case could go before two judges. Judge A strongly believes in a right to life, and that abortions are murder in the eyes of God. Judge B strongly believes that the mother has an absolute right to abort a fetus at any time. To sharpen the problem, suppose, further, that the trial is without a jury (a "bench" trial) and that the facts are undisputed. The doctor is charged with deliberate manslaughter, a Class A felony with a statutory penalty of 5 to 25 years. Now consider the contexts in which the case could arise:

A. The time is 1950, and the state in which this case takes place has a statute explicitly prescribing that any doctor who performs an abortion commits the felony of manslaughter. The fetus is aborted when it is in its *first* month. What *should* Judge A decide? What *should* Judge B decide? If you have different answers to these two questions, how do you justify the difference?

B. The time is the present, and the state in which this case takes place has no abortion statute, but it does have a manslaughter statute. The fetus is aborted when it is in its *first* month. What *should* Judge A decide? What *should* Judge B decide? If you have different answers to these two questions, how do you justify the difference?

C. Same situation as in B. above, but the fetus is aborted when it is in its *fifth* month. What *should* Judge A decide? What *should* Judge B decide? If you have different answers to these two questions, how do you justify the difference?

Law and the Modern Mind[42]

Jerome Frank

A survey was made of the disposition of thousands of minor criminal cases by the several judges of the City Magistrate's Court in New York City during the years 1914 to 1916 with the express purpose of finding to what extent the "personal equation" entered into the administration of justice. It was disclosed that "the magistrates did differ to an amazing degree in their treatment of similar classes of cases." Thus of 546 persons charged with intoxication brought before one judge, he discharged only one and found the others guilty, whereas of the 673 arraigned before another judge, he found 531 not guilty. In disorderly conduct cases, one judge discharged only 18% and another discharged 54%. "In other words, one coming before Magistrate Simons had only 2 chances in 10 of getting off.

---

[42] P. 112 (1930). Frank, you will recall, later became a federal judge.

If he had come before Judge Walsh he would have had more than 5 chances in 10 of getting off." In vagrancy cases, the percentage of discharges varied from 4.5% to 79%. When it came to sentences, the same variations existed. One judge imposed fines on 84% of the persons he found guilty and gave suspended sentences to 7%, while one of his fellows fined 34% and gave suspended sentences to 59%.

New Yorker Cartoon

Two judges are walking down the steps of the courthouse in their flowing black robes. One of them is speaking to the other. The caption reads: "Days when I'm feeling rotten I sentence 'em all to ten years. Days when I'm feeling good, I sentence every one of 'em to six months. It all averages out."

Philosophy, Jurisprudence, and Jurisprudential Temperament of Federal Judges[43]

Ruggiero J. Aldisert[44]

H.L.A. Hart discussed the importance of ascertaining the conventional morality of an actual social group, referring to "standards of conduct which are widely shared in a particular society, and are to be contrasted with the moral principles or moral ideals which may govern an individual's life, but which he does not share with any considerable number of those with whom he lives."[45] Perhaps this is the most critical aspect of our inquiry. The judge must screen out personal bias, passion, and prejudice, and attempt always to distinguish between a personal cultivated taste and general notions of moral obligations. These standards of conduct reflect an obligation to respect rules of society. They are, in Hart's formulation, primary rules of obligation because of "the serious social pressure by which they are supported, and by the considerable sacrifice of individual interest or inclination which compliance with them involves."[46] Wellington said that the way in which one learns about the conventional morality of society "is to live in it, become sensitive to it, experience widely, read extensively, and ruminate, reflect, and analyze situations that seem to call moral obligations into play."[47]

Yet the attempt to base a decision on social consensus is fraught with peril and, in the interpretation of constitutional precepts, may be inappropriate. A classic example of judges mistaking the public consensus is the position perennially espoused by Justices

---

[43] 20 IND. L. REV. 453, 483-84 (1987).

[44] Chief Judge, U.S. Court of Appeals for the Third Circuit.

[45] H.L.A. HART, THE CONCEPT OF LAW 165 (1961).

[46] Id.

[47] Wellington, *Common Law Rules and Constitutional Double Standards: Some Notes on Adjudication*, 83 YALE L.J. 221, 246 (1973).

William J. Brennan, Jr., and Thurgood Marshall in the death penalty cases. Their concurring opinions in *Furman v. Georgia*[48] argued that the death penalty was unconstitutional "cruel and unusual punishment" because it was out of step with contemporary community values. Yet the rush of state legislatures to impose the death penalty since their 1972 statements shows a clarity of community reaction completely opposite to their statements.[49]

To some extent, adherence to the principle of neutrality in judicial decisionmaking provides a check against the temptation to substitute personal for social values. Professor Kent Greenawalt has observed:

> Serious moral choices typically involve some conflict between an action that would serve one's narrow self-interest and an action that would satisfy responsibilities toward others. The dangers of bias are extreme; either we value too highly our own interest or over-compensate and undervalue it. The discipline of imagining similar situations in which we are not involved or play a different role more nearly enables us to place appropriate values on competing considerations.[50]

---

[48] 408 U.S. 238 (1972).

[49] Moreover, a Gallup Poll taken in November 1985 disclosed that three out of four Americans favored the death penalty, seventeen percent opposed it, and eight percent were undecided. N.Y. TIMES, Nov. 28, 1985, at 20, col. 3.

[50] Greenawalt, *The Enduring Significance of Neutral Principles,* 78 COLUM. L. REV. 982, 997 (1978).

Mills v. Wyman

20 Mass. (3 Pickering) 207
Supreme Judicial Court of Massachusetts, 1825

[The defendant's son, age 25, was suddenly taken sick on his return from a voyage at sea. He was poor and in distress. The plaintiff, a stranger to him, helped him and gave him board and nursing care for fifteen days. Four days later, after the plaintiff had incurred these expenses, the father (the defendant in this case) wrote a letter to the plaintiff promising to pay him all his expenses. But the father did not follow through, and the plaintiff now brings an action in assumpsit (contract).]

PARKER, C.J. The rule that a mere verbal promise, without any consideration, cannot be enforced by action, is universal in its application, and cannot be departed from to suit particular cases in which a refusal to perform such a promise may be disgraceful.

The promise declared on in this case appears to have been made without any legal consideration. The kindness and services towards the sick son of the defendant were not bestowed at his request. The son was in no respect under the care of the defendant. He was twenty-five years old, and had long left his father's family. On his return from a foreign country, he fell sick among strangers, and the plaintiff acted the part of the good Samaritan, giving him shelter and comfort until he died. The defendant, his father, on being informed of this event influenced by a transient feeling of gratitude, promises in writing to pay the plaintiff for the expenses he had incurred. But he has determined to break this promise, and is willing to have his case appear on record as a strong example of particular injustice sometimes necessarily resulting from the operation of general rules.

What a man ought to do, generally he ought to be made to do, whether he promise or refuse. But the law of society has left most of such obligations to the *interior* forum, as the tribunal of conscience has aptly been called. Is there not a moral obligation upon every son who has become affluent by means of the education and advantages bestowed upon him by his father, to relieve that father from pecuniary embarrassment, to promote his comfort and happiness, and even to share with him his riches, if thereby he will be made happy? And yet such a son may, with impunity, leave such a father in any degree of penury above that which will expose the community in which he dwells, to the danger of being obliged to preserve him from absolute want. Is not a wealthy father under strong moral obligation to advance the interest of an obedient, well disposed son, to furnish him with the means of acquiring and maintaining a becoming rank in life, to rescue him from the horrors of debt incurred by misfortune? Yet the law will uphold him in any degree of parsimony, short of that which would reduce his son to the necessity of seeking public charity.

Without doubt there are great interests of society which justify withholding the coercive arm of the law from these duties of imperfect obli-gation, as they are called; imperfect, not because they are less binding upon the conscience than those which are called perfect, but because the wisdom of the social law does not impose sanctions upon them.

A deliberate promise, in writing, made freely and without any mistake, one which may lead the party to whom it is made into contracts and expenses, cannot be broken without a violation of moral duty. But if there was nothing paid or promised for it, the law, perhaps wisely, leaves the execution of it to the conscience of him who makes it. It is only when the party making the promise gains something, or he to whom it is made loses something, that the law gives the promise validity.

For the foregoing reasons we are all of the opinion that the nonsuit directed by the Court of Common Pleas was right, and that judgment be entered thereon for costs for the defendant.[51]

---

[51] Thus, the plaintiff not only lost the case, but also was ordered to pay for the defendant's court costs. [-Eds.]

Doing What Comes Naturally[52]

Stanley Fish

It is this picture that underwrites much of the thinking in legal circles about the activity of judging. What judges do, at least when they are doing their jobs properly, is set their personal feelings aside and come to their decisions by consulting the rule (of law) they have accepted as a bridle on their wills. Thus Kenney Hegland[53] cites a famous contract case (*Mills v. Wyman*) in which Chief Justice Parker of the Massachusetts Supreme Court, finding himself faced with a defendant whose actions he abhors nevertheless rules for him because the law he has sworn faithfully to execute bids him do so. Hegland takes this as a particularly perspicuous example of the operation of independent constraints on "personal predilections," an example which, he claims, refutes the "deconstructionist position that legal doctrine does not constrain judicial decision."

As Hegland sees it, the opposition is clear: "personal predilections" versus the constraint of doctrine, and equally clear is the larger opposition of which this one is an instance: civilization and order versus the anarchy of the individual will. But is it really so clear as that? Not if one interrogates the opposition at a basic level and asks, as a starter, what exactly is a "personal predilection"? Where does it come from? In order for the opposition

---

[52] 10–13 (1989).

[53] Professor Hegland teaches law at the University of Arizona. [-Eds.]

to work with the force (a nice word) Hegland intends, personal predilections or preferences must come from nowhere, must originate in the self in a way unrelated to social and public norms; otherwise the opposition would be blurred. But how could such a preference even form apart from some conventional system of thought or mores in relation to which it was possible and thinkable? In the case Hegland cites, although Judge Parker is repelled by a man who breaks a promise to someone who cared for his dying son, he decides that since the promise was not supported by "consideration" (the Good Samaritan did not bargain for payment) it is not legally binding. But it hardly makes any sense to say that Parker's distaste for this ingrate is a "personal predilection"; rather it is a sentiment that forms part of a conventionally established system of obligation which Parker has internalized just as he has internalized the legal doctrine that now trumps his conventional sentiment. The conflict he feels is not between a normative obligation and "mere preference," but between two normative obligations one of which carries the day because it is central to the role he is now playing. Indeed, there is no such thing as a "mere preference" in the sense that makes it a threat to communal norms, for anything that could be experienced as a preference will derive from the norms inherent in some community.

The conclusion only appears to be paradoxical: all preferences are principled, that is, they are intelligible and doable only by virtue of some principled articulation of the world and its possibilities; but by the same token all principles are preferences, because every principle is an extension of a particular and *contestable* articulation of the world and none proceeds from a universal perspective (a contradiction in terms.[54]) When Judge Parker holds for the defendant because no consideration attached to his promise, he speaks from a vision of public life that is anything but neutral and impersonal. In that vision contracting parties begin in what has been called an "equality of distrust" and are presumed to be bargaining for advantage; actions of altruism and simple faith are not recognized except as aberrations that the law will neither respect nor protect. In the eyes of some these "principles" of contract are obviously *un*principled, although for others (including, presumably, Judge Parker), they are necessary to the healthy functioning of a free market. In short, one person's principles are another person's illegitimate ("mere") preferences, and any characterization of a dispute or a choice that puts the principles on one side and the "personal predilections" on the other is itself interested and (in the sense defined above) personal. In the (certain) event that some characterization will prevail (at least for a time) over its rivals, it will do so because some interested assertion of principle has managed to *forcefully* dislodge the other (equally interested) assertions of principle. It is in this sense that force is the sole determinant of outcomes, but the sting is removed from this conclusion when force is understood not as "pure" or "mere" force (phenomena never encountered) but as the urging (perhaps in the softest terms) of some point of view, of some vision of the world replete with purposes, goals, standards, reasons—in short, with everything to which force is usually

---

[54] Fish means here that no person can possibly attain a "universal perspective" because no person can stand outside the universe, in which he or she is immersed, and view the universe as a whole. Hilary Putnam agrees; he calls the universal perspective the "God's-eye view" by way of emphasizing that no human can have such a perspective. [-Eds.]

opposed in the name of principle.

Once the opposition between principle and force has been deconstructed, any number of issues begin to look very different, including the issue of constraints. Constraints... are what is supposedly required to prevent a self composed of desire from going its own (unprincipled) way; but if desires (or preferences) cannot have shape independently of some normative vision, the self that is composed of desires is, ipso facto, composed of constraints, and no *additional* constraints are needed to give it a direction it already has. This is perhaps the most surprising and counterintuitive consequence of the denial of independent constraints (which is one and the same with the denial of literal meaning); rather than leaving us in a world where the brakes are off, it situates us in a world where the brakes—in the form of the imperatives, urgencies, and prohibitions that come along with any point of view (and being in a point of view is not something one can avoid)—are always and already on. When Judge Parker sits down to consider *Mills v. Wyman,* he is in no sense "free" to see the facts in any way he pleases; rather his very first look is informed (constrained) by the ways of thinking that now fill his consciousness as a result of his initiation into the professional community of jurists. That is to say, he looks with judicially informed eyes, eyes from whose perspective he cannot distance himself for a single second except in order to slip into another way of seeing, no less conventional, no less involuntary. At no time is he free to go his "own way" for he is always going in a way marked out by the practice or set of practices of whose defining principles (goals, purposes, interdictions) he is a moving extension, and therefore it would be superfluous of him to submit his behavior to principles other than the ones that already, and *necessarily* constrain him.

Concluding Questions

1. In what ways do Lubet (after *Murphy* in the previous section) and Fish agree? How do they differ? (This is a hard question!)

2. Does judicial bias toward the content of the law exist? Is it as important a problem for justice as judicial bias toward parties? Are the two always (sometimes?) separate and distinct?

3. Do we want judges to be biased in favor of existing law? Would we want them to be biased against? Should the answer depend on whether existing law is just? Should the answer depend on whether the judge believes existing law will produce a just result?

4. What does "bias in favor of existing law" mean? What does Fish say? Does existing law itself create the possibility of bias? Or is a judge simply "constrained" (as Fish would put it) to decide in the way the legal community expects, and then simply "fill in" the legal principles to justify that decision?

5. Is judicial decisionmaking ultimately a matter of power? Justice? Both? Neither?

Group Justice Versus Individual Justice: Category Problems

CHAPTER FOUR

We have been dealing so far with bias and prejudice as it comes up in procedural contexts in the courtroom. Now we begin to look at substantive law. As you read the cases and materials in this and the next chapter, the larger questions you should keep in mind include: When is it fair to attribute group characteristics to a member of the group? Are we doing justice to an individual if we attempt to do justice to a group? What does it mean to do justice to a group? Can we separate the individual from the group when we want to do justice to the individual?

McFarland v. Smith
611 F.2d 414

United States Court of Appeals,
Second Circuit
Oct. 29, 1979

Steven Lloyd Barrett, New York City (The Legal Aid Society, Federal Defender Services Unit, New York, N.Y., on the brief), for petitioner-appellant.

Kenneth R. Fisher, Rochester, N.Y. (Lawrence T. Kurlander, Monroe County Dist. Atty., Rochester, N.Y. on the brief), for intervener-appellee.

Before VAN GRAAFEILAND, NEWMAN and KEARSE, Circuit Judges.

NEWMAN, Circuit Judge:

This is an appeal from a denial of a petition for a writ of habeas corpus brought by a state prisoner to challenge his conviction essentially on the ground that his constitutional rights were denied by the prosecutor's inclusion of improper racial remarks in the summation.

Petitioner was found guilty by a jury of criminal sale of a controlled substance (heroin) in the second degree, N.Y. Penal Law § 220.41, and sentenced on June 2, 1976 in the New York Supreme Court (Monroe County) to a term of eight years to life. The Appellate Division affirmed without opinion and the New York Court of Appeals denied permission to appeal. A petition for a writ of habeas corpus was denied on May 30, 1978 by the United States District Court for the Western District of New York.

At trial, the State's case depended almost entirely on the testimony of Patricia Dorman, a Rochester undercover police officer. She testified that she purchased $450 worth of heroin from petitioner in the bedroom of a second-floor apartment. She recognized petitioner as a person she had known in high school and had since seen occasionally. The defense case depended entirely on the testimony of petitioner's friend, Isaac Singletary. He testified that he and petitioner had come to the apartment house to see two prostitutes with whom they had earlier made a date. According to Singletary, he and petitioner went upstairs to the second-floor apartment together with a Puerto Rican man who had entered the building just after they did. Singletary further testified that he waited in a front room, petitioner used the bathroom, and the Puerto Rican man entered the bedroom along with a Black woman (Dorman) and another Puerto Rican man. Singletary heard a brief discussion in the bedroom, after which the Black woman left the building. Singletary said petitioner emerged from the bathroom, they both asked the Puerto Ricans where the girls were, and when they were told there were no girls, both left. The inference from Singletary's testimony was that Dorman had purchased narcotics from the first Puerto Rican male, and not from petitioner.

Not surprisingly the summation of defense counsel contended vigorously that Officer Dorman's version was false and Singletary's version was true.

In the course of the prosecutor's summation the following occurred:

> MR. PAPPALARDO [the prosecutor]. The officer herself being, by the book[1] a young woman, black woman, by the way this Defendant is black also.
>
> MR. KING [defense counsel]. Objection to the racial connotation of individuals.
>
> THE COURT. Of course I'll instruct the jury now they shall not take into consideration to any extent and use that against any individual race, color, creed makes no difference whatsoever. You may continue.

---

[1] Later in his summation the prosecutor explained that in characterizing Officer Dorman as someone who goes "by the book," he meant that she follows correct procedure for an undercover officer in insisting that she has the purchased narcotics in her hands before she pays out any money. (Tr. at 371–72).

> MR. PAPPALARDO. I'll also instruct the jury—
>
> MR. KING. Objection.
>
> THE COURT. Yes, that's improper. You cannot instruct the jury.
>
> MR. PAPPALARDO. Excuse me, I seem to be interrupted before I finish my statement because the interruption is what the People believe the People's position, as in every single case, it makes no difference what color the Defendant is. I'll finish my point. Don't you convict anyone on color or race. It makes no difference. It makes no difference to me. I hope it makes no difference to Mr. King and anybody else, but the fact is that Officer Dorman is black and the Defendant is black. That's a fact. That's a fact like you consider any other fact. If she's lying she's lying against a member, a person that [sic] is black.
>
> MR. KING. Objection.
>
> THE COURT. Overruled.
>
> MR. PAPPALARDO. That is a proper consideration for you to examine, to think about and now she's lying against another black person. You think about it because that's what Mr. King is telling you that she's lying. Someone she knows and that's [sic] a member of her own race. You use your common sense to think about that.

The prosecutor thus urged the jury to credit Officer Dorman's testimony on the theory that the probability of truthfulness was increased by the circumstances that a Black person was testifying against another Black person. The trial judge's overruling of defense counsel's objection assured the jury that the Court accepted the propriety of this argument.

In *United States ex rel. Haynes v. McKendrick*, 481 F.2d 152 (2d Cir. 1973), this Court ruled that racial remarks in a prosecutor's summation can constitute a violation of a defendant's right under the Due Process Clause to a fair trial. Judge Oakes' opinion drew upon the line of fair trial cases beginning with *Moore v. Dempsey*, 261 U.S. 86 (1923), and the line of equal protection cases beginning with *Strauder v. West Virginia*, 100 U.S. 303 (1879), and noted that when racial prejudice is injected into a criminal trial, "the due process and equal protection clauses overlap or at least meet...."

The Office of the Monroe County District Attorney, which has intervened to uphold petitioner's conviction, contends that the racial remarks of the prosecutor, while "imprudent," were not racial slurs. The remarks in *Haynes* involved racial slurs, and the District Attorney argues that only remarks of that category are appeals to racial prejudice that can render a conviction invalid under the Fourteenth Amendment.

Neither *Haynes* nor the lines of authority on which it drew set the constitutional limits for improper prosecution argument at racial slurs. Race is an impermissible basis for any adverse governmental action in the absence of compelling justification. When a prosecutor's summation includes racial remarks in an effort to persuade a jury to return a guilty verdict, the resulting conviction is constitutionally unfair unless the remarks are abundantly justified. To raise the issue of race is to draw the jury's attention to a characteristic that the Constitution generally commands us to ignore. Even a reference that is not derogatory may carry impermissible connotations, or may trigger prejudiced responses in the listeners that the speaker might neither have predicted nor intended.

This is not to say that every race-conscious argument is impermissible. Indeed, in *Haynes* defense counsel, with apparent court approval, had attacked identification testimony on the ground that the eyewitness, being White, was unlikely to be able to discern distinguishing characteristics of the face of the criminal, who was Black. These remarks were race-conscious, but neutral, since presumably an argument could be made with equal force that a Black eyewitness would have difficulty discerning the features of a White criminal. And there is some basis for accepting the validity of both contentions. Chance, Goldstein & McBride, *Differential Experience and Recognition Memory for Faces*, 97 J. Soc. Psych. 243 (1975); Malpass, *Racial Bias in Eyewitness Identification*, 1 Personality & Soc. Psych. Bull. 42 (1974); Malpass & Kravitz, *Recognition for Faces of Own and Other Race*, 13 J. Personality & Soc. Psych. 330 (1969); Shepherd, Deregowski & Ellis, *A Cross-Cultural Study of Recognition Memory for Faces*, 9 Int'l J. Psych. 205 (1975). But given the general requirement that the race of a criminal defendant must not be the

basis of any adverse inference, any reference to it by a prosecutor must be justified by a compelling state interest. The issue in this case is whether the racial remarks, even if not overt racial slurs, were sufficiently justified to be countenanced.

Since the prosecutor in this case did not spell out his reasoning, one is left to consider what possible lines of reasoning might support a valid argument that the testimony of Officer Dorman is entitled to some degree of enhanced probability of truthfulness because her race is the same as the defendant's.

The analysis may begin by recognizing the obvious fact that from any group, racial or otherwise, some persons called as witnesses will testify helpfully to a defendant and some will testify accusingly.[2] It may well be that testimony is more frequently helpful than accusing when the testimony is given within group lines (witness and defendant members of the same group) than when testimony is given across group lines (witness and defendant not members of the same group). Two circumstances would seem to support this thesis. First, alibi and character witnesses normally come from those with whom the defendant spends time, and there is a reasonable likelihood that members of his group are a disproportionately large segment of his friends and associates. Victims and bystander witnesses who testify accusingly are less likely to be drawn disproportionately from the defendant's group (though for some crimes, victims may be). Second, when testimony is given within rather than across group lines, the incidence of helpful testimony may be further increased because of lying. Of course, of all witnesses who testify helpfully, some percentage are lying, reflecting at least whatever extent mendacity is prevalent in the total population. But in the category of helpful testimony within group lines, an extra increment of lying might occur because of the tendency of some small percentage of the members of any group to lie in an effort to be

---

[2] The percentage of each group that testifies accusingly may not be the same, but the differences do not matter to this analysis.

helpful to a fellow member of their group.[3]

The prosecutor in this case might have believed that both of these circumstances operate to make the incidence of helpful testimony higher within group lines than across them, and conversely that the incidence of accusing testimony is lower within group lines than across them. In other words, if 100 instances are randomly selected where a witness and a defendant are members of the same group, and another 100 instances are randomly selected where a witness and a defendant are not members of the same group, the percentage of witnesses giving accusing testimony may well be lower in the first 100 than in the second 100.

If this is what the prosecutor believed (and was urging the jury to believe), the premise might be sound, but the conclusion—that Officer Dorman's accusing testimony is more likely to be credible because given within group lines rather than across them—is completely illogical. All the premise indicates is that testimony within group lines, compared to testimony across group lines, is less likely to be *accusing*. But this premise provides no basis whatever for reaching any conclusion as to the likelihood that accusing testimony within group lines is *credible*. Specifically, it provides no logical basis for concluding that accusing testimony within group lines is more likely to be truthful than accusing testimony across group lines. Reduced frequency of occurrence is no indicator of credibility. The pertinent analysis is not a comparison of the *incidence* of accusing testimony

within and across group lines, but a comparison of the *truthfulness* of accusing testimony within and across group lines.

As with witnesses giving helpful testimony, some percentage of all witnesses giving accusing testimony are lying. But when accusing testimony within and across group lines is compared, another circumstance may well be at work that might affect the likelihood of credibility. This is prejudice—the hostility of some few members of any group against members of a different group to such a degree that they are willing to accuse falsely. It may well be that prejudice increases the probability of lying when accusing testimony is given across group lines to a greater degree than when accusing testimony is given within group lines. To whatever extent this is so, the converse effect would be to increase the probability of truthfulness when accusing testimony is given within group lines to a greater degree than when accusing testimony is given across group lines.

If the prosecutor was basing his argument on this reasoning, his argument might have some slight logical validity,[4] but is nonetheless constitutionally impermissible for two reasons. First, the degree of validity is highly uncertain and may well be extremely slight. It is one thing to permit race-conscious arguments to be made when comparing the reliability of facial identifications within and across racial lines, but quite another to permit such arguments with respect to comparative rates of false accusations. While there is some reason to believe that identifications are

---

[3] There is no need in this case to decide whether the incidence of such helpful lying within group lines is of sufficient certainty and extent and sufficiently race-neutral to be the basis of a permissible argument by a prosecutor that helpful defense testimony should be disbelieved because a defendant and his witnesses are members of the same group. Whatever the infirmities of such a summation . . . , it poses issues different from those that arise in this case where the prosecutor argues that *accusing* testimony should be believed because the defendant and a prosecution witness are members of the same group. To the extent that the jury may have taken the prosecutor's remark as a veiled suggestion to disbelieve Singletary's helpful testimony, the vice of injecting improper racial considerations into an assessment of Officer Dorman's accusing testimony was compounded, as Judge Kearse's concurring opinion points out.

[4] In some contexts, another phenomenon may be at work that would lessen or even totally undercut any logical validity the prosecutor's argument might otherwise have. This is the tendency among members of some groups to be so personally embarrassed by wrongdoing by members of their group that they are overly quick to condemn. To whatever extent that phenomenon might increase the rate of mistaken accusations within group lines compared to accusations across group lines, it would be expected to manifest itself only in circumstances where the witness was perceiving ambiguous events and too quickly and erroneously concluding that wrongdoing was occurring. It is difficult to imagine that this phenomenon would have any bearing on the relative incidence of deliberately false accusations within group lines compared to deliberately false accusations across group lines.

more reliably made within racial lines than across them, there is no comparable basis for confidence in comparisons about false accusations. A race-conscious argument is not constitutionally permissible unless the basis for it has a sufficiently high degree of reliability to warrant the risks inevitably taken when racial matters are injected into any important decision-making. A major risk here is that the jury will totally fail to follow the narrow reasoning process that lends any possible validity to the prosecutor's argument and instead simply be influenced adversely to the defendant because of the prosecutor's reference to his race. A further risk is that the jury will wrongly conclude that the argument draws its validity from the previously discussed premise concerning the reduced incidence of accusing testimony within group lines. If the jury accepts that reasoning, it will be accepting an argument that is, as previously pointed out, completely illogical.

There is a second reason for disallowing the argument, to whatever extent it might have logical validity. The increased credibility of accusations within group lines compared to accusations across group lines results, if at all, from the degree to which some members of one group are so prejudiced against another group that they are willing to make false accusations. When a prosecutor argues for enhanced likelihood of credibility because the accusation is within group lines, he is asking the jury to give his witness some extra credit simply because the witness is lacking the prejudice that might prompt a witness of another group to accuse falsely. The credibility of the state's witness should depend on an assessment of many pertinent factors, but the state should not be entitled to have its witness's credibility enhanced simply because they are not members of a group that might be prejudiced against the defendant.

This point can best be appreciated by contemplating the minor premise the prosecutor would have to explain to the jury in order to develop his reasoning fully. If a Black officer is logically entitled to any enhanced credibility when testifying against a Black defendant, it can only be because White police officers are more likely than Black police officers to give false accusing testimony against a Black defendant. If the difference is true at all, it presumably is true for all police departments, including Officer Dorman's. If to the prosecutor's knowledge some White offi-

cers of her department would falsely accuse a Black defendant, such an outrageous circumstance surely cannot be a constitutionally valid basis for enhancing the credibility of this witness for the prosecution.

Furthermore, to whatever extent prejudice increases the incidence of false accusing testimony across compared to within group lines, this circumstance supports an argument that is not race-neutral. As the intervenor acknowledged at oral argument, it is inconceivable that a prosecutor would argue to a jury that one reason to believe the accusing testimony of a police officer is that both the officer and the defendant are White.

These considerations lead to the conclusion that the prosecutor's argument is constitutionally impermissible. It invokes race for a purpose that is either illogical or of very slight and uncertain logical validity and does so at a distinct risk of stirring racially prejudiced attitudes. The evils of racial prejudice lurk too frequently throughout the administration of criminal justice. They must be condemned whenever they appear. The Constitution forbids the racial remarks in the summation that preceded petitioner's conviction.

The District Attorney contends that if constitutional error occurred, it was harmless beyond a reasonable doubt. See *Chapman v. California,* 386 U.S. 18 (1967). As both the prosecutor and defense counsel recognized, the case against the defendant depended on the credibility of Officer Dorman as opposed to the defendant's witness, Singletary. The corroborating details of the prosecution's case confirmed a narcotics sale and petitioner's presence at the apartment house, facts he did not contest, but did not significantly prove that petitioner was the seller. When the District Attorney contends that the case against the petitioner was strong, he is assuming the truth of Officer Dorman's testimony. A constitutional error that taints the proper assessment of her credibility cannot be considered harmless.

The judgment is reversed and the cause remanded with instructions to issue a conditional writ discharging the petitioner from custody unless the District Attorney within sixty days files with the District Court a statement of intention to retry petitioner and thereafter proceeds to retrial with reasonable promptness.

KEARSE, Circuit Judge (concurring):

I concur in the result and in most of Judge

Newman's opinion but would add the following observations.

The prosecutor urged the jury to believe the testimony of Officer Dorman because she was Black, the defendant was Black, and Dorman's testimony was accusatory. The immediate implication of the prosecutor's statement was twofold. First, it suggested that an accusation by a Black witness is more likely to be truthful if made against a Black defendant than if made against a White defendant. Second, it suggested that testimony of a Black witness with respect to a Black defendant is more likely to be truthful if it accuses him than if it supports him.

In my view, therefore, the prosecutor's appeal not only may have led the jury to credit unduly Officer Dorman's testimony, but also may have led the jury to believe that Singletary, the sole witness in support of the defendant, was more likely to be lying— not because he and the defendant were friends but because he and the defendant were Black....

The overall effect of the prosecutor's remarks was to imply that Black persons, as contrasted with White persons (the district attorney's office admits it is inconceivable that a prosecutor would make a statement of this kind about a White witness and a White defendant), can be expected to allow racial considerations to affect their testimony. I suspect that this invidious premise, rather than the level of incidence of intra-group accusation, is what was in the prosecutor's mind when he said, "If she's lying she's lying against a member, a person that [sic] is black," and what he conveyed to the jury when he urged, "You use your common sense to think about" whether "she's lying against another black person."

VAN GRAAFEILAND, Circuit Judge, dissenting:

In voting to reverse, my two colleagues set themselves against a competent and eminently fair New York State Supreme Court Judge, five Appellate Division Judges, the Chief Judge of the New York Court of Appeals, and a United States District Court Judge, all of whom were satisfied that petitioner had a fair trial. Although I agree completely with my colleagues that appeals to racial prejudice have no place in a courtroom, I find no such appeal in this case. I therefore cast my lot with the eight judges who felt the same way.

In *Rose v. Mitchell,* 99 S.Ct. 2993 (1979), Mr. Justice Blackmun said:

> For we also cannot deny that, 114 years after the close of the War Between the States and nearly 100 years after *Strauder*, racial and other forms of discrimination still remain a fact of life, in the administration of justice as in our society as a whole.

This was not a startling or unusual statement. Similar pronouncements have issued on countless occasions from the media, the pulpits of every church, and the courts; and, in many instances, the police have been the special target of criticism. See, *e.g.*, J. Decker, *Police Sensitivity and Responsiveness to Minority Community Needs: A Critical Assessment*, 12 Valparaiso Law Review 467 (1978). It is unlikely that any juror could have avoided the influences of these constant reiterations.

In the light of all this what calumny did the young prosecuting attorney utter which deprived petitioner of his constitutional right to due process? He suggested that the jury might take into consideration the fact that petitioner and the police witness were high school classmates and members of the same race. The majority say that this attempt to refute the defendant's claim of frame-up and eliminate any possible claim of racial prejudice created a "distinct risk of stirring racially prejudiced attitudes." I disagree. Unless mere reference to the obvious fact that both petitioner and the police officer were black is prejudicial per se, *but see Iva Ikuko Toguri D'Aquino v. United States,* 192 F.2d 338, 371 (9th Cir. 1951), the prosecutor's remarks were not of such a nature as to foment racial prejudice against anyone.

It may be that if this were an appeal from one of our own district courts, we would find the prosecutor's comments to be a digression from the proof. However, "not every trial error or infirmity which might call for application of supervisory powers correspondingly constitutes a 'failure to observe that fundamental fairness essential to the very concept of justice.'" *Donnelly v. DeChristoforo,* 416 U.S. 637 (1974). Unless there has been a "denial of fundamental fairness, shocking to the universal sense of justice," *Betts v. Brady,* 316 U.S. 455 (1942), this Court should not interfere with the state's conduct of a criminal trial. When such denials occur, proof of their existence does not require erudite discussions of such things as group lines, frequencies, and percentages. I dissent.

Notes and Questions

1. McFarland was sentenced to a prison term of eight years to life for selling $450 worth of heroin to an undercover police officer. Does that sentence seem disproportionately severe? The crime did not involve physical violence, such as rape or murder, or immediate danger to others, such as arson, yet it received a sentence equal in severity to them. Does the sentence reflect society's attempt to take a hard line in the "war on drugs" more than an attempt to mete out exact justice to McFarland?

Should McFarland be given the "benefit of the doubt" on the question whether the prosecutor's statements were unfair *because* of the stiff sentence? Note that the only evidence against him is Officer Dorman's testimony. She takes no significant personal risk: If the jury decides that she lied, the only consequence will be that McFarland is acquitted and *not* that she has any risk of being indicted for perjury. But if the jury decides she was telling the truth—*and* if in fact she was lying—McFarland goes to prison for eight years to life.

2. Judge Van Graafeiland, dissenting, said that "mere reference to the obvious fact that both petitioner and the police officer were black" is not prejudicial *per se*. Do you agree?

3. Judge Van Graafeiland also observes that he might have agreed with Judge Newman had the case come to the Second Circuit as an appeal from one of the federal district courts. A United States Court of Appeals, he argues, should be far more hesitant to "interfere with the state's conduct of a criminal trial" using the writ of habeas corpus.

His hesitancy stems from the fact that the federal government and the states function as separate sovereign entities, except insofar as the Constitution of the United States imposes restraints and obligations which states have agreed will bind them by virtue of their ratification of the Constitution. The cases Judge Van Graafeiland cites are those in which a petitioner has asked a federal court to issue a writ of habeas corpus freeing the petitioner from illegal custody by a *state* official. The federal writ of habeas corpus serves, amongst other purposes, to commence an inquiry by a federal court into a claim of illegality in the detention of the petitioner by a state.

Whether Judge Van Graafeiland's application of the law of habeas corpus to McFarland's conviction should persuade us is a complicated matter we shall not address.[5] It is worthwhile, however, to note a theme found by one historian of habeas, which is similar to Justice Stone's remarks on plain error quoted in *Rojas*:[6]

> The writ's greatness derives from its function of inquiring into the legality of an individual's confinement. Although the definition of 'legality' has changed to meet the demands of a developing concept of liberty, the purpose of the writ has remained the same for several

---

[5] See P. Bator, P. Mishkin, D. Shapiro, H. Wechsler, Hart and Wechsler's The Federal Courts and the Federal System, ch. 10 (2d ed. 1973); R. Sokol, Federal Habeas Corpus, (2d ed. 1969).

[6] W. Duker, A Constitutional History of Habeas Corpus 3 (1980).

hundred years. Its purpose is neither to compensate the prisoner for past injustice nor to penalize the policeman or judge whose behavior gives rise to the proceeding. Further, it is not concerned with the correction of all errors preceding the challenged confinement. Rather, the purpose of habeas corpus is to insure the integrity of the process resulting in imprisonment. Although it is put into operation by a particular prisoner, whose incentive is his own release, its objective is institutional reform. Habeas corpus is the structural reform mechanism of the criminal justice system, functioning to provide an avenue to vindicate substantive rights.

4. Judge Newman agrees that some race-conscious arguments are permissible. In *Haynes*, defense counsel attacked identification testimony on the ground that an eyewitness, being white, was unlikely to be able to discern distinguishing characteristics of the face of the accused, who was black. Judge Newman reasoned that these race-conscious remarks were neutral, "since presumably an argument could be made with equal force that a Black eyewitness would have difficulty discerning the features of a White criminal." Do you agree with the reasoning?

What if an argument could *not* be made with equal force that a black eyewitness would have difficulty discerning the features of a white criminal? Suppose psychological and sociological evidence demonstrated that black eyewitnesses are just as able as white witnesses to discern the features of a white criminal. Should that be relevant?

Suppose you are the attorney for a black who is accused of armed robbery. A white eyewitness has testified for the prosecution that he saw your client from across the street fleeing the scene of the crime. You are convinced that your client was not at the scene of the crime, and that he is a victim of misidentification. If the psychological and sociological literature shows that white witnesses are unlikely to discern distinguishing characteristics of the face of a black person, why *can't* you introduce such an argument to discredit the prosecution's witness? Is the argument race-conscious, hence prejudicial? If the scientific literature does not show a comparable disability on the part of black witnesses, could you bring up the point to impeach a white witness?

5. In the hypothetical in Question 4, assume the trial judge rules in your favor on the general point that the race-conscious argument is permissible. Should you be allowed to raise it for the first time during your closing argument? That is when Prosecutor Pappalardo raised his own race-conscious argument in *McFarland*.

What is the race-conscious "argument" after all? Is it an argument? A presumption? Doesn't its argumentative validity depend upon its truthfulness? Isn't the argument permissible *only* if the relevant psychological and sociological literature supports the underlying generalization that white witnesses have difficulty discerning facial characteristics of black persons?

If we are talking about *facts*—psychological characteristics that are or are not true of persons—then how could the matter fairly be brought up in closing argument? During the attorneys' summation at the close of a trial, it is impermissible to bring up new evidence. The summation is what its name implies: summation of and "fair comment" upon evidence brought out at trial. Isn't the proper time and place to introduce facts the trial itself and not closing argument?

On the other hand, shouldn't counsel be allowed in their closing arguments to appeal to generalizations that "everybody knows"? The jury is, after all, supposed to use "common sense." Shouldn't counsel be allowed to appeal to it?

6. Assuming we conclude that the generalizations are facts that must be introduced into evidence, the proper way would be to put an expert on the stand—a sociologist or psychologist—to testify about the generalization. Then opposing counsel could present evidence rebutting the testimony of the expert. Or, opposing counsel could present evidence that *despite* the generalization, *this particular witness* does not have the disability. For example, the witness could be asked to look at the audience at the trial, then close his eyes and describe the facial characteristics and differences between two black persons seated in the audience.

Isn't it fair that opposing counsel should get a chance to rebut a proposition based on expertise, and to show that the race-conscious characteristic raised at trial does not happen to be true for this witness?

Would it not have been much easier for Judge Newman to hold simply that race-conscious arguments can be made during closing arguments so long as the prosecutor, at the trial, establishes through expert testimony the empirical and statistical soundness of the race-conscious argument? Of course, "expert testimony" has a notorious reputation for being unhelpful. Is it not true that you can often find an "expert" to assert any side of any proposition?[7]

7. What argument does Judge Newman call "completely illogical"? What premises does Judge Newman assign to the argument? Starting from these premises, is the argument illogical? Does Judge Newman come to agree that the argument is logical? Shouldn't Judge Newman have attacked the premises? How? Does Judge Kearse attack them?

8. Why should the prosecutor's *reference* to the defendant's race influence the jury the way Judge Newman imagines? Isn't the jury *looking at* the defendant? Surely the jury isn't being told something *new* about the defendant by the prosecutor (unlike *Rojas*).

9. Judge Newman finds it "outrageous" to think that across-group police officers would testify falsely. Isn't he *compelled* to that conclusion by the very premises that he set up in the first place, that across-group accusers might testify falsely to the same extent that within-group helpers might testify falsely? Why, then, does he suddenly find the conclusion outrageous when he focuses on the police, but not when he focuses on the likes of McFarland and Singletary?

10. Was the state *lucky* that it lost this case on appeal? Suppose it had won on the

---

[7] According to John Langbein: "I sometimes serve as an expert in trust and pension cases, and I have experienced the subtle pressures to join the team—to shade one's views, to conceal doubt, to overstate nuance, to downplay weak aspects of the case that one has been hired to bolster. Nobody likes to disappoint a patron; and beyond this psychological pressure is the financial inducement." Langbein, *The German Advantage in Civil Procedure,* 52 U. Chi. L. Rev. 823, 835 (1985). Elaborating on the difference between the American system and that practiced on the European continent, Langbein writes: "Experts help courts draw inferences based upon specialized knowledge—for example, inferring speed from skid marks or paternity from genetic evidence. In any legal system, courts will rely upon expert assistance in evaluating such evidence. Continental legal systems diverge sharply from ours on how to select and instruct experts. In our system, adversary selection and instruction of partisan experts is the overwhelmingly dominant pattern. In Continental systems, including the German, judicial control of fact-gathering leads to court selection and instruction of neutral experts." Langbein, *Trashing The German Advantage,* 82 Nw. U.L. Rev. 766, 775 (1988).

ground that Prosecutor Pappalardo's remarks were permissibly race-conscious. Wouldn't that open the door for defendants in all future cases involving across-group accusing police officers to argue that the police officers are probably lying? Wouldn't that hurt law-enforcement much more than the single loss would ever hurt the state in the *McFarland* case? Does this explain why Judge Newman did not say, as he could, that McFarland was unconstitutionally deprived of the opportunity to test the truthfulness of Officer Dorman?

11. Imagine the following conversation between Pappalardo and his associates in the District Attorney's office prior to the McFarland trial:

> PROSECUTOR PAPPALARDO. Obviously we're going to put on an accusing witness—Officer Dorman—and the defense is going to put on a helpful witness—probably his friend Singletary. But our witness is a within-group accusing witness who is inherently more credible. If McFarland wants a witness that would match ours in credibility, he's going to have to call an across-group helpful witness.
>
> ASSISTANT PROSECUTOR. But how can McFarland do that? If his friend Singletary was there at the scene, he has to call Singletary. He can't call somebody else. He can't go out and get a friend of his who is white and suborn him by inducing him to commit perjury. He's stuck with Singletary because Singletary was there.
>
> PROSECUTOR PAPPALARDO. Fine. That's McFarland's problem. If Singletary were white, McFarland would be better off. But he's black, so McFarland is in trouble. We were very smart to get blacks on the police force, and now we're reaping the benefits of that policy. Our arresting officer is black and we can tell the jury that they can rely on her testimony because she is black and the defendant is black.
>
> ASSISTANT PROSECUTOR. Is that a fair argument for us to make?
>
> PROSECUTOR PAPPALARDO. It's our job to argue as strongly as possible for conviction. We just make our best arguments. The rest is up to the jury.

Has our imaginary Pappalardo given a complete and satisfactory answer to the Assistant Prosecutor's question?

12. Was justice done to the State? To McFarland?

Comment on Justice and Common Sense

The prosecutor in *McFarland* told the jurors: "You use your common sense to think about that." The "common sense" the prosecutor wanted the jurors to use—the argument implicit in his appeal to "common sense," but which he did not wish to spell out—suggests the following propositions:

(1) Officer Dorman and McFarland were classmates (knew each other) in high school; both are black.

(2) If you knew nothing about two people except that they were high school classmates, you would bet that they feel well disposed toward each other; similarly, if you knew nothing about two people but that they are "members" (already a loaded word) of the same race, you assume they have a disposition not to make accusations against each other of the sort Officer Dorman made against McFarland.

(3) The dispositions stemming from her two "memberships"—in McFarland's high school class and his race—affected Officer Dorman as she testified.

(4) Hence, Officer Dorman's "memberships" enhance the credibility of her accusations against McFarland.

Assuming these four propositions present a fair version of the prosecutor's hidden argument, we can learn several lessons about common sense by closely studying the propositions.

1. Ambiguity[8]

The propositions are riddled with ambiguity. In her concurrence Judge Kearse underscores one: Did the prosecutor mean to say that the disposition not to make accusations against a member of one's own race affects only black people or people of all races? Would it be better to substitute a different expression for "black people"—"people of any race who have experienced oppression"? Judge Newman emphasizes a second ambiguity: Does the disposition not to make accusations govern true accusations or false? And a third: Are people *less* disposed to make accusations against members of the same race (feeling solidarity with them), or *more* disposed (feeling threatened by their unlawful or shameful behavior)?

Can you think of any appeal to common sense that does *not* contain ambiguities? The prosecutor in *McFarland* undoubtedly had the ability to resolve the ambiguities by spelling out his argument. Yet a person may choose to maintain ambiguities for one of at least two major reasons.

First, one might want to make an argument people resent acknowledging to be persuasive. The prosecutor's first ambiguity—black people versus people of all races—conceals an argument of this sort. People hearing an explicit argument might very well act contrary to feelings they would have had were the argument implicit. They seize the occasion of explicit argument to show both themselves and others that they have resisted the argument. Ambiguity allows one to make arguments people believe but do not like hearing. Perhaps a good term for this is an *insinuating argument*.

Second, one might want to make an argument which must compete with an opposing or collateral argument that also makes sense. Consider whether people are well or ill disposed towards members of the same race who are an embarrassment. Both positions likely reflect the real dispositions of a variety of people. They might even reflect dispositions in conflict all at once within a single person. Yet the prosecutor's ambiguity allows him to ignore competing arguments.

2. Stereotyping

More troubling than the ambiguities in the prosecutor's hidden propositions is the implicit condition that we know nothing about Dorman and McFarland but certain stere-

---

[8] A good way to remember the difference between "ambiguity" and "vagueness" is to note that nearly everyone's first name is ambiguous. The names Paul and Dorothy refer ambiguously to many persons with those names. There is nothing "vague" about a first name, but it is "ambiguous." On the other hand, good examples of "vagueness" are attributes, such as heavy, light, tall, short, wide, and narrow.

otypes—high school classmate, black—about which common sense is supposed to draw conclusions. Some of us have fond feelings about the "idea" of "high school classmate." But others of us don't have such feelings, and we probably can recall some high school classmates whom we would rather not recall. Moreover, does fond feeling about the idea, assuming we have it, tell us about actual feelings we have toward individual classmates? Does it hold up in every situation? Surely, class reunions are calculated to incite such feelings. But would the feelings matter much if the classmates were competing for something they both want? If the classmate had an official duty?

The crucial problem with "common sense" reasoning about single characteristics such as "high school classmate" or "black" is that it lulls us into believing we know something about a person or situation which we do not, in fact, know. Officer Dorman may have hated McFarland in high school. Or she may not have known him. She may be more concerned with obtaining convictions of those she arrests than about racial affiliation. To say that people have positive associations surrounding the word "high school classmate" is not to say that they feel fond of this or that person who happens to be a classmate, especially since reasoning according to the naked characteristic tells us nothing about the context in which we are supposed to be judging the effect of the characteristic.

Even if the context is appropriate—and it is dubious whether membership in the same high school class would affect an arresting officer one way or the other—the effect of most characteristics is only statistical. Where it is the *effect* of a characteristic, not the characteristic itself, which is at issue, then the best we can say is that occurrence of the characteristic makes incidence of an effect likely. This statement might be enough to convince us of the incidence of an effect on the basis of the occurrence of the characteristic. But we could just as well insist on further information about the effect itself that would help us judge whether or not the effect in fact follows as it does in the majority of the occurrences of the characteristic.

So, we should want to know additional facts about the relationship between Dorman and McFarland in high school, if the prosecutor really wants to get into it. To say they were high school classmates is to pose a question rather than to give an answer. Yet "common sense" works the other way.

3. Suppression of Conflict

Common sense assumes a "sense" that is "common." Common sense assumes that any conflict between two persons involves one person whose vision of justice and whose behavior accord with the vision and behavior of the great mass of right-thinking people, and another whose vision and behavior do not. Often—often enough to cast doubt on the utility of the assumption—conflict results from competing visions of justice, each held by large, but not dominant, masses of people. It may be valid to speak of "common senses" in a vast, complex and heterogeneous society such as ours, but surely not "common sense," at least not in cases which lead to sustained conflict which cannot be resolved without litigation. One might even conclude that cases in which it is valid to speak of a single "common sense" get resolved short of litigation, so that every reported opinion deals with a conflict which common sense failed to resolve. The lawyer's expertise takes over, one might say, where common sense fails.

Coda

The three characteristics of "common sense"—ambiguity, stereotyping, and suppression of conflict—share a theme in common. The appeal to "common sense" is a rhetorical device by which people making arguments at once refuse to present further information about persons or events and either mask or excuse the refusal. "Common sense" can be ignorance applauding itself. It is thinking according to stereotype rather than real deeds and actual character. It suppresses the individuality of the persons and events whose "characteristics" common sense asks us to evaluate. Instead of learning what actually animated Officer Dorman, we are content to speculate about her propensity to lie because she has the same race as McFarland or because they were high school classmates.

On the other hand, we cannot avoid using common sense arguments. Every description of a person or event is stereotype. The purpose of description is to place the person or event into categories which the listener knows from common experiences have nothing to do with the described person or event. Each person or event is descriptively unique only up to the intersection of many such categories. Persons and events cannot be descriptively unique in the way they may possibly be unique in reality. We have juries precisely to give trials a good dose of this sort of common sense. The classic justification for having juries is to inject community standards of sense and reasonableness into the adjudicatory process.

The evil of the appeal to common sense, therefore, cannot lie in the common sense, since common sense is an inevitable component of argument. Is not the evil of the appeal to common sense the appeal itself, since the purpose of the appeal is to stop listeners from looking further for descriptive categories, to distract them from difficulties hovering around the margin of a problem, to present hidden arguments, or to avoid dealing with opposed and collateral arguments? A juror may already know something based on "common sense," but as soon as an attorney at trial explicitly appeals to this "common sense," is there not danger that it will be legitimated and elevated beyond the point of simply reflecting mass thinking? Might it not be elevated to the point where it reflects mass unthinking?

People v. Thomas
514 N.Y.S.2d 91

Supreme Court, Appellate Division,
Second Department
April 6, 1987

Phillip L. Weinstein, New York City (Catherine Grad, New York City, of counsel), for appellant.

Dexter Thomas, pro se.

Elizabeth Holtzman, Dist. Atty. (Barbara D. Underwood, Rosalyn H. Richter, Brooklyn and Richard J. Cutler, New York City, of counsel), for respondent.

Before WEINSTEIN, J.P., and RUBIN,

KOOPER and SULLIVAN, JJ.

MEMORANDUM BY THE COURT.

Appeal by the defendant from a judgment of the Supreme Court, Kings County (Schwartzwald, J.), rendered January 4, 1984, convicting him of criminal possession of a weapon in the third degree, upon a jury verdict, and imposing sentence.

ORDERED that the judgment is reversed, as

a matter of discretion in the interest of justice, and a new trial is ordered.

The defendant, a black man, was arrested by three white undercover police officers after they approached him on the street in a predominantly black and Hispanic neighborhood and observed him place his hand on the butt of a gun secreted in his waistband. The defendant was subsequently charged with criminal possession of a weapon in the third degree. At the trial, the defendant took the stand in his own behalf and testified that he found the gun in a nearby playground and picked it up with the intention of discarding it. He further testified that when the undercover officers—who had not identified themselves—approached him, he believed them to be muggers and placed his hand on the weapon to discourage them from pursuing him. Moreover, although the officers testified that they were wearing badges around their necks during the arrest, the defendant testified that he observed no badges and that it was only after the officers had handcuffed him that he discovered they were policemen.

The defendant's principal defense, as charged to the jury by the court, was the contention that his possession of the weapon had been temporary and innocent. Nevertheless, the prosecutrix, both in her cross-examination of the defendant and subsequently in summation, repeatedly sought to impeach the veracity of the defendant's contention that he believed the arresting officers to be muggers by referring to the officer's race. The prosecutrix first asked defendant, "[w]hen you saw two white guys with badges hanging around their necks jump out of an unmarked car, is it your testimony that you thought they were muggers?" Continuing, the prosecutrix again stressed the race of the officers by asking defendant what he did when he "saw these two white police officers jump out of an unmarked car." She then asked the defendant "[h]as it happened before that three white guys in an unmarked police car pulled up to you and jumped out and jumped you and knocked you down to the ground." The prosecutrix further pursued this line of inquiry by asking the defendant, "[i]s it your testimony that you have been mugged by three white guys in this neighborhood?" and questioning whether he believed "that these three white guys" were going to shoot him. Thereafter, in her summation, the prosecutrix returned to this theme, arguing that, "I would submit to you that

if three white males jumped out of a green Plymouth Volarie [*sic*] in this neighborhood and ran up to you you might tend to think these are not muggers, these could be police officers." Finally, in one of her concluding summation comments, the prosecutrix again urged the jury to consider that when the defendant "saw these three white guys running up to him . . . he was not holding on to his gun or trying to make them think it was a gun or knife to protect himself." The defendant was subsequently convicted of criminal possession of a weapon in the third degree and now appeals. We conclude that the aforementioned remarks deprived the defendant of a fair trial and reverse.

The inference to be drawn from the prosecutrix's thematic references to the officers' race is that a black man in a black neighborhood cannot conceivably be the victim of a crime committed by a white man. Such an appeal to the jury can serve no purpose other than to arouse racially prejudiced attitudes and to undermine the jury's dispassionate and objective consideration of the evidence adduced at trial. Indeed, as the United States Court of Appeals for the Second Circuit has aptly observed, "[e]ven a reference that is not derogatory may carry impermissible connotations, or may trigger prejudiced responses in listeners that the speaker might neither have predicted nor intended" (*McFarland v. Smith,* 611 F.2d 414, 417). This court, moreover, has repeatedly condemned, as divisive and inimical to both democratic and logical principles, arguments which encourage the jury to weigh the evidence by considering the race of a particular witness. As we stated nearly a quarter century ago, "[t]he vice of such an argument is not only that it is predicated on a false and illogical premise but more important it is divisive: it seeks to separate the racial origins of witnesses in the minds of the jury, and to encourage the weighing of evidence on the basis of racial similarity or dissimilarity of the witnesses. The argument offends the democratic and logical principle that race, creed or nationality, in themselves, provide no reason for believing or disbelieving a witness' testimony." *People v. Hearns,* 18 A.D.2d 173.

The prosecutrix's comments impermissibly encouraged the jury to weigh the credibility of the defendant's testimony by considering the race of the arresting officers, and, accordingly, we conclude that the judgment of conviction must be reversed. Although the defendant failed to register objections to the prosecutrix's comments in this case, a review of the errors in the interest of justice is warranted.

Finally, in light of our disposition, we need not address the defendant's remaining contentions.

Notes and Questions

1. The jury in Brooklyn convicted Thomas of criminal possession of a weapon in the third degree, under New York Penal Law § 265.02. The Grand Jury had indicted Thomas under Subdivision Four—possessing a loaded firearm. Thomas apparently did not contest three major premises or, "elements," of the crime: that (1) he was in possession, (2) of a firearm, (3) that was loaded. He testified instead that "he found the gun in a nearby playground and picked it up with the intention of discarding it." Thomas' trial lawyer knew that the judge would instruct the jury to acquit Thomas if they found his possession of the weapon to be "temporary and innocent."[9] To be guilty of criminal possession, judges in New York have reasoned, one must *intend* to possess the weapon illegally—to keep it indefinitely and for the reason that it is a weapon.[10] Intention is a fourth element of the crime, the sole element Thomas contested.

While Subdivision Four does exempt possession of a loaded firearm in the home or place of business, it says nothing about "temporary and innocent" possession—nothing about the element of intention.[11] Though the statute nowhere mentions "intention," every judge in the United States would read it into the statute. Legislators presumably did *not* use the word, because they know how judges read statutes. One simply cannot understand what legislators mean to say in statutes without referring to a host of rules, canons and traditions judges have created in the course of reading and enforcing statutes. Lawyers find these rules, canons and traditions in opinions such as *Thomas,* but also in the unwritten lore of litigation. If legislators object to a rule, canon or tradition, then they must explicitly disavow it; otherwise judges will assume that the legislators do not object to (or even

---

[9] *See* People v. Pendergraft, 50 A.D.2d 531, 374 N.Y.S.2d 669 (1975) (trial judge must charge jury on the justification of "temporary and lawful" possession even when defense doesn't request the charge).

[10] *See* People v. La Pella, 272 N.Y. 81, 4 N.E.2d 943 (1936). Though *La Pella* says that the defense is a "matter of policy," courts have recently noticed that the "innocent nature of the possession negates both the criminal act of possession and the intent with which the act is undertaken when intent is an element of the crime." People v. Almodovar, 62 N.Y.2d 126, 130, 476 N.Y.S.2d 95, 97, 464 N.E.2d 463 (1984). Does the change in reasoning matter?

[11] It also says nothing about exempting possession of a firearm which is licensed, another instance of "innocent," if not "temporary," possession. The licensing statute, New York Penal Law § 400.00, does not explicitly shield licensed possessors from § 265. However, Subdivision 17 of § 400.00 provides that § 265 shall not apply to an offense which also constitutes a violation of § 400.00 by a person holding an otherwise valid license.

support) their perpetuating the rule, canon or tradition.

Even where legislators do disavow a rule, canon or tradition, judges have ways of resisting—of softening or transforming—the disavowal. After all, legislators depend on judges to enforce their statutes.[12] Beyond confirmation of judges who will be faithful to their program, legislators can do little to ensure enforcement of statutes judges consider abhorrent. Since judges in the United States tend to be drawn from the same political strata as legislators, judicial resistance tends to be confined to extraordinary legislation enacted at moments of crisis.

2. Was Thomas' testimony that he believed the undercover officers to be muggers relevant to his defense that his possession of the gun was "temporary and innocent"? (Hint: Would a person whose possession of a weapon begins as "temporary and innocent" subsequently be permitted to use the weapon? If so, under what circumstances?[13] If the questions the prosecutor directed to Thomas about his testimony were not relevant to undermining the theory of the defense, could the questions have nonetheless been relevant? To what? (Hint: Who is the defense's chief witness? How can the jury assess the credibility of that witness?)

3. Thomas subjected himself to a blistering cross-examination when he took the witness stand.[14] Note how cleverly the prosecutor asked him leading questions.[15] She asked, for example:

> Has it happened before that three white guys in an unmarked police car pulled
> up to you and jumped out and jumped you and knocked you down to the ground?

Wasn't this a loaded question? Isn't the prosecutor supposed to try to trip up Thomas, to show the implausibility of his testimony, to convince the jury he is lying? Is it her job to do that? Or, does a public prosecutor have responsibilities different from those of a private attorney—responsibilities to Thomas?

4. Suppose that all twelve persons on the jury in the *Thomas* case were black. Could one then say that the prosecutor appealed to racism?

---

[12] The fact that legislatures depend on courts for enforcement of statutes has led one legal theorist to assert that statutes are mere suggestions—or starting-points—for the real creation of binding legal norms, which takes place in the courthouse during litigation, not in the legislature enacting statutes. See J. GRAY, THE NATURE and SOURCES OF THE LAW (1909).

[13] Amazingly, no case in New York so far has decided this question. A New York court has held that unlawful possession includes possession for the purpose of self-defense, but only incidental to disarming an assailant in the course of a fight. *See* People v. Pendergraft, 50 A.D.2d 531, 374 N.Y.S.2d 669 (1975). Thomas' incident was different. (How?) As one studies-and-practices law (they always go together) one meets up with lots of questions that seem terribly important and screamingly obvious, to which neither statutes nor case-law supplies an answer. It is this experience, more than volumes of jurisprudence, which exposes the artificiality of the positivist claim that law is the command of the sovereign.

[14] Thomas did not have to. In a criminal trial, the defendant has the right to remain silent and the prosecutor cannot argue to the jury that the defendant's silence should count against the defendant. (Though it may seem obvious, it's worth pinning down exactly why Thomas took the stand.)

[15] On cross-examination, an attorney is entitled to ask leading questions. This gives cross-examination more "bite" than direct examination. On the other hand, cross-examination is constrained: A witness can only be cross-examined as to testimony that came up in direct examination.

5. In *McFarland* Judge Newman said that a race-conscious argument about the reliability of identification was permissible, because it works both ways. Suppose in *Thomas* an unmarked police car in a *white* neighborhood pulled up to a white pedestrian who happened to have a concealed gun, and three blacks jumped out of the car. Suppose the white pedestrian is charged with unlawful possession of a firearm, and his defense is that he thought the three blacks were muggers. In fact, they were police.

(a) Could the prosecutor fairly argue that the defendant had no substantial basis for assuming that the three officers were muggers?

(b) Could the defendant fairly point out to the jury that the three men who jumped out of the car were *blacks*? Or would that be a race-conscious argument like the one in *Thomas*, hence unconstitutional?

(c) Would the defendant's argument—that the three men seemed to be muggers—be at all convincing if the defendant were barred from pointing out that the three men were blacks? If your answer is "no," then what is racist about the argument?

(d) Does the element of racism consist in the fact that it is *unlikely* that three blacks jumping out of an unmarked car in a white neighborhood are police officers, whereas it is *likely* that three whites jumping out of an unmarked car in a black neighborhood are police officers? If your answer is "yes," how could the system be remedied? If it is a fact that most police officers are white, how could we ever get the mirror-image case imagined in this Question? Further, isn't the idea that we need mirror-image equality just as unfair here as it was when we examined it in *McFarland*?

6. What, after all, was the prosecutor supposed to do in *Thomas*? Not mention that the three police officers were white? She referred to the neighborhood experience; presumably, she was counting on the fact that the jurors at the trial were familiar with the very neighborhood where Thomas was arrested. She made pointed references to "this neighborhood." Wasn't she counting on the knowledge of the jury that in this neighborhood, it was indeed unlikely that three white men jumping out of a green Plymouth automobile would be muggers? And what about the green Plymouth? Wouldn't most people in the neighborhood be expected to know what kind of unmarked cars the police drive around in? (Often the police department buys cars in large numbers and soon it becomes common knowledge what kind of cars to "look out for" among street-wise people.) Isn't the prosecutor's stress upon *this neighborhood* and *three white guys* and *green Plymouth* an attempt to demonstrate that Thomas is not credible?

7. Recall that after *McFarland* we speculated that the prosecution might well have been *relieved* that it lost the case. Do you think the prosecution in *Thomas* was relieved to lose? If not, is it possible that there is a deep-seated dissimilarity between the two cases rooted in the concept of justice? What would that be?

Consider what would change if instead of "black" and "white" in *Thomas* we substituted the words "rich" and "poor." Suppose three "poor" guys get out of a green Chevy in a rich neighborhood and go up to a rich pedestrian who is carrying a concealed weapon. The three poor guys turn out to be undercover police officers. The pedestrian defends on the ground that he thought they were muggers. Should the defense attorney be barred from arguing that the three guys who jumped out of the car appeared poor, and that the defendant was rich? If not, why is the prosecutor barred from using race in *Thomas*? Isn't race intrinsically part of the evidence she needs to demonstrate that Thomas is lying? If so, in what *sense* is race part of the evidence? That *black persons lie* (as in *McFarland*)? Or, is the prosecutor using race in a race-neutral way?

8. What does the court hold in *Thomas*? What is the court's reasoning? Thomas may be prosecuted again. Suppose that the prosecutor in the second trial attempts to introduce evidence about Thomas' actual state of mind when the three undercover police officers approached him (assuming Thomas repeats his testimony that he thought the officers to be muggers). Would the trial judge, attempting to follow the Second Department's opinion, permit the prosecutor to introduce such evidence? If she would not be permitted, could she effectively contest Thomas' claim? If permitted, what sorts of evidence?

9. Though Thomas' trial lawyer had not objected to the prosecutor's argument, the Second Department overturned Thomas' conviction using the well-established doctrine in New York practice that the Appellate Division in its "discretion" may reverse a judgment and grant a new trial "in the interests of justice," even where the appellant has failed to preserve error by lodging an objection.[16] Is the case for ignoring the failure of Thomas' attorney to object stronger or weaker than the case in *Rojas*?

10. The police arrested Thomas and the Grand Jury indicted him while an indictment against him for attempted murder was pending. The second trial for criminal possession was to take place while he was serving 12 and 1/2 to 25 years for the attempted murder. Thomas' sentence in the first criminal possession trial was 3 to 6 years not to run concurrently with the sentence for attempted murder. Thomas pleaded guilty and admitted to criminal possession before a second trial. The judge imposed a sentence of 3 to 6 years, this time to run concurrently with the sentence for attempted murder.[17]

11. A newspaper account of the *Thomas* decision reports that an official in the Brooklyn District Attorney's office, "who asked not to be identified, said the trial prosecutor, who is black, made the comments to attack Thomas' credibility and not to appeal to racial prejudice."[18] If we knew the race of the trial prosecutor (not to mention her sex), might that affect our view of the propriety of her questions and arguments about the race of the undercover police officers? Should it? How might you use *McFarland* in answering these questions?

12. Note well the anonymity towards which the actors in Thomas' drama were striving. The opinion does not name the officers. Thomas is "the defendant." The prosecutor, at least, is "the prosecutrix", but even she doesn't have a name. The spokesperson for the District Attorney's office asked the newspaper reporter not to identify her. The opinion itself is a "Memorandum by the Court," not an opinion *for* the court signed by a single

---

[16] *See* WEINSTEIN, KORN AND MILLER, NEW YORK CIVIL PRACTICE—CPLR § 5501.11.

[17] This information was obtained in a telephone conversation by one of the authors with Catherine Grad, one of Thomas' attorneys. New York Penal Law § 265.02 makes criminal possession of a weapon in the third degree a class D felony. Articles 55 and 60 of the New York Penal Law set out sentencing.

[18] NEWSDAY, April 4, 1987 at p. 9, col. 2.

judge.[19] The court demands at least partial anonymity (respecting race) for the officers who arrested Thomas.

Many participants in the legal system strive not to be visible to people outside the system. Why? Recall that *justice,* not whom she weighs in the balance, is blindfolded. Perhaps people ought to be "dispassionate and objective" (as the judges in *Thomas* wanted the jury to be). But should they be anonymous?

13. Assuming the facts of *Thomas,* suppose the case occurred 50 years ago in the deep South. Suppose that instead of the prosecutor wanting to bring out the fact that the three men who jumped out of the car were white, the *defendant* wants to mention that fact. The black defendant wants the jury to know that the three men were *white* because he would then be able to show that he had a reasonable fear of physical brutality. Should a reviewing court hold that any attempt by defense counsel to introduce the color of the three men who jumped out of the car is racially prejudicial evidence and should be disallowed?

14. Was justice done to Thomas? To the People?

---

[19] Notice, as you read appellate opinions, when judges sign them and when they attribute them to the court ("per curiam" or "memorandum by the court"). The tradition of opinions for the court signed by a single judge is American and recent. *See* J. Dawson, The Oracles of the Law 85–88 (1968).

Exercise

Imagine that you are representing a black defendant who is charged with aggravated burglary (a felony) and receiving stolen goods (a misdemeanor). Suppose the prosecutor makes an offer of proof of a Police Department Study of the neighborhood where the crime took place; the study contains statistics of crimes according to race. You and the prosecutor meet in front of the judge, out of the hearing of the jury. The judge asks you if you object to the introduction of this evidence.

The relevant facts of your case are as follows. A burglary occurred in a poor-neighborhood television store; a television set was taken, along with cash out of the cash register. The owner of the store was hit over the head and suffered a mild concussion. A man was seen running out of the store carrying a large box. It was dark, and two pedestrians, on the other side of the street, caught a glimpse of the man. The next evening, acting on a tip, the police obtained a search warrant for your client's apartment, knocked and entered. They found your client watching television. The TV set was the one that had been stolen. Your client said that, earlier that day, two men whom he had never before seen drove up in a Cadillac and offered to sell him the TV set for $100. He had $90 in cash on him and they accepted the $90 and gave him the set, which was boxed and brand new.

Your client was arrested for aggravated burglary and receiving stolen goods. The burglary charge is a felony with a five to ten year sentence. Receiving stolen goods is a misdemeanor with up to six months in prison and a fine.

There is an evidentiary rule of inference in your jurisdiction. It says that possession of stolen goods is prima facie evidence of the misdemeanor of knowingly receiving stolen goods to convict the defendant, unless he offers evidence to rebut the inference. Another rule says that possession of stolen goods is evidence that can be taken into account in determining whether the person in possession stole the goods.

Both eyewitnesses were called by the prosecution at the trial. One of them said he wasn't sure but he thought that the man running out of the store was white. The other also said he wasn't sure but he thought the man was black. Neither saw the face or any identifying characteristics, except that the man was of the same general height and build as the defendant. Your client told you that on the evening of the burglary he was asleep in his apartment. He had come home early from work and fallen asleep. He had no alibi witnesses.

In front of the judge, the prosecutor shows you the statistics she wants to introduce into evidence. The statistics relate to crimes in the poor neighborhood only, and of those crimes, only burglaries. They show that over the past ten years:

(1) 85% of all persons arrested for burglary were black.
(2) 80% of all persons convicted for burglary were black.
(3) The neighborhood population as a whole is 50% black, 50% white.
(4) 95% of all persons arrested for burglary were poor (as defined by national poverty standards).
(5) 90% of all persons convicted for burglary were poor.

The prosecutor argues that your client is poor (under the relevant definition) and black and lives in the neighborhood. Since the two eyewitnesses disagree as to the race of the burglar, the statistical evidence is offered to prove that the eyewitness who is more likely to be correct is the one who said he saw a black.

The first thing you ask the prosecutor is whether she has any more evidence that she is going to introduce for the state. She says she does not. You then make a motion for a directed verdict. You argue to the judge that the only evidence against your client consists of the following: the two eyewitnesses who disagree with each other, the fact that your client was found in possession of the stolen television set, the fact that your client lived in the neighborhood and was in the neighborhood on the night in question, and the statistics that the prosecutrix wants to introduce. Even if those statistics are introduced, you argue, there is not enough evidence to satisfy the state's burden of proving that this defendant committed the crime beyond a reasonable doubt.

The judge denies your motion on the ground that your client's possession of the television set, coupled with the prosecution's eyewitness and statistical evidence, are enough for the jury to convict the defendant unless the defendant persuades the jury that his story—about buying the TV set and being asleep at the time of the burglary—is true. You may, of course, choose not to put your client on the stand, as is his right. But then, if the jury's verdict is for conviction, the judge will let the verdict stand as meeting the evidentiary test of guilty beyond a reasonable doubt.

At this point, does it seem to you that the state's statistical evidence is a *crucial element* in the state's case? That without it there may be insufficient evidence as a matter of law to convict your client (i.e., that the judge ought to direct a verdict in your client's favor)? Whatever your conclusion, you know that it is important to keep the statistical evidence out of the case.

How about asking the prosecutor the following question: "Do you intend to introduce the statistics to show that one of the two eyewitnesses is lying?" While the prosecutor is framing an answer to your question, the judge asks you why you are asking that particular question. You reply: "Because if the statistics show that the likelihood of blacks committing burglaries is 80% and whites only 20%, then the witness who said the burglar is white should be given *greater* credibility. That witness, after all, is reporting a comparatively *rarer* event!"

How do you think the prosecutor will reply to your question and to what she has just heard you say to the judge? She might say: "No, I do not intend to introduce the statistics to show which witness is telling the truth. My argument, judge, is simply that the two eyewitnesses have cancelled each other out. They are both honest, they have both reported what they saw, and they disagree. The only reason I'm introducing the statistic is to get at the truth: was the man who robbed the TV store a black man or a white man? I want the jury to know that, in this neighborhood, there's an 80% chance, maybe a 90% chance, that the burglar was a black man and a poor man, like this defendant."

Has she completely answered the question you asked of her? Is it possible that one witness actually saw a black man and the other witness actually saw a white man? What does the word "actually" mean here? That the criminal was black (or white)? Or that the witnesses actually "saw" a black (or white) man? Is it not possible that a certain prejudice crept in to the vision of the eyewitnesses?

Is it not possible that, in dim light, one of the witnesses figured that he must be seeing a black man and hence his vision played a trick on him—he actually saw that which he theorized he would be seeing? Is it not possible, in other words, that the burglar was white, and that one eyewitness saw him as white, and the other eyewitness's theory got in the way of what he was seeing so that he "saw" a black man?

But doesn't this line of reasoning assume the very conclusion you want to prove? Isn't it just as possible that the burglar was black, one of the witnesses saw him as black, and the other eyewitness had a theory that the criminal must be white so he saw the criminal as white? Or is this *not* "just as possible"? What is the probability that, given an indistinct criminal, people on the street would assume that he was black? Isn't that probability related to the generally known statistics about crime in the neighborhood? In other words, if there is a preponderance of black crime in the neighborhood, then aren't eyewitnesses likely to be biased toward the black in "seeing" a fleeing criminal?

Are you happy with this conclusion? If in fact 80% of the burglaries in the neighborhood are committed by blacks, then isn't it reasonable to expect eyewitnesses to expect to see blacks fleeing from TV stores? Why is this "prejudice"? Why isn't it just the normal distribution of probabilities in that neighborhood?

Are you now happy with *this* conclusion? Or do you now want to look at the original statistics themselves? Could it be that many more blacks were arrested for crimes than whites because the police "saw" blacks as more likely to be criminals and hence arrested them more frequently? In other words, the very statistics that the prosecutor wants to use in this case may be the result of a prejudicial selection process!

Look at the statistics again. Out of 100 persons arrested for burglaries, 85 are black and 15 are white. But out of 100 convictions, 80 are black and 20 are white. Are these figures compatible? Yes, because the conviction rate overall is less than the arrest rate. You might have, for example, 100 persons arrested for burglaries, with the following breakdown:

> 85 blacks arrested
> 15 whites arrested
> 48 blacks convicted
> 12 whites convicted
> 40 persons either acquitted or never prosecuted

What do these statistics say to you? Do they say any or all of the following propositions?

(1) Out of the 40 persons who were either acquitted or never prosecuted, 37 were blacks, and only 3 were whites. This shows that the legal system is extremely fair to blacks.

(2) Only 48 out of 85 blacks who were arrested were convicted, for a conviction rate of only 52%. In contrast, 12 out of 15 whites who were arrested were convicted, for a conviction rate of 80%. This shows that the legal system is extremely fair to blacks.

(3) Police are much more suspicious of blacks than they are of whites, and are inclined to arrest many more innocent blacks than they are inclined to arrest innocent whites. This shows that the legal system is extremely unfair to blacks.

(4) If there is a constant chance—say, 3%—of innocent people being convicted, then the higher the proportion of arrests to convictions, the more likelihood there is of convicting innocent people. Since there is a higher proportion of blacks arrested per conviction than whites, the system is extremely unfair to blacks.

(5) The police don't "bother" whites unless they are pretty certain of criminal guilt. But the police "bother" blacks routinely, leading to many more arrests of blacks. This form of harassment, even if the blacks are eventually acquitted, shows that the system is extremely unfair to blacks.

After you read the first two propositions, were you inclined to say that the system is fair to blacks? Did reading the next three change your mind? Or did you come out even?

Now suppose the judge says to you: "Let's take the state's offer of proof item by item. Do you have any objection to the introduction of statistics numbered (3), (4), and (5)?" You have no objection; these appear neutral. (Should you have an objection?) Then the judge asks you about statistic (1). "Yes," you reply. "The fact that 85% of the people arrested for burglary were blacks simply shows prejudice on the part of the police. Nothing is proved by the fact that someone is arrested. Indeed, the next statistic shows that many blacks who are arrested are ultimately let go. So that proves that arrest statistics are unreliable."

The prosecutor then says: "If I leave out the arrest statistics and only prove up the conviction statistics, would you object to that? After all, conviction statistics are conviction statistics. There is no disputing their reliability. If 80% of convicted burglars are black, that means that 80% of burglars are black in this town—as proven by the highest authority we have, namely, the court."

Would you go along with the offer of proof of conviction statistics? Should you?

Suppose you object that *group* characteristics should not be attributed to individuals.

Even if blacks are more likely, in this neighborhood, to commit burglaries than are whites, that doesn't mean that *this defendant* committed a burglary. Right?

But don't we *always* attribute group characteristics to individuals whenever we use statistical evidence? Isn't that what statistics do?

How about omitting all statistical evidence? "Statistics lie," you might say to the court. "Let's only have *real* evidence, not statistical evidence!" What will the court say?

Shouldn't the court say something like the following: There is no such thing as real evidence. All evidence is fundamentally statistical. If an eyewitness sees Adams on the street, the eyewitness' testimony in reality is: "Whenever I see things on the street that bear a likeness to people I know—a likeness that I've observed over many years of observing people and drawing inferences—it usually happens that I am right when I identify those things as people I know, although the probability changes depending upon how many characteristics of those things that I am able to observe." That's just another way of assigning statistical probabilities to observations.

What if you reply: All right, Judge, but in this case the statistics have the effect of prejudicing the jury. By calling attention to race, the prosecutor might be signalling to the jury that it is all right for the jury to vote the way their prejudices tell them to vote. I did not object to the introduction of the statistic on poor people committing crimes, because as to that statistic, it had no real prejudicial value—many of the people on the jury are also poor But I do object to racial prejudice masquerading as statistics.

Yet you can well predict what the judge's answer will be. The judge will remind you of *McFarland*. In that case, race-conscious statistics that justifiably illuminated the evidence were perfectly proper to introduce at trial, so long as probative value outweighed prejudicial value. In the present case, since the statistic of convicted blacks is so high (80%), it helps the prosecution's case. The prosecution is attempting to show that the one eyewitness who said that the man running out of the store was white was probably wrong. It is critically important to the state to show that that eyewitness was probably wrong, because if the eyewitness were probably right, then this defendant would have to be acquitted. Since the evidence is critically important to the state, and since the evidence itself is not problematic (it is based on actual convictions), and since the statistic is so high (80%), its probative value far outweighs its prejudicial value, and hence it should be introduced into evidence.

How would you deal with *McFarland* here? Would you accept it and try a last-ditch argument? It is no good to repeat an argument that you've already made. Nor to rephrase a previous objection. Do you have any new arguments to make before the court rules on the prosecutor's offer of proof?

You have already objected to the arrest statistics. The prosecutor offers to leave those out if you will accept conviction statistics. Can you find anything wrong with using conviction statistics? Suppose the introduction of the conviction statistics in your case is the item that tips the balance, resulting in your client being convicted. What will then happen to the conviction statistics?

Suppose out of 100 persons convicted for burglary, 80 were black. Suppose this statistic is introduced at trial, and your client is convicted. Now the statistic will have to be revised for the next case. Now, out of 101 persons convicted for burglary, 81 were black. The conviction percentage has gone up slightly; now it is 80.1%. If in the next case the statistic is introduced and results in a conviction of a black defendant, the percentage will go up some more. It will keep going up after each conviction.

What's wrong with that? Shouldn't the conviction percentage go up if more blacks are convicted?

Recall our initial premise: It is the very introduction of the conviction statistic that tips the balance against your client. In short, his conviction has been brought about not by any real-world fact about his own case, but by the statistic. The statistic will keep going up the more it is used, until it gets over 90% and starts approaching 95%. People will believe that blacks are increasingly committing more crimes. And yet there will be no real-world evidence of such a proposition, because the accelerating conviction rate is a mere artifact of the introduction of the previous statistics!

Thus, you can argue to the judge that the introduction of the statistic becomes a self-fulfilling prophecy: Blacks are increasingly likely to be convicted for no reason other than the fact that we started with a statistic and kept introducing it in trial after trial as the statistic itself got higher and higher.

Suppose—since this is, after all, an exercise—that the prosecutor agrees with your argument! But now she reaches down deep and comes up with a last-ditch argument to beat yours. She says: "All right, you've proven that if the statistic is introduced in this trial and results in tipping the scales against the defendant, there is a danger that the new statistic—the 80.1% statistic—will be used in the next case, and in the case after that, and so forth. I concede that *future* cases may become contaminated. I concede that *future* cases could result in injustice due to the self-fulfilling prophecy that you have pointed out.

"But," she continues, "we can cross that bridge when we come to it. As far as *this* case is concerned, we took the statistic of 80% convictions out of the recent Police Department study of court records, and it has never been used before. It comes into this trial as a pure, uncontaminated figure of 80%. Your objection, counselor, is based on your fear of future trials. But you can have no objection to using the statistic in *this* trial, which is the only trial that we're talking about. So, I repeat my motion to allow me to introduce the conviction-rate statistic into this trial."

Now what do you say? Assuming that the prosecutor's statement is accurate—that the race-conscious statistic about burglaries has never before been used in a trial in this jurisdiction—is there any way you can challenge her statement that the statistic is uncontaminated? Is there any way you can argue that in fact the statistic already includes a self-fulfilling prophecy? Think back to the argument that all real evidence is only statistical evidence. Think back to the argument that jurors carry around in their heads certain "common sense" notions that are built up over years of observations of real-world data. Is there a way you can argue that what apparently is the most objective of statistics—the *conviction rate of defendants according to race*—is not as objective as it appears?

Group Justice Versus Individual Justice: Equality Problems

CHAPTER FIVE

5.1 Should group justice trump individual justice?

The Bakke Case

Syllabus

The Medical School of the University of California at Davis (hereinafter Davis) had two admissions programs for the entering class of 100 students—the regular admissions program and the special admissions program. Under the regular procedure, candidates whose overall undergraduate grade point averages fell below 2.5 on a scale of 4.0 were summarily rejected. About one out of six applicants was then given an interview, following which he was rated on a scale of 1 to 100 by each of the committee members, his rating being based on the interviewers' summaries, his overall grade point average, his science courses grade point average, his Medical College Admissions Test (MCAT) scores, letters of recommendation, extracurricular activities, and other biographical data, all of which resulted in a total "benchmark score." The full admissions committee then made offers of admission on the basis of their review of the applicant's file and his score, considering and acting upon applications as they were received.

A separate committee, a majority of whom were members of minority groups, operated the special admissions program. The 1973 and 1974 application forms, respectively, asked candidates whether they wished to be considered as "economically and/or educationally disadvantaged"

applicants and members of a "minority group" (blacks, Chicanos, Asians, American Indians). If an applicant of a minority group was found to be "disadvantaged," he would be rated in a manner similar to the one employed by the general admissions committee. Special candidates, however, did not have to meet the 2.5 grade point cutoff and were not ranked against candidates in the general admissions process. About one-fifth of the special applicants were invited for interviews in 1973 and 1974, following which they were given bench-mark scores, and the top choices were then given to the general admissions committee, which could reject special candidates for failure to meet course requirements or other specific deficiencies. The special committee continued to recommend candidates until 16 special admission selections had been made. During a four-year period 63 minority students were admitted to Davis under the special program and 44 under the general program. No disadvantaged whites were admitted under the special program, though many applied.

Respondent Allan Bakke, a white male, applied to Davis in 1973 and 1974, in both years being considered only under the general admissions program. Though he had a 468 out of 500 score in 1973, he was rejected since no general applicants with scores less than 470 were being accepted after respondent's application, which was filed late in the year, had been processed and completed. At that time four special admission slots were still unfilled. In 1974 respondent applied early, and though he had a total score of 549 out of 600, he was again rejected. In neither year was his name placed on the discretionary waiting list. In both years special applicants were admitted with significantly lower scores than respondent's. After his second rejection, respondent filed this action in state court for mandatory, injunctive, and declaratory relief to compel his admission to Davis, alleging that the special admissions program operated to exclude him on the basis of his race in violation of the Equal Protection Clause of the Fourteenth Amendment, a provision of the California Constitution, and § 601 of Title VI of the Civil Rights Act of 1964, which provides, inter alia, that no person shall on the ground of race or color be excluded from participating in any program receiving federal financial assistance.

The trial court found that the special program operated as a racial quota, because minority applicants in that program were rated only against one another, and 16 places in the class of 100 were reserved for them. Declaring that petitioner could not take race into account in making admissions decisions, the program was held to violate the Federal and State Constitutions and Title VI. Respondent's admission was not ordered, however, for lack of proof that he would have been admitted but for the special program.

The California Supreme Court, applying a strict-scrutiny standard, concluded that the special admissions program was not the least intrusive means of achieving the goals of the admittedly compelling state interests of integrating the medical profession and increasing the number of doctors willing to serve minority patients. Without passing on the state constitutional or federal statutory grounds the court held that petitioner's special admissions program violated the Equal Protection Clause. Since petitioner could not satisfy its burden of demonstrating that respondent, absent the special program, would not have been admitted, the court ordered his admission to Davis.

IN THE SUPREME COURT OF THE UNITED STATES

THE REGENTS OF THE UNIVERSITY OF CALIFORNIA,
Petitioner, -vs.-   No. 76–811

ALLAN BAKKE,
Respondent

Washington, D.C. Wednesday, October 12, 1977.

The above-entitled matter came on for argument at 10:01 o'clock a.m., pursuant to notice,

BEFORE:

> WARREN E. BURGER, Chief Justice of the United States
> WILLIAM J. BRENNAN, JR., Associate Justice
> POTTER STEWART, Associate Justice
> BYRON R. WHITE, Associate Justice
> THURGOOD MARSHALL, Associate Justice
> HARRY A. BLACKMUN, Associate Justice
> LEWIS F. POWELL, JR., Associate Justice
> WILLIAM H. REHNQUIST, Associate Justice
> JOHN PAUL STEVENS, Associate Justice

APPEARANCES:

> ARCHIBALD COX, ESQ., Langdell Hall, Cambridge, Massachusetts 02138; on behalf of the Petitioner.
> WADE H. McCREE, JR., ESQ., Solicitor General of the United States, Department of Justice, Washington, D.C. 20530; on behalf of the United States as amicus curiae.
> REYNOLD H. COLVIN, ESQ., Jacobs, Blanckenburg, May & Colvin, 111 Sutter Street, Suite 1800, San Francisco, California 94104; on behalf of the Respondent.

PROCEEDINGS

MR. CHIEF JUSTICE BURGER. The first case on today's calendar is No. 76–811, Regents of the University of California against Bakke.

Mr. Cox, you may proceed whenever you're ready.

ORAL ARGUMENT OF ARCHIBALD COX, ESQ., ON BEHALF OF THE PETITIONER

MR. COX. Mr. Chief Justice, and may it please the Court:

This case, here on certiorari to the Supreme

Court of California, presents a single vital question: whether a state university, which is forced by limited resources to select a relatively small number of students from a much larger number of well-qualified applicants, is free, voluntarily, to take into account the fact that a qualified applicant is black, Chicano, Asian, or native American in order to increase the number of qualified members of those minority groups trained for the educated professions and participating in them, professions from which minorities were long excluded because of generations of pervasive racial discrimination.

The answer which the Court gives will determine, perhaps for decades, whether members of those minorities are to have the kind of meaningful access to higher education in the professions which the universities have accorded them in recent years, or are to be reduced to the trivial numbers which they were prior to the adoption of minority admissions programs.

There are three facts, realities, which dominated the situation that the medical school at Davis had before it, and which I think must control the decision of this Court. The first is that the number of qualified applicants for the nation's professional schools is vastly greater than the number of places available. That is a fact, and an inescapable fact.

In 1975–76, for example, there were roughly 30,000 qualified applicants for admission to medical school; a much greater number of actual applicants; and there were only about 14,000 places. At Davis, there were 25 applicants for every seat in 1973; in 1974, the ratio had risen to 37 to 1. So that the problem is one of selection among qualified applicants, not of ability to gain from a professional education.

The second fact, on which there is no need for me to elaborate, but it is a fact: For generations, racial discrimination in the United States, much of it stimulated by unconstitutional state action, isolated certain minorities, condemned them to inferior education, and shut them out of the most important and satisfying aspects of American life, including higher education and the professions. And the greatest problem—as the Carnegie Commission on Higher Education noted more than ten years ago—the greatest problem in achieving racial justice was to draw those minorities into the professions that play so important a part in our national life.

And then there is one third fact: There is no racially blind method of selection which will enroll today more than a trickle of minority students in the nation's colleges and professions. These are the realities which the University of California at Davis Medical School faced in 1968 and which, say, I think the Court must face when it comes to its decision.

Until 1969, the applicants at Davis, as at most other medical schools, were chosen on the basis of scores on the medical aptitude test, their college grades, and other personal experiences and qualifications, as revealed in the application. The process excluded, virtually, almost all members of minority groups, even when they were fully qualified for places, because their scores, by and large, were lower on the competitive test and in college grade point averages.

There were no black students and no Chicanos in the class entering Davis in 1968. If one puts to one side the predominantly black medical schools, Howard and Meharry, less than 1 percent, eight-tenths of 1 percent, of all medical students in the United States were black in the year '68–69.

In 1969, the faculty at Davis concluded that drawing into the medical college qualified members of minorities—long victimized by racial discrimination—would yield important educational, professional, and social benefits. It then chose one variant of the only possible method to increasing the number. It established what came to be known as the Task Force Program, following the name of a program established by the Association of American Medical Colleges, which would select—there were only fifty in the entering class at that time—which would select eight educationally but fully qualified—select eight educationally or economically disadvantaged, but fully qualified, minority students for inclusion among the fifty-two in the entering class.

The number was increased to 16 when the size of the class was increased to 100. And it was that this step was taken as part of a movement led by the Association of American Medical Colleges which brought the number of black students studying at predominantly white medical schools from less than 1 percent to more than 5 percent; from 211 to 3,000 in a period of ten years.

I want to emphasize that the designation of sixteen places was not a quota, at least as I would use that word. Certainly it was not a quota in the older sense of an arbitrary limit put on the number of members of a non-popular group who would be admitted to an institution which was looking down its nose at them.

THE COURT. It did put a limit on the number of white people, didn't it?

MR. COX. I think that it limited the number of non-minority, and therefore essentially white, yes. But there are two things to be said about that: One is that this was not pointing the finger at a group which had been marked as inferior in any sense; and it was undifferentiated, it operated against a wide variety of people. So I think it was not stigmatizing in the sense of the old quota against Jews was stigmatizing, in any way.

THE COURT. But it did put a limit on their number in each class?

MR. COX. I'm sorry?

THE COURT. It did put a limit on the number of non-minority people in each class?

MR. COX. It did put a limit, no question about that, and I don't mean to infer that. And I will direct myself to it a little later, if I may.

THE COURT. Do you agree, then, that there was a quota of eighty-four?

MR. COX. Well, I would deny that it was a quota. We agree that there were sixteen places set aside for qualified disadvantaged minority students. Now, if that number—if setting aside a number, if the amount of resources—

THE COURT. No, the question is not whether the sixteen is a quota; the question is whether the eighty-four is a quota. And what is your answer to that?

MR. COX. I would say that neither is properly defined as a quota.

THE COURT. And then, why not?

MR. COX. Because, in the first place—because of my understanding of the meaning of "quota". And I think the decisive things are the facts, and the operative facts are: This is not something imposed from outside, as the quotas are in employment, or the targets are in employment sometimes today.

It was not a limit on the number of minority students. Other minority students were in fact accepted through the regular admissions program. It was not a guarantee of a minimum number of minority students, because all of them had to be, and the testimony is that all of them were, fully qualified.

All right. It did say that if there are sixteen qualified minority students, and they were also disadvantaged, then sixteen places shall be filled by them and only eighty-four places will be available to others.

THE COURT. Mr. Cox, the facts are not in dispute. Does it really matter what we call this program?

MR. COX. No. I quite agree with you, Mr. Justice. I was trying to emphasize that the facts here have none of the aspects—that there are none of the facts that lead us to think of "quota" as a bad word. What we call this doesn't matter; and if we call it a quota, knowing the facts, and deciding according to the operative facts and not influenced by the semantics, it couldn't matter less.

Some people say this was a target. I prefer not to call it that either, because "target" has taken on a connotation. But I would emphasize that it doesn't point the finger at any group. It doesn't say to any group: You are inferior. It doesn't promise taking people regardless of their qualifications, regardless of what they promise society, promise the school, or what qualities they have. And I think those things—and that it is not forced, but was really a decision by the school as to how much of its assets, what part of its assets, it would allocate to the purpose that it felt were being fulfilled by having minorities in the student body, and increasing the number of minorities in the profession.

Justice Stevens, let us suppose that the student was—that the school was much concerned by the lack of qualified general practitioners in Northern California, as indeed it was—but I want to exaggerate for illustration a little bit—and it told the admissions committee: Get people who come from rural communities, if they are qualified, and who express the intention of going back there. And the dean of admissions might well say: Well, how much importance do you give this? And the members of the faculty might say, by vote or otherwise: We think it's terribly important. As long as they are qualified, try and get ten in that group.

I don't think I would say that it was a "quota" of ninety students for others. And I think this, while it involves race, of course—that's why we're here—or color, really is essentially the same thing. The decision of the university was that there are social purposes, or purposes aimed in the end at eliminating racial injustice in this country and in bringing equality of opportunity; there will be purposes served by including minority students.

Well, how important do you think it is? We think it's this important. And that is the significance of the number. That's about the only significance.

THE COURT. Mr. Cox, is it the same thing as an athletic scholarship?

MR. COX. Well, I—

THE COURT. So many places reserved for athletic scholarships.

MR. COX. In the sense—I don't like to liken it to that in terms of its importance, but I think there are a number of places that may be set aside for an institution's different aims, and the aim of some institutions does seem to be to have athletic prowess. So that in that sense this is a choice made to promote the school's, the faculty's, choice of educational and professional objectives.

THE COURT. The aim of most institutions—

MR. COX. So I think there is a parallel, yes.

THE COURT. It's the aim of most institutions, isn't it, not just some?

MR. COX. Yes. But they have—of athletic?

THE COURT. Yes.

MR. COX. Well, I come from Harvard, sir.

[Laughter]

MR. COX. I don't know whether it's our aim, but we don't do very well.

THE COURT. But I can remember the time when—Mr. Cox, I can remember the time when you did, even if—

MR. COX. Yes, yes; you're quite right.

[Laughter]

THE COURT. Mr. Cox—

MR. COX. Maybe I better stop. I've had almost—

THE COURT. Mr. Cox, along that line, is there— I suppose athletic scholarships are largely confined, but not entirely confined, to undergraduate schools; largely, perhaps. Is that a difference between the problems that you're presenting, with respect to undergraduate schools and professional graduate schools?

MR. COX. Well, I quite—that was—it's because the purposes, athletic and social purposes, of an undergraduate school are different from those of a professional school that I am refraining from pressing the analogy too far; although I think it's logically accurate, and it helps one's thinking. Well, the objectives of undergraduate education are somewhat broader, somewhat harder to define. On the other hand, it's clear to me that the inclusion of minorities in undergraduate colleges may be at least as important as at a professional school. And indeed, of course, if they are going to get to a professional school, they have to be there.

But I think one finds that the objectives of these programs apply in large part to undergraduate colleges as well as professional schools, so it has the objective of improving education through greater diversity, and is perhaps even more important at an undergraduate school than it is at a professional school.

But I wouldn't minimize its importance at a professional school, and I would emphasize its importance when it comes to membership in the professions, so that the professions will be aware of all segments of society.

I think the objective of breaking down isolation, which is one of the greatest problems in achieving racial justice in this country, is solved by including minorities, I would say, about equally involved.

The objective that impresses itself on my mind, partly because Dean Lowrey testified to it and partly because I am, at least in part, an educator, is the importance of including young men and women at both undergraduate colleges and the medical schools, so that the other, younger, boys and girls may see: Yes, it is possible for a black to go to the University of Minnesota or to go to Harvard or Yale. I know Johnny down the street, and I know Sammy's father; he became a lawyer, and John's father became a doctor. This is essential if we are ever going to give true equality in a factual sense to people, because the existence or non-existence of opportunities, I am sure we all know, shapes people's aspirations when they are very young; and shapes the way they behave; and shapes, in the most pedagogical sense, I suspect, whether they do or don't read a book in the afternoon—

THE COURT. Mr. Cox, what if—

MR. COX. —and they do or don't read in school.

So I think all these apply to both, Mr. Chief Justice, very strongly.

THE COURT. Mr. Cox, what if Davis Medical School had decided that, since the population of doctors in the—among the minority population of doctors in California was so small, instead of setting aside sixteen seats for minority doctors, they would set aside fifty seats, until that balance were redressed, and the minority population of doctors equalled that of the population as a whole. Would that be any more infirm than the program that Davis has?

MR. COX. Well, I think my answer is this—and it's one which I draw upon Judge Hastie for, in an excellent essay he wrote on this subject—that so long as the numbers are chosen, he said, and they are shown to be reasonably adaptable to the social goal—and I'm thinking of the one you mentioned, Justice Rehnquist—then there is no reason to condemn a program because of the particular number chosen. I would say that perhaps— I don't think I have to press for a reasonably related test; I think that here is a much better showing than that.

I would say that as the number goes up, the danger of invidiousness, or the danger that this is being done not for social purposes but to favor one group as against another group, the risk, if you will, of a finding of an invidious purpose to discriminate against is great. And therefore, I think it's a harder case. But I would have to put the particular school in the context of all schools.

There are programs which are designed, for example, to train Indians to go back and teach at Indian reservations; and nobody else is taught in those. I don't think it's unconstitutional when you see it in the total context. But I think that as the number goes up, it raises these dangers, fears, and the possibility of an adverse finding on what might be the factually dispositive question of intent.

It is fair to say, Mr. Justice—and I don't want to slide away from the thing—the Task Force Program reduced the opportunity of a non-disadvantaged, non-minority applicant who was somewhere near the borderline, or below it, to get into Davis, because there were a certain number of places which were allocated for this purpose, just as a certain number of places might be allocated for people who would deliver medical services as general practitioners in the minority area—in a rural area.

The other thing I was going to say—and then I'm through, Mr. Chief Justice—is that, while it is true that Mr. Bakke and some others, under conventional standards for admission, would be ranked above the minority applicant, I want to emphasize that, in my judgment and I think in fact, that does not justify saying that the better, generally better-qualified people were excluded to make room for generally less-qualified people. There's nothing that shows that after the first two years at medical school the grade point averages will make the minority students poorer medical students; and still less to show that it makes them poorer doctors or poorer citizens or poorer people.

It's quite clear that for some of the things that a medical school wishes to accomplish, and that this medical school wished to accomplish, that the minority applicant may have qualities that are superior to those of his classmate who is not minority. He certainly will be more effective in bringing it home to the young Chicano that he too may become a doctor, he too may attend graduate school. He may be far more likely to go back to such a community to practice medicine where he's needed. Forgive me for taking so long.

THE COURT. Mr. Justice Powell referred to a figure of 23 percent minorities. Does that include Orientals in California?

MR. COX. I think it does, yes.

THE COURT. Is there anything—is there a specific finding in this record that Orientals, as one identifiable group, have been disadvantaged?

MR. COX. Well, I think that the decisions of this Court show, perhaps better than anything else, that they have been the victim of *de jure* discrimination over the years.

THE COURT. And what particular holdings do you refer to?

MR. COX. I had in mind *Okyama*. I think that's the most—no, that's not the most recent case. *Takahashi* is such a case. They go back to *Yick Wo*. I am sure there are three or four more Your Honor will think of quickly.

THE COURT. In terms of the professions, Mr. Cox, is there anything in this record to show that there are not a substantial number of Orientals in medicine, in teaching, and in law?

MR. COX. There are no—

THE COURT. Probably higher than in any of the other categories.

MR. COX. I don't think there are any figures in the record, and there are very few figures on minority participation in the professions published, except with respect to black doctors and black medical students. The others—there are some meaningful figures on Chicanos, but the others are very scattered and inadequate.

I would like to direct my attention, if I may, to one important point, and that's again, the significance of the number sixteen. We submit, first, that the Fourteenth Amendment does not outlaw race-conscious programs where there is no invidious purpose or intent, or where they are aimed at offsetting the consequences of our long tragic history of discrimination and achieving greater racial equity.

THE COURT. Mr. Cox, may I interrupt you—

MR. COX. I would think that these—

THE COURT. Mr. Cox, may I interrupt you with a question that's always troubled me? It's the use of the term "invidious," which I've always had difficulty really understanding. You suggested, in response to Mr. Justice Rehnquist, that if the number were fifty rather than sixteen, there would be a greater risk of a finding of invidious purpose. How does one—how does a judge decide when to make such a finding?

MR. COX. Well, I think he has to consider all the facts. They were most recently laid out in Justice Powell's opinion in the *Arlington Heights* case, the sort of thing that he thought the Court should consider.

If Your Honor is asking me what do I mean by "invidious," I mean primarily stigmatizing, marking as inferior—

THE COURT. Let me make my—

MR. COX. —shutting out of participation—

THE COURT. Mr. Cox, let me make my question a little more precise. Can you give me a test which would differentiate the case of fifty students from the case of sixteen students?

MR. COX. I would have to make this turn on a subjective inquiry, I think; but I would also have to look and see what the significance of the fifty students was in the overall context of the community, its educational system, and the state. And I would—I suppose I would be governed partly by purpose and partly by effect, but that would lead me back to purpose.

THE COURT. But in Mr. Justice Rehnquist's example, he was assuming precisely the same motivation that is present in this case: a desire to increase the number of black and minority doctors, and a desire to increase the mixture of the student population. Why would not that justify the fifty?

MR. COX. Well, if the finding is that this was reasonably adapted to the purpose of increasing the number of minority doctors and that it was not an arbitrary, capricious, selfish setting—and that would have to be decided in the light of the other medical schools in the state and the needs in the state—but if it's solidly based, then I would say fifty was permissible. Just as in my example, I said that educating only Indians in a program tailored to training teachers to go back to Indian reservations seems to me to be constitutional. And there are such programs at both private and state institutions.

ORAL ARGUMENT OF REYNOLD H. COLVIN, ESQ., ON BEHALF OF THE RESPONDENT

MR. COLVIN. Mr. Chief Justice, and may it please the Court:

It seems to me that the first thing that I ought to say to this Honorable Court is that I am Allan Bakke's lawyer and Allan Bakke is my client. And I do not say that in any formal or perfunctory way. I say that because this is a lawsuit. It was a lawsuit brought by Allan Bakke up at Woodland in Yolo County, California, in which Allan Bakke, from the very beginning of this lawsuit in the first paper we ever filed, stated the case. And he stated the case in terms of his individual right.

He stated the case in terms of the fact that he had twice applied for admission to the medical school at Davis and twice had been refused, both in the year 1973 and the year 1974. And he stated in that complaint what now, some three and a half years later, proves to be the very heart of the thing that we are talking about at this juncture. He stated that he was excluded from that school because that school had adopted a racial quota which deprived him of the opportunity for admission into the school. And that's where the case started. It started with a suit against the university.

He stated three grounds upon which he felt that he had been deprived of the right to admission to that school; the equal protection clause of the Fourteenth Amendment, the privileges and immunities clause of the Fourteenth Amendment, the privileges and immunities portion of the California Constitution, and Title VI, 42 United States Code 2000(d). And those were the three grounds upon which he placed his complaint from the very beginning.

THE COURT. You spoke, Mr. Colvin, of the right to admission. You don't seriously submit that he had a right to be admitted.

MR. COLVIN. I wanted to get to that, and I quite agree; and let me say it now so that it is out of the way. We have no contention here that Allan Bakke has a constitutional right, or even a statutory right, to be in a medical school. As a matter of fact, I am sure that if the regents of the University of California had decided to close the medical school at Davis, that Allan Bakke couldn't stand up here through his lawyer, or even get beyond the first demurrer in the Superior Court at Woodland, and say: I have a right to go to medical school.

That is not Allan Bakke's position. Allan Bakke's position is that he has a right, and that right is not to be discriminated against by reason of his race. And that's what brings Allan Bakke to this Court.

Now, let me go for just a moment with what happened in the lawsuit, because it is very important that we follow this step by step. The university, at the very beginning, did several things. First, they denied that they had a racial quota. I think that disappeared from the case. Secondly, they denied that Mr. Bakke would have been admitted, even had there been no racial quota. And, as I will indicate at some length, I hope later on, that disappeared from the case.

Let me make a distinction on this quota question, if I may, Your Honor. There are many points in the university's brief where somehow, in order to take the sting out of the word "quota," the word "goal" is used. This is not a quota, they say, but it is a goal. We find that to be a real misuse of language.

THE COURT. Mr. Colvin, to follow up a minute, Justice Powell's question. That really is a matter of characterization, rather than strictly a fact. If I understand it, there were sixteen places set aside for minority applicants. You are certainly free to argue from that what you want to about quotas and goals, but that really goes beyond a strict factual matter.

MR. COLVIN. Well, the factual question, if I may

respond to that just briefly, arises somehow in a different way. And let me illustrate it this way, because it is a factual—there is a factual circumstance involved. And let me try to spell out what I believe that factual circumstance to be.

Normally, if we have a goal, if we have a goal, if we are going to get a number of people in, we select a standard, and then above that standard we admit people in order to qualify. Precisely the opposite is true here. In this case, we have to follow what the factual situation is. Here, we have a quota where the number is first chosen, and then the number is filled regardless of the standard.

And let me say precisely from the record what I mean. When we take Dr. Lowrey's deposition, one of the very first questions asked Dr. Lowrey is this question: What is the standard of admission to the school? And Dr. Lowrey's response is that the standard is that we will interview no one who has a grade point average below 2.5.

Now, let's look at the record on that point. In the year 1973, the people within the quota or specialization program have overall grade point averages which run all the way down to 2.21. That's in '74. In 1973, they run all the way down to 2.11. But the science grade point averages for that group—and I am not giving you averages. I mean to say range. The range runs all the way down to 2.02. That's the grade point average side of it.

THE COURT. Mr. Colvin, you do not dispute the basic finding that everybody admitted under the special program was qualified, do you?

MR. COLVIN. We certainly do dispute it. Not upon the ground that Mr. Bakke is attempting to tell the school what the qualifications are, nor upon the ground that we as his counsel can somehow set up a rule which will tell us who is qualified to go to medical school.

MR. CHIEF JUSTICE BURGER. Mr. Colvin, don't get too far away from the microphone, if you want to stay on the record.

MR. COLVIN. I am sorry. I sometimes think of it as a retreat.

But the point that we are making is this: that the rules as to admission were fixed neither by Bakke nor his attorneys, but were fixed by the school itself. They were the ones who chose grade point averages, and they were the ones who chose MCAT scores as a basis for judging admission. And let me say this about the MCAT scores, because it relates again to the question that I was answering as to the difference between a goal and a quota—

THE COURT. There is nothing in the record to indicate that they chose the 2.5 figure because they felt that anyone with a lesser score would not be qualified either to do the academic work or to practice medicine.

MR. COLVIN. No, but that was their rule. That was their rule, and I think there is a fair inference from the record that there was a reasonable basis for Dr. Lowrey stating that that was the rule of the school.

THE COURT. Yes, it was an administrative basis.

MR. COLVIN. It was an administrative basis, but at least it was their basis.

THE COURT. But then, how does that go—why do you disagree with the proposition that there is nothing in this record to show that any of the special people were qualified to study and to practice?

MR. COLVIN. We simply say that we do not agree, we do not agree that there is a showing that they were qualified. We are not making the argument that they were disqualified, but we are saying: Taking the school's own standards, taking the very thing that the school was talking about, they simply do not measure up on that point.

But let me finish, if I may, because it is hard to finish all of these things. And I do want to comment about the same thing as it applies to the MCAT scores.

You will recall that in Dr. Lowrey's deposition Dr. Lowrey says: "We would be hard pressed"— "We would be hard pressed to admit people to the school if they had MCAT"—Medical College Aptitude Test—"percentiles in science and in verbal which were below 50."

But look at the record in the case. Look at the record in the case. In 1973, the average—not the range, but the average—of the people in the special admissions group was in the 35th percentile in science and in the 46th percentile in verbal. In 1974, the percentile in science—and this is an average and not a range—was 37, and in verbal 34.

Allan Bakke took the test only once and his record is there. You will find it on page 13 of our brief. He scored in the 97th percentile in science and in the 96th percentile in verbal.

The ultimate fact in this case, no matter how you turn it, is that Mr. Bakke was deprived of an opportunity to attend the school by reason of his race. This is not a matter of conjecture. This is a stipulation by the regents of the University of California.

THE COURT. For purposes of this argument, though, do you need to go any further than to assert and convince somebody that he was deprived of an opportunity to compete for one of the sixteen seats because of his race? Do you need to go any further than that?

MR. COLVIN. I am afraid that—

THE COURT. If you don't need to go any further, you certainly are taking up a lot of your time.

MR. COLVIN. I don't want to take up my time, except to say that there is within this record the stipulation of the regents of the University of California that Mr. Bakke was deprived of the opportunity to attend the University of California Medical School at Davis because of the use of the sixteen places by the special admissions program.

THE COURT. Mr. Colvin, may I follow up on Justice White's observation—same as I view this record—the university doesn't deny or dispute the basic facts. They are perfectly clear. We are here— at least I am here—primarily to hear a constitutional argument. You have devoted twenty minutes to laboring a fact, if I may say so. I would like to help, I really would, on the constitutional issues. Would you address that?

MR. COLVIN. Yes, I would like to address—I would like to address the problems that arise with quota and the problems that arise with race, and I would like also to address the alternative which the university suggests.

We have the deepest difficulty in dealing with this problem of quota; and many, many questions arise. For example, there is a question of numbers. What is the appropriate quota? What is the appropriate quota for a medical school? Sixteen, eight, thirty-two, sixty-four, a hundred? On what basis, on what basis is that quota determined?

And there is a problem, a very serious problem of judicial determination. Does the Court leave open to the school the right to choose any number it wants in order to satisfy that quota? Would the Court be satisfied to allow an institution such as the University of California to adopt a quota of 100 percent and thus deprive all persons who are not people within selected minority groups?

THE COURT. Well, what's your response to the assertion of the university that is was entitled to have a special program and take race into account, and that under the Fourteenth Amendment there was no barrier to its doing that, because of the interests that were involved? What's your response to that?

MR. COLVIN. Our response to that is fundamentally that race is an improper classification in this situation. As a matter of fact, the Government in its own brief makes that very point.

THE COURT. Mr. Colvin, what if the university says: We don't want to just aim at the disadvantaged; we want to increase the number of black doctors who are practicing in California? Is that a permissible goal on the part of the university?

MR. COLVIN. To the extent that the judgment is made on whether those doctors are disadvantaged, it is a legitimate means. To the extent—and the Supreme Court of California says this—to the extent that the preference is on the basis of the race, we believe that is an unconstitutional advantage.

THE COURT. Well, do you say, then, it is not a permissible goal on the part of the university to increase the number of black doctors practicing—

MR. COLVIN. We say it is a permissible goal, and if—

THE COURT. If it is a permissible goal, why on earth beat around the bush? Why not simply make a race-oriented selection?

MR. COLVIN. Because the Supreme Court says to the university: You cannot leap to the quota system. What you must first do is to undertake to meet the question of disadvantage where it exists, if it exists.

THE COURT. But the university comes back and says: We are not interested in disadvantage as such; we are interested in blacks.

MR. COLVIN. Yes, but the Supreme Court comes back to the university and says: What you are doing is skipping one step. You are not—What is the reason for this goal? What is the reason why people are saying: We want more Chicano doctors, more black doctors, more Oriental doctors? The reason is, we claim that there was disadvantage. The difficulty is, with a racial classification, is that we are engaging in these broad generalizations that every one of a given race has suffered the same

advantage or the same disadvantage; the same wealth or the same poverty; the same education or the same lack of education.

There are two benefits for a university to look at the question of advantage. And the first of those benefits is that it does not run into a constitutional difficulty. And the second advantage—or the second benefit of looking at the question of disadvantage is that it meets the problem where it exists. It meets it at the point of the individual. It does not generalize. It is not true that all members of a given race have exactly the same experience, the same wealth, the same education. And that's the point that Justice Mosk is making in the California Supreme Court. He says:

> It is inappropriate, whatever your goal is, to jump to the question of making these racial discriminations.

And particularly inappropriate, we say, because the thing happens is that it keeps Mr. Bakke out of medical school, not because of somebody else's race or anything else, but because of Mr. Bakke's race he becomes ineligible himself to enter the medical school. And Mr. Bakke's individual stake in this matter is an important stake.

And I started with the proposition that I am Mr. Bakke's lawyer and Mr. Bakke is my client. He has a right to that protection. He has a right, if he desires, to show that he is one of those who is entitled to enter the medical school. To keep him out because of his race, we submit, is an impropriety. The whole point—

THE COURT. Your client did compete for the eighty-four seats, didn't he?

MR. COLVIN. Yes, he did.

THE COURT. And he lost?

MR. COLVIN. Yes, he did.

THE COURT. Now, would your argument be the same if one, instead of sixteen, seats were left open?

MR. COLVIN. Most respectfully, the argument does not turn on the numbers.

THE COURT. My question is: Would you make the same argument?

MR. COLVIN. Yes.

THE COURT. If it was one?

MR. COLVIN. If it was one and if there was an agreement, as there is in this case, that he was kept out by his race. Whether it is one, one hundred, two—

THE COURT. I didn't say anything about him being—I said that the regulation said that one seat would be left open for an underprivileged minority person.

MR. COLVIN. Yes. We don't think we would ever get to that point—

THE COURT. So numbers are just important?

MR. COLVIN. Numbers are unimportant. It is the principle of keeping a man out because of his race that is important.

THE COURT. You are arguing about keeping somebody out, and the other side is arguing about getting somebody in.

MR. COLVIN. That's right.

THE COURT. So it depends on which way you look at it, doesn't it?

MR. COLVIN. It depends on which way you look at the problem.

THE COURT. It does?

MR. COLVIN. If I may finish. The problem—

THE COURT. You are talking about your client's rights. Don't these underprivileged people have some rights?

MR. COLVIN. They certainly have the right to compete—

THE COURT. To eat cake.

MR. COLVIN. They have the right to compete. They have the right to equal competition. They even have another right, which was given them by the California Supreme Court. They have the right to compete not only upon the basis of grades, they have the right to compete upon the basis of disadvantage. The university, of course, says we will have nothing to do with that. If we can't have a quota, then there is no place for us to go.

Bear in mind that the Supreme Court of the State of California is entirely explicit in its opinion. It says: "We are not"—emphasize "we are not"—

> telling the University of California Medical School that it has to take the hundred people with the highest grade point average or the highest MCAT scores

—or whatever it is—

REBUTTAL ARGUMENT OF ARCHIBALD COX, ESQ.

MR. COX. I think perhaps I can be most helpful by trying to put the very particular points we covered in my argument within a larger framework of my basic thinking. The first main proposition that I would assert is that the racially conscious admissions program at Davis, and any racially conscious admissions program designed to increase the number of minority students at a professional school, is fully consistent with both the letter and the spirit of the Fourteenth Amendment.

And I simply want to add one footnote, to say that when I use the word "race" or "racially conscious," I am not speaking of race the way one would speak of a red-headed man or a man that has some other mark that is sheer happenstance. That isn't the quality of race in our society today. And I am really talking about all of the things that have gone with race and the remnants of those things in terms of current social problems; and race is a shorthand to express them.

The Supreme Court of California was wrong and its judgment should be reversed, because it said that under present circumstances we may not take race into account. That's what Mr. Colvin pitched his case on. That's the proposition he presented below and he presented here.

The judicializing or constitutionalizing, the drawing of courts in the writing of monolithic rules, tends to dampen one of the greatest—abandons one of the greatest sources of creativity in this country; and the opportunity, in dealing with delicate and sensitive and often painful—it is not easy to turn down young men and women. And in dealing with those problems we are advised to take advantage of the fact that there are fifty states. We are advised to take advantage, so far as the legislatures will allow it, of the fact that different campuses, different faculties, are allowed to make up their own minds. And I think if you set a lot of rules that would draw the Federal courts into scrutinizing the details of what is done, it would invite constant litigation and, as I say, it would abandon a source of creativity. It would destroy important autonomy in wrestling with what I, and I am sure all the Court, recognize is an extraordinarily sensitive and difficult problem, but a search for justice for all, to which this country has always been committed, and which I am sure it is.

MR. CHIEF JUSTICE BURGER. Thank you,

gentlemen; the case is submitted.

Regents of the University of California v. Bakke

438 U.S. 265
Supreme Court of the United States
June 28, 1978

Archibald Cox argued the cause for petitioner. With him on the briefs were Paul J. Mishkin, Jack B. Owens, and Donald L. Reidhaar.

Reynold H. Colvin argued the cause and filed briefs for respondent.

Solicitor General McCree argued the cause for the United States as amicus curiae. With him on the briefs were Attorney General Bell, Assistant Attorney General Days, Deputy Solicitor General Wallace, Brian K. Landsberg, Jessica Dunsay Silver, Miriam R. Eisenstein, and Vincent F. O'Rourke.

MR. JUSTICE POWELL announced the judgment of the Court.

. . . . For the reasons stated in the following opinion, I believe that so much of the judgment of the California court as holds petitioner's special admissions program unlawful and directs that respondent be admitted to the Medical School must be affirmed. For the reasons expressed in a separate opinion, my Brothers THE CHIEF JUSTICE, MR. JUSTICE STEWART, MR. JUSTICE REHNQUIST, and MR. JUSTICE STEVENS concur in this judgment.

I also conclude for the reasons stated in the following opinion that the portion of the court's judgment enjoining petitioner from according any consideration to race in its admissions process must be reversed. For reasons expressed in separate opinions, my Brothers MR. JUSTICE BRENNAN, MR. JUSTICE WHITE, MR. JUSTICE MARSHALL, and MR. JUSTICE BLACKMUN concur in this judgment.

Affirmed in part and reversed in part.

I

Allan Bakke is a white male who applied to the Davis Medical School in both 1973 and 1974.

In both years Bakke's application was considered under the general admissions program, and he received an interview. His 1973 interview was with Dr. Theodore C. West, who considered Bakke "a very desirable applicant to [the] medical school." Despite a strong benchmark score of 468 out of 500, Bakke was rejected. His application had come late in the year, and no applicants in the general admissions process with scores below 470 were accepted after Bakke's application was completed. There were four special admissions slots unfilled at that time, however, for which Bakke was not considered. After his 1973 rejection, Bakke wrote to Dr. George H. Lowrey, Associate Dean and Chairman of the Admissions Committee, protesting that the special admissions program operated as a racial and ethnic quota.

Bakke's 1974 application was completed early in the year. His student interviewer gave him an overall rating of 94, finding him "friendly, well tempered, conscientious and delightful to speak with." His faculty interviewer was, by coincidence, the same Dr. Lowrey to whom he had written in protest of the special admissions program. Dr. Lowrey found Bakke "rather limited in his approach" to the problems of the medical profession and found disturbing Bakke's "very definite opinions which were based more on his personal viewpoints than upon a study of the total problem." Dr. Lowrey gave Bakke the lowest of his six ratings, an 86; his total was 549 out of 600. Again, Bakke's application was rejected. In neither year did the chairman of the admissions committee, Dr. Lowrey, exercise his discretion to place Bakke on the waiting list. In both years, applicants were admitted under the special program with grade point averages, MCAT scores, and benchmark scores significantly lower than Bakke's.

III

[T]he parties fight a sharp preliminary action over the proper characterization of the special admissions program. Petitioner prefers to view it as establishing a "goal" of minority representation in the Medical School. Respondent, echoing the courts below, labels it a racial quota.[1]

This semantic distinction is beside the point: The special admissions program is undeniably a classification based on race and ethnic background. To the extent that there existed a pool of at least minimally qualified minority applicants to fill the 16 special admissions seats, white applicants could compete only for 84 seats in the entering class, rather than the 100 open to minority applicants. Whether this limitation is described as a quota or a goal, it is a line drawn on the basis of race and ethnic status.

Petitioner urges us to adopt for the first time a more restrictive view of the Equal Protection Clause and hold that discrimination against members of the white "majority" cannot be suspect if its purpose can be characterized as "benign."[2] The

clock of our liberties, however, cannot be turned back to 1868. [Citing cases] It is far too late to argue that the guarantee of equal protection to all persons permits the recognition of special wards entitled to a degree of protection greater than that accorded others.[3]

Once the artificial line of a "two-class theory" of the Fourteenth Amendment is put aside, the difficulties entailed in varying the level of judicial review according to a perceived "preferred" status of a particular racial or ethnic minority are intractable. The concepts of "majority" and "minority" necessarily reflect temporary arrangements and political judgments. As observed above, the white "majority" itself is composed of various minority groups, most of which can lay claim to a history of prior discrimination at the hands of the State and private individuals. Not all of these groups can receive preferential treatment and corresponding judicial tolerance of distinctions drawn in terms of race and nationality, for then the only "majority" left would be a new minority of white Anglo-Saxon Protestants. There is no principled basis for deciding which groups would merit "heightened judicial solicitude" and which would

---

[1] Petitioner defines "quota" as a requirement which must be met but can never be exceeded, regardless of the quality of the minority applicants. Petitioner declares that there is no "floor" under the total number of minority students admitted; completely unqualified students will not be admitted simply to meet a "quota." Neither is there a "ceiling," since an unlimited number could be admitted through the general admissions process. On this basis the special admissions program does not meet petitioner's definition of a quota.

The court below found—and petitioner does not deny—that white applicants could not compete for the 16 places reserved solely for the special admissions program. 18 Cal. 3d, at 44, 553 P.2d, at 1159. Both courts below characterized this as a "quota" system.

[2] In the view of Mr. Justice Brennan, Mr. Justice White, Mr. Justice Marshall, and Mr. Justice Blackmun, the pliable notion of "stigma" is the crucial element in analyzing racial classifications. The Equal Protection Clause is not framed in terms of "stigma." Certainly the word has no clearly defined constitutional meaning. It reflects a subjective judgment that is standardless. All state imposed classifications that rearrange burdens and benefits on the basis of race are likely to be viewed with deep resentment by the individuals burdened. The denial to innocent persons of equal rights and opportunities may outrage those so deprived and therefore may be perceived as invidious. These individuals are likely to find little comfort in the notion that the deprivation they are asked to endure is merely the price of membership in the dominant majority and that its imposition is inspired by the supposedly benign purpose of aiding others. One should not lightly dismiss the inherent unfairness of, and the perception of mistreatment that accompanies, a system of allocating benefits and privileges on the basis of skin

color and ethnic origin. Moreover, Mr. Justice Brennan, Mr. Justice White, Mr. Justice Marshall, and Mr. Justice Blackmun offer no principle for deciding whether preferential classifications reflect a benign remedial purpose or a malevolent stigmatic classification, since they are willing in this case to accept mere post hoc declarations by an isolated state entity—a medical school faculty—unadorned by particularized findings of past discrimination, to establish such a remedial purpose.

[3] Professor Bickel noted the self-contradiction of that view:

"The lesson of the great decisions of the Supreme Court and the lesson of contemporary history have been the same for at least a generation: discrimination on the basis of race is illegal, immoral, unconstitutional, inherently wrong, and destructive of democratic society. Now this is to be unlearned and we are told that this is not a matter of fundamental principle but only a matter of whose ox is gored. Those for whom racial equality was demanded are to be more equal than others. Having found support in the Constitution for equality, they now claim support for inequality under the same Constitution." A. Bickel, The Morality of Consent 133 (1975).

not.[4] Courts would be asked to evaluate the extent of the prejudice and consequent harm suffered by various minority groups. Those whose societal injury is thought to exceed some arbitrary level of tolerability then would be entitled to preferential classifications at the expense of individuals belonging to other groups. Those classifications would be free from exacting judicial scrutiny. As these preferences began to have their desired effect, and the consequences of past discrimination were undone, new judicial rankings would be necessary. The kind of variable sociological and political analysis necessary to produce such rankings simply does not lie within the judicial competence—even if they otherwise were politically feasible and socially desirable.

Moreover, there are serious problems of justice connected with the idea of preference itself. First, it may not always be clear that a so-called preference is in fact benign. Courts may be asked to validate burdens imposed upon individual members of a particular group in order to advance the group's general interest. *United Jewish Organizations v. Carey,* 430 U.S., at 172–173 (Brennan, J., concurring in part). Nothing in the Constitution supports the notion that individuals may be asked to suffer otherwise impermissible burdens in order to enhance the societal standing of their ethnic groups. Second, preferential programs may only reinforce common stereotypes holding that certain groups are unable to achieve success without special protection based on a factor having no relationship to individual worth. See *DeFunis v. Odegaard,* 416 U.S. 312, 343 (Douglas, J., dissenting). Third, there is a measure of inequity in forcing innocent persons in respondent's position to bear the burdens of redressing grievances not of their making.

By hitching the meaning of the Equal Protection Clause to these transitory considerations, we would be holding, as a constitutional principle, that judicial scrutiny of classifications touching on racial and ethnic background may vary with the

ebb and flow of political forces. Disparate constitutional tolerance of such classifications well may serve to exacerbate racial and ethnic antagonisms rather than alleviate them. Also, the mutability of a constitutional principle, based upon shifting political and social judgments, undermines the chances for consistent application of the Constitution from one generation to the next, a critical feature of its coherent interpretation. In expounding the Constitution, the Court's role is to discern "principles sufficiently absolute to give them roots throughout the community and continuity over significant periods of time, and to lift them above the level of the pragmatic political judgments of a particular time and place." A. Cox, The Role of the Supreme Court in American Government 114 (1976).

If it is the individual who is entitled to judicial protection against classifications based upon his racial or ethnic background because such distinctions impinge upon personal rights, rather than the individual only because of his membership in a particular group, then constitutional standards may be applied consistently. Political judgments regarding the necessity for the particular classification may be weighed in the constitutional balance, *Korematsu v. United States,* 323 U.S. 214 (1944), but the standard of justification will remain constant. This is as it should be, since those political judgments are the product of rough compromise struck by contending groups within the democratic process. When they touch upon an individual's race or ethnic background, he is entitled to a judicial determination that the burden he is asked to bear on that basis is precisely tailored to serve a compelling governmental interest. The Constitution guarantees that right to every person regardless of his background.

---

[4] As I am in agreement with the view that race may be taken into account as a factor in an admissions program, I agree with my Brothers Brennan, White, Marshall, and Blackmun that the portion of the judgment that would proscribe all consideration of race must be reversed. But I disagree with much that is said in their opinion.

IV

The special admission program purports to serve the purposes of: "reducing the historic deficit of traditionally disfavored minorities in medical schools and in the medical profession," Brief for Petitioner 32; (ii) countering the effects of societal discrimination;[5] increasing the number of physicians who will practice in communities currently underserved; and (iv) obtaining the educational benefits that flow from an ethnically diverse student body.

If petitioner's purpose is to assure within its student body some specified percentage of a particular group merely because of its race or ethnic origin, such a preferential purpose must be rejected not as insubstantial but as facially invalid. Preferring members of any one group for no reason other than race or ethnic origin is discrimination for its

own sake. This the Constitution forbids. [Citing cases]

The State certainly has a legitimate and substantial interest in ameliorating, or eliminating where feasible, the disabling effects of identified discrimination. The line of school desegregation cases, commencing with *Brown,* attests to the importance of this state goal and the commitment of the judiciary to affirm all lawful means toward its attainment. In the school cases, the States were required by court order to redress the wrongs worked by specific instances of racial discrimination. That goal was far more focused than the remedying of the effects of "societal discrimination," an amorphous concept of injury that may be ageless in its reach into the past.

We have never approved a classification that aids persons perceived as members of relatively victimized groups at the expense of other innocent individuals in the absence of judicial, legislative, or administrative findings of constitutional or statutory violations. [Citing cases] After such findings have been made, the governmental interest in preferring members of the injured groups at the expense of others is substantial, since the legal rights of the victims must be vindicated. In such a case, the extent of the injury and the consequent remedy will have been judicially, legislatively, or administratively defined. Also, the remedial action usually remains subject to continuing oversight to assure that it will work the least harm possible to other innocent persons competing for the benefit. Without such findings of constitutional or statutory violations, it cannot be said that the government has any greater interest in helping one individual than in refraining from harming another. Thus, the government has no compelling justification for inflicting such harm.

Hence, the purpose of helping certain groups whom the faculty of the Davis Medical School perceived as victims of "societal discrimination" does not justify a classification that imposes disadvantages upon persons like respondent, who bear no responsibility for whatever harm the beneficiaries of the special admissions program are thought to have suffered. To hold otherwise would be to convert a remedy heretofore reserved for violations of legal rights into a privilege that all institutions throughout the Nation could grant at their pleasure to whatever groups are perceived as victims of societal discrimination. That is a step we have never approved.

---

[5] A number of distinct subgoals have been advanced as falling under the rubric of "compensation for past discrimination." For example, it is said that preferences for Negro applicants may compensate for harm done them personally, or serve to place them at economic levels they might have attained but for discrimination against their forebears. Greenawalt, Judicial Scrutiny of "Benign" Racial Preference in Law School Admissions, 75 Colum. L. Rev. 559, 581–586 (1975). Another view of the "compensation" goal is that it serves as a form of reparation by the "majority" to a victimized group as a whole. B. Bittker, The Case for Black Reparations (1973). That justification for racial or ethnic preferences has been subjected to much criticism. *E.g.,* Greenawalt, *supra,* at 581; Posner, The DeFunis Case and the Constitutionality of Preferential Treatment of Racial Minorities, 1974 Sup. Ct. Rev. 1, 16–17. Finally, it has been argued that ethnic preferences "compensate" the group by providing examples of success whom other members of the group will emulate, thereby advancing the group's interest and society's interest in encouraging new generations to overcome the barriers and frustrations of the past. Redish, Preferential Law School Admissions and the Equal Protection Clause: An Analysis of the Competing Arguments, 22 UCLA L. Rev. 343, 391 (1974). For purposes of analysis these subgoals need not be considered separately.

Racial classifications in admissions conceivably could serve a fifth purpose of fair appraisal of each individual's academic promise in the light of some cultural bias in grading or testing procedures. To the extent that race and ethnic background were considered only to the extent of curing established inaccuracies in predicting academic performance, it might be argued that there is no "preference" at all. Nothing in this record, however, suggests either that any of the quantitative factors considered by the Medical School were culturally biased or that petitioner's special admissions program was formulated to correct for any such biases. Furthermore, if race or ethnic background were used solely to arrive at an unbiased prediction of academic success, the reservation of fixed numbers of seats would be inexplicable.

Petitioner identifies, as another purpose of its program, improving the delivery of health-care services to communities currently underserved. It may be assumed that in some situations a State's interest in facilitating the health care of its citizens is sufficiently compelling to support the use of a suspect classification. But there is virtually no evidence in the record indicating that petitioner's special admissions program is either needed or geared to promote that goal.[6] The court below addressed this failure of proof:

> [T]here are more precise and reliable ways to identify applicants who are genuinely interested in the medical problems of minorities than by race. An applicant of whatever race who has demonstrated his concern for disadvantaged minorities in the past and who declares that practice in such a community is his primary professional goal would be more likely to contribute to alleviation of the medical shortage than one who is chosen entirely on the basis of race and disadvantage. In short, there is no empirical data to demonstrate that any one race is more selflessly socially oriented or by contrast that another is more selfishly acquisitive. 18 Cal.3d, at 56, 553 P.2d, at 1167.

The fourth goal asserted by petitioner is the attainment of a diverse student body. This clearly is a constitutionally permissible goal for an institution of higher education. Academic freedom, though not a specifically enumerated constitutional right, long has been viewed as a special concern of the First Amendment. The freedom of a university to make its own judgments as to education includes the selection of its student body. . . . The atmosphere of "speculation, experiment and creation"—so essential to the quality of higher education—is widely believed to be promoted by a diverse student body. As the Court noted in *Keyishian,* it is not too much to say that the "nation's future depends upon leaders trained through wide exposure" to the ideas and mores of students as diverse as this Nation of many peoples.

Thus, in arguing that its universities must be accorded the right to select those students who will contribute the most to the "robust exchange of ideas," petitioner invokes a countervailing constitutional interest, that of the First Amendment. In this light, petitioner must be viewed as seeking to achieve a goal that is of paramount importance in the fulfillment of its mission.

It may be argued that there is greater force to these views at the undergraduate level than in a medical school where the training is centered primarily on professional competency. But even at the graduate level, our tradition and experience lend support to the view that the contribution of diversity is substantial. In *Sweatt v. Painter,* 339 U.S., at 634, the Court made a similar point with specific reference to legal education:

> The law school, the proving ground for legal learning and practice, cannot be effective in isolation from the individuals and institutions with which the law interacts. Few students and no one who has practiced law would choose to study in an academic vacuum, removed from the interplay of ideas and the exchange of views with which the law is concerned.

Physicians serve a heterogeneous population. An otherwise qualified medical student with a particular background—whether it be ethnic, geographic, culturally advantaged or disadvantaged—may bring to a professional school of medicine experiences, outlooks, and ideas that enrich the training of its student body and better equip its graduates to render with understanding their vital service to humanity.

Ethnic diversity, however, is only one element in a range of factors a university properly may consider in attaining the goal of a heterogeneous student body. Although a university must have wide discretion in making the sensitive judgments as to who should be admitted, constitutional limitations protecting individual rights may not be disregarded. Respondent urges—and the courts below have held—that petitioner's dual admissions program is a racial classification that impermissibly infringes his rights under the Fourteenth Amendment. As the interest of diversity is compelling in the context of a university's admissions program, the question remains whether the program's racial classification is necessary to promote this interest.

---

[6] The only evidence in the record with respect to such underservice is a newspaper article. Record 473.

V

The experience of other university admissions programs, which take race into account in achieving the educational diversity valued by the First Amendment, demonstrates that the assignment of a fixed number of places to a minority group is not a necessary means toward that end.... [R]ace or ethnic background may be deemed a "plus" in a particular applicant's file, yet it does not insulate the individual from comparison with all other candidates for the available seats. The file of a particular black applicant may be examined for his potential contribution to diversity without the factor of race being decisive when compared, for example, with that of an applicant identified as an Italian-American if the latter is thought to exhibit qualities more likely to promote beneficial educational pluralism. Such qualities could include exceptional personal talents, unique work or service experience, leadership potential, maturity, demonstrated compassion, a history of overcoming disadvantage, ability to communicate with the poor, or other qualifications deemed important. In short, an admissions program operated in this way is flexible enough to consider all pertinent elements of diversity in light of the particular qualifications of each applicant, and to place them on the same footing for consideration, although not necessarily according them the same weight. Indeed, the weight attributed to a particular quality may vary from year to year depending upon the "mix" both of the student body and the applicants for the incoming class.

This kind of program treats each applicant as an individual in the admissions process. The applicant who loses out on the last available seat to another candidate receiving a "plus" on the basis of ethnic background will not have been foreclosed from all consideration for that seat simply because he was not the right color or had the wrong surname. It would mean only that his combined qualifications, which may have included similar nonobjective factors, did not outweigh those of the other applicant. His qualifications would have been weighed fairly and competitively, and he would have no basis to complain of unequal treatment under the Fourteenth Amendment.[7]

---

[7] The denial to respondent of this right to individualized consideration without regard to his race is the principal evil of petitioner's special admissions program. Nowhere in the opinion of Mr. Justice Brennan, Mr. Justice White, Mr. Justice Marshall, and Mr. Justice Blackmun is this denial even addressed.

It has been suggested that an admissions program which considers race only as one factor is simply a subtle and more sophisticated—but no less effective—means of according racial preference than the Davis program. A facial intent to discriminate, however, is evident in petitioner's preference program and not denied in this case. No such facial infirmity exists in an admissions program where race or ethnic background is simply one element—to be weighed fairly against other elements—in the selection process. A court would not assume that a university, professing to employ a facially nondiscriminatory admissions policy, would operate it as a cover for the functional equivalent of a quota system. In short, good faith would be presumed in the absence of a showing to the contrary in the manner permitted by our cases.[8] [Citing cases]

In enjoining petitioner from ever considering the race of any applicant, however, the courts below failed to recognize that the State has a substantial interest that legitimately may be served by a properly devised admissions program involving the competitive consideration of race and ethnic origin. For this reason, so much of the California court's judgment as enjoins petitioner from any consid-

---

[8] Universities, like the prosecutor in *Swain,* may make individualized decisions, in which ethnic background plays a part, under a presumption of legality and legitimate educational purpose. So long as the university proceeds on an individualized, case-by-case basis, there is no warrant for judicial interference in the academic process. If an applicant can establish that the institution does not adhere to a policy of individual comparisons, or can show that a systematic exclusion of certain groups results, the presumption of legality might be overcome, creating the necessity of proving legitimate educational purpose.

There also are strong policy reasons that correspond to the constitutional distinction between petitioner's preference program and one that assures a measure of competition among all applicants. Petitioner's program will be viewed as inherently unfair by the public generally as well as by applicants for admission to state universities. Fairness in individual competition for opportunities, especially those provided by the State, is a widely cherished American ethic. Indeed, in a broader sense, an underlying assumption of the rule of law is the worthiness of a system of justice based on fairness to the individual. As Mr. Justice Frankfurter declared in another connection, "[justice] must satisfy the appearance of justice." *Offutt v. United States,* 348 U.S. 11, 14 (1954).

eration of the race of any applicant must be reversed.

VI

With respect to respondent's entitlement to an injunction directing his admission to the Medical School, petitioner has conceded that it could not carry its burden of proving that, but for the existence of its unlawful special admissions program, respondent still would not have been admitted. Hence, respondent is entitled to the injunction, and that portion of the judgment must be affirmed.

DISSENT:

Opinion of MR. JUSTICE BRENNAN, MR. JUSTICE WHITE, MR. JUSTICE MARSHALL, and MR. JUSTICE BLACKMUN, concurring in the judgment in part and dissenting in part....

Davis' articulated purpose of remedying the effects of past societal discrimination is, under our cases, sufficiently important to justify the use of race-conscious admissions programs where there is a sound basis for concluding that minority underrepresentation is substantial and chronic, and that the handicap of past discrimination is impeding access of minorities to the Medical School.

Properly construed ... our prior cases unequivocally show that a state government may adopt race-conscious programs if the purpose of such programs is to remove the disparate racial impact its actions might otherwise have and if there is reason to believe that the disparate impact is itself the product of past discrimination, whether its own or that of society at large. There is no question that Davis' program is valid under this test.

Certainly, on the basis of the undisputed factual submissions before this Court, Davis had a sound basis for believing that the problem of underrepresentation of minorities was substantial and chronic and that the problem was attributable to handicaps imposed on minority applicants by past and present racial discrimination. Until at least 1973, the practice of medicine in this country was, in fact, if not in law, largely the prerogative of whites. In 1950, for example, while Negroes constituted 10 of the total population, Negro physicians constituted only 2.2% of the total number of physicians. The overwhelming majority of these, moreover, were educated in two predominantly Negro medical schools, Howard and Meharry. By 1970, the gap between the proportion of Negroes in medicine and their proportion in the population

had widened: The number of Negroes employed in medicine remained frozen at 2.2% while the Negro population had increased to 11.1%. The number of Negro admittees to predominantly white medical schools, moreover, had declined in absolute numbers during the years 1955 to 1964. The statistical information was compiled by Government officials or medical educators, and has been brought to our attention in many of the briefs. Neither the parties nor the amici challenge the validity of the statistics alluded to in our discussion.

Moreover, Davis had very good reason to believe that the national pattern of underrepresentation of minorities in medicine would be perpetuated if it retained a single admissions standard. For example, the entering classes in 1968 and 1969, the years in which such a standard was used, included only 1 Chicano and 2 Negroes out of the 50 admittees for each year. Nor is there any relief from this pattern of underrepresentation in the statistics for the regular admissions program in later years.

Davis clearly could conclude that the serious and persistent underrepresentation of minorities in medicine depicted by these statistics is the result of handicaps under which minority applicants labor as a consequence of a background of deliberate, purposeful discrimination against minorities in education and in society generally, as well as in the medical profession. From the inception of our national life, Negroes have been subjected to unique legal disabilities impairing access to equal educational opportunity. Under slavery, penal sanctions were imposed upon anyone attempting to educate Negroes. After enactment of the Fourteenth Amendment the States continued to deny Negroes equal educational opportunity, enforcing a strict policy of segregation that itself stamped Negroes as inferior ... that relegated minorities to inferior educational institutions, and that denied them intercourse in the mainstream of professional life necessary to advancement. See *Sweatt v. Painter,* 339 U.S. 629 (1950). Segregation was not limited to public facilities, moreover, but was enforced by criminal penalties against private action as well. Thus, as late as 1908, this Court enforced a state criminal conviction against a private college for teaching Negroes together with whites. *Berea College v. Kentucky,* 211 U.S. 45....

The second prong of our test—whether the Davis program stigmatizes any discrete group or individual and whether race is reasonably used in light of the program's objectives—is clearly satisfied by the Davis program.

It is not even claimed that Davis' program in any way operates to stigmatize or single out any discrete and insular, or even any identifiable, non-minority group. Nor will harm comparable to that imposed upon racial minorities by exclusion or separation on grounds of race be the likely result of the program. It does not, for example, establish an exclusive preserve for minority students apart from and exclusive of whites. Rather, its purpose is to overcome the effects of segregation by bringing the races together. True, whites are excluded from participation in the special admissions program, but this fact only operates to reduce the number of whites to be admitted in the regular admissions program in order to permit admission of a reasonable percentage—less than their proportion of the California population[9]—of otherwise underrepresented qualified minority applicants.

Nor was Bakke in any sense stamped as inferior by the Medical School's rejection of him. Indeed, it is conceded by all that he satisfied those criteria regarded by the school as generally relevant to academic performance better than most of the minority members who were admitted. Moreover, there is absolutely no basis for concluding that Bakke's rejection as a result of Davis' use of racial preference will affect him throughout his life in the same way as the segregation of the Negro schoolchildren in *Brown I* would have affected them. Unlike discrimination against racial minorities, the use of racial preferences for remedial purposes does not inflict a pervasive injury upon individual whites in the sense that wherever they go or whatever they do there is a significant likelihood that they will be treated as second-class citizens because of their color. This distinction does not mean that the exclusion of a white resulting from the preferential use of race is not sufficiently serious to require justification; but it does mean that the injury inflicted by such a policy is not distinguishable from disadvantages caused by a wide range of government actions, none of which has ever been thought impermissible for that reason alone.

In addition, there is simply no evidence that the Davis program discriminates intentionally or unintentionally against any minority group which it purports to benefit. The program does not establish a quota in the invidious sense of a ceiling on the number of minority applicants to be admitted. Nor can the program reasonably be regarded as stigmatizing the program's beneficiaries or their race as inferior. The Davis program does not simply advance less qualified applicants; rather, it compensates applicants, who it is uncontested are fully qualified to study medicine, for educational disadvantages which it was reasonable to conclude were a product of state-fostered discrimination. Once admitted, these students must satisfy the same degree requirements as regularly admitted students; they are taught by the same faculty in the same classes; and their performance is evaluated by the same standards by which regularly admitted students are judged. Under these circumstances, their performance and degrees must be regarded equally with the regularly admitted students with whom they compete for standing. Since minority graduates cannot justifiably be regarded as less well qualified than nonminority graduates by virtue of the special admissions program, there is no reasonable basis to conclude that minority graduates at schools using such programs would be stigmatized as inferior by the existence of such programs.

We disagree with the lower courts' conclusion that the Davis program's use of race was unreasonable in light of its objectives. As petitioner argues, there are no practical means by which it could achieve its ends in the foreseeable future without the use of race-conscious measures. With respect to any factor (such as poverty or family educational background) that may be used as a substitute for race as an indicator of past discrimination, whites greatly outnumber racial minorities simply because whites make up a far larger percentage of the total population and therefore far outnumber minorities in absolute terms at every socio-economic level. For example, of a class of recent medical school applicants from families with less than $10,000 income, at least 71% were white.[10]

---

[9] Negroes and Chicanos alone constitute approximately 22% of California's population. This percentage was computed from data contained in Census, supra n. 49, pt. 6, California, sec. 1, 6–4, and Table 139.

[10] This percentage was computed from data presented in B. Waldman, Economic and Racial Disadvantage as Reflected in Traditional Medical School Selection Factors: A Study of 1976 Applicants to U.S. Medical Schools 34 (Table A–15), 42 (Table A–23) (Association of American Medical Colleges 1977).

Of all 1970 families headed by a person *not* a high school graduate which included related children under 18, 80% were white and 20% were racial minorities. Moreover, while race is positively correlated with differences in GPA and MCAT scores, economic disadvantage is not. Thus, it appears that economically disadvantaged whites do not score less well than economically advantaged whites, while economically advantaged blacks score less well than do disadvantaged whites. These statistics graphically illustrate that the University's purpose to integrate its classes by compensating for past discrimination could not be achieved by a general preference for the economically disadvantaged or the children of parents of limited education unless such groups were to make up the entire class.

Finally, Davis' special admissions program cannot be said to violate the Constitution simply because it has set aside a predetermined number of places for qualified minority applicants rather than using minority status as a positive factor to be considered in evaluating the applications of disadvantaged minority applicants. For purposes of constitutional adjudication, there is no difference between the two approaches. In any admissions program which accords special consideration to disadvantaged racial minorities, a determination of the degree of preference to be given is unavoidable, and any given preference that results in the exclusion of a white candidate is no more or less constitutionally acceptable than a program such as that at Davis. Furthermore, the extent of the preference inevitably depends on how many minority applicants the particular school is seeking to admit in any particular year so long as the number of qualified minority applicants exceeds that number. There is no sensible, and certainly no constitutional, distinction between, for example, adding a set number of points to the admissions rating of disadvantaged minority applicants as an expression of the preference with the expectation that this will result in the admission of an approximately determined number of qualified minority applicants and setting a fixed number of places for such applicants as was done here.

Accordingly, we would reverse the judgment of the Supreme Court of California holding the Medical School's special admissions program unconstitutional and directing respondent's admission, as well as that portion of the judgment enjoining the Medical School from according any consideration to race in the admissions process.

MR. JUSTICE MARSHALL.

I agree with the judgment of the Court only insofar as it permits a university to consider the race of an applicant in making admissions decisions. I do not agree that petitioner's admissions program violates the Constitution. For it must be remembered that, during most of the past 200 years, the Constitution as interpreted by this Court did not prohibit the most ingenious and pervasive forms of discrimination against the Negro. Now, when a State acts to remedy the effects of that legacy of discrimination, I cannot believe that this same Constitution stands as a barrier.

I

Three hundred and fifty years ago, the Negro was dragged to this country in chains to be sold into slavery. Uprooted from his homeland and thrust into bondage for forced labor, the slave was deprived of all legal rights. It was unlawful to teach him to read; he could be sold away from his family and friends at the whim of his master; and killing or maiming him was not a crime. The system of slavery brutalized and dehumanized both master and slave.[11]

The denial of human rights was etched into the American Colonies' first attempts at establishing self-government. When the colonists determined to seek their independence from England, they drafted a unique document cataloguing their grievances against the King and proclaiming as "self-evident" that "all men are created equal" and are endowed "with certain unalienable Rights," including those to "Life, Liberty and the pursuit of Happiness." The self-evident truths and the unalienable rights were intended, however, to apply only to white men. An earlier draft of the Declaration of Independence, submitted by Thomas Jefferson to the Continental Congress, had included among the charges against the King that

[he] has waged cruel war against human

---

[11] The history recounted here is perhaps too well known to require documentation. But I must acknowledge the authorities on which I rely in retelling it. J. Franklin, From Slavery to Freedom (4th ed. 1974) (hereinafter Franklin); R. Kluger, Simple Justice (1975) (hereinafter Kluger); C. Woodward, The Strange Career of Jim Crow (3d ed. 1974) (hereinafter Woodward).

nature itself, violating its most sacred rights of life and liberty in the persons of a distant people who never offended him, captivating and carrying them into slavery in another hemisphere, or to incur miserable death in their transportation thither.

Franklin 88. The Southern delegation insisted that the charge be deleted; the colonists themselves were implicated in the slave trade, and inclusion of this claim might have made it more difficult to justify the continuation of slavery once the ties to England were severed. Thus, even as the colonists embarked on a course to secure their own freedom and equality, they ensured perpetuation of the system that deprived a whole race of those rights.

The implicit protection of slavery embodied in the Declaration of Independence was made explicit in the Constitution, which treated a slave as being equivalent to three-fifths of a person for purposes of apportioning representatives and taxes among the States. Art. I, § 2. The Constitution also contained a clause ensuring that the "Migration or Importation" of slaves into the existing States would be legal until at least 1808, Art. I, § 9, and a fugitive slave clause requiring that when a slave escaped to another State, he must be returned on the claim of the master, Art. IV, § 2. In their declaration of the principles that were to provide the cornerstone of the new Nation, therefore, the Framers made it plain that "we the people," for whose protection the Constitution was designed, did not include those whose skins were the wrong color. As Professor John Hope Franklin has observed, Americans "proudly accepted the challenge and responsibility of their new political freedom by establishing the machinery and safeguards that insured the continued enslavement of blacks." Franklin 100.

The enforced segregation of the races continued into the middle of the 20th century. In both World Wars, Negroes were for the most part confined to separate military units; it was not until 1948 that an end to segregation in the military was ordered by President Truman. And the history of the exclusion of Negro children from white public schools is too well known and recent to require repeating here. That Negroes were deliberately excluded from public graduate and professional schools—and thereby denied the opportunity to become doctors, lawyers, engineers, and the like—

is also well established. It is of course true that some of the Jim Crow laws (which the decisions of this Court had helped to foster) were struck down by this Court in a series of decisions leading up to *Brown v. Board of Education,* 347 U.S. 483 (1954). See, *e.g., Morgan v. Virginia,* 328 U.S. 373 (1946); *Sweatt v. Painter,* 339 U.S. 629 (1950); *McLaurin v. Oklahoma State Regents,* 339 U.S. 637 (1950). Those decisions, however, did not automatically end segregation, nor did they move Negroes from a position of legal inferiority to one of equality. The legacy of years of slavery and of years of second-class citizenship in the wake of emancipation could not be so easily eliminated.

II

The position of the Negro today in America is the tragic but inevitable consequence of centuries of unequal treatment. Measured by any benchmark of comfort or achievement, meaningful equality remains a distant dream for the Negro.

A Negro child today has a life expectancy which is shorter by more than five years than that of a white child.[12] The Negro child's mother is over three times more likely to die of complications in childbirth,[13] and the infant mortality rate for Negroes is nearly twice that for whites. The median income of the Negro family is only 60% that of the median of a white family,[14] and the percentage of Negroes who live in families with incomes below the poverty line is nearly four times greater than that of whites.[15]

When the Negro child reaches working age, he finds that America offers him significantly less than it offers his white counterpart. For Negro adults, the unemployment rate is twice that of whites,[16] and the unemployment rate for Negro teenagers is nearly three times that of white teen-

---

[12] U.S. Dept. of Commerce, Bureau of the Census, Statistical Abstract of the United States 65 (1977) (Table 94).

[13] *Id.,* at 70 (Table 102).

[14] U.S. Dept. of Commerce, Bureau of the Census, Current Population Reports, Series P–60, No. 107, p. 7 (1977) (Table 1).

[15] *Id.,* at 20 (Table 14).

[16] U.S. Dept. of Labor, Bureau of Labor Statistics, Employment and Earnings, January 1978, p. 170 (Table 44).

agers.[17] A Negro male who completes four years of college can expect a median annual income of merely $110 more than a white male who has only a high school diploma.[18] Although Negroes represent 11.5% of the population,[19] they are only 1.2% of the lawyers and judges, 2% of the physicians, 2.3% of the dentists, 1.1% of the engineers and 2.6% of the college and university professors.[20]

The relationship between those figures and the history of unequal treatment afforded to the Negro cannot be denied. At every point from birth to death the impact of the past is reflected in the still disfavored position of the Negro.

In light of the sorry history of discrimination and its devastating impact on the lives of Negroes, bringing the Negro into the mainstream of American life should be a state interest of the highest order. To fail to do so is to ensure that America will forever remain a divided society....

IV

While I applaud the judgment of the Court that a university may consider race in its admissions process, it is more than a little ironic that, after several hundred years of class-based discrimination against Negroes, the Court is unwilling to hold that a class-based remedy for that discrimination is permissible. In declining to so hold, today's judgment ignores the fact that for several hundred years Negroes have been discriminated against, not as individuals, but rather solely because of the color of their skins. It is unnecessary in 20th-century America to have individual Negroes demonstrate that they have been victims of racial discrimination; the racism of our society has been so pervasive that none, regardless of wealth or position, has managed to escape its impact. The experience of Negroes in America has been different in kind, not just in degree, from that of other ethnic groups. It is not merely the history of slavery alone but also that a whole people were marked as inferior by the law. And that mark has endured. The dream of America as the great melting pot has not been realized for the Negro; because of his skin color he never even made it into the pot.

These differences in the experience of the Negro make it difficult for me to accept that Negroes cannot be afforded greater protection under the Fourteenth Amendment where it is necessary to remedy the effects of past discrimination. In the *Civil Rights Cases,* [109 U.S. 3 (1883)] the Court wrote that the Negro emerging from slavery must cease "to be the special favorite of the laws." 109 U.S., at 25; see *supra,* at 392. We cannot in light of the history of the last century yield to that view. Had the Court in that decision and others been willing to "do for human liberty and the fundamental rights of American citizenship, what it did . . . for the protection of slavery and the rights of the masters of fugitive slaves," 109 U.S. at 53 (Harlan, J., dissenting), we would not need now to permit the recognition of any "special wards."

It is because of a legacy of unequal treatment that we now must permit the institutions of this society to give consideration to race in making decisions about who will hold the positions of influence, affluence, and prestige in America. For far too long, the doors to those positions have been shut to Negroes. If we are ever to become a fully integrated society, one in which the color of a person's skin will not determine the opportunities available to him or her, we must be willing to take steps to open those doors. I do not believe that anyone can truly look into America's past and still find that a remedy for the effects of that past is impermissible.

MR. JUSTICE BLACKMUN....

It is worth noting, perhaps, that governmental preference has not been a stranger to our legal life. We see it in veterans' preferences. We see it in the aid-to-the-handicapped programs. We see it in the progressive income tax. We see it in the Indian programs. We may excuse some of these on the ground that they have specific constitutional protection or, as with Indians, that those benefited are wards of the Government. Nevertheless, these preferences exist and may not be ignored. And in the admissions field, as I have indicated, educational institutions have always used geography, athletic ability, anticipated financial largess, alumni pressure, and other factors of that kind.

I add these only as additional components on

---

[17] *Ibid.*

[18] U.S. Dept. of Commerce, Bureau of the Census, Current Population Reports, Series P–60, No. 105, p. 198 (1977) (Table 47).

[19] U.S. Dept. of Commerce, Bureau of the Census, Statistical Abstract, *supra*, at 25 (Table 24).

[20] *Id.*, at 407–408 (Table 662) (based on 1970 census).

the edges of the central question as to which I join my Brothers BRENNAN, WHITE, and MARSHALL in our more general approach. It is gratifying to know that the Court at least finds it constitutional for an academic institution to take race and ethnic background into consideration as one factor, among many, in the administration of its admissions program. I presume that that factor always has been there, though perhaps not conceded or even admitted. It is a fact of life, however, and a part of the real world of which we are all a part. The sooner we get down the road toward accepting and being a part of the real world, and not shutting it out and away from us, the sooner will these difficulties vanish from the scene....

Notes and Questions

1. Wholly apart from statutory or constitutional considerations, which attorney—Cox or Colvin—made the better "justice" argument?[21] Does your answer depend upon whether you believe more in justice for groups or justice for individuals? What justice argument could Cox have made to counter Colvin's?

2. Wholly apart from statutory or constitutional considerations, did the Supreme Court majority or the Supreme Court dissenters make the better "justice" argument? Does your answer depend upon whether you believe more in justice for groups or justice for individuals?

3. Consider the following hypothetical:

A state sets up a licensing procedure for automobile drivers. First, a license is awarded to any applicant who passes a driver's test with a score of 70% or better (and pays a fee and meets other criteria, such as being a resident of the state—these other qualifications will be omitted in the further discussion of this problem). These drivers will be called Group A. Second, a license is awarded to any member of a minority or underprivileged group who scores above 40% in the driver's test; we will call these drivers Group B. Both groups A and B get exactly the same license.

(a) Should a member of Group A be able to sue the licensing board for discrimination? Is there any "quota" system here?

(b) Should a driver who gets a score of 60%, but is not a member of a minority or underprivileged group, be able to sue the licensing board for discrimination in not awarding him a license? Is there any "quota" system here?

(c) Suppose a pedestrian is hit by a car driven by a member of Group B. Should the pedestrian be allowed to bring up in court the fact that the driver scored less than 70% on the driver's test and therefore is presumably not a good driver?

(d) What statistics would "count" in justifying the state's licensing scheme: (i) That most of the people who administer the driving tests are white majority

---

21 For a thorough review of the contemporary positions on the justice of affirmative action, see M. ROSENFELD, AFFIRMATIVE ACTION AND JUSTICE: A PHILOSOPHIC AND CONSTITUTIONAL INQUIRY (1991). In addition to the usual liberal paradigms for analyzing questions of distributive and corrective justice (libertarianism, utilitarianism, contractarianism, and egalitarianism), Rosenfeld deploys a conception drawn from Habermas and Kohlberg: justice as reversible reciprocity.

persons? (ii) That minority and underprivileged drivers are a lower percentage of all drivers than minority and underprivileged persons are a percentage of all citizens? (iii) That minority and underprivileged young persons come from families that are not likely to have cars, and so they have less familiarity with driving than do other people and hence should be allowed a lower score on the driving test?

(e) What policy considerations would "count" in justifying the state's licensing scheme: (i) The state wants to reduce the preponderance of minority and under-privileged persons riding the buses and subways by making it easier for many of them to drive cars? (ii) The state wants more minority and underprivileged drivers of cars to serve as "role models" for other members of those groups? (iii) It's part of the reparations society is paying and should be paying for the pre-Civil War slavery system?

(f) Can it be argued that a score of 40% on the drivers' test is enough for "competence" as a driver? (This is the same as saying that there is a "threshold" of driving competence at a given score level.) If so, why does the state have a score of 70% for the majority of driving applicants? Do they want to keep down the number of cars on the road? Is it likely that states would restrict the number of cars for no reason other than to reduce traffic? Doesn't the state get a substantial part of its revenue from the automotive culture (license fees, registration fees, sales tax on new and used car sales, gasoline tax, tolls)? On the other hand, what if the state simply wants to reduce the number of *accidents*? Suppose it finds an inverse correlation between the score on the drivers' test and the number of auto-mobile accidents? (Thus, if the passing score were raised from 70% to 80%, the number of automobile accidents would go down.) Does this make it harder to justify the Group B drivers?

4. The hypothetical in Question 3 is, of course, different in many respects from the medical-school admissions scheme at Davis in the *Bakke* case. In what *important* and *relevant* aspects is it *similar* to *Bakke*?

5. Is there a "threshold" of medical competence or legal competence in medical schools or law schools? Do the schools compete for entering students with the best test scores and college credentials *not* because those students are the only ones with enough talent to become doctors or lawyers, but simply because they will probably be *better* and *more successful* doctors and lawyers than other candidates for admission?

6. When we think of a person as a member of a class, do we consciously think of how many classes any given person is a member of? Mr. X may be a member of:

—the class of all white anglo-saxon protestants;
—the class of all red-heads;
—the class of all former boy scouts;
—the class of all Republicans;
—the class of all persons who wear eye glasses;
—the class of all persons who have ever been in an automobile accident;
—the class of all persons whose signature is illegible;
—the class of all women who like beer;

—the class of all poets;

—the class of all persons born on Christmas day.

Depending on how we define a given class, we can invent an endless list of classes to which we belong. Is our individuality simply a product of the intersection of *all* the classes to which we belong? Certainly it is impossible for any two persons to belong to exactly the same classes (even identical twins belong to at least two different classes: the class of first-born identical twins and the class of all second-born identical twins). If we add up all the conceivable classes to which we belong, can there be anything left that we could call our "own" personality? Does it matter?

Consider, however, the position of a party to a lawsuit. Won't that party necessarily be considered a member of a class of persons by the judge who is deciding the case? The judge, after all, wants to decide the case in such a way that it will both accord with existing precedent and serve as a good precedent for future cases. But isn't the only way to determine the precedent-value of the case to consider the parties as members of a class of potential persons with the same legal problem?

Isn't the class of persons *with the same legal problem* the inevitable class that every litigant is made a member of—whether the litigant likes it or not?

If so, can the judge possibly avoid deciding the case by reference to the class or category in which the litigant falls? Or to put the matter bluntly, is the individual-vs.-group distinction, and the possible bias that accompanies it, an inherent part of all litigation?

5.2 Should individual justice trump group justice?

City of Los Angeles Department of Water and Power v. Manhart

435 U.S. 702
Supreme Court of the United States
April 25, 1978

STEVENS, J., delivered the opinion of the Court, in which STEWART, WHITE, and POWELL, JJ., joined, in all but the retroactivity ruling, of which MARSHALL, J., joined, and in the retroactivity ruling of which BURGER, C.J., and BLACKMUN and REHNQUIST, JJ., joined. BLACKMUN, J., filed an opinion concurring in part and concurring in the judgment. BURGER, C.J., filed an opinion concurring in part and dissenting in part, in which REHNQUIST, J., joined. MARSHALL, J., filed an opinion concurring in part and dissenting in part. BRENNAN, J., took no part in the consideration or decision of the case.

David J. Oliphant argued the cause for petitioners. With him on the briefs were Burt Pines and J. David Hanson.

Robert M. Dohrmann argued the cause for respondents. With him on the brief were Kenneth M. Schwartz, Laurence D. Steinsapir, Howard M. Knee, and Katherine Stoll Burns.

Briefs of amici curiae urging reversal were filed by James A. Redden, Attorney General, Al J. Laue, Solicitor General, and William F.

Hoelscher, Assistant Attorney General, for the State of Oregon; and by Harry L. Du Brin, Jr., for the New York State Teachers' Retirement System.

Briefs of amici curiae urging affirmance were filed by Solicitor General McCree for the United States et al; by Ruth Bader Ginsburg for the American Civil Liberties Union et al; by Jonathan R. Harkavy for the American Nurses' Assn.; by Marguerite Rawalt for the Association for Women in Mathematics; and by John A. Fillion for the International Union, United Automobile, Aerospace & Agricultural Implement Workers of America.

MR. JUSTICE STEVENS delivered the opinion of the Court.

As a class, women live longer than men. For this reason, the Los Angeles Department of Water and Power required its female employees to make larger contributions to its pension fund than its male employees. We granted certiorari to decide whether this practice discriminated against individual female employees because of their sex in violation of § 703(a) (1) of the Civil Rights Act of 1964, as amended.[22]

For many years the Department has administered retirement, disability, and death-benefit programs for its employees. Upon retirement each employee is eligible for a monthly retirement benefit computed as a fraction of his or her salary multiplied by years of service. The monthly benefits for men and women of the same age, seniority, and salary are equal. Benefits are funded entirely by contributions from the employees and the Department, augmented by the income earned on those contributions. No private insurance company is involved in the administration or payment of benefits.

Based on a study of mortality tables and its own experience, the Department determined that its 2,000 female employees, on the average, will live a few years longer than its 10,000 male employees. The cost of a pension for the average retired female is greater than for the average male retiree because more monthly payments must be made to the average woman. The Department therefore required female employees to make monthly contributions to the fund which were 14.84% higher than the contributions required of comparable male employees. Because employee contributions were withheld from paychecks, a female employee took home less pay than a male employee earning the same salary.[23]

There are both real and fictional differences between women and men. It is true that the average man is taller than the average woman; it is not true that the average woman driver is more accident prone than the average man. Before the Civil Rights Act of 1964 was enacted, an employer could fashion his personnel policies on the basis of assumptions about the differences between men and women, whether or not the assumptions were valid.

It is now well recognized that employment decisions cannot be predicated on mere "stereotyped" impressions about the characteristics of males or females. Myths and purely habitual assumptions about a woman's inability to perform certain kinds of work are no longer acceptable reasons for refusing to employ qualified individuals, or for paying them less. This case does not, however, involve a fictional difference between men and women. It involves a generalization that the parties accept as unquestionably true: Women, as a class, do live longer than men. The Department treated its women employees differently from its men employees because the two classes are in fact different. It is equally true, however, that all individuals in the respective classes do not share the characteristic that differentiates the average class representatives. Many women do not live as long as the average man and many men outlive the average woman. The question, therefore, is

---

[22] The section provides:

"It shall be an unlawful employment practice for an employer—

"(1) to fail or refuse to hire or to discharge any individual, or otherwise to discriminate against any individual with respect to his compensation, terms, conditions, or privileges of employment, because of such individual's race, color, religion, sex, or national origin. . . ."

78 Stat. 255, 42 U.S.C. § 2000e-2 (a)(1).

---

[23] The significance of the disparity is illustrated by the record of one woman whose contributions to the fund (including interest on the amount withheld each month) amounted to $18,171.40; a similarly situated male would have contributed only $12,843.53.

whether the existence or nonexistence of "discrimination" is to be determined by comparison of class characteristics or individual characteristics. A "stereotyped" answer to that question may not be the same as the answer that the language and purpose of the statute command.

The statute makes it unlawful "to discriminate against any *individual* with respect to his compensation, terms, conditions, or privileges of employment, because of such *individual's* race, color, religion, sex, or national origin." The statute's focus on the individual is unambiguous. It precludes treatment of individuals as simply components of a racial, religious, sexual, or national class. If height is required for a job, a tall woman may not be refused employment merely because, on the average, women are too short. Even a true generalization about the class is an insufficient reason for disqualifying an individual to whom the generalization does not apply.

That proposition is of critical importance in this case because there is no assurance that any individual woman working for the Department will actually fit the generalization on which the Department's policy is based. Many of those individuals will not live as long as the average man. While they were working, those individuals received smaller paychecks because of their sex, but they will receive no compensating advantage when they retire.

It is true, of course, that while contributions are being collected from the employees, the Department cannot know which individuals will predecease the average woman. Therefore, unless women as a class are assessed an extra charge, they will be subsidized, to some extent, by the class of male employees. It follows, according to the Department, that fairness to its class of male employees justifies the extra assessment against all of its female employees.

But the question of fairness to various classes affected by the statute is essentially a matter of policy for the legislature to address. Congress has decided that classifications based on sex, like those based on national origin or race, are unlawful. Actuarial studies could unquestionably identify differences in life expectancy based on race

or national origin, as well as sex.[24] But a statute that was designed to make race irrelevant in the employment market . . . could not reasonably be construed to permit a take-home-pay differential based on a racial classification.[25]

Even if the statutory language were less clear, the basic policy of the statute requires that we focus on fairness to individuals rather than fairness to classes. Practices that classify employees in terms of religion, race, or sex tend to preserve traditional assumptions about groups rather than thoughtful scrutiny of individuals. The generalization involved in this case illustrates the point. Separate mortality tables are easily interpreted as reflecting innate differences between the sexes; but a significant part of the longevity differential may be explained by the social fact that men are heavier smokers than women.[26]

Finally, there is no reason to believe that Congress intended a special definition of discrimination in the context of employee group insurance coverage. It is true that insurance is concerned with events that are individually unpredictable, but that is characteristic of many employment decisions. Individual risks, like individual performance, may not be predicted by resort to classifications proscribed by Title VII. Indeed, the fact that this case involves a group insurance program highlights a basic flaw in the Department's fairness argument. For when insurance risks are grouped, the better risks always subsidize the poorer risks. Healthy persons subsidize medical benefits for the less healthy; unmarried workers subsidize the pensions

---

[24] For example, the life expectancy of a white baby in 1973 was 72.2 years; a nonwhite baby could expect to live 65.9 years, a difference of 6.3 years. See Public Health Service, IIA Vital Statistics of the United States, 1973, Table 5–3.

[25] Fortifying this conclusion is the fact that some States have banned higher life insurance rates for blacks since the 19th century. See generally M. James, The Metropolitan Life—A Study in Business Growth 338–339 (1947).

[26] See R. Retherford, The Changing Sex Differential in Mortality 71–82 (1975). Other social causes, such as drinking or eating habits—perhaps even the lingering effects of past employment discrimination—may also affect the mortality differential.

of married workers;[27] persons who eat, drink, or smoke to excess may subsidize pension benefits for persons whose habits are more temperate. Treating different classes of risks as though they were the same for purposes of group insurance is a common practice that has never been considered inherently unfair. To insure the flabby and the fit as though they were equivalent risks may be more common than treating men and women alike;[28] but nothing more than habit makes one "subsidy" seem less fair than the other.

An employment practice that requires 2,000 individuals to contribute more money into a fund than 10,000 other employees simply because each of them is a woman, rather than a man, is in direct conflict with both the language and the policy of the Act. Such a practice does not pass the simple test of whether the evidence shows "treatment of a person in a manner which but for that person's sex would be different." It constitutes discrimination and is unlawful unless exempted by the Equal Pay Act of 1963 or some other affirmative justification. . . .

The Department argues that reversal is required by *General Electric Co. v. Gilbert,* 429 U.S. 125. We are satisfied, however, that neither the holding nor the reasoning of *Gilbert* is controlling.

In *Gilbert* the Court held that the exclusion of pregnancy from an employer's disability benefit plan did not constitute sex discrimination within the meaning of Title VII. . . . [T]he Court first held that the General Electric plan did not involve "discrimination based upon gender as such." The two groups of potential recipients which that case concerned were pregnant women and nonpregnant persons. "While the first group is exclusively female, the second includes members of both sexes." 429 U.S., at 135. In contrast, each of the two groups

of employees involved in this case is composed entirely and exclusively of members of the same sex. On its face, this plan discriminates on the basis of sex whereas the General Electric plan discriminated on the basis of a special physical disability.

The Department challenges the District Court's award of retroactive relief to the entire class of female employees and retirees. . . .[29] [W]e conclude that it was error to grant such relief in this case. Accordingly, although we agree with the Court of Appeals' analysis of the statute, we vacate its judgment and remand the case for further proceedings consistent with this opinion.

It is so ordered.

MR. JUSTICE BLACKMUN, concurring in part and concurring in the judgment.

A program such as the one challenged here does exacerbate gender consciousness. But the program under consideration in *General Electric* [*Gilbert*] did exactly the same thing and yet was upheld against challenge.

The Court's distinction between the present case and *General Electric*—that the permitted classes there were "pregnant women and nonpregnant persons," both female and male, seems to me to be just too easy.[30] It is probably the only distinction that can be drawn. For me, it does not serve to distinguish the case on any principled basis. I therefore must conclude that today's decision cuts back on *General Electric*. I do not say that this is necessarily bad. If that is what Congress has chosen to do by Title VII—as the Court today with such assurance asserts—so be it. I feel, however, that we should meet the posture of the earlier cases head on and not by thin rationalization that seeks to distinguish but fails in its quest.

MR. CHIEF JUSTICE BURGER, with

---

[27] A study of life expectancy in the United States for 1949–1951 showed that 20-year-old men could expect to live to 60.6 years of age if they were divorced. If married, they could expect to reach 70.9 years of age, a difference of more than 10 years. *Id.,* at 93.

[28] The record indicates, however, that the Department has funded its death-benefit plan by equal contributions from male and female employees. A death benefit—unlike a pension benefit—has less value for persons with longer life expectancies. Under the Department's concept of fairness, then, this neutral funding of death benefits is unfair to women as a class.

---

[29] We consider the retroactivity branch of *Manhart* in Question 3 at the end of Section 7.2. [Eds.]

[30] It is of interest that Mr. Justice Stevens, in his dissent in *General Electric,* strongly protested the very distinction he now must make for the Court. It is not accurate to describe the program as dividing "potential recipients into two groups—pregnant women and nonpregnant persons." The classification is between persons who face a risk of pregnancy and those who do not. 429 U.S., at 161–162, n. 5.

whom MR. JUSTICE REHNQUIST joins, concurring in part and dissenting in part.

Gender-based actuarial tables have been in use since at least 1843, and their statistical validity has been repeatedly verified. The vast life insurance, annuity, and pension plan industry is based on these tables. As the Court recognizes, it is a fact that "women, as a class, do live longer than men." It is equally true that employers cannot know in advance when individual members of the classes will die. Yet, if they are to operate economically workable group pension programs, it is only rational to permit them to rely on statistically sound and proved disparities in longevity between men and women. Indeed, it seems to me irrational to assume Congress intended to outlaw use of the fact that, for whatever reasons or combination of reasons, women as a class outlive men.

The Court's conclusion that the language of the civil rights statute is clear, admitting of no advertence to the legislative history, such as there was, is not soundly based. An effect upon pension plans so revolutionary and discriminatory—this time favorable to women at the expense of men—should not be read into the statute without either a clear statement of that intent in the statute, or some reliable indication in the legislative history that this was Congress' purpose.

The reality of differences in human mortality is what mortality experience tables reflect. The difference is the added longevity of women. All the reasons why women statistically outlive men are not clear. But categorizing people on the basis of sex, the one acknowledged immutable difference between men and women, is to take into account all of the unknown reasons, whether biologically or culturally based, or both, which give women a significantly greater life expectancy than men. It is therefore true as the Court says, "that any individual's life expectancy is based on a number of factors, of which sex is only one." But it is not true that by seizing upon the only constant, "measurable" factor, no others were taken into account. All other factors, whether known but variable—or unknown—are the elements which automatically account for the actuarial disparity. And all are accounted for when the constant factor is used as a basis for determining the costs and benefits of a group pension plan.

This is in no sense a failure to treat women as "individuals" in violation of the statute, as the Court holds. It is to treat them as individually as it is possible to do in the face of the unknowable length of each individual life. Individually, every woman has the same statistical possibility of outliving men. This is the essence of basing decisions on reliable statistics when individual determinations are infeasible.

Of course, women cannot be disqualified from, for example, heavy labor just because the generality of women are thought not as strong as men—a proposition which perhaps may sometime be statistically demonstrable, but will remain individually refutable. When, however, it is impossible to tailor a program such as a pension plan to the individual, nothing should prevent application of reliable statistical facts to the individual, for whom the facts cannot be disproved until long after planning, funding, and operating the program have been undertaken.

Notes and Questions

1. Is the "discrimination" in *Manhart* simply the overt classification according to gender? Suppose instead of "women" the Department had asked of the applicants for the pension program, "are you or have you ever been biologically capable of becoming pregnant?" Would/should that make a difference? How did the Court react to this type of argument in the General Electric case that the Court Cited?

2. The *Manhart* case concerned pensions and annuities. The two work roughly the same way. Both provide the insured, upon retirement, with a set monthly income. If a woman has a longer life expectancy than a man, the insurer will accordingly expect to be paying her a higher total of monthly payments. Hence—simply because of the fact that she is a woman—the insurer will want to charge her a higher contribution amount toward her pension program while she is employed.

If instead a woman bought life insurance, would she also be expected to pay a higher rate? No, because life insurance is only paid when the insured dies, and since an insured woman has a longer life expectancy, the insurance company will be able to put off paying her for a longer period of time than it would have to pay an insured man. Thus, a woman should be able to purchase life insurance at a lower rate than would a man.

Now that *Manhart* has required the State of California to charge equal contributions from men and women for annuities, should the law require life insurance companies to raise their rates for women?

Consider also drivers' insurance. At the same age levels for young drivers (under 25), women drivers have fewer accidents than men drivers. As a result, automobile insurance is cheaper for women than for men. Does *Manhart* now require that automobile insurance rates for women be raised?[31]

Might the total result of the elimination of gender-based classifications make insurance more expensive for women? Should the Supreme Court be barging into this complex area of insurance on the basis of a single case?

3. Sometimes individuals purchase unique insurance for themselves—such as a model insuring her face, or a pitcher insuring his arm. The insurer in such a situation evaluates all the characteristics (risk-proneness, lifestyle, etc.) of the insured, and determines an insurance premium for the insured to pay. If the premium reflects the exact discounted risk of the insured event, then the only reason the individual will take out the insurance is that he or she is more risk-averse than the insurance company—for, economically speaking, there is no net benefit in the insurance for either the insurer or the insured. However, if the insurance company sets a premium that exceeds the exact discounted risk of the insured event, then it will make an actuarial profit on the transaction, although it will be a poor business deal for the insured person. If the insured person is highly risk-averse, he or she may want the insurance anyway. In addition, there may be publicity value (a famous actress insures her legs, enabling her press agent to say that she has "million-dollar legs.")

4. Most insurance is not of the "unique" sort, but rather is a form of group insurance. For example, automobile insurance is based on the insurance company's calculation that it will in the aggregate pay out an expected dollar amount of claims if it insures all drivers. If an individual driver does not get into an accident, she will not complain that she made a bad bargain; rather, she will be glad to have avoided being injured.

Why don't insurance companies simply insure all drivers at the same rate, treating them all as "persons" under the law. Suppose insurance company A does precisely this, charging every driver, say, $400 a year. Then suppose insurance company B wishes to compete with A. B decides to have two groups of insured persons: male drivers under 25 years old who are charged $500 a year, and all other drivers who are charged $300 a year. What now

---

[31] "One study showed that if sex were eliminated as a variable, young female drivers' automobile insurance rates would increase 26% and young male drivers' rates would decrease 6% (females are only 24% of the youthful driving population)." Abraham, *Efficiency and Fairness in Insurance Risk Classification,* 71 VA. L. REV. 403, 439 (1985), citing National Ass'n of Ins. Comm'rs, D–3 Advisory Comm., Private Passenger Automobile Insurance Risk Classification 26 (1979).

happens to the competition between A and B?

Clearly the male drivers under 25 years of age will flock to company A and sign up for A's insurance at $400 a year, because it is less than B's rates by $100. All other drivers will flock to company B, because B's rates are significantly cheaper for them.

Now, if B is right in choosing its class—that is, if B's overall accident payouts are significantly less because there are no male drivers under 25 years of age who have signed up with B, then B will profit considerably. But A has lost its careful drivers, and is saddled only with the riskier drivers who are under 25 years old and are male. Its payouts will skyrocket.

Thus we see that it was eminently rational for company B to make the group distinction, and irrational for company A to maintain its one-class program in the face of B's two-class program. A could go bankrupt quickly unless it changes to B's system. Normal market forces dictate that, as soon as a rational classification is discovered by any insurance company, all other insurance companies in the same field will—almost immediately—adopt the same classification.[32]

5. Consider the lower insurance rates for teen-age male drivers whose grades in high school are B or higher. Why should insurance companies have invented a classification for driving, where above-B gets a lower rate and below-B is charged a higher rate? What does academic excellence have to do with the risk of automobile accidents? See if you can list two or three factors that would make this a rational classification.

6. Suppose an automobile insurance company makes a classification based on the religion of the insured, and deliberately charges a higher rate to persons of a particular religion. Should the courts step in and invalidate such a classification? Won't market forces do the same thing? Recall Question 3: there the classification worked because it was related to accident-proneness. Here, if a company makes a classification that is not related to accident-proneness, it will lose out in the competition with other insurers. The persons of the religious group charged the higher rates will go to competing insurers, and if they are good drivers (which is our assumption, because we are saying that the classification is not related to accident-proneness), they will increase the profitability of the insurance company that they go to, whereas the insurance company that discriminated against them will lose a group of good drivers and hence will be hurt in terms of profitability.

Thus, insurance companies are trying to maximize their profit, we should expect them to make classifications that are related to the risk they are insuring against, and to avoid all other classifications.

What if a given classification is related to the insured risk, but also happens to be a discriminatory classification? Isn't that the situation in the *Manhart* case?

---

[32] Note that the more immediately all the other companies adopt the same classification, the less incentive exists for any one company to invent the classification. Inventing a rational classification involves research and overhead time, which is costly. Hence, it is possible that some rational classifications are not made at all. For instance, there was a time when life insurance rates were the same for women as for men. This was irrational given the disparity in longevity, but until one company implemented the classification change, the others had no real incentive to investigate or institute it. In some respects, the *Manhart* case may have been motivated by a reaction against past discriminatory insurance practices toward women.

7. How do you deal with the "individual vs. group" argument in *Manhart* that even though women as a class might live longer than men, this is not necessarily true of any given individual woman—hence it is unfair to charge an individual woman a rate based upon group characteristics?

Wouldn't the same argument be true if a company only had female employees? Some individual employees will live longer than the group average, some less long. Aren't the latter being overcharged?

Is the "individual vs. group" argument simply a misreading of what is meant by group insurance? Don't the "lucky" individuals always subsidize the "unlucky" individuals within any group insurance system? If so, why does the *Manhart* court seem to think that the argument changes if there is a gender distinction between groups?

8. Consider the questions and issues raised in the following transcript of a classroom discussion.

Classroom Dialogue

Cardozo Law School, New York City, October 22, 1986
Course in JUSTICE (experimental course)
Professor Arthur Jacobson, Yeshiva University
Professor Anthony D'Amato, Northwestern University

PROF. JACOBSON. Let's say we discover that there's a category of persons in a group medical insurance plan for which the insurance, in a statistical predictive sense, would cost more. In other words, they are more likely to draw from the pot, statistically. Let's say, women on medical insurance because women have more medical problems if you define pregnancy and birth as a female medical problem, okay? That's another hot case now in California. Why should women pay more for medical insurance because they have all the problems associated with reproductive systems?

PROF. D'AMATO. Are you saying it's unfair only to men who aren't pregnant? Have they came up with a California male who's pregnant?

PROF. JACOBSON. Right.

PROF. D'AMATO. I always knew they were innovative out there in California.
(LAUGHTER)

PROF. JACOBSON. Actually I prefer the pregnancy problem because, first of all, you find it much more difficult to argue that one, emotionally.
(LAUGHTER)

Second of all, I think it's clearly for the benefit of the species, right, that women are doing this for us, uh, whatever you want to call it. There's a clear sort of species benefit argument there which even the most hard-boiled, mean-spirited, economistic male probably could buy, all right?

(LAUGHTER)

Now, let's say the group decides that we're not going to saddle women with that burden and charge them more for the insurance fund. Even though it would be economically rational to do so. So, all the Court is saying in *Manhart,* it seems to me, is that we the public have made such a decision and have voted a statute that says even though this would be a category where it would be economically rational to charge women more, we have decided that the Department cannot do so. They cannot use that category.

PROF. D'AMATO. But why should an insurance company—or a group of persons that decides to set up a group insurance plan—do that which is economically irrational?

STUDENT. For all the reasons Professor Jacobson said.

PROF. D'AMATO. Fine. Then my point is: if instead the group decides to do that which is economically *rational,* how can the Court say that they are discriminating against women?

ANOTHER STUDENT. I think the pregnancy example—the pregnancy cases—the voluntary ones as opposed to the involuntary ones like how long you live—maybe the involuntary ones are a product of voluntary factors like supposedly whether you smoke, whether you drink—

ANOTHER STUDENT. You know bringing in pregnancy, it's more of a, you know, it takes two—you know that somewhere there's a man, a man involved, and it's more likely that that pers—that that man is involved in the female and—

(LAUGHTER)

that no matter which way you carved the benefits, whether you say that women are going to pay more or that men are going to pay the same, it will probably be going to end up the same if they're in a family structure. So—

PROF. JACOBSON. In other words, if you have a female wage earner and a male wage earner, if one is getting screwed, the other will balance it out in your argument.

(LAUGHTER)

STUDENT. However, you know that if you do certain things you will get pregnant whereas you know, you can be sure about, it's more than likely—

PROF. JACOBSON. If you smoke you're more likely to die sooner than if you don't smoke.

STUDENT. And insurance reflects other factors like whether you smoke or not or, they require a physical exam, and to an extent, by allowing that voluntary act to be a burden on other people, you're creating like an involuntary servitude in fact on men because they don't—

PROF. JACOBSON. Well, that's the individualist argument, that's correct. That is the individualist argument. Does anybody have a counter to that?

PROF. D'AMATO. You made it yourself. It's the group argument. You're saying that if people want to purchase insurance, the government can come along to the men in the group and say to them, "You're being unfair to women," and levy a tax on the men that consists of a transfer payment—a subsidy from the men in the group to the women in the group, so that when the annuities are paid out the women as a whole can get more money out than they put in.

PROF. JACOBSON. First of all, I agree with you that it's a transfer payment. The insurance scheme as a whole is a transfer payment. In your system, the transfer payments go to the persons who suffer the insurable event. You think it's fair that they should get the money. The logical consequence of your statement is that we should all pay if we all believe in the justice of the transfer payment. So in your scheme, justice consists of paying the persons who suffer the insured event. In my scheme, justice consists also of paying groups that are discriminated against.

PROF. D'AMATO. Why is that just?

PROF. JACOBSON. It's like the Soviet Union which has state insurance and state insurance only for the vicissitudes of life and I think that may be correct. In other words, I think the system of private insurance may be simply an anachronism.

PROF. D'AMATO. Then maybe we should address the problem at the level of capitalism versus socialism.

PROF. JACOBSON. However, I could defend the system of private insurance. Under either system we'd still have the problem of who should pay.

PROF. D'AMATO. Now you seem to be agreeing with me that the case may not have been correctly decided.

PROF. JACOBSON. Oh no. There was a statute, whether you believe the statute was correct or not, I believe that the statute clearly forbids using gender as a category in the annuity plan.

PROF. D'AMATO. Why? The statute forbids using gender as a category for discrimination, and what I'm saying is that there is no discrimination here because the relevant question is "Who lives longer?" and the answer is women. There is nothing "discriminatory" about that, except that the insurance scheme has to make certain distinctions based on membership in groups that have certain actuarial life expectancies.

PROF. JACOBSON. Is a longer life expectancy the same kind of distinction as ability to become pregnant? Yes?

STUDENT. I think you made the argument before which was that women bearing children is done for the betterment of the whole world—

ANOTHER STUDENT. That's a decision society makes and either way—

PROF. JACOBSON. Who is society? Can you tell me his phone number?

STUDENT. It's a majority, it's the majority who make the decisions. It's the people who make the decisions. It's the Congress who enacts the statute or the Supreme Court who decides the case.

PROF. D'AMATO. I suggest that it's the society of all the people who want to get together and have insurance and this is your group. Of course it's a group because insurance is a group phenomenon. What we're really saying is that everybody in this group is going to contribute to a pot so that those individuals who are adversely affected are going to be paid by those who aren't adversely affected.

PROF. JACOBSON. Okay how about this? Right now the pensions are done employer by employer. What if all women got together, instead of employer by employer—all women decided to get together and insure themselves? Or, vice versa, all men said, "The hell with the women, they live longer. We'll get together, cut them out and have the men's annuity."

PROF. D'AMATO. Fine, that's what's good about this system that we have—that we can do that—whereas in the Soviet Union—which is the system you seem to prefer—they can't do that.

(LAUGHTER)

PROF. JACOBSON. I don't believe we're free to do that, either. It may be unconstitutional under the *Manhart* case.

PROF. D'AMATO. Look, we have people in this country who are high-risk drivers who can't get insurance. There's nothing wrong with those high-risk drivers all getting together and setting up their own insurance company and insuring themselves. They will soon discover that they will have to pay high premiums because every one of them is a high-risk driver. But surely that's fair! That's what we want. It's just that the insurance company, by proxy, is doing the same thing when it charges these people higher insurance rates. There's no evil insurance company gouging people here. The Department in the *Manhart* case was not acting out of evil or discriminatory motives. It was charging women higher rates because it knows that it will have to make more annuity payments to them than to men.

PROF. JACOBSON. Okay, so it doesn't matter whether it's state or private?

PROF. D'AMATO. That's right.

PROF. JACOBSON. Because every—any rational person will come to the same result?

PROF. D'AMATO. That's roughly what happens.

PROF. JACOBSON. The Soviet Union reference is a canard, at that point.

PROF. D'AMATO. If the Soviet Union charges bad drivers more money, they would be operating like a private enterprise. But they probably don't do that. Marxism itself—for all the long and complicated writings of Marx and Engels—reduces to a two-word theory: universal insurance. Marxism simply says that everyone will be insured—to each according to his needs. And to convince the reader, Marx and Engels plug in every social value you can think of—not just the nondiscriminatory ones you like. It's an arbitrary paternalistic system. As soon as we start plugging in social values, we have to (a) justify the values, and (b) answer "Where do you draw the line?" How about political affiliations, for example? Sooner or later that will come up. Once you open the door to making arbitrary distinctions, you're off interfering with the system for political ends. In *Manhart,* the people whose ox is being gored are the males who are paying higher insurance rates—who are being told that as to this characteristic, male versus female, the Supreme Court is not going to let the insurance company be rational.

PROF. JACOBSON. Economically rational.

PROF. D'AMATO. Right—economically rational, which means the Supreme Court is forcing males to engage in involuntary transfer payments to females. But the transfer payments are justified because nice people, like Professor Jacobson, think that women should get a break.

PROF. JACOBSON. All right, as long as you are accusing me of being a collectivist, let me take it all the way. How about the notion, which I think would be a communist notion, that to divide up the human group at all is to bite the apple that leads to shame. In other words, you are not permitted to create any categories because as soon as you create a category, you're departing from the pure notion of insurance which is that we all should pay for the misfortunes of a single one. In other words, the only legitimate category is the group versus the individual.

PROF. D'AMATO. Fine. I'll bite. I'm glad you asked that question. "Why divide up the human being at all according to categories?" And then ask, "Why should the government divide people up into categories?" For me, the evil here is when the government—the Supreme Court, Washington, D.C.—when they divide people into categories, that's the evil. But when people get together, voluntarily without any government involved, and divide themselves up into categories, I believe that's all right because other people can choose to go into other categories. For example, if you want to set up your own religion, and I don't like it, I don't have to join yours—I can set up my own. What's bad is when the government sets up a religion. That's what's happening in this case—the government is engaging in forced categorization. It's true that in this case they're dissolving a category, men against women, not setting one up, but it amounts to exactly the same thing. They're saying the category shall now and forever be "people" and not "men or women." The government is not going to let private groups make certain kinds of classifications. And if you allow the government to get away with it, tomorrow they will tell you that the new category is "Republicans or Democrats," and each group will have to pay the same total taxes, so if you voted for the losing party in the last election your individual tax rate will be higher because your group total has to come out the same as that of the other party. And next year it will be "vegetarians," and someday "Communist Party members" and—

PROF. JACOBSON. Wait a—

PROF. D'AMATO. —and you're into the category business by official decree and that's what I'm against.

PROF. JACOBSON. First of all, I reject the idea that there's a slippery slope. The statute is very clear and very limited. The Civil Rights Act of 1964 says that we shall not discriminate and these are the fundamental American principles.

PROF. D'AMATO. Natural origin is okay though, right? Because we discriminate that way in our immigration laws.

PROF. JACOBSON. I'm not sure if it's okay.

PROF. D'AMATO. Well, that's what I'm saying, it's not okay but we discriminate in our immigration laws—we have country-by-country immigration quotas that favor certain countries having certain racial and ethnic groups and discriminate against other countries—but the Supreme Court hasn't even entertained the thought of striking it down.

PROF. JACOBSON. That's a different problem.

PROF. D'AMATO. No it isn't. It's a part of the same policy that you're defending.

PROF. JACOBSON. No, it's a separable problem. To say how should we treat citizens—

PROF. D'AMATO. Oh?

PROF. JACOBSON. —and then to say, "Well, you can't—"

PROF. D'AMATO. Now who's making distinctions? Who's dividing people into citizens and non-citizens? Why aren't they all just "people"—like your men and women?

PROF. JACOBSON. No, fine, look. These are intellectually separable issues.

PROF. D'AMATO. No they're not. You're making arbitrary divisions. "Citizen" is one of the most arbitrary decisions you can make.

PROF. JACOBSON. Citizen is not arbitrary inasmuch as it defines who is and who is not a member of the polity for the purposes of our laws.

PROF. D'AMATO. Oh. Now I get it. Once you use the word "polity" the difference suddenly becomes clear.

PROF. JACOBSON. Would you let anybody in the world vote in the United States?

PROF. D'AMATO. If they pay U.S. taxes, yes.

PROF. JACOBSON. Oh my God!

PROF. D'AMATO. I thought the Supreme Court was your highest authority.

PROF. JACOBSON. What a remarkable claim!

PROF. D'AMATO. Why not? If they're contributing to the society, why shouldn't they be able to have a voice in it?

PROF. JACOBSON. So you're eliminating the nation-state?

PROF. D'AMATO. Yes, it's the worst governmentally imposed category of them all.

PROF. JACOBSON. Welcome to the Soviet Union!

(LAUGHTER)

The Empty Idea of Equality[33]

Peter Westen

Relationships of equality (and inequality) are derivative, secondary relationships; they are logically posterior, not anterior, to rights. To say that two persons are the same in a certain respect is to presuppose a rule—a prescribed standard for treating them—that both fully satisfy. Before such a rule is established, no standard of comparison exists. After such a rule is established, equality between them is a "logical consequence" of the established rule. They are then "equal" in respect of the rule because that is what equal means: "Equally" means "'according to one and the same rule.'" They are also then entitled to equal treatment under the rule because that is what possessing a rule means: "To conform

---

33 95 HARV. L. REV. 537, 548–50, 571–77 (1982).

to a rule is (tautologically) to apply it to the cases to which it applies." To say that two people are "equal" and entitled to be treated "equally" is to say that they both fully satisfy the criteria of a governing rule of treatment. It says nothing at all about the content or wisdom of the governing rule.

It might be thought that, while relationships of equality logically follow substantive definitions of right, equality may also precede definitions of right. Thus, it might be thought that a substantive right of persons to be treated with human respect is itself a product of an antecedent judgment that all persons are equal. That is not so. To see why, consider how one would go about deciding whether monstrously deformed neonates or human embryos or stroke victims in irreversible comas should be treated as "persons" for purposes of the right to respect. In trying to make the decision, one gets nowhere by intoning that all persons are equal, because the very question is whether the three candidates are indeed "persons" within the meaning of the rule. Nor does it do any good to say that likes should be treated alike, because the very question is whether the three candidates are indeed alike for purposes of human respect. Rather, one must first identify the trait that entitles anyone to be treated with respect and then ascertain empirically whether the trait appears in one or more of the three candidates. If the candidates possess the relevant trait, they become "persons" within the meaning of the rule and hence entitled to respect. If they lack the relevant trait, they are not "persons," not equal to persons, and not to be treated like persons for purposes of the rule.

[I]f the equal protection clause embodies the idea that likes should be treated alike and if that idea truly entails a rebuttable presumption in favor of treating all persons alike, it therefore follows that the equal protection clause contains a rebuttable presumption in favor of treating people alike—a presumption rebuttable only by a showing of "rational" reasons for treating people differently. In short, so the argument goes, any person who wishes to challenge a state regulation that treats him differently from others may invoke the equal protection clause and, by doing so, place the burden on the state to show rational grounds for treating him differently.

The so-called "presumption" of equality raises two separate problems: (1) the rebuttable presumption in favor of treating people alike is neither logically derivable from nor consistent with the idea that "likes should be treated alike"; and (2) the presumption of equality is essentially meaningless.

The first problem is that none of the plausible interpretations of the presumption of equality can be derived logically from the idea of equality. If the proposition that "all people are in some sense alike" means that all people are *morally* alike in all relevant respects (and if that is a coherent thing to say), it does not follow that all people should be treated alike until rational reasons are given for treating them differently. After all, if persons who are alike should be treated alike and if all persons are morally alike, it follows that all persons should *always* be treated alike; if all persons are truly alike in every moral respect, there could never be any reason—much less any rational reason—for treating them differently. The command to "treat likes alike" is absolute, while the presumption of equality is a lesser prima facie command, a command rebuttable by a showing of "rational reasons" for treating people differently. One cannot derive a prima facie command from an absolute command. If, on the other hand, "all people are in some sense alike" means that all persons are empirically and morally alike in certain significant respects, it does not follow that the state has an obligation to treat them alike in *all* respects. On the contrary, if all people are alike in some particular respect, the most that follows is that all people must be treated alike in the particular respect—and in that respect alone—in which they are alike.

Of course, it could be that people are alike in only certain respects but that the presumption functions as a procedural rule for reaching correct decisions in the face of uncertainty about particular cases. A presumption of equality in that event would have to be based on one of two assumptions. First, we might assume ignorance of whether the respects in which people are morally alike are more numerous or more significant than the respects in which they are unalike. Yet in that case, a presumption of equality would be logically inconsistent with the idea that likes should be treated alike. The presumption expresses a *preference* for treating people "alike" as opposed to "unalike." The idea of equality, in contrast, expresses no preference for "like" treatment as opposed to "unlike" treatment. In requiring that likes be treated alike, it necessarily also requires that unlike be treated unalike. This is so because to say that two people are "alike" for purposes of claiming certain treatment means that they both possess whatever quality or qualities are prescribed for that treatment by existing rules, and thus are both entitled to the treatment; and to say that two people are "unalike" means that one of them *lacks* a quality prescribed by rules for that treatment, and thus is not entitled to the treatment. The very rules of treatment that render some people "alike" (and thus require they be treated alike) logically render other people "unalike" (and require they be treated unalike). As far as equality is concerned, therefore, when one is ignorant as to whether people are likely to be alike in morally significant respects, a presumption in favor of treating people alike is as unjustified as a presumption in favor of treating them *un*alike; each presumption creates an unjustified risk that it will deny people the treatment to which they are actually entitled.

The same procedural rule, however, could be based on a second assumption. The presumption of equality could express a judgment that people are alike in more morally significant respects than they are unalike. Put another way, the presumption could be that, in instances of uncertainty, there is greater moral danger in treating persons unalike than in treating them alike. Such a presumption, however, cannot be derived from the general proposition that likes should be treated alike. Instead, it would have to derive from particular experience that distinctions between persons are either *usually* unjustified or sufficiently grave to outweigh the harm of *usually* doing the opposite. Because the principle that "likes should be treated alike" does not itself entail the idea that people are alike in more morally significant respects than they are unalike, any presumption of the latter kind must derive its substance from outside the idea of equality.

The second, and more serious, problem with the presumption of equality is that it is totally indeterminate. For one thing, just as the presumption of equality itself contains no standards for distinguishing "like" from "unlike" objects, neither can it distinguish "like" from "unlike" treatments. Furthermore, because every rule treats people alike in some respects and unalike in others, the presumption cannot fill its "core function" of distinguishing rules that require justification from those that do not. Finally, even if the presumption could definitely identify rules requiring justification, the presumption itself contains no standards for distinguishing "good" from "bad" reasons for treating people unalike, and so it cannot tell an actor when the presumption is rebutted. For all three reasons, the presumption remains meaningless as a moral norm. . . .

What does all this mean for rationality review under the equal protection clause? It means that rationality review cannot be justified or defended as a distinctive attribute of equality. That is not to say that the state may enact regulatory classifications that are "rationally unrelated" to "legitimate state interest[s]." The pros and cons of rationality review are matters of substantive constitutional value that must be decided on their own merits. The point is that, if rationality review has merit, it is not because the state is constitutionally obliged to have rational reasons for treating people "unalike" (as opposed to "alike") but because the state is obliged to have rational and legitimate reason for *every* way in which it treats people. Whatever merit rationality review has must ultimately derive not from notions of equality but from notions of substantive due process.

Is Equality a Totally Empty Idea?[34]

Anthony D'Amato

Let us suppose that a state legislature decides to restrict motorists' use of gasoline by enacting a statute allowing drivers to purchase gasoline only on weekdays if their license plate is odd-numbered and only on weekends if their license plate is even-numbered. The even-numbered drivers, constituting about half the motorists in the state, will thus effectively be restricted to purchasing gasoline on Saturdays, or in other words will have one fifth the opportunity to purchase of the drivers who have odd-numbered plates. We can assume that this statute is not an attempt to reduce lines at service stations (actual statutes have done this by, for example, allowing odd-numbered plates to purchase gasoline on odd-numbered days), but rather to cut down on total gasoline consumption. We can further assume that the legislature calculated that the great difficulty of purchase now imposed upon even-numbered drivers will reduce total gasoline consumption by the desired amount in that state.

Suppose now that the even-numbered drivers bring a class-action suit to declare the statute unconstitutional. Have they been denied substantive due process? No, because the means selected by the legislature to reduce gasoline consumption is rationally related to its goal. In fact, it is probably cheaper than the alternative of issuing ration points to all drivers. Moreover, since the legislature could have stopped the sale of gasoline in the state entirely, cutting back on sales by the means chosen was well within the legislature's power.

Instead, the only real complaint that the even-numbered drivers have is that they have not been treated equally with the odd-numbered drivers. Here one can imagine Professor Westen saying, "But they are not equal—they are different in precisely the difference articulated by the legislature, namely, that they possess license plates that are divisible by 2 whereas the other drivers do not possess such plates." To be sure, this is, logically speaking, a difference. But the fact is that the "difference" selected by the legislature was a random

---

[34] 81 MICH. L. REV. 600 (1983).

one; it was arbitrary. If people are subject to arbitrary classifications, they are not being treated equally. Only if the classifications are nonarbitrary can we agree with Professor Westen that the "equality" rhetoric falls out, because *then* the classification *defines* the relevant difference such that the two groups should now be treated "unalike."

Professor Westen has responded to my hypothetical case by formulating a prescriptive standard that he believes is logically anterior to any concept of equality:

> The state shall not pursue its ends by imposing a great burden on one class of persons where it could fully achieve its ends by imposing a considerably lesser burden on that or another class of persons.[35]

However, his standard is not, and cannot be, a logical presupposition of the idea of equality.

To simplify the analysis, let us assign a burden of 5 to my class of drivers with even-numbered license plates, representing the five days of the week that they cannot purchase gasoline, and a burden of 1 to the odd-numbered class. Professor Westen's standard would require a reduction on the burden of the even class by, for example, lowering it from 5 to 2. But then, in order to fully achieve the state's ends of a reduction in the availability of gasoline, there must be an increase on the odd class from 1 to 4. Thus:

> *Original hypothetical:*
> 5 (even class) + 1 (odd class) = 6
> *Westen's standard, first application:*
> 2 (even class) + 4 (odd class) = 6

However, it is now apparent upon inspection that the new arrangement continues to violate the Westen standard, although from the opposite direction. We must apply the standard again, this time reducing the burden on the odd class and increasing it on the even class. If we had no idea of the concept of equality, we would be required to continue applying the standard indefinitely, until at some point we would hit upon an equilibrium position where there can be no further violation of the statutory standard:

> *Westen standard, final application:*
> 3 (even class) + 3 (odd class) = 6

In brief, the concept of equality is inherent in Westen's standard. The standard is simply a cumbersome way of saying that the two classes of persons must receive equal protection under the law.

Yet one might object that the procedure of successive applications of the standard until equality is reached shows that the standard is anterior to the concept of equality. This objection cannot be maintained, however, due to a hidden assumption in the very procedure I described of successive applications of the standard. For the only way we know what direction to move in making reductions and increases in burdens is to have a concept of equality in mind. The only way we can know that one burden is "great" and another burden is "considerably lesser," to use the words in Professor Westen's standard, is to compare the

---

[35] Westen, *The Meaning of Equality in Law, Science, Math, and Morals: A Reply,* 81 MICH. L. REV. 604 (1983).

burdens. But comparison presupposes a measure of equality, for we cannot know that one burden is greater than another unless we first have a concept of when the two burdens are equal.

Professor Westen's standard, therefore, is logically posterior to the concept of equality. If we start with the Equal Protection Clause, then a standard such as Professor Westen's, which he attempts to ground in substantive due process, can be given operative content.

5.3   The claim to be treated as a group

The cases we have considered so far in this chapter concern claims by individuals whom society treats as a group. In *Bakke* the claim was that the legal system as well ought to treat disadvantaged minorities as a group for remedial purposes. In *Manhart* the claim was that the legal system ought to *prohibit* the group treatment. Now we turn to individuals whom society does *not* treat as a group over relevant purposes, and who claim that the legal system ought to treat them as a group for those purposes. We present two representative samples. The first—the handicapped—are individuals who wish to be treated as a group for preferential treatment in public facilities, such as education and public accommodations. The second are two sets of individuals society has historically treated as a group for some purposes, but who wish the legal system to accord them recognition as a group for other purposes. As you read this section consider whether each group is asking for "extra" justice.

The Foundations of Justice: Why the Retarded and the Rest of Us Have Claims to Equality[36]

Robert M. Veatch

Eddie Conrad is a ten-year-old boy born with multiple deformities; his mental retardation is considered to have preceded birth. He has a hearing impairment probably related to chronic ear infection in early childhood, visual impairment possibly resulting from too high a concentration of oxygen administered at birth, and a speech impairment apparently inexplicable either in terms of his hearing or palate difficulties.

The immediate problem for his parents is that Eddie is to be transferred from a private to a public school and will be placed in a classroom for multi-handicapped children. In the private school, he had been receiving twenty minutes of speech therapy three times a week from the speech therapist and twice a week from a graduate intern. The therapist recommends that an intensive program be continued, and independent evaluations by the public school therapist indicate that such a rate of intensive therapy would be of benefit to the child— although both evaluators concede in the opinion that Eddie's speech will never be normal. The benefit to the child will be to improve articulation, which is not sufficiently clear that others can, with some effort, understand him. No one believes that the therapy will eradicate the problems, however.

---

[36] Pp. 3–4 (1986).

The public school system in the county where Eddie lives provides one speech therapist whose decision as to which children she will see is based on (a) need and (b) the possibility of benefit from the service. The therapist has selected this child as one she will see, but she can schedule him for only one twenty-minute session per week.

The parents have obtained from the division of special education the following facts: there is only one speech therapist for the school system; there are no funds for hiring another; P.L. 94–142 assures that "all handicapped children have available to them...a free appropriate public education that emphasizes special education and related services designed to meet their unique needs. The term 'special education' includes corrective and other supportive services including speech pathology and audiology, psychological services, physical and occupation therapy, recreation, and medical and counseling services (for diagnostic and evaluation purposes)." U.S. Stat., v. 89, 94th Cong., 1st Sess. 773–96 (1975). Legal counsel has advised the family that grounds exist for filing suit against the school system.

The parents have also learned that because of funding difficulties the county school board has cut both art and music from the elementary school curriculum. If these cuts do not resolve the budget difficulties, the school board's next step will be to eliminate physical education in the elementary schools followed by elimination of art, music, and—as a last resort—physical education from the high school curriculum. The parents believe that they would win a case on behalf of their handicapped child. They also realize that winning the suit would result in the hiring of a second speech therapist, but would also entail the sacrifice of the physical education teacher for the elementary schools. Eddie's parents believe their primary obligation is to their child, yet they also feel they have an obligation to support art, music, and physical education in the elementary school curriculum.[37]

The Republic[38]

Plato

[Plato's Republic, as we saw in Chapter 1, is the classic statement of the ideal or just state. There is a strict allocation of functions according to talent and ability. Those good at making shoes will become shoemakers; those who excel at physical sports will become soldiers; those who are the most intelligent will be the rulers of the state. All healthy and strong babies are to be well cared for and nurtured so as to ensure the flourishing of the state. What about children who are born inferior or defective?]

SOCRATES. And as the offspring are born, won't they be taken over by the officers established for this purpose—men or women, or both, for presumably the offices are common to women and men—and ...

---

[37] Although the author does not indicate whether this is a real case or one that is made up from composite examples, it is clear that such a case could very well arise. [Eds.]

[38] THE REPUBLIC OF PLATO 460b (Allan Bloom trans. 1968).

GLAUCON. Yes.

SOCRATES. So, I think, they will take the offspring of the good and bring them into the pen[39] to certain nurses who live apart in a certain section of the city. And those of the worse, and any of the others born deformed, they will hide away in an unspeakable and unseen place, as is seemly.

GLAUCON. If the guardians' species is going to remain pure.

Note

G.M.A. Grube has noted that "[t]here can be no doubt that Plato is here recommending infanticide by exposure for these babies, a practice which was quite common even in classical times. Presumably the point of exposure rather than direct infanticide was that the responsibility was felt to be thrown upon the gods, for the child might be saved, as Oedipus was."[40]

Equal Treatment and Compensatory Discrimination[41]

Thomas Nagel

The greatest injustice in this society, I believe, is neither racial nor sexual but intellectual. I do not mean that it is unjust that some people are more intelligent than others. Nor do I mean that society rewards people differentially simply on the basis of their intelligence; usually it does not. Nevertheless, it provides on the average much larger rewards for tasks that require superior intelligence than for those that do not. This is simply the way things work out in a technologically advanced society with a market economy. It does not reflect a social judgment that smart people *deserve* the opportunity to make more money than dumb people. They may deserve richer educational opportunity, but they do not therefore deserve the material wealth that goes with it. Similar things would be said about society's differential reward of achievements facilitated by other talents or gifts, like beauty, athletic ability, musicality, etc. But intelligence and its development by education provide a particularly significant and pervasive example.

---

[39] A place where lambs, kids, and calves were raised. This whole passage compares the mating and procreation of men to those of animals. The sacred marriages apparently take their standard, not from the gods, but from the beasts.

[40] PLATO, REPUBLIC 122, n. 6 (G.M.A. Grube trans. 1974).

[41] 2 PHILOSOPHY AND PUBLIC AFFAIRS 357 (1973).

Questions

1. If Eddie Conrad's parents sued the county school board for failing to comply with P.L. 94–142, and the school board defended on the ground that compliance would result in cutting physical education from the curriculum, how should the judge decide the case? Should the judge "weigh" the detriment to many students in not having physical education training against the benefit to a small minority of handicapped or mentally retarded children in getting special services? Should the judge ask for expert evidence? If so, evidence of what? Should evidence be introduced as to the qualitative impact upon Eddie Conrad to have speech therapy compared with a possibly lesser impact spread quantitatively across more students of getting training in physical education? Would your answer be different if, instead of physical education, the proposed cuts would be in music and art education in high schools?

2. If the judge is a utilitarian, is it not arguable that the total good is maximized by providing art, music, and physical education instruction to all normal students rather than helping a single disadvantaged boy? But doesn't Eddie Conrad have, in Veatch's words, "an unusual need to make him more like the other children"?[42] If all normal students are deprived of art, music, and physical education, and Eddie receives speech therapy, would the result be that he is better off than any of the normal students? Could you argue to the judge that, even with speech therapy, no normal student would want to trade places with Eddie? Would you then be open to the counter-argument that your argument is unfair because it is not the normal students' fault that Eddie is the way he is? Would it be open to you to distinguish between unfairness and injustice? Could you argue that injustice to Eddie is more important than unfairness in making comparisons?

3. Could an argument be made to the judge that invokes the Aristotelian ideal of justice—that equals should be treated equally and unequals unequally? Should Eddie Conrad be argued to deserve equal treatment? If so, would that not deprive him of any claim to "special services"? What if you argue that Eddie is an "unequal"? If he is an "unequal," in what manner should he be treated unequally? Is it clear that if he receives *less* than his fellow students, he will be treated unequally? Is it also clear that if he receives *more* than his fellow students he will be treated unequally? Then what should it be—less or more? What could Aristotle have had in mind? Does Aristotle's position help or hurt your argument?

4. Plato's vision of unequal treatment for Eddie Conrad is extreme. Eddie would receive *infinitely less* than anyone else; indeed, he is to be destroyed in infancy by being put away in an "unseen place." As Veatch points out,

> there is evidence to indicate that in Rome [at the time of the Roman Empire], the Tiber River was the 'mysterious place' which served as repository for defective infants. Such attitudes are not surprising when viewed within the context of a culture in which even the

---

[42] R. Veatch, The Foundations of Justice: Why the Retarded and the Rest of Us Have Claims to Equality 100 (1986).

infanticide of mentally healthy infants was condoned as an acceptable means of population control.[43]

Even if "not surprising," are such "attitudes" just?

5. Is the liberal principle of "equality of opportunity" open to all persons just when applied to Eddie's situation? Is it not a mockery of justice to say that Eddie has the same opportunity as anyone else to compete for admission to college or for a job? Can the principle of "equality of opportunity" be saved if we amend it by saying that all handicapped persons must be given a "handicap" (as poor golfers are given extra swings) so that competition among persons for scarce resources such as college education or jobs are not influenced by biological factors?

6. Consider the following case reported by Veatch:

Jamie Fisk, an eleven-month-old child suffering from biliary atresia and in need of a liver transplant, received a cadaver organ after her father, an articulate medical administrator, appealed to his Senators, Congressmen, the White House, the American Medical Association, and the American Academy of Pediatrics, all of whom then helped publicize his daughter's need for a liver donation for transplant. No one can question the integrity and dedication of a father who would go to such efforts for his daughter. [But] the father's unique social position and skill in reaching the media gave his daughter an unequal opportunity for access to a life-saving liver transplant in comparison with other similarly situated infants whose parents were not in a position to generate this publicity.[44]

Was it unfair for the media to publicize Jamie's case? Could a less articulate father who also has a child in Jamie's condition sue the hospital that intends to make the liver transplant for Jamie on the ground that a scarce resource should not be allocated because of the extraneous factor of a father's skill in public relations? Should a court hear that case?

7. The title of Veatch's book suggests his major argumentative position. What do you think of his argument, which he spells out as follows?

The natural lottery distributes mental and physical assets in what appears to be a random way with people receiving all manner of assets. Each of us is deficient to some extent in all natural abilities. No one is perfectly intelligent, perfectly strong, perfectly beautiful, or perfectly dispositioned. We are all handicapped. An egalitarian system of justice would provide compensation—medical or educational services—necessary to give us a chance at equality, and it would provide them with priority going to those with the greatest deficits....

The Eddie Conrads of the world will get more specialized educational intervention than others, but some of the rest of us will benefit (or have our loved ones benefit) in other ways and at times we cannot imagine. More critically, the way we view the world changes if one opts for the egalitarian assumptions.... The we/they dichotomy collapses. Since we are all handicapped, we are all beneficiaries.[45]

---

[43] *Ibid.*, at 22.

[44] *Ibid.*, at 125.

[45] *Ibid.*, at 167.

Law, Legislation, and Liberty[46]

Friedrich A. Hayek

The transition from the negative conception of justice as defined by rules of individual conduct to a 'positive' conception which makes it a duty of 'society' to see that individuals have particular things, is often effected by stressing the rights of the individual. It seems that among the younger generation the welfare institutions into which they have been born have engendered a feeling that they have a claim in justice on 'society' for the provision of particular things which it is the duty of that society to provide. However strong this feeling may be, its existence does not prove that the claim has anything to do with justice, or that such claims can be satisfied in a free society.

There is a sense of the noun 'right' in which every rule of just individual conduct creates a corresponding right of individuals. So far as rules of conduct delimit individual domains, the individual will have a right to his domain, and in the defence of it will have the sympathy and the support of his fellows. And where men have formed organizations such as government for enforcing rules of conduct, the individual will have a claim in justice on government that his right be protected and infringements made good.

Such claims, however, can be claims in justice, or rights, only in so far as they are directed towards a person or organization (such as government) which can act, and which is bound in its actions by rules of just conduct. They will include claims on people who have voluntarily incurred obligations, or between people who are connected by special circumstances (such as the relations between parents and children). In such circumstances the rules of just conduct will confer on some persons rights and on others corresponding obligations. But rules as such, without the presence of the particular circumstances to which they refer, cannot confer on anyone a right to a particular sort of thing. A child has a right to be fed, clad, and housed because a corresponding duty is placed on the parents or guardians, or perhaps a particular authority. But there can be no such right in the abstract determined by a rule of just conduct without the particular circumstances being stated which determine on whom the corresponding obligation rests. Nobody has a right to a particular state of affairs unless it is the duty of someone to secure it. We have no right that our houses do not burn down, nor a right that our products or services find a buyer, nor that any particular goods or services be provided for us. Justice does not impose on our fellows a general duty to provide for us; and a claim to such a provision can exist only to the extent that we are maintaining an organization for that purpose. It is equally meaningless to speak of right in the sense of a claim on a spontaneous order, such as society, unless this is meant to imply that somebody has the duty of transforming that cosmos into an organization and thereby to assume the power of controlling its results.

Since we are all made to support the organization of government, we have by the principles determining that organization certain rights which are commonly called political rights. The existence of the compulsory organization of government and its rules of organ-

---

[46] Vol. 2, THE MIRAGE OF SOCIAL JUSTICE 101–103 (1976).

ization does create a claim in justice to shares in the services of government, and may even justify a claim for an equal share in determining what government shall do. But it does not provide a basis for a claim on what government does not, and perhaps could not, provide for all. We are not, in this sense, members of an organization called society, because the society which produces the means for the satisfaction of most of our needs is not an organization directed by a conscious will, and could not produce what it does if it were.

The time-honoured political and civil rights which have been embodied in formal Bills of Right constitute essentially a demand that so far as the power of government extends it ought to be used justly. As we shall see, they all amount to particular applications of, and might be effectively replaced by, the more comprehensive formula that no coercion must be used except in the enforcement of a generic rule applicable to an unknown number of future instances. It may well be desirable that these rights should become truly universal as a result of all governments submitting to them. But so long as the powers of the several governments are at all limited, these rights cannot produce a duty of the governments to bring about a particular state of affairs. What we can require is that so far as government acts it ought to act justly; but we cannot derive from them any positive powers government ought to have. They leave wholly open the question whether the organization for coercion which we call government can and ought in justice be used to determine the particular material position of the several individuals or groups.

Questions

1. Would Hayek require the abolition of public education? If not, does his argument suggest any solutions to the problem of the handicapped?

2. Does the case for affirmative action necessarily depend on the positive conception of justice that Hayek condemns?

The New Indian Claims and Original Rights to Land[47]

David Lyons

Early in its constitutional career, in 1790, Congress passed the Indian Nonintercourse Act, which requires that all transfers of lands from Indians to others be approved by the federal government. The Act was modified from time to time over the next forty-odd years, but it was not changed in any relevant respect, and it remains in effect today.[48] Its purpose is clear. It was meant to guarantee security to Native Americans against fraudulent acqui-

---

47 4 SOCIAL THEORY & PRACTICE 249, 249–51, 262, 266–71 (1977)

48 25 U.S.C.A § 177.

sition by others of the Indians' allotments of land. Such guarantees were plainly needed. By 1790, expropriation had been practiced by Europeans for nearly two centuries. Fraudulent land acquisitions by colonists had been a source of friction between them and the British government, which occasionally leaned towards protecting Native Americans. Security for Indian land was an important bargaining point during the Revolutionary War, when Indian support or at least neutrality was desperately needed by the rebellious colonists. The Nonintercourse Act of 1790 pledged federal security for Indian land holdings. Under it, the federal government is bound to act as guardian or trustee, overseeing all transfers of Indian lands, including those to states and other branches of government as well as to private parties.

Several suits that have recently been initiated by American Indian tribes for recovery of lands held by them when the Nonintercourse Act took effect in 1790 invoke this law. It is alleged that certain transactions by which lands were subsequently lost to them are invalid because federal approval was neither sought nor obtained in those cases. Those historical facts have not been contested.

It does not follow—either legally or morally—that all of the land in question must be returned to the Indians. But an observer might well suppose that some, at least, of the lands should be restored to them. I wish to examine that idea, not only to help us in determining what justice requires, but also to evaluate some lines of reasoning in support of and in opposition to it. For the most natural arguments that might initially be advanced on both sides of the issue—arguments that appear to be implicit in the rhetoric already surrounding these cases—center on what we, following Robert Nozick,[49] might call "historical" considerations affecting social justice.

I wish to suggest that property rights may be even more unstable than has so far been argued. Let us expand on an example that Nozick uses. Suppose that we are occupants of an isolated island. We have arranged to use the land and all its other resources among ourselves, and we live comfortably, with some less perishable goods set aside for rainless seasons. One day, a party of castaways from a shipwreck are washed up on our shore. They are uninvited but also involuntary guests. There is no prospect for their safe removal, and they have no resources beyond their capacity to work. But they are also unaggressive. What are we to do? Nozick would agree that we may not drive them back into the sea just because they come with no rights to anything on our island. Nor may we merely allow them to stay without sharing our resources with them. It is incumbent on us to share with them—whether we like the idea or not—even if that means that we enjoy a lowered standard of living as a consequence.

Let us now consider a variant of our example. Suppose that the castaways who arrive upon our shore are not friendly and cooperative but aggressive and domineering. We try to be hospitable but they do not reciprocate. They cheat us, kill many of us, and force the survivors to reside in a small area of the island, away from our homes, while they appropriate a disproportionately large part, including the most desirable sectors, for themselves.

What does justice call for in such a case? It cannot require less for us than it would

---

[49] See Robert Nozick, Anarchy, State, and Utopia 149–231 (1974).

have done in our original example, when it required that we share with the newcomers. We too have a right to a fair share of the island's resources. If justice requires more, then it may well include compensation from the piratical invaders for the wrongs we have suffered at their hands. We may be too weak to secure our rights; but that does not invalidate our claims.

Suppose that we are too weak and that we pass from the scene without justice being done. Once we are dead, it is impossible to compensate *us* for the wrongs *we* have suffered. Likewise, once the invaders die away, the wrongdoers cannot contribute to any rectification that justice may require.

Consider now the claims of our descendants, and for this purpose imagine two alternative (or possibly successive) historical developments. In the first continuation of our island's story we imagine that our descendants continue to be subjugated, cheated, and denied a fair share of the island's resources, and continue to reside in that portion of the island that was earlier assigned to us, their departed ancestors. They too have valid claims, analogous to those we had that were never respected. For justice requires that they receive not only a fair share of the island's resources but also, we may assume, compensation for the wrongs they themselves have suffered in being deprived during their lifetime of that fair share.

In the second continuation of our island's history, we imagine that enlightenment finally spreads across the island. The descendants of the piratical invaders come to live in harmony with our own descendants, so that no one is deprived of a fair share of the island's resources. Can we assume that any of our descendants, in this happy sequel to our unhappy history, have additional claims against the others on the island, the descendants of the piratical invaders? I do not see how we can. If the generation in question has been deprived of no part of its own fair share of the island's resources, if they suffer no continuing disadvantage owing to the legacy of the former system on the island, what relevant matter might have been overlooked? The wrong that was done to us, the wrong that was never rectified, cannot now be corrected. That part of history is irrelevant to their current claims.

It is important to see now that similar considerations apply to the former case, the first and less happy continuation of our current example. Our subjugated descendants have claims to a fair share of the island's resources and to compensation for wrongs done them by a system on the island that deprives them of that fair share. That system and thus their deprivation and their claims are rooted, *causally and historically*, in the wrongs that we, their ancestors, suffered at the hands of the invaders. But this is not to say that their claims are *normatively* derived from ours, that they inherited our original rights, or that their claims for compensation are claims for correction of wrongs that were done to us, as distinct from wrongs that have been done to them.

My metaphor and its moral may by now be obvious. Let the island be America and the original islanders Native Americans, to whom all the land may be said initially to belong. If those who had landed on these shores had been impoverished outcasts from Europe, unaggressive and cooperative, with no resources save their labor power and no place else to go, it would have been incumbent on their hosts not only to share their resources with them but also to reshape their social arrangements to accommodate the new members of their universe. For the purpose of this general point, it makes no difference how the original occupants of the land had used it, how they had divided it up, how they conceived of property rights, whether they held it individually or collectively, and so on.

That is not, of course, the way things happened, and so history developed much more like the unhappy history in the example. Native Americans by and large tried to be hospitable to their uninvited and unexpected guests, but the guests did not generally reciprocate. To be sure, some of the guests were impoverished, some were outcasts, some were unable to leave once they had arrived, and some, perhaps, would have been prepared to form an integrated society or to settle contentedly on limited tracts set aside for them by their hosts. But too many acted rather as invaders, slavers, and conquerors, who proceeded by force and by fraud to appropriate the land and to eliminate or drive out the people living here.

I do not wish to deny any of this or to minimize the wrongs that were done. I most especially do not mean to deny or to minimize the valid claims of Native Americans living today. My point is that their claims are unlikely to derive normatively from their ancestors' original rights. The original rights of Native Americans were no more sacrosanct than anyone else's. From the fact that they had morally defensible claims two hundred or four hundred years ago it cannot be inferred that those claims persist. But the initial argument assumes just that; it assumes that circumstances had no effect on those rights.

Native Americans have systematically been discriminated against in our society. They have a valid claim to a fair share of its resources as well as to social and economic opportunities. They also have a valid claim to compensation for unjust deprivation that the *current* generation has suffered from past injustices. But it is highly doubtful that they have any special claims based upon their distant ancestors' original occupation of the land. For circumstances have significantly changed. After the European dispossession of the Indians, waves of impoverished immigrants arrived on these shores in little better shape than castaways from a shipwreck. Most of the occupants of America today have had little, if anything, to do with dispossession of Native Americans. This does *not* mean that they have no complicity in a pattern of unjust deprivation of *current* Native Americans, for which compensation is required. But that is another matter entirely, and a much more complex matter too.

I suggest, therefore, that the current Indian land claims be viewed, not as invoking an original right to the land, a right that has been passed down to current Native Americans and that now needs to be enforced, but rather as an occasion for rectifying current inequities (some of which, of course, may trace back causally to the dispossession of Native Americans and the aftermath).

Now that I have made my major points, I must try to note some complications.

One set of complications turns upon the fact that the current Indian claims are being made on behalf of tribes rather than private persons. Tribes originally held the land, and a tribe, like a nation, can hold a right over generations. This has some bearing on the current claims. It does not affect my main point, which was not just that inheritance is suspect but more generally that moral rights to land are inherently unstable or variable with circumstances. We cannot assume that rights held generations ago, even if they were held by tribes, have persisted to this day. But this aspect of the cases is relevant to claims invoking the notion of *compensation* for wrongs done. Some past wrongs can no longer be corrected, but some can. It may be impossible to compensate the ancestors of current

Native Americans for wrongs that they suffered long ago, but it may be possible to compensate tribes for past wrongs done them. If the *tribes* were wronged, those wrongs may well have involved violations of original rights, even if those rights did not survive the changing circumstances and did not persist into the current generation. If tribes can indeed be wronged, and such wrongs are subject to compensation, then the current claims can be supported by related considerations: this sort of argument transcends the valid claims of current Native Americans for compensation in view of wrongs done to them as individual human beings. I do not wish to deny such possibilities here. They require careful and systematic examination.

The tribal character of the current claims is relevant in other respects too, which raise complex and difficult issues. I have noted, for example, that one aim of the current suits appears to be not mere ownership of the land but control over its development. There is the prospect of conflict between the interests of Native Americans in preserving undeveloped land and the others who wish to develop it, build on it, live and work on it. This is not like the conflict between conservationists and developers. For the Native Americans involved are seeking to rebuild a way of life that turns upon certain ways of dealing with the land, and an issue here is the right to inhibit development (which may involve sorely needed jobs, and not just profits) based on the right to secure a culture.

That brings us to a central argument favoring the current claims. And it is important to support the current claims, since radical steps have been threatened to undermine them, including retrospective legislation.

One thing that makes the claims under the Nonintercourse Act so important is that they appear to be legally well-founded. Unlike past calls for reparations for black Americans, in view of the legacy of slavery and discrimination, the current claims under the Nonintercourse Act turn upon existing law. Radical new legislation or executive action is not needed to sustain them.

But it may reasonably be urged that these cases test the sincerity of our historical commitments. The federal government long ago assumed "fiduciary" responsibility for securing Indian lands and protecting Native American interests. It has however adhered to the law chiefly when that worked to the Indians' disadvantage. Now, when at last Native Americans have marshalled the legal resources to secure some lost benefits, the threat is that the law will not be followed. Evenhanded fairness would seem to require that the federal government live up to its past commitments and not retroactively change the rules just when it would undermine Indian interests to do so.

Beyond this, it may dutifully be observed that justice would not be done simply returning all the lands in question to the tribes now claiming them. This would impose enormous burdens on small home owners and small businesses without sufficient reason. It seems, in any case, that undeveloped land is the primary target of the tribes, the other land being unavoidably blanketed in under the legal claims. The federal government should work to negotiate a satisfactory settlement. This is what the tribes have been seeking for some time. . . .

Claims under the Indian Nonintercourse Act are different from some other claims that Native Americans may make for recovery of land, since the former turn upon plainly illegal transactions while the latter may involve marginally legal but unjustifiable acts by the federal government. The rhetoric that I have anatomized in this paper does not distinguish between the cases. I do not mean to suggest that the claims are insupportable because the rhetoric is unilluminating. The point is rather that the claims are stronger then the rhetoric may suggest. My purpose here has been to challenge certain ways of thinking about moral rights to property—ways that are typically invoked to secure unjust holdings. Property rights are not sacrosanct. They must bend to the needs and interests of human beings.

Question

In his classic article, *Original Indian Title*,[50] Felix Cohen argues that for the most part European settlers in the United States paid something like fair market value to Indian tribes for their land.[51] For example, he notes that after paying Napoleon 15 million dollars for the cession of political authority over the Louisiana Territory, the United States government paid

> the Indian tribes of the ceded territory more than twenty times this sum for such lands in their possession as they were willing to sell. And while Napoleon, when he took his 15 million dollars, was thoroughly and completely relieved of all connections with the territory, the Indian tribes were wise enough to reserve from their cessions sufficient land to bring them a current income that exceeds each year the amount of our payment to Napoleon.[52]

Cohen suggests that this recognition of Indian property rights by the federal government was of utmost importance in the development of the purchased land, since the government had to develop the land in order to get a return on its investment. He contrasts the situation in the United States with that in South America, Canada, and Australia, where the land *was* stolen, and remained substantially undeveloped during the same era. Cohen questions, also, how much $24 worth of goods in 1626 (the purchase price of Manhattan island) was actually worth then. How much was the cost of delivery of the goods in human life and labor? How much would that $24 be worth today, if invested at prevailing rates of compound interest?[53] How does Cohen's account affect your thinking about Lyons' argument?

The Case for Black Reparations[54]

Boris I. Bittker

Is the case for compensation weakened by the fact that segregation was sanctioned by the "separate but equal" doctrine from 1896, when it was enunciated by *Plessy v. Ferguson*,

---

[50] 32 Minn. L. Rev. 28 (1947).

[51] At the time he wrote the article, Cohen was, it must be said, Associate Solicitor and Chairman, Board of Appeals, U.S. Department of the Interior, and was responsible for Indian affairs in the Department.

[52] *Ibid.,* at 35–36.

[53] At 7% interest annually it would be worth $1.35 trillion.

[54] Pp. 3–4, 12–15, 22–24, 26–29 (1973).

until 1954, when *Plessy* was overruled by *Brown v. Board of Education*? I think not. We need not employ the fiction that this doctrine was itself unconstitutional during its hegemony in order to free ourselves of its influence. "Wisdom too often never comes, and so one ought not to reject it merely because it comes late."[55] If, even though only by hindsight, conduct is seen to be both unconstitutional and abhorrent, the fact that it was thought permissible, neutral, or benign when committed may be a mitigating element in assessing blame or guilt, but it is surely not a reason to refrain from making amends. When Congress acted in 1946 to redress some of the wrongs committed while America was pursuing her manifest destiny by pushing back the Indians, it created an Indian Claims Commission to adjudicate a wide range of claims by Indian tribes. These included not merely claims under treaties that had been violated by the United States but also "claims which would result if the treaties, contracts, and agreements between the [Indian tribal] claimant and the United States were revised on the ground of fraud, duress, unconscionable consideration, mutual or unilateral mistake, whether of law or fact, or any other ground cognizable by a court of equity" and "claims based upon fair and honorable dealings" is a more amorphous standard than courts are ordinarily handed by Congress and they have only just begun to give it tangible form.[56] But as abstractions go, it would be a suitable one for congress to keep in mind in passing on the reasonableness of the demand for black reparations.

Black reparations, then, would serve to redress injuries suffered under a legal system that was held by *Brown v. Board of Education* to violate the Constitution. Moreover, even before the *Brown* case was decided, segregation as actually practiced consistently and deliberately violated the "separate but equal" doctrine of *Plessy v. Ferguson*. Closely related to the pervasive inferiority of segregated facilities for blacks, but geographically more widespread, was the unequal enforcement of the law. Inequalities in the administration of such public functions and services as police protection, government employment, and voter registration were nakedly improper and could not be cloaked by the "separate but equal" doctrine. There are many shortcomings in our treatment of the losers in our society, but none matches this record of institutionalized deprivation of a group's constitutional rights. In this respect, the case for black reparations is even stronger than the case for compensating the victims of poverty or miscarriages of criminal justice.

The case for black reparations, of course, cannot be judged in isolation; though vast, our nation's resources are not unlimited, and there are other meritorious claims. A prominent black opponent of reparations, Bayard Rustin, argues that "as a purely racial demand, its effect must be to isolate blacks from the white poor with whom they have common economic interests."[57] This problem of competition among worthy but insatiable claimants for limited resources is discussed in a later chapter. I will confine myself here to a brief comment on

---

[55] Justice Frankfurter, dissenting Hensley v. Union Planters Nat'l Bank, 335 U.S. 595, at 600 (1949).

[56] The statutory reference is 25 U.S.C. Section 70a (1946). See Miami Tribe v. U.S., 281 F. 2d 202 (Ct. Cl. 1960), cert. denied, 366 U.S. 924 (1961); Osage Nation v. U.S., 97 F. Supp. 381 (Ct. Cl. 1951), cert. denied, 342 U.S. 896 (1951); Wilkinson, *Indian Tribal Claims Before the Court of Claims,* 55 Geo. L.J. 511 (1966).

[57] "The Failure of Black Separatism," Harper's, Jan. 1970, 25, p. 31. He goes on to assert: "It is insulting to Negroes to offer them reparations for past generations of suffering, as if the balance of an irreparable past could be set straight with a handout." See also *supra* note 10.

a common reaction to the demand for black reparations, epitomized by The New York Times when it dismissed James Forman's demands: "There is neither wealth nor wisdom enough in the world to compensate in money for all the wrongs in history." To point out that Forman was asking for the redress of one wrong, not all, is an insufficient response. A better response is the counter-question: Should no wrongs be corrected unless all can be? In both public and private life, we constantly compare competing demands for the redress of injustice, knowing full well that the pit is bottomless, especially since the amelioration of one ill can cause a previously tolerable condition to seem degrading by comparison. This inquiry into black reparations presupposes a society that is prepared to respond to the most meritorious of these claims, rather than dismissing all of them as man's ineluctable fate.

Because "all the wrongs in history" cannot be righted, it is ordinarily wiser to address recent rather than ancient ones. Time is a great physician; if it does not cure an ill, it may at least dissipate its effects. In this spirit, Germany instituted a reparations program after World War II for Jews and other victims of Nazi persecution, even though Egypt was not concurrently paying compensation for what Pharaoh did to the ancient Hebrews. Similarly, the Indian Claims commission is authorized to rectify violations of our treaties with Indian Tribes and to act favorably on claims under the "fair and honorable dealings" standard, even though the tribes presenting the claims may have acquired their territories by conquest from other Indians (before the white man came to America, or between that time and westward push of the United States) and are not simultaneously offering to redress these wrongs.

In these comments on black reparations, I have focused on the wrongs of the recent past, the consequences of which are everywhere to be seen; slavery has figured only because of its continuing influence on black-white relations after the Civil War. As suggested above, had segregation not been enforced by law the residue of slavery might be hard to identify today. If this were so, it would be quixotic to try to remedy the injustices of slavery by compensating today's blacks for the value of slave labor extracted from their ancestors more than a century ago, though compensation in 1865 for the blacks' forced labor would certainly have been appropriate.

Time may also mitigate an injustice because the intended victim has made a virtue of necessity. For the Jews in medieval ghettos and in the Russian Pale Settlement, for example, isolation served as a preservative for their traditions. They enjoyed an intense communal life, free from the values of the world outside; and no scale can balance the Talmud, which they saved, against Voltaire, whom they foreswore. In such a case, compensation for segregation, however viciously motivated, may seem inappropriate when the passage of time has made it impossible to say whether profit or loss predominated. To be sure, there is a similar conflict between centrifugal and centripetal forces among American blacks: "open occupancy" in private housing and low-rent projects in the suburbs may cost the inner city's black-power movement some of its leaders and members; and an integrated school may pursue "ethnic" studies with cool impartiality, but an all-black school may give black studies a place of honor; those who are accepted everywhere may be at home nowhere. The day may come when the lingering effects of official segregation will coincide with voluntary self-separation. Talk of black reparations will then be outmoded. Notwithstanding the isolationist trends in black life today, however, racial discrimination has not proved to be a blessing in disguise. Unless and until it is, the case for compensation cannot be regarded as barred by the passage of time.

Questions

1. Is the case for reparations for former slaves stronger or weaker than the Indian land claims?

2. Once the question of reparations for groups is decided in the affirmative, who will decide (a) which individuals in the "group" will be entitled to share in the compensation (e.g., what about non-native spouses of Indians?), and (b) whether the group can change its mind (e.g., can an Indian tribe decide to sell its land to real estate developers?) Do these questions change your views about group reparations?

Individualized Justice

CHAPTER SIX

6.1   Doing justice through law: The separation thesis

The Prediction Theory of Law[1]

David Moskowitz

Correctness, justice, and wisdom are the three elements of a judicial decision. A correct decision is one that can be justified as an application of a pre-existing legal rule. Since I believe that there are instances in which a departure from the pre-existing law will be justified, it follows that the correctness of a judicial decision can be only a presumptive justification for the decision. Not only must the judge determine what decision is demanded by the pre-existing law, but he must also decide whether its application in the instant case will result in a desirable decision.

The judge should always begin the process of deciding a case by considering what decision would be reached if the pre-existing law were to be applied. Other values, however, must be considered by the judge in deciding a case, and these enter into the decision process because the judge must decide whether or not to exercise his power to change the pre-existing law.

Since a correct decision, I submit, is one that can be justified as an application of a pre-existing legal rule, it follows that an incorrect decision is a decision that cannot be so justified.

I am, of course, assuming that there will be cases in which an incorrect decision would be more desirable than a correct decision. There is nothing odd in this. The fact that I consider the correct decision to be only presumptively justified and not finally justified indicates that I believe that in some cases a correct decision will not be finally justified, though I admit that the use of the term "incorrect" to describe this situation may appear somewhat paradoxical. In other words, assuming that there will be cases in which the judge should change the pre-existing law, he must consider whether he should do so in each particular case.

An incorrect decision will be justified if the incorrect decision is a just or wise decision. In other words, in some cases, a decision that is just or wise or both may be more desirable

---

[1] 39 TEMP. L.Q. 413 (1966).

than a correct decision, and in these cases the court should reach the just and/or wise decision, which in these cases will also be an incorrect decision, rather than the correct decision.

After the judge has discovered what the correct decision in the case before him would be, he should consider whether it would also be a just decision. A just decision is a decision that is a fair, suitable, and right (in the moral sense) solution to the problem before the court, taking into consideration all the claims of the parties in a civil case and all the interests of the defendant in a criminal case. A decision that is just is presumptively justified.

A wise decision is also presumptively justified. A wise decision is one that will result in beneficial social effects. The rule applied to reach a wise decision will result in beneficial social effects either as a controlling force of human behavior within the society or as a guide to future judges. The element of wisdom is concerned with all the social effects of the decision except those resulting from correct or just decisions.

The judge will reach an incorrect decision (i.e., he will not follow the pre-existing law) when the undesirability of the rule outweighs the desirability of adherence to the pre-existing law.

Notes and Questions

1. How does Moskowitz know that there are three and only three possibilities, namely, correct-according-to-preexisting-law, just, and wise? What about other possibilities, such as intuitively right, politically accommodating, ego-gratifying, establishment-supporting? Or prejudicial? Or biased?

2. What if an attorney adopts Moskowitz's categories and argues to the judge, "Your Honor, you ought to reach the incorrect decision in this case and decide the case according to justice and wisdom"? Would this approach not open the door for opposing counsel to argue, "Your Honor, my opponent has conceded that her approach would be incorrect; all I ask is that you decide the case correctly, which means deciding it in favor of my client"?

3. Is Moskowitz advocating a correct theory of law? Does he believe that he is advocating a correct theory? If so, why should he label his own preferred outcome as "incorrect"?

4. Has Moskowitz constructed a trap for himself and then fallen into it? Why does he feel he *needs* a notion of correctness? If law is a prediction of what courts do, then why not just look at what courts do?

5. Note what happens when we define law as a prediction of what courts do. If courts in fact *take justice into consideration* in reaching their decisions, then *justice is part of the law!* Recall that Kelsen insisted upon a sharp distinction between justice and law—yet he ran into difficulties in describing what courts do for the simple reason that judges might not *accept* such a sharp distinction between justice and law. If judges in fact intermingle legal and justice considerations—or simply fail to distinguish sharply between what is legally required and what is dictated by justice—then wouldn't a thoroughly realistic view of "law" mean that we would have to include justice in the very content of law?

Comment on Normative Statements, Morality and Law

All statements (assertions, claims) are either:

1. Descriptive
2. Normative
3. Or both.

Normative statements are either:

1. Moral
2. Prudential
3. Or both.

Moral statements:

1. Apply to speaker and listener equally.
   Query: Is there an exception for people who (sincerely) do not believe the statement?
2. Apply always and everywhere.
3. A person must really comply and not just appear to do so.

Prudential statements:

1. May apply either to speaker or listener or both.
2. May have spacial or temporal limitations or both.
3. A person need not really comply but must appear to comply.

Law is a prudential statement because:

1. Spacial limitation: laws apply only in their jurisdiction.
2. Temporal limitation: past laws and future law scan usually be disregarded.
3. Law applies only to persons who are within (1) and (2), which may include speaker or listener.
4. Apparent compliance is sufficient ("objective" test).
5. No exception for people who do not believe it. (Ignorance of the law is no excuse.)

A legal statement may coincide with a moral statement. In that event, the legal statement ought to be obeyed because:

1. It derives normative power from the underlying coincident moral statement.
2. It is prudential to obey it (or to appear to be obeying it).

A legal statement may clash with a moral statement. In that event, the legal statement *ought* to be disobeyed, for whenever there is a choice between obeying the law or obeying morality, one must obey morality (because that is what morality *means*). If one does not obey "morality," then, to that person, it is not really "morality." Of course, if one disobeys the law in the course of obeying moral imperatives, that disobedience may be highly imprudent (and can result in the penalties that society imposes for violating the law).

Exercise

It is clear that Moskowitz, in the preceding excerpt, wants to depart from positivism's insistence that all cases should be decided solely on the basis of pre-existing law. Yet he acknowledges the force of the positivist position by saying that all cases that are decided on the basis of pre-existing law are "correct" decisions.

Books have been written in an attempt to prove that either positivism or legal realism are complete theories of law, and other books have been written to disprove them. The most we can do here is to examine the conception of law that positivism and realism share, to show how that conception leads to the "Separation Thesis," and then to see whether that conception is adequate.

Although Kelsen crafted his own variant, he clearly belongs to the reigning school of Anglo-American jurisprudence known as "positivism." Positivism has meant a number of things, one of them being the idea that law is a "command" issued by an authoritative source (such as a dictator or a legislature) and enforced by the power of the state. Some positivists have disputed this idea, feeling that it does not seem to account for what courts do: Courts seem to want to "find" the law rather than invent and command it. Yet all positivists—with no exception we have been able to find—have agreed on one central tenet. They adhere to the "Separation Thesis"—the thesis that law is entirely separate and distinct from any value-system such as justice or morality.

The "Separation Thesis" is not always labelled as such. It arises in protean disguises; part of the task of the advocate is to recognize it when it comes up in legal debate. Often it is signalled by the word "irrelevant." When an attorney attempts to point to a consideration that the court ought to take into account, opposing counsel might object on the ground that such a consideration is "irrelevant." Many times when this objection arises, what is really happening is an assertion of the Separation Thesis.

How did the Separation Thesis get started? Positivists contend that law is a fact, and as such, it cannot be the same thing as a normative value. They say that any law can be criticized according to the critic's own values—for example, any person can say that a given law is unjust. But it is still the law, whether just or unjust.

Thus, positivists claim that only confusion results if we try to intermingle law and values. Recall that Kelsen said that law is scientifically determinable; the question of whether it is "justified" is relegated by Kelsen to the realms of "religion and social metaphysics."

At the center of positivism are two basic propositions: (1) a fact cannot logically give rise to a value consideration such as justice, and (2) law is a fact. Because positivism accepts both of these basic propositions, it concludes that law does not necessarily include justice— that justice does not necessarily inform the law. This conclusion is another way of stating the Separation Thesis.

Let us begin by examining critically basic proposition (1), the logical argument that a fact cannot give rise to a value. We will use the logical term "entail" to mean "logically compel" or "give rise to." Consider the following logical argument (syllogism):

1. A fetus is a human life in being.
2. Abortion is an operation that kills a fetus.
3. Abortion is the killing of a human life.

Does the combination of sentences 1 and 2 entail sentence 3? Yes. Sentence 3, the conclusion, is therefore logically "valid." This does not mean that sentence 3 is true. The truth of sentence 3 depends on the truth of sentences 1 and 2. If either 1 or 2 were false, 3 would then be false, even though 3 is logically entailed by 1 and 2. You can see this by the following syllogism:

1A. A fetus is not a human life in being.
2. Abortion is an operation that kills a fetus.
3A. Abortion is not the killing of a human life.

This syllogism is also valid. Sentences 1A and 2 entail conclusion 3A.

In popular debate, however, one can often discern propositions of the following form:

1B. A fetus is a human life in being.
3B. Abortion is an operation that kills a fetus.
4B. One ought not to commit nor allow an abortion.

But it is clear that the "ought" in sentence 4B is not entailed by sentences 1B and 3B. As the philosopher David Hume demonstrated, factual premises cannot entail a moral conclusion. We need another sentence to make the syllogism valid:

2B. One ought not to take a human life.

You might say that sentence 2B is implied in sentence 1B. In other words, you might argue that if we concede that a fetus is a human life in being, we are impliedly asserting sentence 2B. Yet many of the misunderstandings in popular debate may be traced to the assumption that certain premises are implied. It is always best to state one's premises clearly so that we might see exactly whether the stated form is what is implied or meant. Thus, sentence 2B cannot always be true. Human lives are taken in war; human lives are taken when capital punishment is imposed; and sometimes human lives are taken in order to save other human lives. Suppose we revised sentence 2B into the following sentence 2C:

2C. One ought not to take a human life except when absolutely necessary.

If we did, then conclusion 4C would follow:

4C. One ought not to commit nor allow an abortion except when absolutely necessary.

This, of course, is quite a different conclusion from 4B.

We live in a universe of fact. Nature proceeds in its course "red in tooth and claw." Animals kill and eat other animals for food. Volcanoes erupt and wipe out populations; towns can be destroyed by floods; a succession of dry seasons can bring famines that can destroy civilizations. Primitive people used to look at these violent manifestations of nature and interpret them as punishments inflicted by angry gods for evildoing. But our own perspective on these events is simply that we live on a fragile planet in a minor solar system in one of billions of galaxies. Storms and floods occurred throughout the history of earth, long before there were people. The evolution of life up to the era of the dinosaurs seemed to end, long before there were humans, in the strongest form of life, yet sixty million years ago all the dinosaurs perished, perhaps as the result of the impact of a huge meteor that collided with the earth causing debris that darkened the skies for years, creating super-cold conditions that wiped out the dinosaurs.

Nearly everyone agrees with Hume that a mere fact of nature cannot itself entail a value. Just because something exists is no reason why it ought to exist. The AIDS virus exists, but that fact cannot stand as a reason why we should not try to eradicate it. In short, we cannot construct a system of morality simply by looking at the facts in the universe. In order to get to a moral conclusion, we have to *interpret* those facts morally. Of course, once we do so, we are putting morality in our premises; then moral conclusions will be entailed. When we added sentences 2C and 2D above, we were putting moral interpretations into the premises of our syllogisms. Only by doing so could we derive moral conclusions.

Therefore, we have accepted basic proposition (1) of positivism and legal realism: that a fact or facts cannot logically entail moral values such as justice. But we now have to face basic proposition (2) of the realists and positivists, that law is a value-free fact. If law is a fact, then justice cannot necessarily be part of the law. For justice is a moral value, and moral values, as we have seen, cannot logically be entailed by mere statements of fact. Thus, if we are to refute positivism and legal realism, we must attack their basic proposition (2).

Putting law aside for the moment, can we think of any *factual* statement that embodies a value? Hilary Putnam says that the following two are examples of millions of possible statements of that sort:

1) Yeats was a great poet.
2) The Nazis were evil.[2]

Of course, one might *dispute* that Yeats was a great poet, but that does not mean that the statement is not factual.[3]

Is law a fact? Certainly in the following trivial example it is: We might say a particular statute was passed on January 10, 1937, by majority vote in both houses of Congress, and enacted on January 15 when President Roosevelt signed it. That much is a fact. Or we might say that *Smith v. Jones* is a decided case because it appears on page 239 of volume 87 of the Illinois Reports. But aren't these only records of law, or evidences of law? Isn't the law itself a set of immaterial standards, intangible norms, and learned processes of reaching decisions in respect of factual situations? Isn't law a product of the human mind rather than something that exists in the state of nature?

More than that, isn't law addressed to the shaping and controlling of human behavior? Doesn't it exist only because of its efficacy in making an impact upon the decisions that we choose in everyday life? We make some decisions, and avoid others that we could have made, because of the pervasive influence of "the law." Law thus exerts an immaterial, but nevertheless potent, impact upon our decisional processes. True, law does not control our decisions; sometimes people simply disobey the law. But there would be no point in studying law if it did not have an influence upon human behavior.

Influences upon our behavior may nevertheless be morally neutral. The weather influences our behavior, yet it is a morally neutral phenomenon (except, perhaps, in the minds of primitive societies). Law, simply considered as an influence upon our behavior, may be justice-neutral.

---

[2] H. PUTNAM, THE MANY FACES OF REALISM 63 (1987)

[3] One can dispute the statement "At the present moment, there are exactly 13,783,982 red-headed persons living in the United States," but it is nevertheless a *factual* statement.

But justice and morality come into the picture because law is enforced by human beings. If Jones disobeys the law, the police may step in and arrest Jones. Or Smith may sue Jones. As a result of the arrest or lawsuit, Jones may be forced to pay a penalty. This penalty may be forcibly extracted from Jones by the sheriff. And behind the sheriff stands the armed might of the state. Hence, in the enforcement of law, some human beings (judges, sheriffs, the army) may forcibly interfere in the lives of other human beings (those who violate the law).

Now we have more than an abstract "influence" upon behavior. We have actual, or potential, physical interference by some human beings in the lives of other human beings. When some human beings thus purport to interfere in the freedom of other human beings, they typically demand justificatory arguments in support of that interference.

To see how justificatory arguments are implicated, consider the following case:

> Jones is driving in the right-hand lane of a two-way street when suddenly a child darts out in front of him from behind a parked car. Braking the car would not halt it in time to save the child, so Jones swings his car into the left-hand lane and avoids hitting the child. A police officer, observing the incident, stops Jones and issues him a ticket for driving illegally on the wrong side of the street.

If Jones asks the officer why she is giving him a ticket under the circumstances, the officer might reply, "because the law in this country is that you have to drive in the right lane." According to H.L.A. Hart, a leading positivist, "where rules exist, deviations from them are not merely grounds for a prediction that hostile reactions will follow or that a court will apply sanctions to those who break them, but are also a reason or justification for such reaction and for applying the sanctions."[4] Thus, for Hart, the police officer has actually given Jones a reason why he is getting a ticket. The reason is, simply, that there is a legal rule prohibiting driving in the left lane.

Such a "reason" is hardly convincing. To be sure, it may be the officer's only reason. The officer may have learned, at the police academy, to give tickets to drivers who drive in the wrong lane and to "explain" to such drivers that the reason for giving the ticket is that there is a rule of law prohibiting a driver from driving in the left lane. Nor would Jones be any more enlightened if he were to ask the officer why there is such a rule of law and she responded, "because it is printed in my handbook of vehicle regulations." Why is it printed there? "Because," she responds, "the legislature passed the law and ordered that it be printed in my handbook."

These positivist "reasons" appear to be restatements of the positivist assumption that law is a fact. If one asks why the law is as it is, the answer given is a further fact—that the law was duly enacted and so forth. But an entirely different result emerges if we challenge the assumption that the rule cited by the police officer is a mere fact.

We argue as follows: it is true initially that the legislature could have chosen a rule requiring driving in either the right lane or the left lane. In Great Britain, the traffic rule is the left lane, in the United States and on the European continent, the rule is the right

---

4 H. Hart, The Concept of Law 82 (1961).

lane. Certainly the initial choice of either right or left is a morally neutral choice. There is nothing in anyone's conception of justice that would impel a choice of either the right lane or the left lane. (Similarly, to take another neutral-seeming law, the rule that a will in order to be valid must be witnessed by three persons unrelated to the testator could just as easily have been a rule requiring four witnesses, or two.)

The critical fact is that the legislature chose one lane or the other instead of simply saying nothing and thus allowing drivers to drive in either lane at will. Thus we must ask ourselves why the legislature chose a particular lane as an alternative to choosing nothing at all. And here is where moral values come in: the legislature was attempting to minimize accidents and the loss of life by providing for an orderly system of automotive traffic. The overriding purpose of the legislation is to minimize losses of life and property.

To put the matter another way, Jones should not ask why the legislature chose to prohibit driving in the left lane, but why the legislature chose to confine driving to one lane only. The answer is that the legislature decided that to do so would minimize accidents. The legislation, therefore, is not morally neutral. Rather, it embodies a moral principle— the principle of guiding human conduct in such a manner as to minimize harm to others. (Similarly, we should ask not why a legislature chose to require three witnesses to a will, but why witnesses at all are needed. The answer again is a justice principle: that family members and relatives sometimes may have what amounts to coercive power over a testator, and so to effectuate the testator's real and uninhibited choice regarding the disposition of his or her property, the law requires that the signing of the will be witnessed by several persons unrelated to the testator.)

Jones therefore has a good argument to make to the traffic-court judge when he contests his ticket: "Your Honor, the purpose of traffic regulations is to minimize losses to lives and property. Once in a while a situation can arise where compliance with the traffic laws would have the immediate and foreseeable effect of harming another person. If a reasonable alternative exists so that harm to that person can be avoided without endangering other persons, and if that alternative requires a driver to disobey a traffic regulation, then in such a case it would be contrary to the purpose of traffic regulations as a whole if the driver were not relieved of the duty to comply with the particular traffic regulation in question. By briefly driving on the left hand side of the road, I avoided running over a child."

Is there any way that the positivist might still argue that the traffic regulation in question is morally neutral? By rigidly invoking the Separation Thesis, a positivist judge might rule as follows: "Mr. Jones, there is no doubt in my mind that you did the morally correct thing in avoiding the child. All of us should act at all times in accordance with our own sense of justice and morality. But the traffic regulation that applies to your case makes no exceptions for going into the opposite lane to avoid accidents. My duty is to apply the law as it is written, not as I would want it to be written. As it is written, it requires drivers to drive in the right-hand lane. The penalty for disobedience is a fine of $50. I have no discretion in the matter; I have to apply the law that the legislature has enacted. I cannot say that you obeyed the law; clearly you disobeyed it. Of course you disobeyed it for a good reason. And so I say to you, Mr. Jones, $50 is a small price to pay for saving the life of a child. I find you guilty; please see the clerk to arrange for payment of the fine."

Is the judge's response satisfactory? Does it constitute a full justification for the imposition of the $50 fine? Jones could reply as follows: "Your honor, I can afford to pay the $50, but as a matter of principle I intensely dislike being convicted of a misdemeanor, even a very small one such as this. I try to obey the law. I think that I did obey the law when I avoided hitting the child, because I was obeying the traffic regulations as a whole, and not any particular regulation, and the traffic regulations as a whole are designed to avoid accidents. What I did was avoid an accident. I can't see how that is illegal."

This argument may not convince a positivist judge, who can reply: "If the legislature wanted to pass a statute that simply said, 'Drive in such a way as to avoid accidents,' the legislature would have done so. Instead, the legislature decided to make specific traffic regulations. My job is to apply these specific regulations, which is what I have done in your case."

But would the following argument make a difference? Jones says: "Your Honor, if you impose fines on all drivers who swing temporarily into the left lane to avoid hitting a darting child or a pedestrian who has negligently entered the street, you will eventually teach the public to drive only in the right lane no matter what the cost, because the public as a whole wants to obey the law. And the result of training drivers never to cross the median strip and go into the left lane will inevitably be cases where drivers run over children or other pedestrians."

The positivist judge cannot dispute this argument, because she knows that law does have an impact upon behavior—an impact that in some cases overrides a person's moral impulses. Not everyone will disobey the law in order to vindicate a moral principle; many people if faced with such a dilemma will comply with the law. So the judge is forced to answer as follows: "If what you say does occur, Mr. Jones, the legislature will hear about it, and will be forced, under public pressure, to amend the traffic regulation so as to provide an exception to the right-hand-lane rule. When they enact an exception that allows drivers to go into the left lane temporarily in order to avoid hitting a darting child, then I will faithfully apply that exception to cases such as yours. But until then, you have violated the law."

The judge, in short, is willing to risk sacrificing the lives of several children to bring pressure on the legislature to modify their rule. But why should the judge have such a narrow conception of her own duty in the matter? Why should the judge feel duty-bound to apply a law which, under her own theory, is simply a value-free fact? What conception does she have of the office of judge that would lead her to accept the death of one or more children as a price for getting the law changed? What moral force exists in a value-free law that would override the judge's moral responsibility to unnamed innocent children? Would the legislature itself want judges to apply rules so rigidly? Would the legislature be happy reading about a driver who failed to drive around a darting child because the driver felt constrained to comply with the legislature's rule? Would a legislator who participated in the making of such a rule recognize the fairness of such an application? Or would the legislator instead criticize the judge in Jones' case for teaching the community such a mechanical interpretation of the law?

There is no adequate reason why the judge should feel an obligation to apply a value-free rule when its application can result in the potential death of innocent children who might dart into the street. And that is why most judges, in practice, would find Jones not guilty. Indeed, it is why most police officers would not give Jones a ticket in the first place. Our example has been a peculiar one, designed to test the underpinnings of positivist theory. While it brings out the need for enforcers of the law to have justificatory arguments, the example fortunately is not representative of real-world situations of judicial behavior.

We see in this example that positivism itself is a self-actualizing theory. If a judge starts with the premise that laws are morally neutral, she may consistently arrive at a result such as finding Jones guilty even while praising his moral courage in violating the law. But such a premise also requires the judge to attempt to shift the responsibility for tragic applications of the law to the legislature. Such a shifting of responsibility comes at the cost of encouraging—by the rigid application of rules—a number of unavoided tragic accidents. Is there any good reason for a judge to constrict herself so much, to wear moral blinders, just to enforce a law which the judge says is value-free (and being value-free must be indifferent as to whether it is enforced or not)?

If there is no good reason for a judge to do that, then can there be any good reason to adopt the Separation Thesis in the first place? The Separation Thesis is not a description of law; rather, it is simply a first premiss, a postulate. (Did Kelsen *prove* it or did he simply *assert* it?) May we not reject the Separation Thesis if, for us, it fails to explain judicial behavior?

Even a law as seemingly neutral as the traffic regulation requiring driving in the right-hand lane turns out not to be morally neutral. Can any law at all ever be value-free? Law regulates human conduct and serves to justify the imposition of penalties upon people for behavior contrary to law. Since law has this overwhelming, comprehensive purpose, and since a justificatory reason always seems to be necessary to account for why judges and sheriffs apply and enforce the law, may we not conclude that arguments of justice are intrinsic to the law? In other words, may we not conclude that the Separation Thesis is invalid?

Note that we never said that all laws have to be just; there may be unjust laws. We have only asserted the non-existence of morally neutral laws. We saw, in Chapter 3, Judge Devlin wrestling with the question whether to enforce laws that regulate private behavior. To Judge Devlin, such laws were certainly value-laden. He addressed himself to the question of whether judges should enforce such laws in two cases: when a majority of the public supported such legislation, and when a majority of the public no longer supported such legislation even though it remains on the books. But in neither of these cases did Judge Devlin claim that the laws were value-neutral, or that justice did not enter into the picture of what a judge should do in a case where enforcement of the laws was at issue.

Let us consider the positivists' argument that a legislature can enact any statute it pleases. Nevertheless, there are constraints upon a legislature. In a democracy, legislators want to be reelected; in an undemocratic state, they at least want to avoid antagonizing the public to the point of revolution. Moreover, legislators have a stake in keeping public order. Their own positions and personal power would be nil in a state of anarchy or chaos. Order cannot be kept at gunpoint; if police were needed to keep close guard upon every citizen all the time, then a second phalanx of police would be needed to ensure that the first group did their jobs, and so on to a third level of enforcement; the result is an infinite regress. Rather, the intrinsic sense of stability—or, we contend, of justice—is what makes most legislation acceptable to the public. Societies are stable largely to the extent that the public perceives that the legal order is, on the whole, just.

None of this is to argue that each and every piece of legislation must be perceptively just. For one thing, even in a just society we will likely have a difference between macro-justice and micro-justice. Micro-justice is the impossible ideal: every rule and regulation is itself just. Macro-justice, on the other hand, recognizes that some rules and regulations will be unjust to some groups, and others will be unjust to other groups. The system is in a state of macro-justice if all these injustices more or less cancel each other out. For instance, a progressive income tax may appear to be unjust to high-income taxpayers. But the system may also have a sales tax, which is for the most part regressive and hence impacts disproportionately upon the lowest-income taxpayers. The combination of the two taxes, each unfair but to a different group, might have a canceling-out effect when considered from a macro-perspective.

Another possibility is that some laws will be unjust without destroying the over-all contention that justice is at the basis of legislation in general. Suppose Oregon passes a vehicle safety act that specifically exempts lumber-carrying trucks. These trucks, which sometimes are the equivalent length of three buses, carry enormous logs from lumber camps to processing mills. A victim of an accident caused by a lumber truck that was unable to stop in the normal time that other vehicles could stop would probably say that it was unjust to exempt these trucks from the safety regulations. The victim might also be able to point to special-interest lobbying that led to the exemption passed by the state legislature for the lumber industry. Would that mean that the exemption was unjust? Not necessarily. The public might be sufficiently dependent economically on the lumber industry to make it fair for the public to decide to absorb some vehicular accidents rather than pass legislation that might make it competitively impossible for the lumber industry in Oregon to stay in business.

Whether we are considering legislation or judicial precedents, "justice" seems to have formed a part of their creation and hence "justice" seems relevant in interpreting their applicability to the issue at hand. The Separation Thesis, after all, is not itself a Law embodied in our Constitution. Rather, it is simply a theory of law. It has a certain immediate appeal—because it is easier for people to consider that the world of facts and the world of values are two different worlds, than to engage in the intellectually more difficult task of understanding that they are simply two perspectives on one world—the world we actually have. When we look at the legal world, we see that laws are *incomplete* if we interpret them solely as facts, and equally *incomplete* if we interpret them solely as values. The Separation Thesis requires us to distinguish between two things that are aspects of the same phenomenon—something akin to distinguishing between procedure and substance in the law when we know that procedure and substance are constantly and inevitably interacting with each other all the time.

Fortunately, we are not required to accept the Separation Thesis. But since many people—especially judges—subconsciously accept some degree of separation between law and justice, we have to make a special effort to recognize the Separation Thesis when it is being played like background music, and to argue effectively for a change of tune.

In light of this Exercise, consider the following Juvenile Court case.

In the Interest of Alice and Betty S.[5]

Circuit Court of Cook County, Illinois, Juvenile Division
May 1, 1991

Judge R. Morgan Hamilton, presiding.

THE COURT. Ladies and Gentlemen, the Court has reviewed the testimony presented in this case and all of the evidence offered as well including the Social Investigation, the thoroughly detailed and comprehensive Supplemental Social Investigation, all of the records in the court file.

I have read them all many times and spent a number of hours reviewing that evidence.

As a result the Court has considered the following, which I want to read in the record, so you will understand on what my decision is based.

Court considered the Supplemental Social, dated November 9th, 1990, which indicates that Alice was born February 2nd, 1984, Betty was born May 13th, 1980;

That these children have four siblings. Their birth dates, there appears to be a typographical error, but what is stated in the Supplemental Social, the birth dates of siblings is September 21st, 1975, June 21st, 1978, July 26th, 1978, and September 21st, 1975.

This document indicates that there has been, the testimony was there was a sib named Carol on July 10th, 1988. At that time she was three years old.

The death was due to thermo burns due to scalding and was determined to be homicide by the mother's boyfriend;

That mother was present when Carol was scalded, and that the boyfriend left Carol in the tub and took mother to work, took the siblings in this case—these two minors—to school, then to day care respectively, and that according to Betty the mother and her boyfriend told these

---

minors to lie about how Carol had been burned.

Supplemental Social indicates the mother hit the minors with her hands, stick, belt, electric cord on the face and body; that the mother hit Carol in the head with a stick, knife handle, board;

That there were 12 scars on the top of Carol's head. They were untreated and they were deep scars;

That Carol also had old, untreated bone fractures to her right arm, right leg, and that these were untreated;

That Carol had bruises and abrasions to her face due to blunt trauma, and that on November 6th, 1986 at the age of 20 months—which is prior to this case coming into court—Carol had been found to be dehydrated with abrasions on both shoulders and both of her feet were broken;

That Carol had slept and ate on the floor, stayed all day in a bedroom and on the floor and was sometimes not allowed use the bathroom;

That the minors were left alone at home often;

That Carol had been sexually abused;

That Betty had been sexually abused;

That Alice had been sexually abused;

That the father had stated to the preparers of that document that women bring only tragedy in his life;

That the father leaves for work at 6:00 a.m.;

That the father sometimes works late and comes home around 11:00 p.m., sometimes as often as three nights per week;

That the mother visits these minors every week and brings activities to share with them;

That the minors always look forward to the visits with the mother;

That on November 8th, 1990 the minors discussed foster home placement with their mother;

That the father's home has an empty bedroom that is designated as the minors' room;

That the father has no child care plan;

That the mother has a history of being involved with abusive men.

At Page 32 it is noted specifically father stated to DCFS[6] that "the only way a woman will obey and respond to a man is by beating her up"; and also at this same page that father is a hard worker but a marginal provider for his sons;

That his home is scarcely furnished;

That the meals are not balanced, there is not enough food, and the boys do not obey the father as per the father's own statements;

That the father loves all of his children but there is no communication between father and the minors;

That the father speaks badly of the mother to the boys and to Alice and Betty and that the boys despise their mother;

That the father does not have much to offer to the minors in the way of parenting, nurturing, and care and the recommendation was that the mother was to continue to have two hours of supervised visits weekly, father to have unsupervised weekend visits as soon as he sets up a bedroom with a door and beds for the minors.

In the addendum to the Supplemental Social, dated January 22, 1991, Court reviewed that the father was on a waiting list for a Hispanic homemaker, that the recommendation was for parenting classes for both parents;

That the mother has good interaction with the minors during the visits and that they are two hours in length and supervised on a weekly basis;

That on January 22th, 1991 DCFS made an unannounced home visit to the father's home, found the home to be disorganized—there were piles of clothes on the floor, closet, and bedroom;

That there was not enough food, no milk, meat or fresh food, no cereal, or just no bed for the minors, no child care plan, no emergency plan;

Court reviewed the Home report dated November 8th, 1990 which reported that Alice had a fear of bath tubs, that she had to have Betty close, that she never asked about her mother or father;

That asking for help for her was difficult;

That Alice feels that mistakes can be deadly, and;

That now she is no longer afraid of the dark

---

6 Department of Children and Family Services, State of Illinois. [Eds.]

or baths;

That report stated regarding Betty that Betty says that her mother was there when Carol was burned.

Court reviewed the Psychological Evaluation of the mother dated November 25th, 1989. That report states that the maternal grandfather sold the mother to the father at age 15;

That the mother was raped and hit by the father;

That she married the father;

That the mother denied sex abuse of the girls and that the mother left the father due to physical and emotional abuse.

This report signed by Dr. Carlos Acosta, Ph.D., recommended family therapy, weekend visits with the mother, parenting skills program, and a possible return to the mother in six months.

Court reviewed the Psychological Evaluation of the father dated November 23rd, 1989 and in that report father denies that he bought or raped the mother and states that he only hit the mother once.

The four boys appear to be happy, living with the father.

The boys are hostile against the mother.

The minors enjoy the father's visit. Father appears to try his best within his limitations.

Father accepts the challenge of the examiner to change his attitude—excuse me, to change the attitude of the boys toward their mother.

The recommendation in this report prepared by Dr. Carlos Acosta, Ph.D., was parenting skills, family therapy, for the boys to meet with the mother, for weekend visitation with the father and the brothers and a possible return to the parents in six months.

Court reviewed the reports from Dr. Acosta—one dated November 9th, 1990, which stated that the parents were not ready to take the minors, that they deny their part in the tragedy and one dated June 26th, '90 stating Betty says she is no longer scared of males.

Report indicated mother and father feel very angry with each other; that father is having good control of the boys at this point and that in the father's home there are five males and this is intimidating.

I made no notes concerning the report dated December 11th 1989. I did read it.

Court reviewed the report dated March 6th, 1990, still Dr. Acosta's report, which stated there was individual therapy for the mother, family therapy for the father, and the boys and children's therapy with the minors.

He referred to mother's history of abuse that was so intense that it requires long-term therapy.

He stated that the minors are angry about the parents because the parents did not take good care of them.

Court reviewed Dr. Acosta's report April 5th, 1991 stating mother is now able to accept responsibility, some aspects of abuse, and that marital therapy has begun;

That the father had difficulty accepting that his wife has rights and something to say for the good of the family and that the father resented marital therapy, but he is cooperating;

That Dr. Acosta reviewed his plan of six months of marital therapy to be followed by family therapy.

I also considered the testimony of all witnesses who testified on our witness stand and made some suggestions and interim findings to all parties on the last court date and following a conference in chambers and everyone's decision to rest my findings are as follows:

That it is in the best interest of Alice and Betty that they have unsupervised weekly day visits with their mother;

That the initial length of those visits be actual time spent between mother and minors of two hours;

That the length of the unsupervised visits with the mother may be increased from two hours per visit up to a maximum of eight hours per visit at DCFS discretion and without further court order.

However, the length of the visits, once they are increased, may not be decreased or suspended or terminated without a court order.

I find that unsupervised visits by the mother should begin immediately subject to whatever you have all worked out in this draft order and that mother shall insure that no males are present at any of the visits except members of the family who have been screened by DCFS and I find a violation of the no males present requirement may result in a return to supervised visits.

I find it is in the best interest of these minors that this court review mother's visitation in three months without the need for a Supplemental Petition for that reason and that these visits may be modified at that time.

You have had—You have all had an opportunity to see the Order Miss O'Brien has handed to me?

MS. KAVANAGH. Yes.

MS. ROSAS. Yes.

THE COURT. You are all satisfied with the wording here?

MS. KAVANAGH. As I indicated the State poses an objection.

THE COURT. Miss Kavanagh, it is appropriate to stand up, and then I will recognize you.

MS. KAVANAGH. As I indicated earlier the State is not in agreement as to mother based upon—

THE COURT. Miss Kavanagh, this is not an agreed Order. This is an Order of the Court based on everyone resting and the findings of the court and all of the testimony and all of the evidence heard.

It will not be entered as an agreed Order. It will be entered as an Order of this Court.

MS. KAVANAGH. Your Honor, as I indicated earlier in August of '90 the Court made a finding of unfitness in that mother actively participated and inflicted abuse on not only these minors but really herself.

I believe the Court was very clear in that finding.

As such my understanding is that Section 802-23 mandates that custody shall not be restored until such time as a hearing is held and the Court enters an Order finding that mother is in fact fit.

I understand that the court is not restoring custody at this point to mother; therefore, we have not proceeded in the matter of the fitness hearing.

However, it is the State's position that the court is effectively restoring a limited custody to the mother and I believe in the spirit of 802-23 that goes towards protecting the children in that it requires the parent who has been found unfit to go forward and present evidence showing that the children in fact will be safe.

It is the State's position, your Honor, that based upon the testimony presented to this court of Dr. Acosta he was clear that he would not recommend unsupervised visits; that in his opinion if an abuse situation were to occur and mother was sole supervisor he did not know if she would be able to protect the children.

For that reason, Judge, I would ask the court to clarify as to whether or not you are finding—your finding on unfitness stands.

I would also like to make clear to the Court and for the record the reason why the State is in disagreement as to unsupervised visits.

I believe the facts on this case were heinous and I believe the issue—it is clear the mother has issues to work on.

Until those issues are worked out we are concerned as to the safety of the children.

I believe at this point the evidence has not shown that those children will be safe during unsupervised visits.

THE COURT. I am satisfied that the evidence has shown quite the contrary; that the mother has always been appropriate during each and every visit that she has had with the children.

Not only has she been appropriate but cooperated fully with the Service Plan and always been—has done everything she has been asked to do.

She has also made progress in accepting her responsibility for what has happened to her children and that she will be safe during visitation and I do not equate custody with visitation otherwise we would need only one word—custody or visitation.

I want to refer to my notes.

MS. KAVANAGH. Judge, just to clarify—

THE COURT. No, no. Now it is my turn. You have had your turn.

I am looking at Dr. Acosta's testimony on April 16th under Cross Examination by the mother.

It states that the minors have been in therapy with him for two years, that they are always there together, they are always there for one hour every week;

That he has had a conversation with Betty regarding visits with the mother and she enjoys meeting with her mother;

That he would need to ask her if she wants longer visits with the mother;

That Alice enjoys visits with the mother;

That in the last six months minors went to a family event with the mother—they went to the mother's graduation and they were very proud of this mother;

That he had a conversation with Betty right after the graduation four or five months ago when Betty was proud of and felt good of the mother;

That the minors would benefit from more family outings with the mother and mother would benefit from rules and I have made rules;

That he is with the mother for one hour a week and has spent approximately 100 hours with her and she has improved with her understanding of responsibilities and made great improvement;

That she has complied with all of his recommendations;

That she has followed all of his recommendations and he believes she will continue to comply and the minors would benefit from longer visits with the mother starting with April 16th, the date of the inquiry, and that the mother would also benefit from longer visits with the minors.

While he was not prepared to recommend unsupervised visits I have to look at the total picture, Miss Kavanagh, which I have done and having looked at the total picture I am satisfied that on my terms, following my Order these minors will be safe with their mother.

Now, let's address the issue of fitness.

Before the minors can be returned to their mother's care there must be a fitness hearing.

There has been none.

So, my findings in regards to fitness to be the custodial parent stands.

In terms of ability to care during a two-hour visitation which DCFS has the authority to increase I am satisfied she is fit for those visitations.

That is separate and apart from fit to be the custodial parent as I interpret the statute.

Was there any other issue you wanted to address?

MS. KAVANAGH. No, Judge. You are therefore stating mother is fine and fitness stands?

THE COURT. In regards to custody yes. Court will vacate the previously entered temporary custody order, advise all of the parties that if you are dissatisfied with the Court's decision then you do have the right to appeal that decision and to do so you must file appropriate papers with the Court within the prescribed period of time.[7]

---

[7] As this coursebook went to press, the editors have been informed that the State of Illinois has filed an appeal in this case. [Eds.]

Notes and Questions

1. Two months *before* Judge Hamilton's decision in the case you have just read, one of her earlier child custody cases was reversed by an Illinois appeals court.[8] In that prior case, Judge Hamilton had taken a four-year-old child out of a foster home and remitted the child to the exclusive private guardianship and custody of the child's grandmother. The Appellate Court reversed, saying in part:

> It is well established that the paramount consideration in all guardianship and child custody cases is the best interest of the child. The best interest of the child takes precedence over even a natural parent's superior right to custody of his child. Section 1-2(3)(c) of the Juvenile Court Act specifically states that "the parents' right to the custody of their child shall not prevail when the court determines that it is contrary to the best interests of the child." Ill. Rev. Stat. 1989, ch. 37, par. 801-2(3)(c).

The Appellate Court found that Judge Hamilton's judgment was "contrary to the manifest weight of the evidence," and remitted the child back to the foster home.

2. Immediately *after* Judge Hamilton's decision, columnist Mike Royko wrote a column in the form of a letter to Chief Judge Harry Comerford, headed "Why is This Judge in Juvenile Court?"[9] Here are some quotations from Royko's column:

> When you have a few minutes, will you explain why in the hell you have someone like Judge Morgan Hamilton sitting in Juvenile Court?
>
> As you know—and if you don't, you should—Mrs. T. stood by in 1988 when her boyfriend poured boiling water over her 3-year-old daughter. [Carol] died.
>
> Mom didn't . . . go to prison. The prosecutors had hoped that she would testify against Leonardo and didn't bring charges against her. When Leonardo copped a plea, her testimony was unnecessary, and she was off the hook.

Royko then says Judge Hamilton's order giving the mother unsupervised visiting privileges is usually followed by the mother asking that she be declared fit and getting her children back. Royko ends by calling upon Judge Comerford to transfer Judge Hamilton to a "more suitable court," like Traffic Court. He ends with a threat: that if Judge Comerford does not act, Royko will remind the voters "the next time there is an election for judges."

Royko's column appeared in the Chicago Tribune's morning edition. By the end of the same day, Judge Comerford had acted. He transferred Judge Hamilton out of Juvenile Court to the First Municipal District. In a Chicago Tribune news story the following morning,[10] the presiding judge of the First Municipal District was quoted as reporting that

---

[8] The case is In the Interest of Violetta B. v. Joe Ann Stanciel, 210 Ill. App. 3d 521, 568 N.E.2d 1345 (Ill. App. lst Dist. 4th Div. 1991)

[9] CHICAGO TRIBUNE, May 3, 1991, at p. 3.

[10] *Juvenile Court Judge Under Fire for Decisions is Transferred,* CHICAGO TRIBUNE, May 4, 1991, at p. 5.

Judge Hamilton told Judge Comerford "that she has had it with following the law and getting hammered for it and said, 'Send me somewhere where I can follow the law and not get hammered.'" The news story also quotes an unidentified lawyer who practiced before Judge Hamilton, who said that Judge Hamilton "tried to force families to stay together under almost any circumstances, regardless of what the children felt."

Then a news commentator on Channel 5, Attorney Virginia Martinez, scolded Royko for being cruel to a judge. She said, "Judges are required to make tough decisions. We cannot allow them to be sitting ducks for commentators who ignore a judge's entire record and ignore the facts of a particular case to present a slanted picture to incite public outrage."

Royko replied a few days later.[11] He said that Martinez was right in saying that Royko incited public outrage about the case. He said that as long as Juvenile Court is "going to go on giving abused children as much respect as laboratory rats, I'm going to go on inciting public outrage. And Ms. Martinez and Channel 5 can take that and stick it in their earphones."

A few days later, the Chicago Daily Law Bulletin presented a lead story reporting a "flurry of criticism" by local bench and bar groups of the transfer of Judge Hamilton.[12] The groups included the Illinois Judicial Council, the Chicago Council of Lawyers, and various juvenile law specialists. The newspaper quotes a letter to Judge Comerford from the Chicago Council of Lawyers:

> There is concern that your failure to support a judge who took an unpopular position will discourage other judges from reaching difficult decisions, even if they are following the law. . . . By deferring to Mr. Royko's opinion, you have unfortunately contributed to an atmosphere in which judges cannot follow the dictates of the law without fear that an unpopular decision will lead to reassignment.

Royko shot back in a subsequent column: "I think they're overreacting. I don't write about judges often enough to cause them all to sit around trembling. And when I do write about them, hordes of lawyers usually leap to their defense."[13]

3. Was Judge Hamilton following "the dictates of the law," as the Chicago Council of Lawyers put it? Or should the above-quoted letter from the Chicago Council be interpreted as saying that *whatever* judges decide, they are deciding according to the dictates of the law?

4. Are child custody cases different from other legal disputes? Do they depend so much upon the demeanor of the prospective custodians that only a sitting judge can decide which of the contending parties should be entitled to custody over a child? Even if the "demeanor" evidence is so important, can we be sure that judges will correctly interpret and understand that evidence?

5. Is the remark attributed to Judge Hamilton—that she was "hammered" for "fol-

---

[11] *Judge's Defender Got One Thing Right,* Chicago Tribune, May 10, 1991, at p. 3.

[12] *Bar Groups Criticize Transfer of Judge From Juvenile Court,* Chicago Daily Law Bulletin, May 14, 1991, at p. 1.

[13] *Judge's Defenders Man the Ramparts,* Chicago Tribune, May 17, 1991, at p. 3.

lowing the law"—an implicit admission by the Judge that she had to give the mother unsupervised visitation rights over Alice and Betty *even though she might not have done so if she had unfettered discretion in the matter*? If so, what does that tell us about the Separation Thesis?

Comment on Judges and Justice Arguments

We have seen that it is not easy to *prove* that justice is part of the law in the sense that a judge is *required* to consider justice arguments in reaching a decision. Yet we can not overlook one critically important empirical fact: many if not most judges routinely do consider justice arguments in reaching their decisions on the law. They do so either directly or indirectly, as we have been seeing throughout this coursebook. Thus we may have a situation where judicial behavior is at variance with currently prevailing theories of law— at least to the extent that some version of Kelsen's thesis reflects the present consensus. If so, the situation is encouraging. It charges us with the task of finding a theory of law that adequately describes the judicial behavior that takes place in the real world. If positivism does not do so, so much the worse for positivism.

But although many judges routinely consider justice arguments, or refer to their own theories of what is fair and just, in reaching decisions, some may do so uneasily. They may believe that they are going beyond the law. If this is what they believe, then their own legal philosophies correspond with positivism even if they overtly disclaim a positivistic bent. Furthermore, they will always be open, in a given case, to the argument "Your Honor, we have the law on our side; the other side is talking about justice, and while we are all in favor of justice, that is a question for the legislature in enacting new laws and not a question for a judge in applying the law that the legislature has already enacted." Such an argument is rhetorically powerful if the judge is a positivist or is heavily influenced by the positivist rhetoric that has pervaded Anglo-American jurisprudence for the last hundred years.

It is, therefore, crucial that any attorney who wants to argue a "justice" position must ground that position in a thorough understanding of the way to refute the Separation Thesis. For if the judge has a mental picture that separates law and justice, it will be extremely difficult if not impossible to convince the judge to follow the dictates of justice instead of the dictates of law. The only litigative strategy that has any chance of success is to argue the invalidity of the Separation Thesis itself.

Thus an argumentative method that succeeds in refuting—or more than that, in demolishing—the Separation Thesis is a necessary part of the equipment of attorneys who argue cases before courts. The Exercise you just completed can be of critical importance in your own preparation for legal argument in court, because if you are prepared with a way to recognize the Separation Thesis when it appears in covert disguise in the course of debate, and additionally are prepared with a way to combat it, you may be more efficacious as a practitioner of law.

Moreover, the Exercise may in time have the impressive consequence of becoming self-validating. If judges in particular and legal scholars in general become convinced that the Separation Thesis is incorrect, judges will increasingly become more overt in using "justice" arguments and fairness considerations in their opinions, and will lose their sense of uneasiness when importing justice factors into their decisions. This increasing overtness may serve to make law more predictable (and hence more just to people who want to know what the law is so that they can engage in rational planning), because it will bring out into the open the justice considerations that are presently operating *sub rosa*.

As judges (or future judges, of which you may be one) understand the problems with the Separation Thesis, they may become increasingly impatient with arguments such as the one given above. They will respond: "Your argument would make sense if law were one thing and justice another, but in fact there is no such separation." Finally, justice arguments may become an increasingly important part of the legal preparation of all attorneys, irrespective of which side of a case they are on. Arguing a case will include structuring the argument to comport with underlying principles of justice that are latent in the rules of law at issue in the case. Each side will want to demonstrate that if the law at issue is properly interpreted, justice will require a favorable decision.

Thus, knowing how to refute the Separation Thesis may be of critical importance in helping to shape as well as validate present judicial behavior. This Exercise is not the last word in refuting the Separation Thesis—it is a mere beginning—for the task of perceiving the relation of law and justice is the task of a professional lifetime.

6.2   Doing justice apart from law: The heritage of equity

A History of English Law [14]

Sir William Holdsworth

The distinction between the strict rule of law and modifications of that law on equitable or moral grounds is a distinction well known to many systems of law; and it was familiar to English lawyers from the twelfth century onwards. It is not therefore the distinction between law and equity which is peculiar to English law. What is peculiar is the vesting of the administration of law and equity in two quite separate tribunals. The result has been that the distinction between law and equity has in England been given a sharpness and a permanence which it possesses in no other legal system.

[All the] common law tribunals ceased to administer equity. Litigants, if they wanted equity, were driven to a tribunal the procedure of which had remained free from the technical rules which governed the procedure of the common law courts; and so cases which called for equity went to the Council and later to the Chancery. The precocious fixity attained by the rules of the common law had caused the administration of equity to be handed over to a tribunal which had come to be perfectly distinct from any of the common law courts. And this is the origin of the most unique feature of English as contrasted with, for instance,

---

[14] Vol. I, 446, 449 (7th ed., A. Goodhart and H.G. Hanbury eds. 1956).

Roman equity. The Roman praetor urbanus administered both law and equity; and therefore it was easier to fuse the two systems: the Chancellor and the common law judges were distinct and often rival authorities.

An Introduction to English Legal History[15]

J.H. Baker

By Tudor times it was a trite saying that the Chancery was not a court of law but a court of conscience. Developments in the system of pleading and discussing cases en banc had by then generated the modern conception of law as a body of rules applicable to given sets of facts. The chancellor, by way of contrast, was not concerned with rules but with individual cases. He combined the role of judge and jury, and in delving as deeply as conscience required into the particular circumstances before him he did not distinguish fact and law. Inevitably the chancellor's justice was seen as something superior to the less flexible justice of the [law courts]. Indeed, if proceedings in other courts were in themselves unconscionable, the chancellor would issue injunctions to stop them. This transcendent justice acquired the name "equity."

Equity was a classical notion, defined by Aristotle as "a correction of law where it is defective owing to its universality." The idea was well known to medieval scholars. Glanvill mentions it as an ingredient in the common law, and throughout the year-book period it was applied to the interpretation of statutes. But it was a particularly apt term for the function of the chancellor. As early as 1468, a temporary keeper of the great seal was charged to determine all matters in Chancery "according to equity and conscience."[16] Generations later, Lord Ellesmere explained that the reason why there was a Chancery was "that men's actions are so diverse and infinite that it is impossible to make any general law which may aptly meet with every particular and not fail in some circumstances. The office of the chancellor is to correct men's consciences for frauds, breaches of trust, wrongs and oppressions of what nature soever they be, and to soften and mollify the extremity of the law."[17]

The shift from "conscience" to "equity" was more than a change of vocabulary. It is not certain how medieval chancellors reached their decisions, but "conscience" has a subjective ring to it; guided no doubt by their training in theology and Canon law, they were driven back onto their own consciences. The clerical chancellors were exercising the temporal counterpart of the confessional. In the early sixteenth century we hear grumbles amongst the lawyers about such an arbitrary function, and the dissatisfaction came to a head under Cardinal Wolsey (Chancellor from 1515 to 1529), who had no academic training at all. Wolsey delighted in putting down lawyers, had an arrogant confidence in his own untutored

---

[15] Pp. 89–92 (2d ed. 1979).

[16] XI RYMER'S FOEDERA 579 (G. Holmes & R. Sanderson ed.).

[17] Earl of Oxford's Case (1615), 1 Rep Ch 1 at 6.

common sense, and in his desire to please plaintiffs too often left a sense of injustice. The chancellor's jurisdiction had visibly become another system of secular justice, sharing all the failings of human institutions; and the decisions of an unlearned chancellor, unacquainted with the reasoning of the common law, easily offended at least the lawyers' sense of fairness. A strong reaction to the arbitrariness of the Chancery appeared in a treatise written by an anonymous "serjeant-at-law" shortly after Wolsey's death. The serjeant "marvelled" that the chancellor should presume to interfere by subpoena with the king's law, which was the inheritance of the subject. Conscience was a variable standard, for "divers men, divers consciences"; and it offended the rule of law. The serjeant went so far as to assert that the chancellor's jurisdiction was founded on ignorance of the merits of the common law, and that it was contrary both to reason and the law of God.[18]

The rift was partly closed by Wolsey's successor, Sir Thomas More (1529–33), the first chancellor since the fourteenth century to have been trained in the inns of court. More had earlier written that to allow even a good judge to follow his own whim would defeat the principle that justice must be seen to be done, and would leave people in a condition of slavery.[19] He nevertheless thought the common law was too "rigorous," and he not only exercised the equitable jurisdiction but continued the practice of inhibiting common law actions by injunction. When the judges complained, he invited them to dinner and told them that it belonged to their own discretion "to mitigate and reform the rigour of the law"; if they would do so, he promised he would issue no more injunctions. The judges declined the offer, because, as More later told his biographer, "they may by the verdict of the jury cast off all quarrels from themselves upon them, which they account their chief defence".[20] The judges had no wish to become involved in decisions of fact, and therefore could not tackle questions of conscience.[21] In truth the judges did introduce some equity into the law by means of actions on the case; but their flat rejection of More's proposal destined equity to develop in England as a system separated from the common law. Until More's time it could still be argued that equity or conscience operated in all courts, albeit to an extent which varied with the degree to which individual circumstances could be revealed to the court. As late as 1550 it was said by the King's Bench that "conscience is *aequum et bonum*, which is the basis of every law." But thereafter equity would increasingly be regarded as the peculiar prerogative of the Court of Chancery. As a consequence, equity itself became a kind of law, in the sense of a body of rational principles, and the original rationale of the chancellor's bill jurisdiction was forgotten.

---

[18] Replication of a Serjaunte at the Lawe [c. 1530] in F. Hargrave (Ed) LAW TRACTS (1787), pp. 321–331.

[19] From RESPONSIO AD LUTHERUM, as translated in 94 SS81.

[20] W. ROPER, THE LYFE OF SIR THOMAS MOORE (E.V. Hitchcock edn, 1935), pp. 44–45.

[21] Much of the conservatism of the law judges in that era can be explained by the fact that they were personally liable for rendering judgments contrary to the law if the appellant could so prove on appeal. Indeed, the way appeals were normally taken in those days was to sue the trial judge. [Eds.]

Edwards v. Allouez Mining Co.

38 Mich. 46
Supreme Court of Michigan
January 9, 1878

COOLEY, J. This is an injunction bill, and the facts are very simple. Defendant at a cost of some sixty thousand dollars erected a stamp mill on the banks of Hill creek in the year 1874, and has since been operating it for copper mining purposes. As a result of its operations large quantities of sand are carried down by the waters of the stream and deposited on the bottom lands below. The evidence leads to the belief that it would be impossible to carry on the mining operations of the defendant with profit unless this is permitted. The year following the erection of defendant's mill, complainant purchased a piece of land through which the creek runs a short distance below the mill, and upon which the mill as operated was depositing sand. The land was not purchased for use or occupation, but as a matter of speculation, and apparently under an expectation of being able to force defendant to buy it at a large advance on the purchase price. It was offered to defendant soon after the purchase, and though no price was named, the valuation which has been put upon it by complainant and his witnesses is from three to five times what it cost him, and this perhaps gives some indication what his expectations were. The real value of the land except as a convenience in the business of defendant would seem to have been small. When defendant declined to purchase, this bill was filed. The prayer is that defendant be restrained from running or depositing its stamp sand on complainant's land, and from polluting the waters of the stream by its operations. This is a short statement of so much of the case as is material to what follows. The circuit judge refused the injunction prayed for, but ordered a reference to a jury for an assessment of damages.

There is no doubt that the operations of defendant, whether they inflict any serious injury on complainant or not, amount in effect to an appropriation of that portion of his property upon which sand is being deposited. [Citing cases] It follows and is beyond question that complainant sustains a legal injury for which he is entitled to suitable redress. The only question on this record is, whether he is entitled to the special redress he

seeks, namely, an injunction.

An injunction is not a process to be lightly ordered in any case. Where the effect will be to present to the owners of a valuable mill the alternative either to purchase complainant's lands at his own price or to sacrifice their property, any court having the power to order it ought very carefully to scrutinize the case and make sure that equity requires it. In theory its purpose is to prevent irreparable mischief; it stays an evil the consequences of which could not adequately be compensated if it were suffered to go on. [Citing cases] "There is no power," says Mr. Justice Baldwin, "the exercise of which is more delicate, which requires greater caution, deliberation and sound discretion, or is more dangerous in a doubtful case than the issuing of an injunction. It is the strong arm of equity, that never ought to be extended unless to cases of great injury, where courts of law cannot afford an adequate or commensurate remedy in damages." *Bonaparte v. Camden etc., R. R. Co.*, Baldw., 218. All the cases referred to show that the court looks beyond the actual injury to contemplate the consequences, and however palpable may be the wrong, it will still balance the inconveniences of awarding or denying the writ, and adjudge as these may incline the judicial mind. [Citing cases] Even in the case of a palpable violation of a public right to the annoyance of an individual, he must show the equity which requires this summary interference as the only adequate means of obtaining justice.

What is the irreparable injury which is done or threatened in this case? We can see very plainly what it is in the case of many nuisances, and the equity of this particular remedy is then very manifest. If one man creates intolerable smells near his neighbor's homestead, or by excavations threatens to undermine his house, or cuts off his access to the street by buildings or ditches, or in any other way destroys the comfortable, peaceful and quiet occupation of his homestead, he injures him irrevocably. No man holds the comfort of his home for sale, and no man is willing to accept in lieu of it an award of damages. If equity could not enjoin such a nuisance the writ ought to be dispensed with altogether, and the doctrine of irreparable mischief might be dismissed as meaningless. A nuisance which affects one in his business is less in degree, but it may still be irreparable, because it may break up the business, destroy its good will and inflict damages which are incapable of measurement because the elements of reasonable certainty are not to be obtained for their computation. Even in the case of unoccupied land a nuisance may threaten irreparable injury, where it is devoted in its purchase to some special use, or where the person causing the nuisance is irresponsible, and in some other cases which need not here be specially mentioned.

The land injured in this case was bought by the complainant with a preconceived purpose to force a sale of it upon the defendant. He did not want it for a homestead or for business property, but for the money he could compel the defendant to pay for it. It may be said that no one is concerned with the motives of another in making a lawful purchase, or in doing any other lawful act; and this is true as a rule, but it is not true universally. Wherever one keeps within the limits of lawful action, he is certainly entitled to the protection of the law, whether his motives are commendable or not; but if he demands more than the strict rules of law can give him, his motives may become important. In general it must be assumed that the rules of the common law will give adequate redress for any injury; and when the litigant avers that under the circumstances of his particular case they do not, and that therefore the gracious ear of equity should incline to hear his complaint, it may not be amiss to inquire how he came to be placed in such circumstances. If a man invites an injury, he may still have his redress in the courts of law, but his prayer for the special interposition of equity on the ground that what he invited and expected was about irreparably to injure, would not be likely to trouble the judicial conscience very much if it were wholly ignored.

The land having been bought to make money from by sale, a legal award of damages for an injury to it, is in furtherance of the purpose of the purchase, and therefore a suitable and a just redress. Defendant is not alleged to be irresponsible, and a jury it is supposed will award all that is reasonable. If complainant wants more than is reasonable, he has a right to obtain it under the rules of law, but he cannot demand the aid of equity in a speculation. If in speculative language

he has a corner in real estate, there is no greater reason why he should have the assistance of an injunction to aid his schemes than there would be if on the produce exchange he had effected a corner in grain. Without the writ in either case he may be the sufferer, but he suffers nothing for which damages cannot compensate him. The elements of irreparable injury are entirely wanting to his case.

Our conclusion is that the circuit court gave the complainant all he was entitled to when the case was sent to a jury. The decree must therefore be affirmed with costs.

GRAVES, J. I concur in affirming the decree.

CAMPBELL, C.J. It appears without doubt in this case that defendants, without color or claim of right, are keeping up a continuous series of invasions upon complainant's freehold by using a running stream as a means of transporting sand upon his bottom land in quantities sufficient to bury it. The same course of conduct defiles and silts up the stream, rendering it useless to him for any purpose of business or convenience. It is equivalent in mischief to taking away or destroying his property in the land and his rights in the water.

I cannot concur in the doctrine that any one's rights of this kind are subject to judicial discretion. The rights to equitable relief, where that is the only adequate remedy, are as absolute as to legal relief. The one remedy is no more sacred than the other, and no more capable of lawful denial. If the defendants were to take possession of the land in question by putting a tenant upon it, no power would exist any where to deny complainant his possessory remedy. Where the same sort of wrong is done by indirect assumption of possession so that all the advantages of actual possession are enjoyed by the wrongdoer without going in person upon the soil, there is no reason for denying the only remedy which can secure to complainant the future enjoyment of his own estate, which would not as justly authorize the refusal of a possessory remedy in the other case. And no remedy at law is adequate for such a grievance as is here complained of, because no legal remedy can secure complainant the use of his own property.

It is not claimed, and there is certainly no ground for claiming, that there is any equitable estoppel. Defendants have never acted on any belief that they had a right to do what they are doing. They have always known they were wrongdoers, and have simply presumed on the patience of their neighbors, and neglected to purchase what they could originally have purchased if they had chosen. Neither does the proof show any very serious difficulty in the way of avoiding the mischief, although I do not regard this as at all essential.

It is not denied by complainant that he purchased the land for speculative purposes. As every one has a right to do this if he chooses, it cannot in any way lessen his claims to protection. It would be, I think, a very dangerous principle to hold that a civil wrong can be lessened by the motives of the party injured, so long as he has done no wrong himself. The property of one man is as much entitled to protection as that of another—not because he brought it or intends to use it without selfish motives, but because it is property. Any attempt to discriminate would, in my opinion, leave private interests subject to a discretion which no man could calculate upon, and make the judicial conscience the only arbiter of every one's rights. Some courts may have acted on this notion, but it seems to me that such precedents are unjust, and are not consistent with law or equity as we have received them under our constitutional guaranties of protection to person and property.

I think the court below should have granted a perpetual injunction as prayed.

MARSTON, J., did not sit in this case.

Notes and Questions

1. Consider whether Judge Cooley would have issued an injunction in the following cases:

(a) Plaintiff owned the land for ten years prior to erection of the mill.

(b) Plaintiff purchased the land speculatively after erection of the mill, but did not bring suit until after he had owned the land for ten years.

(c) Plaintiff purchased the land speculatively after erection of the mill, but then decides to build a vacation home on the land.

(d) Plaintiff, a city stockbroker, inherited the land one year after erection of the mill from his parent who had homesteaded the site and who committed suicide as a consequence of the degradation of the property.

(e) Plaintiff had purchased the land prior to erection of the mill in the mistaken belief that defendant would need to purchase the land in order to have sufficient acreage to erect the mill.

2. Zechariah Chafee, Jr. roundly condemned *Allouez* in his Thomas M. Cooley lectures at Michigan Law School:[22]

George Washington and John Marshall made a good deal of money out of land speculation. Why then is it wicked? If there be a proper defense in this case, it is not the clean hands maxim at all. What both opinions were groping for was some solution of the problem of balance of convenience. There is considerable authority that if copper mining was much more valuable to the region than farming bottom lands, then the mine owner was entitled to a sort of informal eminent

---

[22] Z. CHAFEE, JR., SOME PROBLEMS OF EQUITY 96–97 (1950).

domain through which he could use the downstream land for his debris on paying a reasonable lump sum compensation. On this theory, an injunction would be denied, not only to [Edwards], but also to X, his grantor who owned the bottom lands when the nuisance began.

However, the *Allouez* decision seems to rest on the proposition that X can enjoin the mining company, but cannot transfer this right with the land. Judge Cooley does not see that the long-time effect of such a proposition is to punish any person in the position of X. Although he is the clean-handed victim of a deliberate tort, he will have a great deal of difficulty in selling his land. Who wants to pay money for a pile of constantly increasing debris? So the tort-victim is forced to win an injunction suit before he sells, in order to get any sort of price. He may be very reluctant to engage in such an expensive litigation. Suppose he finds a buyer who is willing to take over this burden along with the land. The possibility of such a deal is cut off by the *Allouez* doctrine.

3. A great part of Chancellor Chafee's lectures was devoted to debunking the "clean hands" maxim, the very maxim Judge Cooley used but did not state in *Allouez*:[23]

> The most amusing maxim of equity is 'He who comes into Equity must come with clean hands.' It has given rise to many interesting cases and poor jokes. The maxim has been regarded as an especially significant manifestation of the ethical attitude of equity as contrasted with the common law. Pomeroy, for instance, argues that the principle involved in this maxim is "merely the expression of one of the elementary and fundamental conceptions of equity jurisprudence."[24] Pomeroy's theory is that chancery has power to force a defendant to comply with the dictates of conscience as to matters outside the strict rules of law. Correspondingly, it will not interfere on behalf of a plaintiff whose own conduct in this connection has been contrary to conscience. In other words, since equity tries to enforce good faith in defendants, it no less stringently demands the same good faith from plaintiffs.
>
> Although it is a pity to take this beautiful statue off its lofty pedestal, I propose to show that the clean hands doctrine does not definitely govern anything, that it is a rather recent growth, that it ought not to be called a maxim of equity because it is by no means confined to equity, that its supposed unity is very tenuous and it is really a bundle of rules relating to quite diverse subjects, that insofar as it is a principle it is not very helpful but is at times capable of causing great harm.

Test Chancellor Chafee's assertion against the following case.

---

[23] *Id.* at 1–2.

[24] 2 Pomeroy § 398.

McCune v. Brown

648 S.W.2d 811

Court of Appeals of Arkansas

March 30, 1983

Davidson, Horne, Hollingsworth, Arnold & Grobmyer, Little Rock, for appellant.

Eichenbaum, Scott, Miller, Crockett, Darr & Hawk, P.A. by Frank S. Hamlin and Leonard L. Scott, Little Rock, for appellee.

CLONINGER, Judge.

On August 28, 1981, appellee, W.G. Brown, Sr., filed a complaint in equity against the appellant, Billie Jean McCune, seeking a temporary restraining order to keep appellant from removing any of the contents of a safety deposit box leased to her at Worthen Bank & Trust Company in Little Rock, Arkansas. The contents of the box consisted of 650 gold Kruggerands, 13 Mexican pesos and one double eagle gold piece valued at approximately $250,000. The gold was placed in appellant's safety deposit box on December 12, 1978, at a time when appellee was involved in a divorce proceeding with his wife. Appellee admitted at trial that he had transferred the gold to appellant, his daughter, in an attempt to defeat his ex-wife's rights to the property.

The chancellor held that appellee had proved his right to possession of the gold and therefore was entitled to it pursuant to Ark.Stats.Ann. § 34-2101 et seq. (Repl.1962 and Supp.1981). The chancellor found that appellee had not made a completed gift of the gold and further held that appellee was not estopped from asserting his claim to the gold. From the decision of the chancellor, appellant now brings this appeal, alleging three points for reversal.

Appellant's first point for reversal is that the court erred in not finding that appellee was estopped from asserting any claim to the gold. As appellant points out, this case is very similar to a recent case decided by this court, *Melvin v. Melvin*, 270 Ark. 522, 606 S.W.2d 90 (Ark.App.1980). In *Melvin*, the chancellor made a property division in a divorce proceeding whereby he awarded the husband a Winnebago motor home. On appeal the wife argued that the Winnebago was not marital property which the chancellor could divide because it was a gift to her before marriage. The chancellor had found

that the transfer of title to the Winnebago to his present wife was solely an attempt to keep his former wife from receiving it in an earlier divorce proceeding. The chancellor further found that the general understanding at the time of the transfer was that it would be transferred back to the husband at some time subsequent to the divorce.

On appeal, the Arkansas Court of Appeals found that the evidence supported the court's finding that the husband intended no gift of the Winnebago to his present wife. However, the court further found that the husband was estopped from asserting any claim to the Winnebago. The court recognized that the transfer was made to preclude any possible claim by appellee's former wife. The court analogized this situation to one in which a husband conveys property to his wife in order to defraud his creditors. A conveyance made to defraud creditors is still good between the parties. *Maupin v. Gaines*, 125 Ark. 181, 188 S.W.2d 552 (1916). He does not come into court with clean hands. See *McClure v. McClure*, 220 Ark. 312, 247 S.W.2d 466 (1952).

We agree with appellant that the facts of this case are very similar to the facts in *Melvin*, *supra*. However, we find that the *Melvin* case is in conflict with previous cases decided by the Arkansas Supreme Court in the application of the clean hands maxim. In *Batesville Truck Line, Inc. v. Martin*, 219 Ark. 603, 243 S.W.2d 729 (1951), the Arkansas Supreme Court held that the clean hands doctrine must, in order to defeat a suit, have an immediate and necessary relation to the equity which the complainant seeks to enforce against the defendant. Further, the party complaining of the wrong must have been injured thereby to justify the application of the principle of unclean hands. The purpose of the maxim is to secure justice and equity, and not to aid one in an effort to acquire property to which he has no right.

In the instant case, we find that there was evidence to support the chancellor's decision that appellee was not estopped from asserting his interest in the gold. We hold that this case is governed by the rule in *Batesville Truck Line*, *supra*, and to the extent that *Melvin v. Melvin, supra*, is in conflict, that case is overruled. In order to justify application of the clean hands maxim, appellant must prove that she was somehow injured thereby. Further, a chancellor may balance the equities between the parties in determining whether or not to apply the maxim.

Here, the evidence strongly suggests that appellant knew why the gold was being transferred to her. Although she testified that appellee had made an unconditional gift of the gold to her, the chancellor chose to believe appellee and his witnesses who testified that the gold was transferred to appellant for the purpose of keeping it from his former wife and appellant understood that the gold was to be transferred back to him some time after the divorce. The findings of a chancellor will not be disturbed on appeal unless they are found to be clearly erroneous or against a clear preponderance of the evidence; and, inasmuch as a preponderance of the evidence depends heavily on the credibility of the witnesses, the appellate court defers to the superior position of the chancellor in this regard. . . . We find no error in the chancellor's ruling on this issue.

Questions

1. The case you have just read is an "equity" case because the plaintiff has asked for a temporary restraining order. Since the TRO would impose a direct duty upon the defendant personally, it is traditionally part of the "equity" side of the Arkansas courts even though those courts, like the courts in most states, have merged equity and law.

Since the plaintiff defrauded his former wife by transferring the Kruggerands to his daughter and making it appear that his daughter had title to them, why should an equity court now intercede on his behalf in his lawsuit against his daughter? Isn't the court "rewarding" fraud in this case?

2. If your answer to the latter question is "yes," is this a case of predominantly male judges awarding a suspect decision to a male who has previously defrauded his wife and now is trying to get the Kruggerands back from his daughter? Is this rampant male chauvinism at work?

3. What does justice have to say about this case? Suppose that the plaintiff's former wife reads in the newspapers or in the court reports that Brown has *admitted* that he transferred the gold in order to defeat her rights to the property? She will see—by the very report of the case (a public document) that her former husband has admitted defrauding her! Since this is, presumably, her first notice of the fraud, the statute of limitations will only begin running now.

Suppose that the former wife now wants to recover her property interest in the Kruggerands. In the case you have just read, which is a case by her former husband against the daughter, whom does the former wife want to win the case? Whom will she be rooting for? Her former husband? Or the daughter?

Does your answer to these questions *change your opinion* about the justice of the court's decision?

6.3 Doing justice under the merger of law and equity

A Century of the New Equity[25]

Leonard J. Emmerglick

Commencing in 1845 the states, led by Texas, began to abandon their separate equity courts.

The principal human want for which people turn to the courts in a free society is justice shaped and fashioned to the facts of the individual case—individualized justice. As we abandoned separate equity courts, designed to provide such justice, administrative tribunals were created to meet the need, and they have flourished. Attached to the executive department of government, the administrative tribunal derives from our system of constitutional checks and balances a natural opposition to the judicial branch. Similarly, the English Court of Chancery grew up in opposition to courts of law. The individual turned to the Chancellor for protection against the law. The separate and independent Court of Chancery stood in opposition to strict law, and for that reason was able to individualize justice. The object of administrative adjudication, like that of equity, is to give effect to the peculiar, special circumstances in each case.

Separate equity courts were given up because equity had been made into a body of rigid doctrines which were applied quite as mechanically as the strict common law. Equity had become a sterile system and showed a progressive decadence as an agency able to individualize justice. "The introduction of the common-law theory of binding precedents and the resulting case-law equity . . . that made equity a system must in the end prove fatal to it. In the very act of becoming a system it becomes legalized, and in becoming merely a competing system of law insures its ultimate downfall."[26] Since equity had become "legalized," it was assumed that the usefulness of the separate court was exhausted. But the increasing resort to administrative adjudication which has followed merger is living proof that the task of the separate equity court had not been completed. There was needed, not less, but more freedom to exercise judicial discretion. The human need for justice is not met by providing certainty and predictability. It requires also the ameliorating exercise of discretion. When the courts deemphasize the importance of judicial discretion other agencies are devised to provide something equivalent to it. In the twelfth and thirteenth centuries the common-law courts administered equity. These courts were closely identified with the King, and thus their action was marked by the exercise of broad discretion. By the fourteenth century the common-law courts gained an establishment quite independent of the King. The discretionary character of their justice had largely evaporated. And so a new agency was created to meet the insistent need for individualized justice grounded in the exercise of discretion. That agency, of course, was the Court of Chancery. It too permitted discretion to evaporate, but this time the attempted correction took the form of reverting to the method

---

[25] 23 TEX. L. REV. 244 (1945), reprinted in SELECTED ESSAYS ON EQUITY 53–55 (E. Re ed. 1955).

[26] Pound, *The Decadence of Equity* (1905), 5 COL. L. REV. 20, 25.

of the twelfth century.

With each merger of law and equity in the Anglo-American legal systems there ceased to be a court which stood in opposition to strict law. In cases where individualized justice could properly be attempted the individual had to go to court which stood for both strict law and opposition to it. A court which was obliged to preserve and cultivate the common law was to determine upon what principles the common law should be opposed and defeated. The movement for merger of equity into law discounted this in its preoccupation with the belief that law and equity do not conflict, that equity is nothing more than a body of more enlightened principles of conduct which could be smoothly mortised into the common law. The doctrine of "no conflict" was accepted by Maitland, Langdell, and Ames. That there is very real conflict between law and equity is more generally recognized today. A judgment of a common-law court creates rights in the plaintiff. A decree in equity, operating *in personam*, imposes duties upon the defendant. From this fundamental difference, as well as from equity's principles, drawn from morals and applied in opposition to common-law rules, conflict results. Equity compels the defendant to forego the exercise of legal rights where fairness, good faith and conscience dictate that they should not be enforced.[27]

---

[27] For an example of the price we pay for losing equity, see Jacobson, *The Equitable Administration of Long-Term Relations: An Appreciation of Judge Clark's Opinion in Parev Products* JUDGE CHARLES EDWARD CLARK (P. Petruck ed. 1991). Jacobson criticizes recent contract theorists for using implied terms and tort concepts to fashion rigid, unimaginative remedies for disputes between parties to long-term relations. Judge Clark, the father of merger in federal courts, approached long-term relations as a chancellor administers a trust, deploying novel equitable remedies. [Eds.]

Goldsmith v. Goldsmith

145 N.Y. 313
Court of Appeals of the State of New York
March, 1895

FINCH, J. The findings in this case show a situation which permits the application of an equitable remedy. They establish that Mrs. Goldsmith, while the owner and in possession of a house and lot known as the Myrtle avenue property, met with an accident which incapacitated her for its further care and management, and induced her to commit it to her son, the defendant, Leopold. That son was of age but unmarried and lived with the family, which further consisted of four children, three daughters and one son, all of them, with perhaps a single exception, minors, and two of them under ten years of age. The Myrtle avenue property furnished a home for the family which was supported partly by the rental of a portion of the house, partly by the husband and father, and to some extent by the labor of Annie, the eldest daughter, upon whom the household management devolved after the disability of the mother. The means of the family were narrow and limited. The home which they occupied was very essential to their comfort and support, but even that was incumbered by a mortgage, the annual interest of which was a charge upon their resources. In this state of affairs the findings show that the mother conveyed the house and lot to her son, Leopold, upon a promise on his part to hold it for the benefit of the other four children in common with himself, and give to them their shares in it. He paid no consideration for it beyond the promise thus made. It was a further part of the arrangement that he should have all the accruing rents, but should pay the interest on the mortgage and the taxes on the property, and was to have his board in the family without charge. In pursuance of this arrangement the deed was executed and delivered, and Annie herself took it to the clerk's office for record. It is quite evident that this was an arrangement founded upon the relation of mother and son, and brothers and sisters, involving the trust and confidence growing out of that relation, and intended as a settlement of the family affairs. It furnished a home for all in which they were to have a common right, and which was to be for their joint benefit. The deed was made in February, 1887. The mother died in March of the next year. The plan originally adopted was carried out during her life and for some considerable time after her death. The daughters furnished Leopold with his board without compensation or charge, as was arranged, and occasionally paid out small sums for ordinary repairs of the house. A time came when Leopold sold the Myrtle avenue property, and with a portion of the proceeds bought a house and lot on De Kalb avenue. There is evidence that on this occasion he was asked to take the deed in the name of all the children interested, but objected on the ground that it would be troublesome and inconvenient, and promised to execute a separate paper acknowledging and securing their rights in the property. Soon after he totally repudiated the agreement, and claimed to be the sole and absolute owner of the property, and now defends against the children, insisting that the agreement, if made, was void for uncertainty, and because it rested solely in parol.

There was enough of evidence to warrant the finding that Leopold at the time of the conveyance promised his mother that he would hold the property in trust for the plaintiffs herein. What he said on that occasion was expressed in somewhat different terms by different witnesses, but the substance of all of it concurred in the promise that he would hold the legal title for the benefit of the plaintiffs. That agreement was reflected in the action of both parties for some years after it was made, and induced the plaintiffs to do what otherwise they would not have done, and furnish Leopold his board without charge. The conduct of the latter in now denying the rights of the plaintiffs operates as a manifest fraud upon them and upon the purpose of the dead mother in seeking to provide for her children. It would be a reproach to equity if it proved unable to redress such a wrong.

It may be granted that no express trust was created, and that the judgment cannot be sustained on that ground, but we think the case is one in which equity will raise out of the situation, from the grouped and aggregated facts, an implied trust to prevent and redress a fraud, and which trust will be enforced. The general rule was declared, in *Wood v. Rabe,* (96 N.Y. 425, 426), to be, that when a person, through the influence of a confidential relation, acquires title to property or obtains an advantage which he cannot conscientiously retain, the court, to prevent the abuse of confidence, will grant relief. It was added that, while the fraud must be something more than the mere breach of a verbal agreement, yet, where the transaction is one between parent and child, and involves the greatest confidence on one side and the greatest influence on the other, the case is one side and the greatest influence on the other, the case is one in which equity may properly intervene. One of the findings in this case is "that at the time said deed was delivered the defendant understood that his mother reposed confidence in him, and with that understanding accepted the conveyance and the confidence of his mother." There is no room to doubt the truth of that finding. There was not only involved the relation of mother and son, but that of brothers and sisters, for whose benefit the agreement was made. The absence of a formal writing grew out of that very confidence and trust, and was occasioned by it, as was also the subsequent performance by the children of the condition to furnish board without pay. Upon the whole transaction, therefore, including the confidential relation of the parties and its nature as a family arrangement very much beyond a mere business relation, we think it was competent for a court of equity to impress upon the property and its proceeds an implied trust for the benefit of the children.

We think, therefore, that there was no error in awarding the relief, and that the judgment and order appealed from should be affirmed, with costs.

All concur.

Judgment affirmed.

Questions

1. Would the case have been decided differently if the arrangement had not included free board for Leopold from his sisters? What if the sisters stopped giving Leopold free board as soon as their mother died?

2. After the sisters and brother won their share of Leopold's property by virtue of the court's decision, must the sisters continue to provide free board to Leopold? Must Leopold continue to pay the mortgage and taxes? Must all the siblings live together even if they no longer can stand each other? Do these questions suggest the intricacy of the original context of the mother's conveyance of the property to Leopold? When that context no longer exists, is it appropriate for a court to make rulings that tend to presume the continuation of that context? Should the law treat family relationships in a somewhat special way—for example, not the way the law would treat a corporation or partnership?

3. It appears that Mrs. Goldsmith made a deliberate decision not to seek the help of a lawyer when she made her arrangement with Leopold. Does this suggest that she might not have wanted to hold Leopold strictly to the arrangement if future circumstances changed? Or does it suggest simply that she was ignorant of the legal consequences of her plans?

3. We are told that, historically, equity courts came into the picture in the Fourteenth Century to correct the legalistic excesses of the law courts. But is it not something quite different to argue that equity courts should correct the legal mistakes of people who are ignorant of the law?

5. Consider the purpose of the Statute of Frauds: to discourage fraudulent claims based on conflicting allegations of the existnece of, and provisions of, oral contracts or trusts. Does the *Goldsmith* decision tend to undermine the Statute of Frauds? If so, where is the true "equity" here? Is it equitable to enforce the Statute of Frauds, or to undermine it?

6. After reading about the Separation Thesis one might have gotten the impression that equity was the justice side of the legal system, and law the law side. Do these questions suggest that law and justice cannot be artifically separated by a procedural device, such as the fourteenth century innovation of separating equity courts from law courts? Do law and equity simply present different versions of justice? Does the merger of law and equity change the picture, or does it simply reintroduce an artifical distinction? Is it *ever* possible to separate law and justice?

Sharp v. Kosmalski

40 N.Y.2d 119

Court of Appeals of the State of New York

June 15, 1976

GABRIELLI, J. Plaintiff commenced this action to impose a constructive trust upon property transferred to defendant on the ground that the retention of the property and subsequent ejection of the plaintiff therefrom was in violation of relationship of trust and confidence and constituted unjust enrichment. The Trial Judge dismissed plaintiff's complaint and his decision was affirmed without opinion by the Appellate Division.

Upon the death of his wife of 32 years, plaintiff, a 56-year-old dairy farmer whose education did not go beyond the eighth grade, developed a very close relationship with defendant, a school teacher and a woman 16 years his junior. Defendant assisted plaintiff in disposing of his wife's belongings, performed certain domestic tasks for him such as ironing his shirts and was a frequent companion of the plaintiff. Plaintiff came to depend upon defendant's companionship and, eventually, declared his love for her, proposing marriage to her. Notwithstanding her refusal of his proposal of marriage, defendant continued her association with plaintiff and permitted him to shower her with many gifts, fanning his hope that he could induce defendant to alter her decision concerning his marriage proposal. Defendant was given access to plaintiff's bank account, from which it is not denied that she withdrew substantial amounts of money. Eventually, plaintiff made a will naming defendant as his sole beneficiary and executed a deed naming her a joint owner of his farm. The record reveals that numerous alterations in the way of modernization were made to plaintiff's farmhouse in alleged furtherance of "domestic plans" made by plaintiff and defendant.

In September, 1971, while the renovations were still in progress, plaintiff transferred his remaining joint interest to defendant. At the time of the conveyance, a farm liability policy was issued to plaintiff naming defendant and her daughter as additional insureds. Furthermore, the insurance agent was requested by plaintiff, in the presence of defendant, to change the policy to read "J. Rodney Sharp, life tenant. Jean C. Kosmalski, owner." In February, 1973, the liaison between the parties was abruptly severed as defendant ordered plaintiff to move out of his home and vacate the farm. Defendant took possession of the home, the farm and all the equipment thereon, leaving plaintiff with assets of $300.

Generally, a constructive trust may be imposed "[w]hen property has been acquired in such circumstances that the holder of the legal title may not in good conscience retain the beneficial interest" (*Beatty v Guggenheim Exploration Co.*, 225 NY 380, 386; 1 Scott, Trusts [3d

ed], § 44.2, p 337; 4 Pomeroy's Equity Jurisprudence [5th ed], § 1053, p 119). In the development of the doctrine of constructive trust as a remedy available to courts of equity, the following four requirements were posited: (1) a confidential or fiduciary relation, (2) a promise, (3) a transfer in reliance thereon and (4) unjust enrichment. [Citing cases]

Most frequently, it is the existence of a confidential relationship which triggers the equitable considerations leading to the imposition of a constructive trust. Although no marital or other family relationship is present in this case, such is not essential for the existence of a confidential relation (see *Muller v Sobol*, 277 App Div 884 [meretricious relationship]; Bogert, *op. cit.*, § 482, pp 136–147; 1 Scott, *op. cit.*, p 339). The record in this case clearly indicates that a relationship of trust and confidence did exist between the parties and, hence, the defendant must be charged with an obligation not to abuse the trust and confidence placed in her by the plaintiff. The disparity in education between the plaintiff and defendant highlights the degree of dependence of the plaintiff upon the trust and honor of the defendant.

Unquestionably, there is a transfer of property here, but the Trial Judge found that the transfer was made "without a promise or understanding of any kind." Even without an express promise, however, courts of equity have imposed a constructive trust upon property transferred in reliance upon a confidential relationship. In such a situation, a promise may be implied or inferred from the very transaction itself. As Judge CARDOZO so eloquently observed: "Though a promise in words was lacking, the whole transaction, it might be found, was 'instinct with an obligation' imperfectly expressed (*Wood v. Duff-Gordon*, 222 N.Y. 88, 91)" (*Sinclair v Purdy*, 235 NY 245, 254 (1923) [Citing other cases]. In deciding that a formal writing or express promise was not essential to the application of the doctrine of constuctive trust, Judge CARDOZO further observed in language that is most fitting in the instant case:

> Here was a man transferring to his sister the only property he had in the world. . . . He was doing this, as she admits, in reliance upon her honor. Even if we were to accept her statement that there was no distinct promise to hold for his benefit, the exaction of such

a promise, in view of the relation, might well have seemed to be superfluous." (*Sinclair v. Purdy, supra,* p. 254).

More recently, in *Farano v Stephanelli* (7 AD2d 420, 425), Chief Judge BREITEL, then writing for the Appellate Division, First Department, followed the *Sinclair* approach stating that the decision to invoke the remedy of constructive trust "need not be determined exclusively by whether or not the defendant daughters expressed in so many words a promise to reconvey the properties to the father if he should ask". Indeed, in the case before us, it is inconceivable that plaintiff would convey all of his interest in property which was not only his abode but the very means of his livelihood without at least tacit consent upon the part of the defendant that she would permit him to continue to live on and operate the farm. I would therefore reject the Trial Judge's conclusion, erroneously termed a finding of fact, that no agreement or limitation may, as a matter of law, be implied from the circumstances surrounding the transfer of plaintiff's farm.

The salutary purpose of the constructive trust remedy is to prevent unjust enrichment and it is to this requirement that I now turn. The Trial Judge in his findings of fact, concluded that the transfer did not constitute unjust enrichment. In this instance also, a legal conclusion was mistakenly labeled a finding of fact. A person may be deemed to be unjustly enriched if he (or she) has received a benefit, the retention of which would be unjust (Restatement, Restitution, § 1, Comment *a*). A conclusion that one has been unjustly enriched is essentially a legal inference drawn from the circumstances surrounding the transfer of property and the relationship of the parties. It is a conclusion reached through the application of principles of equity. Having determined that the relationship between plaintiff and defendant in this case is of such a nature as to invoke consideration of the equitable remedy of constructive trust, it remains to be determined whether defendant's conduct following the transfer of plaintiff's farm was in violation of that relationship and, consequently, resulted in the unjust enrichment of

the defendant. This must be determined from the circumstances of the transfer since there is no express promise concerning plaintiff's continued use of the land. Therefore, the case should be remitted to the Appellate Division for a review of the facts. In so doing I would emphasize that the conveyance herein should be interpreted "not literally or irrespective of its setting, but sensibly and broadly with all its human implications" (*Sinclair v Purdy*, 235 NY 245, 254, *supra*). This case seems to present the classic example of a situation where equity should intervene to scrutinize a transaction pregnant with opportunity for abuse and unfairness. It was for just this type of case that there evolved equitable principles and remedies to prevent injustices. Equity still lives. To suffer the hands of equity to be bound by misnamed "findings of fact" which are actually conclusions of law and legal inferences drawn from the facts is to ignore and render impotent the rich and vital impact of equity on the common law and, perforce, permit injustice. Universality of law requires equity.

Accordingly, the order of the Appellate Division should be reversed and the case remitted to that court for a review of the facts, or, if it be so advised, in its discretion, to order a new trial in the interests of justice.

Chief Judge BREITEL and Judges WACHTLER and FUCHSBERG concur with Judge GABRIELLI; Judges JASEN, JONES and COOKE dissent and vote to affirm in the following memorandum: In view of the affirmed findings of fact that the appellant knowingly and voluntarily conveyed his property without agreement or condition of any kind, express or implied, and with full knowledge of their legal effect, it cannot be said that a constructive trust should be imposed as a matter of law. Although we are sympathetic to the appellant who has been doubly aggrieved by the loss of his wife and property, we are limited to considerations of questions of law and, in light of the factual findings, would affirm.

Order reversed and the case remitted to the Appellate Division, Fourth Department, for further proceedings in accordance with the opinion herein, with costs to abide the event.

Questions

1. Isn't the notion of "constructive trust" simply a form of words that achieves a result the court believes is required by the justice of the situation? If so, what is the justice of the situation?

2. Do we *need* the notion of "constructive trust" to resolve this case? Might not the court have made more of the insurance provision that read "J. Rodney Sharp, life tenant," as a contemporaneous written reservation to the deed that was agreed to by both sides?

3. Is this a case of an uneducated farmer who became besotted with a shrewd school teacher who was only out for money? He executed a deed conveying his farm to her, and a year and a half later, she ordered him to move out of his home and vacate the farm. Is the court correct in concluding that "it is inconceivable that plaintiff would convey all of his interest in property which was not only his abode but the very means of his livelihood without at least tacit consent upon the part of defendant that she would permit him to continue to live on and operate the farm"?

4. Are there any *facts* that you can *imagine* that would change the picture dramatically, that could have gone unstated by the court? If you were attorney for the school teacher, what kinds of facts would you look for? Consider the following categories:

> (a) Your client may have contributed domestic services to the farmer that, in the aggregate, were worth the entire value of the farm;
>
> (b) The farmer may have beaten or otherwise physically abused your client;
>
> (c) The farmer was a self-made millionaire who knew exactly what he was doing despite the fact that he had only a grade-school education;
>
> (d) Your client refused the farmer's offer of marriage clearly and distinctly, and never encouraged him in the slightest about the prospect of marriage.

Of course, we are only *imagining* possible facts. But maybe the attorney for the school teacher spent all of his or her time researching "constructive trust" doctrines and paid no attention to facts that could have turned the situation around for the school teacher. We don't know what actually happened. But the POINT is that many cases—maybe most cases, maybe all cases—can be won *on the facts*. The attorney who fails to investigate the facts thoroughly is not doing "justice" to his or her client, and can hardly expect to receive "justice" from the court.

5. Or, suppose there are no mitigating facts in favor of the school teacher. Suppose that the court's opinion fairly summarizes all the relevant facts in the situation (admittedly, an unlikely possibility). What then? What argument can the school teacher use?

Can she show that the court's approach is hopelessly *paternalistic*? The farmer is, after all, an adult of 56 years of age. Why doesn't the court simply give effect to the legal transactions entered into by the farmer, without second-guessing them? Suppose the farmer were to wake up one morning from a dream where God appeared and told him to deed his entire farm to the Seventh Day Adventists, retaining only $300 for himself, and then travel from town to town preaching salvation to sinners. If the farmer were to deed his entire farm to the Seventh Day Adventists, would a subsequent court refuse to validate the deed? Most likely, any court would say that the farmer is free to do with his property as he pleases—indeed, that is almost the *definition* of private property. So why, if a transfer without consideration to a religious or charitable organization is valid, should the court disallow a transfer to a person like the school teacher who has in fact performed valuable domestic services for the farmer?

Do you like this "paternalistic" characterization? Would you say that a court *never* should be paternalistic? Would you say that a court should *never* protect a person from the legal consequences that he or she intended?

Simonds v. Simonds

45 N.Y.2d 233
Court of Appeals of the State of New York
July 11, 1978

Chief Judge BREITEL.

Plaintiff Mary Simonds, decedent's first wife, seeks to impress a constructive trust on proceeds of insurance policies on decedent's life. The proceeds had been paid to the named beneficiaries, defendants Reva Simonds, decedent's second wife, and their daughter Gayle. Plaintiff, however, asserts as superior an equitable interest arising out of a provision in her separation agreement with decedent. Special Term granted partial summary judgment to plaintiff and impressed a constructive trust to the extent of $7,000 plus interest against proceeds of a policy naming the second wife as beneficiary, and the Appellate Division affirmed. Defendant Reva Simonds, the second wife, appeals.

The separation agreement required the husband to maintain in effect, with the wife as beneficiary to the extent of $7,000, existing life insurance policies or, if the policies were to be canceled or to lapse, insurance policies of equal value. The issue is whether that provision entitles the first wife to impress a constructive trust on proceeds of insurance policies subsequently issued, despite the husband's failure to name her as the beneficiary on any substitute policies once the original life insurance policies had lapsed.

There should be an affirmance. The separation agreement vested in the first wife an equitable right in the then existing policies. Decedent's substitution of policies could not deprive the first wife of her equitable interest, which was then transferred to the new policies. Since the proceeds of the substituted policies have been paid to decedent's second wife, whose interest in the policies is subordinate to plaintiff's, a constructive trust may be imposed.

On March 9, 1960, decedent Frederick Simonds and his wife of 14 years, plaintiff Mary Simonds, entered into a separation agreement which, on March 31, 1960, was incorporated into an Illinois divorce decree granted to plaintiff on grounds of desertion. The agreement provided, somewhat inartfully: "The husband agrees that he will keep all of the policies of Insurance now in full force and effect on his life. Said policies now being in the sum of $21,000.00 and the Husband further agrees that the Wife shall be the beneficiary of said policies in an amount not less than $7,000.00 and the Husband further agrees that he shall pay any and all premiums necessary to maintain such policies of Insurance and if for any reason any of them now existing the policies shall be cancelled or be caused to lapse. He shall procure additional insurance in an amount equal to the face value of the policies having been cancelled or caused to lapse." Thus, the husband was to maintain, somehow, at least $7,000 of life insurance for the benefit of his first wife as a named beneficiary.

On May 26, 1960, less than two months after the divorce, decedent husband married defendant Reva Simonds. Defendant Gayle Simonds was born to the couple shortly thereafter.

Sometime after the separation agreement was signed, the then existing insurance policies were apparently canceled or permitted to lapse. It does not appear from the record why, how, or when this happened, but the policies were not extant at the time of decedent husband's death on August 1, 1971. In the interim, however, decedent has acquired three other life insurance policies, totaling over $55,000, none of which named plaintiff as a beneficiary. At his death, decedent had one policy in the amount of $16,138.83 originally issued in 1962 by Metropolitan Life Insurance Company, a second policy for $34,000 issued in 1967 through decedent's employer by Travelers Insurance Company, and a third policy for $5,566 issued in 1962 by the Equitable Life Assurance Society of Iowa. The first two policies named Reva Simonds, defendant's second wife, as beneficiary, and the third policy named their daughter. Hence, at the time of decedent's death he had continuously violated the separation agreement by maintaining no life insurance naming the first wife as a beneficiary.

The first wife, on March 11, 1972, brought an action against the second wife for conversion of $7,000 and to recover $13,600 in back alimony payments. This action was dismissed, essentially on the ground that the causes of action alleged could properly be brought only against decedent's estate, not against the second wife. The estate, however, is insolvent.

Subsequently, the first wife brought this action against both the second wife and the daughter, seeking to impose a constructive trust on the insurance proceeds to the extent of $7,000. A second cause of action, dealing with alimony arrears, is not involved on this appeal. Special Term granted partial summary judgment to the first wife and imposed a constructive trust on the proceeds in the hands of the second wife. A unanimous Appellate Division affirmed in a thoughtful and scholarly opinion by Mr. Justice Richard D. Simons.

There is no question that decedent breached his obligation to maintain life insurance with his first wife as beneficiary. Consequently, the first wife would of course be entitled to maintain an action for breach against the estate. The estate's insolvency, however, would make such an action fruitless. Thus, the controversy revolves around plaintiff's right, in equity, to recover $7,000 of the insurance proceeds.

Born out of the extreme rigidity of the early common law, equity in its origins drew heavily on Roman law, where equitable notions had long been accepted (see 1 Pomeroy, Equity Jurisprudence [5th ed], §§ 2–29. "Its great underlying principles, which are the constant sources, the never-failing roots, of its particular rules, are unquestionably principles of right, justice, and morality, so far as the same can become the elements of a positive human jurisprudence" (*id.*, § 67, at p 90). Law without principle is not law; law without justice is of limited value. Since adherence to principles of "law" does not invariably produce justice, equity is necessary (Aristotle, Nicomachean Ethics, Book V, ch 9, pp 1019–1020 [McKeon, ed Oxford: Clarendon Press, 1941]). Equity arose to soften the impact of legal formalisms; to evolve formalisms narrowing the broad scope of equity is to defeat its essential purpose.

Whatever the legal rights between insurer and insured, the separation agreement vested in the first wife an equitable interest in the insurance policies then in force. An agreement for sufficient consideration, including a separation agreement, to maintain a claimant as a beneficiary of a life insurance policy vests in the claimant an equitable interest in the policies designated. [Citing cases] This interest is superior to that of a named beneficiary who has given no consideration, notwithstanding policy provisions permitting the insured to change the designated beneficiary freely.

This is not to say that an insurance company may not rely on the insured's designation of a beneficiary. None of this opinion bears on the rights or responsibilities of the insurer in law or equity.

Obviously, the policies now at issue are not the same policies in existence at the time of the separation agreement. But it has been held that mere substitution of policies, or even substitution of insurance companies, does not defeat the equitable interest of one who has given sufficient consideration for a promise to be maintained as beneficiary under an insurance policy. [Citing cases]. The persistence of the promisee's equitable interest is all the more evident where the agreement expressly provides for a change in policies, and in effect provides further that the promisee's right shall attach to the new policies.

For a certainty, the first wife's equitable interest would be easier to trace if the new policies were quid pro quo replacements for the original policies. The record does not reveal whether this was so. But inability to trace plaintiff's equitable rights precisely should not require that they not be recognized, much as in the instance of damages difficult to prove (cf., e.g., *Randall-Smith v 43rd St. Estates Corp.*, 17 NY2d 99, 105–106). The separation agreement provides nexus between plaintiff's rights and the later acquired policies. The later policies were expressly contemplated by the parties, and it was agreed that plaintiff would have an interest in them. No reason in equity appears for denying plaintiff that interest, so long as no one who has given value for the policies or otherwise suffered a detriment is involved. The second wife's innocence does not offset the wrong by the now deceased husband.

The conclusion is an application of the general rule that equity regards as done that which should have been done (2 Pomeroy, Equity Jurisprudence [5th ed], §364; see, e.g., *Wallace v First Trust Co., of Albany*, 251 App Div 253, 256). Thus, if an insured, upon lapse or cancellation of insurance, followed by replacement with new insurance, has a contractual obligation to designate a particular person as beneficiary, equity will consider the obligee as a beneficiary.

In this case, the first wife's interest in the original policies extended as well to the later acquired policies. The husband, upon lapse or cancellation of the earlier policies, had by virtue of the separation agreement an obligation to name her as beneficiary on the later policies, an obligation enforceable in equity despite the husband's failure to comply with the terms of the separation agreement. Due to the husband's failure to do what he should have done, the first wife acquired not only a right at law to sue his estate for breach of contract, a right now worthless, but also an equitable right in the policies, a right which, upon the husband's death, attached to the proceeds. [Citing cases]

And, since the first wife was entitled to $7,000 of the insurance proceeds at the time of the husband's death, she is no less entitled because the proceeds have already been converted by being paid, erroneously, to the named beneficiaries. [Citing cases] Her remedy is imposition of a constructive trust.

In the words of Judge Cardozo, "[a] constructive trust is the formula through which the conscience of equity finds expression. When property has been acquired in such circumstances that the holder of the legal title may not in good conscience retain the beneficial interest, equity converts him into a trustee" (*Beatty v Guggenheim Exploration Co.*, 225 NY 380, 386). Thus, a constructive trust is an equitable remedy. It is perhaps more different from an express trust than it is similar (5 Scott, Trusts [3d ed], § 461). As put so well by Scott and restated at the Appellate Division, "[the constructive trustee] is not compelled to convey the property because he is a constructive trustee; it is because he can be compelled to convey it that he is a constructive trustee" (*id.*, § 462, at p 3413).

More precise definitions of a constructive trust have been termed inadequate because of the failure to recognize the broad scope of constructive trust doctrine (*id.*, at p 3412). As another leading scholar has said of constructive trusts, "[t]he Court does not restrict itself by describing all the specific forms of inequitable holding which will move it to grant relief, but rather reserves freedom to apply this remedy to whatever knavery human ingenuity can invent" (Bogert, Trusts and Trustees [2d ed rev, 1978], § 471, at p 29).

Four factors were posited in *Sharp v Kosmalski* (40 NY2d 119, 121). Although the factors are useful in many cases constructive trust doctrine is not rigidly limited. For a single example, one who wrongfully prevents a testator from executing a new will eliminating him as beneficiary will be held as a constructive trustee even in the absence of a confidential or fiduciary relation, a promise by the "trustee', and a transfer in reliance by the testator (see, e.g., *Latham v Father Divine*, 299 NY 22, 26–27). As then Judge Desmond said in response to the argument that a breach of a promise to the testator was necessary for imposition of a constructive trust (at p 27), "[a] constructive trust will be erected whenever necessary to satisfy the demands of justice * * * [I]ts applicability is limited only by the inventiveness of men who find new ways to enrich themselves unjustly by grasping what should not belong to them".

It so happens, as an added argument, if it were necessary, that the four factors enumerated in *Sharp v Kosmalski* are perceptible in this case: a promise, a transfer in reliance on the promise, the fiduciary relation between decedent and his first wife, and the "unjust enrichment" of the second wife. Because decedent and plaintiff were husband and wife, there is a duty of fairness in financial matters extending even past the contemplated separation of the spouses. Hence, a separation agreement based on one party's misrepresentation of financial condition is voidable.

It is agreed that the purpose of the constructive trust is prevention of unjust enrichment (*Sharp v Kosmalski*, 40 NY2d 119, 123, *supra*; Restatement, Restitution, § 160; 5 Scott, Trusts [3d ed], § 462.2).

Unjust enrichment, however, does not require the performance of any wrongful act by the one enriched. [Citing cases] Innocent parties may frequently be unjustly enriched. What is required, generally, is that a party hold property "under such circumstances that in equity and good conscience he ought not to retain it" (*Miller v Schloss*, 218 NY 400, 407; see *Sharp v Kosmalski*, 40 NY2d 119, 123, *supra*; *Sinclair v Purdy*, 235 NY 245, 253–254). A bona fide purchaser of property upon which a constructive trust would otherwise be imposed takes free of the constructive trust, but a gratuitous donee, however innocent, does not.

The unjust enrichment in this case is manifest. At a time when decedent was, certainly, anxious to remarry, he entered into a separation agreement with his wife of 14 years. As part of the agreement, he promised to maintain $7,000 in life insurance with the first wife as beneficiary. Later he broke his promise, and died with insurance policies naming only the second wife and daughter as beneficiaries. They have collected the proceeds, amounting to more than $55,000, while the first wife has collected nothing. Had the husband kept his promise, the beneficiaries would have collected $7,000 less in proceeds. To that extent, the beneficiaries have been unjustly enriched, and the proceeds should be subjected to a constructive trust.

Moreover, the second wife's complaint, if that it be, over the distinction drawn below between her daughter and herself is to no avail.

The first wife's equitable interest attached to all the substituted insurance policies, whether they named the second wife or the daughter as beneficiary. At the time each substituted policy was issued, decedent had an obligation to make the first wife a beneficiary. None of the named beneficiaries can escape the superior equitable interest of the first wife by pointing to other policies. True, plaintiff might also be entitled to impose a constructive trust on the policy naming the daughter as beneficiary. But that provides no cause for prorating the constructive trust. The beneficiaries are jointly and severally liable, if the analogy applicable to express trusts be applied (3 Scott, Trusts [3d ed], §§ 258–258.3). Plaintiff's choice not to appeal the dismissal against the daughter should not bar her from collecting in full against the second wife, who may have a right of contribution against the daughter, a question not before the court and not passed on (cf. *id.*).

The issues in this case should not generate significant controversy. The action is in equity, and the equities are clear. True, some courts have decided the issues differently (*Rindels v Prudential Life Ins. Co. of Amer.*, 83 NM 181; *Lock v Lock*, 8 Ariz App 138, 143; see, also, *Larson v Larson*, 226 Ga 209, 211). Those cases, however, rely heavily on formalisms and too little on basic equitable principles, long established in Anglo-American law and in this State and especially relevant when family transactions are involved. "A court of equity in decreeing a constructive trust is bound by no unyielding formula. The equity of the transaction must shape the measure of relief" (*Beatty v Guggenheim Exploration Co.*, 225 NY 380, 389 [CARDOZO, J.], *supra*).

Accordingly, the order of the Appellate Division should be affirmed, with costs.

Judges JASEN, GABRIELLI, JONES, WACHTLER, FUCHSBERG and COOKE concur.

Order affirmed.

Questions

1. Had the husband kept *no* life insurance after the divorce, would the New York Court of Appeals have traced the first wife's equitable interest to other assets? What if, for example, the husband's only asset at death were a house, held in joint tenancy with the second wife? What if, in addition to the house, he left a pension with a substantial death benefit to the second wife? What if the second wife relied on these assets for her support? What if the child of the second marriage were a minor?

2. Exactly how were the second wife and the daughter "unjustly enriched"? Judge Breitel says that, "Had the husband kept his promise, the beneficiaries would have collected $7,000 less in proceeds." Is Judge Breitel begging his own question?

3. The Court of Appeals talked extensively about equity. Did all the talk lead the court to the right result?

4. The merger of law and equity may have led to an impoverishment of resort to equitable principles in ordinary litigation. Scholars and judges, not trained in equity, tend to think that literalness in the application of statutes and precedents is what law is all about. In a way, the purpose of this coursebook has been to show that principles of justice invariably interact with principles of law, even if the principles of justice are not explicitly stated. Do you think that greater attention to the rich tradition of equity courts would (a) make the justice considerations in a given case more explicit, or (b) improve the quality of judicial decisions?

Justice at the Intersection of Law and Procedure

CHAPTER SEVEN

7.1 Prospectivity

The Sunburst Case

This may seem like one of the driest cases you've ever read. Appearances can be deceiving. You may find it to be one of the most fascinating and intellectually challenging cases in the world of law. As you read the opinion, you might want to make a chronological table of what happened: when did all the events (all the rulings, all the holdings in all the cases) occur in relation to each other? This should be of considerable help in interpreting the case.

Great Northern Ry. Co. v. Sunburst Oil & Refining Co.

287 U.S. 358
Supreme Court of the United States
December 5, 1932

Mr. Justice CARDOZO delivered the opinion of the Court.

Sunburst Oil & Refining Company, the respondent (shipper), brought suit against petitioner (carrier), Great Northern Railway Company, to recover payments claimed to be overcharges for freight. The charges were in conformity with a tariff schedule approved by the Railroad Commission of Montana for intrastate traffic. After payment had been made, the same commission which had approved the schedule held, upon a complaint by the shipper, that the rates so approved were excessive and unreasonable. In this action to recover the excess so paid, the shipper recovered a judgment which was affirmed upon appeal by the Supreme Court of Montana. The question, broadly stated, is whether the annulment by retroaction of rates valid when exacted is an unlawful taking of property within the Fourteenth Amendment. A writ of certiorari brings the case here.

By a statute of Montana the Board of Railroad Commissioners is empowered to fix rates of carriage for intrastate shipments. The rates thereby established are not beyond recall. They may be changed by the board itself on the complaint either of shipper or of carrier, if found to be unreasonable. In an action against the board, they may be set aside upon a like showing by a judgment of the court. Until changed or set aside, they "shall prima facie be deemed to be just, reasonable, and proper." Revised Codes of Montana §§ 3796, 3809, 3810.

The meaning of the statute was considered by the Supreme Court of Montana in a cause determined in May, 1921. *Doney v. Northern Pacific Railway Co.*, 60 Mont. 209, 199 P. 432. A shipper of lumber brought suit against a carrier to recover transportation charges which were alleged to be unreasonable, though they were in accordance with the published tariff. He did this without a preliminary application to the board to modify the schedule. He did it without a preliminary suit in which the board, being brought into court as a defendant, would have opportunity to sustain the schedule and resist the charge. The court held that, until one of these preliminary conditions had been satisfied, no action for restitution could be maintained against the carrier. It coupled that decision with the statement that, upon compliance with one or other of the conditions, the excess, thus ascertained, might be the subject of recovery.

The procedure there outlined was followed by respondent Sunburst. It filed a complaint with the board to the effect that the existing tariff for the carriage of crude petroleum distillate was excessive and unreasonable, in that the rate of 20½ cents was based upon an estimated weight of 7.4 pounds per gallon, whereas the actual weight is not more than 6.6 pounds per gallon. The board sustained the complaint. In doing so it ruled, in conformity with the decision in the *Doney* case, that the published schedule prescribed the minimum and the maximum to which carrier and shipper were required to adhere while the schedule was in force, but that by the true construction of the statute the duty of adherence was subject to a condition or proviso whereby annulment or modification would give a right of reparation for the excess or the deficiency. The revision of the tariff was followed by this suit against the carrier, and later by a judgment by the Supreme Court of Montana in favor of the shipper which is now before us for review.

The Supreme Court of Montana held that the ruling in the *Doney* case was erroneous and would not be followed in the future; that a rate established by the Commission had the same effect as one established by the Legislature; that the statute giving power to the Commission or the court to declare a rate unreasonable was not to be read as meaning that a declaration of invalidity should apply to intermediate transactions; but none the less that the ruling in the *Doney* case was law until reversed and would constitute the governing principle for

shippers and carriers who, during the period of its reign, had acted on the faith of it. We are thus brought to the inquiry whether the judgment thus rendered does violence to any right secured to the petitioner by the Federal Constitution.

[EDITOR'S NOTE: Justice Cardozo's statement of what the Montana Supreme Court interpreted the *Doney* case to mean—"that a statute giving power to the Commission or the court to declare a rate unreasonable was not to be read as meaning that a declaration of invalidity should apply to intermediate transactions"—perhaps should be clarified here. Consider that there are two distinct kinds of allegations a shipper can make of the carrier's charges—(a) that they are excessive, or (b) that the rates are unreasonable. (a) "Excessive" charges come about when the carrier charges more than it was entitled to charge under the rates fixed by the Board. When that happens, the shipper can bring a judicial action for a refund. (b) "Unreasonable" rates are those rates, fixed by the Board, that for some reason or other are alleged to be unreasonable. In the *Doney* case, the shipper brought a judicial action. It was unclear from its Complaint whether it was alleging (a) or (b) or both. The court dismissed the Complaint on the ground that the shipper should have gone to the Board first and followed all the procedures that Justice Cardozo summarized. The court then went on, in dictum, to suggest that the Board had the power in the first instance to find either (a) or (b). Then, some years later in the Sunburst Case, the Montana Supreme Court realized that it had misled everyone in the *Doney* Case. Indeed, Judge Galen, who wrote both the *Doney* opinion and the *Sunburst* opinion, said in *Sunburst*: "Having written that opinion for the court [in *Doney*], the author hereof expresses apology for having misled the profession, and welcomes this opportunity to correct the error made in interpreting our statutes." The error Judge Galen made in *Doney* was to mix up (a) and (b). He now held that *Doney* was correct only insofar as (a) was concerned: a shipper is always entitled to complain that the charges levied by the carrier were in excess of the Board's published rates. But as to (b), Judge Galen held that *Doney* should have said that there can be no finding—neither by the Board nor by a court—that a shipper is entitled to a refund on the ground that a published rate is unreasonable. True, the Board or a court can find that a given rate is unreasonable—because the statute says that it can—but this only means that the Board should thereupon change the rate and make it reasonable. Think of the Board as a mini-legislature. If a legislature finds that one of its statutes is unreasonable, it can change the statute. Similarly, the Board can change its rates. But all those changes only have prospective application. If tomorrow the legislature of your state says that a motorist must stop at the yellow signal (instead of proceeding with caution), that does not mean that you can be arrested for having gone through a yellow signal a month ago. All legislative changes only have prospective application. It follows that a shipper is not entitled to a refund based on a finding that a given fixed rate is unreasonable. As Judge Galen explained, "It truly would be an anomalous situation, were the commission [the Board], acting as a quasi-judicial tribunal, permitted to find that a carrier had violated the law because it charged a rate prescribed by the commission itself, acting in its legislative capacity." Rather, if the shipper does succeed in proving that a rate is unreasonable, the Board will change the rate for the future (and in that way, perhaps, help the shipper as far as its future business is concerned). But whatever the shipper has already paid the carrier under the published rates cannot be affected by a finding that the rates are unreasonable. This, then, is what Justice Cardozo meant when he said that a declaration by a court or by the Board that a rate is unreasonable does not apply to "intermediate transactions."]

The subject is likely to be clarified if we divide it into two branches. Was a federal right infringed by the action of the trial court in adhering to the rule imposed upon it in the *Doney* case by the highest court of the state? If there was no infringement then, did one come about later when the Supreme Court of Montana disavowed the rule of the *Doney* case for the future, but applied it to the past?

1. The trial court did not impair a federal right by giving to a statute of the state the meaning that had been ascribed to it by the highest court of the state, unless such impairment would have resulted if the meaning had been written into the statute by the Legislature itself. But plainly no such consequence would have followed if that course had been pursued. The *Doney* case was decided, as we have seen, in 1921. The transactions complained of occurred between August, 1926, and

August, 1928. Carrier and shipper understood at that time that the rates established by the Commission as the delegate of the Legislature were provisional and tentative. Valid for the time being the rates indubitably were, a prop for conduct while they stood, but the prop might be removed, and charges, past as well as present, would go down at the same time. By implication of law there had been written into the statute a notice to all concerned that payments exacted by a carrier in conformity with a published tariff were subject to be refunded if found thereafter, upon sufficient evidence, to be excessive and unreasonable. The Constitution of the United States would have nothing to say about the validity of a notice of that tenor written in so many words into the body of the act. Carrier and shipper would be presumed to bargain with each other on the basis of existing law. The validity of the notice is no less because it was written into the act by a process of construction. The inquiry is irrelevant whether we would construe the statute in the same way if the duty of construction were ours and not another's. Enough for us that the construction, whether we view it as wise or unwise, does not expose the court that made it to the reproach of withholding from the carrier the privileges and immunities established by the Constitution of the nation.

2. If the carrier did not suffer a denial of due process through the action of the trial court in subjecting the published tariff to the doctrine of the *Doney* case then standing unimpeached, the petitioner, to prevail, must be able to show that a change was brought about through something done or omitted by the Supreme Court of Montana in deciding the appeal.

We think the posture of the case from the viewpoint of constitutional law was the same after the decision of the appeal as it was after the trial. There would certainly have been no denial of due process if the court in affirming the judgment had rendered no opinion or had stated in its opinion that the *Doney* case was approved. The petitioner is thus driven to the position that the Constitution of the United States has been infringed because the *Doney* case was disapproved, and yet, while disapproved, was followed. Adherence to precedent as establishing a governing rule for the past in respect of the meaning of a statute is said to be a denial of due process when coupled with the declaration of an intention to refuse to adhere to it in adjudicating any controversies growing out of the transactions of the future.

We have no occasion to consider whether this division in time of the effects of a decision is a sound or an unsound application of the doctrine of *stare decisis* as known to the common law. Sound or unsound, there is involved in it no denial of a right protected by the Federal Constitution. This is not a case where a court, in overruling an earlier decision, has given to the new ruling a retroactive bearing, and thereby has made invalid what was valid in the doing. This is a case where a court has refused to make its ruling retroactive, and the novel stand is taken that the Constitution of the United States is infringed by the refusal.

We think the Federal Constitution has no voice upon the subject. A state in defining the limits of adherence to precedent may make a choice for itself between the principle of forward operation and that of relation backward. It may say that decisions of its highest court, though later overruled, are law none the less for intermediate transactions. Indeed, there are cases intimating, too broadly, that it *must* give them that effect; but never has doubt been expressed that it *may* so treat them if it pleases, whenever injustice or hardship will thereby be averted.

[EDITOR'S NOTE: Justice Cardozo's reference to averting injustice was the explicit basis of the Montana Supreme Court's holding. Judge Galen found that it would be unjust to deprive Sunburst of a refund because Sunburst shipped its oil in reliance on the procedure suggested in *Doney* that it could obtain a refund if it successfully argued to the Board that the rate was unreasonable. And Judge Galen found that such a holding in favor of Sunburst would also not be unjust to the carrier: "In our opinion, in all justice and fairness it cannot be said that the carrier has, as a result, been injured, for it must have appreciated its liability under the holding of this court in the *Doney* case." Indeed, Judge Galen found in the facts of the Sunburst case evidence that the carrier appreciated its potential liability: "Furthermore, it appears that in reliance upon the holding in the decision in that case [*Doney*] negotiations were under way by which the carrier proposed to make settlement with the shipper [Sunburst] allowing reparation to the extent that the rates charged by the carrier under the published tariff at the time the shipments were made were found by the board of railroad commissioners to be unreasonable." Yet *Doney* was

incorrect, and therefore it must be overruled now. "If we were permitted to adhere to the erroneous construction of the statute announced in the *Doney* case, greater mischief would follow than can possibly result from the operation of the statute as now, we think, correctly interpreted. Justice is in consequence done in this case without injury because of our previous holding." Now, back to Justice Cardozo's opinion:]

On the other hand, a state may hold to the ancient dogma that the law declared by its courts has a Platonic or ideal existence before the act of declaration, in which even the discredited declaration will be viewed as if it had never been, and the reconsidered declaration as law from the beginning. The alternative is the same whether the subject of the new decision is common law or statute. The choice for any state may be determined by the juristic philosophy of the judges of her courts, their conceptions of law, its origin and nature. We review, not the wisdom of their philosophies, but the legality of their acts. The state of Montana has told us by the voice of her highest court that, with these alternative methods open to her, her preference is for the first. In making this choice, she is declaring common law for those within her borders. The common law as administered by her judges ascribes to the decisions of her highest court a power to bind and loose that is unextinguished, for intermediate transactions, by a decision overruling them. As applied to such transactions, we may say of the earlier decision that it has not been overruled at all. It has been translated into a judgment of affirmance and recognized as law anew. Accompanying the recognition is a prophecy, which may or may not be realized in conduct, that transactions arising in the future will be governed by a different rule. If this is the common-law doctrine of adherence to precedent as understood and enforced by the courts of Montana, we are not at liberty, for anything contained in the Constitution of the United States, to thrust upon those courts a different conception either of the binding force of precedent or of the meaning of the judicial process.

The judgment of the Supreme Court of Montana is accordingly

Affirmed.

Notes and Questions

1. It is important to note at the outset that this is a case of intrastate commerce, and hence does not get to the U.S. Supreme Court on the basis of the federal commerce clause. What, then, is the constitutional issue here? The carrier (the Railroad) argued that it was deprived of Due Process of Law under the Fourteenth Amendment. The relevant provision of Section 1 of Amendment 14 reads:

> nor shall any State deprive any person of life, liberty, or property, without due process of law...

Since a corporation had long been regarded as a "person" under the Fourteenth Amendment, the Railroad could cite this clause to claim that Montana deprived it of property without due process of law.

When was Montana supposed to have done that? When the carrier was forced to pay Sunburst an amount equivalent to the "overcharges"? By what agency did Montana do that? By either the trial court or the Montana Supreme Court? How? This is a harder question. Was it by virtue of what either of those courts *did*? Or by virtue of what either of those courts *said*? How does Justice Cardozo answer these questions?

2. Why was the Montana Board of Railroad Commissioners set up in the first place? Why did the legislature give it the power to fix railroad rates? Unregulated, railroads were likely to give preferential rates to big shippers while discriminating against small shippers. Economists might say that this is perfectly normal behavior; those who ship in volume are entitled to a discount. But many small shippers did not see it that way. They felt that they were the victims of discrimination. Because there were many small shippers, they were able to organize into effective lobbying groups and convince state legislatures to help them out against the giant railroads. Moreover, legislators may have felt that encouraging small business was in the state's interest, and hence there was a public economic rationale for railroad rate-determination. In any event, many states set up rate-fixing agencies.

In the Sunburst case, we saw that the Board set rates according to quantity and unit weight. Thus, for example, if a single shipper wanted to ship a valuable oil painting on the railroad, she would be charged according to its weight (and bulk), but not according to its value. The railroad would only be able to charge a modest shipping fee, instead of the monopoly price it might prefer to charge if it could take into account the value of the painting, the customer's necessity of shipping it, the lack of shipping alternatives, and the shipper's poor bargaining power.

3. The Montana Board was set up in a quite different way from the federal agency, the Interstate Commerce Commission. The ICC's procedure was to have the carrier set the rates in the first instance. Then the ICC could act as a quasi-judicial body. A shipper could come in to the ICC to complain that the rates set by the carrier were unreasonable. The shipper would present evidence, and the carrier would defend its rates. If the ICC held for the shipper, it could order the carrier not only to change the rates, but also to pay reparations to the shipper. The reparations would include a refund of the excess amount paid plus damages but also might include a penalty if the carrier's rates were unconscionable. In sharp contrast, the

Montana legislature set up its Board of Commissioners to fix rates. Thus, the Board is a quasi-legislative body. Since it is charged with fixing reasonable rates, the Montana Supreme Court in the *Sunburst* case held that its rates are to be deemed reasonable. Hence, if the Board were to change its rates, that change would have prospective effect only. The fact that a rate is changed does not mean that the previous rate was unreasonable.

***

Exercise

The actual charge in *Sunburst* for the shipment of crude petroleum distillate was based on the total number of gallons shipped (a figure which was not in dispute) times the tariff rate of 20.5 cents per hundred pounds. Sunburst in fact shipped 266 cars of petroleum distillate between August 1926 and August 1928. It figured, and the court found, that if the correct weight of 6.6 pounds per gallon were used instead of the estimated weight of 7.4 pounds per gallon, the carrier would have had to charge Sunburst $3,262.25 less than what it in fact charged Sunburst. When Sunburst shipped the oil, it had no choice; it paid that extra $3,262.25 to the carrier.[1]

But the published tariffs of the Montana Board of Railroad Commissioners not only listed tariff rates; it also listed estimated weights. For example, a list might have looked something like this:

Description of Item	Est. Weight	Shipping Rate
Homogenized Milk	3.5 lb./gal.	12 cents/100 lb.
Skimmed Milk	4.0 lb./gal.	14 cents/100 lb.
Crude Petrol. Dist.	7.4 lb./gal.	20.5 cents/100 lb.

Does this chart show a fixed ratio between weight and rate? There is a *correlation* between weight and rate, but not a precise ratio. Why? Clearly, from the shipper's point of view, *volume* is just as important as *weight*. The number of tanker cars that are filled up by whatever liquid is shipped is indeed significant to the carrier. A very light liquid will use just as much volume as a very heavy liquid. But also significant is the weight of the liquid shipped; the engine has to burn more fuel to carry the additional weight.

Ratemakers might consider other factors in the calculation of rates. If it is easier for the carrier to clean out a tank car that has carried milk than it is to clean a car that has carried oil, the extra labor costs for carrying the oil might make the rates for oil higher than milk. Also, if the oil is combustible, extra fire precautions and fire insurance might require higher rates for oil over milk. In addition, there might be a public policy encouraging the shipment of milk as a food necessity; this might induce the Board to lower the milk rates.

What if volume were the only factor that mattered? Then one tanker car full of milk should have the same shipping rate as one tanker car full of oil; the milk should have to pay

---

[1] How big a claim was $3,262.25 in 1932, the year of the Supreme Court's decision in Sunburst? In the next year 1933, the average income of independent-practitioner attorneys in the Mountain State region of the United States was $2,489. If salaried attorneys are included, the figure drops to $2,065.

20.5 cents per gallon. If we assume that weight is the only factor that mattered, then Homogenized Milk should have slightly less than half the rate of oil; the Homogenized Milk should have to pay only 10 cents per gallon. We don't know what rates the Montana Board actually fixed for these items, but from our hypothetical chart, we can see that the rate charged for Homogenized Milk is between the "volume" rate and the "weight" rate.

What are the different kinds of items in the above chart?

1) type of commodity
2) pounds
3) gallons
4) cents

Of these, is there any one that is superfluous? If we are dealing with a liquid commodity, then all we need to know is the cents per gallon for the type of commodity it is. The weight per gallon is unnecessary information—unnecessary both to carrier and to shipper. It is like the color of the commodity; we don't need to know the color, or the edibility, or any other such information. So long as we know the type of commodity, we look down the chart until we find its rate—measured as cents per hundred gallons—and then both carrier and shipper know what the freight should be charged.

So, if the weight were not listed in the chart, would Sunburst have been deprived of pertinent information? Obviously not; whatever the weight was, Sunburst was going to be charged 20.5 cents per hundred pounds. (If Sunburst wanted to know the weight, it could simply weigh the oil.) Would the Railroad have been deprived of pertinent information? Obviously not; the Railroad's "bottom line" is the tariff rate it can charge Sunburst per hundred pounds of oil that Sunburst ships. No matter what the estimated weight, and no matter what the actual weight, the carrier will charge 20.5 cents per hundred pounds if the item that is shipped is crude petroleum distillate. Thus, upon reflection, both the "estimated weight" on the chart and the real weight are of no pertinent interest either to Sunburst or to the Railroad.

But wasn't the fight in the *Sunburst* case over excessive and unreasonable weights? Didn't Sunburst object to the Montana Board—successfully—that it was entitled to a refund because the actual weight of the oil was less than the estimated weight? Or are appearances deceiving?

We know that the attorneys for Sunburst, appearing before the Montana Board on a claim that the tariff charged was unreasonable, built their case upon the fact that the real weight of the oil was less than the weight that the Montana Board listed as the estimated weight. Sunburst claimed that it was entitled to a refund of $3,262.25 because of this fact. We can imagine that the attorneys for the Railroad did not dispute the fact that the real weight of the oil was less than the estimated weight. Then what did the attorneys argue to the Montana Board on behalf of the Railroad?

Could the attorneys for the Railroad have argued that the question of weight was irrelevant? We have already worked through the steps to reach a conclusion that estimated weights and real weights are indeed irrelevant. Yet the attorneys for the railroad were faced with the political reality that the Montana Board itself published the estimated weights. Would it have been easy for the attorneys to say to the Board that all the estimated weights it has published and has been publishing for all these years are totally irrelevant?

Imagine the following dialogue:

RAILROAD ATTORNEY. We claim that the question of weight is irrelevant.

BOARD MEMBER. What? We take weights into account in fixing rates. How could they possibly be irrelevant?

RAILROAD ATTORNEY. You take many things into account—volume, nature of the goods shipped, and weight.

BOARD MEMBER. Yes, and those are all listed. Our list indicates the nature of the item shipped, its estimated weight, and the shipping rate according to volume. So I still ask, how can you say weight is irrelevant?

RAILROAD ATTORNEY. It's obviously not irrelevant to the thought processes you went through in arriving at the final volume shipping rate. But once you've arrived at that final shipping rate, at that point it is irrelevant. This is a political body, an agency of the state. You are charged with fixing reasonable rates in order to foster the economic development of Montana and to avoid discrimination among shippers. You publish final tariff rates. No one should be able to come in and pick out and isolate one single factor that went into your decision, challenge it, and expect you to change the final tariff.

BOARD MEMBER. Why not, if we've made a mistake?

RAILROAD ATTORNEY. We're not claiming you made a mistake. Sunburst isn't claiming you made a mistake. You estimated the weight of crude petroleum distillate to be 7.4 pounds per gallon. No one is claiming that that was erroneous. It was, after all, just an estimate. So you figured the total tariff, taking into account—among many factors—the estimated weight of crude petroleum distillate. And that's it. The fact that the real weight of Sunburst's shipment is less than the estimated rate has nothing to do with this case. Suppose the real weight turned out to be more than the estimated rate. We couldn't come here and argue that Sunburst has to pay us extra. We're bound by the 20.5 cents per hundred pounds. So, if we're bound, why isn't Sunburst?

SUNBURST ATTORNEY. If the real weight had turned out to be more, you'd be here so fast arguing for an increase that it would make everyone's head spin.

RAILROAD ATTORNEY. We've never done that. Not once, ever, in our entire corporate history.

SUNBURST ATTORNEY. Maybe it's because you've never checked the real weight.

RAILROAD ATTORNEY. Why should we? It's irrelevant.

SUNBURST ATTORNEY. That's not the reason. The reason is because it's expensive for you to check weights, so you don't.

BOARD MEMBER. Now, now, let's not get into a fight over who should have done what. The fact is we've got a case here. Sunburst is complaining that we set our rates too high. I know—because I remember when we did it—that we got our best estimate of the weight, and we used that number to help set the final rate. So now, if it turns out that our estimate was too high, I don't see why Sunburst isn't entitled to a refund.

RAILROAD ATTORNEY. My point is—even if you had the actual weights when you fixed the tariffs, that is, even if you used 6.6 pounds per gallon instead of 7.4, so that your list of tariffs would say "estimated weight 6.6 pounds per gallon," you still might have arrived at the shipping rate of 20.5 cents. Because estimated weight was only one factor that went into your decision about the ultimate shipping weight.

BOARD MEMBER. If that's true, then why do you suppose we publish the estimated weight? Under your theory, we might as well have left it off the chart, since it doesn't matter.

RAILROAD ATTORNEY. Well, frankly, I don't know why you publish the estimated weight. Whatever you put down for the estimated weight doesn't make any difference to Sunburst or to us, so I don't know why you do it.

BOARD MEMBER. And you probably don't know why I'm going to vote against you in this matter. And maybe you'll never know. But that's what I'm going to do unless you come up with a better argument than that one.

Does this strike you as a plausible scenario? Can we say that the railroad attorney is using "legal logic" and the board member is using "political logic"? Even if we could, what difference would it make?

Who has the more emotionally appealing case—Sunburst or the Great Northern Railway? Who is more likely to win before the Montana Board? Who did win? Of course, Sunburst's attorneys did not have an easy time of it. They had to convince the Board that the Board's published rates on crude petroleum distillate tariffs were unreasonable. The Board may not have liked to hear the charge that it was unreasonable. (On the other hand, the Board may have felt that once in a while it is a good idea to reverse itself on a rate matter, in order to demonstrate that it is responsive to complaints from companies such as Sunburst.)

If you were the attorney for the railroad, and you lost the issue before the Board, would you abandon your argument about the irrelevancy of weights when you got to the trial court? Or, on losing in the trial court, would you abandon your argument when you got to the Montana Supreme Court? Isn't your argument one of principle—that factors, such as weight, that go into an agency determination should not be singled out and challenged after the final rates are announced? Doesn't your argument boil down to a claim that the agency's powers are in reality legislative powers—that the power to fix rates is a delegation of legislative power from the legislature (which does not have time itself to have hearings on rate-determinations) to the agency? Thus, if the agency's published tariffs are legislative in nature, wouldn't you argue—and keep arguing at every level you can—that nobody should be heard to second-guess the final result on the ground that one of the factors that went into it turned out to be incorrect? Isn't the railroad's attorney correct in claiming that *even if* the Montana Board had used as an estimated weight the 6.6 number instead of the 7.4 number, they *still* might have come out with a tariff rate of 20.5 cents per gallon?

Anyway, the Board turned out to be unsympathetic to the railroad's argument, so the attorneys for the railroad tried a different tack. They argued that the Board's published rates cannot be declared unreasonable by the very Board that fixed the rates in the first place. We return to our imaginary dialogue:

BOARD MEMBER. Why can't we find that our own rates are unreasonable?

RAILROAD ATTORNEY. Because you set them up in the first place. They must be deemed reasonable as a matter of law.

BOARD MEMBER. You mean we can't make a mistake?

RAILROAD ATTORNEY. That's right. As a matter of law, there is a conclusive presumption that you cannot make a mistake.

BOARD MEMBER. Sounds like hogwash to me. Anyone can make a mistake. I can make a mistake. You can make a mistake. In fact, counsel, you've already made a lot of mistakes.

RAILROAD ATTORNEY. I'm sorry that you see it that way.

SUNBURST ATTORNEY. The Board is only being realistic. It sets its rates as best it can. But once in a blue moon, it makes a mistake. It thinks that crude petroleum distillate weighs 7.4 pounds per gallon when in fact it weighs 6.6 pounds per gallon. That's just a plain mistake. The fair thing to do when you make a mistake is to acknowledge it and rectify it. And not hide behind conclusive presumptions and whatnots.

BOARD MEMBER. Sounds right to us.

SUNBURST ATTORNEY. It's not only right, but it's required by law. The statute that set up this Board says in so many words that this Board is entitled to find its own rates unreasonable and change its rates either by its own initiative or upon the complaint of either the shipper or the carrier.

BOARD MEMBER. That's right. That's the statutory language. Sunburst is correct again, as usual.

By now the railroad attorneys are feeling despondent. They call time out and go into a huddle. And they come up with a third strategy:

RAILROAD ATTORNEY. We'd like to argue that even if the Board can find its own rates to be unreasonable, and even if the Board does find its own rates to be unreasonable, nevertheless we relied on those rates and it would be unfair to us to make us pay a rebate to Sunburst.

BOARD MEMBER. Why, if the rates were unreasonable?

RAILROAD ATTORNEY. Because we relied on them, even if they were unreasonable.

BOARD MEMBER. What business do you have relying on unreasonable rates?

RAILROAD ATTORNEY. What business do you have fixing unreasonable rates?

BOARD MEMBER. We are rapidly losing patience with you, counsel. Are you nearly finished?

RAILROAD ATTORNEY. I just want to add that you should ignore the *Doney* case in this regard.

BOARD MEMBER. I see. At the end of an absolutely terrible presentation, you come in with the clincher. You want us to ignore judicial precedent. I've heard a lot about the arrogance of these big railroads, but I wouldn't have believed it until today.

RAILROAD ATTORNEY. The *Doney* case is just plain wrong. Sooner or later the courts will realize their mistake and overrule it.

BOARD MEMBER. And pigs will fly.

SUNBURST ATTORNEY. And railroads will charge fair rates.

BOARD MEMBER. And every Tom, Dick, and Harry can ignore judicial rulings because the courts just might overturn them.

SUNBURST ATTORNEY. The railroads are crushing everybody in this state, they might as well usurp the functions of the Supreme Court.

BOARD MEMBER. How much did you say the railroad owes you?

SUNBURST ATTORNEY. $3,262.25 plus interest and costs.

BOARD MEMBER. Well, we can't give it to you as much as we'd like to. You've got to go to district court and sue for a rebate. But we'll give you this much. We hold that our rates were unreasonable and excessive, and should have been changed to the basis of 6.6 pounds per gallon.

So now the parties march off to the district court. Sunburst has a favorable ruling from the Board—that the rates charged were unreasonable. The carrier has a portfolio of arguments, all of which did not work when presented to the Board. What happened in court?

Justice Cardozo has told us what happened in the Montana courts. The railroad's argument that the *Doney* case was wrongly decided was accepted by the court. The court also accepted the railroad's argument that the Board had no power to award rebates to the shipper. More than that, the court accepted the railroad's argument that the court itself could not award rebates to the shipper if the shipper's contention was that the Board's fixed rates were unreasonable. (Recall that a shipper is entitled to a rebate if the carrier's charges were "excessive"—that is, in excess of the fixed rates.)

At this point, having had all its arguments—and more—accepted by the court, the lawyers for the railroad must have begun their victory celebration. But wait—the Montana court holds that Sunburst is entitled to its refund!

Imagine that both sets of attorneys have booked nearby restaurants for a victory party. The news of what the court decided comes in. Which side should go ahead with its victory celebration? Who won this case? The railroad won all the legal issues, and Sunburst won all the money damages it asked for in the first place. Who is entitled to celebrate? And what should be celebrated? Have you ever encountered a case where it was hard to tell who won? Of course, there are many cases where each side wins a little—for example, in a divorce case one party might win on the alimony issue and the other on the custody issue, and it is hard to say who "won." But in the Sunburst case, the railroad seems to have won every legal issue in the case, and yet lost on the bottom-line issue of damages. How was this possible? What happened to Due Process of Law?

We will come back to this Exercise after we have read a pair of Alaska cases. They may throw some light on what may have been going on in *Sunburst*.

City of Fairbanks v. Schaible

375 P.2d 201

Supreme Court of Alaska

Aug. 10, 1962

DIMOND, Justice.

Druska Schaible died of asphyxia on November 23, 1957, during a fire in the Lathrop building where she and her husband had an apartment. As her executor her husband brought a wrongful death action under an Alaska statute against the City of Fairbanks. In a case tried by the court judgment in the sum of $50,000 was entered for the executor against the City.

On this appeal there are several questions presented for review, the two principal ones being (1) whether the City enjoys immunity from tort liability in this area; and (2) if there is no immunity, whether negligence was established.

Despite sharp criticism of the doctrine of municipal immunity from tort liability, the limitations designed by courts to permit a municipality to be held liable in certain circumstances have not gone so far as to include fire-fighting activities. Except for negligent operation of fire equipment on the public streets, where liability has been imposed on the theory of nuisance, it appears to be the rule without exception that a fire department maintained by a municipal corporation belongs to the public or governmental branch of the municipality, and that the municipality is not liable for injuries to persons or property resulting from negligence connected with the department's operation or maintenance. The apparent reason for not making exception to the immunity doctrine in this area is the fear that extensive losses might bankrupt a municipality, and the thought that such losses could better be distributed through the medium of private insurance.

In this jurisdiction the question is governed by a statute which has long been part of the law of Alaska. Congress enacted a law in 1884 to provide a civil government for Alaska. Section 7 provided—

> That the general laws of the State of Oregon now in force are hereby declared to be the law in said district, so far as the same may be applicable and not in conflict with the provisions of this act or the laws of the United States.

At that time Oregon's general laws included a civil code, enacted on October 11, 1862, and made effective June 1, 1863. Section 347 permitted an action to be maintained against any county, incorporated town, school district, or other public corporation of like character either upon a contract made by such county or other public corporation in its corporate character, "or for an injury to the rights of the plaintiff, arising from some act or omission of such county or other public corporation." In 1869 the Oregon Supreme Court held in McCalla v. Multnomah County that under this statute a county was liable for damages in tort arising from failure to keep a bridge in repair. In 1886 the court referred to the fact that the principle of the McCalla case had been followed for over 17 years by numerous adjudications respecting the liability of municipal corporations, and recognized that under the statute a municipality had no immunity from tort liability for an act or omission in the exercise of either its governmental or proprietary functions. This was the status of the law respecting municipal tort liability in Oregon in 1884 when Congress made provision for a civil government for Alaska. It then became the law in Alaska by reason of the well established rule that a statute adopted from another state, which has been construed by that state's highest court, is presumed to be adopted with the construction thus placed upon it.

Specifically, we hold here that the City of Fairbanks, which maintains a fire department, may be held liable for injuries resulting from negligence connected with the department's fire-fighting activities. Section 56-2-2 (1949) in plain language imposes liability "for an injury to the rights of the plaintiff arising from some act or omission" of the City. There is nothing in the statute which suggests that liability in the operation and maintenance of a city owned fire department is to be excepted, and we are not justified in reading any such exception into the law.

The City relies heavily on City of Fairbanks v. Gilbertson, 262 F.2d 734 (9th Cir. 1959), where the Court of Appeals for the Ninth Circuit, in affirming a decision of the territorial district court, held that the mantle of municipal immunity covers a fire-fighting activity of the City of Fairbanks. The statute involved (section 56–2–2) was ignored by both the district court and the court of appeals. The early decisions of the Oregon Supreme Court construing this law were not mentioned. Without giving reasons or citing legal authorities, the City merely states that we must take the law of that case as if it had been announced by this court on the day this court was created.

Section 56–2–2 (1949), which we have held imposes liability on a municipal corporation, was totally ignored in the Gilbertson opinion. Whether it was considered in reaching that decision, we do not know. Assuming it had not been considered, we cannot speculate as to whether a different result would have been reached if the history and meaning of that statute had been examined. In any event, it would make no difference here. The Supreme Court of the State of Alaska is not bound by the Ninth Circuit decision in Gilbertson.

The trial court found that the fire department's failure to rescue decedent and its affirmative action in preventing others from saving her amounted to negligence, and that this was the proximate cause of her death. From a review of the evidence we conclude that these findings were not clearly erroneous, and therefore decline to set them aside.

Mrs. Schaible's death was, of course, a tragic event. But even more tragic was the fact, as clearly appears from the evidence, that in all likelihood she would have been saved had it not been for certain acts and omissions of the City.

We start at the point where Mrs. Schaible, cut off from escape through the hallway and stairs because of fire and smoke, was standing by an open window of her apartment awaiting rescue. A fireman climbed up a 24 foot ladder he had placed against the building in an attempt to reach decedent's window, but it was discovered that the ladder was about eight to ten feet too short. Efforts were then made to place a 12 foot ladder on top of the 24 foot one, but this was found to be impracticable. The fire department had one 50 foot ladder, which would have been long enough, but it was apparently being used to evacuate tenants from the other side of the building.

We do not decide that the lack of an additional ladder of sufficient length would alone be sufficient evidence upon which to base a finding of negligence; for other circumstances show that the fire department stepped out of its traditional role of simply doing the best it could to fight the fire and save lives. It assumed a particular obligation to save Mrs. Schaible's life, and then failed to fulfill that obligation by not using other available means to effect her rescue.

While a fireman was backing down the ladder after an unsuccessful attempt to reach decedent's window, he said to her: "Don't jump, we'll get you out." Efforts were then apparently made to find a longer ladder but they were in use elsewhere. In the meantime no attempt was made to rescue decedent with a fire net. No attempt was made to place an available fire truck against the building and place a 24 foot ladder on top of it in order to gain the additional few feet needed to reach decedent's window. From ladders too short to reach other apartment windows, ropes had been thrown to other persons awaiting rescue. But this wasn't done for Mrs. Schaible. The fireman who had reached the top of the 24 foot ladder, and was only from eight to ten feet from the window, made no attempt to deliver a rope to Mrs. Schaible. In fact, he couldn't remember whether "there was ropes on the rig or not."

The City was guilty not only of failure to use common sense methods to rescue decedent. It was also guilty of affirmatively preventing rescue by others. Some spectators had obtained an extension ladder of sufficient length to reach decedent's window. They raised the ladder and started to extend it, and then were ordered by the City's fire inspector to get away from the building. When they refused to obey, they were driven off by fire hoses turned on them by orders from the inspector. A bystander named Anderson climbed the ladder, put his head and shoulders in the window, grabbed Mrs. Schaible by her foot and attempted to pull her over to the window. He tried to get a fireman to give him a rope and help get her out the window. But instead of getting the assistance he asked for, he was ordered to get off the ladder. It was Anderson's belief that Mrs. Schaible was not dead at that time.

The evidence is sufficient to sustain the trial court's finding of negligence. This is not merely a case where the court in retrospect and using hindsight has determined that the City might have done things differently in its overall method of fighting the fire. This is a case where the City specifically induced reliance on the skill and authority of its fire department to rescue decedent, and then failed to use due care to carry out its mission. It affirmatively took over the rescue mission, and excluded others from taking action which in all probability would have been successful. It thus placed decedent in a worse position than when it took complete charge of rescuing her, and became responsible for negligently bringing about her death.

We hold that in this case the City is liable for the negligence of its fire department. However, since there were decisions of the territorial district court which may have led municipalities in Alaska to rely upon a doctrine of immunity from tort liability in the exercise of governmental functions, in order to avoid hardship on the municipalities the rule we state in this case shall apply only to actions arising out of occurrences after the date of this opinion.

The judgment is affirmed as to the City of Fairbanks.

Questions

1. Did BOTH sides win this case? The executor won a $50,000 judgment against the City of Fairbanks. But didn't the City of Fairbanks win more than that? Didn't the City win *sovereign immunity* with respect to all cases where the cause of action arose prior to the date of entry of judgment in the *Schaible* case? (As for causes of action that arise after the entry of judgment in *Schaible,* the City is on notice that it had better take out municipal liability insurance.)

2. Another way of asking "who won?" is to ask, "did either party have any reason to complain?" Certainly the executor had no reason to complain about the $50,000 damage award. What about the City of Fairbanks? Are you sure?

Scheele v. City of Anchorage

385 P.2d 582

Supreme Court of Alaska

October 11, 1963

AREND, Justice.

We are asked in this case to apply retrospectively the rule we laid down in City of Fairbanks v. Schaible, that a municipal corporation in Alaska does not enjoy immunity from tort liability in the exercise of either proprietary or governmental functions.

The plaintiff-appellant complained in the court below that on September 29, 1960, she had suffered personal injuries arising out of police brutality following her arrest. The city and two of its police officers, who had been named with it as defendants, answered denying the charge of brutality and alleging that the plaintiff's injuries were self-inflicted while she was in a state of extreme intoxication. The city subsequently moved for a summary judgment in its favor on the theory that a municipality is not liable for the acts of its employees while engaged in a governmental function.

On December 11, 1961, the trial court ordered that the case should remain in pretrial conference status until this court had rendered a decision in the Schaible case. That decision was published on August 10, 1962. On October 5, 1962, the trial court granted the city's motion for summary judgment and the plaintiff appealed. The trial court in granting the motion was influenced, no doubt, by the following paragraph appearing in City of Fairbanks v. Schaible:

> We hold that in this case the City is liable for the negligence of its fire department. However, since there were decisions of the territorial district court

which may have led municipalities in Alaska to rely upon a doctrine of immunity from tort liability in the exercise of governmental functions, *in order to avoid hardship on the municipalities the rule we state in this case shall apply only to actions arising out of occurrences after the date of this opinion.* [Emphasis added.]

We look upon what we said in the Schaible case, regarding the prospective effect of that decision as obiter dictum, since it was not necessary to the decision in the case. Being obiter dictum it is not binding upon us in this case. Not until it was raised in the instant case have we had the question squarely before us whether the rule in Schaible should be applied retrospectively or prospectively only. Now that we have been enlightened by briefs and arguments of counsel in the case presently before us and have had the benefit of further research and more mature consideration of our own, we are convinced that the dictum in the passage quoted above from our opinion in Schaible was erroneous and we, therefore, disavow it.

In the oft cited case of Great No. Ry. v. Sunburst Oil & Ref. Co., the United States Supreme Court held that there is no federal constitutional objection to a state's highest court making a choice for itself in overruling an earlier decision, whether the new rule declared by it shall operate prospectively only or shall apply also to past transactions. The Court went on to explain:

> The alternative is the same whether the subject of the new decision is common law or statute. The choice for any state may be determined by the juristic philosophy of the judges of her courts, their conceptions of law, its origin and nature. We review, not the wisdom of their phi-

losophies, but the legality of their acts.

What we said as obiter dictum in the Schaible case was prompted by a feeling we entertained at the time we wrote the opinion that it would work a hardship upon municipalities to suddenly pluck from them the mantle of municipal immunity and subject them to liability for torts committed by them in the exercise of governmental functions at times when they may have been relying upon the doctrine of such immunity. The hardship upon municipalities which we had in mind was a financial one occasioned by their failure to protect themselves with liability insurance. It seems to us now that we might just as readily have assumed that the cities, or at least some of them, did not rely upon the doctrine of immunity, for they had the 1958 decision in Lucas v. City of Juneau, 168 F.Supp. 195 (D. Alaska 1958), to guide them. In that case Judge Kelly stated that, if the City of Juneau had been found negligent in the operation of an ambulance as a governmental function, it might have been held liable under the provisions of section 56–2–2 (1949) which provides:

> An action may be maintained . . . for an injury to the rights of the plaintiff arising from some act or omission of [the City].

So we conclude and now hold that the substantive defense of governmental immunity abolished by the decision in the Schaible case is also abolished for the instant case and for all other pending cases, those not yet filed which are not barred by the statute of limitations, and all future cases of action. Accordingly, the summary judgment entered in this case below is reversed and set aside and the case is remanded to the trial court for further proceedings not inconsistent with this opinion.

Reversed and remanded.

Notes and Questions

1. As in the *Sunburst* case, it is important to keep all the important dates in chronological order. Here is a list of relevant dates in the two cases you have just read:

1949. Section 56–2–2 enacted.
1957. Mrs. Schaible dies of asphyxia.
1958. Decision in *Lucas v. City of Juneau.*

1959. Decision in *City of Fairbanks v. Gilbertson* (federal, 9th circuit)

1960. Idellar Scheele's allegations of police brutality.

1962. Decision in *City of Fairbanks v. Schaible*.

1963. Decision in *Scheele v. City of Anchorage*.

2. Clearly Mrs. Schaible's (that is, her estate's) cause of action arose in 1957. The Alaska Supreme Court held in 1962 that her executor was entitled to damages. The Court also held that, for all causes of action arising *after* 1962, municipalities would have liability. Finally, the Court stated that municipalities would have sovereign immunity from all causes of action arising *prior* to 1962 *except* Mrs. Schaible's.

Why did the court single out Mrs. Schaible for special consideration? Everyone else whose cause of action arose prior to 1962 would get nowhere suing an Alaskan city. But Mrs. Schaible was different. Why? Was her case especially unjust? How could the court know whether there would be injustices in other cases?

3. As we saw, when the next case of injustice—allegations of police brutality—came up, the court found itself in a dilemma. It had stated very clearly in *Schaible* that causes of action arising prior to 1962 would be disallowed—except for Mrs. Schaible's. Yet Idellar Scheele's cause of action arose prior to 1962, and she was the alleged victim of police brutality. Would it not be unjust to exclude her? On the other hand, didn't the City of Anchorage rely on the Alaska Supreme Court's own statement in *Schaible* that the City would be immune precisely in cases like Idellar Scheele's?

4. But how *could* the City of Anchorage—or any other Alaskan city—have *relied* on the statement of immunity in *Schaible* when any causes of action that would have been immunized by *Schaible* had already arisen by the time that the *Schaible* decision was announced?

5. Did the court in *Scheele* suddenly discover Section 56–2–2 (1949), which had been overlooked by all previous courts? Check back to the *Schaible* case. Section 56–2–2 (1949) is cited *throughout* the *Schaible* case! Then why did the court reach a different result?

6. Or *was* the result different? Consider:

(a) The injured plaintiff won in *Schaible;*

(b) The injured plaintiff won in *Scheele*.

Does this suggest that the City lost both cases? Consider Question 2 following *Schaible*.

7. What did *Schaible* hold? The court said "We hold..." and went on to state what it held. Did the court accurately state what it held?

8. Consider again the statute, Section 56–2–2 (1949). Did it mean one thing when it was enacted in 1949, another thing when the *Schaible* court construed it in 1962, and a different thing when the *Lucas* court construed it in 1958? Was the *Scheele* court in 1963 then free to pick any of these constructions it wanted? Yet how can the same statute change its meaning at all?

9. Can we say that the same statute always had the same meaning, but that the *Schaible* court must have made a mistake when it said that, for all cases except Mrs. Schaible's case, where the cause of action arose prior to the decision in *Schaible* there would be sovereign immunity of municipalities? How could the court have said such a thing *in the face of Section 56–2–2*? Was the *Schaible* court saying that Section 56–2–2 meant one thing as far as the executor in that case was concerned, and something else for all cases when the cause of action arose before the decision in *Schaible*? If so, how could a court say that, when the statute itself hasn't changed?

10. Does Justice Cardozo's jurisprudential point, which you read in the *Sunburst* case, now make more sense? Recall that Justice Cardozo said:

> A state in defining the limits of adherence to precedent may make a choice for itself between the principle of forward operation and that of relation backward. It may say that decisions of its highest court, though later overruled, are law none the less for intermediate transactions.... On the other hand, a state may hold to the ancient dogma that the law declared by its courts has a Platonic or ideal existence before the act of declaration, in which even the discredited declaration will be viewed as if it had never been, and the reconsidered declaration as law from the beginning. The alternative is the same whether the subject of the new decision is common law or statute. The choice for any state may be determined by the juristic philosophy of the judges of her courts, their conceptions of law, its origin and nature. We review, not the wisdom of their philosophies, but the legality of their acts.

Do you agree with this statement of the issues involved? How did the Supreme Court "review... the legality of their acts"? Was it lawful for the Montana Supreme Court to award damages to Sunburst?

Exercise

All three cases—*Sunburst, Schaible,* and *Scheele*—have been concerned, more or less explicitly, with doing justice to the parties. The *Sunburst* case was perhaps the most explicit in this regard. But is it not also clear, from the way the court stated the facts, that the *Schaible* case was one that cried out for justice in the face of extraordinarily callous behavior on the part of the fire department? And is it not also clear that in *Scheele* the allegation of police brutality also cried out for corrective justice?

Yet how can we account for the fact that the *Schaible* court cut out claims like Idellar Scheele's? How could the judges of the Alaska Supreme Court have singled out Mrs. Schaible for special treatment, while saying that all other causes of action that arose before or after Mrs. Schaible's and up to the date of the judgment in Mrs. Schaible's case—that all those other causes of action would be dismissed on the ground of sovereign immunity? Isn't that almost the very definition of injustice to all those other persons—to treat them differently from Mrs. Schaible even though the statute is the same?

Imagine that you are a clerk to a judge on the Alaska Supreme Court during the consideration of Mrs. Schaible's case. The judge tells you that he has made up his mind on the following points:

> (a) He thinks it is fair to put all municipalities on notice that, from the date of the decision in 1962 on, they will be liable in tort actions.

> (b) He also thinks it is fair that, up to the date of the decision in 1962, any cause of action in tort should be dismissed on the ground of sovereign immunity because municipalities have relied on the *Gilbertson* decision.

However, the judge wants your guidance on what he should do about Mrs. Schaible. Should her case be thrown out because it is the same as all the other cases in (b)? Or is her case an exception to all those cases in (b), such that it should be treated as if it fell under category (a)? What considerations can you come up with?

Are these some of the considerations that came to your mind?

(1) It would be unjust to treat Mrs. Schaible differently from everyone else whose cause of action arose prior to 1962.

(2) The judge is unjust in distinguishing between (a) and (b). The entire (b) category should be dropped.

(3) It would be unjust *not* to treat Mrs. Schaible differently from everyone else whose cause of action arose prior to 1962 because her lawyer was responsible for opening up the possibility of lawsuits against municipalities for everyone whose cause of action arises after 1962. We need to reward plaintiffs like Mrs. Schaible for straightening out the law.

(4) It is unjust to draw the line at causes of action that arose prior to 1962. It would be fairer to allow the new liability rule for all cases that have not reached a final decision prior to 1962, such as Idellar Scheele's case.

Suppose you present this list to the judge, and he says: "As for your second point, forget it. As for your fourth point, you don't understand the underlying reason. We have to protect municipalities which did not take out insurance in reliance on the *Gilbertson* immunity decision. So the relevant time is when the cause of action arose, because that's the only time to which the insurability factor applies. As for point three, you raise an interesting question. Maybe it would be very mean of us not to reward plaintiffs like Mrs. Schaible's executor. Those lawyers came in, wrote briefs, filed papers, argued orally, and actually convinced us that Alaskan municipalities are liable in tort. We can hardly say to them that they convinced us, but that we are not going to apply the rule in their own case."

Now we have enough considerations to turn our attention back to *Sunburst*.

Is it not true that a very important justice consideration in the law is its reliability and predictability? Can't we say, of any judicial decision, that whatever it does, at least it should clarify the law so that future similar cases won't have to go through the same lengthy arguments and future concerned parties will know what the law is? Isn't it fair to *both* sides in a dispute or potential dispute that they can look at a previous similar case and figure out what the law is? Aren't they entitled to notice about what the law provides? Aren't they entitled to plan their actions by taking into account the underlying law? Let us now test these questions.

Let us imagine that the next case after *Sunburst* is a case that is almost identical on its facts.

Trans-Ephemeral Ry. v. Moonburst

Imaginary Court of Montana
February 30, 1935

D'Amato, J., delivered the opinion of the court:

In 1933, the year following the decision of the United States Supreme Court in the *Sunburst* case, respondent Moonburst shipped 266 cars of refined rotgut distillate on petitioner's railroad at 20.5 cents per hundred gallons. Moonburst alleged that if the correct weight of 6.6 pounds per gallon were used instead of the Montana Board's estimated weight of 7.4 pounds per gallon, the carrier would have had to charge Moonburst $3,262.25 less than what it in fact charged Moonburst. When Moonburst shipped the distillate, it had no choice; it paid that extra $3,262.25 to the carrier.

Moonburst's attorneys went before the Montana Board and charged that the fixed rates were unreasonable and excessive.[2] Even though the attorneys for the railroad argued strenuously that our previous decision in *Sunburst*, which was ratified in full by the Supreme Court of the United States, stated as plainly as it could possibly state that the Board was wholly without statutory authority to determine that its own rates were unreasonable, the Board went ahead and held that the rates applied to Moonburst were indeed unreasonable. Moonburst then brought an action in the district court for a refund against the railroad. Again, the attorneys for the railroad argued strenuously that our previous decision in *Sunburst*, which was ratified in full by the Supreme Court of the United States, stated as plainly as could possibly be stated that no court had statutory authority to issue a rebate on the ground of unreasonable rates. Nevertheless, the district court, persuaded by the oratory of Moonburst's attorneys, went ahead and awarded Moonburst $3,262.25 plus interest and costs. The railroad now appeals to this court.

Upon mature reflection, we now see that all we actually held in *Sunburst* was that Sunburst was entitled to a refund based on the unreasonableness of the fixed rates as determined by the Montana Board. Everything else we said—including our comments that neither the Board nor the district court had any power to give rebates based on unreasonable rates—was purely dicta.

We also believe that we were right in *Sunburst* on the question of the power of the Board and the district court. They simply do not have the power to give a shipper a rebate based on the unreasonableness of the fixed rate. At best, the Board may change rates for the future. It has no retroactive power; it is not like a court of law. Hence, there is no basis in law for the Board or for the district court to award Moonburst a refund in the present litigation.

Yet Moonburst had a right to rely on what we did in *Sunburst* and not on what we said in *Sunburst*. A holding is quite different from a dictum. Our judicial power consists in deciding cases, not in pontificating our notions of what the law should be in any case other than the case at hand. What we said about the lack of power in the Montana Board and in the district court to give shippers a refund was wholly dicta, since it could not possibly have been

---

[2] Moonburst hired the same lawyers who had been successful before the Board in the *Sunburst* litigation.

necessary to the result we reached—a result which gave to Sunburst that which we said Sunburst could not have.

We have to be fair and just to Moonburst as we were fair and just to Sunburst.

A majority of this court therefore decides that Moonburst is entitled to its refund. However, this is the very last time we will ever make an exception. The Montana Board and the courts simply lack the legal power to give refunds, period. We cannot give that which we lack the power to give. We make a single exception for Moonburst because Moonburst relied on *Sunburst*. But no one in the future can rely on *Moonburst*, because we are explicitly saying that *Moonburst* is unreliable from now on.

The decision of the court below is AFFIRMED.

Jacobson, J., delivered a dissenting opinion:

I dissent. More than that, I am disgusted.

The majority thinks it has settled this issue. But I happened to have overheard at lunch a few days ago that a new case is going to come this way fairly shortly. It is called *Starburst*. Starburst has already convinced the Montana Board that it was right in *Sunburst* and *Moonburst*. So what do we say to Starburst when it bursts upon our scene? "Sorry, but we told you in *Moonburst* to forget it. Enough is enough."

How can we say that to poor little Starburst? Isn't Starburst entitled to justice also? How can we reasonably distinguish between Moonburst and Starburst?

I can just see it now. The majority, when Starburst arrives here, will say,

This is it. This is the very last one. Never again will we make any exceptions. We make an exception for Starburst because it says that it was relying on our holding in *Moonburst*. True, we held in *Moonburst* that the shipper could get a refund, so technically everything else we said in *Moonburst* was dicta. But we can't possibly go on like this. We really do not have the judicial power to give refunds for unreasonable rates. The legislature never gave us that power. So, after *Starburst*, we can never do it again. AND THIS TIME WE REALLY MEAN IT. *WE UNDERLINE THE FACT THAT, NEVER AGAIN WILL A SHIPPER BE ABLE TO GET A REFUND FROM ANY MONTANA COURT WHATSOEVER.*

And then, what? Along comes Cloudburst and demands *Starburst* treatment. What will the majority then say in *Cloudburst*? Will it say something like:

All right for now. Cloudburst gets its refund. But next time, if any attorney comes here asking for an exception, we will hold that attorney in contempt of court.

And will the next attorney, representing Jailburst, say that the contempt of court threat was merely dicta? Will he issue that statement from prison?

Our problem began when we tried to be fair to Sunburst. We should have thrown Sunburst out of court. A little unfairness can go a long way—maybe toward ultimate fairness to all.

Notes and Questions

1. Do you side with the majority or the dissent in *Moonburst*? Or with neither? What would your opinion be?

2. With everyone agreeing that we have to be fair, and with the facts not at all in dispute, why should we have such paradoxically sharp differences of opinion? Is this an anomaly in the legal system?

3. What has happened to predictability? If you were advising Moonburst, what would you predict on the basis of *Sunburst*? Assuming the imaginary decision in *Moonburst,* what would you predict if your client was Starburst? At some point would you say, "These judges are going to stick to what they say rather than what they do, and cut off this *Sunburst* business. They're just going to throw the next case out on the ground that there is no judicial power to give a refund." Suppose you expect the Montana court to do exactly that? Still, the question is, When? At the time of *Moonburst*? *Starburst*? *Cloudburst*?

4. What has happened to justice? Are these cases *too hard* to deliver justice to the parties? Has the law painted itself into an intricate corner from which legal escape is impossible?

5. The cases we have studied so far have dealt with changes in the law that were supposed to take place after the decision. The opposite side of the coin consists of cases where the question is the retroactive effect to be given a decision. Actually, we got a glimpse of this problem in *Scheele*. But the problem in *Scheele* centered around a statute, and statutory meaning is supposed to be timeless. What if it had centered around a constitutional provision? Suppose a court is convinced that a constitutional provision should be re-interpreted, but is afraid that doing so would create substantial problems of retroactivity? What sorts of problems could be created? This is the subject of the next section of this Chapter.

7.2 Retroactivity

Linkletter v. Walker

381 U.S. 618
Supreme Court of the United States
June 7, 1965

Mr. Justice Clark delivered the opinion of the Court.

In *Mapp v. Ohio,* 367 U.S. 643 (1961), we held that the exclusion of evidence seized in violation of the search and seizure provisions of the Fourth Amendment was required of the States by the Due Process Clause of the Fourteenth Amendment. In so doing we overruled *Wolf v. Colorado,* 338 U.S. 25 (1949), to the extent that it failed to apply the exclusionary rule to the States. This case

presents the question of whether this requirement operates retrospectively upon cases finally decided in the period prior to *Mapp*. The Court of Appeals for the Fifth Circuit held that it did not, and we granted certiorari in order to settle what has become a most troublesome question in the administration of justice. We agree with the Court of Appeals.

The Petitioner was convicted in a Louisiana District Court on May 28, 1959, of "simple burglary." After he was booked and placed in jail, other officers took his keys, entered and searched his home, and seized certain property and papers. Later his place of business was entered and searched and seizures were effected. These intrusions were made without a warrant. The State District Court held that the arresting officers had reasonable cause for the arrest under Louisiana law and finding probable cause to search as an incident to arrest it held the seizures valid. The Supreme Court of Louisiana affirmed in February 1960.

On June 19, 1961, *Mapp* was announced. Immediately thereafter petitioner filed an application for habeas corpus in the United States District Court. After denial there he appealed and the Court of Appeals affirmed. It found the searches too remote from the arrest and therefore illegal but held that the constitutional requirement of exclusion of the evidence under *Mapp* was not retrospective. Petitioner has two points: (1) that the Court of Appeals erred in holding that *Mapp* was not retrospective; and (2) that even though *Mapp* be held not to operate retrospectively, the search in his case was subsequent to that in *Mapp*, and while his final conviction was long prior to our disposition of it, his case should nevertheless be governed by *Mapp*.

Initially we must consider the term "retrospective" for the purposes of our opinion. A ruling which is purely prospective does not apply even to the parties before the court. *Great Northern R. Co. v. Sunburst Oil & Refining Co.,* 287 U.S. 358 (1932). However, we are not here concerned with pure prospectivity since we applied the rule announced in *Mapp* to reverse Miss Mapp's conviction. That decision has also been applied to cases still pending on direct review at the time it was rendered. Therefore, in this case, we are concerned only with whether the exclusionary principle enunciated in *Mapp* applies to state court convictions which had become final[3] before rendition of our opinion.

At common law there was no authority for the proposition that judicial decisions made law only for the future. Blackstone stated the rule that the duty of the court was not to "pronounce a

new law, but to maintain and expound the old one." 1 Blackstone, Commentaries 69 (15th ed. 1809). This Court followed that rule in *Norton v. Shelby County,* 118 U.S. 425 (1886), holding that unconstitutional action "confers no rights; it imposes no duties; it affords no protection; it creates no office; it is, in legal contemplation, as inoperative as though it had never been passed." The judge rather than being the creator of the law was but its discoverer.

On the other hand, Austin maintained that judges do in fact do something more than discover law; they make it interstitially by filling in with judicial interpretation the vague, indefinite, or generic statutory or common-law terms that alone are but the empty crevices of the law. Implicit in such an approach is the admission when a case is overruled that the earlier decision was wrongly decided. However, rather than being erased by the later overruling decision it is considered as an existing juridical fact until overruled, and intermediate cases finally decided under it are not to be disturbed.

The Blackstonian view ruled English jurisprudence and cast its shadow over our own as evidenced by *Norton v. Shelby County, supra.* However, some legal philosophers continued to insist that such a rule was out of tune with actuality largely because judicial repeal ofttime did "work hardship to those who [had] trusted to its existence." Cardozo, Address to the N. Y. Bar Assn., 55 Rep. N.Y. State Bar Assn. 263, 296–297 (1932). The Austinian view gained some acceptance over a hundred years ago when it was decided that although legislative divorces were illegal and void, those previously granted were immunized by a prospective application of the rule of the case. *Bingham v. Miller,* 17 Ohio 445 (1848).

And in 1932 Mr. Justice Cardozo in *Great Northern R. Co. v. Sunburst Oil & Refining Co.,* 287 U.S. 358, applied the Austinian approach in denying a federal constitutional due process attack on the prospective application of a decision of the Montana Supreme Court. He said that a State "may make a choice for itself between the principle of forward operation and that of relation backward." Mr. Justice Cardozo based the rule on the avoidance of "injustice or hardship" citing a long list of state and federal cases supporting the principle that the courts had the power to say that decisions though later overruled "are law none the less for intermediate transactions."

---

[3] By final we mean where the judgment of conviction was rendered, the availability of appeal exhausted, and the time for petition for certiorari had elapsed before our decision in *Mapp v. Ohio.*

One form of limited retroaction which differs somewhat from the type discussed above is that which was established in *United States v. Schooner Peggy*, 1 Cranch 103 (1801). There, a schooner had been seized under an order of the President which commanded that any armed French vessel found on the high seas be captured. An order of condemnation was entered on September 23, 1800. However, while the case was pending before this Court the United States signed an agreement with France providing that any property captured and not "definitively condemned" should be restored. Chief Justice Marshall said:

> It is in the general true that the province of an appellate court is only to enquire whether a judgment when rendered was erroneous or not. But if subsequent to the judgment and before the decision of the appellate court, a law intervenes and positively changes the rule which governs, the law must be obeyed, or its obligation denied ... [and] where individual rights ... are sacrificed for national purposes ... the court must decide according to existing laws, and if it be necessary to set aside a judgment ... which cannot be affirmed but in violation of law, the judgment must be set aside.

Under our cases it appears (1) that a change in law will be given effect while a case is on direct review, *Schooner Peggy, supra,* and (2) that the effect of the subsequent ruling of invalidity on prior final judgments when collaterally attacked is subject to no set "principle of absolute retroactive invalidity" but depends upon a consideration of "particular relations ... and particular conduct ... of rights claimed to have become vested, of status, of prior determinations deemed to have finality"; and "of public policy in the light of the nature both of the statute and of its previous application." *Chicot County Drainage Dist. v. Baxter State Bank,* 308 U.S. 371, at 374.

Thus, the accepted rule today is that in appropriate cases the Court may in the interest of justice make the rule prospective.

While the cases discussed above deal with the invalidity of statutes or the effect of a decision overturning long-established common-law rules, there seems to be no impediment—constitutional or philosophical—to the use of the same rule in the constitutional area where the exigencies of the situation require such an application. It is true that heretofore, without discussion, we have applied new constitutional rules to cases finalized before the promulgation of the rule. Petitioner contends that our method of resolving those prior cases demonstrates that an absolute rule of retroaction prevails in the area of constitutional adjudication. However, we believe that the Constitution neither prohibits nor requires retrospective effect. As Justice Cardozo said, "We think the federal constitution has no voice upon the subject." *Great Northern R. Co. v. Sunburst Oil & Refining Co.,* 287 U.S. 358, 364 (1932) (referring to state court's prospective overruling of prior decision).

Once the premise is accepted that we are neither required to apply, nor prohibited from applying, a decision retrospectively, we must then weigh the merits and demerits in each case by looking to the prior history of the rule in question, its purpose and effect, and whether retrospective operation will further or retard its operation. We believe that this approach is particularly correct with reference to the Fourth Amendment's prohibitions as to unreasonable searches and seizures. Rather than "disparaging" the Amendment we but apply the wisdom of Justice Holmes that "[t]he life of the law has not been logic: it has been experience." Holmes, The Common Law 5 (Howe ed 1963).

Since *Weeks v. United States,* 232 U.S. 383 (1914), this Court has adhered to the rule that evidence seized by federal officers in violation of the Fourth Amendment is not admissible at trial in a federal court. In 1949 in *Wolf v. Colorado, supra,* the Court decided that while the right to privacy—"the core of the Fourth Amendment"— was such a basic right as to be implicit in "the concept of ordered liberty" and thus enforceable against the States through the Fourteenth Amendment, "the ways of enforcing such a basic right raise questions of a different order. How such arbitrary conduct should be checked, what remedies against it should be afforded, the means by which the right should be made effective, are all questions that are not to be so dogmatically answered as to preclude the varying solutions which spring from an allowable range of judgment on issues not susceptible of quantitative solution." At 27–28.

The Court went on to say that the federal exclusionary rule was not "derived from the explicit requirements of the Fourth Amendment.... The decision was a matter of judicial implication." Since "we find that in fact most of the English-speaking world does not regard as vital to such protection the exclusion of evidence thus obtained, we must hesitate to treat this remedy as an essential ingredient of the right." While granting that "in practice" the exclusion of evidence might be "an effective way of deterring unreasonable searches," the Court concluded that it could not "condemn as falling below the minimal standards assured by the Due Process Clause a State's reliance upon other methods which, if consistently enforced, would be equally effective." The continuance of the federal exclusionary rule was excused on the ground that the reasons for it were more "compelling" since public opinion in the community could be exerted against oppressive conduct by local police far more effectively than it could throughout the country.

The "asymmetry which *Wolf* imported into the law," was indicated by a decision announced on the same day, *Lustig v. United States,* 338 U.S. 74 (1949), holding that evidence given to federal authorities "on a silver platter" by state officers was not excludable in federal trials. *Wolf's* holding, in conjunction with the "silver platter" doctrine of *Lustig,* provided wide avenues of abuse in the *Weeks'* exclusionary rule in the federal courts. Evidence seized in violation of the Fourth Amendment by state officers was turned over to federal officers and admitted in evidence in prosecutions in the federal courts.

In 1960 the Court's dissatisfaction with the "silver platter" doctrine, led to its rejection in the leading case of *Elkins v. United States,* 364 U.S. 206. The Court tightened the noose of exclusion in order to strangle completely the use in the federal courts of evidence illegally seized by state agents. It was in *Elkins* that the Court emphasized that the exclusionary rule was "calculated to prevent, not to repair. Its purpose is to deter—to compel respect for the constitutional guaranty in the only effectively available way—by removing the incentive to disregard it."

Mapp was announced in 1961. We affirmatively found that the exclusionary rule was "an essential part of both the Fourth and Fourteenth Amendments" and the only effective remedy for the protection of rights under the Fourth Amendment; that it would stop the needless "shopping around" that was causing conflict between federal and state courts; withdraw the invitation which

Wolf extended to federal officers to step across the street to the state's attorney with their illegal evidence, thus eliminating a practice which tended to destroy the entire system of constitutional restraints on which the liberties of the people rest; that it would promote state-federal cooperation in law enforcement by rejecting the double standard of admissibility of illegal evidence which tends to breed suspicion among the officers, encourages disobedience to the Constitution on the part of all the participants and violates "the imperative of judicial integrity."

We believe that the existence of the *Wolf* doctrine prior to *Mapp* is "an operative fact and may have consequences which cannot justly be ignored. The past cannot always be erased by a new judicial declaration." *Chicot County Drainage Dist. v. Baxter State Bank,* 308 U.S., *supra,* at 374. The thousands of cases that were finally decided on *Wolf* cannot be obliterated. The "particular conduct, private and official," must be considered. Here "prior determinations deemed to have finality and acted upon accordingly" have "become vested." And finally," public policy in the light of the nature both of the . . . [*Wolf* doctrine] and of its previous application" must be given its proper weight. In short, we must look to the purpose of the *Mapp* rule; the reliance placed upon the *Wolf* doctrine; and the effect on the administration of justice of a retrospective application of *Mapp.*

It is clear that the *Wolf* Court, once it had found the Fourth Amendment's unreasonable Search and Seizure Clause applicable to the States through the Due Process Clause of the Fourteenth Amendment, turned its attention to whether the exclusionary rule was included within the command of the Fourth Amendment. This was decided in the negative. It is clear that based upon the factual considerations heretofore discussed the *Wolf* Court then concluded that it was not necessary to the enforcement of the Fourth Amendment for the exclusionary rule to be extended to the States as a requirement of due process. *Mapp* had as its prime purpose the enforcement of the Fourth Amendment through the inclusion of the exclusionary rule within its rights. This, it was found, was the only effective deterrent to lawless police action. Indeed, all of the cases since *Wolf* requiring the exclusion of illegal evidence have been based on the necessity for an effective deterrent to illegal police action. We cannot say that this purpose would be advanced by making the rule retrospective. The misconduct of the police prior to *Mapp* has already occurred and will not be corrected by releasing the prisoners involved. Nor would it add harmony to the delicate state-federal relationship of which we have spoken as part and parcel of the purpose of *Mapp*. Finally, the ruptured privacy of the victims' homes and effects cannot be restored. Reparation comes too late.

Again and again this Court refused to reconsider *Wolf* and gave its implicit approval to hundreds of cases in their application of its rule. In rejecting the *Wolf* doctrine as to the exclusionary rule the purpose was to deter the lawless action of the police and to effectively enforce the Fourth Amendment. That purpose will not at this late date be served by the wholesale release of the guilty victims.

Finally, there are interests in the administration of justice and the integrity of the judicial process to consider. To make the rule of *Mapp* retrospective would tax the administration of justice to the utmost. Hearings would have to be held on the excludability of evidence long since destroyed, misplaced or deteriorated. If it is excluded, the witnesses available at the time of the original trial will not be available or if located their memory will be dimmed. To thus legitimate such an extraordinary procedural weapon that has no bearing on guilt would seriously disrupt the administration of justice.

It is urged, however, that these same considerations apply in the cases that we have applied retrospectively in other areas, notably that of coerced confessions, and that the *Mapp* exclusionary rule should, therefore, be given the same dignity and effect. Coerced confessions are excluded from evidence because of "a complex of values," including "the likelihood that the confession is untrue"; "the preservation of the individual's freedom of will"; and "[t]he abhorrence of society to the use of involuntary confessions." But there is no likelihood of unreliability or coercion present in a search-and-seizure case. Rather than being abhorrent at the time of seizure in this case, the use in state trials of illegally seized evidence had been specifically authorized by this Court in *Wolf*. Finally, in each of the three areas in which we have

applied our rule retrospectively[4] the principle that we applied went to the fairness of the trial—the very integrity of the fact-finding process. Here, as we have pointed out, the fairness of the trial is not under attack. All that petitioner attacks is the admissibility of evidence, the reliability and relevancy of which is not questioned, and which may well have had no effect on the outcome.

Nor can we accept the contention of petitioner that the *Mapp* rule should date from the day of the seizure there, rather than that of the judgment of this Court. The date of the seizure in *Mapp* has no legal significance. It was the judgment of this Court that changed the rule and the date of that opinion is the crucial date. In the light of the cases of this Court this is the better cutoff time.

All that we decide today is that though the error complained of might be fundamental it is not of the nature requiring us to overturn all final convictions based upon it. After full consideration of all the factors we are not able to say that the *Mapp* rule requires retrospective application.

Affirmed.

Mr. Justice Black, with whom Mr. Justice Douglas joins, dissenting.

The Court of Appeals held, and this Court now concedes, that the petitioner Linkletter is presently in prison serving a nine-year sentence at hard labor for burglary under a 1959 Louisiana State Court conviction obtained by use of evidence unreasonably seized in violation of the Fourth and Fourteenth Amendments. On June 19, 1961, we decided *Mapp v. Ohio*, 367 U.S. 643, in which the

---

[4] In *Griffin v. Illinois*, the appeal which was denied because of lack of funds was "an integral part of the [state's] trial system for finally adjudicating the guilt or innocence of a defendant." 351 US 18. Precluding an appeal because of inability to pay was analogized to denying the poor a fair trial. In *Gideon v. Wainwright*, we recognized a fundamental fact that a layman, no matter how intelligent, could not possibly further his claims of innocence and violation of previously declared rights adequately. Because of this the judgment lacked reliability. In *Jackson v. Denno*, the holding went to the basis of fair hearing and trial because the procedural apparatus never assured the defendant a fair determination of voluntariness. In addition, Mr. Justice White expressed grave doubts regarding the ability of the jury to disregard a confession found to be involuntary if the question of guilt was uncertain.

Court specifically held that "all evidence obtained by searches and seizures in violation of the Constitution is, by that same authority, inadmissible in a state court." Stating that this Court had previously held in *Wolf v. Colorado* that the Fourth Amendment was applicable to the States through the Due Process Clause of the Fourteenth Amendment, this Court in *Mapp* went on to add:

> In short, the admission of the new constitutional right by *Wolf* could not consistently tolerate denial of its most important constitutional privilege, namely, the exclusion of the evidence which an accused had been forced to give by reason of the unlawful seizure. To hold otherwise is to grant the right but in reality to withhold its privilege and enjoyment.

Despite the Court's resounding promises throughout the *Mapp* opinion that convictions based on such "unconstitutional evidence" would "find no sanction in the judgments of the courts," Linkletter, convicted in the state court by use of "unconstitutional evidence," is today denied relief by the judgment of this Court because his conviction became "final" before *Mapp* was decided. Linkletter must stay in jail; Miss Mapp, whose offense was committed before Linkletter's, is free. This different treatment of Miss Mapp and Linkletter points up at once the arbitrary and discriminatory nature of the judicial contrivance utilized here to break the promise of *Mapp* by keeping all people in jail who are unfortunate enough to have had their unconstitutional convictions affirmed before June 19, 1961.

Miss Mapp's Ohio offense was committed May 23, 1957; Linkletter's Louisiana offense occurred more than a year later—August 16, 1958. Linkletter was tried in Louisiana, convicted, the State Supreme Court affirmed, and a rehearing was denied March 21, 1960, all within about one year and seven months after his offense was committed. The Ohio Supreme Court affirmed Miss Mapp's conviction March 23, 1960, approximately two years and 10 months after her offense. Thus, had the Ohio courts proceeded with the same expedition as those in Louisiana, or had the Louisiana courts proceeded as slowly as the Ohio courts, Linkletter's conviction would not have been "finally" decided within the Court's definition of "finally" until within about 10 days of the time

Miss Mapp's case was decided in this Court—which would have given Linkletter ample time to petition this Court for virtually automatic relief on direct review after the *Mapp* case was decided. The Court offers no defense based on any known principle of justice for discriminating among defendants who were similarly convicted by use of evidence unconstitutionally seized. It certainly cannot do so as between Linkletter and Miss Mapp. The crime with which she was charged took place more than a year before his, yet the decision today seems to rest on the fanciful concept that the Fourth Amendment protected her 1957 offense against conviction by use of unconstitutional evidence but denied its protection to Linkletter for his 1958 offense. In making this ruling the Court assumes for itself the virtue of acting in harmony with a comment of Justice Holmes that "[t]he life of the law has not been logic: it has been experience." Justice Holmes was not there talking about the Constitution; he was talking about the evolving judge-made law of England and of some of our States whose judges are allowed to follow in the common law tradition. It should be remembered in this connection that no member of this Court has ever more seriously criticized it than did Justice Holmes for reading its own predilections into the "vague contours" of the Due Process Clause. But quite apart from that, there is no experience of the past that justifies a new Court-made rule to perpetrate a grossly invidious and unfair discrimination against Linkletter simply because he happened to be prosecuted in a State that was evidently well up with its criminal court docket. If this discrimination can be excused at all it is not because of experience but because of logic—sterile and formal at that—not, according to Justice Holmes, the most dependable guide in lawmaking.

Interesting as the question may be abstractly, this case should not be decided on the basis of arguments about whether judges "make" law or "discover" it when performing their duty of interpreting the Constitution. This Court recognized in *Chicot County Drainage District v. Baxter State Bank,* 308 U.S. 371, 374, an opinion in which I joined, that "an all-inclusive statement of a principle of absolute retroactive invalidity cannot be justified." And where state courts in certain situations chose to apply their decisions to the future only, this Court also said that, "the federal constitution has no voice" forbidding them to do so. *Great Northern R. Co. v. Sunburst Oil & Ref.*

Co., 287 U.S. 358, 364. In stating this Court's position on the question, the opinion in the *Chicot County* case recognized that rights and interests may have resulted from the existence and operation of a statute which should be respected notwithstanding its later being declared unconstitutional.

Doubtless there might be circumstances in which applying a new interpretation of the law to past events might lead to unjust consequences which, as we said in *Chicot,* "cannot justly be ignored." No such unjust consequences to Linkletter, however, can possibly result here by giving him and others like him the benefit of a changed constitutional interpretation where he is languishing in jail on the basis of evidence concededly used unconstitutionally to convict him. And I simply cannot believe that the State of Louisiana has any "vested interest" that we should recognize in these circumstances in order to keep Linkletter in jail. I therefore would follow this Court's usual practice and apply the *Mapp* rule to unconstitutional convictions which have resulted in persons being presently in prison.

As the Court concedes, this is the first instance on record where this Court, having jurisdiction, has ever refused to give a previously convicted defendant the benefit of a new and more expansive Bill of Rights interpretation. I am at a loss to understand why those who suffer from the use of evidence secured by a search and seizure in violation of the Fourth Amendment should be treated differently from those who have been denied other guarantees of the Bill of Rights. Speaking of the right guaranteed by the Fourth and Fifth Amendments not to be convicted on "unconstitutional evidence," the Court said in *Mapp,* only four years ago, that:

> ... we can no longer permit that right to remain an empty promise. Because it is *enforceable in the same manner and to like effect* as other basic rights secured by the Due Process Clause, we can no longer permit it to be revocable at the whim of any police officer who, in the name of law enforcement itself, chooses to suspend its enjoyment. *Our decision, founded on reason and truth, gives to the individual no more than that which the Constitution guarantees him. . . .* 367 U.S., at 660. (Emphasis supplied.)

There are peculiar reasons why the *Mapp* search and seizure exclusionary rule should be given like dignity and effect as the coerced confession exclusionary rule.

Yet the Court today by a chain of circuitous reasoning degrades the search and seizure exclusionary rule to a position far below that of the rule excluding evidence obtained by coerced confessions. The result is that this departure from the philosophy of *Mapp* denies Linkletter a right to challenge his conviction for an offense committed in August 1958 while it leaves Miss Mapp free because of an offense she committed in 1957.

The Court says that the exclusionary rule's purpose of preventing law enforcement officers from making lawless searches and seizures "will not at this late date be served by the wholesale release of the guilty victims." It has not been the usual thing to cut down trial protections guaranteed by the Constitution on the basis that some guilty persons might escape. There is probably no one of the rights in the Bill of Rights that does not make it more difficult to convict defendants. But all of them are based on the premise, I suppose, that the Bill of Rights' safeguards should be faithfully enforced by the courts without regard to a particular judge's judgment as to whether more people could be convicted by a refusal of courts to enforce the safeguards. Such has heretofore been accepted as a general maxim. In answer to an argument made in the *Mapp* case, that application of the exclusionary rule to the States might allow guilty criminals to go free, this Court conceded that:

> In some cases this will undoubtedly be the result. . . . The criminal goes free, if he must, but it is the law that sets him free. Nothing can destroy a government more quickly than its failure to observe its own laws, or worse, its disregard of the charter of its own existence.

Little consolation can be gathered by people who languish in jail under unconstitutional convictions from the Court's statement that "the ruptured privacy of the victim's homes and effects cannot be restored. Reparation comes too late." Linkletter is still in jail. No State should be considered to have a vested interest in keeping prisoners in jail who were convicted because of lawless conduct of the State's officials. Careful analysis of the Court's opinion shows that it rests on the premise that a State's assumed interest in sustaining convictions obtained under the old, repudiated rule outweighs the interests both of the State and of the individuals convicted in having wrongful convictions set aside. It certainly offends my sense of justice to say that a State holding in jail people who were convicted by unconstitutional methods has a vested interest in keeping them there that outweighs the right of persons adjudged guilty of crime to challenge their unconstitutional convictions at any time. No words can obscure the simple fact that the promises of *Mapp* and *Noia* are to a great extent broken by the decision here. I would reverse.

Questions

1. Do you agree with Justice Black that, where constitutional rights are involved, they cannot be given to one person and denied to another similarly situated person?

2. But if your answer to the first question is Yes, how far would you extend it? You probably would extend it to Linkletter, whose evidence was unconstitutionally seized by the police *a year after* Mapp's evidence was seized. Since Mapp's case was reversed, surely Linkletter's should be reversed. But what about all the persons in prison who were convicted on illegally seized evidence *before* Linkletter and *before* Mapp? Should all of those persons be released? (A new trial would not be practically feasible for many of these "stale" cases, for all the reasons suggested by the Court in its majority opinion.) Doesn't the constitutional rule apply to *them* fully as well as it applies to Mapp and Linkletter?

3. If your answer to the first question is No, was it *easy* for the Court to deny retroactivity when illegally seized evidence is involved? Why? Is it because new trials would be practically difficult for the government to win? Is it because illegally seized evidence has nothing to do with the fairness of a trial? (*Why* should it be fair to convict someone on illegally seized evidence?) Or is it because the exclusionary rule serves primarily a deterrent (i.e., forward-looking) purpose and hence should not be applied retroactively?

Desist v. United States

394 U.S. 244
Supreme Court of the United States
March 24, 1969

Mr. Justice Stewart delivered the opinion of the Court.

The petitioners were convicted by a jury in the District Court for the Southern District of New York of conspiring to import and conceal heroin in violation of the federal narcotics laws. An important part of the Government's evidence consisted of tape recordings of conversations among several of the petitioners in a New York City hotel room. The tapes were made by federal officers in the adjoining room by means of an electronic recording device which did not physically intrude into the petitioners' room. Because there was no "trespass" or "actual intrusion into a constitutionally protected area," the District Court and the Court of Appeals rejected the petitioners' argument that this evidence was inadmissible because the eavesdropping had violated their rights under the Fourth Amendment. The convictions were affirmed, and we granted certiorari to consider the constitutional questions thus presented.

Last Term in *Katz v. United States,* 389 U.S. 347, we held that the reach of the Fourth Amendment "cannot turn upon the presence or absence of a physical intrusion into any given enclosure." Noting that the "Fourth Amendment protects people, not places," we overruled cases holding that a search and seizure of speech requires some trespass or actual penetration of a particular enclosure. We concluded that since every electronic eavesdropping upon private conversations is a search or seizure, it can comply with constitutional standards only when authorized by a neutral magistrate upon a showing of probable cause and under precise limitations and appropriate safeguards. The eavesdropping in this case was not carried out pursuant to such a warrant, and the convictions must therefore be reversed if *Katz* is to be applied to electronic surveillance conducted before the date of that decision. We have concluded, however, that to the extent *Katz* departed from previous holdings of this Court, it should be given wholly prospective application. Accordingly, and because we find no merit in any of the petitioners' other challenges to their convictions, we affirm the judgment before us.

Ever since *Linkletter v. Walker,* 381 U.S. 618, established that "the Constitution neither prohibits nor requires retrospective effect" for decisions expounding new constitutional rules affecting criminal trials, the Court has viewed the retroactivity or nonretroactivity of such decisions as a function of three considerations. As we most recently summarized them in *Stovall v. Denno,* 388 U.S. 293,

> The criteria guiding resolution of the question implicate (a) the purpose to be served by the new standards, (b) the extent of the reliance by law enforcement authorities on the old standards and (c) the effect on the administration of justice of a retroactive application of the new standards.

Foremost among these factors is the purpose to be served by the new constitutional rule. This criterion strongly supports prospectivity for a decision amplifying the evidentiary exclusionary rule. Thus, it was principally the Court's assessment of the purpose of *Mapp v. Ohio,* which led it in *Linkletter* to deny those finally convicted the benefit of *Mapp*'s extension of the exclusionary rule to the States:

> all of the cases . . . requiring the exclusion of illegal evidence have been based on the necessity for an effective deterrent to illegal police action. . . . We cannot say that this purpose would be advanced by making the rule retrospective. The misconduct of the police . . . has already occurred and will not be corrected by releasing the prisoners involved.

The second and third factors—reliance of law enforcement officials, and the burden on the administration of justice that would flow from a retroactive application—also militate in favor of applying *Katz* prospectively. *Katz* for the first time explicitly overruled the "physical penetration" and "trespass" tests enunciated in earlier decisions of this Court. Our periodic restatements of those tests confirmed the interpretation that police and courts alike had placed on the controlling precedents and fully justified reliance on their continuing validity.

Although there apparently have not been many federal convictions based on evidence gathered by warrantless electronic surveillance, we have no cause to doubt that the number of state convictions obtained in reliance on pre-*Katz* decisions is substantial. Moreover, the determination of whether a particular instance of eavesdropping led to the introduction of tainted evidence at trial would in most cases be a difficult and time-consuming task, which, particularly when attempted long after the event, would impose a weighty burden on any court. It is to be noted also that we have relied heavily on the factors of the extent of reliance and consequent burden on the administration of justice only when the purpose of the rule in question did not clearly favor either retroactivity or prospectivity. Because the deterrent purpose of *Katz* overwhelmingly supports nonretroactivity, we would reach that result even if relatively few convictions would be set aside by its retroactive application.

The petitioners argue that even if *Katz* is not given fully retrospective effect, at least it should govern those cases which, like the petitioners', were pending on direct review when *Katz* was decided. Petitioners point out that in *Linkletter,* the only other case involving the retroactivity of a Fourth Amendment decision, the Court held *Mapp* applicable to every case still pending on direct review on the date of that decision.

All of the reasons for making *Katz* retroactive also undercut any distinction between final convictions and those still pending on review. Both the deterrent purpose of the exclusionary rule and the reliance of law enforcement officers focus upon the time of the search, not any subsequent point in the prosecution, as the relevant date. Exclusion of electronic eavesdropping evidence seized before *Katz* would increase the burden on the administration of justice, would overturn convictions based on fair reliance upon pre-*Katz* decisions, and would not serve to deter similar searches and seizures in the future.

In sum, we hold that *Katz* is to be applied only to cases in which the prosecution seeks to introduce the fruits of electronic surveillance conducted after December 18, 1967.[5] Since the eavesdropping in this case occurred before the date and was consistent with pre-*Katz* decisions of this Court, the convictions must be

Affirmed.

Mr. Justice Douglas, dissenting.

It is a mystery to me why *Katz v. United States,* 389 U.S. 347, which was given retroactive effect to petitioner Katz will not be given retroactive effect to petitioner Desist and his co-petitioners. That does not seem to me to be the administration

---

[5] The dissenting opinion of Mr. Justice Fortas suggests that our holding today denies "the benefit of a fundamental constitutional provision, and not merely of court-made rules implementing a constitutional mandate." To the contrary, we simply decline to extend the court-made exclusionary rule to cases in which its deterrent purpose would not be served. The exclusionary rule "has no bearing on guilt" or "the fairness of the trial." Linkletter v. Walker, 381 U.S., at 638.

Of course, Katz himself benefited from the new principle announced on that date, and, as our Brother Douglas observes, to that extent the decision has not technically been given wholly prospective application. But, as we recently explained in Stovall v. Denno, 388 U.S. 293 (1967), the fact that the parties involved in the decision are the only litigants so situated who receive the benefit of the new rule is "an unavoidable consequence of the necessity that constitutional adjudications not stand as mere dictum." Whatever inequity may arguably result from applying the new rule to those "chance beneficiaries" is "an insignificant cost for adherence to sound principles of decision-making."

of justice with an even hand. I would understand today's ruling if in *Katz* we had announced a new constitutional search-and-seizure rule to be applied prospectively in all cases. But we did not do that; nor did we do it in other recent cases announcing variations of old constitutional doctrine. The most notorious example is *Miranda v. Arizona,* 384 U.S. 436, where, as I recall, some 80 cases were presented raising the same question. We took four of them and held the rest and then disposed of each of the four, applying the new procedural rule retroactively. But as respects the rest of the pending cases we denied any relief. Yet it was sheer coincidence that those precise four were chosen. Any other single case in the group or any other four would have been sufficient for our purposes.

Mr. Justice Harlan, dissenting.

In the four short years since we embraced the notion that our constitutional decisions in criminal cases need not be retroactively applied, *Linkletter v. Walker,* 381 U.S. 618, we have created an extraordinary collection of rules to govern the application of that principle. We have held that certain "new" rules are to be applied to all cases then subject to direct review, *Linkletter v. Walker, supra,* certain others are to be applied to all those cases in which trials have not yet commenced, *Johnson v. New Jersey,* 384 U.S. 719 (1966), certain others are to be applied to all those cases in which the tainted evidence has not yet been introduced at trial, *Fuller v. Alaska,* 393 U.S. 80 (1968); and still others are to be applied only to the party involved in the case in which the new rule is announced and to all future cases in which the proscribed official conduct has not yet occurred. *Stovall v. Denno,* 388 U.S. 293 (1967).

Upon reflection, I can no longer accept the rule first announced two years ago in *Stovall v. Denno,* and reaffirmed today, which permits this Court to apply a "new" constitutional rule entirely prospectively, while making an exception only for the particular litigant whose case was chosen as the vehicle for establishing that rule. Indeed, I have concluded that *Linkletter* was right in insisting that all "new" rules of constitutional law must at a minimum be applied to all those cases which are still subject to direct review by this Court at the time the "new" decision is handed down.

Matters of basic principle are at stake. In the classical view of constitutional adjudication, which I share, criminal defendants cannot come before this Court simply to request largesse. This Court is entitled to decide constitutional issues only when the facts of a particular case *require* their resolution for a just adjudication on the merits. We do not release a criminal from jail because we like to do so, or because we think it wise to do so, but only because the government has offended constitutional principle in the conduct of his case. And when another similarly situated defendant comes before us, we must grant the same relief or give a principled reason for acting differently. We depart from this basic judicial tradition when we simply pick and choose from among similarly situated defendants those who alone will receive the benefit of a "new" rule of constitutional law.

The unsound character of the rule reaffirmed today is perhaps best exposed by considering the following hypothetical. Imagine that the Second Circuit in the present case had anticipated the line of reasoning this Court subsequently pursued in *Katz v. United States,* concluding—as this Court there did—that "the underpinnings of *Olmstead* and *Goldman* have been so eroded by our subsequent decisions that the 'trespass' doctrine there enunciated can no longer be regarded as controlling." Would we have *reversed* the case on the ground that the principles the Second Circuit had announced—though identical with those in *Katz*— should not control because *Katz* is not retroactive? To the contrary, I venture to say that we would have taken satisfaction that the lower court had reached the same conclusion we subsequently did in *Katz*. If a "new" constitutional doctrine is truly right, we should not reverse lower courts which have accepted it; nor should we affirm those which have rejected the very arguments we have embraced. Anything else would belie the truism that it is the task of this Court, like that of any other,1 to do justice to each litigant on the merits of his own case. It is only if our decisions can be justified in terms of this fundamental premise that they may properly be considered the legitimate products of a court of law, rather than the commands of a super-legislature.

Re-examination of prior developments in the field of retroactivity leads me irresistibly to the conclusion that the only solid disposition of this case lies in vacating the judgment of the Court of Appeals and in remanding this case to that court for further consideration in light of *Katz*.

Mr. Justice Fortas, dissenting.

The decision today in *Desist v. United States* applies to only the limited number of cases where the constitutionally forbidden wiretap or eavesdropping occurred prior to December 18, 1967. It was on that day that we decided *Katz v. United States,* 389 US 347. The Court in effect grants absolution to police invasions of individual privacy by wiretaps and electronic devices not involving physical trespass, as long as the unconstitutional conduct took place before *Katz*. It holds that only from and after *Katz* will it apply the Fourth Amendment's command without reference to whether a physical trespass was involved. The significance of the decisions is not only that they deprive a relatively few convicted persons of their constitutional rights, but also that they diminish the Constitution; they imply that the availability of constitutional principle can be the subject of judicial choice in circumstances which, I respectfully submit, are far from compelling. I cannot agree.

In the present cases, the Court decides that the lawfulness of wiretaps and electronic eavesdropping occurring before December 18, 1967, will be controlled by *Olmstead v. United States,* a decision that the Court agrees is a false and insupportable reading of the Constitution. The Court holds that the Fourth Amendment meant something quite different before *Katz* was decided than it means afterwards; that Katz and persons whose rights are violated after the date of that decision may have the benefit of the true meaning of the constitutional provision, but that those who were victims before *Katz* may not.

In *Desist v. United States,* the federal case decided today, the federal agents attached the "uninvited ear" of the microphone to the outer instead of the inner panel of the double door separating their hotel room from that of the petitioners. Because of this distinction, their conduct is today held to be immunized from Fourth Amendment attack. *Olmstead* would sanction the differentiation. If the microphone had been attached to the inner panel, or if the agents had used a device that impinged by 1 1000th of an inch upon the room rented by petitioners, *Olmstead* would not have sanctified the result.

This distinction is, of course, nonsense, as I suppose most rational persons would agree; and I am unwilling to suppose that if the majority in *Olmstead* had foreseen the ensuing development and uninhibited use of electronic devices for searching out and seizing the words of others, it would have nevertheless allowed the perimeter of physical property rights to limit the Fourth Amendment's protection of citizens' privacy from unseen invasion.

In any event, there is no doubt that *Olmstead* was thoroughly repudiated by this Court long before December 18, 1967, when *Katz* was decided. *Katz* is not responsible for killing *Olmstead*. Prior cases had left the physical-trespass requirement of *Olmstead* virtually lifeless and merely awaiting the death certificate that *Katz* gave it. They demonstrated to all who were willing to receive the message that *Olmstead* would not shield eavesdropping because it took place outside the physical property line.

Only those police officials and courts whose devotion to wiretapping and electronic surveillance is so intense as to induce them to exploit those techniques until the last spade of earth is shoveled on the doctrinal corpse have continued to rely on *Olmstead*. It is not the least of the unfortunate consequences of today's decisions that they validate this kind of foot-dragging. They reward those who fought the battle for uncontrolled police eavesdropping to the bitter end, despite the clear, though undelivered, verdict. They add this Court's approval to those who honor the Constitution's mandate only where acceptable to them or compelled by the precise and inescapable specifics of a decision of this Court. And they award dunce caps to those law enforcement officers, courts, and public officials who do not merely stand by until an inevitable decree issues from this Court, specifically articulating that which is clearly immanent in the fulfillment of the Constitution, but who generously apply the mandates of the Constitution as the developing case law elucidates them. The full realization of our great charter of liberty, set forth in our Constitution, cannot be achieved by this Court alone. History does not embrace the years needed for us to hold, millimeter by millimeter, that such and such a penetration of individual rights is an infringement of the Constitution's guarantees. The vitality of our Constitution depends upon conceptual faithfulness and not merely decisional obedience. Certainly, this Court should not encourage police or other courts to disregard the plain purport of our decisions and to adopt a let's-wait-until-it's-decided approach.

Since *Katz* itself recognized that *Olmstead* had been "eroded by our subsequent decisions" and that we had "since departed from the narrow view on which [it] ...rested," how can the Court now say that because *Katz* overruled *Olmstead* it "was a clear break with the past"? The issue presented by *Desist* is *not* whether the petitioners will be given the benefit of *Katz*. The issue is *not* whether *Katz* is "retroactive." The issue is whether *because* in *Katz* we formally announced that the "reach of [the Fourth Amendment] ...cannot turn upon the presence or absence of a physical intrusion into any given enclosure," persons claiming the benefit of this principle prior to that date must be denied its protection. It is, I submit, entirely appropriate to state the issue in these terms because there can be no doubt whatever that if the present cases had been presented to this Court a day, a year, or a number of years before *Katz*, we would have held that the petitioners' constitutional rights had been violated, and that the petitioners were entitled, like any other citizens, to their constitutional rights. In these circumstances, I utterly fail to see how today's decisions can be justified. It is indeed a paradox that *Katz*, whose role it was to bury the corpse of *Olmstead*, is here being used to revive it.

Questions

1. Note that in *Linkletter* the Court announced that new constitutional rules need not be given retroactive effect to persons whose cases became final prior to the Court's new determination, but that persons whose cases were still on direct appeal *could* benefit from the new constitutional rule. Then *Desist* comes along and says that a new rule need *not* be applied to persons whose cases are still in the process of direct appeal. Is the Court slowly chipping away the idea of treating equally situated people equally? Is it doing so for reasons of administrative convenience? The Justices of the Supreme Court are, after all, government employees. If anyone is part of the "establishment," they are. Can it be said that they are simply protecting the government in these cases at the expense of individual defendants?

2. If your answer to this last question is Yes, consider the alternative. If the Court were *bound* to apply all new rules retroactively, then might the same "administrative considerations" lead the Court to be very stingy about ever announcing a new rule? Or to put this question another way, isn't the *possibility* of *non-retroactivity* itself an important factor in encouraging the Court to announce new extensions of human rights and liberties under the Constitution?

3. But isn't Justice Harlan's logic irrefutable? Re-read his hypothetical case. Is it not totally convincing? Apparently it was not totally convincing to the majority of the Court. (But the majority of the Court did not address Justice Harlan's hypothetical, and they certainly did not answer it.)

Griffith v. Kentucky

479 U.S. 314
Supreme Court of the United States
January 13, 1987

Justice BLACKMUN delivered the opinion of the Court.

These cases concern the retrospective application of *Batson v. Kentucky,* 476 U.S. 79 (1986). In *Batson,* this Court ruled that a defendant in a state criminal trial could establish a prima facie case of racial discrimination violative of the Fourteenth Amendment, based on the prosecution's use of peremptory challenges to strike members of the defendant's race from the jury venire, and that, once the defendant had made the prima facie showing, the burden shifted to the prosecution to come forward with a neutral explanation for those challenges. In the present cases we consider whether that ruling is applicable to litigation pending on direct state or federal review or not yet final when *Batson* was decided. We answer that question in the affirmative.

Petitioner Randall Lamont Griffith, a black person, was indicted in 1982 in the Circuit Court of Jefferson County, Ky. (the same court where Batson was tried), on charges of first degree robbery, theft by unlawful taking, and being a persistent felony offender in the second degree. On the first day of trial, the prosecution and defense attorneys conducted *voir dire* examination of the jury venire and exercised their peremptory challenges. The prosecution used four of its five allotted challenges to strike four of the five prospective black jurors. The defense used eight of its allotted nine challenges to strike prospective white jurors. There were two duplicate strikes. The two extra jurors who remained because of the duplicate strikes, one of whom was a black person, then were removed by random draw. thus, no black person remained on the jury.

Defense counsel expressed concern that Griffith was to be tried by an all-white jury. He asked the court to request the prosecutor to state his reasons for exercising peremptory challenges against the four prospective black jurors. The request was refused. Counsel then moved for discharge of the panel, alleging that the prosecutor's use of peremptory challenges to remove all but one of the prospective black jurors constituted a violation of Griffith's Sixth and Fourteenth Amendment rights. The court denied the motion. The jury returned a verdict of guilty on the charge of first degree robbery and fixed petitioner's punishment at 10 years' imprisonment. The jury then found petitioner guilty of being a persistent felony offender, and enhanced his sentence to 20 years' imprisonment.

Griffith timely filed here a petition for a writ of certiorari. While his petition was pending, this

Court decided *Batson v. Kentucky.*

Twenty-one years ago, this Court adopted a three-pronged analysis for claims of retroactivity of new constitutional rules of criminal procedure. See *Linkletter v. Walker,* 381 U.S. 618 (1965). In *Linkletter,* the Court held that *Mapp v. Ohio,* which extended the Fourth Amendment exclusionary rule to the States, would not be applied retroactively to a state conviction that had become final before *Mapp* was decided. The Court explained that "the Constitution neither prohibits nor requires retrospective effect" of a new constitutional rule, and that a determination of retroactivity must depend on "weigh[ing] the merits and demerits in each case." The Court's decision not to apply *Mapp* retroactively was based on "the purpose of the *Mapp* rule; the reliance placed upon the [previous] doctrine; and the effect on the administration of justice of a retrospective application of *Mapp.*" See also *Stovall v. Denno,* 388 U.S. 293, (1967) (retroactivity depends on "(a) the purpose to be served by the new standards, (b) the extent of the reliance by law enforcement authorities on the old standards, and (c) the effect on the administration of justice of a retroactive application of the new standards").

The rationale for distinguishing between cases that have become final and those that have not, and for applying new rules retroactively to cases in the latter category, was explained at length by Justice Harlan in *Desist v. United States,* 394 U.S., at 256 (dissenting opinion).

In Justice Harlan's view, and now in ours, failure to apply a newly declared constitutional rule to criminal cases pending on direct review violates basic norms of constitutional adjudication. First, it is a settled principle that this Court adjudicates only "cases" and "controversies." See U.S. Const., Art. III § 2. Unlike a legislature, we do not promulgate new rules of constitutional criminal procedure on a broad basis. Rather, the nature of judicial review requires that we adjudicate specific cases, and each case usually becomes the vehicle for announcement of a new rule. But after we have decided a new rule in the case selected, the integrity of judicial review requires that we apply that rule to all similar cases pending on direct review.

As a practical matter, of course, we cannot hear each case pending on direct review and apply the new rule. But we fulfill our judicial responsibility by instructing the lower courts to apply the new rule retroactively to cases not yet final. Thus, it is the nature of judicial review that precludes us from "[s]imply fishing one case from the stream of appellate review, using it as a vehicle for pronouncing new constitutional standards, and then permitting a stream of similar cases subsequently to flow by unaffected by that new rule."

Second, selective application of new rules violates the principle of treating similarly situated defendants the same. See *Desist v. United States,* 394 U.S., at 258–259 (Harlan, J., dissenting). As we pointed out in *United States v. Johnson,* the problem with not applying new rules to cases pending on direct review is "the *actual inequity* that results when the Court chooses which of many similarly situated defendants should be the chance beneficiary" of a new rule. Although the Court had tolerated this inequity for a time by not applying new rules retroactively to cases on direct review, we noted: "The time for toleration has come to an end."

In *United States v. Johnson,* our acceptance of Justice Harlan's views led to the holding that "subject to [certain exceptions], a decision of this Court construing the Fourth Amendment is to be applied retroactively to all convictions that were not yet final at the time the decision was rendered." The exceptions to which we referred related to three categories in which we concluded that existing precedent established threshold tests for the retroactivity analysis. In two of these categories, the new rule already was retroactively applied: (1) when a decision of this Court did nothing more than apply settled precedent to different factual situations, and (2) when the new ruling was that a trial court lacked authority to convict a criminal defendant in the first place.

The third—category where a new rule is a "clear break" with past precedent—is the one at issue in these cases. We described it in *United States v. Johnson,* 457 U.S., at 549–550:

> [W]here the Court has expressly
> declared a rule of criminal procedure
> to be 'a clear break with the past,'
> *Desist v. United States,* 394 U.S., at
> 248, it almost invariably has gone on
> to find such a newly minted principle
> nonretroactive. In this . . . type of case,
> the traits of the particular constitu-
> tional rule have been less critical than
> the Court's express threshold determi-

nation that the "'new" constitutional interpretatio[n] . . . so change[s] the law that prospectivity is arguably the proper course.' Once the Court has found that the new rule was unanticipated, the second and third *Stovall* factors—reliance by law enforcement authorities on the old standards and effect on the administration of justice of a retroactive application of the new rule—have virtually compelled a finding of non-retroactivity.

Thus, we recognized what may be termed a "clear break exception." Under this exception, a new constitutional rule was not applied retroactively, even to cases on direct review, if the new rule explicitly overruled a past precedent of this Court, or disapproved a practice this Court had arguably sanctioned in prior cases, or overturned a longstanding practice that lower courts had uniformly approved.

The question whether a different retroactivity rule should apply when a new rule is a "clear break" with the past, however, is squarely before us in the present cases. In *Allen v. Hardy,* a case which was here on federal habeas, we said that the rule in *Batson* "is an explicit and substantial break with prior precedent" because it "overruled [a] portion of *Swain*." We therefore now reexamine the rationale for maintaining a "clear break" exception to the general proposition that new rules governing criminal procedure should be retroactive to cases pending on direct review. For the same reasons that persuaded us in *United States v. Johnson* to adopt different conclusions as to convictions on direct review from those that already had become final, we conclude that an engrafted exception based solely upon the particular characteristics of the new rule adopted by the Court is inappropriate.

First, the principle that this Court does not disregard current law, when it adjudicates a case pending before it on direct review, applies regardless of the specific characteristics of the particular new rule announced. The Court recognized in *United States v. Johnson* that the fact that a new rule is a clear break with the past is relevant primarily because it implicates the second and third *Stovall* factors of reliance by law enforcement officials and the burden on the administration of justice imposed by retroactive application. But even if these factors may be useful in deciding whether convictions that already have become final should receive the benefit of a new rule, the "clear break" exception, derived from the *Stovall* factors, reintroduces precisely the type of case-specific analysis that Justice Harlan rejected as inappropriate for cases pending on direct review.

Second, the use of a "clear break" exception creates the same problem of not treating similarly situated defendants the same. James Kirkland Batson, the petitioner in *Batson v. Kentucky,* and Randall Lamont Griffith, the petitioner in the present Kentucky case, were tried in Jefferson Circuit Court approximately three months apart. The same prosecutor exercised peremptory challenges at the trials. It was solely the fortuities of the judicial process that determined the case this Court chose initially to hear on plenary review. Justice POWELL has pointed out that it "hardly comports with the ideal of 'administration of justice with an even hand,'" when "one chance beneficiary—the lucky individual whose case was chosen as the occasion for announcing the new principle—enjoys retroactive application, while others similarly situated have their claims adjudicated under the old doctrine." *Hankerson v. North Carolina,* 432 U.S. 233 (1977). See also *Michigan v. Payne,* 412 U.S. 47, 60 (1973) (MARSHALL, J., dissenting) ("Different treatment of two cases is justified under our Constitution only when the cases differ in some respect relevant to the different treatment"). The fact that the new rule may constitute a clear break with the past has no bearing on the "actual inequity that results" when only one of many similarly situated defendants receives the benefit of the new rule.

We therefore hold that a new rule for the conduct of criminal prosecutions is to be applied retroactively to all cases, state or federal, pending on direct review or not yet final, with no exception for cases in which the new rule constitutes a "clear break" with the past. Accordingly, in [*Griffith*], the judgment of the Supreme Court of Kentucky is reversed, and the case is remanded to that court for further proceedings not inconsistent with this opinion.

It is so ordered.

Justice POWELL, concurring.

I join the Court's opinion, and consider it an important step toward ending the confusion that has resulted from applying *Linkletter v. Walker,*

381 U.S. 618 (1965), on a case-by-case basis.

As the cases we decide today involve only the retroactivity of decisions pending on direct review, it was not necessary for the Court to express an opinion with respect to habeas corpus petitions. As I read the Court's opinion, this question is carefully left open until it is squarely presented. It is to be hoped that the Court then will adopt the Harlan view of retroactivity in cases seeking relief on habeas petitions. Under that view, habeas petitions generally should be judged according to the constitutional standards existing at the time of conviction.

Justice WHITE, with whom THE CHIEF JUSTICE and Justice O'CONNOR join, dissenting.

Last Term this Court decided that the rule announced in *Batson* should not apply on collateral review of convictions that became final before the decision in *Batson* was announced. In reaching this judgment, the Court weighed the three factors that it has traditionally considered in deciding the retroactivity of a new rule of criminal procedure: """"(a) the purpose to be served by the new standards, (b) the extent of the reliance by law enforcement authorities on the old standards, and (c) the effect on the administration of justice of a retroactive application of the new standards.""""" (Citing *Stovall v. Denno,* 388 U.S. 293 (1967)). No Justice suggested that this test is unworkable. The question, then, is why the Court feels constrained to fashion a different rule for cases on direct review. The reasons the Court offers are not new, and I find them as unpersuasive today as I have in the past:

> It is the business of a court, the majority reasons, to treat like cases alike; accordingly, it is unfair for one litigant to receive the benefit of a new decision when another, identically situated, is denied the same benefit. The majority's concerns are no doubt laudable, but I cannot escape the conclusion that the rule they have spawned makes no sense.
>
> Although the majority finds it intolerable to apply a new rule to one case on direct appeal but not to another, it is perfectly willing to tolerate disparate treatment of defendants seeking direct review of their convictions and prisoners

attacking their convictions in collateral proceedings. As I have stated before, it seems to me that the attempt to distinguish between direct and collateral challenges for purposes of retroactivity is misguided. Under the majority's rule, otherwise identically situated defendants may be subject to different constitutional rules, depending on just how long ago now-unconstitutional conduct occurred and how quickly cases proceed through the criminal justice system. The disparity is no different in kind from that which occurs when the benefit of a new constitutional rule is retroactively afforded to the defendant in whose case it is announced but to no others; the Court's new approach equalizes nothing except the numbers of defendants within the disparately treated classes. *Shea v. Louisiana,* 470 U.S. 51, 62–64 (1985) (WHITE, J., dissenting).

The Court's invocation of fairness also overlooks the fact that it is a fortuity that we overruled *Swain v. Alabama,* 380 U.S. 202 (1965), in a case that came to us on direct review. We could as easily have granted certiorari and decided the matter in a case on collateral review, such as *Allen v. Hardy.* In that case, the principle of treating like cases alike would dictate that all cases on collateral review receive the benefit of the new rule. I trust that the Court would not go that far in letting the tail wag the dog: good judgment would—I hope—win out over blind adherence to the principle of treating cases alike. Yet today the Court acts as if it has no choice but to follow a mechanical notion of fairness without pausing to consider "sound principles of decision-making," *Stovall v. Denno,* 388 U.S., at 301.

For the foregoing reasons, I would adhere to the approach set out in *Stovall v. Denno,* and recognize no distinction for retroactivity purposes between cases on direct and collateral review. But even if I saw some merit in applying the Harlan approach to cases on direct appeal, I would nonetheless preserve the exception for "clear breaks" recognized in *United States v. Johnson,* 457 U.S. 537 (1982). Under our precedent, "a decision announcing a new standard 'is almost automatically nonretroactive' where the decision 'has explicitly overruled past precedent.'" *Allen v. Hardy.* As the majority in *Johnson* explained:

> Once the Court has found that [a] new rule was unanticipated, the second and third *Stovall* factors—reliance by law enforcement authorities on the old stan-dards and effect on the administration of justice of a retroactive application of the new rule—have virtually compelled a finding of non-retroactivity.
>
> I respectfully dissent.

Notes and Questions

1. What does the majority mean when it says "The time for toleration is at an end"? The non-retroactivity rule was, after all, the Court's *own* rule. If there were any inequities to "tolerate," weren't they inequities of the Court's own making? Is the Supreme Court so impressed with itself that it "tolerates" its own mistakes until it decides that the time for "toleration is at an end"?

2. Is Justice White, dissenting, persuasive when he argues that there is no real difference between applying a rule retroactively to cases on *direct* appeal and to cases on *indirect* appeal (i.e., "collateral" appeal or "habeas corpus" cases)? If he is right that there is no principled difference, do you agree with him that, therefore, Griffith should be *denied* the benefit of the *Batson* rule? But, then, what's the difference between *Griffith* and *Batson*? They were both tried in the same court by the same prosecutor, and they were both the victims of unfair peremptory challenges of the jury. What principled difference can Justice White see between *Griffith* and *Batson?*

3. Retroactivity is frequently an issue in contexts other than the constitutional rights of criminal defendants. In *Los Angeles Department of Water & Power v. Manhart* (Chapter 5, Section 2), Justice Stevens refused to apply the holding to the plaintiff class in that case—all present or former female employees of the Department. Recall the holding: By charging female employees more for mandatory retirement annuities than male employees the Department *had* discriminated against individual female employees because of their sex. The District Court had allowed a "retroactive" money recovery to the plaintiffs in *Manhart*. By refusing to give the plaintiffs in *Manhart* an award, the Supreme Court is depriving the *very* plaintiffs (and their lawyers) of the benefit of the rule of law that they put money, time and effort into establishing. They brought the suit for their own benefit, knowing full well that those coming after them would benefit as well. Now they find out that they will not benefit at all. Consider Justice Stevens' reasoning:

> In *Albemarle Paper Co. v. Moody,* 422 U.S. 405, the Court reviewed the scope of a district court's discretion to fashion appropriate remedies for a Title VII violation and concluded that "backpay should be denied only for reasons which, if applied generally, would not frustrate the central statutory purposes of eradicating discrimination throughout the economy and making persons whole for injuries suffered through past discrimination." *Id.,* at 421.
>
> The *Albemarle* presumption in favor of retroactive liability can seldom be overcome, but it does not make meaningless the district courts' duty to determine that such relief is appropriate. For several reasons, we conclude that the District Court gave insufficient attention to the equitable nature of Title VII remedies.

Although we now have no doubt about the application of the statute in this case, we must recognize that conscientious and intelligent administrators of pension funds, who did not have the benefit of the extensive briefs and arguments presented to us, may well have assumed that a program like the Department's was entirely lawful. The courts had been silent on the question, and the administrative agencies had conflicting views. The Department's failure to act more swiftly is a sign, not of its recalcitrance, but of the problem's complexity. As commentators have noted, pension administrators could reasonably have thought it unfair—or even illegal—to make male employees shoulder more than their "actuarial share" of the pension burden. There is no reason to believe that the threat of a backpay award is needed to cause other administrators to amend their practices to conform to this decision.

Nor can we ignore the potential impact which changes in rules affecting insurance and pension plans may have on the economy.... Risks that the insurer foresees will be included in the calculation of liability, and the rates or contributions charged will reflect that calculation. The occurrence of major unforeseen contingencies, however, jeopardizes the insurer's solvency and, ultimately, the insured's benefits. Drastic changes in the legal rules governing pension and insurance funds, like other unforeseen events, can have this effect. Consequently, the rules that apply to these funds should not be applied retroactively unless the legislature has plainly commanded that result.

There can be no doubt that the prohibition against sex-differentiated employee contributions represents a marked departure from past practice. Although Title VII was enacted in 1964, this is apparently the first litigation challenging contribution differences based on valid actuarial tables. Retroactive liability could be devastating for a pension fund.[6]

Not one word about the effects on Manhart and the fellow members of her class! It is one thing to lose a case (the plaintiffs surely *lost* in one sense); quite another to have the justice of your position completely ignored in the court's explanation of its position.

Now consider Justice Marshall's dissent on the retroactivity result:

The Court here does not assert that any findings of the District Court were clearly erroneous, nor does it conclude that there was any abuse of discretion. Instead, it states merely that the District Court gave "insufficient attention" to certain factors in striking the equitable balance.

The first such factor mentioned by the Court relates to the "complexity" of the issue presented here, which may have led some pension fund administrators to assume that "a program like the Department's was entirely lawful," and that the alternative of equal contributions was perhaps unlawful because of a perceived "unfair[ness]" to men. The District Court found, however, that petitioners "should have been placed on notice" of the illegality of requiring larger contributions from women on April 5, 1972, when the Equal Employment Opportunity Commission

---

[6] 435 U.S., at 719–22.

amended its regulations to make this illegality clear.

The other major factor relied on by the Court involves "the potential impact . . . on the economy" that might result from retroactive changes in "the rules" applying to pension and insurance funds. According to the Court, such changes could "jeopardiz[e] [an] insurer's solvency and, ultimately, the insureds' benefits." As with the first factor, however, little reference is made by the Court to the situation in this case. No claim is made by either petitioners or the Court that the relief granted here would in any way have threatened the plan's solvency, or indeed that risks of this nature were not "foresee[n]" and thus "included in the calculation of liability" and reflected in "the rates or contributions charged." No one has suggested, moreover, that the relatively modest award at issue—involving a small percentage of the amounts withheld from respondents' paychecks for pension purposes over a 33-month period—could in any way be considered "devastating." And if a "devastating" award were made in some future case, this Court would have ample opportunity to strike it down at that time.

Respondents in this case cannot be "made whole" unless they receive a refund of the money that was illegally withheld from their paychecks by petitioners. Their claim to these funds is more compelling than is the claim in many backpay situations, where the person discriminated against receives payment for a period when he or she was not working. Here, as the Court of Appeals observed, respondents "actually earned the amount in question, but then had it taken from them in violation of Title VII."[7]

Unlike the majority, Justice Marshall does consider the effect on the plaintiffs, in terms of the *strength* of their claim. Presumably the *practical* effect of not getting an award was as minimal on plaintiffs as having to pay an award would have been on the Department. Had the practical effect on plaintiffs (or on the Department) been grave, would the majority have stuck by its guns?

4. Clearly, the Supreme Court is a long way from figuring out a logical position regarding retroactivity. More recent cases have not helped very much. In *Teague v. Lane,* 489 U.S. 288 (1989), a plurality of the Supreme Court adopted Justice Harlan's view that new constitutional rules of criminal procedure generally should not be applied retroactively to cases on collateral review. The plurality affirmed its understanding that such new rules must be applied retroactively to cases still on direct review. But Justice White's criticism—that this is a distinction without a principled difference—still hovers in the air.

In *American Trucking Associations, Inc. v. Smith,* 110 S. Ct. 2323 (1990), the Court held that a taxpayer was not entitled to a refund when the taxing statute was in a later case declared unconstitutional. Here there was no administrative inconvenience of holding new trials, etc., that figured prominently in the criminal cases we have examined. The state government that levied the tax could have easily been ordered by the Supreme Court to refund the tax to all taxpayers who paid it. But the Supreme Court denied retroactive effect

---

[7] 435 U.S., at 729–33.

to the unconstitutional tax.

There will surely be more Supreme Court decisions in the next few years that take up the perplexing question of retroactivity. But our purpose in this Chapter has neither been to present some issues in constitutional law nor to predict where the Supreme Court may be going in this complex area of law. Rather, we have looked at some representative (and intrinsically interesting) cases from a "justice" perspective. In this light, we ask the following questions as a conclusion to the present Chapter:

(a) What role have justice considerations played in the unsteady evolution of the Supreme Court's retroactivity jurisprudence?

(b) Is this an area where, even if there is agreement that fairness is the operative rule of decision, the Justices cannot reasonably agree upon what is fair?

(c) Can fairness and justice be decided in the abstract, so as to lay down a rule for all future retroactive application of new constitutional decisions? What would that rule be? If you cannot give that rule precise content, would you take the position that no one can possibly give it precise content?

(d) We see the Supreme Court in these cases acting as a common-law court, taking the cases one at a time and trying to work out principles of fairness. Yet why doesn't the process get itself resolved? In most areas of the common law, courts eventually work out rules that are more or less stable. But in this area of retroactivity, even as highly competent a court as the Supreme Court of the United States has obvious difficulty in working out rules that hold the promise of stability over time. Indeed, we see a Court collectively changing its mind, fearlessly overruling itself when the occasion seems to call for a change.

(e) Is it possible that, in principle, *every* common law adjudication involves retroactive application of a rule?

(f) Are the retroactivity cases (and the *Sunburst-Moonburst* line as well) so intrinsically complicated that their complexity outruns any judge's conception of fairness? Is a rule of justice impossible in these cases? If so, is that a problem?

(g) Finally, if "justice" cannot be reduced to a rule or a formula in the prospectivity and retroactivity cases, does that mean that "justice" is not a useful argument for the attorneys who litigate such cases? Or, on the contrary, is "justice" the *only* useful argument?

Justice on Trial

CHAPTER EIGHT

United States v. Alstoetter

Nuremberg Military Tribunals
Case III (Nuremberg, Germany 1949)

JUDGE OSWALD ROTHAUG, DEFEN-
DANT:

[Judge Rothaug was one of l6 defendants tried
together by Branch III of the International Military
Tribunal at Nuremberg in 1947. The counts against
each defendant varied, but were drawn from four
overall counts: (1) participation in a common
design and conspiracy to commit war crimes and
crimes against humanity; (2) war crimes; (3) crimes
against humanity; and (4) membership in criminal
organizations. Rothaug was indicted under counts
(2), (3), and (4).

While most books written about the Nuremberg trials have focused upon the main war-crimes
trial at Nuremberg in September 1946 involving the
top 22 captured leaders of the Nazi Party—including Goering, Doenitz, Keitel, Ribbentrop, Hess,
Speer, and Rosenberg—there were over 3,000 war-
crimes prosecutions of German defendants in various countries in Europe following the Second
World War. (In addition, the Military Tribunal for
the Far East conducted many additional trials of
Japanese defendants.) The main trial of the Nazi
leaders resulted in a Judgment that upheld the
legality under international criminal law of the four
counts summarized above. Thus, by the time of
Judge Rothaug's trial in 1947, there was little room
left for the defendant to argue that the proceedings
themselves were legally suspect.

Yet, Judge Rothaug's trial, in particular,
raised an issue that was new in the Nuremberg
prosecutions: whether a judge could be guilty for

doing his job as a judge in the Third Reich. The
intense moral and intellectual dilemma had to be
faced by the judges on the court who had to reach
a judgment in Judge Rothaug's case. How can one
judge find another judge guilty for being a judge?
This dilemma became the subject of a dramatic
motion picture, *Judgment at Nuremberg,* with
Spencer Tracy playing the role of the American
judge on the court. The movie, although overly
long by today's standards, is well worth viewing,
if the viewer is willing to make some concessions
regarding historical accuracy. Hollywood obviously
took "license" with the facts in order to heighten
the dramatic effect, but was very true to the emotional content of the trial.

Oswald Rothaug was born on May 17, l897.
His education was interrupted from 19l6 to 19l8
while he was in the army. He passed the final law
examination in 1922 and the State examination for
the higher administration of justice in 1925.

Rothaug was a member of the National
Socialist Jurists' League and the National Socialist
Public Welfare Association. In his affidavit he
denied belonging to the SD. However, the testimony
of Elkar and his own admission on the witness
stand establishes that he was an "honorary collab-
orator" for the SD on legal matters. He was a
member of the Leadership Corps of the Nazi Party.

In December 1925 he began his career as a
jurist, first as an assistant to an attorney in Ans-
bach and later as an assistant judge at various
courts. In 1927 he became public prosecutor in

Hof in charge of criminal cases. From 1929 to 1933 he officiated as counsellor at the local court in Nuremberg. In June 1933 he became Senior Public Prosecutor in the public prosecution in Nuremberg. Here he was the official in charge of general criminal cases, assistant of the Chief Public Prosecutor handling examination of suspensions of proceedings and of petitions for pardon. From November to April 1937 he officiated as counsellor of the district court in Schweinfurt. He was legal advisor in the civil and penal chamber and at the Court of Assizes, as well as chairman of the lay assessors' court. From April 1937 to May 1943 he was director of the district court in Nuremberg, except for a period in August and September of 1939 when he was in the Wehrmacht. During this time he was chairman of the Court of Assizes, and Chief Justice of the Nuremberg Special Court.

From May 1943 to April 1945 he was Senior Public Prosecutor of the People's Court in Berlin. Here, as head of Department I he handled for a time cases of high treason in the southern Reich territory, and from January 1944 cases concerning the undermining of public morale in the Reich territory.

One of the cases Rothaug presided over was the Katzenberger Case in 1942. The report of the case, which follows, is a document that was introduced in evidence against Rothaug:]

The Katzenberger Case

13 March 1942

Nuremberg Special Court

Judge Rothaug, Presiding Judge:

In the name of the German People:

The Special court for the district of the Court of Appeal in Nuremberg with the District Court Nuremberg-Fuerth in the proceedings against Katzenberger, Lehmann Israel, commonly called Leo, merchant and head of the Jewish religious community in Nuremberg, and Seiler, Irene, owner of a photographic shop in Nuremberg, both at present in arrest pending trial, the charges being racial pollution and perjury—in public session of 13 March 1942, in the presence of—

> The President—Dr. Rothaug, Senior Judge of the District Court;
> Associate Judges—Dr. Ferber and Dr.
> Hoffmann, Judges of the District Court;
> Public Prosecutor for the Special Court—
> Markl:

Findings

1. The defendant Katzenberger is fully Jewish and a German national; he is a member of the Jewish religious community.

As far as his descent is concerned, extracts from the birth registers of the Jewish community at Massbach show that the defendant was born on 25 November 1873 as the son of Louis David Katzenberger, merchant, and his wife Helen née Adelberg. The defendant's father, born on 30 June 1838 at Massbach, was, according to an extract from the Jewish registers at Thundorf, the legitimate son of David Katzenberger, weaver, and his wife Karoline Lippig. The defendant's mother Lena Adelberg, born on 14 June 1847 at Aschbach, was, according to extracts from the birth register of the Jewish religious community of Aschbach, the legitimate daughter of Lehmann Adelberg, merchant, and his wife, Lea. According to the Thundorf register, the defendant's parents were married on 3 December 1867 by the district rabbi in Schweinfurt. The defendant's grandparents on his father's side were married, according to extracts from the Thundorf register, on 3 April 1832; those of his mother's side were married, according to an extract from the register of marriages of the Jewish religious community of Aschbach, on 14 August 1836. . . .

The defendant Katzenberger came to Nuremberg in 1912. Together with his brothers, David and Max, he ran a shoe shop until November 1938. The defendant married in 1906, and there are two children, ages 30 and 34.

Up to 1938 the defendant and his brothers, David, and Max, owned the property of 19 Spittlertorgraben in Nuremberg. There were offices and storerooms in the rear building, whereas the main building facing the street was an apartment house with several apartments.

The codefendant Irene Seiler arrived in 1932 to take a flat in 19 Spittlertorgraben, and the defendant Katzenberger has been acquainted with her since that date.

2. Irene Seiler, née Scheffler, is a German citizen of German blood.

Her descent is proved by documents relating to all four grandparents. She herself, her parents, and all her grandparents belong to the Protestant Lutheran faith. This finding of the religious background is based on available birth and marriage certificates of the Scheffler family which were made part of the trial. As far as descent is concerned therefore, there can be no doubt about Irene Seiler, nee Scheffler, being of German blood.

The defendant Katzenberger was fully cognizant of the fact that Irene Seiler was of German blood and of German nationality.

On 29 July 1939, Irene Scheffler married Johann Seiler, a commercial agent. There have been no children so far.

In her native city, Guben, the defendant attended secondary school and high school up to Unterprima [eighth grade of high school], and after that, for 1 year, she attended the Leipzig State Academy of Art and Book Craft.

She went to Nuremberg in 1932 where she worked in the photographic laboratory of her sister Hertha, which the latter had managed since 1928 as a tenant of 19 Spittlertorgraben. On 1 January 1938, she took over her sister's business at her own expense. On 24 February 1938, she passed her professional examination.

3. The defendant Katzenberger is charged with having had continual extra-marital sexual intercourse with Irene Seiler, née Scheffler, a German national of German blood. He is said to have visited Seiler frequently in her apartment in Spittlertorgraben up to March 1940, while Seiler visited him frequently, up to autumn 1938, in the offices of the rear building. Seiler, who is alleged to have got herself in a dependent position by accepting gifts of money from the defendant Katzenberger and by being allowed money from the defendant Katzenberger and by being allowed delay in paying her rent, was sexually amenable to Katzenberger. Thus, their acquaintance is said to have become of a sexual nature, in particular, sexual intercourse occurred. They are both said to have exchanged kisses sometimes in Seiler's flat and sometimes in Katzenberger's offices. Seiler is alleged to have often sat on Katzenberger's lap. On these occasions Katzenberger, in order to achieve sexual satisfaction, is said to have caressed and patted Seiler on her thighs through her clothes, clinging closely to Seiler, and resting his head on her bosom.

The defendant Katzenberger is charged with having committed this act of racial pollution by taking advantage of wartime conditions. Lack of supervision was in his favor, especially as he is said to have visited Seiler during the black-out. Moreover, Seiler's husband had been called up, and consequently surprise appearances of the husband were not to be feared.

The defendant Irene Seiler is charged with having, on the occasion of her interrogation by the investigating judge of the local Nuremberg Court on 9 July 1941, made deliberately untrue statements and affirmed under oath that this contact was without sexual motives and that she believed that to apply to Katzenberger as well.

Seiler, it is alleged, has thereby become guilty of being a perjuring witness.

[The applicable statutes are:

Law for the Protection of German Blood and Honor, §2:

Sexual intercourse (except in marriage) between Jews and German nationals of German or German-related blood is forbidden.

Decree Against Public Enemies:

Section 2
Crimes During Air Raids

Whoever commits a crime or offense against the body, life, or property, taking advantage of air raid protection measures, is punishable by hard labor of up to 15 years, or for life, and in particularly severe cases, punishable by death.

*   *   *   *   *   *   *

Section 4
Exploitation of the State of War a Reason for More Severe Punishment

Whoever commits a criminal act exploiting the extraordinary conditions caused by war is punishable beyond the regular punishment limits with hard labor of up to 15 years, or for life, or is punishable by death if the sound common sense of the people requires it on account of the crime being particularly despicable.]

The defendants have said this in their defense—

The defendant Seiler—When in 1932 she arrived in the photographic laboratory of her sister in Nuremberg, she was thrown completely on her own resources. Her sister returned to Guben, where she opened a studio as a photographer. Her father had recommended her to the landlord, the defendant Katzenberger, asking him to look after her and to assist her in word and deed. This was how she became closely acquainted with the Jew Katzenberger.

As time went on, Katzenberger did indeed become her adviser, helping her, in particular, in her financial difficulties. Delighted with the friendship and kindness shown her by Katzenberger she came to regard him gradually as nothing but a fatherly friend, and it never occurred to her to look upon him as a Jew. It was true that she called regularly in the storerooms of the rear house. She did so after office hours, because it was easier then to pick out shoes. It also happened that during these visits, and during those paid by Katzenberger to her flat, she kissed Katzenberger now and then and allowed him to kiss her. On these occasions she frequently would sit on Katzenberger's lap which was quite natural with her and had no ulterior motive. In no way should sexual motives be regarded as the cause of her actions. She always thought that Katzenberger's feelings for her were purely those of a concerned father.

Basing herself on this view she made the statement to the investigating judge on 9 July 1941 and affirmed under oath, that when exchanging those caresses neither she herself nor Katzenberger did so because of any erotic emotions.

The defendant Katzenberger—He denies having committed an offense. It is his defense that his relations with Frau Seiler were of a purely friendly nature. The Scheffler family in Guben had likewise looked upon his relations with Frau Seiler only from his point of view. That he continued his relations with Frau Seiler after 1933, 1935, and 1938, might be regarded as a wrong [*Unrecht*] by the NSDAP. The fact of his doing so, however, showed that his conscience was clear.

Moreover, their meetings became less frequent after the action against the Jews in 1938. After Frau Seiler got married in 1939, the husband often came in unexpectedly when he, Katzenberger, was with Frau Seiler in the flat. Never, however, did the husband surprise them in an ambiguous situation. In January or February 1940, at the request of the husband, he went to the Seiler's apartment twice to help them fill in their tax declarations. The last talk he ever had in the Seiler apartment took place in March 1940. On that occasion Frau Seiler suggested to him to discontinue his visits because of the representations made to her by the NSDAP, and she gave him a farewell kiss in the presence of her husband.

He never pursued any plans when being together with Frau Seiler, and he therefore could not have taken advantage of wartime conditions and the blackout.

II

The court has drawn the following conclusions from the excuses made by the defendant Katzenberger and the restrictions with which the defendant Seiler attempted to render her admissions less harmful:

When, in 1932, the defendant Seiler came to settle in Nuremberg at the age of 22, she was a fully grown and sexually mature young woman. According to her own admissions, credible in this case, she was not above sexual surrender in her relations with her friends.

In Nuremberg, when she had taken over her sister's laboratory in 19 Spittlertorgraben, she entered the immediate sphere of the defendant Katzenberger. During their acquaintance she gradually became willing, in a period of almost 10 years, to exchange caresses and, according to the confessions of both defendants, situations arose which can by no means be regarded merely as the outcome of fatherly friendliness. When she met Katzenberger in his offices in the rear building or in her flat, she sat often on his lap and, without a doubt, kissed his lips and cheeks. On these occasions Katzenberger, as he admitted himself, responded [to] these caresses by returning the kisses, putting his head on her bosom and patting her thighs through her clothes.

To assume that the exchange of these caresses, admitted by both of them, were on Katzenberger's part the expression of his fatherly feelings, on Seiler's part merely the actions caused by daughterly feelings with a strong emotional accent, as a natural result of the situation, is contrary to all experience of daily life. The subterfuge used by the defendant in this respect is in the view of the court simply a crude attempt to disguise as sentiment, free of all sexual lust, these actions with their strong sexual bias. In view of the character of the two defendants and basing itself on the evidence submitted, the court is firmly convinced that sexual motives were the primary cause for the caresses exchanged by the two defendants.

Seiler was usually in financial difficulties. Katzenberger availed himself of this fact to make her frequent gifts of money, and repeatedly gave her sums from 1 to 10 reichsmarks. In his capacity as administrator of the property on which Seiler lived and which was owned by the firm he was a partner of, Katzenberger often allowed her long delays in paying her rental debts. He often gave Seiler cigarettes, flowers, and shoes.

The defendant Seiler admits that she was anxious to remain in Katzenberger's favor. They addressed each other in the second person singular.

According to the facts established in the trial, the two defendants offered to their immediate surroundings, and in particular to the community of the house of 19 Spittlertorgraben, the impression of having an intimate love affair.

The witnesses Kleylein, Paul and Babette; Maesel, Johann; Heilmann, Johann; and Leibner, Georg observed frequently that Katzenberger and Seiler waved to each other when Seiler, through one of the rear windows of her flat, saw Katzenberger in his offices. The witnesses' attention was drawn particularly to the frequent visits paid by Seiler to Katzenberger's offices after business hours and on Sundays, as well as to the length of these visits. Everyone in the house came to know eventually that Seiler kept asking Katzenberger for money, and they all became convinced that Katzenberger, as the Jewish creditor, exploited sexually the poor financial situation of the German-blooded woman Seiler. The witness Heilmann, in a conversation with the witness Paul Kleylein, expressed his opinion of the matter to the effect that the Jew was getting a good return for the money he gave Seiler.

Nor did the two defendants themselves regard these mutual calls and exchange of caresses as being merely casual happenings of daily life, beyond reproach. According to statements made by the witnesses Babette and Paul Kleylein, they observed Katzenberger to show definite signs of fright when he saw that they had discovered his visits to Seiler's flat as late as 1940. The witnesses also observed that during the later period Katzenberger sneaked into Seiler's flat rather than walking in openly.

In August 1940, while being in the air-raid shelter, the defendant Seiler had to put up with the following reply given to her by Oestreicher, an inhabitant of the same house, in the presence of all other inhabitants: "I'll pay you back, you Jewish hussy." Seiler did not do anything to defend herself against this reproach later on, and all she did was to tell Katzenberger of this incident shortly after it had happened. Seiler has been unable to give an even remotely credible explanation why she showed this remarkable restraint in the face of so strong an expression of suspicion. Simply pointing out that her father, who is over seventy, had advised her not to take any steps against Oestreicher does not make more plausible her restraint shown in the face of the grave accusation made in public.

The statements made by Hans Zeuschel, assistant inspector of the criminal police, show that the two defendants did not admit from the very beginning the existing sexual situation as being beyond reproach. The fact that Seiler admitted the caresses bestowed on Katzenberger only after having been earnestly admonished, and the additional fact that Katzenberger, when interrogated by the police, confessed only when Seiler's statements were being shown to him, forces the conclusion that they both deemed it advisable to keep secret the actions for which they have been put on trial. This being so, the court is convinced that the two defendants made these statements only for reason of opportuneness intending to minimize and render harmless a situation which has been established by witnesses' testimony.

Seiler has also admitted that she did not tell her husband about the caresses exchanged with Katzenberger prior to her marriage—all she told him was that in the past Katzenberger had helped her a good deal. After getting married in July 1939 she gave Katzenberger a "friendly kiss" on the cheek in the presence of her husband on only one occasion, otherwise they avoided kissing each other when the husband was present.

In view of the behavior of the defendants toward each other, as repeatedly described, the court has become convinced that the relations between Seiler and Katzenberger which extended over a period of 10 years were of a purely sexual nature. This is the only possible explanation of the intimacy of their acquaintance. As there were a large number of circumstances favoring seduction no doubt it is possible that the defendant Katzenberger maintained continuous sexual intercourse with Seiler. The court considers as untrue Katzenberger's statement to the contrary that Seiler did not interest him sexually, and the statements made by the defendant Seiler in support of Katzenberger's defense the court considers as incompatible with all practical experience. They were obviously made with the purpose of saving Katzenberger from his punishment.

The court is therefore convinced that Katzenberger, after the Nuremberg laws had come into effect, had repeated sexual intercourse with Seiler, up to March 1940. It is not possible to say on what days and how often this took place.

The Law for the Protection of German Blood defines extramarital sexual intercourse as any form of sexual activity apart from the actual cohabitation with a member of the opposite sex which, by the method applied in place of actual intercourse, serves to satisfy the sexual instincts of at least one of the partners. The conduct to which the defendants admitted and which in the case of Katzenberger consisted in drawing Seiler close to him, kissing her, patting and caressing her thighs over her clothes, makes it clear that in a crude manner Katzenberger did to Seiler what is popularly called "*Abschmieren*" [petting]. It is obvious that such actions are motivated only by sexual impulses. Even if the Jew had only done these so-called "*Ersatzhandlungen*" [sexual acts in lieu of actual intercourse] to Seiler, it would have been sufficient to charge him with racial pollution in the full sense of the law.

The court, however, is convinced over and above this that Katzenberger, who admits that he is still capable of having sexual intercourse, had intercourse with Seiler throughout the duration of their affair. According to general experiences it is impossible to assume that in the 10 years of his tête-à-têtes with Seiler, which often lasted up to an hour, Katzenberger would have been satisfied with the "*Ersatzhandlungen*" which in themselves warranted the application of the law.

III

Thus, the defendant Katzenberger has been convicted of having had, as a Jew, extramarital sexual intercourse with a German citizen of German blood after the Law for the Protection of German Blood came into force, which according to section 7 of the law means after 17 September 1935. His actions were guided by a consistent plan which was aimed at repetition from the very beginning. He is therefore guilty of a continuous crime of racial pollution according to sections 2 and 5, paragraph 11 of the Law for the Protection of German Blood and German Honor of 15 September 1935.

A legal analysis of the established facts shows that in his polluting activities, the defendant Katzenberger, moreover, generally exploited the exceptional conditions arising out of wartime circumstances. Men have largely vanished from towns and villages because they have been called up or are doing other work for the armed forces which prevents them from remaining at home and maintaining order. It was these general conditions and wartime changes which the defendant exploited. As

he continued his visits to Seiler's apartment up to spring 1940, the defendant took into account the fact that in the absence of more stringent measures of control his practices could not, at least not very easily, be seen through. The fact that her husband had been drafted into the armed forces also helped him in his activities.

Looked at from this point of view, Katzenberger's conduct is particularly contemptible. Together with his offense of racial pollution he is also guilty of an offense under section 4 of the decree against public enemies. It should be noted her that the national community is in need of increased legal protection from all crimes attempting to destroy or undermine its inner solidarity.

On several occasions since the outbreak of war the defendant Katzenberger sneaked into Seiler's flat after dark. In these cases the defendant acted by exploiting the measures taken for the protection in air raids and by making use of the black-out. His chances were further improved by the absence of the bright street lighting which exists in the street along Spittlertorgraben in peacetime. In each case he exploited this fact being fully aware of its significance, thus during his excursions he instinctively escaped observation by people in the street.

The visits paid by Katzenberger to Seiler under the cover of the black-out served at least the purpose of keeping relations going. It does not matter whether during these visits extramarital sexual intercourse took place or whether they only conversed because the husband was present, as Katzenberger claims. The motion to have the husband called as a witness was therefore overruled. The court holds the view that the defendant's actions were deliberately performed as part of a consistent plan and amount to a crime against the body according to section 2 of the decree against public enemies. The law of 15 September 1935 was promulgated to protect German blood and German honor. The Jew's racial pollution amounts to a grave attack on the purity of German blood, the object of the attack being the body of a German woman. The general need for protection therefore makes appear as unimportant the behavior of the other partner in racial pollution who, however, is not liable to prosecution. The fact that racial pollution occurred at least up to 1939-1940 becomes clear from statements made by the witness Zeuschel to whom the defendant repeatedly and consistently admitted that up to the end of 1939 and the beginning of 1940 she was used to sitting on the Jew's lap and exchanging caresses as described above.

Thus, the defendant committed an offense also under section 2 of the decree against public enemies.

The personal character of the defendant likewise stamps him as a public enemy. The racial pollution practiced by him through many years grew, by exploiting wartime conditions, into an attitude inimical to the nation, into an attack on the security of the national community during an emergency.

This was why the defendant Katzenberger had to be sentenced, both on a crime of racial pollution and of an offense under sections 2 and 4 of the decree against public enemies, the two charges being taken in conjunction according to section 73 of the penal code.

In the view of the court the defendant Seiler realized that the contact which Katzenberger continuously had with her was of a sexual nature. The court has no doubt that Seiler actually had sexual intercourse with Katzenberger. Accordingly the oath given by her as a witness was to her knowledge and intention a false one, and she became guilty of perjury under sections 154 and 153 of the penal code.

IV

In passing sentence the court was guided by the following considerations:

The political form of life of the German people under national socialism is based on the community. One fundamental factor of the life of the national community is the racial problem. If a Jew commits racial pollution with a German woman, this amounts to polluting the German race and, by polluting a German woman, to a grave attack on the purity of German blood. The need for protection is particularly strong.

Katzenberger practiced pollution for years. He was well acquainted with the point of view taken by patriotic German men and women as regards racial problems and he knew that by his conduct the patriotic feelings of the German people were slapped in the face. Neither the National Socialist Revolution of 1933, nor the passing of the Law for the Protection of German Blood in 1935, neither the action against the Jews in 1938, nor the outbreak of war in 1939 made him abandon this activity of his.

As the only feasible answer to the frivolous

conduct of the defendant, the court therefore deems it necessary to pronounce the death sentence as the heaviest punishment provided by section 4 of the decree against public enemies. His case must be judged with special severity, as he had to be sentenced in connection with the offense of committing racial pollution, under section 2 of the decree against public enemies, the more so, if taking into consideration the defendant's personality and the accumulative nature of his deeds. This is why the defendant is liable to the death penalty which the law provides for such cases as the only punishment. Dr. Baur, the medical expert, describes the defendant as fully responsible.

Accordingly, the court has pronounced the death sentence. It was also considered necessary to deprive him of his civil rights for life, as specified in sections 32–34 of the penal code. When imposing punishment on the defendant Seiler, her personal character was the first matter to be considered. For many years, Seiler indulged in this contemptible love affair with the Jew Katzenberger. The national regeneration of the German people in 1933 was altogether immaterial to her in her practices, nor was she in the least influenced when the Law for the Protection of German Blood and Honor was promulgated in September 1935. It was, therefore, nothing but an act of frivolous provocation on her part to apply for membership in the NSDAP in 1937, which she obtained.

When by initiating legal proceedings against Katzenberger the German people were to be given satisfaction for the Jew's polluting activities, the defendant Seiler did not pay the slightest heed to the concerns of State authority or to those of the people and decided to protect the Jew.

Taking this over-all situation into consideration the court considered a sentence of 4 years of hard labor as having been deserved by the defendant.

An extenuating circumstance was that the defendant, finding herself in an embarrassing situation, affirmed her—as she knew—false statement with an oath. Had she spoken the truth she could have been prosecuted for adultery, aiding, and soliciting. The court therefore reduced the sentence by half despite her guilt, and imposed as the appropriate sentence 2 years of hard labor. (Sec. 157, par. I, No. 1, of the Penal Code.)

On account of the lack of honor of which she was convicted, she had to be deprived of her civil rights too. This has been decided for a duration of 2 years.

The 3 months the defendant Seiler spent in arrest pending trial will be taken into consideration in her sentence.

Costs will be charged to the defendants.

[Signed] ROTHAUG

DR. FERBER

DR. HOFFMANN

Certified:

Nuremberg, 23 March 1942

The Registrar of the Office of the Special
Court for the district of the Nuremberg Court
of Appeal with the District Court Nuremberg-
Fuerth

[Stamp]

District Court   [Illegible signature]

Nuremberg-Fuerth   Justizinspektor

[Editor's Note: The above document was introduced into evidence before the Nuremberg Military Tribunal. We turn now to the litigation itself:]

Opening Statement on Behalf of Defendant Rothaug

DR. KOESSL. May it please the Tribunal. If I correctly understand the unuttered yet cogent logic of the charges listed in the indictment, the effect and example of that legal system to which the prosecution tries to attach the stigma of a criminal government institution begins with the Rothaug case. The evidence against him, out of proportion considering the entire framework of the indictment, is in contrast to his mere functional position, based on his activities as judge and prosecutor. . . .

[T]he activity of a judge at the Special Court or a Reich public prosecutor is limited to the application of the law which is based on the official Reich legislation in the field of criminal law. I shall demonstrate that this Reich legislation in all its harshness has, in its purpose, neither lost nor limited its character of purely criminal law and that, on this point, it has not been misinterpreted as clearly proved by the literature on the subject and the jurisdiction by the supreme judicial authorities and others.

Here must be proved a fact evident in itself, namely that judges and prosecutors in the same position as Rothaug were never and in no context expected to have objects alien to the field of crim-

inal law in carrying out their official duties.

Records of sentences already submitted and others still to be submitted will prove that this had in no way been intended.

This touches on the legal question, whether official functions resting on the official Reich legislation which, up to this very moment, is covered in international law by the principle of nationality and sovereignty, functions which were carried out in public, may be conceived as actions of persecution on racial, religious, or political grounds and may be treated as being on the same level as actions which were carried out secretly and without control, and which could be recognized as wrong already by their cruelty and severity by every person concerned as offending against justice and law.

Here, I wish to convince the court that offenses of the latter kind, if they ever did happen within the legal sphere, could and should only be known to the immediate participants but not to persons who held positions like the defendant Rothaug.

In the concrete reflection on the relationship to the law of the position of judges and likewise prosecutors, it is of decisive importance to elucidate in public law that the German judge, under any regime, had merely to examine whether a law had been announced in accordance with rules and regulations, whereas an examination from other points of view was outside his jurisdiction. In this context it is further necessary to elucidate the significance and import of the judge being subject to the law and the meaning of a sentence in the sense of German public law, especially in relationship to the legislative and executive power in an authoritarian state, thus to the governing power.

Here we cannot omit to clarify the basic legal principles and corresponding regulations which determine this relationship or to prove the practical application based on files. Thus, the question of the judge's subjection to the law calls for a clarification of the consequences on his task resulting thereof. It necessitates the recognition of the law as a form of expression of justice, as part of the legal system and as immediate emanation of the ruling state doctrine at any given time, as well as the recognition of the judge's actual position in this legal system. Therefore, it is also necessary to show in a condensed form the general basis and principle of the legal doctrine which since 1933 was decisive for the German judge in establishing the intentions of the law in a concrete individual case.

The accusations which have been made in general or in individual cases concerning Rothaug's method of handling proceedings or which have been connected with such proceedings become meaningless or lose in importance if their explanation is tackled in general from the angle of the correct basic procedure regulations or from the available records of individual proceedings. This leads, as a matter of course, to a basic discussion of the individual cases which have been particularly stressed by the prosecution, and which lie in the direction of the prosecution's main thrust. No one knows better than the judge the human inadequacy and fallibility, because by the very nature of his profession he deals with that aspect of life. Thus, he would be the last to believe himself immune from human error, least of all at a time of intellectual revolution and under the effect of the very highest wartime pressure. Nevertheless, I beg the Tribunal not to think me presumptuous if I try to prove that the sentences pronounced by the Special Court at Nuremberg were in keeping with the basic principles of jurisdiction of the Reich courts, and that among thousands of cases only very rarely one has been successfully contested or otherwise amended. . . .

[Editor's Note: In the voluminous evidence introduced at the Nuremberg trials was included the "Judges' Letters" issued by the Reich Minister of Justice, Dr. Thierack, sent to all German judges and public prosecutors. In Thierack's words, "these Judges' Letters shall mainly contain decisions which I deem to be especially worthy of interest, because of their findings or argumentations. By these decisions I want to show how better findings could and ought to have been arrived at. . . . The contents of the letters are confidential; they are handed to each judge and public prosecutor by the chief against receipt."

The first volume of Letters was issued in October 1942, months *after* the Katzenberger Case. Nevertheless, they tended to show to the Tribunal the context of criminal trials at the time. They tended to show the exhortations upon judges by the Reich Minister of Justice. Only the case as described by the Reich Minister, and only his comments on that case, are reproduced here. However, the case we include here was one that had occurred in 1940 and may have been familiar to Judge Rothaug. Do you think that this evidence, introduced by the Prosecution, helps the case against Judge Rothaug? Or would it be useful to his defense?]

Introduced into Evidence Against Defendant Rothaug:

Refusal by a School Child to Give the German Salute
Decree by the Court of Guardians of
21 September 1940

An 11-year-old girl is conspicuous in school through continuously refusing the German salute. She bases this on her religious convictions and cites in explanation some passages from the Bible. In matters concerning the Fuehrer she appears altogether disinterested.

The parents, who also have a 6-year-old daughter, approve of this behavior of the child and obstinately decline to influence the child to the contrary. They also refuse to give the German salute and point to the passage in the Bible, "Do nothing with an upraised hand for it displeases the Lord." They adhere to this in spite of advice by the court and the director of the school. The mother refuses altogether to discuss it with the child. The father is willing to do so, but says that the child should decide herself. The parents prove themselves to be adversaries of the National Socialist State also in other respects. They possess no swastika flag. They did not enter their child for the Hitler Youth: they were expelled from the National Socialist Public Welfare Association, because they will not support the collections, despite an adequate income of the man. Nevertheless they deny being adversaries of the movement. The juvenile board suggested that the parents should be deprived of the right to bring up the two children on account of their attitude.

The guardianship court refused to carry out this proposal and merely made an order for supervision by a probation officer.

In the explanation, the court stated that it had not been proved that the parents were adversaries of the National Socialist movement or that they really had fought against it; they were merely "not sympathetic to the movement and not willing to promote it."

It was stated furthermore that "the parents are only in so far responsible for their attitude toward the National Socialist movement as they act contrary to the relevant penal laws." The parents must realize that the children must be brought up in the National Socialist spirit and that the schools have instructions to educate them in that spirit. If the parents are not willing to bring up their children in that spirit themselves, or if they believe that their religious views do not allow them to bring up their children in that spirit, the least that must be demanded from them is not to oppose National Socialist education at school. Owing to the fact that the child is well brought up in other respects and that—judging from the court's personal impression—the parents are "of absolutely reliable character," it may be assumed that in future they will not give the school any trouble with respect to education.

The court of appeal rescinded the decision of the guardianship court and deprived the parents of the right to look after their children, as they are not fit to bring them up.

Opinion of the Reich Minister of Justice

The judge at the guardianship court in his decision misunderstood the principles of National Socialist education of youth.

Today, the education of German youth is based on the home, the school, and the Hitler Youth (law regarding the Hitler Youth of 1 December 1936). They have to cooperate and each of them has to carry out that part of the educational task allotted to him by the community. The aim of this joint work consists in educating the young people in body, in mind, and morally in the National Socialist spirit for service to the nation and for the community.

This aim can be reached only by joint cooperation of the home, the school, and the Hitler Youth. Any opposition to and any deviation from this education endanger the common aim. An essential part of this education as well as a particular responsibility have been laid into the hands of the parents. They are united with the child by ties of blood. The child lives close to them and constantly looks to the habits and the example of the parents. To educate means to guide. To guide means to set an example by your way of life. The child models his way of life on the example of his parents. What the child hears and sees there, especially in early youth, it becomes accustomed to by degrees and accepts it as a rule of life. Therefore, the educational aim of the National Socialist State can only be achieved if the parents, conscientiously and aware of their responsibility, give their child in thought and deed a model example for its behavior in the community life of our nation. To this education of German man or woman belongs also

the imparting of respect and awe for the symbols of the State and the movement at an early stage. Here, too, the community expects active cooperation on the part of the parents. A reserved neutral attitude is as harmful as attacking the National Socialist idea. Thus, indifference to the training of a patriotic member of the national community means neglect of duty on the part of the parents and endangers the educational aim for the child, even if this is not immediately apparent in each case. For this reason, it is not enough that in the present case the parents will not oppose the school in the future; they are supposed to cooperate actively in their children's education as a whole. Thus, the responsibility of the parents does not start where its violation becomes punishable. The child is often being endangered if the parents consciously oppose the educational work of the community. That was the case here. Who continue to refuse the German salute on account of erroneous religious beliefs, who separates himself from the great social work of construction of national socialism without any reason, and who purposely withholds his children from the Hitler Youth and never takes advice, of him it can no longer be said that he merely "does not sympathize" with the movement and does not promote it. He attacks it by his opposition and is its adversary. This is proved by his convictions and by his inner attitude.

Thus, the judge of the guardianship court ought to have deprived them of the right to look after their children simply by consideration of the fact that parents, who openly profess the ideas of the "Jehovah's Witnesses," are not fit to educate their children in the spirit of national socialism.

Editor's Digression: What Was Happening in the United States

[Not mentioned at the Nuremberg prosecution of Judge Rothaug were the following developments in the United States at roughly the same time that the Katzenberger Case was developing in Germany. In the year 1940 of the decision in the German guardianship court, the United States Supreme Court handed down a decision in a case of a 12-year-old girl and her 10-year-old brother who were expelled from the public schools of Minersville, Pennsylvania, for refusing to pledge allegiance to the American flag as part of the daily school exercise. Their father had to put them into private schools, and because of the financial burden, sued the school authorities to enjoin them from contin-

uing to exact participation in the flag-salute ceremony as a condition of his children's attendance
in public school. The family were "Jehovah's Witnesses." Mr. Justice Frankfurter, for the majority
of the Court, said that "The ultimate foundation
of a free society is the binding tie of cohesive
sentiment," and that "National unity is the basis
of national security." The Court upheld the right
of the school board to expel the students. *Minersville School District v. Gobitis*, 310 U.S. 586 (1940).
The decision was overruled three years later in *West
Virginia State Board of Education v. Barnette*, 319
U.S. 624 (1943), with Justice Frankfurter dissenting.[1]]

*Introduced into Evidence Against
Defendant Rothaug:*

Newspaper Report of the Katzenberger Trial

The Nuremberg newspaper, *Der Stuermer*, for
April 2, 1942, contained an article about the Katz-
enberger trial, entitled "DEATH TO THE RACE
DEFILER," excerpts from which are as follows:

Sentenced to Death! (p. 3, col. 1)

When the court reenters the courtroom
to announce the verdict one can already see
from the earnest looks of the judges that the
fate of the Talmudic criminal has been sealed.
As a race defiler and public parasite
Katzenberger is sentenced to death.
The co-defendant Irene S. gets 2 years
hard labor and loss of civil rights for perjury.
President of the District Court of Appeal R.
points to words in the findings of the verdict,
which prove to what extent the German judges
are imbued with the tremendous importance
of the racial laws. The president brands the
depravity of the defendant and stamps him
as an evil public parasite. "Racial defilement
is worse than murder! Entire generations will
be affected by it into the remotest future!"
President of the District Court of Appeal R.
in his speech also refers to the guilt of Jewry

in this war. "If today German soldiers are
bleeding to death, then the guilt falls upon
that race which from the very beginning
strived for Germany's ruin, and still hopes
today that the German people will not emerge
from this struggle." In the case of Katzenberger the court had to pronounce the death
sentence. The physical destruction of the per-
petrator was the only possible atonement.

The end (p. 3, col. 1)

With the findings of the verdict the sentence of the Special Court has become effective.

*Why the "Stuermer" describes the Katzen-
berger trial in detail* (p. 3, col. 2)

* * * * * * * *

The Jew Katzenberger was sentenced to
death as a race defiler and public parasite.
This sentence (it is not the first of this kind
in the Reich) was pronounced in Nuremberg
and thus honors the city whose name was
bestowed upon the racial laws of 15 September 1935. For the "Stuermer" however, this
sentence signifies a special satisfaction, because it was the "Stuermer" which, in a
special edition of the year 1938, had demanded the death penalty for race defilers.

* * * * * * * *

If today Jewish race defilers are really
sentenced to death, then this proves that the
"Stuermer" has been a good prophet for
many years.

**Extracts From the Testimony of Defendant
Rothaug: Direct Examination**

DR. KOESSL (Counsel for defendant Rothaug). It
has been asserted that you had coupled together
the Katzenberger and Seiler proceedings in order
to exclude the Seiler woman as a witness. What
was the situation there?

DEFENDANT ROTHAUG. Under the German
Code of Procedure, there are always as many penal
proceedings pending as there are defendants. Under
certain conditions, such penal proceedings can be
tried together for the purpose of uniform trial and
decision. That is what we call joinder of penal
cases. That joinder may be decided by the court,
concerning cases which are pending with it separately. But such joinder may be established by the

---

[1] For further details on *Gobitis* and *Barnette* and
a critical asssessment of the issues raised by these and
other cases, see G. FLETCHER, LOYALTY (Oxford University Press, forthcoming 1992). Fletcher's book is one
of the rare philosophic accounts of loyalty.

prosecution itself by one combined indictment. That was what was done in the Katzenberger-Seiler case. The prosecution, by filing one indictment for both defendants, had already established the joinder prior to the files reaching the court. The joinder of the two cases was therefore neither due to a file prepared by me, nor to a file prepared by the court.

DR. KOESSL. Would it have been possible for the prosecutor to proceed differently?

DEFENDANT ROTHAUG. Naturally. He could have filed separate indictments. The question was merely whether that would have been correct from the technical point of procedure.

DR. KOESSL. What are the legal provisions on which a joinder of penal cases is based at the Special Court?

DEFENDANT ROTHAUG. A joinder is based on article XV, section 2 of the competency order.

DR. KOESSL. When do the conditions exist for a joinder, such as demanded by the law?

DEFENDANT ROTHAUG. Such conditions can arise from all sorts of situations. They exist in particular if one offense developed from another offense, and if the judgment has to be based on the same facts. That was the case in the Katzenberger-Seiler affairs, which we have been discussing.

DR. KOESSL. What was the reason for the prosecutor to connect the two cases?

DEFENDANT ROTHAUG. Both cases, as is proved clearly by the opinion of the court, had to be decided on the basis of the same facts. Therefore, a joinder was altogether natural and corresponded to the customary treatment such as was applied in other cases as well.

DR. KOESSL. What was the legal nature of such joinder?

DEFENDANT ROTHAUG. It was purely a measure of expediency.

DR. KOESSL. Is a defendant entitled to ask for not combining his case with that of another defendant because in the case of a joinder he loses evidence?

DEFENDANT ROTHAUG. The defendant does not have such a claim. According to the general legal doctrine, which existed prior to 1933, a joinder is admissible even if, as a result of a joinder, one

codefendant can no longer appear as a witness. But if it is decisive that the codefendant should appear as the witness, the two cases can be separated after all so as to have an opportunity to examine the codefendant as a witness. But that is left entirely to the discretion of the court, and the defendant has no claim to have that question decided in one definite way.

DR. KOESSL. When several penal cases are combined, does that mean that all possibility is excluded to examine one of the codefendants in the same proceedings as a witness? I would like you to supplement your previous answer and to tell us whether it is possible temporarily to separate proceedings.

DEFENDANT ROTHAUG. Such temporary separation is allowed expressly by jurisdiction. Therefore, during one proceeding, temporarily a separation can be ordered. One codefendant can be examined as a witness, and after he has been examined the case can be recombined.

DR. KOESSL. Did anybody at any time—be it the prosecutor, the defense counsel, or the defendant—during the trial make a motion to separate proceedings?

DEFENDANT ROTHAUG. Such a motion was not made either at the trial or outside of it by anybody. Not even the mere idea of doing that was ever mentioned, and the reason was that at that time nobody regarded the joinder of the two cases as a defect.

DR. KOESSL. In the case under discussion, was it likely that the chances of the two defendants might be affected by joining their cases?

DEFENDANT ROTHAUG. As I have stated before, the legal position of the defendants could not be affected, and their chances were not affected either. If one had thought that their chances might be affected, I think in that case the two defense counsel would have made a motion to have the two proceedings separated. If one wishes to judge the situation properly, one has to bear in mind the following: that is to say, one has to think of the situation such as it would have been if the Seiler woman had not been a codefendant but a witness. In that case, she would have made no different statements at the trial than she had made at her interrogation under oath before the investigating judge, for she made the same statements as a codefendant, and we had to discuss her statements under oath before the investigating judge from every point of view for the purpose of the verdict. What difference would there have been, as far as our judgment was concerned, if she had repeated the same statements at the trial in her capacity as a witness? The real problems of the proceedings would and could not have been affected in any way by that.

* * * * * * * * *

PRESIDING JUDGE BRAND. Were tickets issued for admission to the trial?

DEFENDANT ROTHAUG. Yes, Your Honor.

DR. KOESSL. I shall come back to those tickets later. What importance had to be attributed to the fact that a trial was held in front of such a large public?

DEFENDANT ROTHAUG. Under the German Code of Penal Procedure, the fact that the public is admitted to a trial constitutes one guaranty that the proceedings will be conducted in an orderly manner.

DR. KOESSL. Did Katzenberger have a defense counsel?

DEFENDANT ROTHAUG. Yes, he had.

DR. KOESSL. Was that defense counsel a Jew?

DEFENDANT ROTHAUG. Yes, he was.

DR. KOESSL. Did the Seiler woman have a defense counsel, too?

DEFENDANT ROTHAUG. Yes, she had.

DR. KOESSL. What sort of a man was the defense counsel for Seiler? Was he a National Socialist, or what was he?

DEFENDANT ROTHAUG. I knew him. He wasn't a National Socialist for certain. My impression was that he was entirely uninterested in politics and devoted to his profession.

* * * * * * * * *

DR. KOESSL. Now, we're going to examine the statements by the witness Seiler. The statements by the witnesses Ferber, Seiler, and Dr. Baur are criticizing your method of conducting the Katzenberger case.

According to the testimony of the witness Seiler, you addressed the audience and said—"The Jews are our misfortune. It is the fault of the Jews that this war happened. Those who have contact with the Jews will perish through them. Racial

defilement is worse than murder, and poisons the blood for generations. It can only be atoned by exterminating the offender."

Did you make remarks of that kind, or of a similar nature, or what exactly did happen?

DEFENDANT ROTHAUG. That expression— "The Jews are our misfortune" or "It is the fault of the Jews that the war happened," or "Those who have contact with the Jews will perish through them"—those expressions are well known slogans from the *Stuermer*, which I think appeared in large letters in every issue of the *Stuermer.*

PRESIDING JUDGE BRAND. Mr. Witness, the only question before you is whether you used, in substance, the language which was attributed to you. You may answer that question. We are not concerned with who else used the same language.

DEFENDANT ROTHAUG. Neither on duty nor in my private life did I use such generalizations, but the facts which have been discussed here, and which were mentioned in that issue of the *Stuermer*, concerning all that I would like to give my view on one point. That is the question as to war guilt. I can remember more or less exactly—and that idea is also mentioned in the opinion of the judgment in the same way in which I expressed it at the trial. Naturally, it was not the purpose of the trial to prove that it was the fault of the Jews that war had broken out. The point was, however, this. As is known, both defendants tried to make the situations which incriminated them appear more harmless, as if their relations had been everyday matters. And in that connection, I remember that I put it to Katzenberger that, particularly here in Nuremberg, he must have known that such relations were particularly dangerous even if the relations had been harmless, because, ever since 1933, he had observed the developments, and then, finally, war had broken out and the Jews were held responsible for the war, and all these events should have caused him to be wise and to abandon relations which were bound to endanger him, even if those relations had been only harmless-and if they had been harmless it would, after all, have been easy to abandon them. . . .

DR. KOESSL. Witness, you came to the explanation of the connections where you have made the so-called speeches to the audience. Will you explain the purpose and the connections for making these so-called speeches?

DEFENDANT ROTHAUG. I base myself on the

fact that the reason for the trials being public according to the German rules of procedure was that the conscience of law should be strengthened and that the population should be educated in the meaning of the laws. Our sphere dealt with entirely new legislation, new in consideration of the basis on which it was founded and of its purposes; for that reason—and of course one has to consider that this new legislation provided severe and most severe consequences, and that makes it understandable why I—and that was with approval of all interested offices of the administration of justice—was of the position that it was necessary to bring as quickly and as effectively as possible this legislation before the population in order to warn them because that warning in a certain sense is a justification of the severe sentence, particularly the extent of the sentence; and that explains why I had the intention to conduct my trials before the public and as many people as possible and as broadly as possible. That also explains why it was not only my intention to describe the bare legal facts but the offenses regardless in what field they were committed and to explain them from the point of view of the doctrine of the State and from the points of view of the legal system and political point of view. The guiding thought for me was that it was our duty, and at the same time, our justification before the public, to explain that the sentence pronounced in any individual case was the direct consequence of the legislation provided therefore. It has to be added that fundamentally according to German rules of procedure, the sentence can only be based on the entirety of the trial; that is to say, that all points of view which are concerned with the penalty or the extent of penalty have to be discussed in all details during the trial because that alone puts the defendant in a position to recognize the main points which may be directed against him; and I also want to emphasize that at no time were lectures made for their own purpose, but that such statements were made in connection with the testimony of the defendant or the witnesses at the time and at the place where it seemed proper.

DR. KOESSL. Ferber charges you generally, and particularly, in the case Katzenberger.

DEFENDANT ROTHAUG. I intended to add, that it is therefore quite certain that at that session I also stated my opinion concerning the problem of race defilement on the basis of the doctrine of the State and on the basis of the legal system, and on the basis of our political and legal foundations. That I also discussed the danger in the manner that these things were regarded at that time according to the legal situation, the danger arising from the mixture of races to coming generations, that I consider to be a fact. What words I used and what thoughts I may have expressed in detail in discussing these matters, that, of course, I could no longer tell today. But what I object to is the assertion that these may have been statements of the level of the "*Stuermer*;" and with absolute certainty I should like to exclude the possibility that in that connection I demanded any physical destruction. That, according to the law, would not have been possible. That, of course, based on the fact of the war which went far beyond any racial point of view.

* * * * * * * *

DR. KOESSL. The witness Seiler in her direct examination testified that she and the defendant Katzenberger had denied under oath at various times those relations. Was Katzenberger heard under oath?

DEFENDANT ROTHAUG. No, he was not heard under oath. That was not admissible under German law because German law holds that the defendant had to be entirely free to use all possibilities for his defense. That is considered a certain guarantee to aid in finding the truth.

DR. KOESSL. The witness Seiler also stated in her direct examination that the judge, Rothaug, used the assumption of her guilt as the basis for the entire conduct of the trial. The reason for the discrimination in her opinion had been that Rothaug did not want to hear any answer. Did you examine the witness Seiler thoroughly?

DEFENDANT ROTHAUG. Of course, she was examined thoroughly, and I may point out—and that can be found also from reading the opinion—that this was a so-called case of circumstantial evidence, that a large number of individual situations of more or less importance were compiled in order to make it possible to reconstruct the circumstances which were of importance for the evaluation; and it was always like that, and it was no different in this Katzenberger-Seiler case, that I discussed with the defendants every phase and every little detail; not only in order to completely clarify any particular action, that of course, was the main purpose; but beyond that it was of importance to establish what the point of view of the defendants was, and how they described matters; that is the reason why that matter took a day and a half, and in addition to that, after the examination of every witness who offered something new, again the two defendants were heard thoroughly concerning the new situation. At any rate the evidence which was taken as the basis for the judgment, was discussed in all possible detail.

* * * * * * * *

DR. KOESSL. Among the judges concerned during the deliberations, was there any doubt about the guilt of Katzenberger?

DEFENDANT ROTHAUG. I remember the deliberations very well. That conference was peaceful as could be; for in the course of the trial, which lasted a day and a half, the entire occurrence, as far as the facts were concerned based upon the statements of the defendants and on what the witnesses testified to, had developed into such a clear picture that there could not have been any differences of opinion; and, after a very short time—and I remember that very well also—we arrived at a decision and actually started to write the judgment down, but considering the importance of the case, we extended the time for deliberations so that the impression should not be given that we wanted to pronounce a hasty decision. There were no difficulties at all, the reason being that the facts themselves were of compelling logic, and that anything else which was the consequence of the facts just arose from them logically and in the way one had to evaluate those things at that time, and of course, we could not evaluate it based upon any different philosophy.

DR. KOESSL. Which motions were made by the defense counsel?

DEFENDANT ROTHAUG. I would like to say with certainty that one of the defense counsel, without being able to tell who it was, made an attempt in the direction of a lenient sentence, and he was trying to combat its evaluation as a serious case, but there was no doubt left about the basic facts in the case. That is the way I remember the case, and it must have been like that; and that was also manifest by the calm deliberations where no points of argument came in existence.

DR. KOESSL. Was any one of the associate judges of a different opinion concerning the extent of punishment? Did any one of them vote against the

death penalty, for instance?

DEFENDANT ROTHAUG. The core of the question from the very beginning was the following.

PRESIDING JUDGE BRAND. Let me ask you a question. Did all of the judges vote for the death penalty? Answer yes or no.

DEFENDANT ROTHAUG. Yes, absolutely.

PRESIDING JUDGE BRAND. Next question.

DR. KOESSL. At that time, among the jurists around you—but those who were not in direct contact with the case—were there any discussions about that sentence?

DEFENDANT ROTHAUG. In no way at all. That sentence was never criticized in any way or considered doubtful by jurists who were not connected with the case which would normally be possible.

Final Statements of the Defendants

PRESIDING JUDGE BRAND. The record will show that the defendants have already had the opportunity to testify at length under oath, and they are now accorded the privilege, in each instance, of making an unsworn statement for the benefit of the Tribunal.

DEFENDANT ROTHAUG. I served my country throughout my life and in whatever position I was assigned to, in faithfulness, with a pure heart, and without malice. Seen from my present position you might consider this wrong, and you could say I and all those who surrounded me should have been more suspicious of developments as they took place. This prognosis in retrospect is just as convincing as it is cheap. Nobody in our position at that time could be of the opinion that the State which we served could be accused of being altogether illegal and that the war that it waged was a war of aggression, as is demonstrated today to all the world. Therefore, it is no accident and no excuse that, apart from defending myself against the flood of personal defamations which I received from the circle of my previous friends and assistants, I am now anxious to prove to you that both in the service as a judge and prosecutor, I applied the laws of my country in the manner in which they were intended, to the best of my conscience and belief. We were guided by the practice of the Reich Supreme Court and went the same way which was taken by the remaining 60 to 80 Special Courts in the Reich. We were not specialists in crimes against humanity, and no proof has been furnished in any

single case that, in any connection, we had applied
an illegal method.

Opinion and Judgment of the Military Tribunal

THE DEFENDANT ROTHAUG:

The defendant is charged under counts two,
three, and four of the indictment. Under count
four he is charged with being a member of the
Party Leadership Corps. He is not charged with
membership in the SD. The proof as to count four
establishes that he was *Gauwalter* of the Lawyers'
League. The Lawyers' League was a formation of
the Party and not a part of the Leadership Corps
as determined by the International Military Tribunal in the case against Goering, et al.

As to counts two and four of the indictment,
from the evidence submitted, the Tribunal finds the
defendant not guilty. The question of the defendant's guilt as to count three of the indictment
remains to be determined.

Sometime in the first half of the year 1941
the witness Groben issued a warrant of arrest
against Katzenberger, who was accused of having
had intimate relations with the photographer Seiler.
According to the results of the police inquiry, actual
intercourse had not been proved, and Katzenberger
denied the charge. Upon Groben's advice, Katzenberger agreed that he would not move against
the warrant of arrest at that time but would await
the results of further investigation. These further
investigations were very lengthy, although Groben
pressed the public prosecutor for speed. The police,
in spite of their efforts, were unable to get further
material evidence, and it became apparent that the
way to clarify the situation was to take the sworn
statement of Seiler, and this was done.

In her sworn statement she said that Katzenberger had known both her and her family for
many years before she had come to Nuremberg
and that his relationship to her was a friendly and
fatherly one and denied the charge of sexual intercourse. The evidence also showed that Katzenberger had given Seiler financial assistance on various occasions and that he was administrator of
the property where Seiler lived, which was owned
by a firm of which he was a partner. Upon Seiler's
statement, Groben informed Dr. Herz, counsel for
Katzenberger, of the result and suggested that it
was the right time to move against the warrant of
arrest.

When this was done, Rothaug learned of it

and ordered that the Katzenberger case be transferred from the criminal divisional court to the
Special Court. The first indictment was withdrawn,
and another indictment was prepared for the Special Court.

The witness Markl states that Rothaug dominated the prosecution, especially through his close
friendship with the senior public prosecutor, Dr.
Schroeder, who was the superior of Markl.

The indictment before the Special Court was
prepared according to the orders of Rothaug, and
Katzenberger was not charged only with race defilement in this new indictment, but there was also
an additional charge under the decree against public
enemies, which made the death sentence permissible. The new indictment also joined the Seiler
woman on a charge of perjury. The effect of joining
Seiler in the charge against Katzenberger was to
preclude her from being a witness for the defendant,
and such a combination was contrary to established
practice. Rothaug at this time told Markl that there
was sufficient proof of sexual intercourse between
Seiler and Katzenberger to convince him, and that
he was prepared to condemn Katzenberger to death.
Markl informed the Ministry of Justice of Rothaug's intended procedure against Katzenberger
and was told that if Rothaug so desired it, the
procedure would be approved.

Prior to the trial, the defendant Rothaug
called on Dr. Armin Baur, medical counsellor for
the Nuremberg Court, as the medical expert for
the Katzenberger case. He stated to Baur that he
wanted to pronounce a death sentence and that it
was, therefore, necessary for the defendant to be
examined. This examination, Rothaug stated, was
a mere formality since Katzenberger "would be
beheaded anyhow." To the doctor's reproach that
Katzenberger was old, and it seemed questionable
whether he could be charged with race defilement,
Rothaug stated:

It is sufficient for me that the swine said
that a German girl had sat upon his lap.

The trial itself, as testified to by many witnesses, was in the nature of a political demonstra-
tion. High Party officials attended, including Reich
Inspector Oexle. Part of the group of Party officials
appeared in uniform.

During the proceedings, Rothaug tried with
all his power to encourage the witnesses to make
incriminating statements against the defendants.
Both defendants were hardly heard by the court.

Their statements were passed over or disregarded. During the course of the trial, Rothaug took the opportunity to give the audience a National Socialist lecture on the subject of the Jewish question. The witnesses found great difficulty in giving testimony because of the way in which the trial was conducted, since Rothaug constantly anticipated the evaluation of the facts and gave expression to his own opinions.

Because of the way the trial was conducted, it was apparent that the sentence which would be imposed was the death sentence.

After the introduction of evidence was concluded, a recess was taken, during which time the prosecutor Markl appeared in the consultation room and Rothaug made it clear to him that he expected the prosecution to ask for a death sentence against Katzenberger and a term in the penitentiary for Seiler. Rothaug at this time also gave him suggestions as to what he should include in his arguments.

The reasons for the verdict were drawn up by Ferber. They were based upon the notes of Rothaug as to what should be included. Considerable space is given to Katzenberger's ancestry and the fact that he was of the Mosaic faith, although that fact was admitted by Katzenberger. Such space is also given to the relationship between Katzenberger and Seiler. That there was no proof of actual sexual intercourse is clear from the opinion. The proof seems to have gone little farther than the fact that the defendant Seiler had at times sat upon Katzenberger's lap and that he had kissed her, which facts were also admitted. Many assumptions were made in the reasons stated which obviously are not borne out by the evidence. The court even goes back to the time prior to the passage of the law for the protection of German Blood and Honor, during which Katzenberger had known Seiler. It draws the conclusion, apparently without evidence, that their relationship for a period of approximately 10 years, had always been of a sexual nature. The opinion undertakes to bring the case under the decision of the Reich Supreme Court that actual sexual intercourse need not be proved, provided the acts are sexual in nature. . . .

We have gone to some extent into the evidence of this case to show the nature of the proceedings and the animus of the defendant Rothaug. One undisputed fact, however, is sufficient to establish this case as being an act in furtherance of the Nazi program to persecute and exterminate Jews. That

fact is that nobody but a Jew could have been tried for racial pollution. To this offense was added the charge that it was committed by Katzenberger through exploiting war conditions and the blackout. This brought the offense under the ordinance against public enemies and made the offense capital. Katzenberger was tried and executed only because he was a Jew. As stated by Elkar in his testimony, Rothaug achieved the final result by interpretations of existing laws as he boasted to Elkar he was able to do.

This Tribunal is not concerned with the legal incontestability under German law of these cases above discussed. The evidence establishes beyond a reasonable doubt that Katzenberger was condemned and executed because he was a Jew; and Durka, Struss, and Lopata met the same fate because they were Poles. Their execution was in conformity with the policy of the Nazi State of persecution, torture, and extermination of these races. The defendant Rothaug was the knowing and willing instrument in that program of persecution and extermination.

From the evidence it is clear that these trials lacked the essential elements of legality. In these cases the defendant's court, in spite of the legal sophistries which he employed, was merely an instrument in the program of the leaders of the Nazi State of persecution and extermination. That the number the defendant could wipe out within his competency was smaller than the number involved in the mass persecutions and exterminations by the leaders whom he served, does not mitigate his contribution to the program of those leaders. His acts were more terrible in that those who might have hoped for last refuge in the institutions of justice found these institutions turned against them and a part of the program of terror and oppression.

The individual cases in which Rothaug applied the cruel and discriminatory law against Poles and Jews cannot be considered in isolation. It is of the essence of the charges against him that he participated in the national program of racial persecution. It is of the essence of the proof that he identified himself with this national program and gave himself utterly to its accomplishment. He participated in the crime of genocide.

Again, in determining the degree of guilt the Tribunal has considered the entire record of his activities, not alone under the head of racial persecution but in other respects also. Despite protestations that his judgments were based solely upon evidence introduced in court, we are firmly convinced that in numberless cases Rothaug's opinions were formed and decisions made, and in many instances publicly or privately announced before the trial had even commenced and certainly before it was concluded. He was in constant contact with his confidential assistant Elkar, a member of the criminal SD, who sat with him in weekly conferences in the chambers of the court. He formed his opinions from dubious records submitted to him before trial. By his manner and methods he made his court an instrumentality of terror and won the fear and hatred of the population. From the evidence of his closest associates as well as his victims, we find that Oswald Rothaug represented in Germany the personification of the secret Nazi intrigue and cruelty. He was and is a sadistic and evil man.

Under any civilized judicial system he could have been impeached and removed from office or convicted of malfeasance in office on account of the scheming malevolence with which he administered injustice.

Upon the evidence in this case it is the judgment of this Tribunal that the defendant Rothaug is guilty under count three of the indictment. In his case we find no mitigating circumstances; no extenuation.

Defendant OSWALD ROTHAUG, on the count of the indictment on which you have been convicted, this Tribunal sentences you to imprisonment for life.

The Marshal will remove this defendant from the court and will produce the defendant Rudolf Oeschey.

Comment: Under What Law Was Judge Rothaug Convicted?

Very little was said in the trial of Judge Oswald Rothaug or the other fifteen defendants about the legal basis for their indictments. But the legal basis for the jurisdiction of the International Military Tribunal had been briefed and argued the previous year, in 1946, during the Nuremberg trial of the major war criminals (including Goering, Hess, von Ribbentrop, and Alfred Rosenberg). Thus by the time the numerous Nuremberg prosecutions got down to lesser known German leaders such as Judge Rothaug, the legal issues were considered settled.

The four major victorious Allied Powers, namely the United States, Great Britain, France, and the Soviet Union, agreed upon and promulgated "Control Council Law No. 10," which defined the crimes and punishments for the prosecution of war criminals and other similar offenders. This Control Council Law was binding upon various judges who sat on the various Nuremberg courts in the numerous trials that went on from 1946 to 1949. It is unlikely that any judge would have been selected by any of the major powers to serve on any of these courts if that judge was known to be opposed to the legal basis for the trials, or if that judge felt himself (there apparently were no women judges) not bound by Control Council Law No. 10. Nevertheless, it remained open to each judge to satisfy himself that there was a sound basis for the law. No solider was pointing a gun to the head of any judge and saying that the judge must obey Control Council Law No. 10.

The attorneys for the major war criminals in the chief trial in 1946 argued strenuously that Control Council Law No. 10, signed in Berlin on December 20, 1945, was a law that was passed *after* all of the events that were charged against the accused defendants. Hence, its application to the defendants would be *ex post facto* and violative of the basic principle of justice that a person should not be punished for an act that was not criminal at the time it occurred.

Moreover, the attorneys for the defendants pointed out that nothing the defendants did was illegal under the laws of the Third Reich. In fact, not only did the laws of Germany support what Hitler and his cronies did, but indeed Hitler and his cronies embodied the spirit of the laws and gave the laws purpose, direction, and meaningfulness.

How did the Nuremberg Tribunal deal with the charge of *ex post facto* law? The brief analysis which follows has not previously been made, as far as the authors of this Coursebook are aware. One of the authors suggested the analysis in a paper he co-authored with two of his students in 1969,[2] but the analysis was sketchy and not fully developed at the time.

The analysis begins with a sharp distinction between "War Crimes" and "Crimes Against Humanity," two separately defined crimes in Control Council Law No. 10. War crimes included "murder, ill treatment or deportation to slave labour" of civilian populations during war, "murder or ill treatment of prisoners of war," "killing of hostages," "wanton destruction of cities, towns, or villages, or devastation not justified by military necessity." As to these violations of the laws and customs of war, there was no legitimate *ex post facto* argument to be made. For these are traditional crimes under international law. Trials were held, and people were prosecuted for such crimes, in the United States Civil War in the nineteenth century and after World War I, among other instances. The international laws of war apply wherever war is fought; there is no "territorial" exception.

Because of the historical accident that the major war criminals were tried first at Nuremberg, and because most of them were guilty of "War Crimes" in the classical sense,[3] their attorneys did not try hard to separate the "War Crimes" count from the "Crimes Against Humanity" count. They tried lumping them both under their *ex post facto* contention. But because "War Crimes" were not at all instances of *ex post facto* law, their argument was fatally weakened. The net result was that the *ex post facto* argument was undermined *with respect to all of the counts*.

As a result, by the time of the trial against Judge Oswald Rothaug, the judges were already tired of hearing about *ex post facto* laws.

Recall, however, that Rothaug was *acquitted* by the tribunal of the "war crimes" charge. He was *only* convicted for violating "Crimes Against Humanity." Hence, we ought to take a closer look as to that particular count, which resulted in a life sentence for Rothaug. Was it an *ex post facto* law?

"Crimes Against Humanity" is defined in Control Council Law No. 10 as follows:

(c) *Crimes Against Humanity*. Atrocities and offenses, including but not limited to, murder, extermination, enslavement, deportation, imprisonment, torture, rape, or other inhumane acts committed against any civilian population, or persecutions on political, racial or religious grounds whether or not in violation of the domestic laws of the country where perpetrated.

In the United States in any given year there are thousands of murders and rapes, and hundreds of thousands of imprisonments. Are these all subject to the potential jurisdiction of

---

[2] D'Amato, Gould & Woods, *War Crimes and Vietnam: The 'Nuremberg Defense' and the Military Service Resister*, 57 CAL. L. REV. 1055 (1969), reprinted in 3, THE VIETNAM WAR AND INTERNATIONAL LAW 407 (R. Falk ed. 1972).

[3] *Id*. at 1062 (chart of indictments and convictions, showing that 20 defendants out of 22 were convicted of "War Crimes" if they were also convicted of "Crimes Against Humanity").

an international *military* tribunal? As strange as that question sounds with respect to the United States today, how much stranger must it have sounded with respect to murders, rapes, and imprisonments that occurred prior to the passage of Control Council Law No. 10, in 1945?

In the trial of the major war criminals, the judges partially realized the force of the *ex post facto* argument with respect to the count of "Crimes Against Humanity":

> The Tribunal is of the opinion that revolting and horrible as many of these crimes were, it has not been satisfactorily proved that they were done in execution of, or in connection with, any [war crime]. The Tribunal therefore cannot make a general declaration that the acts before 1939 were Crimes Against Humanity within the meaning of [Control Council Law No. 10], but from the beginning of the war in 1939 War Crimes were committed on a vast scale, which were also Crimes Against Humanity; and insofar as the inhumane acts charged in the Indictment, and committed after the beginning of the war, did not constitute War Crimes, they were all committed in execution of, or in connection with, the aggressive war, and therefore constituted Crimes against Humanity. [1 International Military Tribunal, Trial of the Major War Criminals 171 (1947).]

What does this paragraph say? Does it say that "crimes against humanity" suddenly sprang into being in 1939? It certainly says that no alleged crimes against humanity prior to 1939 will be punished at Nuremberg. (Since Judge Rothaug's Katzenberger trial occurred in 1942, that act comes well within the Tribunal's coverage.)

Does the passage say that anything that isn't a war crime but was done by a German after 1939 was committed in connection with the German war effort and hence was a "Crime Against Humanity?" But, then, who would be left out? Would a print shop that printed Hitler's decrees be guilty of a crime? Would a railroad engineer who repaired trains be guilty of furthering the deportation of Jews to the death camps? Would such an engineer be able to defend on the basis that he was very poor at his job, and as a result many trains were delayed?

Of course, those fanciful cases were not the subject of Nuremberg prosecutions. Whatever the breadth of the definition of "Crimes against Humanity," it was never seriously suggested that ordinary German workers should be indicted for assisting in the war effort. Even ordinary German soldiers below the rank of Sergeant were not among the over 3,000 Germans prosecuted in the many post-war trials.

Clearly, then, the victorious Allies used their discretion in selecting Germans to be prosecuted. But "discretion" is a broad term, and "Crimes Against Humanity," as we have seen, is broadly and vaguely defined. The case before us is that of Judge Oswald Rothaug. Why was *he* indicted? Why was *he* convicted?

Now that you have read the pertinent materials on his trial, you are able to form a judgment as to whether Judge Rothaug was, or was not, "guilty" under the charge of "crimes against humanity." You are able to form a judgment as to how that charge ought to be interpreted in Judge Rothaug's case. Even if it is overly broad in respect of some possible cases, was it overly broad in respect of Judge Rothaug?

But the answers to the foregoing questions—however difficult they may be to arrive at— do not end our inquiry. We invite you to consider the following questions.

Questions

1. Judge Rothaug was found guilty of joining Katzenberger and Seiler as defendants, thus precluding Seiler from being an effective witness for Katzenberger. Was it fair for the Military Tribunal to try Judge Rothaug along with fifteen other officials, prosecutors, judges, and administrators?

2. Judge Rothaug was found guilty of stretching the anti-pollution law to cover the facts of the Katzenberger case. Was Control Council Law No. 10 stretched to cover Judge Rothaug?

3. Judge Rothaug felt that the spirit of the Nazi laws called for an activist judge. Does the spirit of the new "Crimes Against Humanity" call for overriding our sense that any criminal *ex post facto* law is *per se* unjust?

4. Was Judge Rothaug convicted in part because he administered an evil law, even though he did not enact that law? Could he defend on the ground that he was only doing his job? Could the judges of the Military Tribunal defend their judgment against Rothaug on the same ground?

5. If Judge Rothaug was convicted because of what he did as a judge, was his conviction the result of what the judges on the Military Court felt bound to do because of their role as judges?

6. Did justice triumph?